Microsoft® Office 2003:
The Complete Reference

About the Authors

Jennifer Ackerman Kettell has taken a long and winding path from aspiring romance author to multipublished computer book author. Side trips along the way have included stints at online services MSN and GEnie, a few cross-country moves, and an endless search for decent bagels west of the Mississippi. Jenn has written and contributed to more than a dozen books on web design, digital photography and graphics, and software applications. Some of her titles include *Dreamweaver 4: The Complete Reference* and *Special Edition Using Dreamweaver MX* (written with Molly Holzschlag). Jenn currently lives in the dry heat of Arizona with her husband, two children, a dog, a couple of hermit crabs, and lots of dust bunnies. You can catch up with Jenn at www.gilajenn.com.

Guy Hart-Davis is the author of *How to Do Everything with Your iPod, Windows XP Professional: The Complete Reference,* and about 20 other computer books. He specializes in Microsoft Office, Windows XP, Visual Basic for Applications, and digital audio.

Curt Simmons (MCP, MCSA, MCSE) is a Microsoft product expert and the author of more than 30 books, including *How to Do Everything with Windows XP, Windows XP Headaches,* and *How to Do Everything with Photoshop Album.* When he is not writing, Curt spends his time with his wife and daughters. Visit Curt on the Internet at www.curtsimmons.com.

Microsoft® Office 2003: The Complete Reference

Jennifer Ackerman Kettell
Guy Hart-Davis
Curt Simmons

McGraw-Hill/Osborne
New York   Chicago   San Francisco
Lisbon   London   Madrid   Mexico City
Milan   New Delhi   San Juan
Seoul   Singapore   Sydney   Toronto

The *McGraw-Hill* Companies

McGraw-Hill/Osborne
2100 Powell Street, 10th Floor
Emeryville, California 94608
U.S.A.

To arrange bulk purchase discounts for sales promotions, premiums, or fund-raisers, please contact **McGraw-Hill**/Osborne at the above address. For information on translations or book distributors outside the U.S.A., please see the International Contact Information page immediately following the index of this book.

Microsoft® Office 2003: The Complete Reference

1234567890 CUS CUS 019876543

ISBN: 0-07-222995-0

Publisher
Brandon A. Nordin

Vice President & Associate Publisher
Scott Rogers

Executive Editor
Jane Brownlow

Acquisitions Editor
Katie Conley

Project Editor
Janet Walden

Acquisitions Coordinator
Tana Allen

Technical Editors
Bill Bruns, Warren Raquel

Copy Editor
Judith Brown

Proofreader
Claire Splan

Indexer
Claire Splan

Composition
Carie Abrew, George Toma Charbak,
Tara A. Davis

Illustrators
Kathleen Fay Edwards,
Melinda Moore Lytle, Lyssa Wald

Series Design
Peter F. Hancik, Lyssa Wald

This book was composed with Corel VENTURA™ Publisher.

For Greg, for everything.
–Jenn

To Rhonda and Teddy.
–Guy

To Dawn, Hannah, and Mattie
–Curt

Contents at a Glance

Part I Common Office 2003 Elements

1	Getting to Know Office 2003	3
2	Customizing the Office Environment	17
3	Managing Files in Office	37
4	Text Tools	55
5	Drawing and Graphics Tools	77

Part II Word Processing

6	Word	105
7	Editing Text	125
8	Document Formatting	145
9	Reusable Formatting with Styles and Templates	161
10	Tables and Columns	181
11	Advanced Page Layout in Word	197
12	Automating Information with Fields	207
13	Managing Long Documents	221
14	Mail Merge, Labels, and Envelopes	237

Part III Spreadsheets

15	Excel	251
16	Formatting Worksheets and Restricting Data	277
17	Calculating with Formulas and Functions	305
18	Viewing and Manipulating Data with Charts and PivotTables	331
19	Creating Excel Databases	357

Part IV   Presentations

20	PowerPoint	377
21	Creating and Editing Slides	389
22	Adding Graphics, Multimedia, and Special Effects to Slides	407
23	Showing Your PowerPoint Presentations	429

Part V   Schedule and Contact Management

24	Outlook	443
25	Outlook E-mail	453
26	Outlook Calendar and Task Lists	467
27	Managing Contacts and Taking Notes	479
28	Scheduling and Planning with Others	487

Part VI   Databases

29	Databases in Access	495
30	Defining and Developing Tables	513
31	Creating Queries	531
32	Forms and Reports	551
33	Building a Database Application	567

Part VII   Web and Print Layout

34	Designing Pages and Sites in FrontPage	581
35	Advanced Management Features and Web Site Publishing	627
36	Creating Publications in Publisher	659
37	Publishing Documents in Publisher	673

Part VIII   Integration and Collaboration

38	Using Office Applications Together	681
39	Using Office on the Web	713
40	Collaboration Using Office Tools and SharePoint Team Services	725

Part IX   Macros and Visual Basic for Applications

41	Creating and Using Office Macros	755
42	Using Visual Basic for Applications with Office	771
43	Putting VBA and Macros to Work	789

Part X Appendixes

A Keyboard Shortcuts 817

B XML: The Underpinnings of Office 2003 829

Index   837

Contents

Acknowledgments xxxv
Introduction xxxvii

Part I   Common Office 2003 Elements

1   Getting to Know Office 2003   3
The Office Suite of Programs   3
    Microsoft Word   4
    Microsoft Excel   6
    Microsoft PowerPoint   6
    Microsoft Outlook   7
    Microsoft Access   8
    Microsoft FrontPage   10
    Microsoft Publisher   11
    Collaborative Tools   12
Installing Office 2003   12
Getting Office Help   15

2   Customizing the Office Environment   17
Customizing Toolbars and Menus   17
    Displaying, Moving, and Customizing Toolbars   18
    Customizing Menus and Context Menus   20
    Controlling the Appearance of a Menu Item or
        Toolbar Button   21
    Customizing Keyboard Shortcuts in Word   21
Setting Smart Tag Options   23
AutoCorrect, Spell Checking, and Grammar Checking   24
    AutoCorrect   24
    Spell Checking   29
    Grammar Checking   31
Improving Accessibility   34
Using Office on Tablet PCs   34

Configuring Options for Pen Input 35
Using the Writing Tools 36

3 Managing Files in Office **37**
Choosing Where to Store Your Files and Templates 37
Coming to Grips with the My Documents Folder 37
Changing the Working Folder for the Office Applications . . 38
Changing the Templates Folders for Word, Excel, and
PowerPoint 39
Using Office over a Network 39
Entering a Universal Naming Convention (UNC) Path 40
Mapping a Network Drive to a Local Drive Letter 40
Disconnecting a Network Drive 42
Browsing with the My Network Places Folder 42
Using Office over the Internet 42
Creating Files 43
Creating a New Default File 43
Creating a File from the New Task Pane 43
Creating a File from a Template in Windows Explorer 45
Creating Your Own Templates 45
Finding Files 45
Performing a Basic File Search 46
Performing an Advanced File Search 47
Working with the Files You Find 49
Using Office's Recovery Options Effectively 50
Understanding What the Recovery Features Do 50
Configuring the Backup and Recovery Options 51
Using Microsoft Office Application Recovery to Close
a Hung Application 51
Recovering a Document 52

4 Text Tools **55**
Entering Text 55
Entering Text with the Keyboard 55
Entering Text via Paste, and Drag and Drop 60
Entering Text via Speech Recognition 61
Entering Text via Scanning and OCR 62
Formatting Text 64
Cutting, Copying, and Pasting 67
Understanding the Windows Clipboard and the
Office Clipboard 67

Using the Office Clipboard 68
Configuring the Office Clipboard 69
Using Paste Special and Smart Tags to Control
Formatting on Pasted Items 69
Selecting Text 70
Selecting Text with the Mouse 71
Selecting Text with the Keyboard 71
Selecting Text with the Keyboard and Mouse 72
Applying Paragraph Formatting 72
Applying Alignment 72
Applying Borders 73
Using Find and Replace 74
Finding Text 74
Finding and Replacing Text 75
Using Wildcard Characters in Searches 75
Application-Specific Find and Replace Features 75

5 Drawing and Graphics Tools **77**
How the Office Applications Handle Pictures 77
Inserting Clip Art 78
Working with Shapes, AutoShapes, and WordArt 82
Starting a Drawing 82
Adding Basic Shapes 83
Adding AutoShapes 84
Adding WordArt Objects to Your Drawings 84
Adding Text to an AutoShape 86
Resizing and Formatting Drawing Objects 87
Positioning Drawing Objects 89
Layering Drawing Objects 92
Specifying Text-Wrapping Options 92
Enhancing Your Documents with Text Boxes 92
Adding Graphics to Your Documents 93
Inserting (Embedding) a Picture 94
Linking a Picture 94
Using Insert and Link in Word and Outlook 95
Cropping a Picture 95
Importing Pictures from Scanners and Cameras 95
Charts and Diagrams 97
When to Use Microsoft Chart for Creating Charts 97
Creating Basic Diagrams 98
Creating Organization Charts 100

Part II   Word Processing

6   Word **105**
Word Task Pane 105
 Hiding the Task Pane 106
Customizing Word Options 107
 View Options 107
 General Options 108
 Edit Options 109
 Print Options 110
 Save Options 111
 Track Changes 112
 Other Options 112
Document Views 112
 Normal View 113
 Web Layout View 113
 Print Layout View 114
 Reading Layout View 114
 Outline View 116
 Splitting the Document Window 117
 Maximizing Screen Space 118
 Zoom 119
Navigating in Word 119
 Keyboard Navigation 119
 Mouse Navigation 120
 Accessing the Document Map 120
 Using the Object Browser 121
Printing Word Documents 122
 Using Print Preview 122
 Printing Thumbnails 122

7   Editing Text **125**
Automatic Text Tools 125
 AutoCorrect 125
 AutoText 126
 Repeating Text 130
Undo and Redo 131
Text Formatting 131
 Changing Case 133
 Drop Caps 134
 Coloring and Highlighting Text 135

Adding Special Characters 135
Bullets and Numbering 137
    Automatic Bullets and Numbering 137
    Using the Bullets and Numbering Tools 139
    Customizing List Formats 140
    Multilevel Outline Lists 141
    Removing Bullets and Numbering 143

8   Document Formatting **145**
Paragraph Formatting 145
    Alignment 145
    Line Spacing 146
    Paragraph Page Flow 148
Indentation 149
    Tabs 150
    Using the Ruler 152
Margins and Page Orientation 153
Page and Section Breaks 154
    Section Breaks 155
Headers and Footers 157
    Varying Headers and Footers 159
Page Numbering 159

9   Reusable Formatting with Styles and Templates **161**
AutoFormatting 161
Paragraph and Character Styles 164
    Applying Styles 166
    Creating Styles 166
    Modifying Styles 168
    Using List and Table Styles 169
Templates 170
    Modifying the Normal Template 171
    Attaching a Template 171
    Creating Your Own Templates 173
    Controlling Access to Styles 174
The Style Gallery 175
Themes 176
    Theme Assets and Liabilities 177
    Applying and Removing Themes 178
    Converting Themes into Templates 178
    Themes Across Applications 180

10 Tables and Columns **181**
Tables 181
Creating Tables 182
    Inserting Tables from the Menu 182
    Inserting Tables from the Toolbar 183
    Drawing Tables 183
    Converting Text to Tables 184
Manipulating Tables 185
    Selecting Table Elements 186
    Inserting and Deleting Columns and Rows 186
    Adjusting Table Properties 186
    Merging and Splitting Cells 188
    Nesting Tables 189
    Splitting Tables 189
    Hiding Grid Lines 189
Formatting Table Content 189
    Table Styles Using AutoFormat 189
    Changing Borders and Shading 190
    Rotating Text 190
    Repeating Headings 191
    Sorting Data 191
    Quick Math Calculations 192
Columns 192
    Using Column Breaks 194
Hyphenation 195

11 Advanced Page Layout in Word **197**
Borders, Boxes, and Shading 198
    Borders 198
    Shading 199
    Horizontal Rules 200
Page Fills and Backgrounds 201
    Page Backgrounds 201
    Watermarks 204
Text Boxes 204
    Overflowing Text Boxes 205

12 Automating Information with Fields **207**
Field Basics 207
    Field Switches 208

Inserting Fields 211
Toggling Field Codes 212
Updating Field Content 213
Common Fields 213
Page Numbering 213
Date and Time 213
Document Properties 214
AutoText Fields 215
Creating Forms 215
Adding Form Fields 216
Web Forms 218
Protecting Your Form 218

13 Managing Long Documents **221**
Outlining 221
Creating an Outline 221
Changing Outline Level Styles 222
Rearranging and Viewing the Outline 223
Using Bookmarks in Long Documents 224
Creating a Master Document 225
Working with Subdocuments 226
Page Numbering Across Documents 227
Generating a Table of Contents 228
Creating an Index 230
Preparing Index Entries 230
Generating the Index 231
Other Types of Tables and Indexes 232
Cross-References 234
Formatting References 235
Adding Footnotes 235

14 Mail Merge, Labels, and Envelopes **237**
Using the Letter Wizard 237
Mail Merges 238
Creating a Database 241
Filtering and Sorting a Database 243
Generating Envelopes 244
E-Postage 246
Creating Labels 246

Part III   Spreadsheets

15   Excel **251**
  Using and Hiding the Task Pane 251
      Hiding the Getting Started Task Pane 252
  Customizing Excel Options 252
      View Options 253
      Calculation Options 254
      Edit Options 255
      General Options 255
      Transition Options 256
      Save Options 256
      Loading and Unloading Add-Ins 256
  Using Worksheets and Workbooks 257
  Understanding the Excel Screen 258
  Navigating in Workbooks and Selecting Objects 258
      Navigating in Worksheets 258
      Selecting Cells and Ranges of Cells 260
      Selecting Worksheets in a Workbook 263
  Entering Data in Your Worksheets 264
      Entering Data Manually 264
      Entering Data by Using Drag and Drop 265
      Entering Data with Paste, Paste Options, and
          Paste Special 265
      Linking Data Across Worksheets or Across Workbooks ... 267
  Improving Your View with Hiding, Splits,
      Extra Windows, Zooming, and Freezing 268
      Hiding a Window 268
      Splitting the Window 268
      Using Extra Windows 269
      Zooming In and Out 269
      Using Freezing to Keep Some Rows and Columns Visible . 269
  Converting from Other Formats 269
  Printing Worksheets 270
      Instant Printing with the Default Settings 270
      Using Print Preview 270
      Setting the Print Area 271
      Setting Page Breaks 272
      Modifying Print Settings 273

16   Formatting Worksheets and Restricting Data   277
Adding, Deleting, and Manipulating Worksheets   277
    Adding, Deleting, Hiding, and Redisplaying Worksheets ...   277
    Moving and Copying Worksheets   278
    Renaming a Worksheet   279
    Changing the Formatting on New Default
        Worksheets and Workbooks   279
Formatting Cells and Ranges   279
    Applying Number Formatting   280
    Understanding Excel's Number Formats   281
    Applying Visual Formatting   287
    Formatting Rows and Columns   288
    Conditional Formatting   289
    AutoFormat   290
    Using Styles in Excel   291
Restricting Data and Protecting Workbooks   293
    Checking Data Entry for Invalid Entries   293
    Protecting Cells, a Worksheet, or Workbook   296
    Protecting a Worksheet   297
    Allowing Users to Edit Ranges in a Protected Worksheet ...   297
    Protecting a Workbook with Passwords   299
Using AutoFill   300
    Creating Custom AutoFill Lists   301
Find and Replace   302

17   Calculating with Formulas and Functions   305
Understanding What Formulas and Functions Are   305
    Components of a Formula   305
    How Excel Handles Numbers   308
    Referring to Cells and Ranges in Your Formulas   308
    Referring to Other Worksheets in Your Formulas   308
    Example of Entering a Formula   309
    Using Range Names and Labels in Formulas   309
    Using Absolute, Relative, and Mixed References   311
    Displaying Formulas   311
    Hiding Your Formulas from Other Users   312
Troubleshooting Formulas   312
    Understanding and Fixing Basic Errors   312
    Fixing Formatting, Operator Precedence, and
        Range-Change Errors   312

Understanding Formula AutoCorrect 314
Configuring Error-Checking Options 314
Checking for Errors Manually 315
Entering Functions 315
Components of a Function 316
Entering a Function 316
Using the Insert Function Dialog Box 317
Nesting One Function Inside Another Function 318
Editing a Function 319
Monitoring Calculations with the Watch Window 319
Working with Array Formulas 319
Goal Seeking 320
Using the Solver 321
Examples of Functions in Action 323
Database Functions 323
Date and Time Functions 323
Financial Functions 324
Logical Functions 325
Information Functions 326
Lookup and Reference Functions 327
Mathematical and Trigonometric Functions 327
Statistical Functions 328
Text Functions 329

18   Viewing and Manipulating Data with Charts and PivotTables ...   331
Working with Charts 331
Components of an Excel Chart 331
Using the Chart Wizard 332
Choosing the Right Type of Chart for Your Data 335
Creating a Chart Instantly Using the Keyboard 336
Editing Charts 336
Formatting Charts 340
Copying Formatting from One Chart to Another 342
Unlinking a Chart from Its Data Source 342
Printing Your Charts 343
Creating Custom Chart Types 343
Working with PivotTables 344
What Is a PivotTable? 345
Running the PivotTable and PivotChart Wizard 346
Creating Your PivotTable 348
Changing the PivotTable 350
Using the PivotTable Toolbar 351
Formatting a PivotTable 351

Changing a Field to a Different Function 352
Choosing PivotTable Options 352
Working with PivotCharts 352
Creating a Conventional Chart from PivotTable Data 353

19   Creating Excel Databases **357**
Creating a Database 357
Entering Data in Your Database 359
Entering Data by Using Standard Techniques 359
Entering and Editing Data with Data Entry Forms 359
Sorting 361
Preparing to Sort Your Database 361
Performing a Quick Sort 361
Performing a Multifield Sort 362
Sorting by a Custom Sort Order 362
Finding and Replacing Data in Databases 363
Filtering 363
Performing Quick Filtering with AutoFilter 363
Creating Custom Filters Manually 365
Linking to an External Database 367
Linking to a Database with the Query Wizard 367
Customizing a Query with MS Query 371
Performing Web Queries 373

Part IV   Presentations

20   PowerPoint **377**
Exploring the PowerPoint Interface 377
Menus in PowerPoint 377
PowerPoint's Toolbars 379
Outline/Slides Pane 381
Work Area 381
Starting a Presentation 382
Using Blank Presentation 382
From Design Template 382
AutoContent Wizard 384
Browsing a Presentation 386
Saving a Presentation 387

21   Creating and Editing Slides **389**
Working with Slides 389
Add a Slide 389

Remove a Slide   390
Reorganize Slides   390
Editing Slides   391
Changing Text   391
Changing Design   391
Changing Layout   392
Formatting Text   392
Formatting Paragraphs   394
Formatting Bullets and Numbering   395
Adjusting a Placeholder Box   397
Managing Placeholder Layout   398
Checking Spelling and AutoCorrect Options   399
Inserting a Table   399
Entering Data   400
Formatting Tables   400
Insert Microsoft Word Table   401
Inserting a Chart   401
Creating a PowerPoint Chart   402
Use a Microsoft Excel Chart   403
Inserting an Organization Chart   403
Inserting a Text Box   404
Inserting an Object   405
Inserting a Hyperlink   405

22   Adding Graphics, Multimedia, and Special Effects to Slides **407**
Insert Clip Art and Photos   407
Insert Clip Art   407
Edit a Clip Art Image   409
Insert a Photo   412
Create a Photo Album   412
Using Draw Tools   414
Modify Shapes   414
Modify Orientation   416
Adjust an AutoShape   417
Make a Shape 3-D   417
Change a Shape's Fill Color   418
Change an AutoShape   419
Edit Line Properties   419
Copy and Paste Shapes   420
Align a Shape   420
Manage Stack Order   420
Create Shapes   422
Draw Basic Shapes   422

Draw an Arc and Other Standard Shapes 423
Group Shapes 423
Insert Text on Shapes 424
Use Connectors 424
Create a Flowchart 425
Configure Action Buttons 426
Inserting Multimedia Content 427

23 Showing Your PowerPoint Presentations **429**
Transitions and Animation 429
Setting Up Transitions 429
Using Animation 431
Getting Ready for Your Presentation 432
Rehearsing Your Presentation 433
Using Hidden Slides 433
Using a Pen/Highlighter 434
Set Up Show Options 435
Printing Speaker Notes and Audience Handouts 436
Add a Header and Footer 436
Configure Print Settings 437
Use Print Preview 437
Print a Presentation 439

Part V Schedule and Contact Management

24 Outlook **443**
A First Look at Outlook 443
Mail 443
Calendar 445
Contacts 445
Tasks 446
Using Outlook's Toolbars 446
Using Categories 448
Data File Management 448
Importing and Exporting Data 450
Archiving Data 451

25 Outlook E-mail **453**
Setting Up a Mail Account 453
Sending and Receiving E-mail 454
Reading E-mail 455
Composing and Responding to E-mail 456
Managing Attachments 457

Configuring E-mail Options 460
    Standard E-mail Options 460
    Using a Signature 461
    Using Stationery 461
    Managing Automatic Send/Receive 462
    Flagging Messages 463
Managing Mail 464
    Using Personal Folders 464
    Managing Junk E-mail 465

26 **Outlook Calendar and Task Lists** **467**
Outlook Calendar 467
    Configuring Appointments 468
    Configuring Meetings 471
    Scheduling an Event 473
    Working with Reminders 473
    Calendar Management 473
Using Tasks 474
    Creating a Task 474
    Assigning a Task 476

27 **Managing Contacts and Taking Notes** **479**
Outlook Contacts 479
    Creating a Contact 479
    Viewing Contacts 482
    Editing Contact Information 482
    Working with Contacts 483
Taking Notes 484
    Creating a Note 484
    Viewing Notes 485
    Changing a Note's Color 485
    Changing Note Preferences 485

28 **Scheduling and Planning with Others** **487**
Sharing Your Calendar 487
    Accessing a Shared Calendar 487
    Hiding Personal Calendar Data 488
    Working with Free/Busy Times 488
Working with Scheduled Meetings and Appointments 489
    Rescheduling a Shared Appointment or Meeting 490
    Changing Meeting Attendees 491
    Send an E-mail to the Meeting or Appointment Organizer .. 491
    Delete a Meeting or Appointment 491

Part VI   Databases

29   Databases in Access **495**

Access Components 495

   The Database Engine 495

   Databases and Projects 497

Creating a Database 497

   Building a Blank Database 497

   Using a Template Wizard 497

   Choosing a File Format 499

   Converting a Database 499

Creating a Project 499

Upsizing a Database 500

   Running the Upsizing Wizard 501

Importing and Exporting Data 501

   Importing Data 502

   Linking Data 503

   Exporting Data 503

Database Objects 504

   Tables 504

   Queries 504

   Forms 505

   Reports 505

   Data Access Pages 505

   Macros 505

   Modules 506

The Database Window 506

   Creating Objects 507

   Editing in Design View 507

Customizing Access 508

   View Tab 509

   General Tab 509

   Edit/Find Tab 510

   Datasheet Tab 510

   Forms/Reports Tab 510

   Pages Tab 510

   Advanced Tab 510

   Tables/Queries Tab 511

30   Defining and Developing Tables **513**

Creating Tables 514

   Using the Table Wizard 514

   Table Design View 516

Entering Fields 517
    Choosing Data Types 518
Setting Field Properties 519
    Primary Keys 519
    Indexes 520
    Input Masks 520
    Format Properties 522
    Default Values 525
    Validation Rules 526
Data Normalization 526
    Non-Normalized Example 527
    Normalized Example 528
    Table Relationships 528

31   Creating Queries **531**
Query Types 531
    Select Queries 531
    Crosstab Queries 534
    Parameter Queries 535
    Action Queries 536
Query Wizards 540
    Simple Query Wizard 541
    Crosstab Query Wizard 542
    Find Duplicates Query Wizard 543
    Find Unmatched Query Wizard 544
Working in Query Design View 545
    Choosing Tables 545
    Choosing Fields 545
    Defining Query Criteria 546
    Performing Calculations 547
SQL Queries 547
    Using SQL as a Record Source 547
    SQL-Specific Queries 549

32   Forms and Reports **551**
Forms 551
    Anatomy of a Form 552
    Creating Forms 552
    Customizing Forms 557
    Linked Forms and Subforms 559
Reports 561
    Report Layout 561

Creating Reports 563
Grouping and Sorting Records 565

33 **Building a Database Application** **567**
Using a Database Application Wizard 567
Templates Home Page 568
Building Applications from Scratch 569
Switchboards 569
The Switchboard Manager 570
Customizing the User Interface 572
Adding Custom Menus and Toolbars 572
Setting Startup Options 572
Locking a Database 573
Making an MDE File 576
Making Data Available 576
Linking to External Data 576
Replicating a Database 577

Part VII **Web and Print Layout**

34 **Designing Pages and Sites in FrontPage** **581**
Creating a New FrontPage Site 581
Choosing a Design Template 583
Deciding on a Structure for Your Site 583
Importing an Existing Web Site 584
Saving Your Web Site 587
Getting Around in FrontPage 588
Working with Pages in FrontPage 592
Creating New Pages 593
Applying a Theme to a Site 594
Working with Text 596
Formatting a Background 598
Using Background Sounds 601
Assigning Page Titles 602
Using Photos and Clip Art 602
Working with the Drawing Toolbar 609
Inserting Web Components 611
Inserting Tables 616
Creating Hyperlinks 619
Creating a New Theme 620
Configuring Theme Colors 621

Working with Custom Font Styles 623
Creating Theme Graphics 625

35 Advanced Management Features and Web Site Publishing **627**
Working with HTML in FrontPage 627
Code and Split-Pane View 628
Working with Tags 628
Controlling Color Coding 629
Finding and Replacing Text and Finding Line Numbers 629
Using Custom HTML 629
Working with Reveal Tags 630
Managing HTML Preferences 630
Working with Forms and Form Input 632
Creating Forms 633
Working with Form Templates 634
Exploring Form Elements 635
Confirmation Page 639
Using the Form Page Wizard 639
Gathering Form Input 642
Managing Browser Compatibility 645
Publishing Sites and Pages 647
Choosing a Web Provider 648
Publishing Your Site 650
Updating Your Site 651
Using Reports to Manage Your Web Site 652
Site Summary 652
Detailed Reports 654
Setting Reports View Options 657

36 Creating Publications in Publisher **659**
Creating Publications with Templates 659
Creating Custom Publications 661
Setting Up Publication Pages 661
Working with Content 665

37 Publishing Documents in Publisher **673**
Printing on Your Home or Office Printer 673
Working with Professional Printers 673
Color Printing 674

Registration Settings 675
Fonts 676
Using Pack and Go 676
Publishing to the Web 677
Web Publishing and Photos 677

Part VIII   Integration and Collaboration

38   Using Office Applications Together **681**
Using the Clipboard 681
Embedding and Linking Objects 682
Understanding the Differences Between
Embedding and Linking 682
Choosing When to Embed and When to Link 683
Verifying Whether an Object Is Linked or Embedded 684
Embedding or Linking an Object 684
Editing an Embedded Object 686
Editing a Linked Object 687
Editing, Updating, and Breaking Links 688
Using Office's XML Capabilities 688
What You're Likely to Do with XML Files 689
Working with XML Documents in Word 689
Creating XML Documents in Word 691
Working with XML Files in Excel 701
Creating XML Files in Excel 703

39   Using Office on the Web **713**
HTML and Round Tripping 713
Understanding the File Formats Available 714
Single File Web Page Format 714
Web Page Format 714
Web Page, Filtered Format 714
Publishing Documents on the Web 715
Using Hyperlinks in Office Documents 715
Choosing Web Options 716
General Tab Options 716
Browsers Tab Options 717
Files Tab Options 718
Pictures Tab Options 718

Encoding Tab Options 718
Fonts Tab Options 718
Saving a File as a Web Page 719
Using Web Page Preview to Check How Your File Looks ... 719
Setting the Page Title 719
Saving a Word Document as a Web Page 719
Saving an Excel Worksheet or Workbook as a Web Page 721
Saving a PowerPoint Presentation as a Web Page 722
Saving an Access Data Access Page as a Web Page 724

40 Collaboration Using Office Tools and SharePoint
    Team Services **725**
Review Tools 725
Tracking Changes in Word Documents 725
Tracking Changes in Excel Workbooks 730
Comparing and Merging Documents in Word 733
Comparing and Merging Changes in PowerPoint 735
Securing Documents 736
Securing Documents with Passwords 737
Specifying an Encryption Type for a Document 737
Removing Personal Information from
    Document Properties 738
Working with Comments 738
How Comments Work 738
Using Comments in Word 739
Using Comments in Excel 739
Using Comments in PowerPoint 740
Sending Documents in E-mail 741
Sending a Document for Review 741
Receiving and Returning a Document Sent for Review 742
Sending and Receiving a Document as an Attachment 743
Sending and Receiving a Word Document or
    Excel Worksheet in a Message 743
Routing a Word Document or Excel Workbook Among
    a Group of People 744
Receiving a Routed Document or Workbook 746
Using SharePoint Team Services 747
Anatomy of a SharePoint Site 747
Understanding Permissions on SharePoint Sites 748
Accessing a SharePoint Site 748
Managing Documents Within SharePoint 748
Synchronizing Documents with SharePoint Sites 750

Part IX   Macros and Visual Basic for Applications

41   Creating and Using Office Macros **755**
Understanding Macros 755
Understanding Office's Macro Virus–Protection Features 756
    Understanding and Setting Security Levels 756
    Digital Signatures 759
Recording Macros 760
Testing and Running Your Macros 762
    Running a Macro from the Macros Dialog Box 763
    Running a Macro from an Interface Item 763
Storing Your Macros 765
    Storing Your Macros in Word 766
    Storing Your Macros in Excel 766
    Storing Your Macros in PowerPoint 767
    Storing Your Macros in Access 767
    Storing Your Macros in Outlook 767
Recording the Sample Macros 767
    Recording the Sample Macro in Word 767
    Recording the Sample Macro in Excel 768

42   Using Visual Basic for Applications with Office **771**
Understanding VBA 771
    Understanding Objects, Properties, and Methods 772
VBA Projects and Their Components 773
    Modules 773
    Userforms 773
    Classes 773
    Procedures, Subprocedures, Macros, and Functions 773
Using the Visual Basic Editor 774
    Launching the Visual Basic Editor 774
    Getting Acquainted with the Visual Basic Editor 774
    Returning to the Host Application 777
    Using the Visual Basic Editor's Features for
        Creating Code 777
Running Code 781
    Design Mode, Run Mode, and Break Mode 781
    Running a Macro from the Visual Basic Editor 781
    Interrupting Code When It's Running 781
    Stepping into a Procedure 782
    Setting a Line of Code to Be the Next Statement 782

Executing Code in the Immediate Window 782
Following the Value of Expressions as Code Runs 783
Managing Your Macros, Modules, Userforms, and Classes 784
Creating a Module, Userform, or Class 784
Copying or Moving a Macro 784
Renaming a Macro or Module 784
Deleting a Macro or Module 784
Copying and Moving Modules, Userforms, or Classes 785
Exporting and Importing Modules, Userforms,
and Classes 785
Examining the Recorded Macros 785
Examining and Editing the Word Macro 785
Examining the Excel Macro 788

43   Putting VBA and Macros to Work **789**
Working with Variables 789
VBA's 12 Types of Variables 789
Declaring and Using a Variable 789
Recommendations for Declaring Variables Effectively 792
Making Decisions with If and Select Case 792
If Statements 792
Select Case Structures 793
Using Message Boxes and Input Boxes 794
Input Boxes 796
Using Loops to Repeat Actions 797
Creating the IsAlphanumeric Function 798
Calling One Procedure from Another Procedure 800
Adding a Reference to Another Project or Application 800
Accessing Another Application 801
Using the Call Stack Window to Track Procedure Calls 802
Creating Dialog Boxes 802
Creating the Userform 803
Adding the Frames 804
Adding the Option Buttons 805
Adding the Check Boxes 805
Creating the Initialize Subprocedure for the Userform 806
Adding the Label and Text Box 807
Adding the Command Buttons 808
Calling the Userform from the Macro 812
Distributing a VBA Project 812
Signing Your VBA Project 812
Locking Your VBA Project 813

Part X Appendixes

A Keyboard Shortcuts 817

B XML: The Underpinnings of Office 2003 829
    What Is XML? 829
    What Is XML For? 830
    What Benefits Does XML Offer? 830
    How XML Is Implemented in Office 831
    XML Terms and Components 832
        XML Files 832
        XML Schemas and DTDs 833
        Namespaces 833
        Elements 834
        Attributes 835
        Comments 835

    Index 837

Acknowledgments

As with all books, this was definitely a group project. Editors Jane Brownlow and Katie Conley brought us all together. Curt Simmons and Guy Hart-Davis, my coauthors, stepped up to the plate and made this book come alive. Tech editors Bill Bruns and Warren Raquel caught my mistakes. Project editor Janet Walden and copy editor Judith Brown made sure all the i's were dotted and t's were crossed. Indexer Claire Splan ensured you'll be able to find everything. David Fugate always knows when I need to look at the big picture.

This is always my kids' favorite page in the book because they get to see their names in print. So for Mandy and Zach, thank you for your patience. For my husband, Greg, thanks for your constant love and support. For my mother, Roberta Ackerman, thank you for everything from driving to kung fu to reviewing my page proofs. And although he's no longer with us, thank you to my father, Leon Ackerman, for instilling in me the determination and humor to tackle anything that comes along.

Finally, I want to thank everyone who enriches the lives of me and my family, making it possible for me to write at all. Much love to Phil Berman and Jeff Rose, Carole and Irwyn Berman, Jennifer Montoya, Colin and Devin Montoya, Ron and Marla Yablon, Suzanne McMinn, Irene and Paulluvi Bahl, Gillian Whitney, and Joshua and David Whitney.

—Jenn Kettell

Thanks to the terrific editorial and production team at McGraw-Hill/Osborne who made great efforts to ensure this book happened, in particular Katie Conley, Janet Walden, Judith Brown, and the tech dynamos Warren Raquel and Bill Bruns.

—Guy Hart-Davis

Thanks to everyone at McGraw-Hill/Osborne for all their hard work and patience. A special thanks goes to Jane Brownlow, Bill Bruns, and Katie Conley for keeping things moving in the right direction. Thanks also to my agent, Margot Hutchison, and my family for their support.

—Curt Simmons

Introduction

Microsoft Office 2003 is a bit of a misnomer. In today's world, word processing, using spreadsheets and databases, and even creating professional-looking publications aren't limited to offices. Everyone from soccer moms to CEOs can find dozens of uses for the programs in Microsoft Office 2003. This version of Office integrates these programs more than ever, saving you time and effort to get the job done.

About Microsoft Office 2003 and This Book

The core of the Microsoft Office System 2003 consists of Word for word processing, Excel for spreadsheets, Outlook for contact and appointment management and e-mail, and PowerPoint for presentations.

Microsoft has bundled the applications that make up the Office System 2003 in several editions. Some of these editions include additional programs such as Access for relational databases and Publisher for brochures and other publications. The applications in your suite, therefore, may not match all of the applications covered in this book. In fact, no edition contains all the applications, and some are not bundled at all.

Here are the current options for the Office applications:

- **Microsoft Office Basic Edition 2003**   Word 2003, Excel 2003, Outlook 2003. This version is available only on new computers.

- **Microsoft Office Standard Edition 2003**   Word 2003, Excel 2003, PowerPoint 2003, and Outlook 2003.

- **Microsoft Office Student and Teacher Edition 2003**   Word 2003, Excel 2003, PowerPoint 2003, and Outlook 2003.

- **Microsoft Office Small Business Edition 2003**   Word 2003, Excel 2003, PowerPoint 2003, Outlook 2003, Publisher 2003, and Outlook 2003 with Business Contact Manager.

- **Microsoft Office Professional Edition 2003**   Word 2003, Excel 2003, PowerPoint 2003, Outlook 2003, Publisher 2003, Outlook 2003 with Business Contact Manager, and Access 2003.

One major change in the bundling of Office is the exclusion of FrontPage. Although FrontPage has been included in the Professional edition of previous versions of Office, it's now being sold only as a stand-alone product. Many Office users will opt to upgrade or purchase this application concurrently with their Office edition, however, because of the ever-increasing importance of having a web presence and the integration between products. Thus, FrontPage is covered in this book.

With the exception of FrontPage, applications that are not currently packaged in any of the suites have not been included in this book. These applications include Visio, OneNote, and Project. InfoPath, although included in the volume-licensed Professional Enterprise edition, is also not covered because of its currently limited audience.

How This Book Is Organized

Microsoft Office 2003: The Complete Reference is divided into ten parts, as follows:

Part I: Common Office 2003 Elements

The first portion of the book introduces the various applications in Office and common elements, such as entering text, spell checking, using find and replace, and adding graphics.

Part II: Word Processing

Word 2003 is the most-used application in the Office suite. Learn how to format and edit text, use styles and templates, add tables, and lay out your text in columns. Working on a large, multichapter document? You'll learn how to let Word generate everything from a table of contents to the index, and even manage your page numbering across several documents.

Part III: Spreadsheets

This section introduces Excel 2003. Discover how to get the most out of this powerful program using formulas and functions. Learn how to create detailed charts, graphs, and PivotTables that give you a different perspective on your data.

Part IV: Presentations

PowerPoint 2003 lets you add graphics, sound, and special effects to make your presentations stand out from the crowd. This program started out as the purview of the business realm, but it's recently entered classrooms from elementary school to college.

Part V: Schedule and Contact Management

If your time is limited and your need to communicate is great, Outlook 2003 manages everything from e-mail to your appointment schedule to your address book. These chapters cover everything from automatically filtering the spam cluttering your Inbox to coordinating your meeting schedule.

Part VI: Databases

Access 2003 is a full-featured database application. Learn how to develop a simple table and query structure, add forms, and generate reports. Then pull it all together by creating a complete database application.

Part VII: Web and Print Layout

If web design is what you have in mind, FrontPage 2003 has everything you need to bring your vision to life. Learn how to create dynamic pages complete with rollover buttons without touching a line of HTML code. Publisher 2003 also produces web pages, along with brochures, business cards, and other print layouts.

Part VIII: Integration and Collaboration

Each of the Office applications is powerful in and of itself. Get them working together, and you have a system that will truly soar. This section shows you how to integrate Office applications. Office also helps you work with others, and these chapters tell you how to collaborate in your own office or on the Web.

Part IX: Macros and Visual Basic for Applications

Office contains solutions for almost anything you need, but you can almost always think of something more. By using macros and Visual Basic for Applications, you can extend the power of Office. This section shows you how.

Part X: Appendixes

Appendix A lists the keyboard shortcuts used in each application. This quick reference can save you time by keeping your hands on the keyboard instead of the mouse.

Appendix B explains XML, the new underpinnings of Office, making the integration of the Office programs better than ever and greatly increasing the adaptability of these applications to new purposes.

Conventions Used in This Book

The following conventions are used in *Microsoft Office 2003: The Complete Reference* in order to make it easier for you to follow the text and instructions:

- *Italic type* introduces a new term or phrase.

- SMALL CAPITAL LETTERS are used for keys to press on the keyboard, such as CTRL-S to save a file. In this example, you would press the S key while holding down the CTRL (CONTROL) key.

- `Monospace font is used for field code and HTML code examples.`

- Menu selections are separated with a pipe (|) symbol, such as File | Save. In this example, click on the File menu, then choose Save from that menu.

PART

I

Common Office 2003 Elements

CHAPTER 1
Getting to Know Office 2003

CHAPTER 2
Customizing the Office
Environment

CHAPTER 3
Text Tools

CHAPTER 4
Drawing and Graphics Tools

Getting to Know Office 2003

Welcome to Microsoft Office 2003. The new version of Office is a great tool, and if you are using Office applications at your work or at home, you have a lot of power at your fingertips. How would you like an easy, integrated way to write documents, publish documents, publish Web pages, manage data, and even keep up with e-mail and your calendar? You can do all of this in Microsoft Office 2003, and that's only the beginning.

This book is designed to be your complete reference to Office 2003. In these pages, you'll learn how to use Office's features and functions and how to get the most from this complex software. Before you get started, however, it's a good idea to take a broad look at the applications available in Microsoft Office, as well as a few tips about installation. We'll cover those issues in this chapter, so let's get started.

The Office Suite of Programs

Office is a *suite* of programs, meaning there are several applications available within the Office family. Rather than trying to create one mammoth application that does everything you might ever want, Office contains a number of applications that focus on certain tasks. However, the good news is that the applications are now very streamlined. The Word interface looks similar to the PowerPoint interface, and so forth. Once you have used one application, you'll have a good idea how to use the next application because they all have the same look and feel.

As a general rule, Office 2003 applications all contain the same interface features. As you can see in Figure 1-1, Word contains menus and toolbars along the top that allow you to access different functions. You see a work area where you actually create your document, and you have a task pane on the right side of the application that gives you a variety of options, depending on what you are doing at the moment. You'll see this same interface time and time again, whether you are working in Word, PowerPoint, FrontPage, and so forth. Also, the buttons and menus you find will be the same or similar between applications. The streamlined approach makes your learning curve less painful and helps integrate all of the Office applications.

So, what is available in the Office suite of applications? The following sections give you a quick overview.

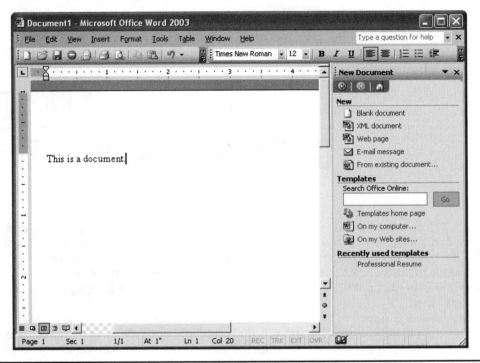

FIGURE 1-1   Word's interface, which shows many of the standard Office interface elements

Microsoft Word

Microsoft's flagship application, Word, has been extremely popular over the years. Word allows you to create a variety of documents and different kinds of files. Many corporations use it as the default word processing program; in fact, this book was written in Word.

Using Word, you can create standard documents that you can format in any way you want. You can control bullets, numbering, fonts, colors, styles—you can even format borders and shading and use backgrounds. You can insert photos, clip art, diagrams, as well as files created in other Office applications. For example, you can cut and paste a web page and place it in a Word document or an Excel chart.

Word also provides you with a number of templates and wizards you can use to create all kinds of documents quickly and easily. Figure 1-2 shows you the Templates window, and as you can see, you can access standard templates as well as different wizards from a variety of categories.

You can then use the template to quickly customize your own content and create a nicely formatted document. As you can see in Figure 1-3, you can create a résumé using the Professional Resume template. Of course, you are free to build documents from scratch, but the template options can save you a lot of time.

Word also contains great collaboration features. You can have several people work on the same document, track their additions and changes, then merge those changes into one

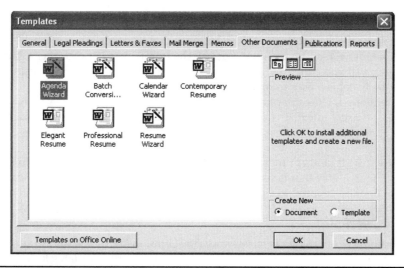

FIGURE 1-2   Word templates available for your use

document. You can also collaborate online and create shared workspace. These features make Word easy and flexible to use in professional environments.

Of course, you can do much, much more with Microsoft Word, and you can learn more about these features and many more in Part II of the book.

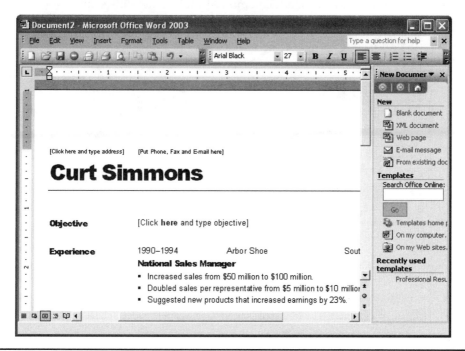

FIGURE 1-3   The Professional Resume template

Microsoft Excel

The popular spreadsheet application, Excel, allows you to create custom workbooks, enter data into a spreadsheet, and basically "crunch" the numbers you need. It is a great way to track business profit and expenses, and create a variety of reports and charts using your data. In other words, Excel is a way to manage data and make it usable.

As we mentioned, Office applications have a streamlined interface. And as you can see in Figure 1-4, the Excel interface is very similar to Word and other applications. You'll find many of the same features, such as table and cell formatting options and team collaboration features.

Excel provides all kinds of mathematical functions and features so you can use and manipulate data in a way that is useful to you. It's a handy but complex application, and Part III of the book is devoted to Excel. You can learn all you need to know in Part III.

Microsoft PowerPoint

Using PowerPoint, you can create slide show presentations with text and graphics, as you can see in Figure 1-5. Choose from any number of PowerPoint templates for an automatic, smooth presentation that maintains font and graphic continuity between slides. You can even insert audio and video clips into your presentations and play them directly on screen in front of a live audience.

PowerPoint gives you the flexibility to create custom presentations using your graphics, or you can use PowerPoint templates and slide layout options that choose a slide design and layout automatically—all you have to do is enter your text, charts, photos, and other multimedia. You can add sound clips that play with your presentations, and you can easily use transitions and slide effects for added emphasis. Like other Office applications, you can

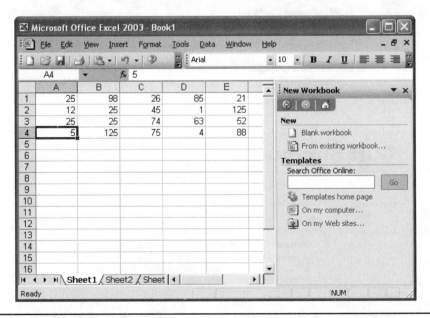

FIGURE 1-4   Excel interface

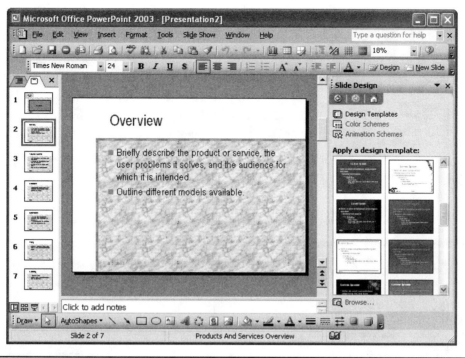

FIGURE 1-5   PowerPoint interface

also use collaborative sharing and a shared workspace so that several people can work on a presentation at the same time. With PowerPoint's Slide Sorter view, you can easily rework presentations and reorganize them just by dragging slides around. If writing presentations isn't your "thing," PowerPoint can help you there too. An AutoContent wizard can help you outline your ideas and basically create a presentation for you, telling you what to say on each bulleted point!

Once you are done, you can save your presentation either for live presentation or online use. There are a number of different Save As options that will meet whatever output needs you may have, as you'll learn in Part IV.

Microsoft Outlook

Outlook has often been called "e-mail software," but in reality, Outlook is a powerful information management program. It not only does your e-mail, but it also allows you to manage contacts, manage your calendar, manage task lists, and much more.

At the heart of Outlook is e-mail. Using Outlook, you can easily send and receive e-mail, attachments, and related data. Outlook 2003 has a more streamlined design, where you can see your mailboxes, such as the Inbox, Outbox, Sent Items, Deleted Items, and other folders you have made, and you can see your currently selected mailbox and any currently selected message. As you can see in Figure 1-6, this approach gives you a single information interface. Outlook keeps track of all your received and sent mail (along with deleted mail), and it has new junk mail filtering capabilities that can help you control annoying spam mail.

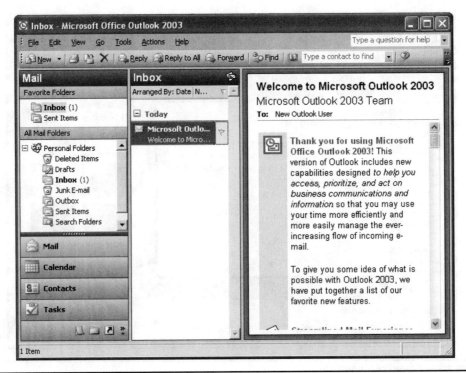

FIGURE 1-6   Outlook—your information interface

Along with e-mail features, Outlook also contains a Calendar feature, shown in Figure 1-7. Use the calendar to enter appointments and events. Outlook can keep up with them for you and notify you before they occur. You can allow other users to manage and update your calendar, and you can import calendar data from different PDAs. You also have Contacts and Tasks features that allow you to easily keep up with people and the tasks that you need to accomplish. Overall, Outlook is personal information management at its best, and you can find out all about Outlook in Part V of this book.

Microsoft Access

One of the problems in businesses has always been the management of information. How do you realistically manage a product catalog that contains over a thousand elements, or how do you maintain business contacts and customer contacts that number in the tens of thousands? The answer is with a database, and Microsoft Access is Office's answer to the database dilemma.

Access is a full-scale database that allows you to create different databases to store information, shown in Figure 1-8. Using the database, you can run queries, create forms and reports, and even publish a database application in a variety of ways. Along with FrontPage, you can make a database available on a web site.

The overall purpose of a database is to contain information, then manipulate that information in a way that is useful, and Access does just that. You can find out all about Access in Part VI of this book.

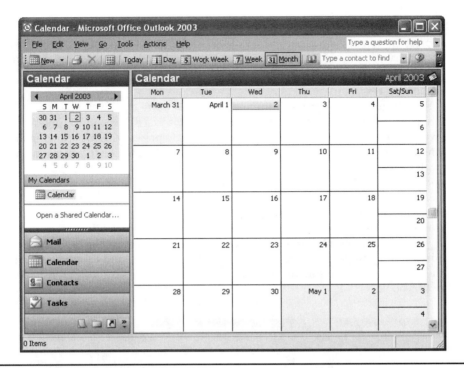

FIGURE 1-7   Outlook's Calendar feature

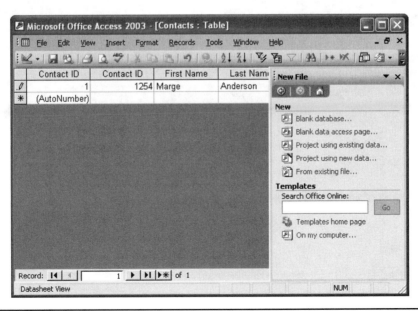

FIGURE 1-8   Access interface

Microsoft FrontPage

FrontPage 2003, shown in Figure 1-9, is a popular web site/web page development program. In FrontPage 2003, Microsoft has included a number of new features that make publishing web sites and pages from FrontPage easier, and we see the official end of "FrontPage Server Extensions" in this revision.

Using FrontPage, you can create entire web sites and individual web pages using a standard "what you see is what you get" (WYSIWYG) interface. Basically, FrontPage works a lot like word processing programs in that you can create pages without knowing HTML. This feature allows professionals and novice web masters alike to create interesting and effective web pages.

The good news about FrontPage is that it is easy for the beginner, but robust enough for the experienced web developer. You can use FrontPage templates and graphics features to quickly create an effective web page, where you basically plug in the information you want. However, advanced users who want to work with code can do so in Code view or even a split pane view, where Code and Design view are combined, as shown in Figure 1-10. Combine these features along with many more helpful publishing options, and FrontPage is a great application for web page and site development. You can learn more about FrontPage in Part VII of this book.

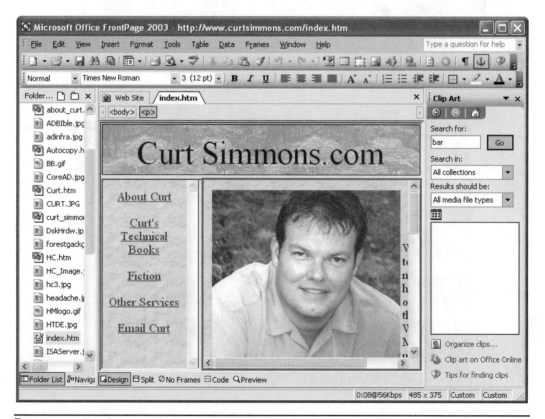

FIGURE 1-9   FrontPage interface

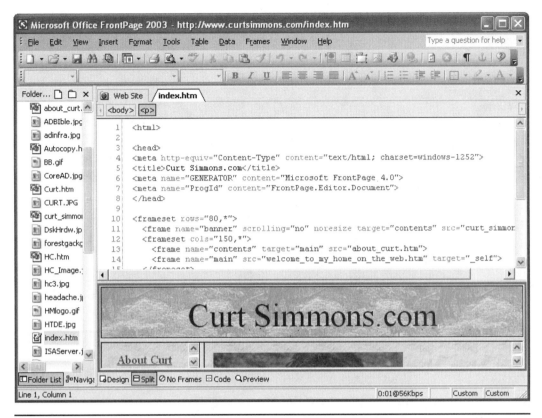

FIGURE 1-10   Split pane view in FrontPage

Microsoft Publisher

Microsoft Publisher is just that—software that allows you to publish information, such as documents and books that are printed, web sites, e-mail newsletters, design sets for calendars and related products, stationery, fund-raiser posters, and many others. All of the mentioned options here can be created from scratch or by using a wizard to guide you through the process.

Let's say that your organization needs to print a 20-page reference manual. The manual includes text and graphics, and you need a way to create a master document that you send to a printer for printing. Publisher is the product you use. Using Publisher, you can create the print and web products you might want, but you can finely control their overall placement and look. As you can see in Figure 1-11, we are creating a custom business card. Using business card paper, we can print these cards, and they will look as good as cards that come from a professional printer.

Publisher gives you a number of options and features, and you can easily cut and paste data between Publisher and other Office applications. Find out more about Publisher in Part VII of the book.

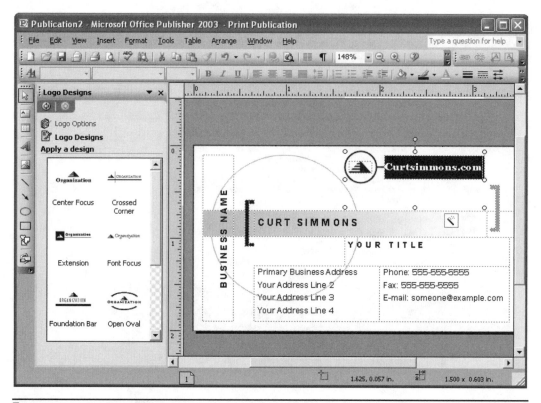

FIGURE 1-11   Publisher interface

Collaborative Tools

There's another aspect of Office we'd like to mention—collaborating with your colleagues. In addition to the tools within the various applications for reviewing, protecting, and e-mailing your work, Office also offers SharePoint Services. You can learn more about this in Part VIII of the book. SharePoint is software designed to work with a company's intranet server. Using SharePoint, you can publish data from FrontPage on the intranet server; but more importantly, SharePoint provides a way for different groups within an organization to work on a project from the web server. In other words, SharePoint provides a single point for shared data, including web data and different forms and databases.

Installing Office 2003

The installation of Office 2003 is rather straightforward. A wizard walks you through the steps and installs and configures the software for you. However, before you start installing Office 2003, make sure that the computer(s) on which you install Office contain the minimum installation requirements. Meeting or exceeding the minimum requirements ensures that Office can be installed and that it will function in a suitable manner.

So, what do you need in order to install Microsoft Office? The following list tells you the minimum requirements.

- A PC with a Pentium 133 MHz or higher processor (or equivalent). A Pentium III is recommended.
- Windows 2000 operating system with Service Pack 3 or later, or Windows XP. Windows XP is recommended.
- 64MB of RAM for the operating system and an additional 8MB of RAM for each Office application that will be run simultaneously. 128MB of RAM is recommended (and in truth, much more is helpful).
- 245MB of hard disk space. Depending on the installation options you choose, you may need more available disk space as well.
- CD-ROM drive.
- Super VGA (800x600) or higher resolution monitor with 256 colors.
- Microsoft mouse or compatible pointing device.
- Tablet PC pen required for capturing digital ink.

NOTE   *The requirements listed are minimum requirements published by Microsoft. Ideally, your computer should exceed these minimum requirements, or you may experience slow performance when using Office applications.*

Once you are sure the computer you want to install Office on meets these minimum requirements, you can start the installation by simply inserting the Office 2003 installation CD and following these steps:

1. On the Office 2003 welcome screen that appears, click Next.
2. On the Product Key window, enter the product key found on the back of your CD case. (The key is not case sensitive.) Once you have entered the key, click the Next.

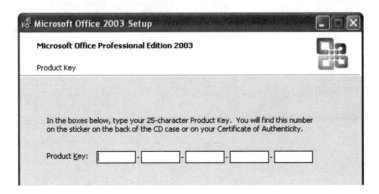

3. On the User Information window, enter your name, initials, and organization (if any), and click Next.

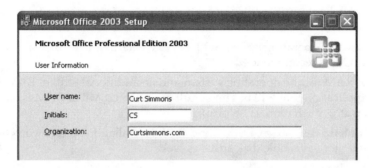

4. The End-User License Agreement window appears. Read the agreement and click the "I accept the terms in the License Agreement" check box, and click Next. Setup will not continue unless you agree with the terms.

5. In the Type of Installation window, the Typical option is selected by default. This installs the most commonly used components. However, you are free to choose a complete installation, minimal, or custom installation. Also notice at the bottom of the page that you can configure a different folder or location for Office to install to. By default, Office installs in C:\Program Files\Microsoft Office. Make your selections and click Next.

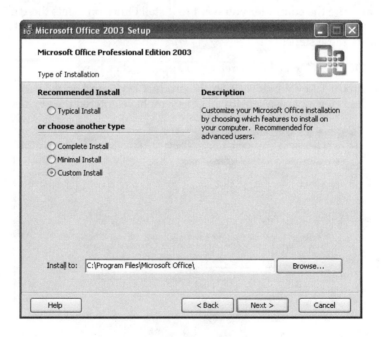

6. If you choose Custom Install in step 5, you'll get a custom installation window where you can choose the applications that you want to install. You can customize different options within those applications as well. Make your selections and click Next.

7. A summary window appears, telling you what is about to be installed. Review the summary window and click Back to make changes, or Install to continue with the installation.

8. The wizard installs Office on your computer. Click Finish when the installation is complete.

NOTE   *At any time, you can change the Office components that are installed. Just insert the installation CD back into the CD-ROM drive. A window will appear allowing you to modify or uninstall. Choose Modify and make any desired changes.*

Getting Office Help

One of the best ways to get help with Microsoft Office is in this book—after all, that's why we wrote it. However, we can't solve every problem you might experience (unless you want

FIGURE 1-12   Example Help window

this book to be the size of a subcompact car). So, what should you do when you have a question or problem with an Office application that you can't solve?

First of all, always check the applications' help files, as shown in Figure 1-12. Just click the Help menu, and you can access local help files as well as help files from Microsoft.com. You can see an entire index of documentation, or you can enter a search to narrow your scope. Any help results come to you in the task pane. Selecting an item in the help files opens a Help window where you can read the topic and print it if you like.

You can also get help directly at http://support.microsoft.com. The Microsoft Support site is a searchable database of known issues and problems that is available for Office as well as other Microsoft products. You may find the answer to specific problems right here. Finally, you can find newsgroups, discussion boards, and other web sites on the Internet that are available to help you. Just type **Microsoft Office** into any search engine to locate helpful sites.

Customizing the Office Environment

To use Office most productively and comfortably, you'll probably need to customize it. This chapter discusses the range of customization options that Office provides. These options include customizing toolbars and menus; setting Smart Tag options; using the AutoCorrect, spell checker, and grammar checker features to improve your documents; setting accessibility options; and using Office on Tablet PCs.

Customizing Toolbars and Menus

Your first step in customizing Office should be to customize toolbars and menus in the applications you use most. You can also customize keyboard shortcuts in Word.

Start by choosing Tools | Customize from Word or PowerPoint (these applications offer the most options) and choosing basic options on the Options tab of the Customize dialog box.

On this tab, you can choose the following options:

- Whether to display the Standard toolbar and Formatting toolbar on one row or on separate rows

- Whether to display full menus immediately all the time, or to display full menus after a short delay of displaying personalized menus (menus that contain the commands you use most frequently)

- Whether to display large toolbar icons (or regular-size toolbar icons)

- Whether to list font names in their font on the Font drop-down menu or in a standard font (which may display faster and which uses less memory)

- Whether to display ScreenTips on toolbars and (in Word, PowerPoint, and Outlook) whether to show shortcut keys in ScreenTips

- Which menu animations to use when displaying menus

Displaying, Moving, and Customizing Toolbars

By default, most of the Office applications display the Standard toolbar and the Formatting toolbar when you open them. You can display any of the other general-purpose toolbars that are available in the application at any time.

Other toolbars are reserved for specific operations. The applications display these toolbars as necessary when you start one of those operations. For example, Outlook displays the E-mail toolbar when you're creating an e-mail; this toolbar isn't available at other times (because you don't need it for other tasks). In some of the applications, you can display most of the toolbars from the Toolbars tab of the Customize dialog box.

The toolbars in the Office applications contain the buttons that Microsoft's usability testers found most useful. You may well prefer to have different buttons on your most-used toolbars. Alternatively, you can create a custom toolbar that contains only the buttons you need.

Displaying and Moving Toolbars

You can toggle the display of a toolbar by choosing View | Toolbars and selecting the toolbar from the submenu, or by right-clicking a displayed toolbar (or the menu bar) and selecting the toolbar from the context menu.

By default, the Office applications display the most-used toolbars in a *docked* position— anchored to one side (usually the top) of the application window. You can reposition a docked toolbar, or the menu bar, by dragging the dotted handle at its left end (in a horizontal configuration) or upper end (in a vertical configuration). When you have two toolbars positioned on the same row (as the Standard and Formatting toolbars are positioned by default), you can resize a toolbar by dragging its handle.

Toolbars and the menu bar can also *float* in the application window. The Office applications automatically display some toolbars as floating rather than docked. You can dock a floating toolbar by dragging it to one of the edges of the application window or by double-clicking its title bar. You can make a docked toolbar float by dragging it into the application window. You can resize a floating toolbar by dragging its borders.

The following illustration shows two docked toolbars and one floating toolbar.

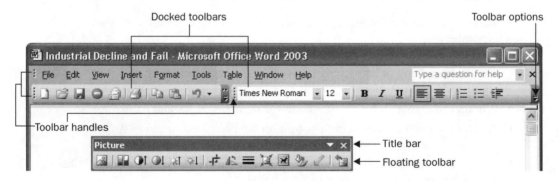

Customizing a Toolbar

Displaying, hiding, and repositioning toolbars only gets you so far. To get the most out of toolbars, you need to customize them. Your aim in customization should be to have those toolbars you display provide all the buttons you need most frequently in your work while taking up as little of your precious screen real estate as possible.

You can customize a toolbar in any of the following ways:

- Click the Toolbar Options button at the right end or lower end, click Add or Remove Buttons, select the toolbar from the submenu if necessary, and then select and deselect the options on the menu of buttons to control which buttons are displayed.

- Hold down ALT, drag a button off a toolbar, and drop it in the document area of the application window to remove it.

- Hold down ALT and drag a button to a new location either on the same toolbar or on another toolbar. Hold down CTRL-ALT and drag to copy a button rather than move it.

- Right-click a displayed toolbar, and choose Customize to display the Customize dialog box, shown on the left in the following illustration. Display the Commands tab, shown on the right, select the appropriate category, and drag the command from the Commands list to the toolbar, menu, or context menu on which you want it to appear.

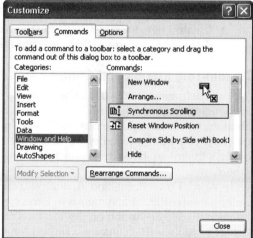

- Click Rearrange Commands on the Commands tab of the Customize dialog box, and use the options in the Rearrange Commands dialog box, shown on the left in the following illustration, to add, delete, or rearrange the buttons on a toolbar or the commands on a menu. Click Add and use the Add Command dialog box, shown on the right in the following illustration, to add a command. Choose the Menu Bar item in the Categories list box to put one of the top-level menus (for example, File, Edit, or View) on the menu or toolbar you're rearranging.

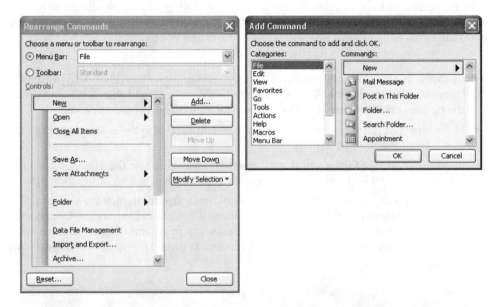

- Create a new toolbar by clicking the New button on the Toolbars tab of the Customize dialog box (shown earlier) and entering the name in the New Toolbar dialog box.

Customizing Menus and Context Menus

You can customize menus in all the Office applications by using the same techniques as for customizing toolbars: use the Rearrange Commands dialog box, or display the Commands tab of the Customize dialog box, and then drag the command to the menu or context menu on which you want it to appear. When you drag the command over a menu, the application displays the menu. Drag the command to the appropriate position on the menu and drop it there.

In Word, PowerPoint, and Access, you can customize the context menus as well. (You can't customize the context menus in Excel or Outlook.) To customize a shortcut menu, select the Shortcut Menus option on the Toolbars tab of the Customize dialog box. The application displays a toolbar that contains a button for each category of context menu offered by the application. Drag a command from the Commands tab of the Customize toolbar to the menu category, then to the menu, then to the appropriate position on the menu, and drop it there. The following illustration shows an example of using the Shortcut Menus toolbar to add the Copy Ink As Text command to the Ink Comment context menu in Word.

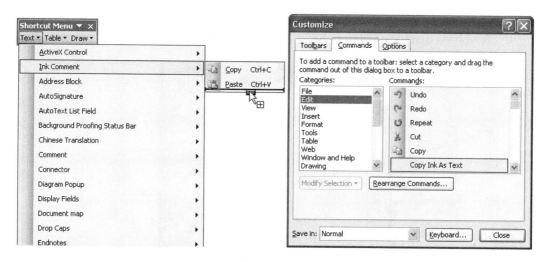

Controlling the Appearance of a Menu Item or Toolbar Button

The Office applications also let you control the appearance of a menu item or toolbar button. To do so, display the Customize dialog box, right-click the toolbar button or menu item you want to affect, and choose the appropriate option from the shortcut menu. (Alternatively, click Modify Selection on the Commands tab of the Customize dialog box and use the resulting menu, or use the Modify Selection command in the Rearrange Commands dialog box.)

These are the main changes you can make:

- Reset a built-in button or menu item to its default settings.

- Delete the button or menu item.

- Change the name for an item that includes text in the display style. Type the name in the Name box. Type an ampersand (&) before the character you want to use as the access key (the hotkey) for the menu item.

- Change the button image by using the Change Button Image submenu, the Edit Button Image command, the Paste Button Image command, or the Reset Button Image command. Use the Copy Button Image command to copy the image from the selected button for use on another button.

- Choose the display style for the item: Default Style (text for menus, button for a toolbar), Text Only (Always), Text Only (in Menus), or Image and Text.

- Assign a hyperlink to the button or command.

Customizing Keyboard Shortcuts in Word

If you're used to working with the keyboard, you may want to customize Office with keyboard shortcuts so that you can work fast without taking your hands off the keyboard. You can do this in Word but not in the other applications.

To customize keyboard shortcuts in Word:

1. Choose Tools | Customize to display the Customize dialog box.

2. Click the Keyboard button on the Commands tab to display the Customize Keyboard dialog box, shown here with customization underway:

3. In the Save Changes In drop-down list, choose the customization context: Normal (the global template), the active document, or the template attached to the active document (if the template is other than Normal).

   - Changes you make in the active document apply only to that document.
   - Changes you make in the template apply to all documents based on that template, unless a document has a setting that overrides it.
   - Changes you make to Normal apply to all documents, unless another global template that's loaded, the active document's template, or the active document itself contains a setting that overrides it.

4. Select the category in the Categories list box, and then select the command in the Commands list box. You can assign keyboard shortcuts to any command, to a macro, to a font, to an AutoText entry, to a style, or to a symbol.

5. Click in the Press New Shortcut Key box, and then press the key combination you want to assign.

6. Check the Currently Assigned To readout to see if this keyboard combination is assigned to another item. If necessary, choose another keyboard combination.

7. Click Assign.

From the Customize Keyboard dialog box, you can click Remove to remove an existing keyboard shortcut, or click Reset All to reset all built-in keyboard combinations to their defaults.

NOTE   *Appendix A lists the most useful keyboard shortcuts in the Office applications.*

Setting Smart Tag Options

Smart Tags are pop-up buttons attached to certain types of information in the main Office applications. When you select the information (for example, a range of cells in Excel) or hover the mouse pointer in the right location, the Smart Tag's action button appears. You can then click the action button to display a menu of options for the item, as shown in these two examples:

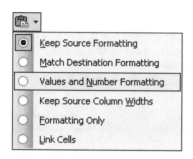

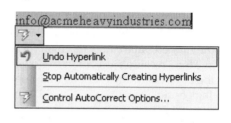

The choices on this menu depend on the item selected. For example, when you paste data in Excel, the Smart Tag offers you choices such as pasting the data, pasting the values, and pasting only the formatting; when you paste text in Word, the Smart Tag offers you choices such as keeping the source formatting, matching the destination formatting, keeping the text only, and displaying the Styles and Formatting task pane so you can apply another style manually.

To configure Smart Tags, choose Tools | AutoCorrect Options, and work on the Smart Tags tab of the AutoCorrect dialog box. The next illustration shows the Smart Tags tabs of the AutoCorrect dialog box for Word (on the left) and Excel (on the right).

These are the key options for controlling Smart Tags:

- To turn off Smart Tags, deselect the Label Data with Smart Tags option or the Label Text with Smart Tags option.

- To control which Smart Tags the application uses, select and deselect the options in the Recognizers list.

- To recheck the current file for Smart Tags, click the Check option (Recheck Document, Check Workbook, Check Presentation).

- To control whether the application embeds Smart Tags in the file, select or deselect the Embed Smart Tags in This Workbook option in Excel or the Embed Smart Tags in This Presentation option in PowerPoint. In Word, click Save Options to display the Save tab of the Options dialog box; then select or deselect the Embed Smart Tags option.

- To control how Smart Tags are displayed in Excel, choose the appropriate option in the Show Smart Tags As drop-down list. In Word, select the Show Smart Tag Active Buttons option to display Smart Tags.

AutoCorrect, Spell Checking, and Grammar Checking

Office includes powerful features for reducing the number of typos you make, alerting you to those typos you do make, and helping you identify and fix problems with your grammar. Three of the most useful features—AutoCorrect, the spell checker, and the grammar checker—are implemented across most of the Office applications.

AutoCorrect

AutoCorrect is an automatic-correction feature that watches as you type and makes corrections when you type characters that match one of its entries. If you've worked with older word processing applications, you may remember glossaries. AutoCorrect's most useful aspect is essentially an automatic form of glossary. Word also includes manual glossaries, which are now called AutoText.

AutoCorrect is implemented in most of the Office applications. Word has the most extensive implementation, including formatted AutoCorrect entries.

Office stores text-only AutoCorrect entries centrally so each application can access them. The entries are stored in the MSO*nnnn*.acl file in the *%userprofile%*\Application Data\Microsoft\Office folder, where *%userprofile%* is the path to your user profile (for example, c:\Documents and Settings\Jane Petersen\Application Data\Microsoft\Office) and *nnnn is the numeric designation for the localization of Office you're using. For example, U.S. English AutoCorrect entries are stored in the MSO1033.acl file.*

TIP   *If you use AutoCorrect extensively, back up your ACL file. If you use multiple computers, you may want to copy the ACL file from one computer to another so you don't need to re-create AutoCorrect entries manually.*

Configuring AutoCorrect

To configure AutoCorrect and create and delete entries, you work in the AutoCorrect dialog box. The number of tabs in the AutoCorrect dialog box depends on the application: five tabs in Word, three in Excel, two in PowerPoint, and a single tab in Access and Outlook. Display the AutoCorrect dialog box as follows:

- In Word, Excel, PowerPoint, and Access, choose Tools | AutoCorrect Options.

- In Outlook, choose Tools | Options, click the Spelling tab, and then click AutoCorrect Options.

NOTE   *By default, Outlook uses Word as its e-mail editor and inherits those of Word's AutoCorrect options that apply to Outlook as well. If you choose not to use Word as your e-mail editor, you need to select the option Use AutoCorrect When Word Isn't the E-mail Editor on the Spelling tab of the Options dialog box in order to use AutoCorrect.*

For each application, AutoCorrect offers five self-explanatory options for correcting two initial capitals, capitalizing the first letter of each sentence, capitalizing the names of days, correcting accidental use of Caps Lock, and replacing text as you type. Setting these options is a matter of personal preference. Many people turn off the Capitalize First Letter of Sentence option because they find it annoying when they're typing notes or composing fragments of sentences.

The key option is Replace Text as You Type, which controls AutoCorrect's main feature— scanning for entries as you type and replacing them with their designated replacement text. You'll seldom want to turn this option off, unless you're using someone else's account on a computer, and you find AutoCorrect unexpectedly replacing text you type.

AutoCorrect also offers the following application-specific options:

- Word, Excel, and PowerPoint offer the Show AutoCorrect Options Buttons option, which provides in-document buttons for undoing corrections and configuring AutoCorrect. (See "Undoing an AutoCorrect Correction," a little later in this chapter.)

- Word and PowerPoint offer the self-explanatory Capitalize First Letter of Table Cells option.

- Word offers the Correct Keyboard Setting option, which detects when the language you're typing is different from the language the text is configured as using and switches to the language you're typing. This option can be useful when you're working on a document in multiple languages.

- Word offers the Automatically Use Suggestions from the Spelling Checker option. If you select this option, AutoCorrect uses the spell checker's suggestion only when AutoCorrect itself has no match and the spell checker provides a single match.

Understanding How AutoCorrect Works

AutoCorrect is mostly intuitive—but not quite.

As you type, AutoCorrect examines each character. When you type a character that typically means you've finished typing a word, AutoCorrect compares the word (or, more precisely, the group of characters) against its list of entries. If the word matches an entry,

AutoCorrect substitutes the replacement text for the word. If the word doesn't match an entry, AutoCorrect checks the word and its predecessor together to see if they match an entry. If so, AutoCorrect substitutes the replacement text. If not, AutoCorrect checks those two words with the word before them—and so on until it has checked all the complete words in the preceding 31 characters, at which point it gives up.

As you'll infer from this, AutoCorrect entries can be up to 31 characters long and can contain spaces and punctuation. The replacement text for an entry can be up to 255 characters long—plenty to enable you to enter a short paragraph or two. (If you try to use more than 255 characters, AutoCorrect warns you that it will need to shorten the replacement text.)

No entry's name should be a real word in any language you use; otherwise AutoCorrect will replace that word each time you try to use it. The exception is if you want to prevent yourself from using a particular word. For example, if the word "purchase" sends your boss into conniptions, you can define AutoCorrect entries to change words based on "purchase" (purchase, purchases, purchased, purchasing, and so on) to their counterparts based on "buy." AutoCorrect will then censor your writing gently and automatically.

AutoCorrect considers various characters to mean you've finished typing a word. As you'd guess, these characters include spaces, punctuation, tabs, carriage returns, line feeds (SHIFT-ENTER), and page breaks (CTRL-ENTER). You might not guess that various symbols (such as % and #) trigger AutoCorrect checks, but they do.

Creating and Deleting AutoCorrect Entries

AutoCorrect comes with a large number of built-in entries that range from simple typos (for example, "abotu" instead of "about"), to basic grammatical mistakes (for example, "may of been" instead of "may have been"), and some symbols (for example, AutoCorrect corrects (c) to a copyright symbol, ©). You can add as many custom entries as you need. You can also replace or delete the built-in entries if you find them inconvenient.

To work with AutoCorrect entries, choose Tools | AutoCorrect Options to display the AutoCorrect dialog box. (In Outlook, choose Tools | Options, click the Spelling tab, and then click AutoCorrect Options.) Then work as follows:

- To add an AutoCorrect entry, type the entry name in the Replace text box and the replacement text in the With text box; then click Add. You can speed up the process in two ways. First, you can paste text you've previously copied into either of these text boxes. Second, you can make AutoCorrect automatically enter the replacement text in the With text box by selecting it in your document, workbook, or other file before issuing the Tools | AutoCorrect Options command.

NOTE   *If an AutoCorrect entry with the same name already exists, AutoCorrect prompts you to decide whether to overwrite it.*

- To delete an AutoCorrect entry, select it in the list box (scroll or type down to it), and click Delete.
- To change the name of an existing AutoCorrect entry, select it in the list to enter its name in the Replace text box and its contents in the With text box. Type the new name and click Add to create a new entry with that name and contents. Then delete the old entry.

In Word, you can also create AutoCorrect entries from misspelled words identified by the spell checker:

- Right-click a word the spell checker has flagged with its red underline, and then choose the correct word from the AutoCorrect submenu.
- From the Spelling and Grammar dialog box, select the correct word in the Suggestions list box, and then click the AutoCorrect button.

When you take either of these actions, Word corrects the term in the text and adds an AutoCorrect entry for it.

Undoing an AutoCorrect Correction

When AutoCorrect makes a correction that you don't want to keep, you can undo it by issuing an Undo command. (For example, press CTRL-Z or click the Undo button.) But if you were typing fast at the time AutoCorrect chose to kick in, you might need to undo a lot of typing (or other editing) before you can undo the AutoCorrect action.

To make corrections easier, Word, PowerPoint, Excel, and Outlook track corrections applied by AutoCorrect. When you hover your mouse pointer over an AutoCorrect correction, the application displays an AutoCorrect Options button that you can click to display a menu of AutoCorrect options. The options vary depending on the AutoCorrect action performed: typical choices are to undo this instance of the correction, to stop auto-capitalizing the first letter of sentences, to stop correcting this AutoCorrect entry (for the future), and to display the AutoCorrect dialog box (Control AutoCorrect Options) so you can adjust other options.

Tips for Using AutoCorrect Effectively

AutoCorrect is wonderful for fixing typos as you type. But if you work extensively with text, consider using AutoCorrect to accelerate your typing by defining AutoCorrect entries for long words, phrases, sentences, or even paragraphs you use frequently.

You can also use AutoCorrect for enforcing consistency. For example, if you work for the Vice President for Sales and Marketing but tend to type the title as "Vice President of Sales and Marketing," create an AutoCorrect entry to change "Vice President of Sales and" to "Vice President for Sales and." AutoCorrect will then correct the error for you automatically when you make it. Note that the phrase is too long to include "Marketing" in the AutoCorrect entry. But this has a hidden benefit—AutoCorrect will fire as you go on to type "Marketing." Otherwise, if the entry included "Marketing," and you typed the wrong phrase and no further, AutoCorrect wouldn't fire.

To continue the previous example, you should create a shorter AutoCorrect entry (called something like "bossjob") that expands to your boss's correct title. The shorter entry will save you keystrokes and capitalization.

If you create many AutoCorrect entries, remembering entries you use less frequently may be a problem. But there's nothing to stop you from creating multiple entries for the same replacement text.

Adding and Deleting AutoCorrect Exceptions

You can also define AutoCorrect *exceptions*—terms that you don't want AutoCorrect to automatically correct. AutoCorrect exceptions work in Word, Excel, PowerPoint, Access, and Outlook. All these applications provide first-letter exceptions (for abbreviations such as Corp. and for similar terms that end with punctuation) and initial-caps exceptions (for example, IDs). Word also provides "other exceptions," which let you define exceptions that fall outside those categories.

To add and delete exceptions, click the Exceptions button on the AutoCorrect tab of the AutoCorrect dialog box, and work in the AutoCorrect Exceptions dialog box.

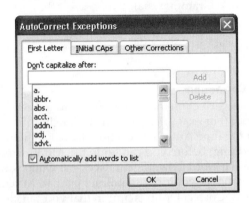

Creating Formatted AutoCorrect Entries in Word

In Word (and in Outlook, when you're using Word as the e-mail editor), you can also create formatted AutoCorrect entries. These can be text entries that contain formatting, entries that consist of graphics, or both. For example, you could create a formatted AutoCorrect entry that included your company name, address, and logo.

NOTE *Word stores formatted AutoCorrect entries in your Normal template (Normal.dot). Avoid creating large numbers of graphical AutoCorrect entries, because doing so can bloat the Normal template and make it slow to load.*

To create a formatted AutoCorrect entry:

1. Enter the text and any graphics in a document, and apply formatting as needed.

2. Select the formatted items and choose Tools | AutoCorrect Options.

3. Make sure the Formatted Text option in the Replace Text as You Type section of the AutoCorrect tab is selected. For a graphic, Word selects this option automatically. For formatted text that doesn't include a paragraph mark, you sometimes need to select it yourself.

4. Type the name for the entry. Don't duplicate the name for an unformatted entry—that's a recipe for confusion.

5. Click OK.

> **TIP**   *If you need to insert signatures in faxes you send from your computer, scan a signature and save it as an AutoCorrect entry so you can enter it quickly. (If you don't have a scanner but your computer can receive faxes, fax yourself a sheet of signatures. Then use a graphics application to cut out the signature that has come through best, and save it as a separate file.)*

Spell Checking

Spelling is a great task for computerization, because any given word is spelled either correctly or incorrectly: there are essentially no gray areas. Office includes a powerful spell checker that enables you to identify and correct any misspelled words in your documents, worksheets, presentations, messages, and databases.

Running a Spell Check

The spell checker is largely self-explanatory. You launch it by clicking the Spelling button on the toolbar, choosing Tools | Spelling and Grammar from the main menu, or pressing F7. The spell checker searches for spelling errors and displays a Spelling dialog box or a Spelling and Grammar dialog box with suggestions and options if it finds errors. The following illustration shows an example of a Spelling and Grammar dialog box and a Spelling dialog box. These dialog boxes enable you to ignore one or all instances of the disputed word, add it to the dictionary, change this instance to one of the words suggested, change all instances to one of the words suggested, and create an AutoCorrect entry to automatically correct the word to one of the words suggested.

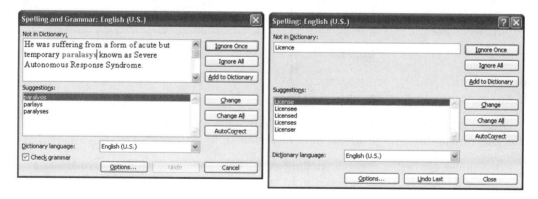

In Word, PowerPoint, and Outlook (when you're using Word as your e-mail editor), the spell checker automatically checks spelling as you type. When a word doesn't match any of the custom dictionaries loaded, the spell checker flags it with a wavy red underline. Right-click an underlined word to see a menu of suggested replacements and options (such as ignoring instances of this word or adding it to your dictionary so it won't be queried in future).

To turn off automatic spell-checking in Word, Outlook, and PowerPoint, choose Tools | Options, deselect the Check Spelling as You Type option on the Spelling tab of the Options dialog box, and click OK. (In PowerPoint, the tab is named Spelling and Style.)

Configuring Spell-Checking Options

Office's default settings for the spell checker work for many people, but you may want to customize them to better suit your needs. The Options dialog box (Tools | Options) gives you fine control over the settings for the spell checker. Depending on the application, you'll find the options on the Spelling & Grammar tab (Word), the Spelling and Style tab (PowerPoint), or the Spelling tab (Excel, Outlook, Access).

The options available depend on the application. The next illustration shows the Spelling & Grammar tab of Word's Options dialog box on the left and the Spelling tab of Excel's Options dialog box on the right.

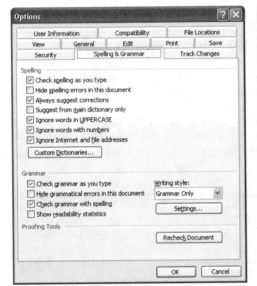
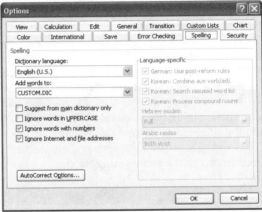

Access and Excel share the same set of options, while Word, PowerPoint, and Outlook offer different options. These are the most important options:

- Choosing whether to check spelling as you type and, if so, whether to hide all spelling errors. These options apply to Word and PowerPoint.

- Ignoring certain categories of text, such as uppercase words, words that include numbers, and Internet and file addresses (in other words, URLs and paths).

- Limiting suggestions to words from the main dictionary (instead of using additional dictionaries of your choice).

- Choosing which dictionary and language to use.

The purpose of most of these options is obvious, and setting them is a matter of personal preference.

NOTE *Word's Spelling and Grammar tab includes a section of Grammar options. These are discussed in an upcoming section.*

Using Custom Dictionaries

The spell checker uses a shared dictionary that's installed by default in the \Program Files\ Common Files\Microsoft Shared\Proof\ folder. (Which dictionary file it is depends on the language you're using.) This dictionary contains a wide range of words for that language, but you may well need to supplement it with special words and technical terms you use in your work. To do so, you can use one or more custom dictionaries.

A custom dictionary is a text file that contains a list of words the spell checker shouldn't query. Office starts you off with a custom dictionary named Custom.dic, which it stores in the %*userprofile*%\Application Data\Microsoft\Proof\ folder. Office's default setting is to add words to this dictionary when you issue an Add command from the spell checker.

To work with custom dictionaries, run Word and choose Tools | Options. On the Spelling & Grammar tab of the Options dialog box, click the Custom Dictionaries button. The Custom Dictionaries dialog box appears:

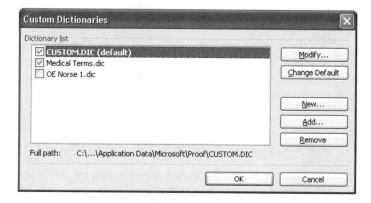

You can then take the following actions as needed:

- To specify which dictionaries to use, select and deselect the appropriate options.
- To make a different dictionary the default, select it and click Change Default.
- To create a new dictionary, click New, specify the name and location, and click OK.
- To remove a dictionary, select it, and then click the Remove button.
- To add an existing dictionary, click Add, navigate to and select the dictionary file, and then click OK.
- To edit a dictionary, select it, click the Modify button, and work in the resulting dialog box. You may want to edit a dictionary to remove incorrect words you've mistakenly added or to add words you know the spell checker will disagree with.

Grammar Checking

Word and Outlook let you check grammar as well as spelling. This is at best a mixed blessing. As you'll know from using it, the English language is extremely complex, flexible, and subtle. Even eloquent people can get horribly tangled up in grammar. Computerized grammar checkers can do even worse, because they don't understand the text they're analyzing—

they just examine the words in the text according to the complex parameters programmed into them and raise objections when they identify text that appears to match problems they've been taught to identify.

CAUTION *The grammar checker is no substitute for an editor—a human editor, that is. If you know your grammar is shaky, at the very least, consider asking a friend or colleague to quickly review any important documents you create. For documents you're publishing, use a professional editor. If you use the grammar checker, evaluate each of its suggestions carefully, because they may be completely wrong and may introduce errors into your documents.*

Turning Grammar Checking Off and On

Grammar checking is turned on by default in Word. The controls for turning grammar checking off and on are in the Grammar section of the Spelling & Grammar tab of Word's Options dialog box (Tools | Options).

These options are easy to understand. You can choose the following:

- Whether to have Word check grammar as you type. The grammar checker flags possible errors with a wavy green underline, but you can also choose to hide the display of grammatical errors. (Most people find that there's no point in checking grammar as you type and suppressing the display of any errors.)

NOTE *Checking grammar as you type requires a fair amount of computing power. By turning off this option, you may be able to improve Word's performance on an underpowered computer.*

- Whether to check grammar when you run a spelling check. Most people who use the grammar checker at all prefer to check grammar during a spelling check rather than as they type.

- Whether to have the grammar checker display readability statistics after completing a grammar check. Some of these statistics—which include average numbers of sentences per paragraph, words per sentence, and characters per word, and the percentage of passive sentences—can be useful: for example, you may realize your sentences or paragraphs are too long on average, or that you use too many passive sentences. The Flesch Reading Ease score and Flesch-Kincaid Grade Level score strike most users as irrelevant.

Running a Grammar Check

If you let Word check grammar as you type, right-click a flagged word or phrase to see suggested changes, as shown next:

Neither of them pay any tax.

To run a manual grammar check, start a spelling check by clicking the Spelling button on the toolbar, choosing Tools | Spelling and Grammar from the menu, or pressing F7. Word then offers grammar suggestions interspersed with the spelling suggestions.

Setting Grammar Options

If you use the grammar checker, choose options to suit your needs. First, on the Spelling & Grammar tab of the Options dialog box, specify what to check by choosing Grammar Only or Grammar & Style in the Writing Style drop-down list. Then click the Settings button and specify the details in the Grammar Settings dialog box.

Improving Accessibility

To make the Office applications easier to use, you may want to do some of the following:

- Change font sizes and colors to make text easier to read.

- Use the Zoom command (View | Zoom) to enlarge the display and make items more readable without changing the font size.

- Increase the size of toolbar buttons (choose Tools | Customize, and select the Large Icons option on the Options tab).

- Create customized toolbars, menus, and shortcut keys as discussed earlier in this chapter.

- Use an IntelliMouse or other wheeled pointing device to scroll and zoom. To scroll, move the wheel. To zoom, hold down CTRL and move the wheel.

- Use Windows accessibility features from the Start | All Programs | Accessories | Accessibility submenu or from the Accessibility Options dialog box (Start | Control Panel | Accessibility Options). For example, you can use Magnifier to zoom the computer screen; use the StickyKeys, FilterKeys, and ToggleKeys features to make Windows and Office more keyboard friendly; or use Narrator to read the contents of documents and interface elements aloud.

TIP   *For further accessibility options, visit the Microsoft Accessibility page on the Microsoft web site (www.microsoft.com/enable/).*

Using Office on Tablet PCs

Office provides fully integrated support for Tablet PC ink and for handwriting recognition. Ink use is mostly restricted to Tablet PCs themselves, although you can select, copy, and paste ink objects on non–Tablet PC computers as well. You can use the handwriting recognition features fully on other PCs—either awkwardly with a conventional mouse or trackball, or more effectively by using a digitizer tablet. You can enter text using handwriting recognition either via the Writing Pad (shown next) or via the Write Anywhere feature.

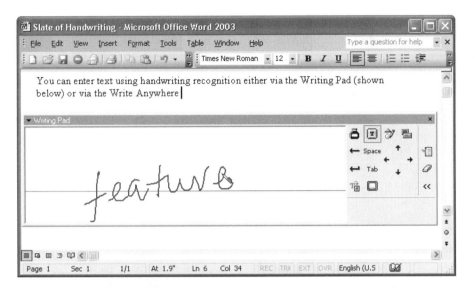

Ink enables you to handwrite notes into or onto Word documents, Excel worksheets, PowerPoint presentations, and Outlook messages. The ink items can become part of the document, or they can be attached as annotations. Depending on the type of work you're doing, you may find one capability more useful than the other. You can search through your handwritten notes, which makes the information in them much more accessible than it would otherwise be.

You can also use ink to create handwritten documents. For example, you might create handwritten slides in PowerPoint to give a presentation an air of informality or spontaneity. Likewise, by using ink, you can create a handwritten document in Word, and send a handwritten e-mail message using Outlook—should you ever need to.

Microsoft has designed Office's ink support to be as easy to understand as possible, so using ink is largely tap-and-go. You'll probably put more effort into configuring options for pen input and handwriting than figuring out how to use ink and handwriting.

Most of the features are implemented via the Language bar, which you can display in Windows XP by right-clicking the notification area and choosing Toolbars | Language Bar. (In Windows 2000, choose Start | Settings | Control Panel, double-click the Text Services icon, click Language Bar, select the option Show the Language Bar on the Desktop, and click OK twice.) The Language bar appears either docked on the taskbar next to the notification area or as a free-floating pane.

Configuring Options for Pen Input

To configure options for pen input and drawing:

1. Right-click the Language bar and choose Settings from the context menu to display the Text Services and Input Languages dialog box. (If the Language bar isn't displayed, display it as described in the previous section.)

2. Select the Writing Pad item or the Write Anywhere item, and click Properties to display the Handwriting Options dialog box.

3. Choose handwriting options, and click OK:

   • The Common tab contains options for specifying the ink color and pen width, configuring recognition, and controlling the toolbar layout.

   • The Writing Pad tab contains options for choosing the background color and number of lines on the writing pad.

4. Select the Drawing Pad item, and click Properties to display the Draw Options dialog box. Choose the pen color and width, and specify the layout for the toolbar.

5. Click OK to close the Draw Options dialog box, and then click OK to close the Text Services and Input Languages dialog box.

Using the Writing Tools

To use one of the writing tools, activate it from the Language bar. Click the icon for the currently selected writing tool, and then choose the other tool from the menu. You can have only one of the writing tools—the Writing Pad, Write Anywhere, the Drawing Pad, and the On-Screen Standard Keyboard or the On-Screen Symbol Keyboard—active at any time. Turning one of these tools on turns off whichever tool was previously active.

The writing tools are largely intuitive to use:

• The Writing Pad (shown earlier) provides a special area for writing, together with one or more lines to help keep your writing straight.

• The Write Anywhere feature lets you input text by scrawling anywhere in the application window.

• The On-Screen Standard Keyboard (shown on the left in the following illustration) has a QWERTY layout, including a Windows key and a Context Menu key; the On-Screen Symbol Keyboard (shown on the right) includes common symbols. Office displays either keyboard as fully opaque when the mouse pointer is over it, turns the keyboard semitransparent when it's inactive, and hides the keyboard when an application that doesn't accept pen input is active.

• The Drawing Pad enables you to create sketches and insert them in your documents.

Managing Files in Office

The Office applications handle file management in similar ways, but how much you leave to defaults and how much you manage independently will depend on your situation. On an intranet, others may manage some of these tasks for you; in a home office, you have full control. This chapter covers the creation and storage options that Office offers. You'll learn what the My Documents folder is and how to change its location; how to change the working folder for each of the Office applications if you don't want to use the defaults; and how to change the templates folders for Word, Excel, and PowerPoint.

Local network and Internet file management is discussed, and you'll learn how to create new files based on templates, how to create templates of your own, and how to track down files that go missing. Finally, we'll show you how to configure Office's recovery options to protect your data against crashes and power outages, and how to recover data from the recovery files.

Choosing Where to Store Your Files and Templates

This section discusses how to specify where to store the files you create and the templates you use in the Office applications. The options open to you will depend on whether you use Office on a standalone PC or on a networked PC.

- On a standalone PC that connects to the Internet, your storage options are a local drive or a web server that's running Microsoft's SharePoint Services. (If your standalone PC doesn't connect to the Internet, your choices are limited to your local drives.)

- On a networked PC, you'll be able to store files on local drives, on network drives, or on SharePoint web servers.

Coming to Grips with the My Documents Folder

Office's default storage location for data files is the folder designated by the My Documents shortcut, which appears directly on the Start menu in Windows XP and on the desktop in Windows 2000 Professional. The My Documents shortcut isn't a regular shortcut to a folder;

instead, it's a virtual folder (technically called a *shell extension*) that points to the location of your My Documents folder in Windows.

The default location for the folder to which the My Documents shortcut refers is the *%userprofile%*\My Documents folder, where *%userprofile%* is the environment variable that points to the path for your user profile. In a default setup, your user profile is stored in the C:\Documents and Settings*username*\ folder. So for a user named Jane Smith, the My Documents shortcut might refer to the C:\Documents and Settings\Jane Smith\My Documents folder.

You can rename the My Documents shell extension by using conventional Windows renaming techniques. (For example, select the My Documents item, press F2, type the new name, and press ENTER.) If you manage your own computer, you can change the folder to which your My Documents shell extension points. Right-click the My Documents item on the Start menu (in Windows XP) or on the desktop (in Windows 2000), and choose Properties from the shortcut menu. On the Target tab of the Properties dialog box, click the Move button, use the Browse for Folder dialog box to specify the folder you want to use, and click OK.

An administrator may have redirected your My Documents folder to a different location. For example, if you're using Office on Windows 2000 Professional or Windows XP Professional on a Windows-based network, an administrator may have redirected the My Documents folder to a network drive so that you automatically save your documents in a location that can be backed up centrally to prevent data loss.

Changing the Working Folder for the Office Applications

By default, each Office application starts with your My Documents folder as the working folder—the folder in which the application suggests saving files and from which the application suggests opening files. You can change the default folder so that each application starts with the working folder that suits you. If necessary, each application can use a different working folder. (Even if not, you need to set each working folder separately unless you want to use the default.)

To change the working folders, choose Tools | Options to display the Options dialog box, and then take the following steps:

- In Word, display the File Locations tab. Select the Documents item in the File Locations list box, and click Modify to display the Modify Location dialog box (a common Open dialog box in disguise). Select the folder and click OK.

- In Excel, display the General tab, and then type or paste the folder path in the Default File Location box.

TIP   *The easiest way to enter the folder path in Excel, PowerPoint, or Access is to open a Windows Explorer window to the folder, display the Address bar if it's not already displayed, select the folder's address, and issue a Copy command (for example, press CTRL-C). You can then paste the copied path into the Options dialog box.*

- In PowerPoint, display the Save tab, and then type or paste the folder path in the Default File Location box.
- In Access, display the General tab, and type or paste the folder path in the Default Database Folder box.

Click OK to close the Options dialog box and apply the change.

Changing the Templates Folders for Word, Excel, and PowerPoint

Word, Excel, and PowerPoint share common templates folders—one templates folder for local templates, and another for workgroup templates. To change the location in which the applications look for these templates:

1. In Word, choose Tools | Options to display the Options dialog box.
2. Click the File Locations tab to display it.
3. Select the User Templates item or the Workgroup Templates option as appropriate.
4. Click Modify, use the Modify Location dialog box to specify the folder, and click OK.
5. Click OK to close the Options dialog box.

The user templates are your templates: Microsoft installs a default set of templates for you, and you can add your own templates to them. The default location for these templates is your *%userprofile%*\Application Data\Microsoft\Templates folder. Other users can't see these templates unless you copy or move them to a shared folder.

The workgroup templates folder is intended for sharing templates with other users who use the same network or the same computer as you do. In a default setup, Office has no workgroup templates path set, so you need to specify the path if you intend to use workgroup templates. (In a corporate environment, an administrator may have designated a workgroup templates folder for you, so you may not need to set one yourself.)

Beyond the user templates folder and the workgroup templates folder, Office keeps its own stash of templates in a subfolder of the Program Files\Microsoft Office\Templates folder. The subfolder's name depends on the localization of Office you're using. For example, for the U.S. English localization, the subfolder is named 1033, the localization code. You can't save templates to Office's templates folder.

Using Office over a Network

Opening a file stored on a network drive can be as easy as opening a file stored on a local drive. To access a network drive, you can map a drive letter to the network drive, use the My Network Places folder to navigate to the network drive, or simply enter the appropriate universal naming convention (UNC) path to connect to the drive. The following sections discuss these options briefly.

When you try to access a network drive, you may need to supply the appropriate username and password in the Connect To dialog box, shown here. Select the Remember My Password option if you want to avoid typing your password each time you access the drive.

Entering a Universal Naming Convention (UNC) Path

For specifying network paths, Windows uses the *universal naming convention* (UNC), a widely used naming scheme. A UNC name starts with two backslashes (\\) followed by the server name, then another backslash, and then the name of the shared folder. For example, in the UNC path \\acmeheavysv303\public, acmeheavysv303 is the server name, and public is the name of the shared folder.

You can connect to a shared folder by entering the folder's UNC in Windows Explorer, in the Run dialog box (Start | Run), or in a common dialog box. (For example, enter the UNC in the File Name text box in the Open dialog box or the Save As dialog box to change to a shared folder.)

Mapping a Network Drive to a Local Drive Letter

Mapping a network drive to a local drive letter is the easiest way of providing constant access to a network drive. To map a network drive:

1. Open a Windows Explorer window:
   - On Windows XP, choose Start | My Computer.
   - On Windows 2000, double-click the My Computer shortcut on the desktop.
2. Choose Tools | Map Network Drive. Windows displays the Map Network Drive dialog box, shown next with options chosen:

3. The Drive drop-down list shows the letter Windows will assign to this network drive. By default, Windows XP assigns the letter Z to the first network mapping and then uses the latest unused letter of the alphabet for subsequent mappings: Y, X, W, and so on. Windows 2000 starts with the first available letter—typically E, F, or G, depending on how many local drives (hard drives, CD drives, DVD drives, and so on) your computer has. You can choose any available letter in the Drive drop-down list.

4. Enter the UNC path in the Folder text box. If you know the path, you can type it or paste it. Usually, it's easiest to click Browse, use the Browse for Folder dialog box to specify the folder, and click OK. Windows then enters the path for you.

5. By default, Windows selects the Reconnect at Logon option, which makes Windows reestablish the mapping to the network drive each time you successfully log on to your computer. In most cases, you'll want to leave this option selected; however, if you want to create a mapping that will last only until you log off the current computing session, deselect this option.

6. Normally, you'll access the network drive under your own logon credentials—in other words, using the username and password with which you logged on to Windows. However, in some cases, you may need to use another username and password to connect to the network drive. In this case, click the Different User Name link, and enter the other username and its password in the Connect As dialog box.

7. Click OK in the Connect As dialog box and Finish in Map Network Drive. If Windows is able to establish the mapping, it may open a Windows Explorer window to the drive.

Disconnecting a Network Drive

To disconnect a network drive:

1. Close all files that you have open on that drive.

2. Open a Windows Explorer window to display your computer's drives:

   - In Windows XP, choose Start | My Computer.
   - In Windows 2000, double-click the My Computer shortcut on your desktop.

3. Right-click the drive and choose Disconnect from the shortcut menu.

Alternatively, open a Windows Explorer window, choose Tools | Disconnect Network Drive, select the drive or drives in the resulting dialog box, and click OK.

Browsing with the My Network Places Folder

You can also use the My Network Places folder to navigate easily to a network drive. Choose Start | My Network Places in Windows XP, or double-click the My Network Places shortcut on your desktop in Windows 2000, to display the My Network Places folder. In Windows XP, click the View Workgroup Computers link in the Network Tasks pane to display local computers that you can connect to. In Windows 2000, use the Entire Network option or the Computers Near Me option to browse the network.

Once you've found the folder you want to use, you can open files that it contains. For quicker access to the folder, map a drive to it:

1. Right-click the folder's icon and choose Map Network Drive from the shortcut menu to display the Map Network Drive dialog box. Windows enters the path to the folder in the Folder box.

2. If necessary, change the drive letter Windows suggests.

3. Click Finish.

Using Office over the Internet

The Office applications can store files directly on a web server, an FTP (File Transfer Protocol) server, or a server running Microsoft's SharePoint Services. This capability can be very useful for working with intranet sites, because you can open a page on an intranet server directly in an Office application, edit or update the page, and then save it. To open a file from a server, you need what's called *read permission*; to save a file to a server, you need *write permission*.

NOTE   *Chapter 40 discusses how to use SharePoint Team Services.*

If you have a fast and reliable Internet connection, you can work with files on Internet servers as well. You *can* also work with files on Internet servers across slower or less reliable connections, but the results tend to be less satisfactory. The problem is that if an Office application is unable even temporarily to write data to the server, it may be unable to save a file. If worse comes to the worst, you may lose any unsaved changes in the file.

For this reason, it's usually best not to work directly with files on Internet servers. Instead, use Windows Explorer or another tool to download a copy of any file you need to open. Then work with the file on your local disk, where you can save changes instantly as often as necessary. When you've finished making changes to the file, or when you've created a new file that you want to place on the Internet server, upload the file. This way, you keep a copy of the file on your local disk at all times, which will help you avoid losing any data.

You can access an intranet server or Internet server via Internet Explorer or another web browser or via a common dialog box (for example, the Open dialog box or the Save As dialog box), but the most convenient way to access a server is to create a network place for it. To do so, run the Add Network Place wizard, and follow through its steps:

1. Choose Start | My Network Places in Windows XP, or double-click the My Network Places shortcut on your desktop in Windows 2000, to display the My Network Places folder.

2. Launch the Add Network Place wizard:

   - In Windows XP, click the Add a Network Place link in the Network Tasks pane.
   - In Windows 2000, double-click the Add Network Place icon.

3. Follow the steps in the wizard to create the network place.

Creating Files

Most of the ways of creating a new file are standard for Windows applications, but there are some wrinkles you'll benefit from understanding.

Each of the applications creates files based on templates—a file that contains the basic information you want to appear in every document of a particular type. For example, a template for creating documents in Word might contain styles and formatting, while a template for an invoice in Excel might contain the full text of the invoice except for those blanks that need to be filled in for each billing.

Creating a New Default File

In Word, Excel, and PowerPoint, the quickest way of creating a new document, workbook, or presentation based on the default settings is to click the New button on the Standard toolbar. (In Word, the button is called New Blank Document.) Clicking this button creates the new file without displaying the New task pane.

This technique doesn't work in Access, however—in Access, clicking the New button displays the New File task pane instead.

Creating a File from the New Task Pane

The standard way of creating a new file based on a template is to display the application's New task pane by choosing File | New. (Alternatively, choose the New task pane from another task pane you already have displayed.) The New task panes—the New Document task pane in Word, the New Workbook task pane in Excel, the New Presentation task pane in PowerPoint, and the New File task pane in Access—provide a series of links for creating a new document from a template:

- Click the Blank link (Blank Document in Word, Blank Workbook in Excel, Blank Presentation in PowerPoint, Blank Database or Blank Data Access page in Access) to create a blank file using the application's default settings. (As mentioned in the previous section, clicking the New button on the Standard toolbar is a quicker way of creating a blank file.)

- Click the On My Computer link to display the Templates dialog box for the application. The tabs of this dialog box show the templates that appear in your personal templates folder, your workgroup templates folder (if one is designated), and in the Office templates folder. The following illustration shows the Templates dialog box for Word.

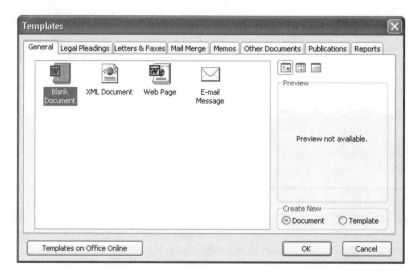

- Click the Templates Home Page link to display the Microsoft Office Templates page on the Microsoft web site in your web browser. Browse to find the template you want, and then download it to your computer. You'll need to install the Microsoft Office Template and Media Control if you don't already have it installed on your PC.

- Click the On My Web Sites link to display the list of web sites in your My Network Places list. Select the site that contains the templates you want.

- Click the From Existing link (From Existing Document for Word, From Existing Workbook for Excel, From Existing Presentation for PowerPoint, or From Existing File for Access) to create a file based on an existing file. The application displays the New from Existing dialog box—for example, Excel displays the New from Existing Workbook dialog box. Navigate to and select the file on which you want to base the new file, and then click the Create New button. The application creates the new file by cloning the specified file—essentially, using the existing file as the template for the new file.

Creating a File from a Template in Windows Explorer

Another method of creating a file based on a template is to open a Windows Explorer window to the folder that creates the template, then double-click the template file. (Alternatively, right-click the template file and choose New from the context menu.) This technique is primarily useful for templates that aren't stored in one of Office's designated templates folders.

Creating Your Own Templates

You can create your own templates to use as the basis for new files of particular types that you need to produce. For example, you might create a template containing the styles and formatting for your company's newsletter, together with macros for standardizing input and laying out the text. Or you might create a PowerPoint presentation that contains the appropriate number of slides, with suitable sample contents, for the training course you give. You could then share these templates with your colleagues so that they could produce these types of files easily in the correct format.

To create a template:

1. Create the file in the usual way.

2. Apply formatting and enter contents as needed by the template. (You can also add macros and customizations to the template.)

3. Choose File | Save As to display the Save As dialog box.

4. Select the appropriate Template choice in the Save As Type drop-down list. The application automatically switches to your personal templates folder. Change to another folder if appropriate—for example, to your workgroup templates folder.

5. Enter the filename for the template and click Save.

NOTE   *When creating a template from scratch in Word, it helps to alert Word to the fact that this will be a template. To do this, select the Template option in the Create New section of the Templates dialog box when specifying the existing template on which to base the new template. Word names the document window Template*n *(for example, Template1) instead of Document*n *and automatically switches to your personal templates folder. It then applies the Document Template file type when you issue the Save command for the template.*

Finding Files

Office integrates tightly with the Search feature in Windows to enable you to round up files you've lost track of. Once you've found files matching the criteria you specify, you can open them, check their properties, or use them as templates for new files.

Searching in Office is implemented through the File Search task panes. You get to choose between the Basic File Search task pane and the Advanced File Search task pane. The Basic File Search task pane assumes you want to search for files containing a particular text string (for example, a key word or key phrase) anywhere in the file or its properties. The Advanced File Search task pane lets you specify exactly where you expect to find what you're searching for (for example, in the Author property of a file), set various conditions, and generally perform a highly detailed search.

Performing a Basic File Search

To perform a basic file search, follow these steps:

1. Choose File | File Search to display the Basic File Search task pane:

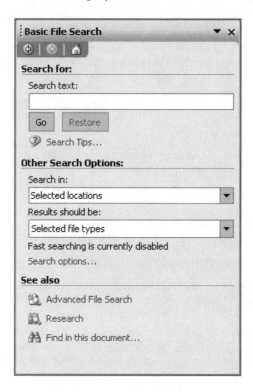

2. In the Search Text box, enter text that will distinguish the file or files you're searching for from other files. This text can appear either in the body of the file (for example, in the text of a Word document or in the text on a PowerPoint slide)

or in the file's properties. For example, if you've associated one or more key words with the file or files you're looking for, enter them in the Search Text box.

Tip *Basic Search automatically uses Office's Find All Word Forms feature, which extends the search to find other forms of a verb or noun you use. For example, if you search for "deny," the search also finds files containing "denies," "denied," and "denying," but not "denial." For further flexibility, you can use the ? and * wildcard characters. The ? represents any single character, so "f?ee" finds words such as "flee" and "free." The * represents one or more characters, so "f*e" finds words such as "fee," "free," and "finance." The * wildcard character is useful in many searches but can sometimes find surprisingly large numbers of files you're* not *looking for.*

---

3. In the Search In drop-down list, select the locations you want to search for the files:

   - The search mechanism offers the choices My Computer (local drives and folders), My Network Places (those of your network places that are searchable), or Outlook (your Outlook folders). You can expand these locations to select their subcomponents.

   - You can select the Everywhere option to search all available locations, but such searches may take a long time.

   - Restrict the search as far as possible to make it run faster and to reduce the number of irrelevant matches returned. For example, if you're sure the file you want is stored on your computer, don't search My Network Places.

4. In the Results Should Be drop-down list, select the options for the file types you want to find. You can choose Anything (all file types), Office Files (or files created by individual applications—for example, Word Files), Outlook Items (or particular types of items—for example, E-mail Messages), or Web Pages.

5. Click Go to perform the search. The search mechanism returns the matches it finds, breaking them down by location.

6. If the search has located the files you want, work with them as described in "Working with the Files You Find," later in this chapter.

If the search hasn't located the files you want, click Modify in the Search Results pane to return to the Basic File Search pane. Change the parameters for the search (for example, search in different locations), and run the search again.

Performing an Advanced File Search

If you know exactly what you need to find, you'll do better to use the Advanced File Search options than to waste time letting the Basic File Search options find tenuous matches for you.

To perform an advanced file search:

1. Choose File | File Search to display the Basic File Search task pane.

2. Click the Advanced File Search link in the See Also area to display the Advanced File Search pane:

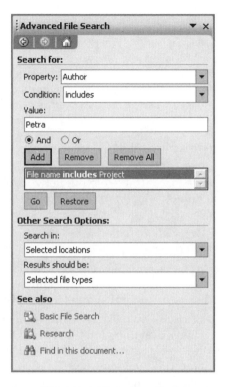

3. Use the controls in the Search For area to specify what to search for:

- Choose the appropriate property in the Property drop-down list. For example, to choose files whose filename includes a certain word, choose File Name in the Property drop-down list. To choose files created by a certain person, choose Author in the Property drop-down list.

- Specify the appropriate condition in the Condition drop-down list. The choices available depend on the property you select. For example, to choose files whose filename includes a certain word, you would select the Includes item in the Condition drop-down list. (In this case, Includes is the only choice.) When searching for files created by a specified author, the Condition drop-down list offers the choices Is (Exactly) and Includes.

- Type the appropriate information (for example, the filename or author name) in the Value box.

- When creating a second or subsequent condition, select the And option or the Or option as appropriate. For example, you could search for files by two separate authors by creating the condition "Author Is (Exactly) Petra Nemmanden" and the condition "Author Is (Exactly) Jack Smith" and selecting the Or option.

- Click Add to add each condition to the list in the list box. After creating conditions, you can use the Remove button to remove a selected condition or the Remove All button to remove all the conditions for a fresh start.

4. In the Search In drop-down list, select the locations you want to search for the files. (See step 3 in the previous list for details.)

5. In the Results Should Be drop-down list, select the options for the file types you want to find. You can choose Anything (all file types), Office Files (or files created by individual applications—for example, Word Files), Outlook Items (or particular types of items—for example, E-mail Messages), or Web Pages.

6. Click Go to perform the search. The search mechanism returns the matches it finds, breaking them down by location.

7. If the search has located the files you want, work with them as described in "Working with the Files You Find," next.

If the search hasn't located the files you want, click Modify in the Search Results pane to return to the Advanced File Search pane. Change the parameters for the search, and run the search again.

Working with the Files You Find

Once you've found files via searching, you can take the following actions by selecting a file's entry and working with the resulting drop-down list:

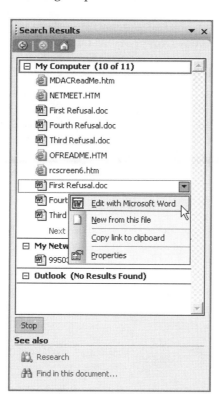

- **Edit with *Application***   Open the file for editing or viewing in the specified application.
- **New from This File**   Create a new file using this file as a template.
- **Copy Link to Clipboard**   Copy the file's full name (the folder path and the filename—for example, D:\Documents and Settings\Petra Nemmanden\My Documents\Third Refusal.doc) to the Clipboard for temporary storage.
- **Properties**   Display the Properties dialog box for the file so that you can easily check the details of the file (for example, fields such as its Author, Keywords, or Comments) to confirm that it's the file you're looking for.

NOTE   *Hover the mouse pointer over an entry in the Search Results pane to display a ScreenTip showing the filename, the full name (the folder path and the filename), and when the file was last modified.*

Using Office's Recovery Options Effectively

The wonders of creating documents on computers have historically been balanced out to an unfortunately large extent by the ease of losing those documents, thanks (or otherwise) to user error, application crashes, operating system crashes, hardware failures (including server or network failures), or power outages. To help you avoid losing data through your own fault, your computer's fault, or that of your network or the electricity supply company, Office includes two recovery features.

The recovery features are impressive, but they're for emergencies only. You should never rely on these features to save your work, because they're not always effective.

Understanding What the Recovery Features Do

The first of Office's recovery features is AutoRecover, which automatically saves recovery copies of files that contain unsaved changes as you work. After a crash or a power outage, you can then try to recover one of the versions that AutoRecover has saved.

The second of Office's recovery features is Microsoft Office Application Recovery, an application for closing down an Office application that has crashed. Microsoft Office Application Recovery can sometimes save data from the crashed application. When the application is relaunched, you can try to recover the data.

Of course, applications shouldn't crash—but of course some do sometimes. To protect your files against crashes, you should save your files frequently. How frequently depends on the type of work you're doing and how much you'd dislike having to repeat it. But you should at least consider saving a file after you've made any significant change. That might mean saving a file once every minute or once every hour.

If you spend three hours putting a complex worksheet together before saving it, you're asking for trouble. AutoRecover may be able to save you from disaster, but you should never rely on AutoRecover. If you're tempted to rely on AutoRecover, try thinking of AutoRecover as akin to a fire sprinkler system—the sprinkler may save your home and its contents from disaster, but you'd probably rather not find out the hard way whether it actually works.

Configuring the Backup and Recovery Options

Word, Excel, and PowerPoint let you configure AutoRecover by using the Save AutoRecover Info Every *NN* Minutes options on the Save tab of the Options dialog box (Tools | Options). The default setting is 10 minutes, but you may want to set a shorter interval if your computer has been unstable. You may also want to turn AutoRecover off if you prefer to save your documents manually every time you make an important change, or if you find that AutoRecover's automatic saves interfere with your work or your concentration. (The status bar displays *Saving AutoRecover Info* and a progress readout during each AutoRecover save.)

Excel offers two extra options for AutoRecover:

- You can control where AutoRecover saves its files by using the AutoRecover Save Location option (also on the Save tab of the Options dialog box). The default location is the *%userprofile%*\Application Data\Microsoft\Excel folder.

- You can disable AutoRecover for a workbook by selecting the Disable AutoRecover option on the Save tab of the Options dialog box.

Using Microsoft Office Application Recovery to Close a Hung Application

Normally, when an application *hangs* (stops responding to the keyboard and mouse), you need to use Windows Task Manager to shut it down. Windows Task Manager closes the application effectively but without finesse. In the process, you lose any unsaved changes in the files open in that application.

Office includes a tool called Microsoft Office Application Recovery for shutting down the Office applications a bit more gently when they crash—and, if you're lucky, saving any unsaved changes in the files that application has open.

When one of the Office applications stops responding:

1. Make sure nothing easily fixable is wrong:
   - Check that you haven't got a modal dialog box open for the application but hidden behind another window.
   - If you're running a VBA macro or program, wait for it to stop. Windows lists an application as Not Responding when it's under VBA's control.
   - Wait for a couple of minutes to see if the application starts responding again.

2. Choose Start | All Programs | Microsoft Office | Microsoft Office Tools | Microsoft Office Application Recovery.

3. In the Microsoft Office Application Recovery window, shown here, select the application that's not responding, and then click Recover Application to try to recover the application.

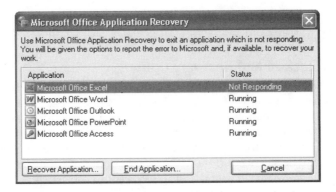

4. If Microsoft Office Application Recovery is able to recover data, you'll see a progress report such as that shown next. The recovery operation may take anything from a few seconds to several minutes, depending on how much data was involved.

5. Windows displays the error-reporting dialog box that invites you to send Microsoft a report on the problem. If Microsoft Office Application Recovery may be able to save some of your work, this dialog box includes an option for recovering your work and restarting the application. Make sure this option is selected, and then click Send Error Report or Don't Send, as appropriate.

6. If the Recover Application option doesn't work, click End Application to end the application forcibly. (Clicking End Application has the same effect as using End Task on the Applications tab of Windows Task Manager.)

Recovering a Document

When an Office application restarts after a crash or after being closed by Microsoft Office Application Recovery or Windows Task Manager, it displays the Document Recovery task pane on the left of the application window. The Document Recovery task pane lists any files the application has recovered, together with original versions of the documents, as shown in the following example.

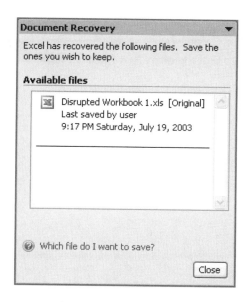

When you hover the mouse pointer over the entry for an available file in the Document Recovery task pane, the application displays a drop-down button on the right side of the entry. Click the button to display the menu, and then choose Open, Save As, Delete (for AutoRecover versions only, not for original files), or Show Repairs.

Once you've opened a document, the menu offers the choices View, Save As, Close, and Show Repairs. The Show Repairs option displays a report showing which errors (if any) were detected and repaired in the file. The Show Repairs dialog box shown here contains an example of repairing a Word document:

After deciding which recovered file to keep, use a Save As command to save it under a different name from the original file. This way, you'll be able to go back to the original file if you subsequently discover that the recovered file has problems you didn't identify when viewing it.

Click Close to close the Document Recovery task pane.

NOTE   *Approach the recovery of documents with as calm a mind as possible. Don't fall sobbing with relief on a recovered document and save it over your old document before making sure it contains usable data without errors.*

CHAPTER 4

Text Tools

Text entry and editing remains an essential part of many jobs using Office—so Office contains plenty of features to make text entry and editing as easy as possible. Most of these features work in a similar way in most of the Office applications.

Office supports several different options for entering text: the keyboard; paste, and drag and drop; speech recognition; and scanning and optical character recognition. Once the text is entered, the key methods of formatting are the Formatting toolbar and Font dialog box. The Office Clipboard is an improvement on the Windows Clipboard, and we'll show you how to use it effectively for cut, copy, and paste operations. You'll need to know the essential maneuvers for selecting text with the keyboard, with the mouse, and with the keyboard and mouse together. You'll also need to know how to apply basic paragraph formatting, such as alignment and borders, and how to use the Find and Replace functionality that the Office applications include to differing degrees.

Entering Text

The keyboard is the most obvious way of entering text, but it's by no means the only way. If you have special needs or just want to try something new, you can "train" your computer to recognize your voice; and if you have a scanner, you can enter text via scanning and performing optical character recognition on documents.

Entering Text with the Keyboard

As you'd expect, the basic means of entering text in the Office applications is the keyboard: to type a *t*, press T; to type a *T*, press SHIFT and T, and so on. If you're using a keyboard layout that reflects your physical keyboard, that's about as difficult as entering characters represented on the keyboard gets. However, if your computer is set to use a keyboard layout that is different from your physical keyboard, or if you need to be able to enter text in two or more languages, read the section "Installing Different Keyboard Layouts or Languages" and the sections that follow it.

Entering Symbols and Special Characters

To enter a character that's not represented on your keyboard, you can use the Symbol dialog box, the character code for the character (if you know it), or a special code that some Office applications use for some characters. The Symbol dialog box is the easiest way to enter the widest range of symbols and special characters.

From any Office application, choose Insert | Symbol to display the Symbol dialog box, shown in Figure 4-1. By default, the Symbol dialog box displays its Symbols tab.

From the Symbols tab of the Symbol dialog box, you can take the following actions:

- Insert a character by double-clicking it or by selecting it and clicking Insert. Select the font type in the Font drop-down list; then either use the Subset drop-down list to navigate to the appropriate subset of characters, or simply scroll through the list.

- Insert a recently used symbol from the Recently Used Symbols list.

- Learn the character code for a character. The ASCII (Decimal) code is the code you can enter by holding down the ALT key, typing a leading 0 (for a three-digit number),

FIGURE 4-1
The Symbols tab and Special Characters tab of the Symbol dialog box

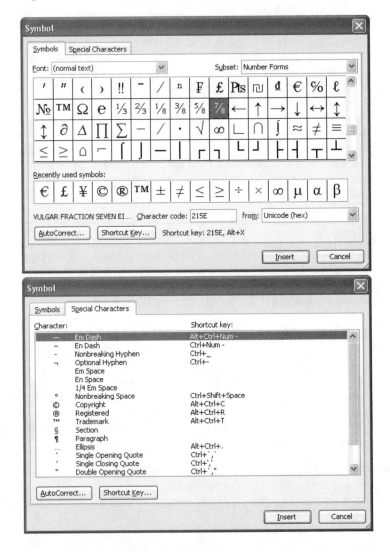

and then typing the number on the numeric keypad on your keyboard. Unless you're good at remembering four-digit numbers, this tends to be the most awkward way to enter symbols and special characters, but it can occasionally be useful.

- Learn the current shortcut key for a character (from the Shortcut Key readout that appears if a shortcut key is assigned), or create a shortcut key by clicking Shortcut Key and working in the resulting Customize Keyboard dialog box.

- Create an AutoCorrect entry for the character by clicking the AutoCorrect button and working in the resulting AutoCorrect dialog box.

TIP   *Creating an AutoCorrect entry for a character can be convenient, but if you always use that character in the same few words, consider creating an AutoCorrect entry for each of those words as well as an AutoCorrect entry for each character.*

When working in Word, Excel, and Outlook, you can use the Special Characters tab (see Figure 4-1) of the Symbol dialog box to insert a short list of widely used symbols, such as em dashes and en dashes, ® and ™ symbols, and nonbreaking hyphens and spaces. From the Special Characters tab, you can create shortcut key combinations and AutoCorrect entries as you can from the Symbols tab. After inserting the characters you want, click the Close button (the X) to close the Symbol dialog box.

Entering Accented and Special Characters with Key Combinations

You can use the Symbol dialog box to enter characters with these special marks called *diacritics*, but if you use them often, it might be easier to memorize the key combinations for them. Word and Outlook let you enter accented and other special characters quickly by using the key combinations shown in the following table:

Diacritic	Characters	Key Combination
Acute accent	Á á É é Í í Ó ó Ú ú Ý ý	CTRL-' *letter* Example: **CTRL-' y** to produce ý
Cedilla	Ç ç	CTRL-, C (capital or lowercase) Example: **CTRL-, C** or **CTRL-, c**
Circumflex	Â â Ê ê Î î Ô ô Û û	CTRL-SHIFT-^ *letter* Example: **CTRL-SHIFT-^ e** to produce ê
Dieresis	Ä ä Ë ë Ï ï Ö ö Ü ü	CTRL-SHIFT-: *letter* Example: **CTRL-SHIFT-: o** to produce ö
(Diphthong)	Æ æ Œ œ	CTRL-SHIFT-& *first letter* Example: **CTRL-SHIFT-& A** to produce Æ
Enye	Ã ã Ñ ñ Õ õ	CTRL-SHIFT-~ *letter* Example: **CTRL-SHIFT-~ n** to produce ñ
Grave accent	À à È è Ì ì Ò ò Ù ù	CTRL-accent *letter* Example: **CTRL-` A** to produce À
O-slash	Ø ø	**CTRL-/ O** or **CTRL-/ o**
Ring	Å å	**CTRL-SHIFT-@ A** or **CTRL-SHIFT-@ a**
(S-zett)	ß	**CTRL-SHIFT-& S**

If you need to use only a few of these key combinations, you'll probably be able to remember them easily enough. But if you find yourself needing to enter the character for only a small group of words, create an AutoCorrect entry for each word so that AutoCorrect does the work for you.

Installing Different Keyboard Layouts or Languages

Using multiple keyboard layouts or multiple languages (or both) in Windows and Office can be confusing because of several variables involved:

- First, there's the language setting that Windows is using—for example, English (United States).
- Second, there's the logical keyboard layout you're using—for example, the US keyboard layout or the United States–Dvorak keyboard layout, which doesn't necessarily match the layout shown on your physical keyboard.
- Third, there's the language that Office thinks you're using for text in the Office applications. You can use multiple languages—for example, you might switch among English, Finnish, and Swedish for business purposes.

To change the language setting or the keyboard layout setting, choose Start | Control Panel | Date, Time, Language, and Regional Options | Add Other Languages. On the Languages tab of the Regional and Language Options dialog box, click Details to display the Text Services and Input Languages dialog box.

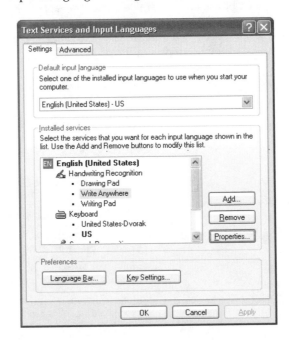

To add another language, or another keyboard layout for a language that's already installed, click Add. In the Add Input Language dialog box that appears, use the options in the drop-down lists to specify the input language and keyboard layout, and click OK.

After installing another input language or layout, use the Default Input Language drop-down list on the Settings tab of the Text Services and Input Languages dialog box to set your default input language and keyboard layout.

Switching Among Languages and Keyboard Layouts

Once you've installed multiple languages or multiple keyboard layouts, Windows XP automatically displays the Language bar at the right end of the taskbar (when the taskbar is displayed horizontally rather than vertically). You can switch among installed languages by clicking the Language icon on the Language bar and choosing the language from the resulting menu. You can switch among installed keyboard layouts for that language by clicking the Keyboard icon on the Language bar and choosing the layout from the resulting menu.

You can also use keyboard shortcuts to switch among installed languages and installed keyboard layouts. Windows XP's default setting is CTRL-SHIFT to toggle or cycle among the input languages and ALT-SHIFT (using the left ALT key) to toggle or cycle among the keyboard layouts. You can customize the keyboard shortcuts by clicking the Key Settings button on the Settings tab of the Text Services and Input Languages dialog box and working in the Advanced Key Settings dialog box.

Installing Office Features Required for Other Languages

To use other languages with Office, you need to install support for them:

1. Choose Start | All Programs | Microsoft Office | Microsoft Office Tools | Microsoft Office 2003 Language Settings.

NOTE   *At this point, Windows may launch the Windows Installer to install the Language Settings tools. If your computer doesn't have the installation source files cached, you'll need to provide your Office System CD or network installation source.*

2. Use the options on the Enabled Languages tab of the Language Settings dialog box to add and remove languages.

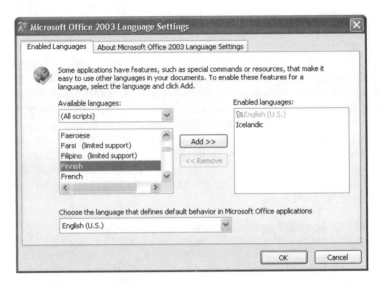

3. In the drop-down list at the bottom of the tab, choose the language you want to use as the default in the Office applications, and click OK.

4. If Office tells you that you'll need to quit and restart all open Office applications before you can use the new language settings, choose whether to let Office close the applications automatically or whether to close them yourself manually. If you let Office close the applications, you'll be prompted to save any unsaved work in the applications.

Entering Text via Paste, and Drag and Drop

You can also enter text via the Paste command and drag and drop:

- Use the Windows Clipboard (which can contain one text item at a time, together with items of other data types) to cut and paste text or to copy and paste text.

- Use the Office Clipboard (which can contain up to 24 text items or other items at a time) to cut and paste text or to copy and paste text.

NOTE   *"Cutting, Copying, and Pasting," later in this chapter, explains how to use the Windows Clipboard and the Office Clipboard.*

- Use drag and drop to move text from one document to another, or from one part of a document to another part.

- Use CTRL-drag and drop to copy text from one document to another, or from one part of a document to another part.

Entering Text via Speech Recognition

Office includes rudimentary voice control (Voice Command mode) and speech recognition. You can use voice control to issue menu, task pane, and dialog box commands in the main Office applications, and speech recognition to enter text in them.

Whether you'll find voice control and speech recognition useful enough for regular use depends on how badly you actually need them. If you have a temporary or permanent disability, voice control and speech recognition can make the difference between being able to use the computer and not being able to. But if you're dreaming of enjoying the future of computing and ultimate ease of use, dream on. Even with plenty of horsepower (say, a Pentium IV running at 2 GHz or higher) and memory (512MB or more RAM), voice control and speech recognition can be slow and less accurate than you'd want.

Before you can use speech recognition, you need to train Office to recognize your pronunciation of words. Choose Tools | Speech | Speech Recognition from one of the main Office applications (for example, Word or Excel), let the Microphone wizard walk you through the process of adjusting your microphone, and then work your way through speech training (see the following illustration) to create your default speech profile. The more you work on your speech profile by diligently correcting mistakes in your dictated documents and by performing more training (run the wizard again), the more accurate speech recognition will get. But it's a slow process.

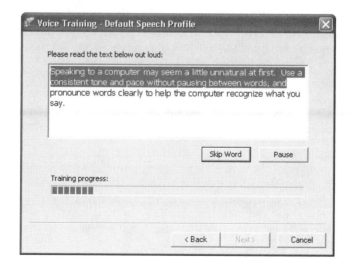

After training, you can begin using voice control and speech recognition. Office displays the Language bar with buttons for switching the microphone on and off, entering Dictation mode, entering Voice Command mode, and other tools:

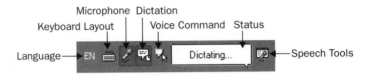

By default, Office makes the Language bar float rather than remaining anchored to the taskbar, which is the way Windows XP automatically displays it when you have multiple languages or multiple keyboard layouts loaded. You can configure the Language bar's behavior by right-clicking it and choosing Settings from the context menu to display the Settings tab of the Text Services and Input Languages dialog box. Click Preferences to display the Language Bar Settings dialog box and choose configuration options that suit you. You can choose to display the Language bar on the desktop, make it transparent when inactive, show additional Language bar icons in the Notification area, include Language bar text labels, and turn off advanced text services.

To make the Language bar float again, right-click it on the taskbar and choose the option Show the Language Bar on the Desktop. If you don't have the Language bar displayed on the taskbar, display the Language Bar Settings dialog box (by clicking Preferences in the Text Services and Input Languages dialog box), and select the Show the Language Bar on the Desktop option there.

To use voice control and dictation:

- To use voice control, click the Voice Command button. You can display a menu by saying its name, and then choose a command on the menu by saying its name. Likewise, you can navigate to a tab in a dialog box by saying the tab's name, select and deselect options, and click buttons using your voice.

- To dictate into the current document, click the Dictation button on the Language bar and dictate the text you want to enter into your document. There may be a lag between your speaking and words appearing on the screen, which can be disconcerting if you're watching as you dictate.

CAUTION *From typing comes the word* typo *for typing error—as you probably well know. Because speech recognition uses only words in its dictionary, it doesn't make typos—but it makes "wordos" and "phrasos" instead, substituting one or more words or a phrase in place of what you intended. Proof your documents carefully for wordos and phrasos, because they can completely change the meaning of the documents, and neither the spelling nor grammar checker can catch them.*

Entering Text via Scanning and OCR

Office includes a scanning tool and a stripped-down optical character recognition (OCR) tool that enable you to use your scanner and computer to automatically turn a hard-copy document to text in Word. From Word, you can copy or move the text to another application as necessary.

To enter text via scanning and OCR:

1. Choose Start | All Programs | Microsoft Office | Microsoft Office Tools | Microsoft Office Document Imaging. Microsoft Office Document Imaging launches.

NOTE   *If the Microsoft Office Document Scanning and Imaging features weren't installed on your computer, the Windows Installer will install them now. If your computer has the installation files cached, the Installer draws the files from the cache; if not, you'll need to supply your Office System CD or network installation source.*

2. Choose File | Scan New Document. The Scan New Document dialog box appears:

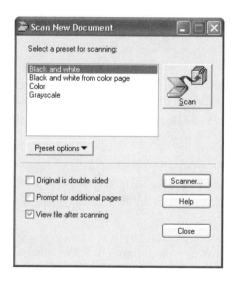

3. In the Select a Preset for Scanning box, choose Black and White, Black and White from Color Page, Color, or Grayscale as appropriate. For scanning plain text, use Black and White.

4. Select or deselect the Original Is Double Sided option, the Prompt for Additional Pages option, and the View File After Scanning option as appropriate.

5. Click Scan. Office initializes the scanner, scans the document, performs OCR on it, and displays the result.

6. Scan further pages if appropriate, and then click Close to close the Scan New Document dialog box.

7. If you want to use only part of the page, click the Select button on the View toolbar (the button with the white arrow) and drag to select the text.

8. Choose Tools | Send Text to Word. Microsoft Office Document Imaging displays the Send Text to Word dialog box:

9. Select the Current Selection option, the Selected Pages option, or the All Pages option as appropriate.

10. The Maintain Pictures in Output option controls whether Microsoft Office Document Imaging includes pictures. Select or deselect this option as appropriate.

11. Click OK. Microsoft Office Document Imaging exports the text to a new Word document, launching Word if necessary.

NOTE *You can also perform the scanning operation in two stages by choosing Start | All Programs | Microsoft Office | Microsoft Office Tools | Microsoft Office Document Scanning to display the Scan New Document dialog box, and then launching Microsoft Office Document Imaging and opening the file.*

After scanning text, run a spell check on the result before using it in your work. OCR can be impressively accurate when scanning clean pages, but closely kerned fonts, nonstandard fonts, or smudges often introduce errors. Some of these can be difficult to spot, especially when the letters *rn* are read as an *m*. A spell check will catch examples that create typos—for example, *Intemet* instead of *Internet*—but if the error produces a real word, you'll need to catch it by sense.

Formatting Text

Basic text formatting works in more or less the same way across all the major Office applications. Because these applications use text in different ways, each offers a different selection of formatting options suitable to its needs. But once you know the basics of font formatting, you can quickly come to grips with the specific font formatting that a particular application offers.

To apply font formatting, use the keyboard or mouse to select the characters you want to affect. (See "Selecting Text," later in this chapter.)

NOTE *In Word and PowerPoint, you can simply click to position the insertion point in a single word to which you want to apply formatting. But for clarity, it's easier if you always select the text you want to affect.*

You can then apply formatting to the selected text by using the Formatting toolbar or the Font dialog box (or, in the case of Excel, the Font tab of the Format Cells dialog box):

- The Formatting toolbar contains a variety of buttons for frequently used formatting, such as font, font size, font color, bold, italic, and underline. In Outlook, these buttons appear on the E-mail toolbar as well as on the Formatting toolbar. Here is the Formatting toolbar from PowerPoint with the font-formatting buttons labeled:

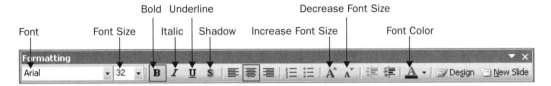

- The Font dialog box (Format | Font) in Word, Outlook, and PowerPoint, and the Font tab of the Format Cells dialog box (Format | Cells or press CTRL-1) in Excel offer a wider selection of font formatting. Figure 4-2 shows the Font tab of the Font dialog box for Word (and for Outlook with Word as the e-mail editor) and the Font tab of the Format Cells dialog box for Excel.

Most of the options in the Font dialog boxes are easy to understand, but the following merit an explanation:

- The Automatic setting for font color makes the application apply a font color that contrasts strongly with the background color. In most cases, the default background color is white, so the default automatic font color is black. If you change the background color to dark brown, for example, the application makes the automatic font color white so it's visible. However, Excel fails to make this change when you format a cell with a dark pattern, and PowerPoint fails to make this change when you format a slide or a text box with a dark background; so in these applications, applying the specific font color you want is a good idea.

- The Text Effects page in Word's Font dialog box (also used for Outlook when Outlook is using Word as the e-mail editor) applies preset animations around the selected text. These animations quickly become annoying and are best used rarely or not at all. If your documents are supposed to wow their readers, let the content do the wowing, not the formatting.

- In Word, you can set the default font, font size, and formatting for future documents based on the Normal template (the default template) by choosing the formatting in the Font dialog box, clicking the Default button, and choosing Yes in the confirmation dialog box that appears.

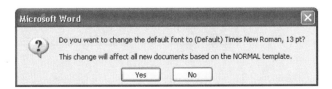

- In Excel, the Normal Font option on the Font tab of the Format Cells dialog box reapplies the font settings of the Normal style to the options in the dialog box.
- In PowerPoint, you can set the default font for new Auto Shapes and text boxes by choosing the details in the Font dialog box, selecting Default for New Objects, and clicking OK.

FIGURE 4-2
Some of the font formatting options in Word (top) and Excel (bottom)

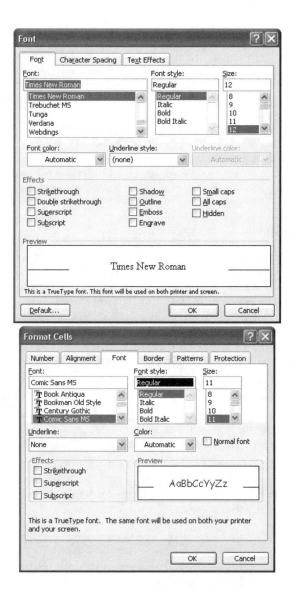

> **NOTE** *In Word and Excel, you can use styles to apply formatting quickly. A* style *is a predefined set of formatting information. Both Word and Excel come with built-in styles that you can use as they are or modify to suit your needs. You can also create custom styles of your own. Chapter 9 discusses how to use styles in Word. "Using Styles in Excel" in Chapter 16 explains how to use styles in Excel.*

Cutting, Copying, and Pasting

The Office applications' implementation of cut, copy, and paste provides you with a powerful tool for copying or moving text and other objects from one file (or part of a file) to another. Understanding the Windows Clipboard and the Office Clipboard will help you perform these operations efficiently and effectively.

Understanding the Windows Clipboard and the Office Clipboard

All versions of Windows, including Windows XP and Windows 2000 Professional, have a built-in feature called the Clipboard for implementing basic cut, copy, and paste functionality:

- You issue a Cut command to remove an object (for example, a word) from the active document or file and place it on the Clipboard.
- You issue a Copy command to place a copy of the currently selected object on the Clipboard.
- You issue a Paste command to insert the current contents of the Clipboard into the active document or file.

The Clipboard can hold several different types of data, including text and graphics, but it can hold only one set of items at once. When you issue another Cut or Copy command, Windows overwrites the contents of the Clipboard for that data type with the new information.

 Windows applications implement cut, copy, and paste via the standard items on the Edit menu and many context menus and on toolbar buttons (shown left to right, Cut, Copy, Paste).

You can also use the standard keyboard shortcuts and alternative shortcuts listed in the following table. Microsoft officially prefers the CTRL-based shortcuts, but many users find the alternative shortcuts easier—so take your choice.

Operation	Standard Windows Shortcut	Other Shortcut
Cut	CTRL-X	SHIFT-DEL
Copy	CTRL-C	CTRL-INS
Paste	CTRL-V	SHIFT-INS

By the time Office 2000 was being designed, the shortcomings of the Windows Clipboard for heavy-duty use had long been apparent: many users needed to be able

FIGURE 4-3
The Office
Clipboard

to copy multiple items before performing a paste operation, and some were prepared to pay for shareware packages that provided enhanced clipboard functionality. So Office 2000 introduced the Office Clipboard, which was implemented as a toolbar and could contain multiple items.

Office XP changed the Office Clipboard from a toolbar to a task pane, and Office 2003 retains the task pane format (see Figure 4-3). With default settings, the Office applications display the Office Clipboard when you perform two or more cut or copy operations, or a mixture of the two, without performing a paste operation between them. If you have the task pane displayed, you can display the Office Clipboard by choosing it from the drop-down menu of task panes. If not, you can display it by choosing Edit | Office Clipboard or by pressing CTRL-C twice in succession.

The Office Clipboard can contain up to 24 items of the same type or of different types. The Office Clipboard in Figure 4-3 shows several items cut and copied to it.

Using the Office Clipboard

The Office Clipboard is easy to use:

- Scroll up and down to see items that don't fit within the display.
- To paste an item, position the insertion point where you want the item to appear, then click the item on the Office Clipboard.
- To paste all items, position the insertion point and click Paste All.
- To clear the Office Clipboard of all its current contents, click Clear All.
- To delete an item, right-click it and choose Delete from the shortcut menu.

Once you start using the Office Clipboard, Office displays a taskbar icon in the notification area by default. The context menu for this icon offers the self-explanatory commands Show Office Clipboard, Clear All, and Stop Collecting. The context menu also has an Options submenu that provides quick access to the configuration options discussed in the next section.

Configuring the Office Clipboard

The Options button at the bottom of the Office Clipboard task pane and the Options menu item on the Clipboard icon in the notification area offer the following configuration options:

- **Show Office Clipboard Automatically**   Controls whether Office displays the Clipboard task pane automatically or at all.

- **Show Office Clipboard when Ctrl+C Pressed Twice**   Controls whether Office displays the Clipboard automatically when you press CTRL-C twice in succession. You might want to turn this option off if you find yourself inadvertently repeating this key combination.

- **Collect Without Showing Office Clipboard**   Controls whether Office displays the Clipboard automatically once you've performed two copy or cut operations without a paste operation between them. Select this option if you don't want the Clipboard task pane taking up screen real estate while you're making a collection of cut or copied items to paste.

- **Show Office Clipboard Icon on Taskbar**   Controls whether Office displays the Clipboard icon on the taskbar.

- **Show Status Near Taskbar when Copying**   Controls whether Office displays an informational pop-up (for example, *Item 12 of 24 Clipboard Items Collected*) over the notification area when you cut or copy an item to the Office Clipboard.

Using Paste Special and Smart Tags to Control Formatting on Pasted Items

By default, when you copy an item to the Clipboard and then paste it into a different location, the Clipboard retains the item's formatting—or at least as much of the formatting as possible. What's retained and what's lost depends on what the item is, what formatting it has, and what types of formatting the destination location supports.

If you copy an item and then paste it back into the same application, all the formatting can be retained (and is, by default). But if you paste the item into another application, some formatting may be lost. For example, if you copy a Word table and paste it into an Excel worksheet, Excel has to figure out how to handle it. The default setting is to paste the contents of the table's cells into cells on the worksheet, retaining as much of their formatting as Excel can handle. But Excel also offers other options, such as pasting the table as an embedded Word object (which retains the formatting it had in the source file), pasting the table as a picture (which is rarely useful), pasting the table's contents as unformatted text, and pasting the entire contents of the table's cells into one cell in Excel and turning the result into a hyperlink.

If you choose, you can control the format in which an item is pasted into an Office application. You can do so by using either the Paste Special dialog box or by using the Paste Options Smart Tag that results from the paste operation. (See "Setting Smart Tag Options" in Chapter 2 for an explanation of Smart Tags.)

To use the Paste Special dialog box (shown next), choose Edit | Paste Special instead of issuing a conventional Paste command. Select the format in which you want to paste the item, and then click OK.

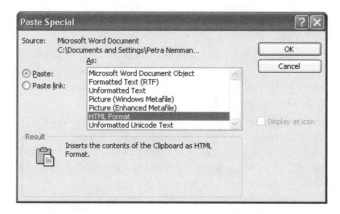

To use the Paste Options Smart Tag, issue a conventional Paste command (for example, press CTRL-V) to paste the item into the destination with the default formatting options. Then click the Smart Tag for the pasted item, and choose the appropriate option from the Smart Tag menu to change the format of the pasted item. The example here shows the options available after copying some Excel cells into a Word document.

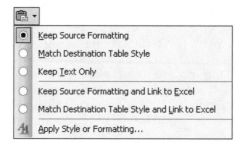

Selecting Text

To format or manipulate text in the Office applications, you typically need to select it first. You can do so by using the mouse, the keyboard, or a combination of the two.

NOTE *Word includes various other techniques for selecting text quickly with the keyboard, the mouse, or both. See Part II and Appendix A.*

Selecting Text with the Mouse

The basic actions for selecting text with the mouse are as follows:

Action	Effect
Double-click	Selects the word you double-click. The word includes a trailing space (if there is one) in Word, Outlook, and PowerPoint, but not in Excel and Access.
Triple-click	Selects the paragraph you triple-click in Word, Outlook, and PowerPoint.
Click and drag	Selects the characters, words, or partial words you drag through. Word and PowerPoint include an option called When Selecting, Automatically Select Entire Word (on the Edit tab of the Options dialog box). This option is selected by default and makes the application select entire words rather than partial words once you've dragged from the starting word to another word. Outlook uses this feature as well when Word is set to be the e-mail editor.

Selecting Text with the Keyboard

Most Office applications support the following keyboard shortcuts for selecting text:

Shortcut	Effect
SHIFT-LEFT ARROW	Selects the next character to the left.
SHIFT-RIGHT ARROW	Selects the next character to the right.
SHIFT-UP ARROW	Selects from the insertion point to the same character position on the previous line, or to the start of the paragraph (if the insertion point is in the first line).
SHIFT-DOWN ARROW	Selects from the insertion point to the same character position in the following line, or to the end of the paragraph (if the insertion point is in the last line or its character position is further along the line than the character position of the last character in the paragraph).
CTRL-SHIFT-LEFT ARROW	Selects from the insertion point to the beginning of the word.
CTRL-SHIFT-RIGHT ARROW	Selects from the insertion point to the end of the word, including any trailing space.
CTRL-A	Selects all the contents of the active object: a text box, header area, or document in Word; a worksheet in Excel; a slide in PowerPoint; and so on.

Shortcut	Effect
CTRL-SHIFT-DOWN ARROW	**Word** and **PowerPoint:** Selects from the insertion point to the end of the paragraph.
CTRL-SHIFT-UP ARROW	**Word** and **PowerPoint:** Selects from the insertion point to the start of the paragraph.
SHIFT-HOME	Selects from the current position to the start of the line.
SHIFT-END	Selects from the current position to the end of the line.
CTRL-SHIFT-HOME	**Word:** Selects from the current position to the start of the document. **Excel:** Selects from the active cell to the start of the worksheet. **PowerPoint:** Selects from the current position to the start of the active shape.
CTRL-SHIFT-END	**Word:** Selects from the current position to the end of the document. **Excel:** Selects from the active cell to the last cell ever used in the worksheet. **PowerPoint:** Selects from the current position to the end of the active shape.

Selecting Text with the Keyboard and Mouse

You can also select text by using the keyboard and the mouse together. These are the three key techniques you should be familiar with:

- In Word, Excel, Outlook, and PowerPoint, click to position the insertion point, hold down SHIFT, and click at the end of the text you want to select.

- In Word, Outlook, and PowerPoint, CTRL-click to select a sentence.

- In Word and Outlook, you can make multiple selections by making the first selection with the mouse, holding down CTRL, and then making further selections with the mouse. Making multiple selections can be useful for applying formatting to several words or phrases at once.

Applying Paragraph Formatting

For readability or emphasis, you'll often need to apply alignment and borders to paragraphs in Word, Outlook, and PowerPoint, to cells in Excel worksheets, and to fields in Access reports.

Applying Alignment

 The easiest way to apply alignment is by using the Align Left, Center, and Align Right buttons, shown here, on the Formatting toolbar.

NOTE *Word also offers a Justify button for justified paragraphs (aligned to both margins).*

You can also apply alignment by using the following keyboard shortcuts in some applications:

Keyboard Shortcut	Alignment
CTRL-L	Left
CTRL-R	Right
CTRL-E	Center

Each application provides additional ways to apply alignment:

- **Word**   From the Indents and Spacing tab of the Paragraph dialog box (Format | Paragraph)
- **Excel**   From the Alignment tab of the Format Cells dialog box (CTRL-1 or Format | Cells). This tab also offers options for controlling vertical alignment.
- **Outlook**   From the Indents and Spacing tab of the Paragraph dialog box (Format | Paragraph) when using Word as the e-mail editor, or from the Paragraph dialog box (Format | Paragraph) when not using Word as the e-mail editor
- **PowerPoint**   From the Format | Alignment submenu

Applying Borders

Word, Excel, and Outlook (using Word as its e-mail editor) provide quick access to border formatting through the Border button on the Formatting toolbar. Click the Border button to apply the currently displayed border type to the selected item, or click the drop-down button and choose the border type from the panel:

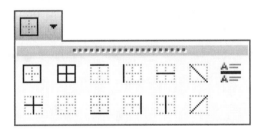

Word, PowerPoint, and Outlook (using Word as its e-mail editor) offer more comprehensive controls for applying borders on the Tables and Borders toolbar, shown next with the border-related buttons labeled. Excel's Borders toolbar offers similar border-formatting options.

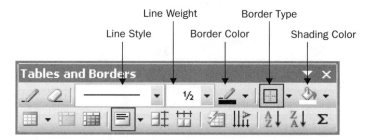

You can also apply border formatting in the following ways:

- **Word and Outlook (using Word as the e-mail editor)**   From the three tabs of the Borders and Shading dialog box (Format | Borders and Shading)
- **Excel**   From the Border tab of the Format Cells dialog box (CTRL-1 or Format | Cells)

Using Find and Replace

Each Office application includes a find and replace feature, but the specifics vary greatly depending on the application's needs: Word has extremely powerful functionality that can find and replace not only text but also formatting; Outlook has marginally less power when it's using Word as its e-mail editor, and only minimal find functionality when it's not using Word; PowerPoint and Excel have correspondingly less power; and Access's implementation of find and replace is limited to those actions required for database work.

Here, we discuss the general principles of find and replace, which are implemented in similar ways in the text-based portions of each application, and we mention options you'll want to investigate when working in particular applications. You'll find coverage of each application's specific find and replace features in the chapters that cover those applications.

Finding Text

To find a particular string of text, follow these general steps:

1. Choose Edit | Find to display the Find dialog box or the Find tab of the Find and Replace dialog box (depending on the application).
2. Enter the string of text in the Find What box. You can reuse a previous search string from the current session of this application by selecting it from the drop-down list.

TIP   *Use a leading space or trailing space (as appropriate) to prevent partial word matches. For example, searching for "uncle" (with no trailing space) also finds words such as "unclear" and "unclean." Adding a trailing space restricts the searches to "uncle" and a space.*

---

3. Choose other options, such as the Match Case option or the Find Whole Words Only option, as appropriate. (Some of these options are application specific.)

4. Click the Find Next button to find the next instance of the string of text. Click Find Next again if necessary.

5. After finding the string you were searching for, click Close to close the Find dialog box or the Find and Replace dialog box.

Finding and Replacing Text

To find and replace text, follow these general steps:

1. Choose Edit | Replace to display the Replace dialog box or the Replace tab of the Find and Replace dialog box (depending on the application).

2. Enter the string of text you're searching for in the Find What box. You can reuse a previous search string from the current session of this application by selecting it from the drop-down list.

3. Enter the replacement string of text in the Replace With box. You can reuse a previous replacement string from the current session of this application by selecting it from the drop-down list.

4. Choose other options, such as the Match Case option or the Find Whole Words Only option, as appropriate. (Some of these options are application specific.)

5. Click the button for the action you want to take:

   - Click Find Next to find the next instance of the search string. You can then click Replace to replace that instance, click Find Next to find the next instance, and so work your way through the file.

   - Click Replace All to replace all instances of the search string with the replacement string instantly.

6. After replacing as many instances as you need, click Close to close the Find dialog box or the Find and Replace dialog box.

Using Wildcard Characters in Searches

To make your searches more powerful, you can use the same wildcard characters—? and *— you used for file searches in Chapter 3. The ? wildcard character represents any single character, so "bl??" finds words such as "blow" and "blab." The * wildcard character represents one or more characters, so "projec*" finds words such as "project," "projects," "projection," and "projections."

Application-Specific Find and Replace Features

Beyond basic find and replace functionality, the individual Office applications offer tailored capabilities that you'll probably want to investigate. Here are some examples:

   - Word enables you to search for and replace formatting. For example, you can search for one style and replace it with another style, or replace all instances of a given font with another font.

   - Word enables you to search for and replace special characters by using the Special pop-up menu from the Find tab or Replace tab of the Find and Replace dialog box.

- Excel enables you to find or replace specified formatting, restrict the search to the active worksheet rather than the entire workbook, and choose whether to match the entire contents of cells rather than matching partial contents.

- Access enables you to specify where to search for the specified item and whether to match the start of the field, the whole field, or any part of the field.

Drawing and Graphics Tools

This chapter explains how to enhance your documents by using the drawing and graphics tools that Office provides. The Office applications use a drawing layer to position graphical objects and text boxes in a document. Understanding this concept helps you to use their graphical features in sophisticated ways.

We'll introduce you to the picture library included with Office, for inserting clip art and other objects in your documents, and explain how to work with shapes, AutoShapes, and WordArt objects. You'll learn how to import graphics into your documents either by embedding or linking them, how to import pictures directly into your documents when necessary, and how to use the Office tools to create modest charts and diagrams (including organization charts).

How the Office Applications Handle Pictures

The key to working effectively with drawing objects in the Office applications is understanding how they're implemented. Although Word documents, PowerPoint presentations, HTML-formatted e-mail messages in Outlook, and Excel worksheets appear to be flat, the applications treat them as consisting of a number of different layers. The primary layers are the text layer (which contains the text) and the drawing layer. The layers are transparent unless they contain an object, so when you look at the document (for example, a Word document) you see the contents of all the layers together, making up the entire appearance of the document.

You can change the order in which the layers appear, so you can change the way that objects appear to be superimposed on each other. For example, in a Word document, you can position a graphic so that it appears behind the text of the document, inline with the text, or in front of the text.

The different layers are easier to see in PowerPoint than in Excel, Word, and Outlook. This is because, when creating or editing a typical presentation in PowerPoint, you work with AutoShape objects; whereas Excel, Word, or Outlook start you off in the text layer and leave you there until you specifically go to work with an object that resides in a different layer—for example, a drawing object in the drawing layer.

The drawing layer effectively works as a very thick layer that consists of as many sublayers as you need. You can create multiple objects in the drawing layer, either keeping them separate from each other or arranging them into groups that you can keep together and manipulate with a single command. You can arrange objects in the drawing layer so that they overlap each other, and you can alter the order in which they appear by moving the objects forward (up the stack of layers, as it were) or backward (down the stack of layers).

To work with objects in the drawing layer, display the Drawing toolbar by choosing it from the View | Toolbars menu or the toolbars context menu. Alternatively, in Word or Excel, click the Drawing button on the Standard toolbar to display the Drawing toolbar, shown in Figure 5-1.

Inserting Clip Art

Office includes a wide selection of graphics, photographs, movie clips, and sounds clip art that you can use freely in your documents. When using these items, exercise discretion and restraint—a unique picture may still be worth the thousand words of the cliché, but a tired piece of clip art may detract from a document rather than enhance it.

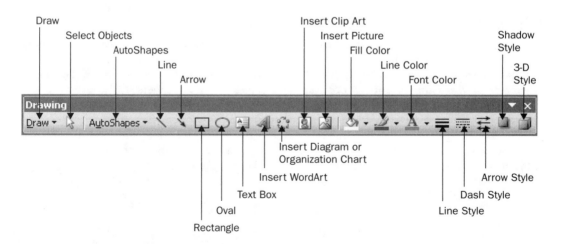

FIGURE 5-1   The Drawing toolbar gives you access to shapes, AutoShapes, and key commands for manipulating graphical objects.

To insert one of Office's included clip art items:

1. Choose Insert | Picture | Clip Art to display the Clip Art task pane. Here it is after a successful search:

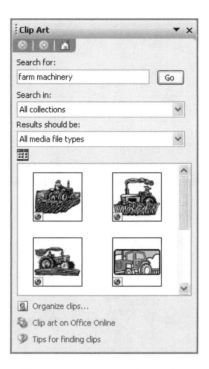

2. Use the Search For box, the Search In drop-down list, and the Results Should Be drop-down list to specify which types of files you're looking for:

   • In the Search For box, specify one or more key words.

   • In the Search In drop-down list, choose which collections to search (or choose Everywhere).

   • In the Results Should Be drop-down list, choose the media types you're interested in: All Media Types, Clip Art, Photographs, Movies, or Sounds.

3. Click Go. Office searches for matching media types and displays them in the pane.

Once you've found a clip that matches your needs, you can take a variety of actions with it. The most basic action is to insert the clip in your document. To do so, click the clip, or click the button that appears when you hover the mouse over it, and choose Insert from the menu. A menu opens, with these options for further actions:

   • **Copy/Paste**   Copies the clip so you can paste it elsewhere.

- **Delete from Clip Organizer** Deletes the clip from all collections in the Clip Organizer. Office makes you confirm the deletion in case you misclicked. This option isn't available for clips that come with Office, only for clips you add.

- **Copy to Collection** Displays the Copy to Collection dialog box so you can add a copy of the clip to another collection—for example, your favorites. This option is useful for making a collection of clips you use often. It is available only for clips stored on local drives.

- **Make Available Offline** Displays the Copy to Collection dialog box so you can download this clip from its online source to one of your collections. This option is available only for online clips.

- **Move to Collection** Displays the Move to Collection dialog box so you can move the clip to another collection. This option is useful for relocating clips in your collections. You can move only clips you add to the collection, not the clips included with Office.

- **Edit Keywords** Displays the Keywords dialog box, in which you can add, modify, or delete the keywords associated with the clip. You can't change the key words for the clips included with Office, only for clips you add.

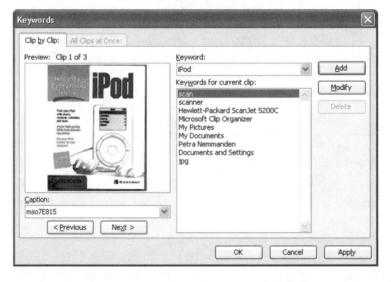

- **Find Similar Style** Searches for clips that have a similar style to the clip from which you issue this command. This option is useful when you need multiple clips in the same style to convey a certain impression in a document. The clips returned by a style search can span an interesting range of subjects and key words.

- **Preview/Properties** Displays the Preview/Properties dialog box, shown next, in which you can view the image and its details. The Paths section of the Preview/Properties dialog box shows you the full path for the image's file and the catalog that contains the image.

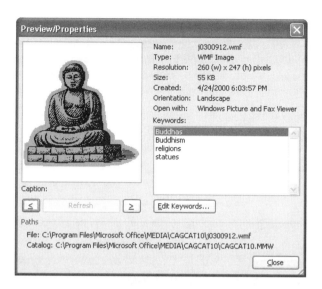

To organize your clips, click the Organize Clips link at the foot of the Clip Art task pane. Office opens the Microsoft Clip Organizer applet:

The first time you open Microsoft Clip Organizer, Office displays the Add Clips to Organizer dialog box. Use the controls in this dialog box to specify whether to search your hard disk now for media files to add to your catalogs. To specify particular folders, click Options. In the resulting Auto Import Settings dialog box, specify which folders to search for media files, and click the Catalog button. Alternatively, click Later to dismiss the Add Clips to Organizer dialog box until the next time you launch Microsoft Clip Organizer. (To prevent the Add Clips to Organizer dialog box from being displayed again, select the Don't Show This Message Again option before dismissing the dialog box.)

These are the key commands for working with Microsoft Clip Organizer:

- To navigate your collections, click the Collection List button and work in the Collection List task pane. To search for clips, click the Search button and use the Search task pane.

- To add clips, choose File | Add Clips to Organizer, and then choose Automatically, On My Own, or From Scanner or Camera from the submenu.

- To edit the key words for a selected clip, choose Edit | Keywords.

- To make your collection of clips take up as little space as possible, choose Tools | Compact.

Working with Shapes, AutoShapes, and WordArt

Office enables you to create drawing objects that fall into three broad categories: shapes (basic shapes), AutoShapes (more complex shapes, with some intelligence built in), and WordArt (pictures made by applying effects to text). We'll cover each of these in the following sections, but we'll start by explaining what happens when you start a drawing in an Office application.

Starting a Drawing

When you click one of the controls on the Drawing toolbar to start creating a drawing, the application prepares to receive drawing input. PowerPoint is perpetually in what amounts to a drawing mode, so it doesn't need to make any change in order to receive drawing input. Excel doesn't need to make any preparation either. But Word and Outlook need to make several changes.

If the active document in Word is in Normal view or Outline view, Word automatically switches the document to Print Layout view so that you can see where the graphic will fall. If the active document is already in Print Layout view, Print Preview, Web Layout view, or Reading Layout view, Word doesn't need to change the view.

Word and Outlook automatically display the *drawing canvas*—a rectangular area that you can use to group multiple drawing objects together into a single drawing—together with the Drawing Canvas toolbar. The Drawing Canvas toolbar contains buttons for fitting the canvas to the contents, expanding the canvas area, setting the drawing to be scalable with the canvas it's on, and controlling text-wrapping options.

At first, the drawing canvas displays the message *Create your drawing here* to make sure you know what it's for. This message disappears as soon as you place a drawing object in the drawing canvas area.

The following illustration shows the drawing canvas in a Word document with a drawing started and key items labeled. You can resize the drawing canvas by dragging one of the handles at its corners or the midpoints of its sides. If you decide not to proceed with the drawing, remove the drawing canvas by clicking its border to select it and then pressing DELETE.

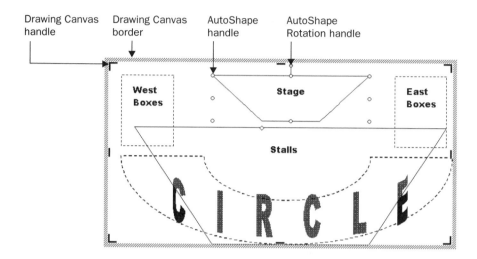

After you finish working on a drawing and click outside the drawing canvas, Word and Outlook hide the drawing canvas. They display the drawing canvas again when you select an object that's placed on the canvas.

Adding Basic Shapes

To add a basic shape to a document, click the appropriate button on the Drawing toolbar to activate the tool, click in the document to position one corner of the shape, and then drag to the size you want the shape to be. When you release the mouse button, the application restores the mouse pointer.

The process could hardly be simpler, but there are four enhancements you'll benefit from knowing about:

- To create the shape so that it is centered on the point where you click and start dragging, instead of having one corner of the shape (or its frame) appear there, hold down CTRL as you click and drag.

- To constrain a rectangle to a square, or to constrain an ellipse to a circle, hold down SHIFT as you click and drag.

- Hold down CTRL-SHIFT to apply both the centering and the constraint.

- To create multiple shapes of the same type (for example, several rectangles), double-click the tool. Then, when you release the mouse button after creating a shape, the tool remains active. Press ESC to toggle the tool off when you've finished creating all the shapes of that type. (Alternatively, click or double-click another tool.)

Adding AutoShapes

To add an AutoShape to a document, click the AutoShapes button on the Drawing toolbar, choose the appropriate category from the AutoShapes menu (shown next), and select the AutoShapes you want.

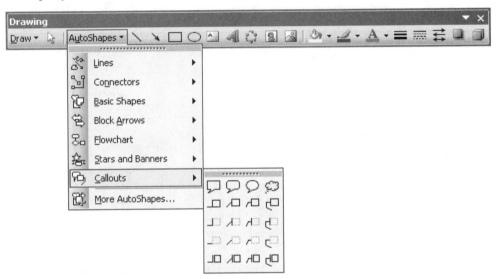

Then click in the document to position one corner of the AutoShape and drag to the size you want the AutoShape to be. When you release the mouse button, the application restores the mouse pointer.

AutoShapes are easy to work with, but it's worth knowing the following:

- The More AutoShapes item on the AutoShapes menu displays the Clip Art task pane with a selection of AutoShapes in it.

- As with basic shapes, you can hold down CTRL to create the AutoShape centered around the point at which you click, hold down SHIFT to constrain a shape, and hold down CTRL-SHIFT to combine the effects.

- To create multiple AutoShapes of the same type, create the first AutoShape, and set any formatting needed. ("Resizing and Formatting Drawing Objects," later in this chapter, discusses how to format AutoShapes.) Then copy the AutoShape and paste in as many copies as you need.

- The AutoShapes in the Connectors category are smart—once you've attached an end of a connector to an object, the connector stays attached even when you move the object. For this to work in Word and Outlook, the objects need to be positioned on the same drawing canvas.

Adding WordArt Objects to Your Drawings

Another element you can add to your drawings is a WordArt object. WordArt is an Office applet for creating text-based designs, such as logos or decorations. WordArt works in Word, Excel, Outlook, and PowerPoint. Like all means of making text more difficult to read, WordArt is best used only when necessary and, even then, only in moderation.

To insert a WordArt object in a drawing:

1. Click the Insert WordArt button on the Drawing toolbar. (Alternatively, choose Insert | Picture | WordArt.) Office displays the WordArt Gallery dialog box:

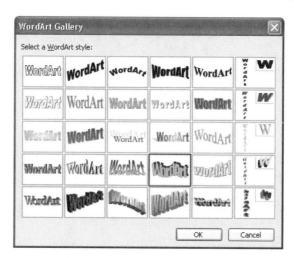

2. Select the style of WordArt item and click OK. WordArt displays the Edit WordArt Text dialog box:

3. Type the text in the Text box.

4. Select the font, font size, and bold and italic as appropriate.

5. Click OK. WordArt closes the Edit WordArt Text dialog box, inserts the WordArt object in your document, and displays the WordArt toolbar. Figure 5-2 shows a WordArt object and the WordArt toolbar.

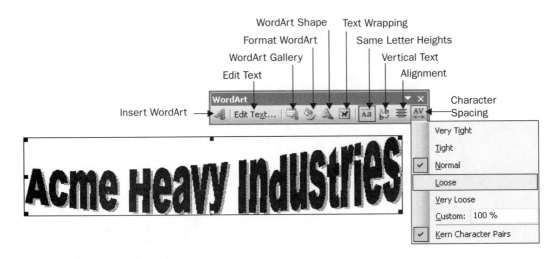

FIGURE 5-2   The WordArt toolbar provides quick access to the commands for manipulating WordArt objects.

Most of the buttons on the WordArt toolbar are easy to understand: te Edit Text button displays the Edit WordArt Text dialog box (alternatively, double-click the WordArt item to display this dialog box); the WordArt Gallery button lets you change the WordArt style applied to the object, and the WordArt Shape button lets you change its shape. The other buttons let you tweak the positioning of the WordArt item, make its letter heights all the same, change the text orientation to vertical, change the alignment, and adjust the character spacing.

You can resize a WordArt object either by clicking the Format WordArt button and working in the resulting dialog box or by dragging one of its handles. You can rotate a WordArt object by dragging its rotation handle.

Adding Text to an AutoShape

You can add text inside just about any AutoShape that has enough space. In practice, this means basic shapes, block arrows, flowcharts, stars and banners, and callouts can contain text—even lightning-bolt AutoShapes and crescent-moon AutoShapes can contain text, but you'll need to place it artfully to keep it clear of the lines. Lines and connectors needn't apply, because they lack sufficient depth to handle the text.

To add text to an AutoShape, right-click the AutoShape and choose Add Text from the shortcut menu. The application displays an insertion point inside the AutoShape. Type the text, select it, and apply formatting by using standard means such as those discussed in the previous chapter.

If you need to add text to a line or connector AutoShape, place a text box or a callout AutoShape next to it, enter the text, and resize the text box or callout to present the text to best advantage (for example, change the width of the text box or callout to rebreak the text lines to a suitable width). Then format the line color for the text box or callout with the No Line option and set the fill color to No Fill.

Resizing and Formatting Drawing Objects

To resize a drawing object to approximately the right size, select the object and drag one of its handles. To resize an object more precisely, right-click it and issue the Format command (for example, Format AutoShape) to display the Format dialog box. Then use the options on the Size tab to specify the height and width either in units (for example, inches) or as a percentage of the original size.

You can format a selected drawing object by using the commands on the Drawing toolbar, by using standard dialog boxes (for example, the Font dialog box), or by displaying the Format dialog box for the object and working with the options on its tabs. The Format dialog box offers quick access to most of the formatting options for the object, so it's usually the fastest way of setting multiple formatting options at once.

The name of the Format dialog box changes to reflect the object you're working with: for an AutoShape, you see the Format AutoShape dialog box; for a text box, you see the Format Text Box dialog box; for a picture, you see the Format Picture dialog box; and for the drawing canvas, you see the Format Drawing Canvas dialog box. These dialog boxes contain the selection of options available to the object. In most of the applications, the options are divided among these six tabs:

- **Colors and Lines** Contains options for specifying the fill color and transparency percentage (how see-through the object is); the line color, style, and weight; and the beginning and ending style for arrows that the object contains.

- **Size** Contains options for specifying the height and width of the object, either using measurements (for example, inches or centimeters) or scale; for locking the aspect ratio of the object (so that you can't change its height without changing the width as well, and vice versa); and for scaling the picture relative to its original size.

- **Layout** Contains options for specifying the wrapping style and the horizontal alignment of the object. The horizontal alignment options aren't available when the object is positioned in line with text (in other words, in the text layer). Click the Advanced button to display the Advanced Layout dialog box, whose two tabs contain options for fine-tuning the object's position and text wrapping.

- **Picture** Available only for graphics. Contains options for cropping the picture; adjusting its color, brightness, and contrast; resetting the picture; and (in PowerPoint) recoloring the picture. Click the Compress button to display the

Compress Pictures dialog box, which contains options for compressing either the selected picture or all pictures in the document.

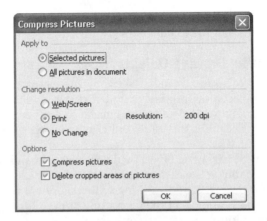

The Web/Screen option uses a resolution of 96 dots per inch (dpi), the maximum that monitors can display; the Print option uses 200 dpi; and the No Change option leaves the current resolution in place. Use the No Change option with the Delete Cropped Areas of Pictures option to remove any portions of the picture you've cropped, thus reducing the file size. Use the Delete Cropped Areas of Pictures option only when you're sure you won't need to undo the cropping.

- **Text Box**   Available only for text boxes and AutoShapes that contain text. Contains options for specifying the internal margins between the edges of the text box and the text it contains, for turning word wrap on and off, and for resizing the AutoShape.

Note   *The Convert to Frame button on the Text Box tab of the Format Text Box dialog box converts the text box to a frame. Frames are an older method of placing text that are largely superfluous these days. You may lose some formatting when converting a text box to a frame.*

- **Web**   Contains a text box for specifying alternative text to be displayed while a web browser is loading the picture, when the picture isn't available, or when the user has chosen not to display pictures. For example, you might supply a text description of the picture so that the user knows what she's missing.

Excel's Format dialog boxes contain no Layout tab or Text Box tab but contain a Properties tab (which lets you specify whether to move and resize the object with cells and whether to include the object in printouts) and a Protection tab for controlling locking on the object and its text.

Positioning Drawing Objects

The Office applications offer many options for positioning drawing objects. You can drag objects roughly into position, nudge them precisely into position, use the Format dialog box to position them by specifying measurements, align one object according to another, and create groups of objects that you can format and move together.

You can also adjust the granularity of the drawing grid and choose whether objects snap to the grid or not.

Dragging and Nudging Objects

The basic method of positioning an object is to select it and drag it to where you want it to appear. Dragging is good for moving objects for medium or long distances, but for short distances or pinpoint placement, you need a steady hand with the mouse.

To move an object a shorter distance, *nudge* it. Select the object and press the appropriate arrow key to move the object one square up, down, left, or right on the underlying grid used by the applications for positioning objects. You can also nudge a selected object by choosing Draw | Nudge and then choosing Up, Down, Left, or Right from the submenu as appropriate, but the arrow keys are so much faster and easier to use that the Nudge submenu is seldom used.

TIP   *All the submenus on the AutoShapes menu, and most of the submenus on the Draw menu, are* tear-off palettes *that you can drag off the menu and use as toolbars. A horizontal line of dots (the handle) at the top of a submenu indicates that it's a tear-off palette. To tear the palette off, click its handle and drag it off the menu. Click the Close button (the X button) button on the palette when you need to close it.*

Configuring and Displaying the Drawing Grid

To get objects in precise locations, you may need to adjust the size of the grid itself and the option controlling whether objects snap to the grid or not. Having objects snap to the grid makes it easy to align them quickly, but you may need to turn off snapping to get objects in exactly the right positions—otherwise, snapping will move them to the grid line nearest where you drop them. You may also want to display the grid lines so that you can see which grid line an object is aligned with.

To adjust the grid, the snapping, and the display of grid lines:

1. Display the appropriate dialog box:
   - Choose Draw | Grid from the Drawing toolbar to display the Drawing Grid dialog box (shown on the left in the next illustration) in Word or Outlook.

- Choose Draw | Grid and Guides to display the Grid and Guides dialog box in PowerPoint (shown on the right).

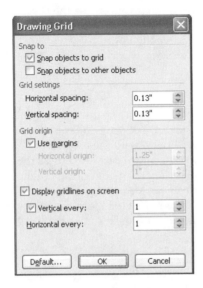

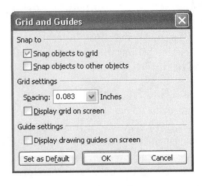

2. Use the controls in the Grid Settings section to change the spacing as required.

NOTE   *You can restore default grid line spacing by clicking the Default button (in Word and Outlook) or the Set as Default button (in PowerPoint). Word and Outlook display a confirmation dialog box; click Yes.*

3. Choose whether to display the grid lines on screen by selecting or clearing the Display Gridlines on Screen option (in Word or Outlook) or the Display Grid on Screen option (in PowerPoint).

4. In the Snap To section, choose whether to snap objects to the grid (the default setting) and whether to snap objects to other objects (this setting is deselected by default).

5. Click OK.

In Excel, you can choose to have objects snap to the grid, to shapes, or to neither. Choose Draw | Snap | To Grid, or Draw | Snap | To Shape from the Drawing toolbar as appropriate.

Positioning an Object Using the Format Dialog Box
Word, Outlook, and PowerPoint also support the following ways of positioning an object:

- In Word and Outlook, right-click the object, display the Format dialog box for it (for example, the Format AutoShape dialog box or the Format Drawing Canvas dialog box); then click the Advanced button on the Layout tab to display the Advanced Layout dialog box. On the Picture Position tab, shown in the following illustration, specify the horizontal alignment and the vertical alignment. If the object is anchored to a text object (for example, a paragraph), choose whether to allow the object to move when the text moves. To position the object precisely on the page, choose the Absolute Position option in the Horizontal section and the Vertical section, and specify Page in the right-hand drop-down list.

- In PowerPoint, right-click the object, display the Format dialog box for it, and use the options on the Position tab to specify the position.

Aligning an Object According to Another Object

Instead of positioning an object by a grid line, you can align an object with another object. To do so:

1. Select the object to which you want to align the other object or objects.

2. Hold down SHIFT and click to select the other objects.

3. Choose Draw | Align or Distribute from the Drawing toolbar, and choose the appropriate command from the submenu. Most of the options are self-explanatory, but the following merit explanation:

   - The Align Center option applies horizontal centering, while the Align Middle option applies vertical centering.

   - The Distribute Horizontally option and the Distribute Vertically option place the objects evenly across the area. These commands are available only when you have selected three or more objects.

Grouping and Ungrouping Objects

When you've selected multiple objects, you can treat them as an informal group—for example, you can drag an object to move all the objects, or apply shared formatting to all the objects at once. To apply formal grouping so that you can quickly work with these objects as a unit in future, issue a Group command from the Draw menu or the Grouping submenu on the context menu. To ungroup grouped objects, issue an Ungroup command. To regroup objects, issue a Regroup command.

Layering Drawing Objects

Drawing objects are layered on a Z-axis (from front to back). To adjust the order in which drawing objects appear, select an object and use the Order submenu on the Draw menu or the context menu to move the object forward or back. Your choices are to bring the object to the front or send it to the back; to bring it forward by one layer or send it backward by one layer; and to bring it in front of the text or send it behind the text.

Specifying Text-Wrapping Options

To control how the text of a document wraps around an object, you set text-wrapping options. You can do so either on the Layout tab of the Format dialog box for the object (shown on the left in the next illustration) or on the Text Wrapping tab of the Advanced Layout dialog box (shown on the right in the illustration). The Text Wrapping tab offers more precise wrapping options. For example, you can choose to wrap text around only one side of the object, and you can specify exact distances to use between the text and the object. To display the Advanced Layout dialog box, click the Advanced button on the Layout tab of the Format dialog box.

Enhancing Your Documents with Text Boxes

If your work includes creating attractive or complex text layouts, you're likely to find the text box a useful tool. You can use text boxes to create short sidebars, notes, highlights, and pull quotes—or simply use text boxes to position text exactly where you want it to appear on a page.

By default, a text box has a thin black line around it, but you can remove this by choosing the No Line option in the Line Color drop-down list on the Colors and Lines tab of the Format Text Box dialog box.

Text boxes in Word and Outlook have more flexibility than text boxes in the other applications. Because a text box is actually a mini-document positioned in the drawing layer, you can put various objects into it, such as tables, graphics, WordArt objects, and AutoShapes.

In Word and Outlook, you can link text boxes together so that the contents of one flow into the contents of the next. This feature can be useful for presenting a linked series of pieces of information (for example, summaries or factoids) to help hold the reader's interest across a series of dense columns or pages. Used wrongly or to excess, this technique can prove supremely irritating to readers, so use it with discretion and due forethought.

To link one text box to another:

1. Right-click the first text box, and choose Create Text Box Link from the context menu. The mouse pointer changes to a complex graphic that denotes pouring text.

2. Click the second text box. (This text box must be empty.) The contents of the first text box are linked to the second text box, so any contents that won't fit in the first text box appear in the second.

3. Link further text boxes as necessary by repeating steps 1 and 2.

After you've linked two or more text boxes, you can navigate through the sequence of text boxes by right-clicking and choosing Next Text Box or Previous Text Box from the shortcut menu. To break a link, right-click and choose Break Forward Link.

Adding Graphics to Your Documents

As you saw earlier in this chapter, the Office applications make it easy to insert clip art in your documents. But clip art is usually decoration, or at best a generic picture to illustrate a concept or an archetype. To actually show your readers or your audience something useful, in most any business or social situation, you'll probably need to insert a specific graphic, such as a custom illustration, a photograph, or a screen capture. Office makes this process easy too.

To add a graphic to a document:

1. Position the insertion point or the active cell where you want the graphic to appear.

2. Choose Insert | Picture | From File. The application displays the Insert Picture dialog box, which is a common Open dialog box with a modest enhancement.

3. Navigate to and select the graphic you want to add.

4. Issue the appropriate command to place the graphic in your document:

   • Click the Insert button to insert the picture in the document. Technically, this is called *embedding*. See the following sections for a discussion of what embedding and linking involve and what their effects and advantages are.

   • Click the Insert drop-down button, and choose Link to File to insert in the document a link to the picture.

   • Click the Insert drop-down button, and choose Insert and Link to insert in the document a copy of the picture in its current state and a link to the source file.

Inserting (Embedding) a Picture

The Insert command in the Insert Picture dialog box *embeds* the specified picture file in the document. Embedding a picture in a document causes the application to save the picture in the document without a link to the document source. Embedding works in all the Office applications and is the basic means of inserting a picture.

The advantage of embedding is that, because the picture is saved in the document, the picture remains available even if you move the document or disconnect the computer so that the picture's source file is no longer available. The disadvantages are that embedding a picture significantly increases the document's size (because the picture's data must be saved in it, either in the original format or in a modified format), and there is no easy way to update the picture if the source file changes: instead, you need to manually replace the embedded picture with the latest version of the picture from the source file.

Linking a Picture

The Link to File command in the Insert Picture dialog box inserts in the document a link to the picture. The picture itself remains in its source file. When the source file is available, the application displays the picture. You can update the link manually or have the application update it automatically to display the latest version of the picture. When the source file isn't available, the application displays a placeholder for the picture instead. The placeholder is a blank square with a small red ✕ on a white square. Because the placeholder is often displayed at a different size than the linked picture, the layout of your documents can suffer.

Linking has two advantages. First, because only the link is saved in the document, not the picture itself, the document's file size increases by only a tiny amount. Linking can greatly reduce the file size of a document that includes many pictures. Second, you can make the document display the latest version of the picture by updating the link.

The disadvantage of linking is that if the source file isn't available, the picture doesn't appear. So if, for example, you need to distribute a Word report that includes pictures, embedding would be a better choice than linking, even though the file size of the document with embedded pictures would be far larger than that of the document with linked pictures.

Tip   *For a document that you distribute on an intranet or extranet, you can use linked pictures effectively by storing the pictures in a shared folder that each recipient of the document can access by using the same folder path. (If the folder path is different, the links won't work.)*

Word, PowerPoint, and Access support linking a picture; Excel doesn't support linking. (Instead, you need to embed the graphics file in Excel.)

Tip   *In a Word document, you can convert a linked picture to an embedded picture by choosing Edit | Links, selecting the link in the Links dialog box, and clicking the Break Link button.*

Using Insert and Link in Word and Outlook

Word and Outlook offer an Insert and Link command designed to give you the best of embedding and linking at the same time. This command embeds a copy of the picture in the document but also creates a link to the source file.

When you update the document (for example, if the document is set to update automatically when it's opened), Word or Outlook tries to use the link to retrieve the current version of the picture in the source file. If the source file isn't available (for example, because your computer is offline), Word or Outlook displays the embedded version of the picture instead.

Cropping a Picture

You can crop a picture (hiding parts of it from display—not cutting them off) in either of two ways:

- Click the Crop button on the Picture toolbar, and use the resulting mouse pointer to drag one of the picture's handles to specify which part of it to crop.

- Choose Format | Picture and use the options in the Crop From section of the Picture tab of the Format Picture dialog box to specify how much to crop from the left, right, top, and bottom of the picture.

Importing Pictures from Scanners and Cameras

Office enables you to import a picture from a scanner or camera directly into a document. This capability can be handy when you need to perform such an import operation directly. But in most cases, you'll get better results by importing the picture via the tools built into Windows (for example, the Scanner and Camera wizard in Windows XP). Then you can crop and improve it in a graphics application, and import the finished file into your document via the Insert | Picture | From File command.

That said, to import a picture from a scanner or camera directly:

1. Position the insertion point where you want the picture to appear. For example, in a Word document, you might create a text box in which to position the picture.

2. Choose Insert | Picture | From Scanner or Camera. Office displays the Insert Picture from Scanner or Camera dialog box:

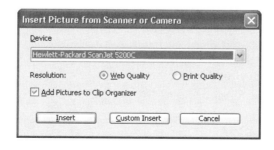

3. Use the Device drop-down list to specify which scanner or camera to use. (If you have only one scanner or camera attached to your computer, Office will probably have selected the right device.)

4. Select the Web Quality option or the Print Quality option to specify the resolution at which to import the picture. Use the Web Quality option for items that will be displayed on screen (whether on the Web or not) and the Print Quality option for items you'll use in printed documents. Print Quality is higher than Web Quality, so print-quality items have a larger file size than web-quality items.

5. Select or deselect the Add Pictures to Clip Organizer option as appropriate.

6. Click Custom Insert. The wizard then leads you through the process of scanning an item with your scanner or downloading an image from your digital camera. For example, if you're using a scanner on Windows XP, you see the Scan Using dialog box, shown here, in which you can specify which type of picture you want to create and how to crop it.

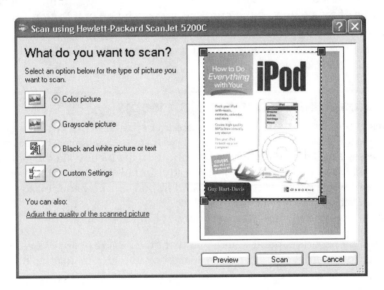

NOTE *You can also use the Insert command instead of the Custom Insert command if you're comfortable using the default scan type with no cropping. For almost all cases, Custom Insert is a better choice.*

7. After performing the scan or acquiring the image from your digital camera, the wizard inserts it in your document.

8. Crop or format the image as needed.

Charts and Diagrams

Before you start reading this section, a quick disclaimer: most people find that the Microsoft Chart applet and the Diagram applet are seldom (if ever) worth using. The Organization Chart applet is more useful, particularly if the organization charts you need to create are modest in scope and number of objects.

When to Use Microsoft Chart for Creating Charts

If you've been following through the commands used so far in this chapter, you've probably noticed the Insert | Picture | Chart command. This command launches the Microsoft Chart applet, which you can use for creating simple charts in your documents. When you issue this command, Microsoft Chart inserts a basic bar chart and displays a datasheet window, which contains the sample data represented in the graph. The following illustration shows the bar chart and datasheet window. You can then change the data and change the chart type to produce a chart that suits your needs.

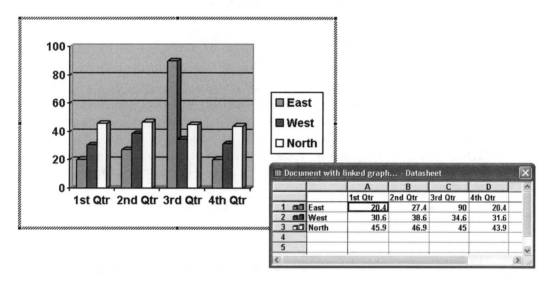

In most cases, Microsoft Chart is barely worth using if you have Office rather than a standalone copy of Word or PowerPoint. This is because Excel provides far more powerful charting capabilities (see Chapter 18 for details). You can include an Excel chart in a Word document, a PowerPoint presentation, or an Outlook e-mail message by copying and pasting a chart from Excel or by using the Insert | Object command and choosing Microsoft Excel Chart in the Insert Object dialog box.

Creating Basic Diagrams

Office includes a Diagram applet that enables you to quickly insert six different kinds of basic diagrams in your documents. Choose Insert | Diagram from the menu to display the Diagram Gallery dialog box, choose the diagram type, and click OK.

These are the types of diagrams you can create:

- **Organization chart**   A chart that represents organizational relationships as a hierarchical structure. Organization charts also have their own command on the Insert | Picture submenu. See the next section for a more detailed discussion of organization charts.

- **Cycle diagram**   A diagram that represents data and labels in a circular layout. Usually used for demonstrating the flow of a process (for example, the cycle of the seasons).

- **Radial diagram**   A diagram that represents information as circles attached by spokes to a central hub.

- **Pyramid diagram**   A diagram that represents information as a series of slices in a pyramid.

- **Venn diagram**   A diagram that represents information as a series of overlapping circles.

- **Target diagram**   A diagram that represents information as a series of concentric circles with labels at the side.

The diagrams are extremely basic—for example, you can't adjust the size of pyramid slices or the amount of overlap in the Venn circles—but they can prove adequate for quick-and-dirty illustrations. Figure 5-3 shows examples of the diagrams, including examples of

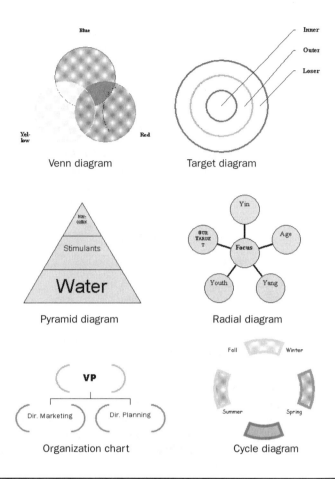

Venn diagram   Target diagram

Pyramid diagram   Radial diagram

Organization chart   Cycle diagram

FIGURE 5-3   With Office's Diagram applet, you can create organization charts and five other types of diagrams.

the clumsiness of Office's diagram tools. For example, notice that there's not enough space in the Venn diagram's labels for the word "Yellow" to appear without breaking. To get around problems like this, use AutoShapes for labeling diagrams when the built-in labels don't work satisfactorily.

The Diagram toolbar, shown in the next illustration with the Layout menu displayed, provides buttons for inserting a new shape (for a new data point), selecting the previous item (Move Shape Backward) or the next item (Move Shape Forward), reversing the layout of the diagram, toggling AutoLayout on and off and resizing the diagram (the Layout menu), applying an AutoFormat, changing the diagram to one of the other types (but not to an organization chart), and applying text wrapping.

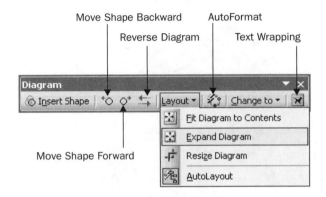

By default, Diagram inserts the diagrams directly in the text layer. Use the Text Wrapping menu to reposition a diagram or to edit its wrap points.

TIP *If Diagram fails to remove a "Click to Add Text" placeholder when you add text to a shape, force an update by adding an extra shape and then deleting it.*

Creating Organization Charts

Office includes an applet for creating organization charts (or *org charts*, as most people refer to them). The Organization Chart applet offers modest features that work well for creating org charts for small companies or departments, but if you need to create one for more than a few dozen people, you should consider a heavier-duty solution, such as Corel iGrafx Flowcharter, NetViz, or Microsoft Visio.

To create an org chart with Organization Chart:

1. Open the application and the file in which you want to create the org chart. (For example, launch Word and open the appropriate HR document.)

2. Choose Insert | Picture | Organization Chart. The application lays out a drawing canvas in the application, creates the stub of an org chart on it, and displays the Organization Chart toolbar. The following illustration shows how it looks in a Word document.

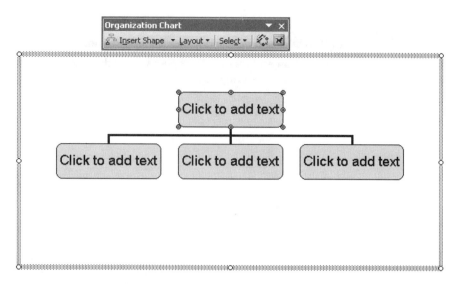

These are the basic actions for creating your org chart from the stub of the org chart:

- Click one of the "Click to add text" boxes and type the text. Format the text as necessary by using standard formatting commands from the toolbar, the menus, or the shortcut menu.

- Delete one of the stub items by selecting it and pressing DELETE. You can't delete the topmost item until you've deleted all its subordinate items.

- Add a subordinate, coworker, or assistant by selecting the shape to which it will be related, then clicking the Insert Shape button and choosing Subordinate, Coworker, or Assistant from the menu.

- Apply a layout by clicking the Layout button and choosing the layout from the menu. From this menu, you can toggle the AutoLayout feature on and off.

CAUTION   *If the AutoLayout feature is switched off, when you add multiple subordinates, coworkers, or assistants, Organization Chart stacks their items one on top of another. This makes it very hard to see what you're doing. The solution is to use AutoLayout while adding items, and then switch it off when you want to lay out your org chart manually.*

- Apply one of Organization Chart's AutoFormats by clicking the AutoFormat button and choosing the format in the Organization Chart Style Gallery dialog box. Many of the designs are intended for on-screen or web display, so if you're creating an organization chart destined to be printed in black and white, make sure the design will look okay.

- Select a level of the org chart, a branch of it, all assistants, or all connecting lines by clicking the Select button and issuing the appropriate command.
- Use the Text Wrapping button and its menu to specify how the org chart should appear in your document—in line with the text, behind the text, in front of the text, and so on.

PART

Word Processing

CHAPTER 6
Word

CHAPTER 7
Editing Text

CHAPTER 8
Document Formatting

CHAPTER 9
Reusable Formatting with
Styles and Templates

CHAPTER 10
Tables and Columns

CHAPTER 11
Advanced Page Layout
in Word

CHAPTER 12
Automating Information
with Fields

CHAPTER 13
Managing Long Documents

CHAPTER 14
Mail Merge, Labels,
and Envelopes

Word

The word processing component in Office 2003 is Word, useful for everything from short letters to lengthy, multichapter manuscripts and mail merges for the masses. Word is used more often than any other application in Office. In fact, many Office users never use the other applications at all, much as they might appreciate having them available "just in case." In some ways, this reliance on Word is justified—features such as the well-hidden calculator can be used with tables in place of simple Excel spreadsheets, and the database features inherent in the mail merge tool can do the job without the need to build an Access database. As you'll see in Chapter 38, however, the true power of Word—and, indeed, all of the Office applications—is their ability to work together.

Word Task Pane

As with all of the Office 2003 applications, one of the most obvious features upon opening Word is the task pane. The task pane provides a home base of sorts offering context-sensitive options for document-related functions. The following panes are available in Word by using the drop-down button in the task pane:

- **Getting Started**
  This pane appears on startup (unless you've deselected this option, as explained in the next section) and lets you open and create documents and access program information from Microsoft. Also available from View | Task Pane.

- **Help** You can search the local help files and get additional support from Microsoft. Also available from Help | Microsoft Word Help.

- **Clip Art**   Search for graphics files organized by collection, file type, and location. Also accessed from Insert | Picture | Clip Art.

- **Research**   You can search specified encyclopedias, thesauruses, and translation tools for more information about selected words. Also available from the Standard toolbar and using Tools | Research.

- **Clipboard**   The Clipboard can hold 24 items that have been copied or cut from any Office application, which can then be pasted elsewhere at a later time. Also available using Edit | Office Clipboard.

- **Search Results**   After initiating a file search (File | File Search), this pane will show the results of the ongoing search. You can continue working on an open document while the search is under way.

- **New Document**   You can choose document creation options based on various formats or templates. Also available from File | New.

- **Shared Workspace**   If you are working with others, you can share a central copy of a document from a SharePoint Team Services web site. Document workspaces are covered in Chapter 40.

- **Document Updates**   This feature works in conjunction with the shared workspace, enabling you to get the most recent version of the document from the server.

- **Protect Document**   These settings enable you to limit what types of edits can be made to a shared document, both in editing and formatting. Also available using Tools | Protect Document.

- **Styles and Formatting**   This pane allows you to apply and modify character and paragraph styles to selected text. Styles are explained in Chapter 9. Also available from the Formatting toolbar (only to apply styles) and Format | Styles and Formatting.

- **Reveal Formatting**   Use this pane to see the formatting applied to selected text or paragraphs. This is somewhat similar to the Reveal Codes feature in WordPerfect. Also available from Format | Reveal Formatting.

- **Mail Merge**   The Mail Merge wizard opens and prompts you through the creation of a database-merged document. Also available from the Mail Merge toolbar and the Tools | Letters and Mailings | Mail Merge Wizard menu.

- **XML Structure**   If you're creating an XML document, you can apply XML elements to the document. Elements from all XML schema attached to the document will appear in the task pane.

Hiding the Task Pane

Unfortunately, the task pane takes up considerable screen real estate, so many users opt to hide it except when using one of the tools just listed. Even if you hide the task pane by default, it will pop up when you access the related features from the toolbars and menus, so you're not losing anything by closing it. To the contrary, you'll be gaining a considerable amount of screen space if you keep it closed.

There are two ways to deal with the task pane. First, if you use it to open or create your documents when entering Word, it will close itself after you've made a selection. To keep the task pane from opening at all upon startup:

1. Select Tools | Options from the main menu.
2. In the View tab, deselect Startup Task Pane.
3. Click OK.

Customizing Word Options

Setting the appearance of the task pane is just one of many Word-specific options that are available to you in the Options dialog box, as shown in Figure 6-1. The purpose of most of these options is obvious, and setting them is a matter of personal preference. Some stand out, however, such as the options discussed next.

View Options

Your use of the View options depends primarily on the structure and purpose of your document. If you're creating a long document with bookmarks to aid in navigation, you may want to show bookmarks. For newsletters with clip art and other pictures, showing picture placeholders is helpful. Other options might appeal (or not) depending on your skill level in Word and your tolerance level of possible distractions popping up on your screen, such as ScreenTips and Smart Tags.

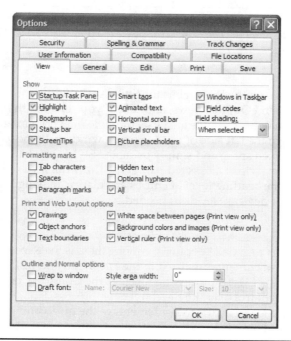

FIGURE 6-1   The Options tabs offer hundreds of customizable features.

Some of the View options are of particular note because they're useful when formatting and editing your document.

Formatting Marks

When you're exploring the View options, it's tempting to set the formatting marks individually. Keep in mind, however, that you can toggle the display of all of these marks using the Show/Hide ¶ button on the Standard toolbar. If you set formatting marks individually, the selected marks will appear regardless of the status of the Show/Hide ¶ button.

NOTE   *One downside to the Show/Hide button is that it displays spaces as midline dots (·) throughout the document, which some people find annoying. A work-around is to use the View options to select only those formatting marks you wish to see, and then leave the Show/ Hide ¶ button alone. Of course, this means those marks will always be displayed. On the rare occasions you're using the ¶ symbol, such as in this paragraph (or in a legal setting), having the paragraph formatting mark always displayed can be equally distracting.*

Print and Web Layout

The Print and Web Layout Options section controls the appearance of the document window in the Print and Web Layout views. Generally, these options are only useful if you're using Word as a publication layout or web design tool. Text boundaries display crop marks around the text space bounded by the document margins. Object anchors show where images and drawings are anchored within the text.

TIP   *Select the White Space Between Pages option to separate pages in Print view. This separation— which is actually dark gray in color—makes it easier to notice page separations when you're working on large documents.*

Style Area Width

The other feature of note on the View tab is the Style Area Width. The style area only appears in the Normal and Outline views, and only if you set a width for it to appear on the screen. When enabled, the style area lists the style of every paragraph in the document in a list down the left side of the document window. In most cases, you're better off saving the screen space and simply using the Style section of the Formatting toolbar to determine the style of a selected paragraph. In Outline view, however, the style area can help you see the heading level of entries at a glance, making it faster to balance outlines and increase or decrease levels as needed.

General Options

The General tab contains a myriad of options. Among them is the Recently Used File list that determines how many documents are listed in the File menu and task pane. If you often receive documents in other word processing formats, the Confirm Conversion at Open option gives you more control over the file conversion process. Finally, the Measurement Units option allows you to use metric measurements or the pixels and picas that are common to the Web. Even if you choose to keep your default measurement units in inches, centimeters, or millimeters, you can set HTML features to be measured in pixels.

If you're coming to Microsoft Word for the first time from a WordPerfect environment, the General tab also has options to access additional help files to ease the transition, as well as viewing options to mimic the old DOS-based WordPerfect display.

TIP *Setting the Recently Used File list to its maximum (nine files) makes it easier to find commonly used documents without having to navigate the Open File dialog box. Maximizing this setting doesn't affect Word's performance at all.*

Edit Options

The Edit options specify how you want Word to respond to certain editing tasks. By default, Word replaces selected text, images, or objects with any new text you enter. To disable this feature, deselect the Typing Replaces Selection option.

The CTRL + Click to Follow Hyperlinks option keeps you from inadvertently firing a link when you intended to edit it. Without this option, it's a bit too easy to mistakenly activate a link when you merely intended to reformat it or remove its linking ability. Chapter 9 explains how to format and access hyperlinks in Word.

When you select Keep Track of Formatting, Word updates your style list to note any differences in formatting as you create your document, adding new pseudo-styles to the list, as shown next, where the title style has two additional pseudo-styles underneath. A pseudo-style is a variation on an applied style, as when you boldface text that's already formatted with a style (such as the Title style) without updating the style itself. In conjunction with this feature, Mark Formatting Inconsistencies will display a Smart Tag if the formatting of a paragraph has been changed from the attached style. Styles are covered in detail in Chapter 9.

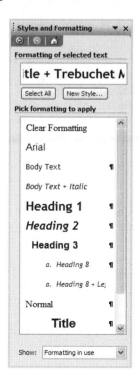

One of the first options that most advanced users disable in the Edit tab is When Selecting, Automatically Select Entire Word. This and the Use Smart Paragraph Selection option can increase rather than decrease the frustrations of making exact selections because they inherently select more than you may have intended.

TIP   *It's easy enough to double-click on a word to select the entire word, while deselecting this option gives you the flexibility to select only the first letter or other characters within a word. Similarly, you can triple-click to select an entire paragraph. In other words, you don't lose anything by disabling these options.*

Default Paragraph Style can be another useful option, especially if you're using a style such as Body Text to format the majority of your document. The drop-down menu lists all of the styles available in the open document.

Print Options

The Print options control the default settings for printing documents. They also offer some control over the printer itself. Background printing and reverse print order both streamline your work flow. Background printing spools the document into memory so you can continue working while printing. If your printer stacks printed pages face-up as they exit the sheet feeder, reverse order printing will print the last sheet first—and so on—so the completed stack is in the proper order.

CAUTION   *If both the Print options and the printer settings are set to print in reverse order, they can cancel each other out. In this situation, Word would spool the pages in reverse order, and the printer would then reverse the spool, defeating the purpose of both settings.*

If you're using European-sized paper, the Allow A4/Letter Paper Resizing option enables Word to automatically reformat your document to print on that paper. This doesn't affect the document itself, just the printed results. In order to actually print on the A4 paper, you'll need to set this as the paper size in the Page Setup dialog box (File | Page Setup). Since this Print option doesn't affect the document, it doesn't hurt anything to keep it selected, just in case you ever need to print on different paper.

The Update Fields and Update Links options can generally be deselected. In most cases, if you're using fields in your document, you'll update them manually before printing, or automatically when saving the document. The same is usually true of documents that are linked to your Word document.

The Print options also control information to be printed in addition to or within the document.

Include with Document

The options in the Include with Document section of the Print tab control the printing of fields and codes that would otherwise be excluded from the hard copy. Printing document properties can be useful for tracking purposes, particularly when searching a network server for outdated files, as the properties list the dates when the document was created and last modified, the title of the document, author, and keywords relating to the file.

Field codes, XML tags, and hidden text can be useful when editing a work in progress, but are not necessarily appreciated in the final work. Conversely, objects or background colors and images may need to appear in the final work, but only waste ink and printing time when reviewing a draft. So you can turn this feature on and off as needed.

Don't confuse the Print options with those found when you select File | Print. If you're planning to do duplex printing or want the document properties page to be printed, these options need to be set in the Print options before you begin the process of printing the document. In the case of duplex printing, your printer hardware must be capable of performing this function, and the printer settings must be configured properly. This varies by printer model, so refer to your printer manual for help.

Save Options

The Save options control the information Word stores in your documents. Arguably the most important option on this tab is the Default Format setting. If you're working in any other, non-Word document (.doc) format on a regular basis, you can change the default to HTML, Word templates (.dot), text (.txt), or one of several other formats. When you save a new document, the default format will be the first option offered in the Save dialog box.

Backup copies and autorecovery are critical. As with any software application, Word is prone to the occasional spontaneous crash. Murphy's Law stipulates this will happen at the most inopportune time, such as when you've typed five pages of the most sparkling prose ever to reach your keyboard. If you have enabled Always Create Backup Copy, Word will move the last saved version of the document into a backup file every time you save a new version. Save AutoRecover Info allows you to set an increment at which recovery information is automatically stored in a separate file. If Word crashes, it will automatically reopen with this file, which may be (but isn't always, depending on how often you save) more current than the last saved file.

NOTE   *Background saves are different from AutoRecover information. The Allow Background Saves option merely allows you to choose File | Save (or* CTRL-S*) and keep working while Word saves the file. It doesn't automatically save the file.*

The Fast Save option (which also appears in PowerPoint) is enticing because it saves only the changes you've made in the document, which makes the save process faster and keeps you working. The downside of using this feature is that you need to ensure that you deselect it at the end of your session to allow Word to save a complete version of your document. If you somehow lose the original, complete file before making another complete save, the fast save is worthless. Because Fast Save tracks lists of changes, your file size can become inordinately large, particularly when editing and making format changes. Unless you're using a particularly slow computer or working with an ungainly document, the standard Save feature is fast enough that it won't cause a significant delay in your work.

Most users will want to deselect the Prompt to Save Normal Template option. When making style changes for a particular document, you're likely to add or change several styles. If you want to be able to access them later, you'll save them in a new template. When prompted to save the Normal template, however, it's too easy to inadvertently save style changes that you won't want to apply to other documents.

When exchanging documents with others, it's possible that they will have a different version of Word, particularly when you're an early adopter of new software. To ensure compatibility, you can set Word to disable any features that were introduced after a specific version. Another option that can be useful when exchanging documents is Embed TrueType Fonts. This option saves the font files used in creating the document along with the document, thus ensuring that the recipient can view the text in the font you intended. This significantly increases the file size of the document, however, so you'll only want to use this option if you're using obscure fonts that are unlikely to be on the recipient's computer.

Track Changes

The options in the Track Changes tab control the color and style of changes to the text. The Balloons options, available in the Print and Web Layout views, place changes in balloons alongside the text so as not to detract from the content itself. The settings for these balloons determine their appearance and placement on the page, as well as how they appear in print. Balloons are shaded in the same colors as in-line changes, so changes to the markup colors will change the balloon appearance. Tracking changes and other review tools are explained in Chapter 40.

Other Options

Most of the other Options tabs contain features that were explained in Chapters 2 and 3, as they're common to all Office applications. Differences of note include the mailing address field on the User Information tab, which can be used when printing envelopes and labels. In the Compatibility tab you can disable specific options for the open document and make font substitutions if a font in the document isn't available on your system. Most of the options on the File Locations tab are just fine in their default settings, but you should make note of the location of your user templates, as that's where new templates you create should be stored.

Of course, as with all Office applications, you can also customize the Word interface by modifying the menus, keyboard shortcuts, and toolbars. Chapter 2 explains how to do this.

Document Views

Word provides several different ways to enter and view your work. Most likely, you'll have a favorite view that you use more often than the others. Each view has points in its favor, however, for certain tasks.

To change views, select from the View menu. Unless you've disabled the horizontal scroll bar at the bottom of the Word window, you'll notice five buttons on the lower-left side of the window. These buttons make it easy to change views without navigating through the menus.

Normal View

Normal view (shown in Figure 6-2) displays the character formatting of a document, but not the positioning. Page formatting items such as headers, footers, and background colors don't appear in Normal view. Graphics will appear, but only after the text to which they're anchored, regardless of alignment, text wrapping, and other settings.

Normal view makes it easy to set styles for each paragraph, thus ensuring consistency throughout the document. To do this, you'll need to set the Style Area Width option in the View options. Don't worry about the actual width setting in the dialog box—you can adjust it manually by dragging the vertical divider between the style area and the document, once you've set even a minimal width in the View options.

Normal view also makes it easy to view and edit section breaks. Section breaks appear as lines across the document, and they're labeled to let you know the nature of the break setting (continuous, next page, odd, or even).

Web Layout View

If you're creating documents for the Web, you'll most likely want to work in Web Layout view (shown in Figure 6-3). This view attempts to duplicate the conditions of the Web, including text wrapping (instead of margin control) and graphics placement.

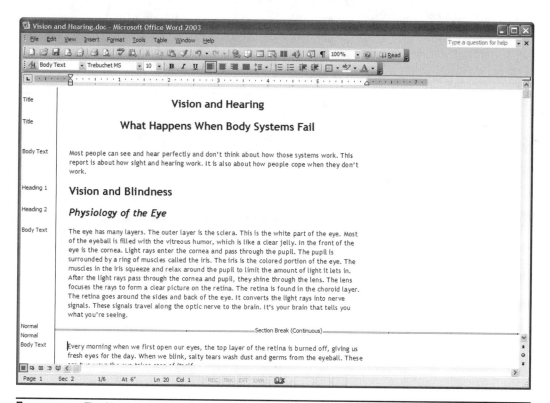

FIGURE 6-2   The Normal view displays paragraph styles on the left.

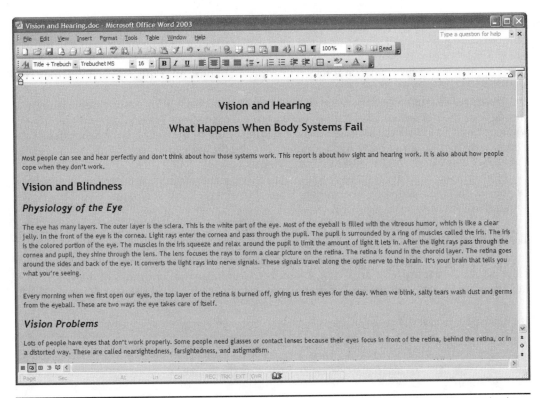

FIGURE 6-3   Web Layout view wraps text to the size of the window and displays the background color
of the page.

NOTE   *Web Layout view doesn't provide a perfect rendering of how your page will appear on the
Web. Variations in computer platforms and browsers will make the document render differently.
When designing for the Web, nothing can replace testing the completed pages in a variety of
browsers.*

Print Layout View

Print Layout view (see Figure 6-4) simulates the printed page. Graphics are rendered in the
proper position, styles are applied, and headers and footers appear. Pages are separated by
visual white space, making it easy to see how text is flowing from page to page.

Reading Layout View

Reading Layout view (Figure 6-5) is a new feature in Office 2003. The purpose of this view
is to eliminate most of the on-screen distractions so the document is easily readable. This is
particularly useful when reviewing and marking up a document. The important review and
editing controls are available, including the Research button to put a thesaurus, foreign

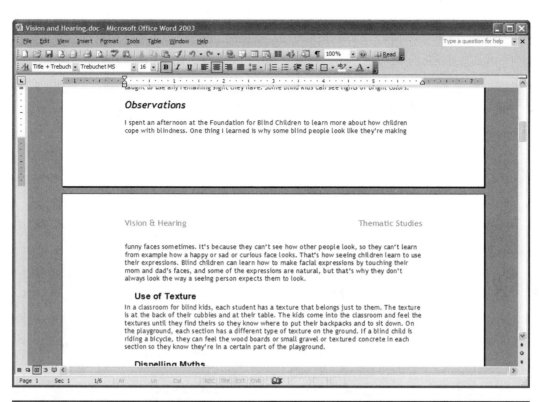

FIGURE 6-4 Although this rendering doesn't do it justice, the page header is clearly visible in Print Layout view.

language translators, and encyclopedias within reach. Text size controls can be used to increase or decrease the text size for easier reading or to fit more content on a page. The Actual Size button displays the actual content of the page, albeit in an unreadable fashion; this setting is useful for seeing where page breaks would normally fall in the document. Since this is primarily a reading view rather than a working view, the Stop Reading button exits the Reading Layout view and returns to the previous working view.

Reading Layout view is extremely useful on tablet PCs because you can read documents easily without printing them out. You can even make handwritten notations in the document.

***

NOTE *The page flow and formatting in Reading Layout view are not accurate representations of the formatted document. The font is larger and lines are shorter to make the pages more readable on screen. Also, headers and footers aren't displayed. To see a true rendering of the document as it will appear in its final form, use the Web Layout or Print Layout views.*

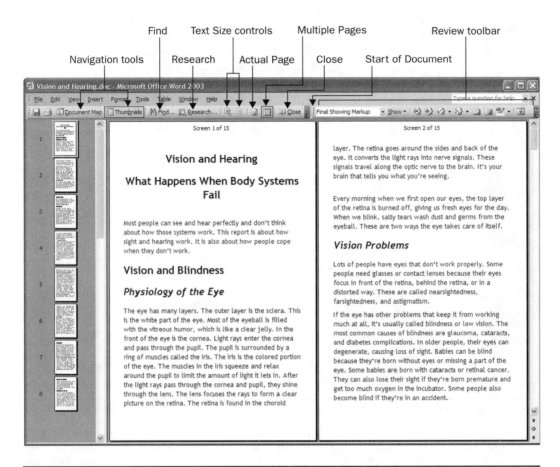

FIGURE 6-5 The new Reading Layout view displays pages in a readable format, but excludes headers and footers.

Outline View

One of the most powerful views is the Outline view (see Figure 6-6). This view is useful in establishing the structure of a document such as a thesis or business plan. The book you now hold in your hands was structured in Outline view. Headings can be promoted or demoted using the Level Promote/Demote tools or the Heading styles. Items can be moved around in the outline by dragging and dropping, and the visible headings can be adjusted to display only certain levels of the outline.

Outline view is also used to control Master Documents, a method for splitting large documents across smaller files while retaining formatting, page numbering, indexing, and table of contents references. This feature is explained in detail in Chapter 13.

Level Promotion/Demotion tools   Master Document tools

Heading style   Show Level controls

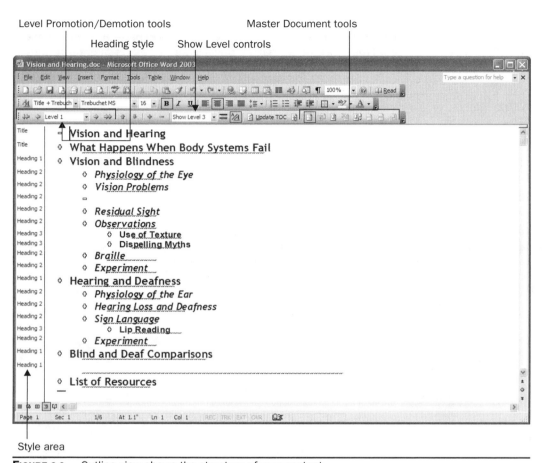

Style area

FIGURE 6-6   Outline view shows the structure of your content.

Splitting the Document Window

When working in a multipage document, you may want to cross-check content you wrote earlier with the material you're currently composing. Rather than scrolling back and forth through the document, it's easiest just to display both sections at the same time.

To split the document window:

1. Choose Window | Split.

2. Position the window divider where you want it on the screen.
   This becomes the horizontal scroll bar for the top pane.

3. Scroll through both panes to locate the content you want.

You can also split the window in order to see the document in two different views at once. Figure 6-7 shows the document in Print Layout view in the top pane and Outline view at the bottom of the screen. This is useful for rearranging sections of material organized by headings.

NOTE   *You cannot use the Reading Layout view in a split pane. If you change to this view while the document window is split, it will return to one pane, even when you choose Stop Reading.*

To return to a single pane, double-click on the horizontal divider between the panes. The single window will reflect the view settings of the top pane.

Maximizing Screen Space

The more features Microsoft adds to Word, the more crowded the document window becomes. Although Reading Layout view makes it easier to read pages on screen, there may still be times when you want to eliminate all the surrounding distractions. Full Screen view eliminates the menus, rulers, toolbars, and title bar, leaving you with a full-screen document and just one button to close the view. To access Full Screen view, choose View | Full Screen. To exit, click the Close Full Screen button. To totally clear the screen, close the Full Screen toolbar; use the ESC key to return to your previous view.

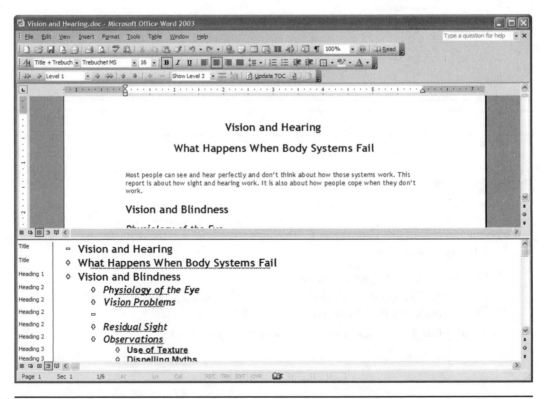

FIGURE 6-7   By splitting the document window you can see two different views at the same time.

TIP   *You can still access the menus in Full Screen view. If you slide your mouse to the top of the screen, the menus will temporarily appear. As soon as you move the mouse pointer away from the top of the screen, the menus disappear again. You can also make specific toolbars appear by right-clicking on the Full Screen toolbar and selecting from the pop-up menu.*

Zoom

Spending hours in front of a computer screen can cause severe eyestrain even with the best monitors. One way of combating this is by increasing the size of the text as it appears on your screen. You can use the Zoom tool to magnify the page up to 500 percent. Likewise, you can minimize the page to as little as 10 percent using the same tool. Zoom is available from the View | Zoom menu or on the Standard toolbar.

Navigating in Word

Navigation in Word can be as simple as pointing and clicking the mouse. Of course, there are several advanced methods of navigating more quickly and accurately through your document.

Keyboard Navigation

Most likely, if you're working in Word, your fingers are on the keyboard more often than not. Lifting your fingers from the keys to the mouse can interrupt your thought process and slow you down. Table 6-1 lists the common keyboard shortcuts for navigation.

TABLE 6-1
Keyboard
Navigation

Navigation	Keyboard Shortcut
Beginning of document	CTRL-HOME
End of document	CTRL-END
Previous screen	PAGE UP
Next screen	PAGE DOWN
Top of current screen	ALT-CTRL-PAGE UP
Bottom of current screen	ALT-CTRL-PAGE DOWN
Switch to other open document	CTRL-F6
Return to previous open document	CTRL-SHIFT-F6
Previous paragraph	CTRL-UP ARROW
Next paragraph	CTRL-DOWN ARROW
Beginning of line	HOME
End of line	END
Previous word	CTRL-LEFT ARROW
Next word	CTRL-RIGHT ARROW

Mouse Navigation

While keyboard navigation may be the most efficient in terms of movement, mouse navigation is the most common because it doesn't require memorizing extensive lists of keystrokes. Here are several tricks that can make mouse navigation even easier:

- If your mouse has a scroll wheel, rotating the wheel will scroll the screen up and down (without changing the insertion point) by two lines at a time.
- Clicking above or below the position slider in the vertical scrollbar on the right will scroll the document up or down by a full screen.
- If you have ScreenTips activated, dragging the position slider in the vertical scrollbar will display page numbers and headings as you scroll through the document.
- To scroll into the left margin in Normal view, hold down SHIFT while clicking the arrow on the left side of the horizontal scrollbar. Hold down SHIFT while clicking the arrow on the right side to remove the margin.

Accessing the Document Map

The Document Map is a little-known tool that provides an outline-style view of your document's structure based on headings and subheadings. At first glance, it would seem that the Document Map serves the same function as splitting the document window between Outline view and one of the other views. The Document Map's true purpose, however, is to aid in navigation (shown in Figure 6-8). Clicking on a heading in the Document Map immediately takes you to that place in the document and repositions the insertion point.

As with Outline view, the Document Map's hierarchical list can be expanded and contracted by clicking on the small boxes beside each parent entry.

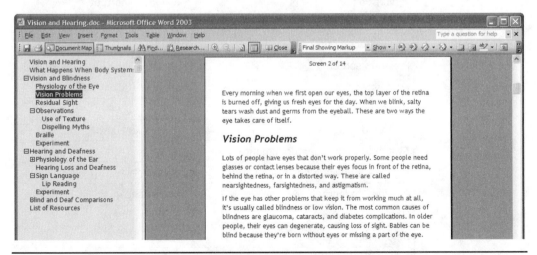

FIGURE 6-8   The Document Map provides a hierarchical representation of the document to aid in navigation.

Using the Object Browser

Even lesser known than the Document Map—but equally as useful—is the Object Browser. The Object Browser is a series of three buttons located underneath the vertical scrollbar on the right side of the document window.

To use the Object Browser:

1. Click the Select Browse Object button between the two arrows.

2. Choose an object type from the pop-up menu. The arrow keys surrounding the Object Browser will change color to highlight them.

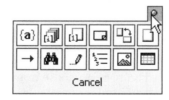

3. Click one of the arrows to move forward or backward through the document.

4. The arrows will move you to the previous or next iteration of the object you selected.

The Object Browser searches for the following items:

- **Field**   Searches for any field codes in the document, such as a date and time stamp.

- **Endnotes and Footnotes**   Searches for endnote or footnote codes in the document. To search for the endnotes or footnotes themselves, begin the search within one of the notes.

- **Comment**   Searches for comments in the document, such as those added by others when they review a document.

- **Section**   Scrolls through section breaks. This feature doesn't discriminate between continuous, page break, or even/odd section breaks.

- **Page**   Scrolls from page to page in the document.

- **Go To**   Allows you to specify other objects for which the Object Browser should search. These include bookmarks, OLE objects, and equations.
- **Find**   Opens the Find and Replace dialog box, then searches for matching criteria.
- **Edits**   Scrolls to the last three places where you modified the document.
- **Heading**   Scrolls from heading style to heading style.
- **Graphics**   Scrolls for pictures and clip art in the document.
- **Table**   Scrolls from table to table.

NOTE   *The Find option of the Object Browser is the same tool as the Find tab of the Find and Replace options on the Edit menu. Find and Replace are covered in Chapter 4.*

Printing Word Documents

Printing in Word is much the same as printing in any other Office application. Given that Word documents are more likely to be printed than any others, however, there are also some extra features to give you more control over your final output.

Remember the Print tab in the Options dialog box earlier in this chapter? Many of the choices you made in that dialog box will be reflected in your output. If you choose to print document properties, they will print on a separate sheet along with your document. If you didn't choose to set this option as a default, however, it's not too late to print document properties—or a list of styles or even keyboard shortcuts—for the current document. To do this:

1. Select File | Print. (Don't use the Print button on the Standard toolbar, as that will bypass the Print dialog box.)
2. In the Print What field (see Figure 6-9), choose from the drop-down list. The default option is to print the document itself.
3. Click OK to print.

Using Print Preview

Unlike Excel, in which the Print Preview option provides your only view of how your worksheet will look on paper, Word has options that minimize the importance of this tool. The Print Layout view is much more useful and provides a larger view of how your document will appear in print. One feature that saves Print Preview from obsolescence, however, is its ability to view multiple pages at once. This is particularly useful when you want to take a fast look at graphics to ensure they're positioned consistently throughout the document.

Printing Thumbnails

When creating a document, logic dictates that you configure the margins, fonts, and other page settings to suit your anticipated final output. If you're printing drafts of the document, however, your print needs are often very different. Documents intended to be printed on 11×17-inch newsletter sheets might be printed in draft mode on 8.5×11-inch paper. In order to conserve paper, you can opt to print multiple document pages on a single sheet of paper.

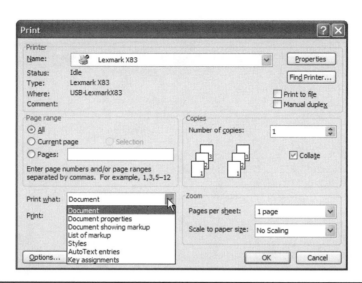

FIGURE 6-9   The Print What field of the Print dialog box, often taken for granted, provides access to several useful lists.

The Zoom options in the Print dialog box are used to adjust these settings. In the first scenario, Scale to Paper Size will resize your document to print on the smaller paper. In the latter case, you can instruct Word to print up to 16 pages on a single sheet. Best of all, neither of these options changes the actual document settings.

Editing Text

The hardest part of using Word is coming up with words to fill that white screen. Unfortunately, no how-to book can do that part for you. However, once you've put your words on screen you can edit them and begin formatting your document; this chapter explains how. If you've skipped around in this book, you might want to review Chapter 4, which explained the methods of entering text into all of the Office applications using the keyboard, scanners, handwriting tools, and even your own voice.

Automatic Text Tools

One of the first things you'll notice when typing in Word is that your text can change before your eyes. Word has several tools to automatically correct, format, or insert the right words at the right time (or at least what it hopes is the right time). As you'll see , although each of these tools can be extremely useful, they do have their flaws.

NOTE *Aside from the tools listed here, you can also use fields to automate text entry and formatting. Fields are covered in Chapter 12.*

AutoCorrect

AutoCorrect was explained in Chapter 2, and it's available in all of the Office applications. Word is the application in which you're most likely to make changes to the AutoCorrect options and add new words, since most of your extensive text entry is generally done in Word.

One of the easiest ways to extend the usefulness of AutoCorrect is in conjunction with the spell-checking features of Word. An overlooked feature of the Spelling context menu and the Spelling and Grammar dialog box is the ability to add to the AutoCorrect list. If you find that you commonly make the same typos repeatedly, adding the words you tend to misspell to the list can save you time. In the Spelling and Grammar dialog box, click on the correct spelling, and then click the AutoCorrect button. If you're correcting spelling in context, words not recognized by the spellchecker will appear with a red underline. Right-click on the underlined word, select AutoCorrect from the context menu, and then choose the correct spelling from the suggestions list. You'll notice this list duplicates the regular spelling suggestions on the context menu. For more information on spelling and grammar checking, see Chapter 2.

Just as AutoCorrect is likely to be most useful in Word, it's also likely to be most annoying here. Judicious use of the AutoCorrect dialog box enables you to turn off features, such as correcting two initial caps, and others that you might not appreciate as you type a particular document. Also remember that the CTRL-Z keyboard shortcut will undo an automatic correction if used immediately after the correction is made, as will accessing the Smart Tag associated with any automatic correction.

AutoText

AutoCorrect uses the same list for all of the Office applications. Word has another correction tool that's application specific, called AutoText. The advantage AutoText has over AutoCorrect is that it can be used for entries that are specific to Word documents or even to a specific Word template. AutoText contains several preformatted entries, grouped in categories and mostly consisting of entries to speed up letter writing (salutations, closings, and reference lines). One of the most powerful features of AutoText is AutoComplete.

AutoComplete

When using Word for the first time, you might be surprised if you start typing the letters **frid** and see a ScreenTip appear prompting you to press ENTER to complete the word *Friday*. This is AutoComplete, which is a subfeature of AutoText. When you start to type a word that has an AutoText entry, Word puts a ScreenTip on the screen after the first four letters to remind you that the entry exists. If you type **octo**, for example, a ScreenTip with "October (Press ENTER to Insert)" appears. If you want to accept the AutoText entry—in this case, replace the "octo" you've typed with "October"—you need to press ENTER (or F3). If you're intending to type the word *octopus*, simply keep typing and ignore the AutoText prompt.

October (Press ENTER to Insert)
octo

Aside from days of the week and months of the year, Word automatically converts your name, company name, and initials into AutoText entries. It obtains this information from the User Information tab in the Tools | Options dialog box. Word will also make AutoComplete entries out of e-mail addresses, mailing addresses, and telephone numbers.

Creating AutoText Entries

One of the advantages of AutoText over AutoCorrect is that you can customize entries for a specific template. Thus, if you're writing about sea life, you can create an AutoText entry for *octopus* in a marine.dot template. This won't appear in other templates, leaving you free to create an entry for *octogenarians* in another document.

octopus (Press ENTER to Insert)
octop

To create an AutoText entry:

1. Type the text of your entry.

2. Select the text.

3. Select Insert | AutoText | New.

4. Name the new entry in the Create AutoText dialog box.

5. Press OK.

In this case, you'd have to type five letters instead of four in order for Word to distinguish it from *October*.

TIP *You can also create an AutoText entry to insert a graphic. Embed the graphic in your document, select it, then follow steps 3-5 in the preceding list. The default name of the entry will be an asterisk (*), but you can change this name to anything you'd like.*

Inserting AutoText

Another method for inserting AutoText entries is through the AutoText menu or toolbar. To open the AutoText toolbar, right-click in the toolbar area, and then select the AutoText toolbar from the context menu. Click on All Entries to select from the list of available AutoText entries. If you access AutoText frequently, the toolbar saves the time of navigating through the menu structure. The toolbar takes up screen real estate, though, so for occasional access, it's best to use the menu option. This is done by selecting Insert | AutoText and then choosing an entry from the categories listed, as shown in Figure 7-1.

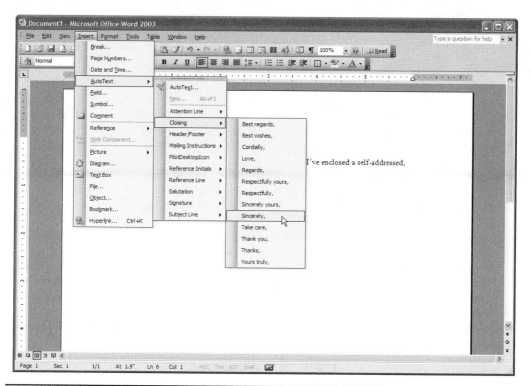

FIGURE 7-1   The AutoText menu is categorized by type of entry.

¿Habla Usted Español?

One little-known feature of the AutoText menu is that it's language sensitive. If you're typing in another language, such as Spanish, the AutoText menu and toolbar will translate the categories and entries into that language. As you can see in the following illustration, the AutoText categories and entries reflect the Spanish language setting of the paragraph, even though the rest of the document is in English. You can use this feature even if the majority of your text is in English (or any other language); just set the language of the paragraph using Tools | Language, and select Insert | AutoText. For more information about changing the language of a document or selection, see Chapter 4.

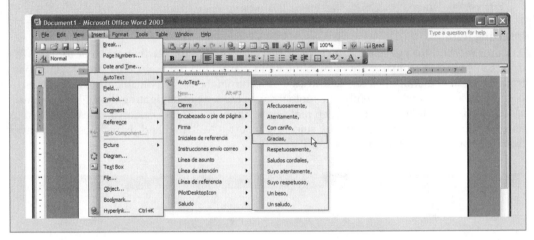

NOTE *Most of the AutoComplete entries don't appear in the AutoText menu. These entries are compiled from other sources, such as your Outlook address book or the User Information in the Options dialog box, and would make the AutoText menu too unwieldy.*

Organizing AutoText Entries

The AutoText entries that are preformatted in Word are sorted into general categories. But how did they get into those categories? The trick lies in using styles (which are covered in detail in Chapter 9). When you create a new AutoText entry, it will automatically be placed into a category named after the style that is applied to the selected text. Moreover, when you insert an entry into a document, the paragraph will be formatted in this style.

Let's look at this in practice. If you create an AutoText entry from a Title style, the new entry will appear in a category labeled Title, as seen in Figure 7-2. If you insert this entry into a document, it will be formatted in the Title style. If this text is inserted into the middle of a paragraph, the style of the entire paragraph will be changed to Title, as well. Even if you later delete the style Title, the category and related AutoText entries will remain, as will the formatting of the style for those entries.

Understanding how AutoText entries are categorized enables you to use the feature to your advantage. To create a new category, simply create a new style with the name you want

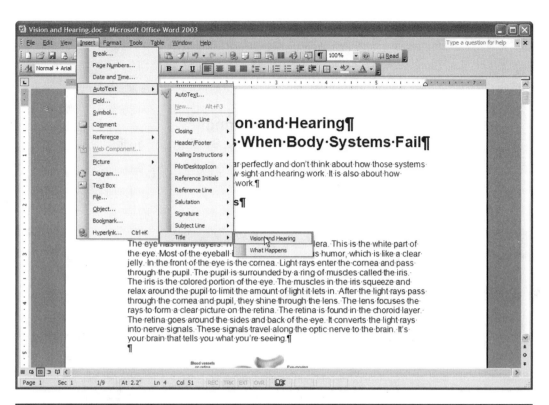

FIGURE 7-2   Creating an entry for the title "Vision and Hearing" automatically places it in the Title category.

for the category, enter the desired text, and then create your new AutoText entry. Once the entry is created, you can delete the style if you wish. Putting this into practice, if you want to make an AutoText category containing medical terminology, first create a style named Medical. Enter a list of terms using this style, and make each term a new AutoText entry. They'll all be filed under a new Medical category.

This also points out the flaws in the AutoText feature. Before creating new AutoText entries, you need to be sure the text is formatted in the style you want it to have in future iterations. In many cases, you'll want to change the style of the selected text before creating the new entry, which makes this process much more awkward. You also need to choose your style names carefully if they're to make sense in the AutoText menu later.

The biggest flaw of AutoText, however, is that organizing your entries into style-related categories can work against you when you want to quickly insert entries later. When you're inserting AutoText into a paragraph that's formatted with the Normal style—or any other style that doesn't have an associated AutoText category—you can see the full list of categories and entries. If the paragraph is formatted in a style that's been used as a category for AutoText entries, however, you're limited to only the entries within the related category. For example, if you create an AutoText entry using the Title category, any time you try to insert an AutoText entry while the insertion point is in a Title style, you'll only be able to insert the entries from the Title category, as seen in Figure 7-3.

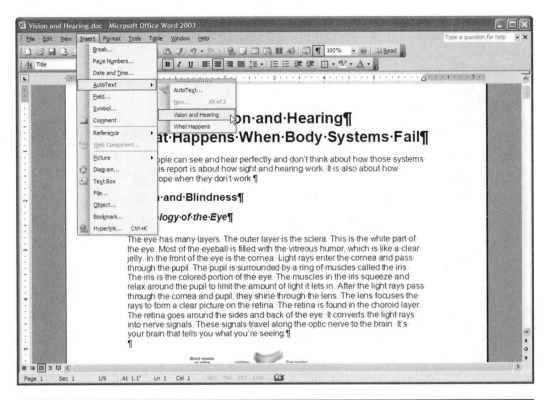

FIGURE 7-3 Argh! Because a Title category has been created in the AutoText menu, the options are limited when trying to insert AutoText into a paragraph formatted with the Title style.

Of course, the complete list of entries is available, but by the time you access the entry you want, you could have typed it. To view the complete list of AutoText entries, select Insert | AutoText | AutoText. This opens the AutoText tab of the AutoCorrect dialog box, which contains an alphabetized, but uncategorized, list of entries. Scroll through the list to find the entry you need, highlight it, and click Insert. This multistep process definitely takes the *Auto* out of AutoText.

This flaw existed in the previous version of Word, and unfortunately hasn't been changed in Word 2003, so we can only assume this is done by design rather than oversight. It severely limits the usefulness of categorizing entries, however. The only way around this problem is *never* to use "real" style names when categorizing your AutoText entries. Always create new style names just to use for categorization, then delete them from the styles list.

Repeating Text

Let's say you're preparing a document that extols the strengths and weaknesses of various products. Each product description needs to follow the same format. An easy way to ensure that every description has the same major headings is to use repeating text. To do this:

1. Type the text. In the case of the product description example, you can enter a list of headings, such as Price, Review, Pros, Cons, each separated with a carriage return.

2. Position the insertion point where you want to repeat what you just typed. In the example, you'd position the cursor below the name of the next product in the list.

3. Press F4 to repeat the text.

4. Repeat steps 2 and 3 as necessary to repeat the same text elsewhere in the document.

As with all the other automated text entry features, repeating text has some flaws. It's important that you don't use the arrow keys while typing your text because this will clear the text queue and start anew. Similarly, you can't apply formatting such as bold or italics—even using the keyboard shortcuts—without clearing the text queue. For repeating straight text, however, this is a quick and handy tool.

Undo and Redo

Nobody's perfect, even with the myriad tools available in Office. When you make a mistake, click the Undo button in the Standard toolbar. If you mistakenly undo a mistake, you can redo it using the Redo button on the toolbar. Both tools are also accessible from the Edit menu or keyboard shortcuts (CTRL-Z to undo, CTRL-Y to redo).

If you look at the Undo and Redo buttons on the toolbar, you'll notice each one has a down arrow next to it. These open drop-down menus containing the history of your document. If you want to undo a series of actions back to a particular point, scroll down the list and click at the point where you want to revert. The undo/redo history remembers changes made before and after saving the document, but only for the current editing session. Once you close the document or exit Word, the history is lost.

Text Formatting

There's more to word processing than getting the words on the screen, of course. Once the skeleton has been created, it's fleshed out by formatting the text to draw the reader's eye to headings or key points. Most of your formatting is done through judicious use of the bold, italic, and underlining options, which were explained in Chapter 4. Consistent formatting is achieved through the use of styles, covered in Chapter 9.

The default font setting in Word is Times New Roman 12 point. Unless you change this default (by updating the Normal.dot template) or are using a different template, this is the font in which your text will initially appear. There are several ways to change the formatting of your text. In Chapter 4, you learned how to change fonts and basic formatting using the Formatting toolbar, which is common to all Office applications (other than Outlook). Some text formatting, however, is only accessible from the Font dialog box.

To access the Font dialog box, shown in Figure 7-4, select Format | Font. Here, you can change the font, font style (bold and italic), and font size, just as you can with the Formatting toolbar. There are some features of note, however.

- **Underline Style**   You have more control over underlining than you do with the standard Formatting toolbar option. You can choose to underline <u>only</u> <u>the</u> <u>words</u> (not spaces) or to format the underline with a <u>double line</u> or various artistic line styles.

- **Superscript and Subscript**   This formatting reduces the size of the characters and puts them above or below the baseline. These are useful when entering chemical formulas, such as H_2O.

- **Strikethrough and Double Strikethrough**   The text is displayed with one or two lines through the middle, giving it the appearance of having been crossed out. This can be used when editing your content, to virtually cross out a block of text without deleting it, such as ~~this block here~~. If you decide to return to your previous wording, it's much easier to reformat the text without the strikethrough than it is to retype it from memory.

- **Small Caps**   Lowercase characters are converted into uppercase, while also reducing the size of the characters. This makes the lowercase characters appear smaller than the uppercase, but with the SAME LETTER STYLE.

FIGURE 7-4   The Font dialog box controls special character effects such as super- and subscript and strikethrough text.

- **Hidden Text** This text is invisible unless you set your View or Print options to display it. Hidden text is useful when you're writing a report and need to submit a draft of the work in progress. You can hide text that hasn't yet been edited and print a clean draft. Meanwhile, you can set your View options to see the hidden text on your screen so you can continue with your work. Just don't forget to deselect the Hidden property of the text before completing the report.

As you select these formatting options, you can get an idea of their effect in the Preview pane at the bottom of the dialog box. Some of the other options—Shadow, Outline, Emboss, Engrave, and All Caps—aren't commonly used, but it's interesting to preview them to see their effect.

The Font dialog box also controls character spacing. In most cases, the default spacing is fine, so you'll rarely need to access this tab. If you're working with large fonts, however, you'll want to control the kerning of the letters. *Kerning* controls the white space between letters, such as between the *A* and the *V* in the word HAVE. At smaller font sizes, kerning isn't very noticeable, but it can be quite dramatic on a larger scale. The Character Spacing tab also offers more precise control over superscripts and subscripts. You can set the position of the characters to be raised or lowered by a set number of points from the baseline. Unlike the regular superscript and subscript options on the Font tab, this positioning can be used if you want to retain the font size of the character and increase or decrease the positioning offset.

In addition to the font formatting options, there are special character formatting tools that can save you time.

Changing Case

One of the most common text entry mistakes is forgetting to turn off the CAPS LOCK key. This can result in a paragraph (or more) of text in capital letters, depending on when you catch it. You can automatically change the text back to lower- or mixed case using the Change Case tool.

The Change Case tool is also useful for putting headings into *title case* (the first letter of each word capitalized, as in a book title) and other purposes. The Change Case tool has several different options, but the results are different depending on whether you access the tool from the keyboard shortcut (SHIFT-F3) or the menu (Format | Change Case). When you Change Case using the menu option, a dialog box offers you the following choices:

- **Sentence Case** This option only works when you select a sentence or paragraph. The first letter of the first word in each sentence is capitalized, while the rest of the sentence is rendered in lowercase. If there are words in initial caps within a sentence, that capitalization is retained. If there isn't any selection, the text remains unchanged.

- **Lowercase** All the characters in the selection are rendered in lowercase. If no selection is made, the word located near the insertion point is changed.

- **Uppercase** All the characters in the selection are rendered in uppercase. If no selection is made, the word located near the insertion point is changed.

- **Title Case** The first character in each word of the selection is capitalized, and all other characters are rendered in lowercase. If no selection is made, the word located near the insertion point is capitalized.

- **Toggle Case**   The case of each character in the selection is toggled, changing uppercase letters to lowercase and vice versa. If no selection is made, the word near the insertion point is toggled.

If you use the SHIFT-F3 keyboard shortcut to change case, only the Title Case, Uppercase, and Lowercase options are available. The keyboard shortcut will toggle through each of these three options in that order, so you need to press the key combination three times to change the text to lowercase.

Drop Caps

If you've ever read an illuminated manuscript, the first letter on the page is much larger than the rest of the text, taking up several lines, with the remaining text in the paragraph wrapping to the right of it. (Another example appears on the first page of each chapter in this book.) This is called a *drop cap*. To create a drop cap in Word, put the insertion point in the paragraph you want formatted, then select Format | Drop Cap. In the Drop Cap dialog box, you can choose how to wrap the rest of the paragraph text around the letter and select formatting options for the letter (see Figure 7-5).

NOTE   *Drop caps only work on the first letter in a paragraph. Even if you select a different word within a paragraph, the drop cap will be applied to the first letter of the first word in the paragraph.*

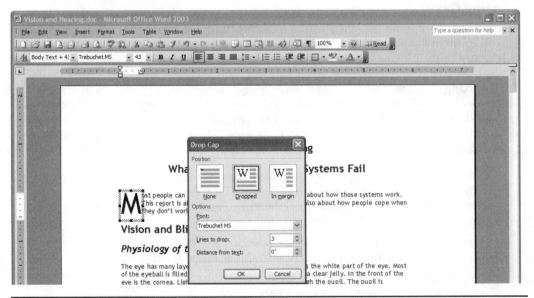

FIGURE 7-5   The options selected in this dialog box determined the appearance of the drop cap in the text.

Coloring and Highlighting Text

There's more to text than black and white. You can add color in two ways. To color the text itself, click on the arrow to the right of the Font Color button on the Formatting toolbar. The drop-down menu displays a rainbow of colors, along with an option to access even more. This feature offers the same result as setting a color in the Font dialog box, but is much faster.

You can also change the background—or highlight—color of the text. Highlighting is most useful when you're editing in a collaborative environment and want to draw the team's attention to particular wording within a paragraph. You can highlight an individual selection by selecting the text, then clicking the Highlight button on the Formatting toolbar.

Highlighting can also be used as a study aid to draw your attention to key facts in a document. In this case, you may want to read the document on screen with the highlighter active so you can mark the text as you read, just as you would with a regular highlighter and a printed page of text. To activate the highlighter:

1. Click the Highlight button on the Formatting toolbar. This activates the highlighting tool, as evidenced by the change in cursor.

2. Select the text you want to highlight. You can manually drag the highlighter across the text or use any of the text selection keyboard shortcuts listed in Chapter 4, such as double-clicking on a word or using SHIFT-END to select the rest of a line.

3. Continue selecting text.

4. Turn off the highlighting tool by clicking on the Highlight button again.

The drop-down menu for the highlighter is much more limited than the Font Color option. Choose a color that allows the text to show through clearly.

Adding Special Characters

Did you wonder when reading the "¿Habla Usted Español?" sidebar earlier in this chapter how to type the inverted question mark and tilde *n*? These are inserted using symbols. Some special characters are so commonly used that they've been preformatted into AutoCorrect. To enter a copyright symbol, for example, you can type **(c)**, and Word will change it into the symbol (©). Others, such as the Spanish characters, are more obscure, and you must use the menus to enter them.

NOTE   *In some cases, these preformatted symbols are one of the annoyances of AutoCorrect. If you're typing an outline with headings such as (c), you'll want to disable the copyright symbol AutoCorrect item. Alternatively, you can use the Smart Tag to remove the AutoCorrection after the fact.*

To insert a special character or symbol:

1. Position the cursor at the insertion point.

2. Select Insert | Symbol. This opens the Symbol dialog box, which contains a character map for the current font.

3. Scroll through the symbols to find the one you need. You can use the Subset drop-down box to look for symbols grouped by type.

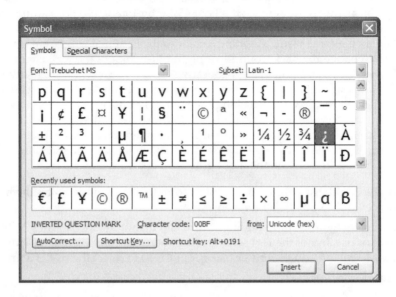

4. Insert the symbol into the document:

   • Double-click on the symbol, or

   • Click on the symbol to select it, and then click Insert.

5. After you click Insert to add a symbol, the Cancel button changes to a Close button. Click that to exit the Symbol dialog box.

Your most recently used symbols appear in a bar across the bottom of the dialog box, making it easier to insert the same symbols later in the document. Sometimes the symbol you need isn't available in your current font. To use symbols from another font—or view the character map for a symbol font such as Webdings—change the Font in the Symbol dialog box.

TIP   *The bottom of the dialog box lists the keyboard shortcut for the selected symbol. If you're using the same symbol repeatedly, make note of the keyboard shortcut, which is usually a combination of the* ALT *key and a four-digit number. This number must be entered from the numeric keypad while* NUM LOCK *is engaged in order for the keypresses to register. Thus, a tilde n is entered by holding down the* ALT *key while entering 0241 on the numeric keypad.*

The Symbol dialog box also contains a tab that lists special characters, such as the em dash (—), nonbreaking spaces, and em spaces. An em dash or em space takes up the same width as the lowercase m character. An en dash or space is the same width as the n character. Nonbreaking spaces are used to insert a space between two words to ensure they aren't split between lines.

Bullets and Numbering

One of the most common methods of formatting text is through the use of bulleted and numbered lists. Everything from a shopping list to an outline for a book report to a business plan can make use of lists.

The approach you take to insert bullets and numbering differs depending on the structure and formatting requirements of the list. The easiest way to create a list is to use automatic bullets and numbering. If your list is more complex, particularly if you want to customize the bullets, starting number, or paragraph formatting, the Bullets and Numbering dialog box and the related toolbar buttons provide more options.

Automatic Bullets and Numbering

Creating a bulleted or numbered list in Word can be as simple as typing the starting number or bullet item, then typing your list. In order to use this feature, you need to enable the Automatic Numbered Lists and Automatic Bulleted Lists options in the AutoFormat As You Type tab of the AutoCorrect Options dialog box (Tools | AutoCorrect Options). With these enabled, you then start on a blank line and do the following:

1. Enter a leading character for the first point of your list. Leading characters can be letters, numbers, or a bullet character, as listed in Table 7-1.

2. For a numbered (or lettered) list, you can also add punctuation to the numbering. If you want the number to be followed by a period, for example, type it after the number. You can also enclose the letter or number in parenthesis or follow it with a hyphen.

NOTE *If you precede a number with a pound symbol (#), the list will not be automatically numbered. Only periods, parenthesis, and hyphens are recognized by AutoFormat.*

---

3. Press SPACE or TAB.

4. Type the text of the entry.

5. Press ENTER. The first entry is automatically formatted, and the next line is numbered or bulleted in sequence.

Whether you use the space or tab to separate the bullet/number from the text, it will be formatted with a tab. If you use a bullet character, it is automatically converted to the corresponding bullet. The list will also be indented, using the current settings of the Bullets and Numbering dialog box.

NOTE *Bullets and list numbers are inserted using fields, not standard text, so they're not edited in the same manner as the list content itself. To modify these fields, you need to use the Bullets and Numbering dialog box, as explained in the next section, "Using the Bullets and Numbering Tools." The field is also automatically updated if you insert items into the middle of a numbered list or add items at the end of a list.*

Bullet or Number Character	Results In
1, 2, 3 (any number)	A numbered list, beginning with the number you enter
A, B, C (any uppercase letter) a, b, c (any lowercase letter)	A numbered list, beginning with the letter you enter
I, II, III (any Roman numeral) i, ii, iii (any lowercase Roman numeral)	A numbered list, beginning with the number you enter
O (the letter, in either upper- or lowercase) * (SHIFT-8)	•
- - (two hyphens)	■
=> (equal sign and right bracket)	⇨
-> (hyphen and right bracket)	→
- (hyphen)	-
— (em dash, using CTRL-ALT-MINUS from the numeric keypad)	—

TABLE 7-1   Bullet and Number Characters Recognized by Word's AutoFormat Feature

When creating bulleted lists on the fly, you can substitute certain characters for the bullets, and Word will automatically convert them to the appropriate symbol, as listed in Table 7-1. You can also start a list with a number or letter other than 1 or A by simply typing that letter or number as the first in the list. You can even start a list with 0 (zero).

CAUTION   *In the unlikely event that you want to start your numbered list with the letter o, it will be automatically converted to a small dot bullet. To get around this, add a period or parenthesis after the letter.*

If you want list items to consist of a lead-in or term and then explanatory text, Word will recognize the formatting of the lead-in and the punctuation used to separate it from the text that follows. As you add to the list, Word automatically applies this formatting, using the delimiting punctuation as the cue to end the extra formatting. As you can see in the following bulleted list, the terms Bullets and Numbered are in bold, separated from the explanatory text with em spaces. You can also use periods, dashes, and colons as delineators.

- **Bullets**   Lists that use symbols to delineate items. These are also called unordered lists because the order of the items generally isn't important. Marketing copy makes use of bulleted lists to highlight key points of a product, but no point is necessarily more important than the others in the list.

- **Numbered**   Lists that use letters or numbers to delineate items. These are also called ordered lists because the order of the items is crucial to their purpose. Step-by-step instructions are numbered so that they are followed in order.

To end a list, press ENTER to go to the next line. Instead of adding text, however, just press ENTER a second time. The paragraph will revert to the normal paragraph formatting, without the bullets or numbering.

NOTE   *Blank lines cannot be automatically formatted as list items since a blank line indicates the end of a list.*

Using the Bullets and Numbering Tools

The AutoFormat feature is handy, but doesn't offer much control over the formatting of lists. The automatic formatting can also be distracting if you're still composing the list items and making changes to the list. Fortunately, you can also apply bullets and numbers after the fact. To turn a series of typed paragraphs into a bulleted or numbered list, select the items and click either the Numbering or Bullets button on the Formatting toolbar. The list will automatically be formatted using the last type of list you used in the document. If a previous list was formatted as A, B, C, the new list will also be lettered. If a previous bulleted list used square bullets, the new list will have the same bullet type.

TIP   *When you create a new numbered list, a Smart Tag will appear to offer the option of restarting the list numbering or to format the list using the Bullets and Numbering dialog box.*

You can also create a list by selecting the items and then choosing Format | Bullets and Numbering. This brings up the Bullets and Numbering dialog box, shown here. The preset bullet and numbering options will work for most situations. To use one of these presets, simply click on it and then on OK.

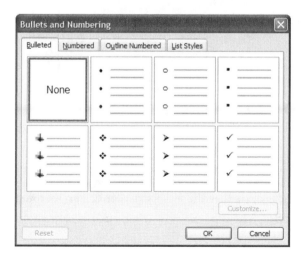

Use the Restart Numbering or Continue Previous List radio buttons at the bottom of the Numbered tab to set the numbering options of a numbered list.

Customizing List Formats

Of course, as with anything, there are always exceptions. If you wish to use a different type of bullet—even a graphic bullet icon—simply customize the list format. To customize a numbered list format:

1. Choose Format | Bullets and Numbering.

2. In the Bullets and Numbering dialog box, choose the Numbered tab.

3. Click on one of the preset list options, other than None.

TIP   *Choose one that you're not likely to use for other lists in the document. When you customize the list, the new formatting will replace this selection on the previews.*

4. Click Customize.

5. Change the settings in the Customize Numbered List dialog box.

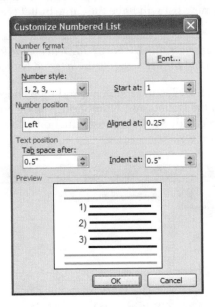

- **Number Format**   The way the number will appear before the list item. You can add a period or parenthesis following the number field. You can also add leading text, such as the word Chapter or Part, before the number field.

- **Number Style**   The type of numbering, such as Roman numerals or lowercase letters.

- **Start At**   The number or letter to start the sequential numbering.

- **Number Position**   Alignment and indentation settings for the numbering.

- **Text Position**   Indentation for the list item.

6. View the Preview window to check the new formatting settings.

7. Click OK.

Bulleted lists are customized in much the same manner. In the Customize Bulleted List dialog box, you can change the bullet character as well as the positioning of the bullet and text. To use a graphic bullet rather than a standard character, click the Picture button, and then select from the Picture Bullet dialog box:

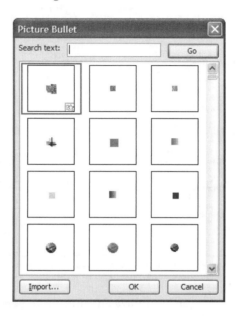

Multilevel Outline Lists

Some lists consist of more than one level of information. For true outlining and formatting tables of contents, you're best served using the Outline view, as explained in Chapter 13. For a hierarchical list within a document, you can create a multilevel list using the Bullets and Numbering tools.

Again, Word offers both an automatic and a manually formatted solution to multilevel lists. If you're automatically formatting your list as you type, you can change the level of a list item by pressing TAB at the beginning of the item to indent it in the hierarchy. The item is automatically numbered in a sublevel format (such as lowercase letters or Roman numerals, depending on the level of the item). Items that follow are formatted in this same subhead format. To return to a major heading, press SHIFT-TAB.

To manually format a multilevel list, type your list, using tabs to demote items as necessary. Then select the list and choose Format | Bullets and Numbering, choose the Outline Numbered tab, and click OK. Again, the presets will usually meet your needs. Items that are preceded by tabs will be formatted as subheads in the list—the more tabs before the item, the lower in the hierarchy. A multilevel list and the Outline Numbered tab of the Bullets and Numbering dialog box are shown in Figure 7-6.

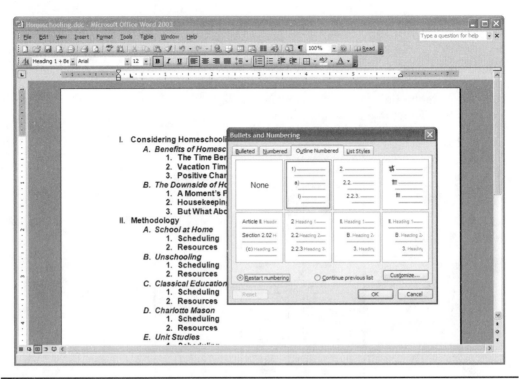

FIGURE 7-6 Major items are formatted numerically, subitems are formatted with lowercase letters, and their subitems with lowercase Roman numerals.

As with other list types, you can customize an outline numbered list. In the Customize Outline Numbered List dialog box, you can customize the appearance, bullet or number type, indentation, alignment, and even the applied style of each level of the outline.

Removing Bullets and Numbering

If you change your mind about formatting paragraphs as a list, you can remove the bullets and numbering—and return the paragraph to the indentation and tab settings for any style that is applied to the text. To do this, select the list items and click the Bullets or Numbering button (whichever is currently applied to the list) on the Formatting toolbar.

You can remove the bullet or numbering of a single item in the list by selecting only that item and clicking the Bullets or Numbering button. Alternatively, position the insertion point at the start of the list item, and press BACKSPACE. This is useful when you want to include a paragraph of explanation about a list item, as such a paragraph wouldn't require a bullet or number. In the case of a numbered list, any items following the selection will be renumbered to continue the list. If you want to restart the numbering, you'll need to do so from the Bullets and Numbering dialog box.

PART II

CHAPTER

Document Formatting

Almost as important as the content of a document is its appearance. The structure of a document lends itself to greater readability, as is the case when margins, page breaks, and indents are used to add white space. Headers, footers, and page numbers make for easier navigation of a document.

Paragraph Formatting

By default, paragraphs are formatted to standard left alignment and single spaced. For most purposes, this is indeed the norm. When it comes to titles, manuscript formatting, and justifying newsletter text, however, the defaults no longer apply. This is where paragraph formatting comes into play.

For Word purposes, paragraphs are denoted with the paragraph symbol (¶) at their end. To view these symbols, select the Show/Hide ¶ button on the Standard toolbar. Although they're often a visual nuisance while composing text, they're quite useful when formatting.

NOTE *The paragraph symbol marks a hard return (pressing the ENTER key). Soft returns (SHIFT-ENTER) are used to start a new line while retaining the formatting of the previous line. For Word purposes, the text on that new line is still considered to be part of the previous paragraph; the line change is noted with a carriage return symbol (↵) rather than ¶. Text after a soft return inherits the same paragraph format and style properties as the preceding text in the paragraph, and will automatically adopt any changes made to that formatting. Also, even if the paragraph is formatted with an indented first line, the line after a soft return will not be indented, because it's a continuation of the same paragraph.*

To modify paragraph formatting, position the cursor within the desired paragraph. Alternatively, you can select the entire paragraph (or paragraphs) using the arrow in the left margin of the document or a keyboard shortcut. You can then change the formatting of the paragraph using either the Formatting toolbar or Format | Paragraph, as described next.

Alignment

Alignment controls the margins to which the paragraph is bound. Left, right, and center alignment are rather apparent. Justify binds the text to both the left and right margins, spacing the text on each line evenly between the margins. All four alignment options are available from the Formatting toolbar:

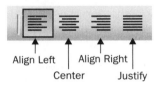

TIP   *If you're using Justify alignment, be sure to end your paragraphs with a hard return. If the last line ends with a soft return, the text will be spread evenly across the line, even if there are only a few words or even characters on that line. The result is visually amateurish and difficult to read.*

Each line can only have one alignment format applied. If you want to have some text left aligned, some centered, and some right aligned—as you might when formatting a header or footer—you need to use tabs to control this formatting. This is covered in "Tabs," later in this chapter.

There is another method of setting paragraph alignment that's not as well known as the toolbar or dialog box. To automatically modify the alignment of a blank line as you type:

1. Position the insertion point on the blank line.

2. Move the cursor to the middle or right side of the line. The I-beam cursor will change as you move across the line, with lines appearing to the left, below (centered), or to the right of the I-beam, showing the alignment of the text.

3. Double-click when the I-beam represents the alignment you desire.

4. Type your text.

CAUTION   *If you double-click at the end of a line of previously entered text, a tab is inserted to center or right-align additional text in the paragraph rather than changing the alignment of the existing text. Also, be certain the I-beam cursor changes to the alignment option you wish; if the lines aren't visible in the cursor, double-clicking is likely to add tab stops rather than changing the alignment.*

Line Spacing

Line spacing can also be controlled on the Formatting toolbar, with options for single, 1.5, double, 2.5, and triple spacing. More commonly, however, line spacing is changed using the Paragraph dialog box (Figure 8-1). The Paragraph dialog box determines not only the spacing between lines, but also the spacing between paragraphs, giving you a great deal of control over the flow of text on the page. You cannot use the Formatting toolbar to control spacing between paragraphs.

TIP   *You can also change alignment in the Paragraph dialog box, but it's faster to use the toolbar if that's all you're changing.*

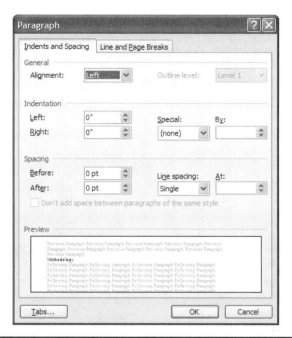

FIGURE 8-1   The Paragraph dialog box provides control over spacing between lines and paragraphs.

There are six options for line spacing in the Paragraph dialog box:

- **Single**   This leaves enough space between lines so the characters don't overlap, but no extra white space. This is the default.

- **1.5**   This leaves a half-line of white space between each line in the paragraph.

- **Double**   This leaves a blank line between each line in the paragraph. The point size of the blank line is the same as the paragraph's text. This is often required when typing a manuscript or term paper for submission.

- **At Least**   This always leaves at least the specified point size in white space between lines, even if the text itself is smaller or larger than that size.

- **Exactly**   This always sizes the line at exactly the point size specified, regardless of the font size.

- **Multiple**   This leaves white space in a multiple of single spacing between lines. For a triple-spaced paragraph, for example, choose Multiple in the Line Spacing field and enter **3** in the At field.

You can also control the amount of white space between paragraphs in the Paragraph dialog box. It's far preferable to control this white space using paragraph formatting rather than extra carriage returns because the formatting gives you control down to the point size. If you have a title at the top of your document, for example, and want to have the first full paragraph ten lines below, you can control this white space using the Spacing options rather than inserting ten empty paragraphs. You can choose to apply this formatting either to the title paragraph or the first body text paragraph. To apply it to the title:

1. Select the title paragraph.
2. Choose Format | Paragraph to open the Paragraph dialog box.
3. On the Indents and Spacing tab, enter a point value in the After field of the Spacing options.
4. Click OK.

To apply the formatting to the body text, follow the same procedure, entering a point value in the Before field in step 3.

TIP *If you're using styles, give some thought to how you'll be using each style before setting spacing options. If you apply 48 points of white space before the body text paragraph and then apply that formatting to the Body Text style, every paragraph will have that white space preceding it. If, instead, you apply the white space to a Title style, you'll probably be happier with the results because the extra white space will only appear where you intended it—after a title. More information about styles can be found in Chapter 9.*

Paragraph Page Flow

One of the biggest annoyances in word processing is when only one line of a paragraph appears at the top or bottom of a page, separated from the remainder of the paragraph. These are called *widows* and *orphans*. At best, they merely look out of place. At worst, they can add an extra page to your document, putting you over page count on a paper or grant proposal.

Widow and orphan control, found on the Line and Page Breaks tab of the Paragraph dialog box (Figure 8-2), will keep a paragraph together if only one line overflows to the top or is left at the bottom of a page.

The other options on this tab are as follows:

- **Keep Lines Together**   Keeps all lines of a paragraph on the same page. This is often used to keep a complete descriptive paragraph on the same page as the graphic it describes.

- **Keep with Next**   Keeps the selected paragraph on the same page as the following paragraph. This is commonly used to keep section headings with their accompanying text. If several paragraphs are linked together using this option, the text will eventually be forced to flow onto another page, at which point the Keep Lines Together and/or Widow and Orphan controls will take precedence to control the positioning of the soft page break.

- **Page Break Before**   Inserts a page break before the selected paragraph, ensuring that it starts a new page. This can be applied to heading paragraphs so each new heading begins on a new page, with the text of that section following.

- **Suppress Line Numbers**   If you have line numbers displayed in the document (File | Page Setup, then choose Line Numbering from the Layout tab), this option will suppress the numbering for the selected paragraph(s). Line numbers are often used when printing HTML code.

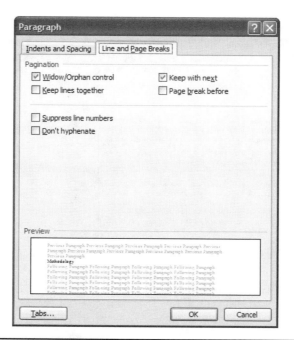

FIGURE 8-2   The Line and Page Breaks tab of the Paragraph dialog box determines the flow of paragraphs from page to page.

- **Don't Hyphenate**   Suppresses hyphenation in the selected paragraph, if Hyphenation is enabled for the document (Tools | Language | Hyphenation, which is explained in Chapter 10). Hyphenation is most often used when working with columns, and suppressing it is sometimes necessary when too many hyphens in a paragraph make it virtually unreadable.

Indentation

Indents control the flow of text within a paragraph by changing the margins of the paragraph, as when quoting a block of text (Figure 8-3). Indents from the left margin can be added from the Formatting toolbar in half-inch increments. You can set indents to a specific length using the Indentation options in the Paragraph dialog box. Right indents and indents of both margins must be set using the Paragraph dialog box.

There are two special forms of indentation. First-line indents are formatted so that the first line of a paragraph is indented from the left margin, while following lines remain the same. The default indent is a half-inch, but you can change this spacing. You can get the same effect using a tab, but indents are more powerful and easier to customize. As you'll see in greater detail in Chapter 9, you can format a Word style to automatically indent the first line of each paragraph.

Hanging indents are the reverse of first-line indents. In a hanging indent, the first line begins at the margin, while the remaining lines of the paragraph are indented by the specified distance. These are most commonly used with bullets and numbered lists, which are covered in Chapter 7.

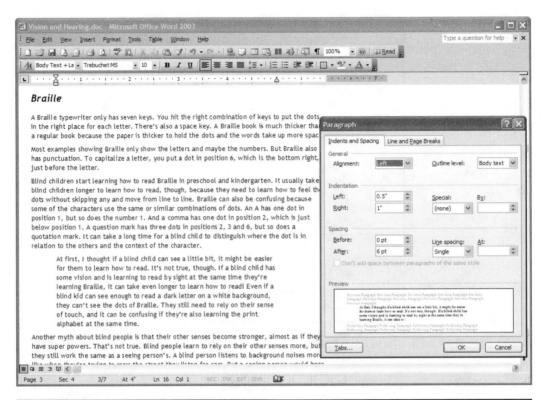

FIGURE 8-3 A paragraph has been indented on both the right and left sides using the settings in the Indentation section of the Paragraph dialog box.

Tabs

A common mistake among novices is to use tabs and indents interchangeably. While tabs can duplicate some of the features of indents, they're not nearly as robust for whole-paragraph formatting. The tab characters can clutter the screen, particularly when you use multiple tabs to position text, making it easy to lose track of exactly what formatting is being applied. Instead, tabs are more useful for single-line paragraphs, such as entries in a table of contents or the header or footer of a document.

Tabs are visually displayed with tab symbols (→), but they are controlled by tab stops. Tab stops determine where the text is positioned on a line following a tab. The default tab stops are left aligned at half-inch intervals between the margins of the document, just like the default indentation stops. As with just about everything in Word, these tab stops can be changed. The Tabs dialog box (shown next) is accessible from the Tabs button in the Paragraph dialog box or from the Format | Tabs menu.

NOTE *If you don't see the tab symbols on your screen, use the Show/Hide ¶ button on the Standard toolbar to make them visible.*

The Tabs dialog box offers several alignment options for tab stops:

- **Left**   This is the default alignment setting. Text following the tab will be left aligned.

- **Center**   Text after the tab will be centered around the tab stop. This is most commonly used to center a page number in a header or footer when there is other text aligned to the left or right around it (thus precluding using the Center paragraph alignment for the entire paragraph).

- **Right**   Text following the tab will be right aligned. This is commonly used in headers and footers to position the page number on the bottom right of the page.

- **Decimal**   Text (in this case, usually numbers) following the tab will be aligned according to the decimal point or period in the text. This option is generally used when aligning a column of numbers. Digits preceding the decimal point are right aligned (thus moving toward the left margin), while digits after the decimal point are left aligned (thus moving toward the right margin).

$$
\begin{array}{rr}
\rightarrow & 72.45\P \\
\rightarrow & 136.87\P \\
\rightarrow & 2.04\P \\
\rightarrow & 332.87\P \\
\text{TOTAL} \quad \rightarrow & 544.23\P \\
\end{array}
$$

- **Bar**   This option doesn't affect text at all. Instead, it draws a vertical bar at the position specified. This was used before Word had options for borders and shading, but it's since been deprecated by these more versatile features.

Tabs can also be set to have leaders. *Leaders* are a series of dots, dashes, or underlines leading from the point where the tab was inserted to the tab stop. These are most commonly used in a table of contents, with dots leading from the chapter name to the page number.

To set a tab stop:

1. Open the Tabs dialog box.

2. Enter the position at which you want to set the tab stop.

3. Set the alignment option for the tab stop.

4. Set the leader options for the tab stop.

5. Click the Set button.

6. Continue setting tab stops, or click OK to exit the Tabs dialog box.

CAUTION *The Increase and Decrease Indent buttons on the Formatting toolbar base their alignment on the tab stops in the document. If you change the default tab stops in the Tabs dialog box, using the Increase Indent button will indent the paragraph along the new default stops. There is a fluke in this, however: the first indent will remain at a 0.5-inch interval, even if the new default is greater than 0.5-inch intervals, but the indent will be less than 0.5 inch if the new default is less than this.*

Using the Ruler

As just mentioned, the tab stops and indentation stops both default at half-inch intervals. This is because the Indent buttons on the toolbar and the tab stops are cued to the same ruler. Changes you make in the Tabs dialog box are reflected on the ruler at the top of the document window. If you can't see the ruler, choose View | Ruler.

The ruler pulls information from several settings into one visual display.

- The margins for the page are shaded on the ruler.

- The margins for the current paragraph are represented by triangles along the bottom of the ruler.

- The left margin for the first line in a paragraph is designated by an inverted triangle. This is usually right above the left paragraph margin marker. In the case of a first-line or hanging indent, the inverted triangle will appear to the right or left of the left margin marker.

- Default tabs are marked with a small hash mark just under the ruler.

- Tab stops that you set manually are displayed on the ruler itself. The symbol on the ruler also tells you the alignment of the tab stop. An L-type symbol signifies left-alignment. A backwards L symbol represents right-alignment. An inverted T symbol is used for center-aligned tabs, while an inverted T with a dot is used for decimal tabs.

You can adjust the paragraph margins, indentation settings, and tab stops by dragging the appropriate marker across the ruler. To manually set a first-line indent, drag only the inverted triangle to the desired location. To adjust the entire left paragraph margin, drag the square box located below the left margin marker. Dragging the square box will adjust both the left paragraph margin and any first-line offset (hanging or indented) at the same time. If the paragraph has already been set with a first-line indent, this indentation will be adjusted relative to the new paragraph margin. As you drag the indentation marker or tab stop, a dotted line will extend into your document, showing you where the stop will fall; this helps you align it to existing content in the document.

You can also use the ruler to set new tabs. To do this:

1. Position the insertion point within the paragraph for which you want to set the tab stops.

2. Select a tab (or indentation) alignment by toggling the button on the left side of the ruler.

3. Click on the ruler to position the tab stop.

4. To remove a tab stop, drag the marker off the ruler. This can only be done with tab stops, not margin markers.

NOTE *Remember that any tab stops you create only apply to the paragraphs that are selected at the time you set them. In order to set tabs for the entire document, you must first Select All.*

As you become familiar with Word, you'll also become more comfortable using tabs and indents appropriately. One of the best uses of both indents and tabs is in bullets and numbering, which are covered in Chapter 7.

Margins and Page Orientation

The boundaries of the content of a document are called *margins*. As explained in the "Paragraph Formatting" section of this chapter, Word allows you to set margins for each paragraph in the document. Any graphics or other objects on the page also have margins, relative to the surrounding content and any borders around the object, as covered in Chapter 11. More important, however, are the overall margins and setup of the entire document. Document and page margins are set in the Page Setup dialog box (File | Page Setup, then click the Margins tab). As shown in Figure 8-4, you can specify the margins for the top, bottom, left, and right of the page. Margins are set in conjunction with the paper orientation and any gutters required to bind the completed document when it is printed.

NOTE *If you view your document in Reading Layout, the margins may appear altered to make the page more readable on screen. The actual margin settings remain intact, however, so the page will print properly.*

Word also allows you to set gutters for each page. A *gutter* is extra white space on the left side or top of the page to allow for binding or hole punching. The margin settings are added to any gutter settings, so if your gutter is 1 inch and your margin is 1.25 inches, the

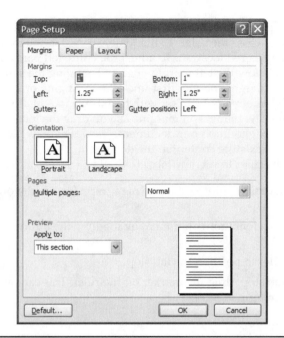

FIGURE 8-4   The Page Setup dialog box controls the printed appearance of the page.

text area will begin 2.25 inches from the edge of the paper. If you're using duplex printing (printing on both sides of the paper), you can change the Multiple Pages option to Mirror Margins so the gutter is on the left side of the front and right side of the back of the page, as in a bound book.

TIP   There's a good reason for using gutters appropriately instead of simply setting a wider left margin. You can bleed text or an image into the margin of a page, but the gutter area remains sacrosanct. Thus, you can have a graphic cross into the margin for visual effect while ensuring the gutter remains to leave adequate room for binding the printed document.

When setting margins, it's important to know the printable space limits of your printer. Some printers can print to the very edge of the page. This is useful when printing business cards. Other printers require a border of up to half an inch around the perimeter of the page. Your printer documentation—or simple experimentation—should provide this information.

At the same time you set your margins, you should also set the paper orientation for the document. Portrait orientation, the default, prints across the short edge and down the long edge. Landscape orientation prints across the long edge of the page.

Page and Section Breaks

It's quite likely, of course, that your document is more than one page in length. Word will automatically add page breaks to control the flow of text from page to page and handle widows and orphans. These page breaks are known as *soft* page breaks because they'll change as you add and delete paragraphs. When you want complete control over where page breaks occur, you'll have to manually insert a *hard* page break or section break. Hard page breaks can be inserted by pressing CTRL-ENTER. You can also insert a page break using Insert | Break, then selecting Page Break. As shown in Figure 8-5, soft page breaks are designated in Normal view with a dotted line. Hard page breaks will state "Page Break" on the dotted line.

While soft page breaks will change as the document is modified—think of them as being linked to the page itself—hard page or section breaks are linked to the paragraph in which they're placed. If you add or delete content, the page break may no longer be as judiciously located, and you'll have to manually remove the break. To do this, select the break marker and press DELETE. To remove all of the hard page breaks in the document, use the Find and Replace tool, as explained in Chapter 4.

Section Breaks

Although page breaks can manually force text onto another page, the layout and orientation of the new page is the same as those preceding it. If you need to change the layout of a page or series of pages, you need to break the document into sections and define the layout of each. Section breaks can be used to set up column layouts (covered in Chapter 10), change

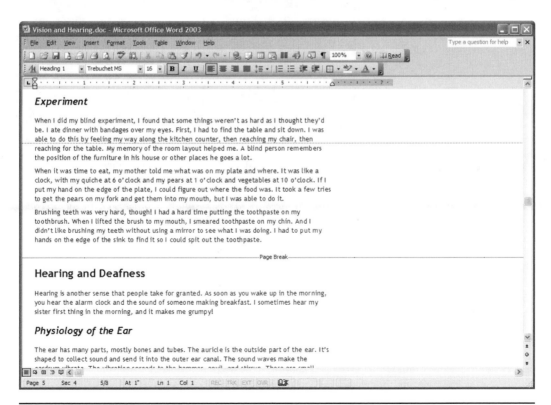

FIGURE 8-5 Word automatically adds soft page breaks; you can insert hard page breaks.

headers or footers in mid-document, or even change the orientation of a page to accommodate an embedded chart or table.

When using section breaks, the first decision to make is what type of break is appropriate:

- **Next Page**   This break starts a new page. It's more powerful than a hard page break because you can change the header and footer of the new section, as well as the page layout, orientation, and paper size.

- **Continuous**   This inserts a section break on the same page as the preceding section. This type of break is used to format columns or add line numbering to a particular portion of the document.

- **Even/Odd Page**   This break starts a new page, inserting a blank page if necessary to ensure the new section begins on an even or odd page. This is most often used to ensure a chapter or section begins on a facing page when it's bound in printed form.

Once you've chosen the type of section break, choose Insert | Break, then select from the list.

To delete a section break, select the Section Break divider and press DELETE.

TIP   *When using Continuous section breaks, especially to create columns, always create an "extra" section break after the content to be affected before changing its layout. By surrounding your columns with section breaks before formatting the actual columns, you've given yourself an escape clause to return to the standard formatting of the document following the columnar diversion. Otherwise, it's a lengthy procedure to add the following section break and then return to a single-column layout that's properly formatted. More information about columns can be found in Chapter 10.*

Whenever you use a section break to force a new page in order to change the page setup, you have the option of applying the changes you make in the Page Setup dialog box to either the whole document or just the selected section. This choice is made in the Preview section of the Page Setup dialog box (on each tab). Again, if the changes to that section are a temporary state—the document will revert to a prior section layout later in the document—add an extra section break that retains that initial layout before making changes to the new section.

Headers and Footers

Headers and footers provide information at the top and bottom of a page that's usually descriptive of the document in some way. The title or chapter name of the document, page numbers, the date—all of these commonly appear in a header or footer. Headers and footers are printed in the margin of the page, at a distance from the edge specified in the Headers and Footers section on the Layout tab of the Page Setup dialog box.

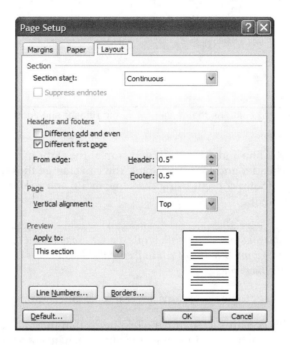

NOTE   *You can insert graphics into a header or footer just as you would elsewhere in the document (see Chapter 11). Keep in mind that if the graphic is large, however, the header or footer will be forced to encroach on the body of the document, which can cause text and graphics to overlap.*

To create a header or footer, select View | Header and Footer. This opens the floating Header and Footer toolbar. Headers and footers are created in Print Layout view (and only visible in same), so Word will automatically switch to this mode if you invoke the Header and Footer feature while in another view. If you're already in Print Layout, you can access a header or footer by double-clicking in that area of the page. The header and footer are grayed out when editing the body of the document; when you open the Header and Footer toolbar, the body text becomes grayed out to enable you to focus on only the header or footer, as shown in Figure 8-6.

Although they're initially empty, Word automatically sets up a header and footer for every section of the document. If you don't add header and footer information, these areas will stay empty and won't affect the final appearance of your document. Headers and footers are preformatted with left paragraph alignment and two tab stops—a center-aligned

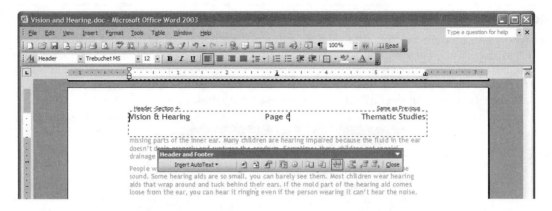

FIGURE 8-6   The dashed box contains the header, while the Header and Footer toolbar floats below.

stop in the middle of the line and a right-aligned stop at the right margin—because those are the most common header and footer settings. You can change these settings, however, and format header and footer content using the same menu and toolbar options you would to format any other content.

NOTE   *The default header and footer styles illustrate a good use of mixed tab stops to format a paragraph. As seen in Figure 8-6, the page number of the document is centered with left- and right-aligned text on either side.*

The Header and Footer toolbar contains several tools and options:

- **AutoText**   This contains a list of AutoText items that might be appropriate for a header or footer, such as the filename, the author's name, and the creation date of the document. These entries are actually fields, which are explained in Chapter 12.

- **Page Numbering**   There are three items on the toolbar to insert and format page numbers. See "Page Numbering," later in this chapter, for information on how to format page numbers.

- **Insert Date and Time**   These options insert fields that will be updated to reflect the current date and time every time you open the document. The time and date when you print the document will appear in the final output.

- **Page Setup**   This opens the Page Setup dialog box to provide access to the layout options. You can elect to have different headers and footers for the first page and/or odd and even pages in the document, as explained in the next section.

- **Show/Hide Document Text**   Selecting this option hides the body of the document completely from view, allowing you to focus solely on the header or footer. This option isn't commonly used, as you'll generally want to see how your header and footer appear within the context of the document as a whole.

- **Same as Previous**   If your document has multiple sections or you've elected to have different headers and footers for various pages, this option instructs Word to inherit the same header and footer as the previous section.
- **Switch Between Header and Footer**   Toggles between the header and footer for that page.
- **Show Previous/Next**   Navigates from section to section, allowing you to configure multiple headers and footers in a row or to view each section's header/footer to ensure they flow as you intended.

Varying Headers and Footers

Whenever you add a section break that forces a new page in the document, another header and footer are added. If the Same as Previous button is selected, the new section will inherit the header and footer of the previous section; otherwise, the new header and footer are blank. In addition to these section headers/footers, Word allows headers and footers to be different on the first page of the document or different according to whether the page is odd or even. To create varying headers and footers for these pages, follow these steps:

1. In Print Layout view, double-click in the header or footer of the first page of the document.

2. Click the Page Setup button to enter the Layout tab of the Page Setup dialog box.

3. Under Headers and Footers, select Different Odd and Even or Different First Page (or both).

4. Click OK to return to the header or footer.

5. Use the Show Previous and Show Next buttons, along with the Switch Between Header and Footer button, to navigate to each of the headers and footers and format them as you wish.

6. Click the Close button on the Header and Footer toolbar to close the toolbar and return to the body of the document.

TIP   *Wait until the structure of your document is fairly stable before adding content to headers and footers. If your document has many sections with different headers and footers, it can be difficult to track which were inherited from other sections and which are unique. As you modify the content of the document, these varying headers and footers can thus become a jumbled mess.*

Page Numbering

The most common piece of information in a header or footer is page numbering, as evidenced by the numbering options contained on the Header and Footer toolbar. To add a page number to a header or footer, position the insertion point where you desire, then click the Insert Page Number button. If you want the header or footer to say "Page *n*" on every page, type the word **Page**, then click the Insert Page Number button. You can also format the page numbering to say "Page *n* of *x*" by typing the word **Page**, clicking the Insert Page Number button, typing the word **of**, then clicking the Insert Number of Pages button.

In most cases, the default numbering and format are acceptable. If you need to start the numbering with a specific number—as when printing a lengthy project comprising several documents—use the Format Page Number button to open the Page Number Format dialog box. This dialog box also allows you to change the numbering to Roman numerals or to follow an outline format linking the page number to the chapter number.

You can also add page numbering to the header or footer without using the toolbar. To do this, choose Insert | Page Numbers. The Page Numbers dialog box appears and you can set the position, alignment, and format here. This is a useful shortcut when this is the only information that will appear in the header or footer, but shouldn't be used in conjunction with other header and footer content because adding the page numbering in this manner can overlap or otherwise change the appearance of existing header or footer content.

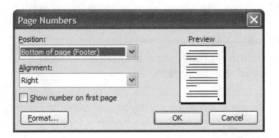

NOTE   *As you scroll through your document, you'll see that page numbering is updated on every page. This may lead you to the mistaken belief that each page has an independent header/footer. In truth, the page number is created by a field designed to update on each page. The actual header or footer is the same for the entire section, so changes you make to one header/footer will affect the entire section.*

Reusable Formatting with Styles and Templates

By applying text and paragraph formatting, you have an amazing level of control over the appearance of your text and its positioning on the page. To create a section heading, you can change the font, increase the font size, make the section title bold, and add 12 points of space between the heading and the underlying text. Applying this formatting repeatedly within a document can consume an inordinate amount of time—unless you make use of styles and templates. Styles can apply several format options at once. Templates contain groups of styles for a particular type of document.

There are two other types of reusable formatting. AutoFormatting operates so automatically, you may not even realize it's there. Themes are used so infrequently, they're often overlooked and their potential is misunderstood.

AutoFormatting

As you can guess from its name, AutoFormatting applies formatting automatically, as you type. The settings for this tool are grouped in a dialog box with the AutoCorrect features, explained in Chapter 7. AutoCorrect focuses on changing spelling and expanding abbreviations while retaining the formatting of the entry, but AutoFormat changes the appearance and formatting of items. AutoFormat contains a specific list of formatting that it will apply. You can enable or disable these entries, but you cannot create new ones. To access the AutoFormat options, choose Tools | AutoCorrect Options, and then click on one of the two AutoFormat tabs.

There are two types of AutoFormat entries. AutoFormat As You Type (Figure 9-1) makes changes to the document as you type. These include changing straight quotation marks to *smart quotes* (quotation marks that curl around adjoining characters) and converting web addresses into hyperlinks. AutoFormat also automatically applies bullets or numbering to lists and controls the format of tables and headings.

Although these are intended as time-saving options—and indeed can be useful in some situations—many of the AutoFormat As You Type options are more annoying than helpful. Unless you're creating a web page or a document to be read on screen, hyperlinks are usually more hassle than help. You can CTRL-click on a hyperlink within a document to load the

FIGURE 9-1
AutoFormat As
You Type makes
formatting
changes to
characters and
paragraphs while
you work.

page in your web browser, which can be useful to check a fact or confirm a URL in the
document, but you usually don't want the hyperlink formatting to appear in your printed
document. Reformatting a web address once it's been converted to a hyperlink requires an
extra step—you must first remove the hyperlink (right-click, then select Remove Hyperlink
from the context menu).

At first glance, the fraction conversion formatting appears useful, until you realize that
it only works for certain fractions, which means your formatting can be inconsistent if you
have several fractions in the document. Replacing dashes with hyphens can also be an
annoyance if you're deliberately using dashes.

Whenever Word makes an AutoFormat change, it will insert a Smart Tag, which enables
you to undo the operation. To undo formatting changes on the fly, use the BACKSPACE key
or press CTRL-Z immediately after the formatting is applied.

The other type of AutoFormat is applied to the entire document when you opt to use
the AutoFormat tool. The options for this AutoFormat (Figure 9-2) are similar to those of the
AutoFormat As You Type, and you can use this to your advantage. If you want more control
over which formatting is applied and when, disable the options in AutoFormat As You Type,
and choose the options you want in the AutoFormat tab. In this way, you can draft your
document and retain your dashes, unformatted links, and manual headings.

Formatting selected in the AutoFormat option is applied using Format | AutoFormat.
The AutoFormat dialog box, shown next, lets you apply the chosen formatting immediately
or in a linear fashion, accepting or rejecting each change. Before clicking OK to proceed,
select the Options button to review the AutoFormat options.

Table 9-1 lists the common types of AutoFormatting entries for both types of automated formatting.

TIP   *Before invoking the AutoFormat command, save your document.*

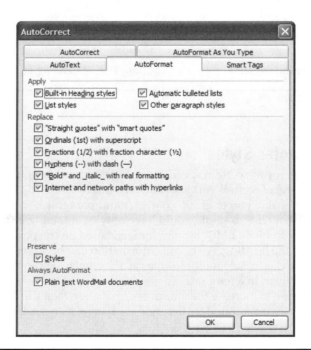

FIGURE 9-2   AutoFormat options are similar to those of AutoFormat As You Type, but can also be set to preserve styles already applied to text.

Entry	Result
1st, 2nd, 3rd, etc.	Superscripts the ordinal characters so they appear as 1st, 2nd, 3rd, etc.
1/2, 1/4, 3/4	Converts the fractions to the associated symbols, ½, ¼, and ¾. This does not work on other fractions, such as 1/8, 1/3, etc.
A web address, such as www.pendragn.com, with or without the http:// prefix	Inserts a hyperlink, which can be fired using CTRL-click.
Bulleted lists formatted with o, *, -, --, en or em dashes (– or —), =>, ->, or a small picture followed by a tab or space	Creates a bulleted list with bullets converted to associated symbols: •, , -, ¦, –, —, ⇨, or →. In the case of a picture, it is used as the bullet.
Numbered lists formatted with 0, 1, I, i, A, or a, followed by a period, hyphen, or parenthesis and a space or tab	Creates a numeric list using the alphanumeric sequence chosen.
Three or more dashes, underlines, equal symbols, quotation marks, or pound symbols in a row	Adds a border to the paragraph.
+---+---+	Creates a table.
-- (two dashes)	Changes to a hyphen.
A short sentence followed by ENTER	Changes to a heading style.

TABLE 9-1   AutoFormat Entries

Paragraph and Character Styles

While AutoFormat can format certain specific character and paragraph instances, it still doesn't provide the level of control you'll want over your documents. This is where styles come into play. Styles enable you to group character and paragraph formatting for specific types of text. A manuscript, for example, could have a style containing instructions to format chapter headings with Trebuchet MS 18-point font, centered on the page with 24 points of space before and after the heading. All of this information can be stored in one style called ChapterHead. Styles can be applied multiple times in a document, and can be used in multiple documents by storing them in a template. Furthermore, if you decide to change the format of the chapter headings—to increase the amount of space between the heading and the body text, for example—you can update the style to change every instance of that style throughout the document.

There are four types of styles:

- **Character styles**   These are used to format characters or words within a paragraph. You use them to apply font settings, borders, and shading to text, but they don't have an effect on the alignment or other paragraph formatting of the text. Character styles can be applied to a selection within a paragraph, rather than the entire paragraph.

- **Paragraph styles** These styles are used to format entire paragraphs. They can contain both character and paragraph formatting. Paragraphs are initially formatted with the Normal style unless another style is applied.

- **List styles** Bulleted and numbered lists can be formatted with a style that applies the same alignment, bullets or numbering, and formatting to multiple lists. You can create list styles for an entire list or just certain levels of a multilevel outline.

- **Table styles** These styles control the format of the borders and alignment of the table itself as well as the style of the table's contents. You can create styles to control the entire table or just portions such as the header row.

There are several ways to access the list of styles for a document. The Formatting toolbar has a drop-down list of styles, located to the left of the font field. This menu is useful if you want to quickly apply a style and are already familiar with the available styles. If you click on the Styles and Formatting button to the left of the list, you can open the Styles and Formatting task pane (Figure 9-3), which offers more information and options to organize and modify styles. This task pane is also accessible by choosing Styles and Formatting from the drop-down task pane list (if the task pane is already open) or choosing Format | Styles and Formatting from the main menu.

FIGURE 9-3
The Styles and Formatting pane displays all available styles, the most common styles, or just those currently in use in the document.

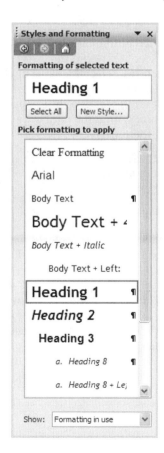

Each type of style has an associated icon, which appears next to the style name in the Styles and Formatting list (both in the Formatting toolbar and the task pane). Character styles have an underlined *a*. Paragraph styles are noted with a paragraph symbol (¶). Table styles have a grid icon. List styles appear with a bulleted list icon.

NOTE *If you create a list style manually instead of using the Bullets and Numbering dialog box (explained in the upcoming section "Using List and Table Styles"), it will be designated as a paragraph style rather than a list style.*

When you use the Styles and Formatting task pane, ScreenTips appear with the formatting of each style as you mouse over them. If you click on the down-arrow as you mouse over a style, you'll be offered the options of modifying, deleting, or updating the style. You can also use this menu to select all text formatted with a particular style.

The Styles and Formatting task pane lists the available formatting by default. These styles are available from the current template (you'll learn more about templates later in this chapter). You can narrow this list down to Formatting in Use, or expand the list to All Styles using the Show option at the bottom of the task pane.

Applying Styles

Some styles will be applied automatically—such as when you type a brief heading, followed by a larger block of text—but most styles will need to be manually applied.

To apply a character style, select the word or characters you want to modify, and then choose a character style from the Styles and Formatting list on the Formatting toolbar or from the Styles and Formatting task pane. To apply paragraph styles, you only have to position the insertion point within the paragraph. You can apply a style to multiple paragraphs by selecting them first.

TIP *If you apply a style by mistake, you can reapply the Normal style by pressing* CTRL-SHIFT-N. *To return a character style to its default state, press* CTRL-SPACEBAR *to reapply the default paragraph font.*

Creating Styles

Word ships with approximately 100 defined styles, covering everything from common headings to HTML code listings. These styles will work for a generic document, but they don't do much in a highly formatted document with a nonstandard font and customized spacing requirements. The preformatted styles are also intended to cover only the most common types of text, such as the date stamp of a business letter. If you're creating a newsletter or manuscript, you may need a particular style that isn't on the default list.

When creating new styles, you can base them on formatting that's already applied to a selected paragraph or create them from scratch in the New Style dialog box, shown next.

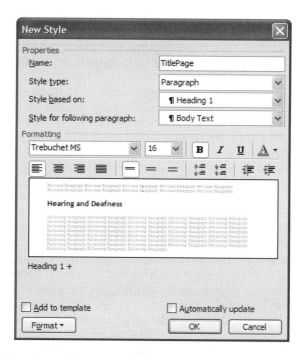

PART II

If you're basing the new style on an existing paragraph, select the paragraph, and then click New Style on the Styles and Formatting task pane. Fill in the new name for the style. The formatting will be selected in the options in the Formatting section of the dialog box, and will also appear in laundry-list form below the preview box.

To create a new style from scratch, click on the New Style option in the Styles and Formatting task pane without selecting any text first. Use the Formatting options in the dialog box to set your font, paragraph formatting, bullets and numbers, and other preferences. Additional formatting control can be found by clicking the Format button and selecting from the menu. The dialog boxes that open from this menu are identical to those that appear in the Format menu when entering text.

Before saving the new style, be sure to set the remaining properties. These are often overlooked, but can be extremely useful. Most importantly, give the style a name you'll remember. There's nothing worse than wanting to apply a style and having to wade through a series of meaningless Style1, Style2, Style3… entries. For Style Based On, you can base the new style on one that already exists. If the font or paragraph alignment of that style changes, the new style will also inherit those changes. The style you apply locally—that is, to the new style you're creating—takes precedence in the inheritance hierarchy. For example, if you base the new style—say you call it "Quotation"—on a BodyText style with 12-point Times New Roman, and you set the new style to have 10-point Bergell, paragraphs with the Quotation style attached will appear in 10-point Bergell. Even if you later change the BodyText style to 14-point Arial, the new style will remain the same.

NOTE   *If you're familiar with cascading style sheets in web design, this hierarchy is nothing new. The closer the style is to the actual text, the greater the priority. A style directly applied to a selection is closer to the text than a style that may have formed its basis.*

The final Properties option controls paragraphs that follow those formatted with the new style. If you press ENTER with the insertion point immediately preceding the paragraph mark, the new paragraph will assume the style you specify in Style for Following Paragraphs. Note, however, that if your insertion point is anywhere else in the paragraph, even if you press ENTER to start a new paragraph, the new paragraph will inherit the style of the old one because the style has already been applied to the contents of the new paragraph. To give an example, you can create a ChapterTitle style with the Style for Following Paragraphs set to BodyText. If you type a chapter title and then press ENTER at the end of the line, the next paragraph will automatically be formatted as BodyText. If you later put the insertion point in the middle of the chapter title and press ENTER, both lines of the title will remain formatted as ChapterTitle.

Also when creating new styles, you need to decide whether the style should become part of the open template or only remain available for the current document. The default is to store the style in the current document. To add it to the template, select Add to Template at the bottom of the New Style dialog box.

Finally, if you check Automatically Update, you can modify the style on the fly. Any changes you make to a paragraph with that style applied will automatically become incorporated into the style itself and be applied to other paragraphs using that style. Again, use care when selecting this option, as it's easy to reformat your document beyond all recognition when you only intended to make changes to a single paragraph.

Modifying Styles

You can modify a style without using the Automatically Update option. To do this, open the Styles and Formatting task pane. Mouse over the style you want to modify, and an arrow will appear, allowing you to open a context-sensitive menu for that style. When you choose Modify, the Modify Style dialog box opens, which looks very similar to the New Style dialog box and contains the same format options.

If you look carefully at the drop-down menu for each style, you'll also notice options that make it easy to locate instances using a particular style. The menu for a Heading 2 style is shown here:

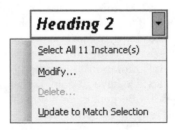

If you're unsure of whether a style is serving a purpose, notice how many instances of it are in your document. Especially if you are going to use the Update to Match Selection option, you should know how many instances exist and how it's being used. A change that might benefit one instance of that style may not be as appealing for other instances. In those cases, it's better to create a new style and apply it where necessary.

Using List and Table Styles

List and table styles appear on the Styles and Formatting task pane, but are usually applied differently from character and paragraph styles. List and table styles are sometimes confusing because they can be applied as paragraph styles directly from the Styles and Formatting task pane or as a multilevel construct from the List Styles or Table AutoFormat options.

List Styles

Paragraphs can be formatted to resemble lists by using list styles. These styles are treated as paragraph styles, but contain bullets or numbering, and are generally indented or offset. You can apply this type of list style manually, such as when you want to format a list to be indented on the order of the List Bullet 2 style (available if you set the Styles and Formatting task pane to show All Styles). List styles can also be formatted automatically when you start a list and then press ENTER to add a new item. The formatting from the first paragraph carries over, and in the case of a numbered list, will increase incrementally. This is covered in greater detail in Chapter 7.

The other type of list style is applied to an entire list. These can be multilevel lists containing a mix of numbers, bullets, and repeated text (such as Chapter 1, Chapter 2, Chapter 3, etc.). List styles are generally created, modified, and applied using the List Styles tab in the Bullets and Numbering dialog box (Format | Bullets and Numbering). Word applies the correct level of the list style based on the level of the text. This is useful when formatting outlines, which are covered in Chapter 13.

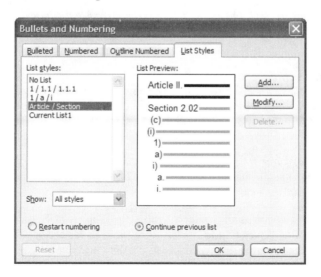

You can add a new list style by clicking the Add button in the List Styles tab. The New Style dialog box, shown next, appears at first glance to be identical to the character and paragraph New Style dialog box, shown earlier. But upon closer look, you'll see several important distinctions. You can apply a list style to a particular level of a list, change the numbering, and specify the bullet symbol or graphical icon for the style.

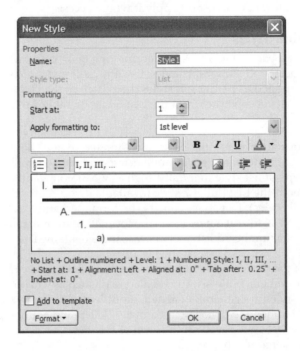

CAUTION *If you create list styles based on heading levels, the heading styles of your entire document will change to reflect those of the list styles.*

Table Styles

Table styles function similarly to list styles. Table styles contain formatting for the borders, shading, and alignment of the cells, columns, and rows of the table, as well as the formatting of the table's contents, all of which are explained in Chapter 10. You can apply a specific table style directly to a column or row of a table.

TIP *A quick method of converting text to a formatted table is to select the text, then choose a table style from the Styles and Formatting task pane. The Insert Table dialog box that appears will allow you to configure the new table.*

You can also add styles to an entire table using the Table AutoFormat tool, also covered in Chapter 10. The dialog boxes to add and modify table styles are similar to the other style dialog boxes except that they primarily focus on borders and shading.

Templates

Whenever you save a document, any styles you used or created in that document are saved, as well. The styles are stored in a template. Every document is based on a template. If you create a new blank document—whether by using the blank document that opens when you start Word, pressing the New Blank Document button in the Standard toolbar, or choosing Blank Document from the New Document task pane—the document is based on the Normal template. Styles you create in a document are only available in that document, but the styles in the Normal template are available in all documents.

Modifying the Normal Template

The Normal template is named normal.dot. This is known as a global template because it's automatically loaded with every document you create or modify in Word. The Normal template contains the most common styles, but the document itself is blank.

When you create new styles, you can opt to add them to the current template. If the only template available is normal.dot, the new style will become part of the global template and thus be available in all your documents. This option has great potential. You can change the Normal style to be Arial instead of Times New Roman, and every document you create from that point on will use Arial as the default font.

Changing the Normal template is also fraught with the potential for undesirable consequences in your documents. Let's say you modify the BodyText style in a document and add it to the template. The changes you made to the font, alignment, and other formatting of the style will now be changed in every document you open. The Bergell body text that looks wonderful on your party invitations won't look as wonderful in your marketing plan.

Attaching a Template

To avoid slipups, you can attach different templates to a document, each created for a specific purpose. Word ships with several preformatted templates for everything from memos to legal pleadings.

Creating a New Template-Based Document

To create a document using a template:

1. Choose File | New to open the New Document task pane. If the task pane is already open, switch to it.

2. Choose to search for a template on your computer, on Microsoft's web site, or on another site. Generally, it's best to stay local and choose a template on your computer.

TIP   *You can download additional templates from the Microsoft site at http://office.microsoft.com/ templates instead of searching for them when you create a document. By downloading the templates before using them, you can file them so they appear in your own folders in the Template dialog box. If you simply open them directly from Word, the template itself isn't saved locally for future use.*

3. In the Templates dialog box, shown in Figure 9-4, choose a template. Many of the templates have a sample that appears in the Preview window to help you choose from among the different variations of letters, faxes, and memos.

4. Click OK.

Viewing some of the packaged templates should give you ideas about what can be contained in a template. Basically, this is just about anything! Templates can contain company logos, form letter text, and headers and footers, as well as styles. They can also

FIGURE 9-4
The Templates dialog box is organized into tabs containing templates of similar type.

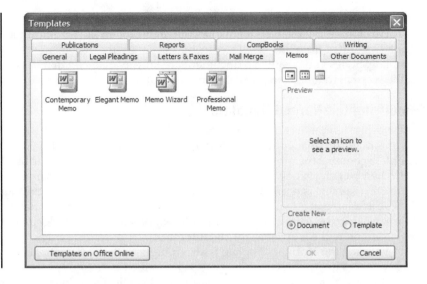

contain macros and new toolbars. You can even add tabs of your own to the Templates dialog box, such as the Writing tab that appears in Figure 9-4, by saving your user-created templates in folders.

Attaching a Template to an Existing Document

In some cases, you'll create the content of a document before choosing a template. You can attach a template to an existing document using the Templates and Add-Ins tool (Tools | Templates and Add-Ins). In the Templates and Add-Ins dialog box, click Attach to open the list of user templates, and select a template. Unlike opening a document in the Templates dialog box, using the Attach Template file picker doesn't give you any preview options.

The Templates and Add-Ins dialog box also contains the Organizer, shown next. This tool allows you to move styles, macros, keyboard shortcuts, and toolbars between templates. If you want to borrow a style from another template without attaching the entire template to the document, use the Organizer to copy the style.

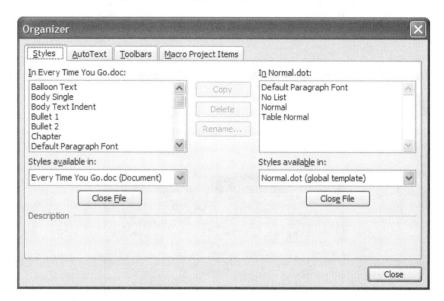

Creating Your Own Templates

If you find yourself creating the same styles over and over again for several documents, you can save time by creating a custom template. A template contains all of the styles associated with a particular type of document. Templates can also contain custom toolbars, macros, keyboard shortcuts, and view settings. A template can even contain standard information and graphics, such as the company logo and the standard To: and From: fields for a company memo or your name and return address for the title page of every manuscript you create.

To create a template:

1. Choose File | New or open the New Document task pane.
2. Choose On My Computer in the Templates options. This will open the Templates dialog box.
3. On the General tab, choose Blank Document.
4. Click the Template button on the lower right of the dialog box.
5. Click OK.
6. Add styles, text, graphics, toolbars, and any other elements you want to include in the new template.
7. Choose File | Save.

The document will automatically be saved as a template (.dot) in the user templates folder. The next time you open the Template dialog box, the new template will appear as an option.

Controlling Access to Styles

If you're working in a collaborative environment—whether it is a marketing team or a school group project—nothing can be more frustrating than having your well-formatted document torn to shreds by another member of the team. You can protect your styles from editing by making them unavailable to other users. You can also prevent users from applying styles to protected text. To control style access:

1. Choose Tools | Protect Document.

2. In the Protect Document task pane, shown in Figure 9-5, select Limit Formatting to a Selection of Styles.

3. Click Settings.

4. In the Formatting Restrictions dialog box, select the styles that can be used in the document. Deselect styles that aren't permitted.

5. Click OK to return to the task pane.

6. In the Editing Restrictions options, set the type of editing that's permitted. You can lock the document so it's only viewable in read only, or you can require all changes to be tracked in Review mode or as comments in the document. Finally, you can limit editing to filling in fields, without providing access to other portions of the document.

7. Click Yes, Start Enforcing Protection.

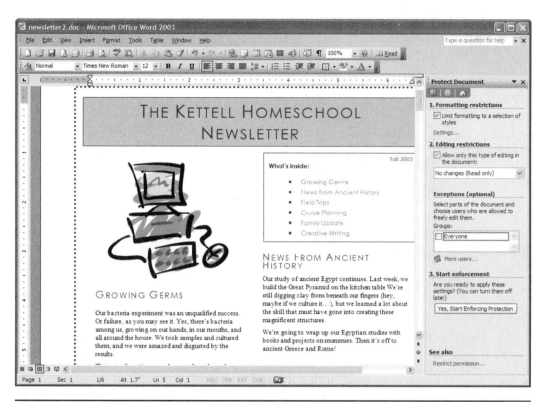

FIGURE 9-5   You can control the styles used in a document and what types of changes can be made in the Protect Document task pane.

8. In the Start Enforcing Protection dialog box, enter an optional password (and confirmation), and then click OK.

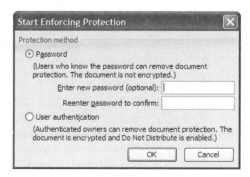

The Style Gallery

When you use several templates and dozens of styles, it's easy to lose track of which formatting is contained in each. Word attempts to organize this information in the Style

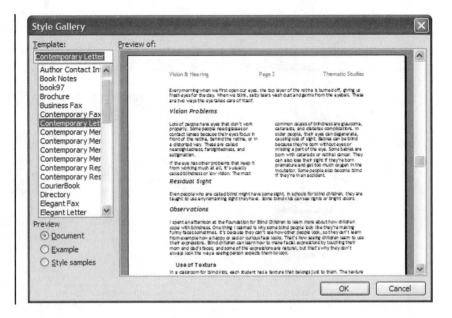

Gallery, shown in Figure 9-6 above. The Style Gallery is well hidden, accessible only as an option in the Theme dialog box (Format | Theme). This lack of visibility may be for the best, as this feature isn't nearly as useful as its name would imply.

The Style Gallery is supposed to provide examples of the styles available in each template, including a rendering of the current document if it is attached to that template. In actuality, however, most of the templates are lacking examples, even among those shipped with Office. Also, if you want to put the styles in a template to work in your document, you need to use the Templates and Add-Ins Organizer to move the styles into the current template. The Style Gallery doesn't offer access to this feature, however, and you must close the Style Gallery before you can open the Organizer.

Themes

Themes are often thought to be related to templates. Although they both contain styles that control the appearance of the document, templates and themes are used for very different purposes. *Templates* are a collection of styles and predesigned elements used to create a document for a particular purpose. *Themes*, on the other hand, are a collection of styles, colors, backgrounds, and graphics used to give a document an overall look.

Themes can be used to give a coordinated appearance to web pages, business cards, brochures, letterhead, and newsletters—the purpose of the document can vary, but all the documents will have a similar look. Themes are somewhat gimmicky, but they can be used to advantage, particularly for someone with a home business who lacks the budget or graphic arts skills to create a custom design.

Theme Assets and Liabilities

An Office theme contains a background image, bullets and icons, and horizontal rules, as shown in Figure 9-7. It also has styles to control the font, size, color, and appearance of text, headings, and hyperlinks. Some themes also have animated graphics, intended for use solely on web pages. Because of the graphic elements, and given that themes originated in FrontPage, many Office experts consider them to be unusable for anything other than web sites. There are other ways to use themes, however, if you understand their strengths and limitations.

Themes Change Templates and Styles

Themes are not templates. If you add a theme to a page that is based on a template, the theme styles will override those of the template. If you later remove the theme, the styles will not revert to the previous template settings, so you'll have to reapply the template to the document or manually modify the styles. If you want to modify a theme, you need to edit it in FrontPage, not in Word. You can, however, create a template based on a theme, as explained in the upcoming "Converting Themes into Templates" section.

The styles for Normal and Headings 1–6 will be changed to match the theme. Tables will also assume the theme properties—borders and text will be color coordinated, and the fonts will match those of the document text. If you change themes, the table properties will also change.

NOTE   *Keep in mind that many of the styles associated with a theme are based on using coordinating colors. If other styles in your document are based on the Normal or a Heading style, they will inherit the color change, while styles not based on Normal or one of the headings may no longer coordinate with the rest of the document.*

FIGURE 9-7
You can add a theme to your document using Format | Theme, then choosing from the extensive list of options.

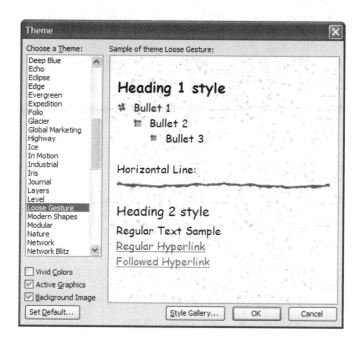

Backgrounds and Graphics

Themes have background colors or images. To see them, use Print Layout view and change your View options (Tools | Options | View tab) to enable Background Colors and Images. If you want to print the background, you also need to enable the same option on the Print tab of the Options dialog box. To see the background but not print it, only enable the option on the View tab, while leaving the Print option at its default (disabled) setting. Remember that backgrounds and graphic bullets use a considerable amount of ink when printing. They may also hinder the readability of your printed document, as the ink bleeds together a bit.

Use Print Preview to see how your document will look without a background, as many of the theme layouts are rather bland without them. Often, text in a bold color or large font looks fine with a background image, but looks unprofessional or oversized without the coordinating background. Remember, most of these themes were designed with web pages in mind, not letterhead or business cards.

Applying and Removing Themes

To apply a theme, choose Format | Theme. As you scroll through the list of themes in the dialog box (refer to Figure 9-7), you can see the elements of each one in the preview box. You can subtly alter the colors for each theme by selecting the Vivid Colors option; this generally just makes the hyperlinks brighter, although in some themes the changes are more significant. If you're using the theme with the intention of printing the final document, you can disable the Active Graphics in the Theme dialog box. You can also disable the Background Image here, if you don't want to control this through the View and Print options. To attach a theme to your document, click OK. As you can see from Figure 9-8, the document assumes the elements of the theme. In this case, Loose Gesture has a textured, sand-colored background and rich accent colors for hyperlinks, bullets, and horizontal rules. The Normal text remains black, making it stand out against the busy background.

Because themes and templates are often put to work in the same document, the Style Gallery is accessible from the Theme dialog box. The Style Gallery lists all of the prepackaged and user-generated templates. You can view a sample of your document with both the selected theme and template attached, giving you a general idea of how it will be formatted with those choices.

It can be fun to play with themes, if only to spark your own ideas. If you apply a theme and later wish to remove it, return to the Theme dialog box (Format | Theme) and select No Theme at the top of the Choose a Theme list. When you click OK, the document will return to the Normal template.

Converting Themes into Templates

Themes are only customizable in FrontPage and are limited to modifications in the Normal and Heading styles, hyperlink styles, background graphics, horizontal rules, and bullets. You can, however, convert a theme into a template, to which you can add other styles, modify the graphics, insert standard text, and make other layout changes. To do this:

1. Select Format | Theme to open the Theme dialog box.

2. Choose a theme from the list.

3. Choose the Vivid Color and other theme options, as desired.

4. Click OK to exit the dialog box and apply the theme to the current document.

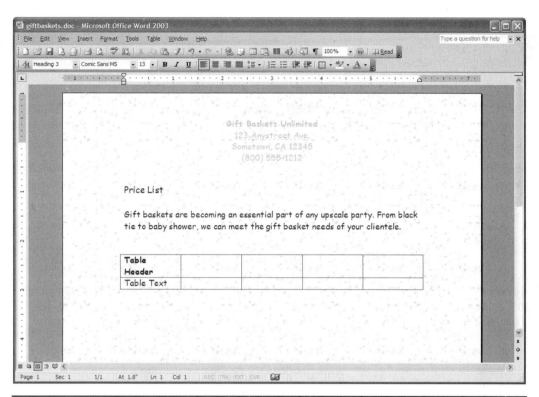

FIGURE 9-8   Loose Gesture theme applied to a document

5. Make modifications to the document as necessary:
   - Change the background image using Format | Background.
   - Change the styles using Format | Styles and Formatting.
   - Add Headers and Footers (View | Header and Footer).
   - Modify the table style with Table | AutoFormat.
   - Insert stock text, such as a return address for letterhead.

6. Choose File | Save (or File | Save As) to open the Save As dialog box.

7. In the Save As Type field, choose Word Template (.dot). The directory will automatically change to store the new template in your templates folder.

8. Name the file and click Save. The new template is saved complete with the background image, styles, and all the other elements of the document.

Keep in mind if you do this that the new template is not associated with the theme upon which it was based. If you make extensive changes to the template, the resulting documents may no longer resemble other documents based on the original theme. Accordingly, if you later change the theme, the template will remain the same.

Themes Across Applications

If you've chosen to use themes to reflect an image for yourself or your company, you'll likely want to use that same image for all of your marketing materials and presentations. Because themes are based on HTML documents and cascading style sheets (both of which, along with FrontPage themes, are covered in Chapter 35), they are all available in FrontPage. If you choose the Layers theme for your letterhead, you can design your web site to match using the Layers theme in FrontPage.

Outlook also makes use of the same theme set. In order to access these themes in Outlook, you need to use Word as your e-mail editor and compose in HTML or rich text format. When you're in the Word editor composing an e-mail, most of the standard Word formatting options are available, including themes. Chapter 25 has more information about Outlook e-mail and stationery.

As mentioned, themes are most useful for business cards, presentations, brochures, and web sites—all documents that are best created in one of the other Office applications. One of the biggest disappointments in this feature, however, is that only 23 of the themes found in Word and FrontPage are available in Publisher, and only 20 are in PowerPoint. Other themes appear in Publisher or PowerPoint, but not in Word and FrontPage. Interestingly, only 17 themes are available in all four applications. To duplicate the other themes in PowerPoint or Publisher, you'll need to copy and paste graphic elements and re-create the text styles manually. If you're already applying a prepackaged theme, chances are you're trying to save time or have fallen in love with one of those designs. In both cases, you're unlikely to want to re-create the theme in PowerPoint or Publisher, should you need to use those applications. And while a choice of 17 themes may be considered more than adequate by some, these are generally the most bold, corporate, or masculine of the bunch. You won't find Poetry or Citrus Punch in either Publisher or PowerPoint. It's unknown why only certain themes were deemed worthy of duplicating in PowerPoint or Publisher—and in some cases, only in one of those applications—while others are unique to Word and FrontPage.

Then again, if you're already creating a unique corporate image using themes, you can plan ahead to create coordinating themes for any of the other applications you're likely to use to generate brochures, newsletters, and other products utilizing that image. All of the images used in themes, including the background graphics, are stored on your hard drive. Background images can be sized to fit everything from business cards to 11×17-inch newsletters. Shapes created in Word or FrontPage can be copied and pasted into Publisher or PowerPoint. And font styles and sizes can be re-created easily in these applications.

For more information on using applications together, see Chapter 38.

Tables and Columns

Judicious use of indents, tabs, and paragraph formatting offers considerable control over the layout of a document. Some types of material require additional formatting, however, to organize it or otherwise control the flow. Tables are used to organize content, whether it be text, graphics, sorted data, or even elements to control page layout. Columns are used to control the flow of content across the page, complete with white space and sometimes vertical lines to increase readability.

Although tables and columns are somewhat dissimilar in functionality, the advent of advanced page layout in web design has caused many people to group these features together. Tables are used extensively in web page layout, and can even be used to simulate columns on a page, leading to some confusion when it comes to applying the same principles to printed page layout. This chapter will explain the limitations and uses of both tables and columns as they relate to Word.

Tables

A table is made up of columns and rows. The intersection of each column and row is a cell. Each cell can contain a unique combination of text, graphics, or even another table (called *nested tables*). Formatting can be applied to the entire table, to columns, to rows, or to individual cells, giving you complete control over every aspect of the layout.

It used to be that tables were strictly used to present tabular data—numbers upon which calculations were performed, such as an invoice or income and expense ledger. Although Word offers a calculator and other tools to manipulate and sort tabular data, this is definitely a weak spot in the application. Fortunately, Excel handles these operations quite nicely, and as explained in Chapter 38, Excel spreadsheets can be embedded into a Word document.

These days, tables are more often used to organize lists of information, such as many of the tables in this book. They're also used in page layout and to create forms, such as invoices or school registration forms. If your document contains a glossary, one column of a table can contain the term, while another lists the definition; the table will retain the alignment of each entry even if the definition is several lines long. You can even create a simple calendar by putting a graphic in the top row of a table, then using the cells below for the days of the month. Notice that the alignment and shading for the row containing the days of the week are different from those of the date cells.

Creating Tables

There are four ways to create a table in Word. Each provides a different level of control over the creation of the initial table format, and each appeals to a different type of user.

Inserting Tables from the Menu

To insert a table from the main menu, choose Table | Insert | Table. The Insert Table dialog box, shown here, allows you to specify how many columns and rows the initial table should contain. You can also choose from the following AutoFit behaviors:

- **Fixed Column Width**   Columns can be set to a specific width. If you choose Auto in this option, the column width will be set to fill the space between the margins. If the margins change, the table settings will remain the same. Once the table is created, the contents of a cell will cause it to increase in size vertically, but the horizontal width of the column will remain constant.

- **AutoFit to Contents**   Once the table is created, the width of the columns will automatically adjust to fit their contents. Thus, a column with only one word in each cell becomes narrower, while a column with cells containing a graphic or longer phrase becomes wider.

- **AutoFit to Window**   Columns are automatically created to fill the space between the margins of the page. If the margins change, the table will change to fit within the new settings.

The AutoFormat option allows you to set a style for the new table as it's being created. Table styles control the appearance and formatting of tables, as explained in the section "Table Styles Using AutoFormat," later in this chapter.

If your document will contain several tables with the same basic configuration, select the Remember Dimensions for New Tables option. This will preserve your settings for other tables.

Inserting Tables from the Toolbar

The second method for inserting tables is with the Insert Table button on the Standard toolbar. If you click on this button, Word will insert a table that is five columns wide and four rows deep. You can create a larger table by dragging the cursor over the columns and rows in the drop-down menu, as shown in Figure 10-1. The AutoFit options you set in the Insert Table dialog box will also be applied to tables created using the toolbar.

Drawing Tables

The third method of creating a table appeals to visual people, but can be frustrating to use. When you draw a table, you can completely customize the layout, creating cells of unequal sizes in a column or row (shown in Figure 10-2) and immediately applying borders and shading to the table.

Before drawing a table, you must be in either Print Layout or Web Layout view; if you're not already in one of those views, Word will automatically change it for you when you select Draw Table. To begin drawing a table, choose Table | Draw Table, or click the Tables and Borders button on the Standard toolbar. Either method will open the Tables and Borders floating toolbar, which contains all the options you need to create the table. Your mouse pointer changes to a pencil to indicate that you're drawing a table. If you make a mistake or want to erase a line, click on the Eraser button on the toolbar, and then click on the line.

When you draw a table, Word automatically aligns your columns and rows to an invisible grid. Larger cells are actually created by automatically merging cells. This is important because you may want to use the Table menu to make adjustments later with the Split and Merge options.

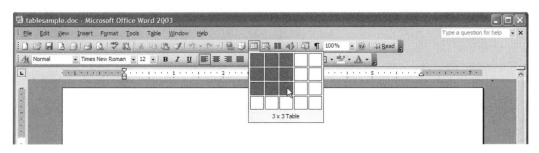

FIGURE 10-1   The Insert Table button on the Standard toolbar allows you to create a table of the dimensions you specify.

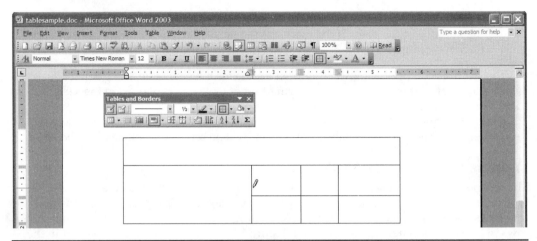

FIGURE 10-2   This table contains four columns and three rows, but many of the cells have been automatically merged as they were drawn.

Using the Draw Table tool is sometimes fraught with frustration. If you don't line up the pencil directly under an existing column divider, Word may insert a new column into the table. At other times, the entire table will shift in unexpected ways.

TIP   *If the idea of drawing tables leaves you uninspired, use one of the Insert Table options and modify the basic table using the options on the Table menu. These are explained in the "Manipulating Tables" section of this chapter.*

Converting Text to Tables

The final method of creating a table involves converting comma- or tab-separated text into a table. To do this:

1. Type your text, separated by paragraphs (ENTER key), commas, tabs, or any other delimiter.

NOTE   *Choose your delimiter with care. If you set the delimiter to an alphanumeric character, any iterations of that character within the text of your table will flow the following text into the next cell.*

2. Highlight the text you wish to convert into a table.

3. Choose Table | Convert | Text to Table.

4. In the Convert Text to Table dialog box, confirm that the Separate Text At option is set to the delimiter for your text.

5. Choose the number of columns for your table. Word automatically determines the number of rows to ensure that every entry in the text is placed into a cell.

6. Click OK.

The Convert Text to Table tool is generally used when you're formatting data that was previously formatted with tabs or commas, such as in a backup of an old database table or spreadsheet.

NOTE *You can also use the reverse command, Table | Convert | Table to Text, to remove the grid lines and convert the table into delimited text. You can choose to use paragraphs, tabs, commas, or a character of your choosing as the delimiter.*

Manipulating Tables

Once you've created an initial table structure, you can enter data (of course, in the case of converting text to a table, the data already exists). All the standard commands and toolbars are available. To move from cell to cell, use the TAB key.

TIP *To enter a tab into a table cell, use CTRL-TAB. To start a new paragraph within a cell, use the ENTER key, as usual.*

You can insert text and graphics inside a table using the same commands and options as you would to insert them elsewhere in the document. This includes using the Copy, Cut, and Paste commands, Insert | Picture, and even Table | Insert | Table (as explained in the section "Nesting Tables" in this chapter).

Often as you're entering data, you'll need to make adjustments to the initial table structure. These changes can be made using the Tables and Borders toolbar or the Table menu.

Selecting Table Elements

In order to make changes to the table structure, you first need to select a column, row, cell, or the entire table. You can do this using the mouse or with the Table menu (Table | Select). The following table tells you how to select the various table elements.

To Select...	Do This
Cell	Click within the cell.
Row	Move the mouse pointer to the left side of the table, and then click on the row when the pointer becomes a white arrow.
Column	Position the mouse pointer over the column, and then click when the pointer changes to a black arrow.
Table	Click on the small box in the upper-left corner of the table.

The column selection arrow can be somewhat elusive, so you may find it easier to click in a cell within the column and use the Table | Select | Column menu option instead.

Inserting and Deleting Columns and Rows

The most common table-related task is adding and removing columns and rows. When you select a column or row in a table, the Insert Table button on the Standard toolbar changes function. The button can be used to quickly insert a column or row. When you click on it, you'll be prompted to insert the new column or row above or below the selection.

You can also use the Table menu to insert columns and rows by choosing Table | Insert, and then selecting from the column and row options. You can insert cells in the same manner; in this case, you'll be asked how to shift the surrounding cells to accommodate the new one.

To delete columns, rows, or cells, use the Table | Delete menu. Again, if you choose to delete a cell, a dialog box will ask you to choose how to shift the remaining cells.

Another way to insert and delete cells is to move them around with the mouse. You can drag table elements within a table, effectively moving a column or row from one spot in the table to another. If you drag a cell, column, or row off the table and then drop it, you'll create a new table.

Adjusting Table Properties

Another common table modification is adjusting the width and height of cells. Again, you can do this using the mouse to manipulate the table borders manually, but you can make more precise (and consistent) adjustments using the Table | Table Properties menu option. The Table Properties dialog box, shown next, allows you to make adjustments to each column and row. Select multiple columns or rows before opening the dialog box to make changes to several columns/rows at once. In the case of row height, you can specify it as an exact measurement or a minimum setting. For column width, you can specify an exact width or a percentage of the table width. Use the Previous and Next buttons to scroll through all the columns and rows of the table to make individual changes without having to toggle between the table and the dialog box.

The Cell tab of the Table Properties dialog box, shown next, enables you to change the width of an individual cell. This option is a bit misleading, however, as changes to the cell width affect the width of the entire column. While you're in this dialog box, you can specify the alignment of text within the cell. By default, text is aligned at the top of each cell, but you can change the alignment to be vertically centered or at the bottom of the cell.

Also within the Cell tab is an Options button. This opens the Cell Options dialog box, which lets you specify the margins within each cell. This is the white space between the cell border and its contents. For text that overflows the default size of a cell, you can choose to wrap the text—which will, in turn, make the row height greater—or resize the text to make it fit within the confines of the cell.

While the Cell tab lets you set the alignment for the contents of individual cells, the Table tab, shown next, controls the alignment for the table itself. You can align a table to the left margin, centered, or the right margin. You can also offset the table from its left alignment by setting the Indent From Left option. You can even control how surrounding text wraps around the table.

NOTE   *AutoFit options take precedence over the Size setting in the Table tab. Thus, changes to the table size may readjust as you add data to the table.*

Merging and Splitting Cells

Some table settings can't be controlled in the Table Properties dialog box. In the case of the calendar example shown earlier in the chapter, the top cell spans the entire width of the table. To do this, you need to merge the cells in the top row. You can merge cells into rows or columns. Select the cells you want to merge, and then choose Table | Merge Cells. You can also merge cells using the Eraser in the Tables and Borders toolbar.

Other situations require dividing one cell into smaller cells, while retaining the structure of the surrounding cells. To do this, highlight the cell and choose Table | Split Cells. The cell will be split evenly into the number of columns or rows you specify in the Split Cells dialog box.

TIP *You don't have to manually merge a group of cells before splitting them into a new configuration. You can highlight a group of cells and choose Table | Split Cells. Select the option Merge Cells Before Split, and the cells will be merged into one large cell, then divided according to the number of columns and rows you specify.*

Nesting Tables

Although you can merge and split cells with wild abandon, sometimes it's simply easier just to insert a table within the cell of a table. To do this, put the insertion point within a cell and choose Table | Insert | Table. Nested tables have the same flexibility as other tables. It's easy to lose track of which cells belong to which tables, though, so edit with care.

Splitting Tables

Sometimes one table just won't do. If you need to divide a table into two separate tables, you can split it. Put the insertion point into the row that will become the first row of the new table, and then choose Table | Split Table. After the table is split, the insertion point is moved to the space between the two tables, allowing you to enter text between the tables.

Hiding Grid Lines

When you create a table, Word provides grid lines to delineate the table structure. These grid lines don't appear in print, but are strictly for your benefit. These are often confused with the table's borders, which are lines that do appear in print and are turned on by default. If you're modifying the borders of a table, you may want to hide the grid lines so they don't cause confusion. To do this, select Table | Hide Gridlines.

Formatting Table Content

Formatting the table structure is just one part of taking control of your tables. You can also control the format of the cell content and the appearance of the table. AutoFormat lets you give the table a consistent appearance without a lot of effort. If you don't find a style you like, you can manually control the borders and shading of the table and its cells. The contents of the table can be rotated, sorted, and tallied. Finally, you can caption the table to provide a useful description of its purpose.

Table Styles Using AutoFormat

As discussed in Chapter 9, you can create styles for tables just as you can for paragraphs, characters, and lists. Table styles include settings for the borders, shading, and background color of cells. The AutoFormat option is available when you insert a new table using the Insert Table dialog box or by using the Table | Table AutoFormat command when you're ready to apply the formatting. In the Table AutoFormat dialog box, you can choose to apply all attributes of a chosen style or just those you require:

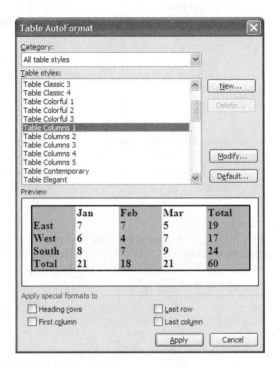

Changing Borders and Shading

Unless you used the AutoFormat option, tables are created with a default half-point border. You can modify the table borders and add a background color (shading) using the Tables and Borders toolbar. As you can see here, the drop-down menu on the Borders button shows the most common border options. The Border Color, Line Style, and Line Weight buttons allow you to control the appearance of border lines.

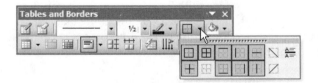

Alternatively, you can use Format | Borders and Shading for more control over the table or individual cells, columns, and rows.

Rotating Text

When creating a table with headings for each row, you can choose to change the direction of the text from horizontal to vertical. To do this, select the affected cells and choose Change

Text Direction from the Tables and Borders toolbar. This option is also available from the context menu (right-click), but is not on the Table menu. If this feature is one you use often, you can add it to the Table menu. See Chapter 2 to learn how to customize menus.

Repeating Headings

Lengthy tables often span multiple pages. In these cases, you can repeat the Heading row of the table to help your readers stay oriented as they read the table content. To do this, select the rows you wish to repeat on each page, and then choose Table | Heading Rows Repeat. You can select more than one row of repeating text, but you must select them all together before using this menu option.

Sorting Data

As mentioned at the beginning of this chapter, Word isn't very well suited for calculating and manipulating data. Still, you can do rudimentary sorts and calculations for those situations where it's not worth firing up another application.

To sort the data in a table, put the insertion point inside the table, and then choose Table | Sort. The Sort dialog box lets you sort text, numbers, or dates. In a multicolumn table, you must specify which column is the primary sort criteria. When the contents of one cell in the column are moved, the other cells in the original row are also adjusted. You can specify more than one column for the sort criteria, as when you want to sort by a Month column, then a Date column. You can also specify whether the data should be sorted in ascending or descending order. Finally, if you've created a heading row in your table, be sure to click the appropriate My List Has setting. We've chosen No Header Row here:

NOTE *Word automatically selects the entire table when completing a sort. If you want to sort only a particular column, select the column before choosing Table | Sort. In the Sort Options dialog box (accessed using the Options button), select Sort Column Only.*

The Sort Options dialog box allows you to use the Sort feature on text that's not contained in a table. Specify the delineation of the list items (tabs, commas, etc.), and the Sort operation will work the same way it does when sorting a table.

Quick Math Calculations

For quick sums of numeric table content, you can use the AutoSum button on the Tables and Borders toolbar. For slightly more involved calculations, use the Table | Formula feature. The Formula dialog box, shown next, allows you to perform Excel-like calculations. To do so, begin each formula with an equal sign, followed by the formula structure. You can refer to specific cells, whereby the intersection of the first column and row is cell A1, the first column and second row is cell A2, and the second column and first row is B1. To refer to a range of cells, use the colon, as in =sum(B5:B18). If you use a formula in an empty cell at the bottom of a column of numbers, Word will automatically assume you want to calculate the sum of all the numbers above it, and will fill in this portion of the dialog box. You can change the entry to calculate the average or perform boolean operations.

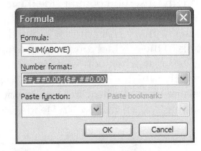

For anything more challenging than a simple sum, you're still better off using Excel. The Insert Microsoft Excel Worksheet button on the Standard toolbar makes it easy to embed a worksheet into your document, giving you all the tools and features of the spreadsheet application within your word processor.

Columns

Columns offer another way to organize the flow of text on a page. If you're creating newsletters in Word, it's important to learn how to control the gutter between columns and how to set column breaks to control how the text flows between columns. You'll also want to know how to change the number of columns within a document or even on a single page.

You can format columns before typing text or apply it to existing text, although I've generally found that it's easiest to enter the text first. If you format the columns first and then need to edit your text, any column breaks you have inserted will become misplaced.

The Columns button on the Standard toolbar provides a quick method for setting column formatting, but doesn't offer much control. Even if you use this method for applying the initial column formatting, you'll find yourself fine-tuning these settings using the method described in the following section. For that reason, it's generally easiest to go straight to the main source and do all your formatting at once.

To apply columns to existing text:

1. Select the text you wish to format in columns. You can choose the whole document or only a portion.

2. Choose Format | Columns.

3. In the Columns dialog box, specify your column settings:

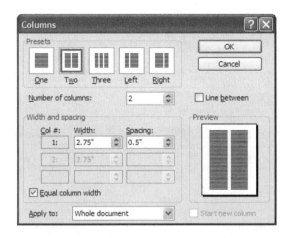

- **Presets**   This sets the number of columns simply by clicking on one of them. The last two options provide for two uneven columns, as you often see in a newspaper.

- **Number of Columns**   If the presets don't suit you, specify the exact number of columns for your layout.

- **Width and Spacing**   The default is for each column to be of equal width, but once you've set the number of columns, you can deselect this option and fine-tune the settings for each one. The Width setting controls the width of the column, while the Spacing setting controls the amount of white space between columns.

- **Apply To**   Regardless of your text selection prior to opening the Columns dialog box, you can apply your new column settings to just the selected text or to the whole document. If you choose to apply the columns to the selected text, you also have the option of starting the columns on the current page or forcing a section break to start the columns on a new page.

- **Line Between**   Check this option to add a vertical line to the gutter between columns, serving as another visual cue.

4. Click OK.

Figure 10-3 shows a page of text divided into two columns with a line divider. The text preceding the column-formatted text is in a single column.

If you formatted only a portion of the document into columns, you'll notice section breaks at the beginning and end of the selection. These breaks are only visible if you have

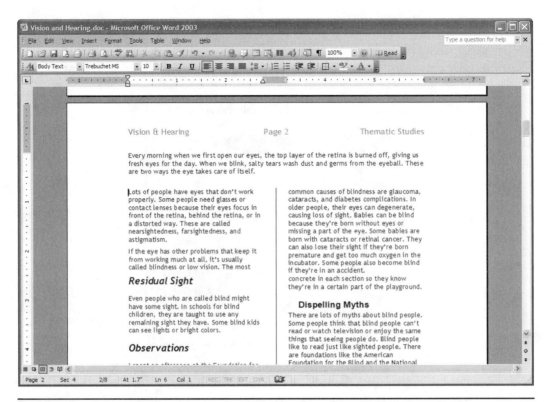

FIGURE 10-3   Only text that was previously selected has been formatted into two columns.

formatting marks displayed (Show/Hide ¶ or the View settings in the Options dialog box). To remove columns, delete the section breaks.

Using Column Breaks

Once you've formatted text into columns, look closely at how the text flows from one column into the next. Be particularly aware of headings that appear at the bottom of one column while their underlying text appears at the top of the next. If you're unhappy with where these column breaks occur, you can manually insert column breaks. To do this, position the cursor where you want the text to break, choose Insert | Break, and pick Column Break.

Because columns divide text into short lines, the vertical flow isn't the only change. If you're using multiple columns, you may find that the horizontal flow of the text is more readable if you justify both the left and right margins of the text. Doing this, however, causes long words at the end of a line to move to the following line, leaving big gaps between words as Word tries to compensate for this extra space. To minimize this, you may need to hyphenate your document.

Hyphenation

There are two ways of hyphenating text in Word. To manually hyphenate a word, simply press the hyphen key on your keyboard; Word will automatically move the characters after the hyphen to another line. Word can also be set to automatically hyphenate text where it deems necessary.

Automatic hyphenation in Word is a mixed blessing. If your text is left aligned, single column—which is most likely the majority of your work—hyphenation is generally more of a nuisance than a help. Jagged right margins are the norm, and you can manually hyphenate long words that leave extraneous white space. The reason automatic hyphenation is troublesome is that it tends to hyphenate as much as possible, which can detract from the readability of your document.

If your text is formatted in columns or right justified, however, hyphenation can control the flow of your text to reduce blocks of white space caused by awkward word wrapping. Even so, you should always review the final document to ensure that the hyphenation isn't overwhelming.

CAUTION *When reviewing your document for hyphenation, don't use the Reading Layout view. This view is intended for increasing readability on screen and is not a true representation of how your printed document will appear. Thus, the hyphenation in Reading Layout may be far different from your final result. Instead, use the Print Layout view, or examine a printed draft of the document.*

To set automatic hyphenation:

1. Go to Tools | Language | Hyphenation.

2. In the Hyphenation dialog box, select Automatically Hyphenate Document:

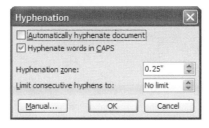

3. Enter the Hyphenation Zone. This is the acceptable amount of space between the end of a line and the right margin. A wider hyphenation zone will result in fewer words being hyphenated and potentially more white space at the end of a line. A narrow hyphenation zone will hyphenate more words in order to decrease the amount of white space at the end of each line.

4. Enter the Limit Consecutive Hyphens To setting. This setting controls how many consecutive lines can be hyphenated. A setting of No Limit gives Word complete control. Setting a low number means that for every one or two lines that are

hyphenated, there must be at least one line without hyphenation. This improves readability.

5. Click OK.

You can also use the Hyphenation dialog box to manually hyphenate the document within the constraints you set. To do this, deselect the Automatically Hyphenate Document option, and then set the Hyphenation Zone and consecutive hyphens limit. When you're ready to hyphenate the document, enter the dialog box once again and click Manual. The end result is the same as using automatic hyphenation, but allows you to create and edit the document without the distraction of hyphen control.

NOTE   *If you need to do a Find and Replace on a hyphenated document, it's best to leave off the hyphens in your search criteria. If you include the hyphen character, only those words matching the exact hyphenation will be found. If you exclude the hyphen in your search criteria, Word will find all instances of the text, including those that are optionally hyphenated.*

Advanced Page Layout in Word

Page layout used to be the purview of professionals. Typesetting, color matching, graphic design, and layout took the skill of trained designers. The equipment necessary to produce publications was well beyond the price reach of the average consumer, or even the average small business. The advent of desktop publishing packages, matched with the lower prices and increased capabilities of inkjet printers, brought page layout closer to home. The most recent versions of Word bring it closer still, right onto your computer.

While Word is still primarily a word processor, you can fire off simple newsletters, business cards, and brochures with ease. A combination of text boxes, drawing tools, and graphics gives you almost complete control over your page layout. This chapter explains how to make the transition from text formatting to publication production.

Knowing When to Use Another Application

Although Word has become increasingly robust in its page layout abilities, it's still a word processor. Precise page layout is best done in a dedicated page layout application, such as Publisher, which is covered fully in Chapters 36 and 37. Desktop publishing packages offer features that are unavailable or, at best, involve multistep work-arounds in Word.

So how do you decide which application to use? Here is a list of the strengths and prime uses for Word and Publisher.

Publisher:

- Templates for greeting cards, brochures, fliers, business cards, menus, text frames, placeholders, and newsletters
- Four-color separation, spot printing, and crop mark support that are all useful when working with a commercial printer or copy shop
- Pixel-precise control over the positioning of text boxes, graphics, and other elements

- Layout guides to assist in element placement
- Font and color schemes
- Automated "Continued on" and "Continued from" features
- Greater control over nonstandard paper sizes

Word:

- More header and footer control
- Tables of contents, cross-references, and indexes
- Easier to create long documents
- Shorter learning curve for those already familiar with word processing tools

Borders, Boxes, and Shading

One of the easiest ways to dress up a document is to create visual separations between key elements. In a magazine, the eye is almost automatically drawn to information that's boxed or shaded to set it apart from the body of an article. You can create those effects in Word using Borders and Shading (Format | Borders and Shading).

Borders

Borders (Figure 11-1) are used to box-in text and graphics. In Word, you can apply the border to all four sides to create a box, or control which sides should be encompassed by

FIGURE 11-1
The Borders tab provides complete control over the style and application of lines and custom borders to each side of the selection.

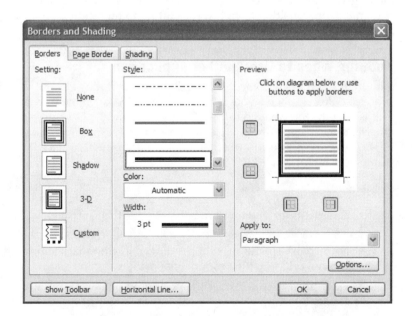

the border. Choose a setting from the options on the left side of the dialog box. Choose Box to completely surround the selection. The Shadow and 3-D settings are preformatted to create those visual effects. The Custom setting permits you to combine different line styles or apply borders only to specified sides of the selection.

Once you've chosen a setting, select a line style, color, and width. If you chose the Box setting, these changes will automatically appear in the Preview pane. For a Custom border, make your line selections, and then click on the appropriate side of the Preview pane to apply the line to that side.

By default, borders are applied with a 1-point margin for the top and bottom lines, and a 4-point margin on the left and right sides. Change the margins by clicking the Options button. The borders for a paragraph are set to the paragraph margins, not the page margins. Thus, if you have indented text inside the border, as in a bulleted or numbered list, the border for those paragraphs will also be indented. In a multiparagraph box, this can break the consistency of the borders, as shown here:

> It's·been·a·busy·month·for·us·here.·This·issue·of·our·
> newsletter·is·chock-full-of·ideas·and·tips.¶
> ¶
> Included·in·this·issue:¶
> ¶
> > •→ In·the·Garden¶
> > •→ Upcoming·Trips¶
> > •→ Recipes¶
> > •→ Creative·Corner¶
>
> ¶
> Read·on!¶
> ¶

You can see that the top paragraphs have an indented right margin, the bulleted list has an indented left margin, and the final paragraphs are set to the page margins. The only way to avoid this problem is to use a text box, which is described later in this chapter, in "Text Boxes."

Borders and shading are applied to tables, cells, and paragraphs rather than the whole page or document. If you want to apply a border to an entire page, click on the Page Border tab of the Borders and Shading dialog box. This tab is identical to the Borders tab except that the border is applied to the entire page or document rather than selected paragraphs.

Shading

The term *shading* in the Borders and Shading dialog box (Figure 11-2) is somewhat misleading. Shading is essentially a background fill of a selection. Apply a color from the Fill box. If you need a wider range of color choices, click the More Colors button.

You can create a patterned fill using the options under Patterns. The percentages refer to how much of the fill area will be filled in with small dots or a pattern of lines—the higher the percentage, the more densely packed the pattern will appear. Word automatically chooses a pattern color to coordinate with the fill color. If you haven't chosen a fill color, the automatic pattern color choice is gray. By combining fill colors, pattern styles, and pattern colors, you can create a wide range of backgrounds for boxed text, or any other text you select. Keep in mind, however, that when you print intense colors and patterns, your text may not be as crisp and readable as it was on screen.

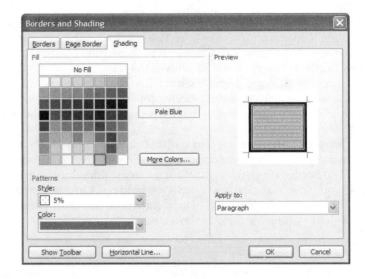

FIGURE 11-2
By combining pattern styles and colors, you can create interesting backgrounds for a selection, but sometimes, what looks good on screen can appear muddied in print.

TIP   *Word is pretty smart when it comes to shading. If you've created a border around a block of text, you can position the insertion point anywhere inside that box before applying the shading, and it will automatically be applied to the entire box. If you make a selection within that box, however, the shading will only be applied to the selected area.*

Horizontal Rules

Sometimes a simple line is enough to break up the vertical space. Word offers several ways to create a horizontal line (called a *rule*) across the page. AutoFormat, covered in Chapter 9, automatically converts certain characters into a rule, as seen in this table:

To Get This Horizontal Rule		Type This Three Times, Followed by ENTER
Single line	————————	Underscore (_)
Double line	————————	Equal (=)
Thin line	————————	Hyphen (-)
Wavy line	∿∿∿∿∿∿∿	Tilde (~)
Thick dotted line	•••••••••••••••	Asterisk (*)
Thick line surrounded by two thin lines	━━━━━━━	Pound (#)

You can also apply a rule using a border line by setting one line of the style and thickness of your choice either above or below the selected paragraph. If you click the Horizontal Line button in the Borders and Shading dialog box, you can choose from a number of custom rules, as shown here:

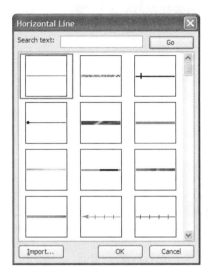

Once a horizontal rule is applied—using any of these methods, including AutoFormat—you can remove it by selecting the paragraph to which it was applied and clicking None in the Borders and Shading dialog box.

Page Fills and Backgrounds

Page fills and backgrounds are most commonly seen when using themes (see Chapter 9), but you can also add them yourself. Keep in mind that the same rules apply to page fills as to shading: too much color can compromise readability in print, so use with care. Page fills, backgrounds, and watermarks are applied to every page in the document.

To add a page fill to a document, choose Format | Background, and then choose a color. The entire page will be filled, not just the area within the margins.

CAUTION   *If your printer cannot print to the edges of the page, you'll have a narrow white border around each page, even though on screen it will appear to be completely filled.*

To remove a page fill, choose Format | Background, then No Fill.

Page Backgrounds

If a solid color fill won't do, you can apply various gradients, patterns, textures, and even pictures to the page background using Fill Effects. To apply an effect, choose Format | Background | Fill Effects. The effects shown on the following pages are available.

- **Gradient**   You can create a custom gradient fill of two or more colors and a variety of angles.

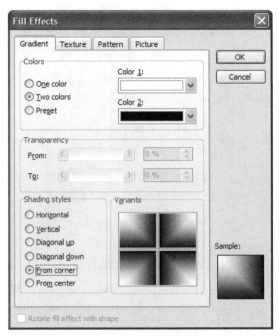

- **Texture**   Choose from one of the presets or your own texture tile.

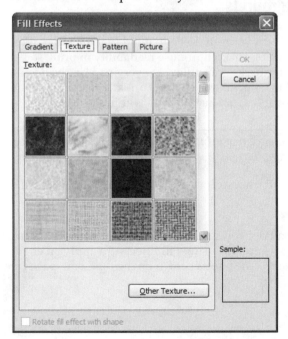

- **Pattern**   Choose from one of the 48 available patterns. You can also choose the two colors of the pattern—foreground and background.

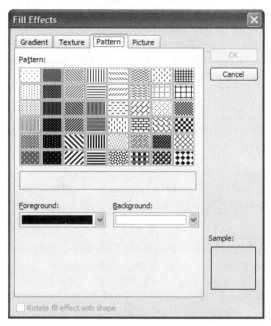

- **Picture**   Select a picture from the clip art that ships with Microsoft or your own resources. Pictures will be automatically resized to fit across the dimensions of the page. You can lock the aspect ratio so the graphic scales evenly.

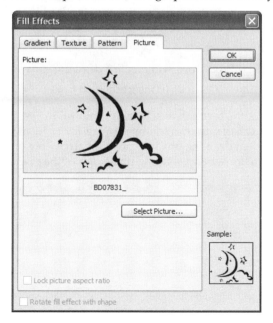

Watermarks

A *watermark* is a logo or text that appears in the background of a page. It's generally a light gray shade so as not to interfere with the document content. In the case of a logo, companies sometimes use watermarks to "brand" their reports or letters. In the case of text, watermarks can be used to mark a document as Confidential, Do Not Copy, or Draft, as shown in Figure 11-3.

To add a watermark, choose Format | Background | Printed Watermark. If you're using a logo, be sure the graphic has already been created. If the logo is too dark, select the Washout option.

TIP   *When using a logo for a watermark, it's best to create the image in grayscale. A color logo used as a watermark will appear in color on the printed page, even if you use the Washout setting.*

For a text watermark, choose from the Text options or type your own entry into the field. You can control the color and opacity of the text, as well as its direction.

Text Boxes

Word processors are very linear in their structure. Each line must contain at least a paragraph mark in order to progress to the next line. Page layout is generally far from linear. Sidebars bleed into the page from the margins. Columns, covered in Chapter 10, change format in the middle of an article. Blocks of text with different indentation are grouped together, which, as discussed in Chapter 8, can wreak havoc with paragraph borders. All of these situations are handled with Word by using text boxes. If you look again at Figure 11-3, you'll see that text boxes, along with page borders, embedded graphics, and shading can turn Word into a robust page layout tool.

A text box is actually a tool on the Drawing toolbar, which was covered in Chapter 5. What makes text boxes unique is that you can use the standard Word formatting options to format the text, even as you use the text box to position it with free reign.

To create a text box:

1. Choose Insert | Text Box. Word will create a drawing canvas at the insertion point.

2. Click inside the drawing canvas to insert the text box.

Drag on the borders of the text box to size it. You can fill the entire drawing canvas with the text box. Move the text box into position by moving the mouse until the pointer changes into a four-sided arrow, then drag the box into position anywhere on the page. You can format the text box with a border and shading using any of the drawing tools.

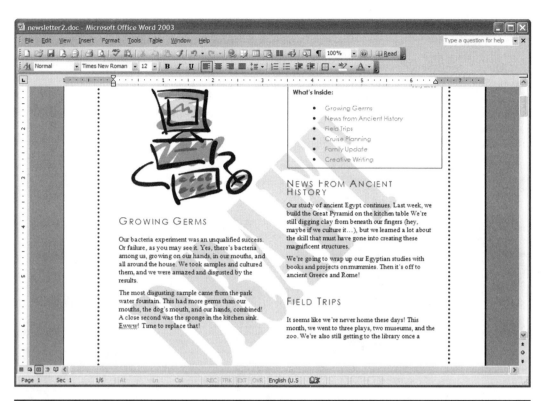

FIGURE 11-3   The Draft watermark appears diagonally across the page in a light gray so that the overlying text can still be read.

Overflowing Text Boxes

When you're using text boxes to format a page, text will sometimes need to flow from one box to another, such as when you're using text boxes to create columns, or text is flowing onto another page. To have content spill from one text box into another:

1. Create both text boxes and fill the first one with your content.

2. Click the Create Text Box Link button on the Text Box toolbar. Alternatively, click on the frame of the text box, right-click to bring up the context menu, and then select Create Text Box Link.

3. The mouse pointer will change into a pitcher, as shown next to "Field Trips" in Figure 11-4. Click inside the next text box to "pour" the overflowing text.

You can repeat these steps as many times as necessary to allow text to flow from text box to text box throughout your document. If you need to break a link, choose Break Forward Link while in the text box preceding the one you want to exclude.

Magazines often use the phrases "continued on" or "continued from" in small print to guide readers from page to page of an article. You can duplicate this in Word using cross-references. These are covered in Chapter 13.

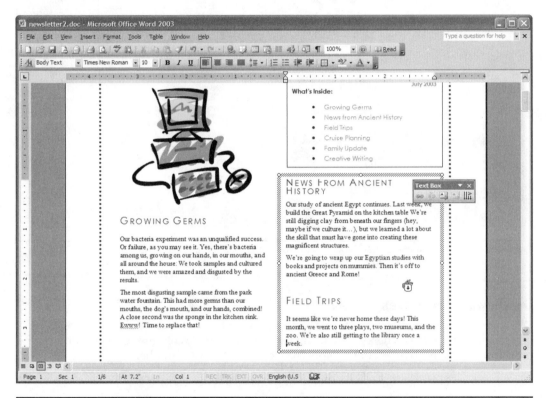

FIGURE 11-4   Flowing text from text box to text box provides more control than standard columns because you can position the text boxes precisely on the page.

Automating Information with Fields

Fields serve many purposes in Word. At the most basic level, they are special codes inserted in a document that allow text to be dynamically generated. Word takes the field code and its optional settings and uses that information to generate the text that actually gets printed. Using fields to automatically generate content for such things as headers and footers allows you to hand that functionality off to Word while you concentrate on more important things, like writing your document content.

In Word, you can use fields directly in a variety of ways. Use fields to display information about the document, such as the author's name, number of pages, or word count. Use them to display the results of a calculation in a formula. You can even use fields as the basis for making a document into a dynamic data entry form.

Field functionality is so powerful and flexible that it's used as the basis for many other Word features, such as table of contents and index building, form data entry, mail merge, and far more. This chapter gives you an overview of some of the more commonly used fields and how to use them in your Word documents.

Field Basics

All fields are inserted into a document using a format called the *field code*. This format consists of special curly braces marking the field and contains the name of the field and the options and formatting for it.

Like a web page, where you normally see the finished page in the browser instead of all the HTML code behind it, Word doesn't display the field codes in the document, but instead displays the text generated by the field—the field results. You can, however, tell Word to display field codes instead of the field results so you can modify the code directly or simply verify that it is correct. Here's an example of a field code that displays the current date in a long format:

```
{ DATE  \@ "dddd, MMMM dd, yyyy" }
```

The field code is surrounded by curly braces. The first word in the field code, in this case DATE, is the type of field. The portions of the field code in quotation marks represent the information that's displayed when the field is rendered, in this case, the day and date. The information following the field name provides specifics about the field, such as what goes in it and how to format the results. The field results of the date field look something like this:

```
Thursday, January 1, 2004
```

Field Switches

Switches are optional instructions, always preceded by a backslash, that specify the properties and options for a field. There are four common ones that can be used with many fields:

- Format (*)
- Numeric picture (\#)
- Date-time picture (\@)
- Lock result (\!)

Format (*)

You use this switch to specify how a field should be displayed. In the case of text fields, it controls the capitalization of the text, as shown in Table 12-1. You add the instruction that specifies how you want the text capitalized. For numeric fields, the switch is used to specify how the number should be displayed, as you can see in Table 12-2.

You can use the standard Word formatting tools to set the style, font, font size, text color, and whether the text is bold, italic and underlined for field results just as you can with standard text. There are, however, certain things to keep in mind. When the selection you apply formatting to contains the entire field results, this formatting will automatically be maintained when the field results are updated. However, when you apply formatting to only a portion of the field results, updating the field may cause that formatting to be lost.

You can prevent this by placing the * MERGEFORMAT switch in the field code. This tells Word to keep the formatting changes when the field is updated. You can add this switch automatically in the Field dialog box by checking the Preserve Formatting During Updates option. Table 12-3 shows the switches that are used to control the formatting of the result text.

Numeric Picture (\#)

More information about how to format numbers is contained in the numeric picture switch, so named because you use symbols in place of the numbers in the format instructions to

Format Instruction	Field Results
* Caps	The first letter of every word is capitalized.
* FirstCap	The first letter of the first word is capitalized.
* Upper	Field results are displayed in all uppercase.
* Lower	Field results are displayed in all lowercase.

TABLE 12-1   Capitalization Format Switches

Format Instruction	Field Results
* alphabetic	Displays the results as alphabetic characters (A instead of 1, B instead of 2). If the word "alphabetic" is lowercase, the alphabetic characters are also displayed in lowercase; if "ALPHABETIC," they are displayed in uppercase.
* Arabic	Displays the results as common ordinal numbers.
* CardText	Displays the results as cardinal text. For example, "50" is displayed as "fifty," and 200 is displayed as "two hundred." Combine with a capitalization switch to control capitalization.
* DollarText	Displays the results as cardinal text with the first two decimal places displayed as a fraction, for example, "One Hundred Thirty and 35/100".
* Hex	Displays the results as a hexadecimal (base 16) number.
* OrdText	Displays the results as ordinal text, for example, { DATE \@ "d" * OrdText } would display a value such as "thirty-first."
* Ordinal	Displays the results as ordinal numerals, for example, { DATE \@ "d" * OrdText } may display "31st."
* roman	Displays the results as Roman numerals. The capitalization of the results is based on the capitalization of the word "roman" in the switch.

TABLE 12-2   Numeric Format Switches

present a picture of how the number should be displayed. In addition to the specific characters representing numbers and formatting, you can add your own text such as currency symbols ($) or percent signs (%). Table 12-4 shows the basic symbols used for numeric pictures.

Date-Time Picture (\@)

The date-time picture format is used to format date fields, using symbols to represent the format and position of numeric and textual values. If not provided, date fields use the default format in the Insert | Date and Time dialog box if one is specified.

Date-time field results can be displayed using either numeric or text values for the components of the date. Various combinations of these instructions—day (d), month (M),

Format Instruction	Field Results
* Charformat	The formatting of the first letter of the field type is used to specify the formatting for the results. For example, { **D**ATE \@ "d" * OrdText * Charformat } will display the date as bold italicized text.
* MERGEFORMAT	When a result is updated, apply any text formatting from the previous result to the new result.

TABLE 12-3   Character Format Switches

Symbol	Field Results
0	Specifies a required digit. If the results do not contain digits in this position in the format string, Word pads with zero. For example, { = 5 \# 00.00 } displays "05.00".
#	Specifies required spacing. If the results do not contain digits in this position in the format string, Word pads the results with a space. For example, { = 5 \# ##0.00 } displays " 5.00".
X	Drops digits to the left of the "x" placeholder when used left of a decimal point. When used after a decimal point, the results are rounded to that place. For example: { = 1234 \# x## } displays "234" { = 1/8 \# 0.00x } displays "0.125" { = 1/8 \# .x } displays ".1"
. (decimal point)	Determines the position of a decimal point. For example, { = 1234.567 \# ##.00 } displays "1234.57".
– (minus sign) and + (plus sign)	Adds a plus or minus sign to positive or negative values. If a minus sign is specified, positive and zero values have a space added.
"positive;negative; zero" and "positive; negative"	Instructs Word to use different formatting for positive, negative, and zero results. The first format is used for positive results, the second for negative results, and the third (if provided) for zero results. For example, { = SUM(Total) \# "##.00;(##.00);**$0**" } displays 1234.57; (1234.57); or **0** depending on the result. The zero field is optional; if you leave it blank, zero results are formatted the same as positive results.

TABLE 12-4   Numeric Switch Symbols

year (y), hours (h), and minutes (m)—are used to build a date-time picture. You can also include text, punctuation, and spaces. For example, the field { DATE \@ "dddd, MMMM d, yyyy" } displays "Friday, November 24, 2000." Table 12-5 shows the symbols used for date-time formatting.

Symbol	Field Results
M	Displays the month as a number. Single-digit months are not displayed with a leading 0 (zero). For example, April is "4".
MM	Displays the month as a number. Single-digit months have a leading 0 (zero) added to them. For example, April is "04".
MMM	Displays the month as a three-letter abbreviation. For example, April is "Apr".
MMMM	Displays the full name of the month: "April"

TABLE 12-5   Date-Time Switch Symbols

Symbol	Field Results
d	Displays the day of the month as a number without a leading 0 (zero) for single digits.
dd	Displays the day of the month as a number with a leading 0 (zero) for single digits, for example, "02".
ddd	Displays the day of the week as a three-letter abbreviation, for example, "Sun," "Mon," etc.
dddd	Displays the full name of the day of the week ("Sunday," "Monday").
yy	Displays a two-digit year, for example, "03".
yyyy	Displays a four-digit year, for example, "2003".
h or H	Displays the hour without a leading 0 (zero) for single-digit hours. An uppercase "H" specifies 24-hour time.
hh or HH	Displays the hour with a leading 0 (zero) for single-digit hours. An uppercase "H" specifies 24-hour time.
m, mm	Displays minutes without a leading 0 (zero) for single-digit results.
mm	Displays minutes with a leading 0 (zero) for single-digit results.
AM/PM and am/pm	Displays A.M. and P.M. The case of the symbol indicates the case of the results. For example, { TIME \@ "h AM/PM" } displays "9 AM".
A/P and a/p	Displays abbreviated A.M. and P.M. values. For example, { TIME \@ "h a/p" } displays "9 a".

TABLE 12-5 Date-Time Switch Symbols *(continued)*

Lock Result (\!)

The final general switch is the lock result switch. This keeps Word from updating a field that is included in the result of a BOOKMARK, INCLUDETEXT, or REF field unless the field result in the original location has changed. Word normally updates fields included in a field result whenever the BOOKMARK, INCLUDETEXT, or REF field is updated.

Inserting Fields

Fields can be inserted into a document in several ways depending on the field type. Many of the most common fields, including date-time and various AutoText fields, can be added directly from the Insert menu. Fields can also be entered from the Field dialog box. Those who have mastered the art of fields and know the field codes by heart can even type them in directly.

Tip *If you know exactly what fields you want to use and don't want to bother taking your hands off the keyboard, just press CTRL-F9 to insert the curly braces, and type in the field code.*

The Field dialog box, shown in Figure 12-1, can be used to insert most Word fields directly. It acts almost like a mini-wizard, showing you the properties and options for any field that you choose. This dialog is handy because even if you don't remember how to add a specific field, you can always do it here. Open the Field dialog box by choosing Insert | Field from the main menu. The dialog box is divided into three sections—selection, properties, and options. The options available in the properties and options sections are dependent on the field chosen from the list.

The Field dialog box allows you to edit fields in two different ways. The simplest way is the default—choose field properties and options from the custom lists for each field. You can also click the Field Codes button to edit the field code directly, with a handy description below the field showing the format and options available for that particular field.

Once a field has been inserted in a document, you can edit it anytime in the Field dialog box by right-clicking on it and choosing Edit.

Toggling Field Codes

You can toggle between field codes and results any time you like, to see how they are formatted. You can use this to modify field properties directly, or simply use it to become more familiar with fields and how they are used in various Word features.

To toggle field codes and results, you set the appropriate option in Word's Options dialog box. Choose Tools | Options, select the View tab, and check Field Codes in the Show section. A more direct way of toggling field codes is to use the keyboard shortcuts. Use ALT-F9 to toggle all field codes, or SHIFT-F9 to toggle only the currently selected field.

TIP *Normally, when you print a document you want field content to be printed instead of the field codes. You can, however, choose to display the field codes themselves when you print. Open the Options dialog box using Tools | Options, click the Print tab, and make sure Field Codes is selected in the Include with Document settings.*

FIGURE 12-1
You can use the Field dialog box to add most fields directly to a document.

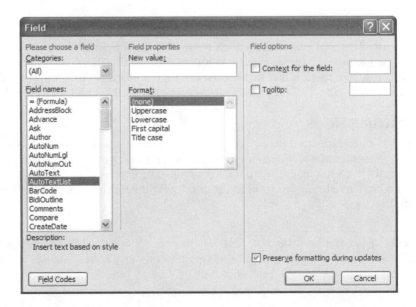

Updating Field Content

It's important to know that Word doesn't automatically update field results as the document is edited, and it doesn't provide a menu option for updating fields. Instead, you must update fields manually. The simplest way to do this is to use the keyboard shortcut. Select the field and press F9. You can also right-click on a field and choose Update Field from the context menu. To update more than one field at a time, or even all fields, select them and use the F9 key.

You can also choose to automatically update all fields in a document when it is printed. Choose Tools | Options to open the Options dialog box, and click the Print tab. Make sure the Update Fields check box is selected.

TIP   *Word's toolbars (with the exception of the seldom-used Database toolbar) do not contain a button for updating form fields, but you can add one to any toolbar you choose. Choose Tools | Customize, and click the Commands tag. Choose the Tools category and drag the icon for Update Fields from the Commands list to the toolbar that is most convenient for you.*

Keeping Fields from Updating

Although in most cases you want fields to be updated automatically, there are times when you may want to make the results from a particular field static so that they can't be updated. For example, you may modify a result by typing directly into it and not want those changes to be obliterated when the field updates. Word provides two ways to prevent fields from updating: locking and unlinking.

- **Locking fields**   This option prevents a field from updating, but gives you the option of unlocking it in the future if you decide it should be updated again. Press CTRL-F11 to lock a field, and CTRL-SHIFT-F11 to unlock it again.

- **Unlinking fields**   This option converts field results to plain text. This is a more drastic step that can't be changed later aside from the Undo command, so only do it if you're sure you won't need the field results updated again. Press CTRL-SHIFT-F9 to unlink field results from the underlying field.

Common Fields

Word allows you to add over 70 fields directly from the Field dialog box, and even more from various places such as the Form and Web Tools toolbars. While an exhaustive description of every single form field allowed is beyond the scope of this chapter, you should know about most of the more commonly used fields.

Page Numbering

Page numbering fields, shown in Table 12-6, are typically used in the header or footer of a document to automatically display the page number, but they can also be used anywhere in a document. Headers and footers have a button to add these fields. Everywhere else you must insert these using the Field dialog box.

Date and Time

Date and time fields can be created directly using the Insert | Date and Time menu. The wide array of formats displayed there are the same as the ones displayed for the DateTime

Field	Description
{ Page }	Displays the current date and time.
{ NumPages }	Displays the total number of pages in the document. Use this to display the position in the document, for example, "Page { Page } of { NumPages }" for "Page 5 of 10".
{ SectionPages }	Displays the total number of pages in a section. You must restart page numbering after a section break if you use this field.

TABLE 12-6　Page Numbering Fields

field in the Field dialog box, so you can use this as a shortcut to add a date-time field. Be sure to check the Update Automatically box, otherwise the date will be added to the page as standard text instead of a field.

Word has several fields for generating date and time results. These are listed in Table 12-7.

While at first glance the { Date } and { Time } switches might seem identical, there are subtle differences. If you have specified a default date or time format in the Date and Time dialog box, both fields use that format. Otherwise, the { Date } field uses the Windows Short Date style (chosen in the Control Panel), while { Time } uses the Windows Time Style setting.

Date-time fields are particularly useful for documents that require frequent updating, such as forms, phone lists, or an employee handbook. Saved or printed copies of the document will always display the date of their creation, making it easy to tell how old the information is.

Document Properties

Document property fields are used to display relevant information about the document. This can include information such as the author's name, or comments that are obtained from the document properties set under File | Properties. There are also dynamically generated document property fields that display statistical information about the document such as the word count. Table 12-8 lists the document property fields.

Field	Description
{ Date }	Displays the current date and time.
{ Time }	Displays the current date and time.
{ CreateDate }	Displays the date the document was created.
{ PrintDate }	Displays the date and time the document was last printed.
{ SaveDate }	Displays the date and time the document was last modified.

TABLE 12-7　Date-Time Fields

Field	Description
{ Author }	Displays the author from the document properties.
{ Comments }	Displays the comments from the document properties.
{ EditTime }	Displays the total amount of time spent editing the document.
{ FileName }	Displays the document's filename.
{ FileSize }	Displays the size of the document in either KB or MB.
{ Keywords }	Displays keywords from the document properties.
{ NumChars }	Displays the number of characters in the document.
{ NumWords }	Displays the number of words in the document.
{ Subject }	Displays the subject from the document properties.
{ Title }	Displays the title of the document from the document properties.

TABLE 12-8   Document Property Fields

Use document property fields for templates or documents that may be created or edited by several people, or for documents where word count or other document information is useful, such as articles, columns, and term papers.

AutoText Fields

An AutoText field is used to insert an AutoText entry into the document. While you can insert AutoText directly into a document, as explained in Chapter 7, the field has the added advantage of automatically updating whenever the AutoText entry changes. To use this field, you must first add the text you want as an AutoText entry using the Insert | AutoText | AutoText dialog box. Then, simply insert an { *AutoText entry* } field into your document wherever you want the text to be displayed, with the text in the brackets replaced with the name of your AutoText entry.

AutoText fields are useful for any arbitrary text that is used frequently, but may change. AutoText can be used to store mailing information, web site addresses, signature files, and more.

Creating Forms

While fields are used behind the scenes to automatically generate a variety of content, they can also take on a more active role. Word's forms use several fields to prompt for user input into an otherwise standardized document. Of course, you can use Word to create standard printed forms designed to be filled out manually, but the dynamic capabilities of Word add an extra dimension. They allow you to create forms that can be filled out using Word itself or on the Web using a browser. To create a data entry form in Word using the standard form fields, do the following:

1. Create a new document or template using the New Document task pane. Templates are often used for forms because they can be used to generate a new document for the filled-in form.

2. Create the document, adding any static text, images, or even non-form-related fields.

3. Insert the desired form fields in the document where you want data entry to occur. See the following section for more information.

4. Protect the form. See the "Protecting Your Form" section at the end of the chapter to see how this is done.

Adding Form Fields

Three form fields are designated specifically for forms. They are an exception to the rule that all fields can be entered in the Fields task pane. Instead, you add form fields to a form using the Forms toolbar. Make the Forms toolbar visible by selecting View | Toolbars | Forms. This toolbar includes buttons for adding the three form fields, as well as a button for setting the field properties, toggling field shading, and protecting the form. The three form fields allow you to add text boxes, drop-down lists, and check boxes to your forms. You can hook these form fields to macros, which allow you to set other form fields to default values based on a choice or to validate user input. A description of these fields and their options follows.

Text Form Fields

The most common form field is the FORMTEXTBOX field. This is the field used for most direct data entry, including text, numbers, dates, and more. Click the Text Form Field button on the Forms toolbar to add a text form field anywhere in your document. Then click the Form Field Options button to set the properties of this field.

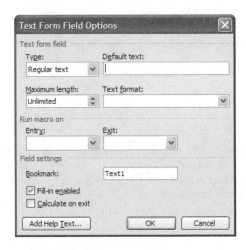

In the Text Form Field Options dialog box, you can choose the type of text that can be entered (text, numeric, dates, or calculation), the maximum length of the field, default text to put in the field, and a format for the text, allowing you to specify capitalization rules.

Drop-Down Form Fields

Drop-down form fields use the FORMDROPDOWN field to provide a list of options for the user to choose from. Click the Drop-Down Form Field button on the Forms toolbar to add one of these fields to your form, and click the Form Field Options button to customize it.

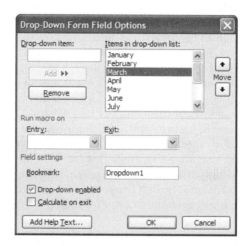

You can add choices to the list by entering them in the Drop-Down Item box, and then clicking the Add button. Additional controls in the Drop-Down Form Field Options dialog box allow you to rearrange or remove items from the list, and choose macros to run on entry and exit from the form.

Check Box Form Fields

Finally, you can add check boxes to the form, using the FORMCHECKBOX field. Check boxes are simple on/off controls, allowing a user to make a choice.

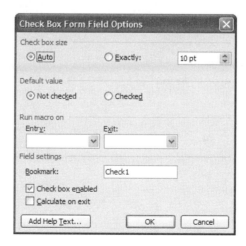

Check box options are limited compared to the other two form fields. You can choose a size for the check box, either based on the document text size or one specifically chosen for the box. You can also choose whether the check box should be checked by default, and whether a macro should run when the field is entered or exited.

Web Forms

In addition to the use of fields from the Forms menu, Word allows you to add various HTML controls to a page using the Web Tools toolbar. This toolbar allows you to add fields for web-specific controls, such as radio buttons, multiline text area controls, and Submit and Reset buttons. Choose View | Toolbars | Web Tools to show this toolbar.

Unlike the traditional Word form fields, which are always viewed in the context of the document or in a printed version, web form fields are submitted to a script on a web server for processing. This generally results in the entered information being stored in a database, or sent in an e-mail, independently of the form. For this reason, HTML form fields require an HTMLName property used to identify the field. Set this value by using the Properties button on the Web Tools toolbar after adding any of the web controls.

The most important field that all web forms need is a Submit button. The Submit button is used to specify a destination for the form, in the action property. Figure 12-2 shows how to set a form action using the Submit button properties. This is a URL that the form is sent to upon completion when a user clicks the Submit button.

TIP   *Even more form controls can be added to forms on the Control Toolbox toolbar. These are ActiveX controls and aren't suited for use in web-based forms because many browsers cannot handle them. Use these strictly for forms designed to be used in Word. They do, however, have a definite advantage in that they can be integrated with VBA applications.*

Protecting Your Form

Once you have created a form, you should protect it from accidental or even deliberate modification. Word allows you to lock a document so that the only change that can be made

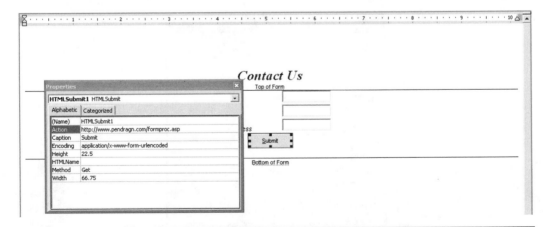

FIGURE 12-2   Unlike traditional Word forms, web-hosted forms require the addition of a Submit button to send the information for processing.

is data entry into form fields. While the Forms toolbar provides a shortcut button for locking a form, the Protect Document task pane can be utilized for more extensive protection options.

Follow these steps to protect a document:

1. Choose Tools | Protect Document to open the Protect Document task pane.

2. Check the Allow Only This Type of Editing in the Document box.

3. Choose Filling in Forms from the list of choices under Editing Restrictions.

4. If your document contains section breaks, a hyperlink will show below the Editing Restrictions drop-down. This opens the Select Sections dialog, where you can choose to protect all or only some sections by checking the ones you want to protect. You can add section breaks to a document by using the Insert | Break menu and choosing one of the section break options.

5. If you have installed the Windows Rights Management client, you can optionally choose users who are allowed to edit the form. Choose them under Exceptions if it is visible.

6. Click Yes, Start Enforcing Protection in the Start Enforcement section. The following dialog box will appear:

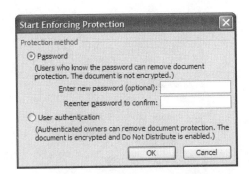

7. In the Start Enforcing Protection dialog box, choose the level of protection you would like. Prevent Accidental Changes will keep casual users from making any changes to the form outside of any form fields. Choose Prevent Intentional or Malicious Changes for stronger protection using encryption.

Managing Long Documents

L ong documents have special considerations. Reports, theses, and manuscripts may all require additional formatting, such as a table of contents, footnotes, and an index. Navigating a 400-page manuscript is unduly cumbersome if it's all in one document. When you break such a document into small segments, however, you need to retain consistent page numbering throughout.

This chapter explains how to manage long documents. It also explains features that are most commonly used with these documents, but can also be applied to shorter works.

Outlining

Most people think of outlines as a note-taking technique best used (and possibly then forgotten) in college. Chapter 7 explained how to use bullets and numbering to create this sort of multilevel outline. Bullets and numbering are useful when you're typing in notes that have already been organized, but they can be awkward to move around without reformatting.

Word offers another outlining tool, the Outline view (first introduced in Chapter 6), that will not only format a multilevel note structure, but will actually organize your outline into headers and body text, as shown in Figure 13-1. Furthermore, this tool can also be used to quickly promote or demote levels, apply styles to each level, and move headings and their underlying subheadings and content throughout the document. Finally, you can use the Outline view to create and maintain Master Documents, which are used to piece small documents into a larger, cohesive whole.

Creating an Outline

To access Outline view, choose View | Outline. As you start typing, every paragraph is assigned to an outline level. The default is, appropriately enough, Level 1. You can promote and demote paragraphs as you type by clicking on the Promote or Demote buttons on the Outlining toolbar (the arrows to either side of the Outline Level indicator, as shown here).

You don't have to select the entire paragraph to promote or demote an entry; simply positioning the insertion point somewhere within the paragraph is enough. You can also

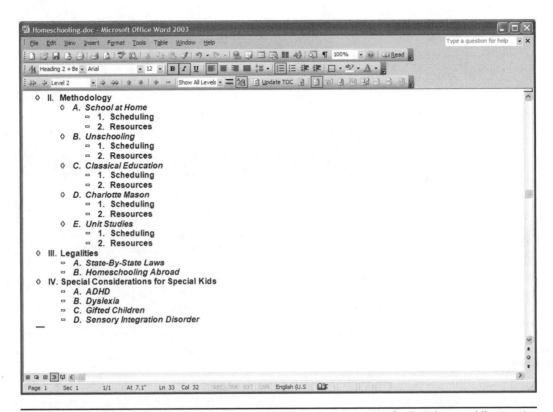

FIGURE 13-1   The Outlining toolbar automatically appears when you enter Outline view, enabling you to control the outline.

use the Outline Level drop-down menu to change to a specific level. This is useful if you want to promote a paragraph back to Level 1 when you're much deeper into the subheadings of the outline.

As you promote and demote paragraphs, notice that the style and formatting change. (Styles are covered in Chapter 9.) By default, each outline level is mapped to the corresponding heading style. There are nine heading/outline levels available in Outline view, plus the Body Text level. Interestingly, the Body Text outline level is formatted to the Normal style by default, instead of the Body Text style. This and the other outline levels can be mapped to different styles, however.

Changing Outline Level Styles

The heading styles all have a distinct appearance by default. These may be fine for a standard document, but can be too bold when you're simply creating an outline. There are two ways to change the formatting of the outline levels. First, you can change the style of the headings, as explained in Chapter 9. This is not always desirable if you want to retain the standard heading styles to format the document. The other option is to apply different styles to the text while retaining the outline level.

Although you can customize an outline quite a bit, there are some limitations. The heading styles (Heading 1, Heading 2, etc.) are always mapped to the corresponding outline level, and cannot be changed to another level. Thus, if you want the title of your document to be formatted in a title style and appear as the top level of your outline, you can't then change Heading 1 to appear as Level 2 in Outline view.

Although it defies logic, you also can't make changes to paragraph formatting within Outline view, even though that's where it would make sense to map other styles to an outline level. Instead, to associate a style (other than the heading styles) with a particular outline level, you must:

1. Choose View | Print Layout (or Normal).
2. Select the paragraph to which you want to apply a particular style and outline level.
3. Apply the style using the Style drop-down menu on the Formatting toolbar or the Styles and Formatting task pane.
4. Choose Format | Paragraph.
5. On the Indents and Spacing tab, select an outline level.
6. Click OK.
7. If the Styles and Formatting task pane isn't already open, click on the Styles and Formatting button on the Formatting toolbar (located to the left of the Style drop-down).
8. Use the drop-down menu for the current style, and choose Update to Match Selection. This will change all instances of that style to appear at the same level in Outline view.

Rearranging and Viewing the Outline

An advantage of Outline view is the ability to move entire sections and subsections in the document. To move an entry, click and drag it to a new location. If you drag an entry that has levels underneath it, the entire section moves with its parent. To move just one paragraph, either select it or position the insertion point within it, and then use the Move Up and Move Down arrows on the Outlining toolbar. To promote or demote a heading with subsections, click on the plus sign to the left of the heading, and use the Promote and Demote buttons; all of the selected subsections will be promoted or demoted accordingly.

You can also change the view of the outline to show only certain levels by choosing from the Show Level drop-down menu on the Outlining toolbar. If your document contains many levels of outlining, changing the view to show only Level 1 and Level 2 heads can be useful when changing the structure of the document. As shown in Figure 13-2, changing the view

---

Combining Outline Tools

One of the most useful changes you can make to an outline is to use bullets and numbering to format it as a multilevel outline. To do this, select the entire outline, choose Format | Bullets and Numbering, and click on the Outline Numbered tab. You'll need to customize the outline option you choose; then click the More button to open the complete list of options. Be sure that each outline level is associated with the appropriate style in the Link Level to Style field.

By combining the Bullets and Numbering tool with the Outline view features, you get the best of all worlds—automatic numbering and the flexibility to move sections and subsections easily throughout the document.

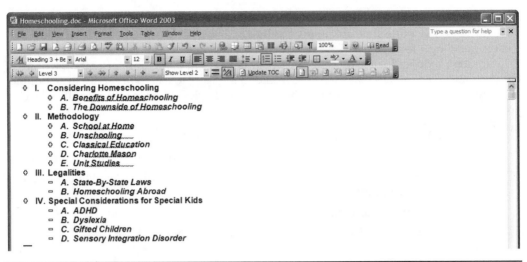

FIGURE 13-2 A lengthy outline becomes more manageable when the view is limited to Level 2 and above.

allows more of the section headings to appear on one screen, making it easier to move things around. When you move or delete headings in this view, any subsections will automatically be affected, as well.

NOTE *Whenever you're wondering where your outline went, check the Show Level to be sure you're getting the complete picture. Although the Show Level is used to control which outline entries are visible, the Outline Level may indicate a heading that's not included in that display. The Outline Level displays the level of the paragraph where the insertion point was positioned before you used the Show Level constraints.*

When viewing only the upper-level headings, you can expand or contract sections of the outline using the Plus and Minus buttons on the toolbar. These are useful when you want to see the subheadings of just a small piece of the outline while keeping the rest of it contracted.

Using Bookmarks in Long Documents

Outline view helps you navigate through a long document by allowing you to view only the major heading levels. When you're editing a document, however, it's helpful to be able to mark your spot directly in the body text and return to the document later. If you're writing a report and need to research an issue before adding key information to the document, a bookmark can mark the spot. Moreover, you can have multiple bookmarks in a single document, each uniquely named to make them easier to use later.

You can create a bookmark either at an insertion point or with a selection of key text, such as a heading or a portion of a paragraph. To create the bookmark, choose Insert | Bookmark, or press CTRL-SHIFT-F5. In the Bookmark dialog box, shown next, give the bookmark a name that will be meaningful to you later; then click Add.

The bookmark will be coded in hidden text. If you can't see the bookmark symbol in your document, choose Tools | Options, click the View tab, and select Bookmarks from the Show options. The symbol is very light gray, so it's hard to notice even when it's visible.

To return to a bookmarked position, choose the Bookmark feature again (either from the menus or with the keyboard shortcut), click on the bookmark name, and click Go To. You can also access the Go To tab of the Find and Replace tool by pressing CTRL-G. In the dialog box, shown here, click on Bookmark, and then choose the bookmark from the drop-down list on the right. After choosing a bookmark in this manner once, the Go To tool will "remember" that you've used it for bookmarks in the past, and the drop-down list will be available immediately.

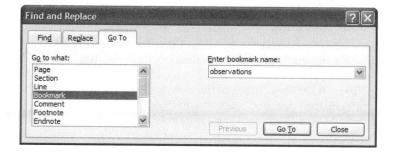

Creating a Master Document

Even with Outline view and Bookmarks available, some documents are just too unwieldy to manage. The more embedded graphics, text boxes, and sheer text you have in a document, the larger the file size. Larger files mean more time accessing your hard drive and filling up your memory.

Master Documents solve this problem by allowing you to break your document into smaller ones while retaining control over page numbering, headers and footers, and even footnotes and tables of contents.

To create a Master Document:

1. Use Outline view to create an outline of the Master Document.

2. Choose a heading style for the subdocuments you want to create. All subdocuments should be referenced in the same style, and it should be a heading style that's not used elsewhere in the Master Document. Label these headings carefully, as they'll become part of the naming of the subdocument files.

3. Select the portion of the outline that contains all the intended subdocument headings, beginning with the first heading that's to be converted into a subdocument.

4. Click the Create Subdocument button in the Outlining toolbar. Every instance of the first heading style in your selection will become a subdocument.

5. Save the Master Document. This will also save the new subdocuments, even though they don't yet have content.

Although the primary purpose of the Master Document is to act as a control panel of sorts for all the subdocuments, you can also add content to the master. You can even convert an existing document into a Master Document by formatting certain text as headings in Outline view, then creating the subdocuments based on those new headings.

CAUTION *If there's one fatal flaw of Master Documents, it's that they're not as portable as they could be. If you move a Master Document and subdocuments to another computer, you need to duplicate the folder structure identically, or the links will break. In other words, the subdocument links won't dynamically update. This makes it virtually impossible to move a Master Document from a local hard disk onto a network drive because the drive letter is invariably different.*

Working with Subdocuments

Master Documents can be used to combine several smaller documents into a cohesive whole. To turn an existing document into a subdocument, position the insertion point on a blank line formatted with the proper heading style. Then click the Insert Subdocument button on the Outlining toolbar. The entire content of the new subdocument is added to the Master Document. You can collapse the subdocuments to make navigating easier.

When you open a Master Document that contains subdocuments, the outline is contracted to show only the subdocument headings, as shown in Figure 13-3. These headings appear as hyperlinks, which are used to open the subdocuments (CTRL-click to fire a hyperlink within Word).

It's important that you always edit a subdocument by launching it from the Master Document. This will ensure that the documents remain linked, and making changes to the whole document will be easier. Launching subdocuments from the Master Document also ensures document integrity and security. If members of a project team are all working on the same Master Document, the subdocuments that are in use must be locked so others can't edit the same document at the same time. The Master Document will automatically lock the files when the subdocuments are contracted or when a subdocument is in use.

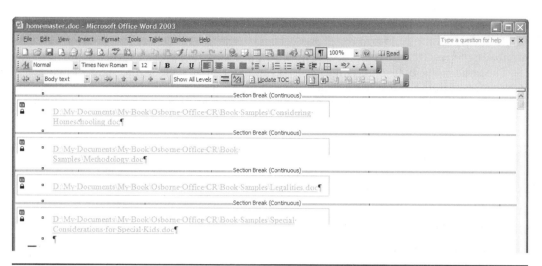

FIGURE 13-3   When opening a Master Document, the subdocuments appear as hyperlinks.

Use the Expand Subdocument button to view or conceal the content of a subdocument within the Master Document. While the subdocuments are contracted, it's easy to rearrange their position in the Master Document by dragging the document icon to the left of the link.

Combining and Splitting Subdocuments

As you create your content, you'll inevitably find that some sections flesh out more than others. To combine two small subdocuments, expand the Master Document to view the content of the subdocuments. Then drag the headings and text from one subdocument into the section markers for another.

The inverse is also true—you'll have some sections that become too unwieldy and need to be broken into smaller pieces. To move a portion of a subdocument into its own subdocument:

1. Expand the Master Document using the Expand Subdocument button.

2. Drag the headings and content you want to split out into an area of the Master Document that's not bounded by an existing subdocument.

3. Select the heading for the new subdocument, and click the Create Subdocument button.

Once the new subdocument has been created, you can move it around in the Master Document to its position in the flow.

Page Numbering Across Documents

When adding information such as page numbering, headers, and footers, remember that anything you add to the whole (the Master Document) will be applied to the whole, while anything you add to a subdocument will only be applied to that piece. Thus, if you want to add page numbers to a document and have the numbering continue from subdocument to subdocument, you should add the page numbers to the Master Document. If you want the numbering to restart with each section, add the page numbering to each subdocument.

The same is true of headers and footers. If you want the first page of the entire document to be different from the rest of the report or manuscript, apply the headers and footers to the Master Document. If you want the first page of each section to be different, add the headers and footers to the subdocuments.

TIP   *Use cut and paste to maintain consistency across subdocuments. Even if you want numbering or headers to restart with each subdocument, you probably still want them to be formatted consistently within the entire work.*

Generating a Table of Contents

Longer documents are not only more challenging for the author to navigate, but they're also more difficult for the reader. A table of contents offers the reader of your printed document the same ease of navigation offered to you by the Outline view when you create the document.

Word can create a table of contents (TOC) automatically, but you'll need to ensure that you work efficiently as you create your document(s). Word uses heading styles to recognize which items to include in the TOC, so you should apply those styles consistently. This is another instance where Outline view is helpful. If you don't want to use heading styles, you should create other styles that you can apply just as consistently, such as a PartName style, a ChapterName style, and a SectionName style.

Think about where you want to position the TOC in your document after it's generated. This isn't necessarily where the TOC will appear after you print the document and put the final hard copy together, however. The TOC itself can throw off your page numbering unless you go to the trouble of formatting the page numbering of the TOC pages differently and restarting the numbering at 1 after it. Some people have an inherent need to keep things in exact order and won't mind the extra work involved. For the rest, put the TOC at the end of the document; you can always rearrange the physical pieces of paper after printing.

NOTE   *If you're creating the document for use on the web, the trick of putting the TOC at the end of the document isn't effective because site visitors don't know where to look in the document. In this case, you'll have to resort to jumping through number hoops. This involves changing the page numbering for the TOC and other introductory content (the title page, acknowledgments page, etc.), usually to lowercase Roman numerals, then reformatting and restarting the numbering when you get to the first chapter. Page numbering and section breaks are covered in Chapter 8.*

You also want to wait until your document is fairly well formed before creating a TOC. It's easy enough to regenerate or update the TOC, but you'll invariably want to "tweak" it, and those changes will be lost every time you update it.

To create a TOC:

1. Put the insertion point where you want the table of contents to be located in the document.

2. Choose Insert | Reference | Index and Tables.

3. Click on the Table of Contents tab:

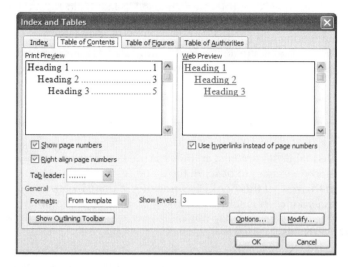

4. Select the alignment and leader options. You can also make a choice from the Formats drop-down box to give the TOC a more professional look.

5. Choose how many levels of the outline should appear in the TOC. By default, three levels are displayed, which is usually plenty of depth to help readers pinpoint the general information they need.

6. If you've formatted your outline using styles other than the heading styles, click Options to associate the correct TOC levels and appropriate styles, as shown here:

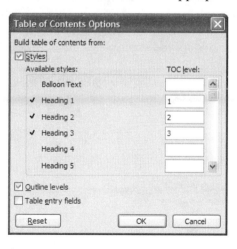

7. Click OK to insert the TOC.

If you waited until your document was complete before creating the TOC, you might only need to review it and make minor adjustments. If your document changes, however, you'll need to update the TOC to ensure the pages still match with their actual location in the document. To update the TOC, position the insertion point within the TOC, and press F9 (or right-click on one of the TOC entries, and choose Update Field from the context menu). A dialog box will prompt you to update either the page numbers or the entire table of contents.

As with page numbering and headers or footers, if you want to generate a table of contents for an entire Master Document, create the TOC within that Master Document. If you want a separate table of contents for each section of the document, create a table of contents within each subdocument. Of course, a table of contents isn't only the purview of Master Documents. You can create a table of contents just as easily for a single document of any length.

Creating an Index

Along with a detailed table of contents, an index is incredibly useful for a long document. Imagine trying to find references to obscure tools and features in this book without an index. Of course, in the case of this book, the indexing is done by a professional indexer. Creating an index on your own is serious business, requiring a lot of manual labor.

Preparing Index Entries

If you know you're going to generate an index for your document, it's best to start compiling entries immediately. As you create the document, keep track of key words that should be indexed. This can be done with old-fashioned pen and paper, but that's just adding a step to the process. There are two other methods that will save time. First, you can simply mark the words and phrases as index entries while you type. To do this:

1. Select the word or phrase.
2. Choose Insert | Reference | Index and Tables.
3. On the Index tab, click the Mark Entry button.
4. In the Mark Index Entry dialog box, the word or phrase you selected will appear in the Main Entry field. If you want to change the wording of the entry, such as to put a person's last name first for index purposes, change the entry in this field.

5. You can add a subentry to break the index down further. If the word or phrase you're entering should be grouped with similar information, create a main entry that encompasses the entire group, and copy the selected word or phrase into the Subentry field.

6. By default, Word will reference the current page on which the index entry appears. If you want to specify a page range instead, you can create a bookmark for a range of pages before marking the index entry, and then select the bookmark within the Mark Index Entry dialog box.

7. Set the format options for the page references.

8. Click Mark to create the entry. If you've already used the term elsewhere in the document and want those instances to be marked as well, choose Mark All.

Many indexes have cross-references to enable readers who are looking up obscure terms to find additional information about the same topic. As you're creating your document, keep a running list of these terms and cross-references. To add them, choose Insert | Reference | Index and Tables, click on the Index tab, and click the Mark Entry button—all without having selected text first. From here, you can enter the term (the main entry) and a cross-reference instead of a page number. It doesn't matter where these index entries are coded into the document because they're not referring to a page number.

Another method for developing an index is to maintain a second file while creating your document. In this file, create a two-column table. As you type words and phrases you'll want to index, enter them in the left column of the table. In the right column, enter any variation in the wording of the entry as it should appear in the index (such as putting the last name of a person first). If you want to create a subentry, type a main entry term in the right column, followed by a colon, and the word or phrase for the subentry.

When you're done creating your document, you should have a complete list of terms and phrases to include in the index, known as a *concordance file*. In the main document, choose Insert | Reference | Index and Tables; then click the Index tab. Instead of manually entering your list, however, click the AutoMark button. Use the Open File dialog box to open the concordance file, and Word will do the rest, searching for each word and phrase you entered in the left column of the file and marking an index entry based on the right-column text.

Generating the Index

After you've prepared all your index terms and phrases—and finished creating the document itself—you can generate the actual index. To do this, position the insertion point where you want the index to appear. This is usually at the end of the document, which is strongly recommended so that the pages of the index don't throw off the page numbering of the rest of the document (as well as the more practical reason that people just expect an index to be at the end). Choose Insert | Reference | Index and Tables; the Index tab should automatically appear because you've been marking the index entries. Choose the formatting options for your index, and click OK.

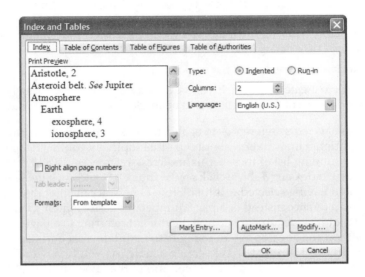

Other Types of Tables and Indexes

The Index and Tables dialog box can generate other types of indexes that are used for more specific purposes. A table of figures is usually only seen in a book with many graphics that need to be cited for copyright reasons. A table of authorities is used in legal documents to cite case law.

The methods for creating these tables are very similar to a table of contents or index. For a table of authorities, highlight the full citation in the text, choose Insert | Reference | Index and Tables, select the Table of Authorities tab, and then click Mark Citation. You can edit the citation, enter the type of citation, and reference any shorter forms of the same citation that appear in the document. To create the table once you're done marking citations, generate it in the same way you create a table of contents or index, by positioning the insertion point where you want the table to appear, then choosing Insert | Reference | Index and Tables. Click to see the Table of Authorities tab, shown next. Set the options to format the table, and click OK.

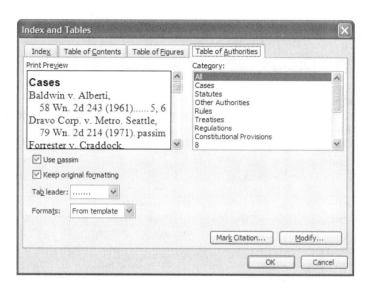

For a table of figures, label each figure with a caption, all formatted with the same style. Choose Insert | Reference | Index and Tables, and then click on the Table of Figures tab, shown here. Select the formatting for the table. Use the Options button to select the style that's been applied to the captions so Word will pick them out of the document. Click OK to insert the table of figures into the document.

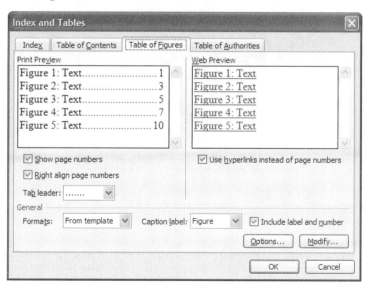

Cross-References

Another useful tool for long documents is cross-referencing. A cross-reference can tell the reader to refer to a different chapter or a figure. The reference can be as specific as a paragraph or page, or as vague as "see above" or "see below."

Word has a powerful cross-reference tool. Not only will it automate these references, but it will update them as the document changes. Cross-references are just another type of field, so every cross-reference in the document can be updated at once simply by pressing F9. Fields are covered in detail in Chapter 12.

It's easy to add cross-references in Word using Insert | Reference | Cross-Reference. There are several types of references, however, and each one works a bit differently:

- **Numbered**   Used to cross-reference numbered paragraphs. If you're using this reference type, you can set the Insert Reference To field to reference the paragraph number within the context of the surrounding paragraph. Thus, if you're in subsection c of paragraph II.C.3 and want to reference subsection b of paragraph II.C.5, the reference would read 5.b. You can also insert the reference to a page number or text within a paragraph.

- **Heading**   Used to cross-reference paragraphs formatted with the heading styles. All of the headings in the document will appear in the For Which Heading list, as shown here:

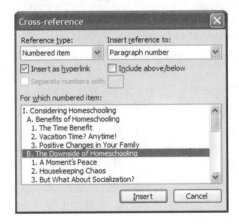

- **Bookmark**   Used to cross-reference text you've marked as a bookmark. This type of reference can refer to either the text of the bookmark or the page or paragraph number where it resides.

- **Footnote/endnote**   Used to reference footnotes or endnotes in the document. The reference can specify the footnote number or the page on which it first appeared.

- **Equation/figure/illustration/table**   Used to refer to figure or other object captions (not the object itself). This option only works if you've inserted your captions using the Insert | Reference | Caption feature, as it inserts a field that the cross-reference accesses for this type of reference.

Formatting References

When adding a cross-reference, you rarely just insert the reference itself. Instead, it's common to lead in with text such as "See" or "as shown in" to maintain the flow of the text. These lead-ins must be typed, along with a space between the wording and the cross-reference field you insert. It's your choice whether to add this text before inserting the cross-reference or after.

The cross-reference field itself is formatted in the same style as the paragraph into which it's inserted. If you want the cross-reference to appear in bold or italic type, select the lead-in text and the field code and apply the formatting.

Adding Footnotes

Long documents such as theses and studies often require footnotes or endnotes. When you think of a document having a table of contents, index, table of figures, cross-references, and now footnotes, it's no wonder the document is so long! Footnotes are important when citing someone else's work, however, so the extra space is justified. The only difference between footnotes and endnotes is that footnotes appear on the same page as the paragraph that refers to it, while endnotes appear in a list at the end of the document.

To add a footnote, position the insertion point where you want the footnote reference to appear, and choose Insert | Reference | Footnote. The Footnote and Endnote dialog box, shown here, lets you specify where the note should appear and the symbol or numbering format. In the rare instance when you want both footnotes and endnotes in the same document, such as when you're using footnotes to point out specific wording in another work and endnotes to list all the referenced works themselves, you can specify that the footnotes use symbols while the endnotes use numbers.

> **TIP**   *If you're using symbols instead of numbers for your footnotes, set the Numbering option to restart each page so the symbols can be recycled on each page. Because a footnote appears on the same page as its reference, this won't confuse your readers.*

After you click Insert in the Footnote and Endnote dialog box, Word inserts a symbol or number to mark the reference point, then moves the insertion point to the bottom of the window so you can enter the footnote text. If you're composing your document in Print view, your notes are typed directly into the document at the insertion point, so you can see how the page is being formatted and flowing while you work. You can also edit a footnote directly from the document in Print view. If you're working in one of the other views, Word opens a separate pane in the window to enter the note text, as shown in Figure 13-4. To edit a footnote from one of these views, double-click on the reference number or symbol to reopen the footnote pane.

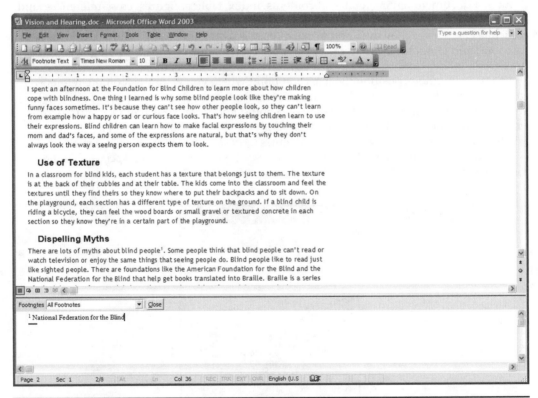

FIGURE 13-4   Entering footnotes in Normal view causes a separate pane to appear at the bottom of the window.

Mail Merge, Labels, and Envelopes

Mail merge is useful for all types of Word users, from the large corporation sending out hundreds of invoices and form letters to the home user creating personalized party invitations. In point of fact, this feature is really misnamed because some of its most creative uses are in documents that have nothing at all to do with mail. Instead, think of it as a database merge, and you'll see all sorts of potential, such as filling in a template for product specifications or creating jewel-box inserts for all the CDs in your collection. You can even create a directory of information from a database table, such as listing all those CDs for a catalog.

Of course, none of this is to say that mail merge isn't optimal for form letters, invoices, and even personalizing the salutation of your annual holiday letter. Combined with the envelope and label tools—and with the addition of a postage service such as e-stamps—Word can take care of everything but sealing the envelope.

Using the Letter Wizard

Whether you're using mail merge to send the same letter to hundreds of people or a note to just one person, it all starts with the letter itself. If creating a letter causes you grief, the Letter wizard can help with the formatting so you can concentrate on the content. The Letter wizard gathers information on the sender, recipient, subject, and enclosures, then inserts that information in the appropriate places in the letter.

The body text of the letter is formatted according to the preferences you set in the wizard. You can choose full block (everything is left aligned), modified block (closing and signature are indented two-thirds into the page), or semi-block format (each paragraph is first-line indented and closing/signature is indented).

The Letter wizard is a template, of sorts, so you can access it by creating a new document based on the Letter Wizard template. To learn how to create a document from a template, see Chapter 9.

You can also use the Letter wizard on an existing document. To do this, choose Tools | Letters and Mailings | Letter Wizard. If you apply the Letter wizard to an existing document, information you enter in the dialog box can overwrite existing information in the letter. The options listed in the Closing field, for instance, might give you an idea of a better way to sign off at the end of the letter; by entering the new closing in the dialog box, it's automatically changed in the document when you click OK.

CAUTION   *The Letter wizard's strength is also often its downfall. If the wizard can't recognize elements of your existing document, it will insert new ones based on the information you enter in the dialog box. Thus, you can wind up with two signature lines or salutations, resulting in a big mess rather than a well-formatted letter. This is especially true if you write a casual letter with slangy closings or add extra blank lines between elements of your letter.*

Mail Merges

When you need to create multiple copies of essentially the same document, yet with customized information in each one, you need to use mail merge. A mail merge uses a new or existing database table to fill in fields in the document while retaining the surrounding content. Mail merge is most commonly used on letters—thus its name—but it's equally handy for other database/word processing tasks.

As you'll learn in Chapter 32, you can create Access database reports to print information stored in a database, and this is preferable for dumps of query results and simple forms. Using mail merge in Word, however, allows you to get more creative, such as typing a multipage newsletter and having the subscriber's address print directly on the back page, thus avoiding the need for labels. You can also use mail merge to print labels for CDs, complete with graphics.

Creating a mail merge begins by choosing Tools | Letters and Mailings | Mail Merge. This opens the Mail Merge task pane, as shown in Figure 14-1. You can invoke this tool on a blank page and wait to be prompted to create the document as you step through the Mail Merge wizard. Or, as shown in the figure, you can begin typing the document before launching the tool. Notice that the salutation is incomplete, and there's no addressee in this letter. If you look closely, the content of the letter itself is also missing the name of the company.

When you begin the mail-merge process, you're asked what type of document you're creating:

- **Letters**   Used when creating a form letter. This is also the document type to use if you're using mail merge for a more creative purpose.
- **E-Mail Messages**   Used to create a form letter that is then automatically sent to a list of e-mail addresses or business faxes, drawn from the Outlook contacts list.

NOTE   *For more information about the Outlook contacts list, see Chapter 27.*

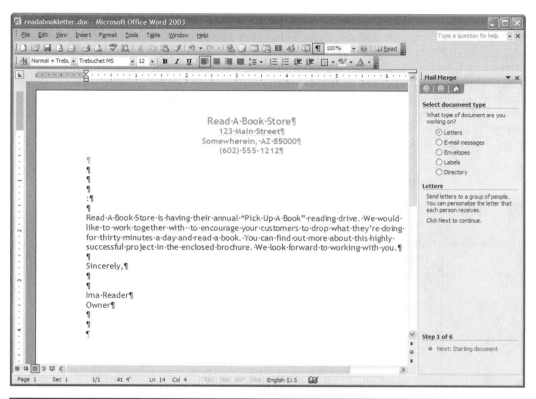

FIGURE 14-1   With mail merge, certain information can be added using fields during the mail-merge process.

- **Envelopes**   Used to create envelopes with mail-merge fields. You can use the same database as the source for this merge, ensuring that you have envelopes for each form letter. You'll be prompted to choose an envelope size in addition to the normal mail-merge steps.

- **Labels**   Used to create mailing labels. You can set the Avery label type or create a custom label, in addition to the other options.

- **Directory**   Used to create a directory listing, such as a company phone list. This option prints multiple records on a page.

After you complete each step of the wizard, click on the Next hyperlink at the bottom of the task pane to proceed to the next step. In step 2, choose whether to base the mail merge on the current document (as in Figure 14-1), on a new document, or on another existing document. The document you select or create here is the boilerplate content; this material will appear in every copy of the merged document.

In step 3, select a data source for the mail merge. If you're using a new list, click the Create hyperlink that appears after clicking the Type a New List radio button. You can also choose an existing database, created in Access or for a previous mail merge, or use the Outlook contacts list. In those cases, you'll be prompted to browse and select a data source. Word opens the table you select and prompts you to choose which records should be included in the merge, as shown here:

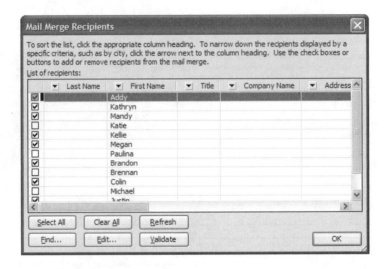

CAUTION   *If you're creating an e-mail merge, screen your list carefully. Spam is a hot-button issue with most people, and there are laws against it in several states. Many e-mail applications even screen for spam based on how many recipients appear in the To:, CC:, or even BCC: lists of a message.*

In step 4, you create or edit your boilerplate, depending on which option you choose in step 1. This is also when you add the field codes to connect the data to the boilerplate. In Figure 14-2, an address block is added to the boilerplate. Use the More Items option in the task pane to insert specific fields, such as referring to a person or company by name in the body of a letter. You can use the same field multiple times throughout the document. Word knows to reuse the same record each time, just as it knows to move to the next record when it reaches the end of the document. As you insert fields, you'll notice the field codes being inserted into the boilerplate. Data fields are formatted using the field name surrounded by double angle brackets, such as <<LastName>>.

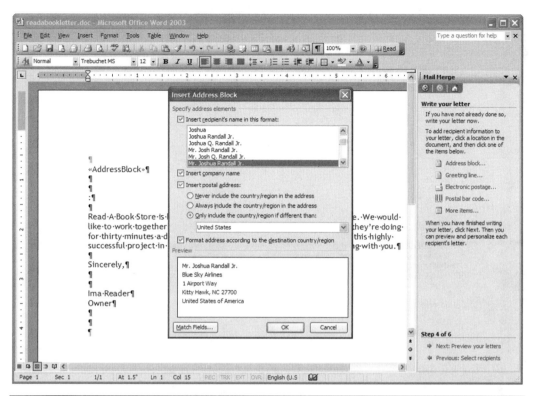

FIGURE 14-2   When adding an address block to a mail-merged document, you have the option of including or excluding information such as titles.

Step 5 displays a preview of the document using one of the records from the data source, as shown in Figure 14-3. This is the time to check the merged content carefully. The most common mistakes in a mail merge are extra punctuation or salutations added when the merged field contains punctuation that already appears in the boilerplate. Also look carefully at the spacing of any data that is inserted within a paragraph. If you want to preview a specific record, use the Mail Merge task pane to scroll through the records. If you notice errors, use the Previous hyperlink to return to a step and edit the document and/or data source.

When all is well, proceed to step 6 to complete the merge and print the new documents. You can print the entire batch at once or edit individual letters to further customize them before printing.

Creating a Database

When you're creating form letters, you're most likely going to use a preexisting database or the Outlook contacts list as a data source. For quick merges, however, such as when creating labels for goody bags for a party, it's faster and easier to create a new database during the

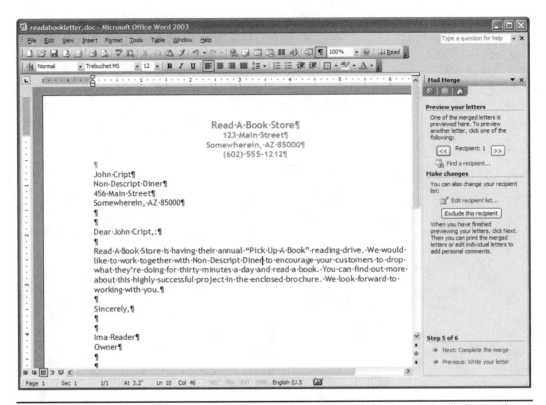

FIGURE 14-3   Don't overlook the preview step of a mail merge, as this is when you're likely to notice mistakes in the formatting of the merged data and the boilerplate document.

mail-merge process. To do this, select Type a New List in step 3 of the wizard. The New Address List dialog box appears:

The standard database fields are included in the dialog box, making it easy to quickly enter information. To add records, click the New Entry button after each record. You can review the entries using the First and Last buttons, the Previous and Next buttons, or by entering a specific record number.

If your data doesn't fit the listed fields, click the Customize button to open the Customize Address List dialog box. In this box, you can enter any field name you need. Click the Add button to create new fields in the Add Field dialog box, then use the Move Up and Move Down buttons in the Customize Address List dialog box to change the order of the fields.

TIP   *If you're creating a quick mail merge that doesn't use the standard address list fields, save time by commandeering one of the default fields for your own purposes. Word will read a CD title just as readily from a field labeled Address as it will from one labeled CDTitle, and you've saved the step of adding a new field to the database. Just be sure you remember which field holds which data!*

Filtering and Sorting a Database

When you edit the recipient list to pare down the records to be used in the data source, every record from the table is listed. You can quickly pare down the records by filtering the database. To do this:

1. In the Mail Merge Recipients dialog box, choose Edit.

2. In the Address List dialog box, choose Filter and Sort.

3. In the Filter and Sort dialog box, select filtering criteria by choosing a field, the boolean operation to be performed on the field's data, and the desired condition.

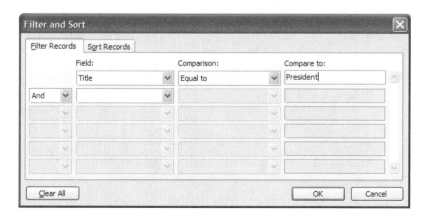

4. Click OK to return to the now-filtered list.

You can also sort the database by following steps 1 and 2 described previously, then clicking on the Sort Records tab, shown next. This doesn't filter out any records, it just sorts them according to the field you specify in the order you require.

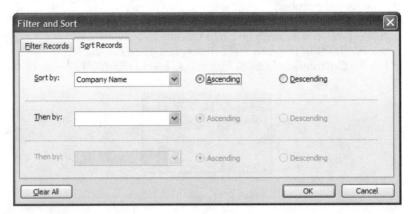

Generating Envelopes

The mail-merge tool is useful when creating customized envelopes based on a data source. If you want to print only one envelope or several envelopes based on the same information, however, it's faster and easier to use the envelopes and labels tool. Choose Tools | Letters and Mailings | Envelopes and Labels.

In the Envelopes tab, enter the recipient's address and your return address. If you want to add electronic postage to the envelope (as explained in the next section), click the check box below the recipient's address.

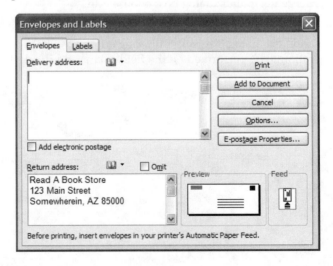

One advantage this tool has over the mail-merge feature is that you can create and print an envelope in a separate dialog box even while another document—such as a letter—is open. You can print directly from the dialog box if you're ready to print out the envelope, or you can click Add to Document to insert the envelope formatting at the beginning of the current document. If you choose the latter, the envelope is formatted in a separate section so the envelope margins and other settings don't affect the rest of the document.

There are several advantages to adding the envelope to the document instead of printing it separately. First, the envelope remains a part of the document, so if you lose the envelope or need to send the same information out again later, it's readily available. You can also use this method to create stock letterhead, adding a blank envelope to the beginning of the document and a blank letter at the end, both formatted with your font, color scheme, and even your logo. In fact, this is the only way to print a logo on your envelopes; you can't add a logo if you print directly from the wizard.

Whether you are printing from the dialog box or intend to add the envelope to the document, you should first click the Options button to ensure the envelope is formatted properly. In the Envelope Options dialog box, set the envelope size according to the standard envelope sizes. The default margins for the address and return address are usually fine, but modify them as needed.

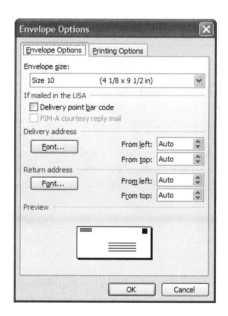

Don't forget to check the Printing Options tab, shown next. Every printer has a unique method for feeding paper, and in the case of envelopes this is critical. If you're unsure which feed option to select, try marking a piece of regular paper with the words Front, Back, Top, and Bottom, then printing a sample envelope.

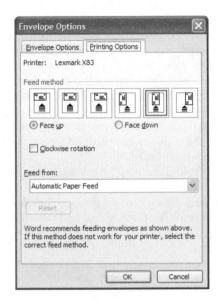

E-Postage

Electronic postage is a relatively new—and often overlooked—option available from the mail merge and envelopes and labels features. In order to use e-postage, you first need to establish an account and purchase postage from a third-party vendor. Stamps.com is one such vendor. To create an account, click on the Add Electronic Postage or E-Postage Properties options in the Envelopes and Labels dialog box. A dialog box will warn you that you must first install e-postage software, and will prompt you to do so immediately. If you opt to install the software, you'll be directed to the Stamps.com web site, where you can establish an account and purchase postage.

CAUTION *Stamps.com is just the latest of many electronic postage vendors. These services charge a monthly fee—usually after an initial trial period—which can be a flat charge or a percentage of the postage you purchase from the service. You'll also pay to purchase postage, even during the trial. Don't purchase more than you'll reasonably use in a short period of time, as these services tend to go out of business or change their rate structure on short notice.*

If you're creating large mail merges, printing postage directly onto the envelopes or labels can be a tremendous time-saver. For the occasional personal letter, however, this can prove to be an expensive option, as you're required to purchase stamps in $10 blocks.

Creating Labels

Labels and envelopes are grouped together in Word because the most common use of labels is for addressing letters and packages. Of course, there are stock labels for dozens of purposes these days, including business cards, placeholders, and ID badges. To create a label, choose Tools | Letters and Mailings | Envelopes and Labels, and then click on the Labels tab. The Labels tab allows you to specify a label type and indicate whether you want to print a single label or a full sheet of the same label.

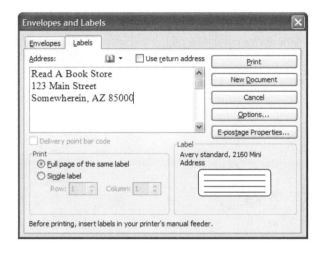

Like the envelopes tool, the labels options allow you to specify a type of label or create a custom type. All of the standard Avery label styles are listed. To see how a specific label is formatted, select that label style from the list, and click Details. From the label style dialog box, you can see how many labels will be printed on a page. More importantly, you can change the margins here, which enables you to fit a bit more information on the label than the defaults allow. Here is an example of the dialog box for a business card:

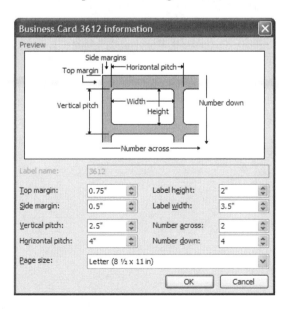

If you're using a nonstandard label, you can add it to the list by clicking New Label in the Label Options dialog box. Give the label a name and set the margins, dimensions, and number of labels to print in each column and row.

TIP *You can create a blank table for creating labels with different information on each label on the sheet. To do this, use the labels tool to specify the label options, and then click New Document. Word will create a blank document with a table to use as a guide for the label margins. Enter your content into the table, being careful not to exceed the line limit for the label type; then print the document.*

PART

Spreadsheets

CHAPTER 15
Excel

CHAPTER 16
Formatting Worksheets and
Restricting Data

CHAPTER 17
Calculating with Formulas
and Functions

CHAPTER 18
Viewing and Manipulating
Data with Charts and
PivotTables

CHAPTER 19
Creating Excel Databases

Excel

Excel is a full-featured spreadsheet application that you can use for a wide variety of purposes: anything from quick calculations, to reports laden with charts, to sophisticated analyses of complex data with many what-if conditions. You can even use Excel to create simple flat-file databases with many records—although for any database of any size and complexity, Access is a much better choice.

This chapter starts by discussing how to configure Excel to suit your needs. It then covers using worksheets, navigating in workbooks, converting spreadsheets in other formats to Excel, customizing Excel with add-ins, and printing workbooks.

Using and Hiding the Task Pane

As with Word, the task pane is displayed by default when you open Excel. By default, the task pane appears docked to the right side of the Excel window, but you can drag it to any other edge of the window to dock it there if you prefer. Alternatively, you can display the task pane floating free anywhere in the Excel window.

The following task panes are available in Excel by using the drop-down button in the task pane:

- **Getting Started**   Unless you've deselected this option (as explained in the next section), this task pane appears on startup and lets you open and create workbooks and access program information from Microsoft. Also available from View | Task Pane and the toolbar shortcut menu.

- **Help**   This lets you search the local help files and get additional support from Microsoft. Also available from Help | Microsoft Excel Help or by pressing F1.

- **Search Results**   After you initiate a file search (File | File Search), this pane will show the results of the ongoing search. You can continue working on your open workbooks while the search is under way.

- **Clip Art**   Use this task pane to search for graphics files organized by collection, file type, and location. Also available from Insert | Picture | Clip Art.

- **Research**   You can search specified encyclopedias, thesauruses, and translation tools for more information about selected words. Also available from the Standard toolbar and using Tools | Research.

- **Clipboard** The clipboard can hold up to 24 items copied or cut from any Office application. You can then paste these items elsewhere later. Also available from Edit | Office Clipboard.

- **New Workbook** This offers workbook-creation options based on various formats or templates. Also available from File | New.

- **Template Help** Custom help content that is included in the template attached to the document you're currently using can be displayed in this task pane.

- **Document Actions** Custom document actions available for the document you're currently using can be displayed in this task pane.

- **Shared Workspace** You use this task pane to share a central copy of a document with others from a SharePoint Team Services web site. Chapter 40 explains document workspaces.

- **Document Updates** This feature works in conjunction with the Shared Workspace, enabling you to get the most recent version of the workbook from the server.

- **XML Source** This task pane displays the schema of the XML data file currently displayed. You can map schema elements to parts of the worksheet by dragging them to the worksheet.

Once you've moved from one task pane to another, you can retrace your steps by clicking the Back button, and go forward again by clicking the Forward button. Click the Home button to display the Getting Started task pane.

Hiding the Getting Started Task Pane

The Getting Started task pane takes up a considerable slice of the Excel window, so many users opt to hide it by default. The upside to hiding the task pane by default is that you gain a considerable amount of screen real estate—and there's no downside, because the task pane will pop up automatically when you access task pane–related features from the toolbars and menus.

There are two ways to deal with the task pane. First, if you use it to open or create your documents when launching Excel, the task pane will close itself after you've made a selection. Second, you can keep the task pane from opening at all when you start Excel:

1. Select Tools | Options from the main menu.

2. On the View tab, deselect Startup Task Pane.

3. Click OK.

Customizing Excel Options

Setting the appearance of the task pane is just one of many Excel-specific options that are available to you in the Options dialog box, as shown in Figure 15-1. The purpose of most of these options is obvious, and setting them is a matter of personal preference. For example, the options on the Color tab let you specify which colors Excel should use, and the options on the International tab let you specify decimal separator characters, thousands separator characters, and more.

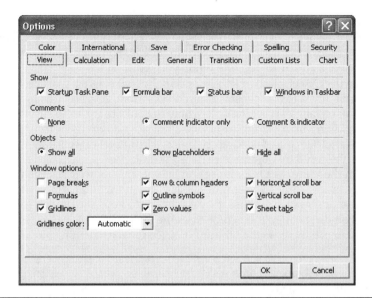

FIGURE 15-1   The View tab controls the appearance of the Excel window and its contents; other Options tabs offer dozens more customizable features.

Some options stand out, however. The following sections discuss the options you're most likely to benefit from understanding and changing.

TIP   *Some of these options are discussed in other chapters rather than in this chapter. "Spell Checking" in Chapter 2 explains the spelling options. "Troubleshooting Formulas" in Chapter 17 explains the error-checking options. "Restricting Data and Protecting Workbooks" in Chapter 16 discusses the security options. "Configuring Chart Options" in Chapter 18 covers the chart options.*

View Options

Your use of these options depends on the type of work you're doing and how you prefer to go about it.

The options in the Show section of the View tab let you specify whether Excel displays the task pane, formula bar, and status bar on startup. (You can toggle the display of these options while working by choosing View | Task Pane, View | Formula Bar, or View | Status Bar.) But the key option is Windows in Taskbar, which controls whether Excel displays a separate taskbar button for each open workbook or a single taskbar button for Excel. Having separate taskbar buttons for each open workbook can enable you to switch from one workbook to another more easily, but some people find the extra clutter on the taskbar outweighs this convenience.

The options in the Comments section let you specify how Excel displays comments attached to cells in worksheets. Your choices are to hide comments and comment indicators, display only comment indicators, or display both comment indicators and comments. The latter setting is primarily useful for worksheets with few comments; worksheets with many comments can get busy with all comments displayed. Displaying only comment indicators is usually a happy medium, but you may want to hide all comment indicators to keep a complex worksheet as clean as possible while you work on it.

The options in the Objects section let you specify how Excel displays objects (for example, pictures and charts) in your worksheets. Your choices are to display the objects, to display placeholders (blank rectangles) that indicate where the objects are, or to suppress the display of all objects. Displaying many complex objects may slow down the scrolling of worksheets, so displaying placeholders may speed up scrolling. Hiding all objects enables you to work in cells otherwise obscured by objects.

The options in the Window Options section let you specify which screen items are displayed in the window: row and column headers, the horizontal and vertical scroll bars, the worksheet tabs, and even grid lines. (If you choose to keep the default setting of grid lines displayed, you can change their color from the automatic color.) By deselecting options you don't need, you can increase the amount of screen real estate for your workbooks.

NOTE *The joker in the Window Options pack is the Formulas option, which controls whether cells that contain formulas display the formula results (the default) or the formulas themselves. You may want to display formulas when constructing or editing a worksheet, but chances are that you'll usually want to display their results.*

Calculation Options

The Calculation options specify how you want Excel to calculate your worksheets. Your choices are automatic calculation of all formulas, automatic calculation of all formulas except those in data tables, or manual recalculation.

For most users, automatic recalculation is best. The exception is if you're using a worksheet complex enough for recalculation to bog your computer down, in which case, the other options are worth investigating. If you choose manual recalculation, you can choose whether Excel recalculates formulas before saving the workbook. Doing so is the default and is usually a good idea, because it helps avoid someone subsequently opening the workbook and not realizing that some formula results aren't up-to-date.

The options in the Workbook Options section let you control whether Excel updates references to formulas that reference other applications, whether to save copies of values contained in linked documents, and more. For most purposes, the default settings are satisfactory.

CAUTION *The Precision as Displayed option on the Calculation tab changes the numbers in the cells to match the precision with which they're displayed. For example, if you're using two decimal places in a worksheet, applying this option would change the numbers in all the cells in the workbook to using two decimal places (including any rounding involved): $44.5593 would change to $44.56, and so on. You'll seldom need to use this option. If you do, experiment first with a copy of your data, because the only way of undoing the change made by Precision as Displayed is to revert to an unaffected copy of the data.*

Edit Options

The Edit options offer fine control over Excel's features for editing columns, rows, and cell contents. Most of the options, such as Edit Directly in Cell and Allow Cell Drag and Drop, are self-explanatory. Some stand out, however, such as the options discussed next:

- Move Selection After Enter lets you specify whether, and in which direction, Excel moves the selection when you press ENTER to apply an entry to a cell. The default is to move down to the next cell. You might prefer to move right (or, rarely, up or left).

- Enable AutoComplete for Cell Values controls whether, when you're entering text in a cell, AutoComplete suggests a matching item from another cell in the column once you've typed enough letters to identify it. For example, if you enter **Madrid** in cell A1, enter **Malaga** in cell A2, and type **mad** in cell A3, AutoComplete suggests "Madrid" to complete that cell. AutoComplete can greatly speed up entering repetitive information in columns. But if you find AutoComplete distracting, deselect this option.

- Extend List Formats and Formulas controls whether Excel applies repeated formats and formulas to new rows that you add to the end of a list. In most cases, this feature saves you time and effort. If not, deselect this option.

General Options

The General options control various aspects of Excel's behavior and are mostly self-explanatory: whether Excel displays tooltips over interface elements, displays the Properties dialog box to prompt you to enter workbook properties when you save a workbook, uses R1C1 reference style (row number, column number) instead of the default A1 reference style, and more.

You may well want to change the following options:

- Set the Recently Used File List option to specify how many files are listed at the bottom of the File menu and in the task pane.

- Adjust the Sheets in New Workbook option to specify how many worksheets each new workbook contains. The default is 3. If you frequently have to add or delete worksheets, adjust the number accordingly. The limits are 0 and 255 sheets.

- Set the standard font and font size for your workbooks.

- Change your default file location (the folder initially used by dialog boxes such as Open and Save As). For example, you might use a network location.

- Edit or change your username.

NOTE *You should understand the At Startup, Open All Files In option even if (as is likely) you choose not to use it. If you enter a path in this box, Excel automatically opens all Excel files (templates, workbooks, and add-ins) stored in that folder on startup. Use this option if you always need to have specific workbooks open or add-ins installed when you're working in Excel.*

Click Web Options to access the Web Options dialog box, which lets you specify default formats for saving worksheets as web pages. Click Service Options to display the Service

Options dialog box for participating in Microsoft's Customer Experience Improvement Program.

Transition Options

The Transition options provide help with moving to Excel from Lotus 1-2-3, including using Lotus 1-2-3 Help and 1-2-3–style navigation keys.

You can also specify the format in which to save your Excel files. For example, you might choose XML Spreadsheet rather than the default Microsoft Excel Workbook.

Save Options

The Save options let you specify whether, how frequently, and where to save AutoRecover information for recovering your work after Excel has crashed.

The default setting is to save AutoRecover information for all workbooks every ten minutes. You can disable AutoRecover for the active workbook by selecting the Disable AutoRecover option.

Loading and Unloading Add-Ins

Excel includes several *add-ins*, optional components that you can load when you need the extra functionality they provide. For example, the Euro Currency Tools add-in provides tools for working with the euro, which can be handy if you do business with Europe.

If you need an add-in frequently, you can always load it. But in general, it's not a good idea to load add-ins unless you need them, because they take up memory and may slow down your computer. So you should load add-ins when you need them, use them, and then unload them when you've finished.

To load or unload an add-in:

    1. Choose Tools | Add-Ins. Excel displays the Add-Ins dialog box:

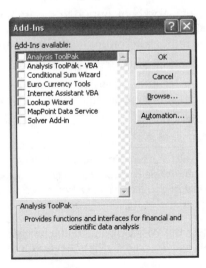

2. Select the options for the add-ins you want to load. Clear the options for any loaded add-ins you want to unload.

3. Click OK.

Once you've loaded an add-in, you can use the features it provides. These features may be implemented as menu commands, toolbar buttons, wizards, and so on.

If your computer has a complete installation of Office, the add-ins will be installed; if it has a custom installation, they may be. If you need to install the add-ins:

1. Choose Start | Control Panel | Add or Remove Programs.

2. Select Microsoft Office 2003 and click Change.

3. Click Add or Remove Features.

4. Select the Choose Advanced Customization of Applications option and click Next.

5. On the Advanced Customization sheet, expand the Excel item, and then expand the Add-ins item.

6. For each add-in you want to load, choose the Run from My Computer option.

7. Click Update to update your installation of Office.

Using Worksheets and Workbooks

Excel's basic unit is the *worksheet*, a grid of cells in which you enter data. Each worksheet consists of 256 columns and 65,536 rows. The intersection of each row and column is a cell, so each worksheet contains 16,777,216 cells.

By default, Excel uses the A1 reference scheme to refer to columns, rows, and cells:

- The columns are designated by letters: A to Z for the first 26 columns, AA to AZ for the next 26 columns, then BA to BZ, and so on. The last column is IV.

- The rows are numbered from 1 to 65536.

- The cells are designated by the column and row. So the first cell on a worksheet is cell A1, and the last cell is IV65536. This designation is called the *cell address*.

Instead of A1, Excel can also use the R1C1 reference format, which uses the letter R and a number to indicate the row and the letter C and a number to indicate the column. For example, cell B2 is R2C2 in R1C1 reference format. You can change to R1C1 format on the General tab of the Options dialog box (Tools | Options).

Excel saves worksheets in *workbook* files. Workbook files use the Microsoft Excel Worksheet file format, which has the .xls file extension. Each workbook can contain either one or more worksheets. Default new workbooks contain 3 worksheets, and can contain up to 256 worksheets. The worksheets are named Sheet1, Sheet2, and so on. You can change these names as needed.

Workbooks make it easy to keep related information on separate sheets that you can access quickly. For example, you might use a separate worksheet to track the sales results for each of your company's sales territories. As you'll see shortly, Excel provides features for entering the same data on multiple worksheets simultaneously, so you can quickly create a group of worksheets that contain the same basic information—for example, the layout of those sales results and associated information. On the top sheet of the workbook, you might put a summary worksheet that presents an executive overview of the sales results. Excel lets you create formulas that link from one worksheet to another, so the sales-territory worksheets could automatically update the summary worksheet.

Understanding the Excel Screen

Figure 15-2 shows the Excel application window with a workbook open and a worksheet displayed. In addition to standard Windows elements such as the task pane (if you choose to display it), menu bar, toolbars, scroll bars, and status bar, Excel has a reference area that shows the active cell's address, a formula bar for entering and editing data and formulas, row and column headings, and worksheet tabs. These items are labeled on the figure.

Navigating in Workbooks and Selecting Objects

Once you have set your options and designed your screen layout the way you want it, you are ready to go to work. We'll look next at how to navigate in worksheets, select objects, work with named ranges, and select worksheets.

Navigating in Worksheets

Most people find the mouse the easiest way of navigating in worksheets: you simply click a worksheet or cell to access it, or use the scroll bars to scroll to different areas of the worksheet. But you can also navigate easily by using the arrow keys and keyboard shortcuts. Keyboard shortcuts are especially effective when you're working in a large worksheet that would require extensive scrolling to navigate.

The following are the most widely used keyboard shortcuts:

Action	Keyboard Shortcut
Move to the specified edge of the data region.	CTRL-UP ARROW, DOWN ARROW, LEFT ARROW, or RIGHT ARROW
Move to the first cell in the row.	HOME
Move to the first cell in the worksheet.	CTRL-HOME
Move to the last cell ever used in the worksheet.	CTRL-END
Move down one screen.	PAGE DOWN
Move up one screen.	PAGE UP
Move to the right by one screen.	ALT-PAGE DOWN
Move to the left by one screen.	ALT-PAGE UP
Scroll the workbook to display the active cell.	CTRL-BACKSPACE
Move to the next worksheet.	CTRL-PAGE DOWN
Move to the previous worksheet.	CTRL-PAGE UP

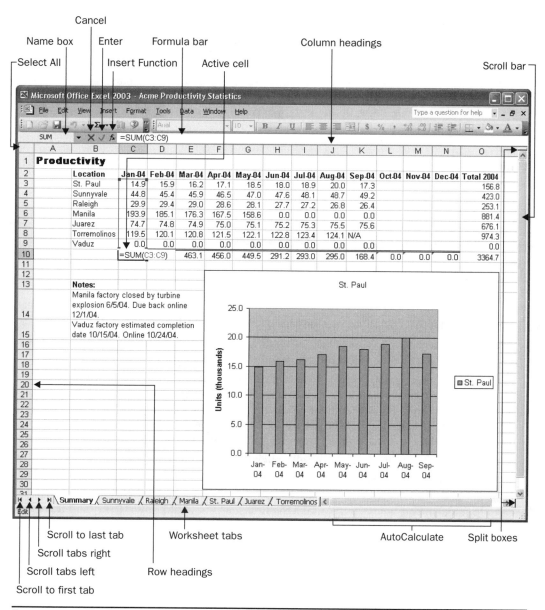

FIGURE 15-2 The Excel application window with a workbook open and a workbook displayed

You can move to a specific cell by typing its address in the name box and pressing ENTER. To move to another worksheet with the mouse, click its tab. If necessary, use the tab scroll buttons to make the tab appear in the list.

Selecting Cells and Ranges of Cells

Much of your work in Excel will be with *ranges* of cells. Excel supports both ranges of contiguous cells and ranges of noncontiguous cells:

- A range of contiguous cells is a rectangle of cells defined by the starting and ending cell addresses, separated by a colon. For example, the range A1:C3 consists of nine cells: the first three cells in the first three columns (or the first three cells in the first three rows, depending on how you look at it).

NOTE   *Technically, a range can consist of a single cell, but most people understand ranges to have two or more cells.*

- A range of noncontiguous cells consists of a collection of cell addresses separated by commas. For example, a range consisting of the cells A1, B2, and C3 would be represented A1,B2,C3. Ranges of noncontiguous cells can include ranges of contiguous cells—for example, A1,B2:C4,D5.

You can select objects in worksheets by using the mouse, the keyboard, or both. These are the basic techniques you need to know:

- To select a cell, click it, or use the arrow keys to move the active cell outline to it.
- To select a row or column, click its heading. Press SHIFT-SPACEBAR to select the row or CTRL-SPACEBAR to select the column the active cell is in.
- To select a contiguous range of cells, click the cell at one corner of the range, and then drag to the other corner. You can drag in any direction—up, down, or diagonally in any direction. This technique works best when the full range of cells appears on screen. If you need to scroll the window to reach the end of the range, you may overrun the far corner of the range. In this case, use the next technique instead.
- To select a contiguous range of cells, click the cell at one corner of the range, scroll if necessary to display the far corner of the range, hold down SHIFT, and click. This technique works well for ranges that run beyond the current window.
- To make multiple selections, make the first selection, hold down CTRL, and then make the other selections.
- To select all the cells in the active worksheet, click the Select All button, the unmarked button at the intersection of the column headings and row headings.

Two other ways of selecting cells and ranges are worth mentioning at this point. The next two sections discuss them.

Naming a Range

To make a range easier to access and identify quickly, you can assign it a name. You can then select the range easily by using the name box's drop-down list or the Go To dialog box; you can quickly apply formatting to the range; and you can use the range's name in calculations rather than having to specify the address.

To assign a name to a range:

1. Select the range.
2. Choose Insert | Name | Define. Excel displays the Define Name dialog box:

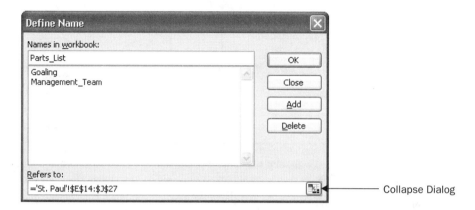
Collapse Dialog

3. To create just this name and dismiss the dialog box, click OK. To create other names, click Add, then enter a new name, use the Collapse Dialog button to identify the range, and click Add again. ("Using the Collapse Dialog Button to Specify Ranges," later in this chapter, explains the use of the Collapse Dialog button.)

From the Define Name dialog box, you can also delete a range name.

TIP *You can also name a range by selecting it, clicking in the name box, typing the name for the range, and pressing* ENTER. *However, using the Define Name dialog box lets you more easily see the other range names you've defined, which can help you implement an orderly naming scheme and avoid duplicating names.*

Using the Go To and Go To Special Dialog Boxes to Select Ranges

For selecting ranges and cells with specific contents, Excel provides the Go To dialog box and the Go To Special dialog box. The Go To dialog box is shown on the left in Figure 15-3 (choose Edit | Go To, or press CTRL-G). It largely duplicates the functionality of the name box, but it also offers you quick access to unnamed ranges you've worked with recently, if you can identify them by their addresses.

Click Special in the Go To dialog box to display the Go To Special dialog box. This dialog box (shown on the right in Figure 15-3) tends to be of more interest than the Go To dialog box, as it enables you to easily select cells that match specific criteria, such as Comments, Conditional Formats, or Data Validation.

Choose the appropriate options (discussed in Table 15-1), and click OK to select the cells with those characteristics. You can then move through the range of cells selected by using ENTER, SHIFT-ENTER, TAB, and SHIFT-TAB.

 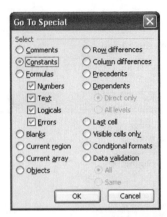

FIGURE 15-3   Use the Go To dialog box (left) to select named ranges or unnamed ranges you've recently worked with, and the Go To Special dialog box to select cells that match specific criteria.

Option	Explanation
Comments	Cells that contain comments
Constants	Cells that contain constant data (text, numbers, or dates) rather than formulas. Select or deselect the Numbers option and Text option under Formulas to specify whether to include numbers and text in the search.
Formulas	Cells that contain formulas rather than constant data. (In other words, the cell's contents begin with =.) Select or deselect the Numbers option, Text option, Logicals option, and Errors option to specify whether to include numbers, text, logical values (TRUE or FALSE), and error values. For example, you might use this option to check all your formulas or to quell errors.
Blanks	Cells that contain no data or formatting. Excel excludes cells after the last cell in the worksheet that contains data.
Current Region	The active cell and all cells around it up to the first blank row and blank column in each direction
Current Array	The active cell and the array it's in
Objects	Text boxes, charts, AutoShapes, and other objects (for example, sounds)
Row Differences	Cells within the selected range whose contents are different from the contents of the comparison cells you specify. Select the range to evaluate, click a cell in the comparison column to make it active, and then select this option from the Go To Special dialog box.
Column Differences	Cells within the selected range whose contents are different from the contents of the comparison cells you specify. Select the range to evaluate, click a cell in the comparison row to make it active, and then select this option from the Go To Special dialog box.

TABLE 15-1   Go To Special Options

Option	Explanation
Precedents	Cells that the active cell refers to. Under the Dependents option, select the Direct Only option (the default) or the All Levels option to specify whether to select direct references only or indirect references as well.
Dependents	Cells that refer to the active cell. Select the Direct Only option (the default) or the All Levels option to specify whether to select direct references only or indirect references as well.
Last Cell	The last cell ever used in the active worksheet
Visible Cells Only	Cells that are visible, not cells that are hidden. Use this option to avoid pasting hidden rows or columns along with visible rows and columns. Select the range, display the Go To Special dialog box, select this option, and then copy the range.
Conditional Formats	Cells that have conditional formatting applied. (See "Conditional Formatting" in Chapter 16.) Under the Data Validation option, choose the All option (the default) to select all cells. Select the Same option to select only those that match the active cell.
Data Validation	Cells that contain data validation rules. Choose the All option (the default) to select all cells. Select the Same option to select only those that match the active cell.

TABLE 15-1   Go To Special Options *(continued)*

Using the Collapse Dialog Button to Specify Ranges

Many of Excel's dialog boxes require you to specify the range to affect. In some cases, you can enter the range automatically by selecting it before displaying the dialog box. Alternatively, you can type the range, but it's easy to get the address wrong. So these dialog boxes contain a Collapse Dialog button, like that shown on the Define Name dialog box (earlier in this chapter), that you can click to collapse the dialog and get it out of the way while you select the range on the worksheet to enter it in the dialog box. You then click the Collapse Dialog button again to restore the dialog.

Selecting Worksheets in a Workbook

You can select worksheets in a workbook as follows:

- Click a worksheet's tab to select it.
- SHIFT-click another worksheet's tab to select all the worksheets between the currently selected worksheet and the one you click.
- CTRL-click another worksheet's tab to add that worksheet to the selection, or CTRL-click a selected worksheet's tab to remove it from the selection.

NOTE   *When multiple worksheets are selected, Excel displays [Group] in the title bar to remind you.*

Excel also offers two keyboard shortcuts for selecting worksheets:

- Press CTRL-SHIFT-PAGE DOWN to select the current worksheet and the next worksheet.
- Press CTRL-SHIFT-PAGE UP to select the current worksheet and the previous worksheet.

Entering Data in Your Worksheets

There are three main ways of entering data in your worksheets: by typing it in manually, by using drag and drop to move or copy existing data, and by pasting in cut or copied existing data. The following sections discuss these ways of entering data.

Entering Data Manually

You can enter data in a cell by selecting the cell, typing the entry, and then pressing ENTER or clicking the Enter button. Pressing ENTER moves the active cell to the next cell in the direction specified by the Move Selection After Enter option on the Edit tab of the Options dialog box. Alternatively, move to another cell by clicking in it, by using one of the arrow keys, or by pressing TAB (to move right), SHIFT-TAB (to move left), or SHIFT-ENTER (to move the opposite way to that given by ENTER).

When entering data, you can work in either the cell itself (the default position of the insertion point) or in the formula bar (by clicking there). Entering data in the cell itself tends to be more straightforward, because you can see where the data will appear in the worksheet and whether it will fit in the cell. Entering data in the Formula bar is useful for long or complex entries for which a lack of space in the cell itself might prove distracting.

Excel also offers the following techniques for speeding up data entry:

- To enter data in a range of cells, select the range, type the entry, and then press CTRL-ENTER.
- To enter data in multiple worksheets at once, click the worksheet tabs to select the worksheets, and then enter the data.

NOTE   *"Using AutoFill" in Chapter 16 explains how to use Excel's AutoFill feature to enter lists and series of data quickly in ranges of cells. Chapter 17 explains how to enter formulas and functions in cells.*

To delete the existing contents of a cell or range, select it and press DELETE.

Understanding Excel's Limited Undo Feature—and Improving It

Unlike Word, which can undo an impressively long sequence of actions, Excel can undo only 16 actions by default—and even those 16 actions won't always be available to you. Some actions in Excel can't be undone, but Excel doesn't warn you before clearing the Undo buffer, so you may find yourself unable to undo actions.

If you're able to edit the Registry on your computer, you can change Excel's number of undo levels. In the HKEY_CURRENT_USER\Software\Microsoft\Office\11.0\

Excel\Options subkey, create a new DWORD value entry, name it UndoHistory, select the Decimal option, and set the value to the number of undo levels you want—anywhere from 0 to 100. Close the Registry Editor; then close and restart Excel to make the change take effect.

To replace the existing contents of a cell, simply create a new entry over it. To edit the existing contents of a cell, double-click it. Alternatively, move to the cell and press F2. You can then edit the text either in the cell itself (the default) or in the formula bar (by clicking there).

Once you're editing the contents of a cell, the LEFT ARROW and RIGHT ARROW keys move the insertion point left and right, so you can't use these keys (or UP ARROW or DOWN ARROW) to move to other cells. Instead, you need to press ENTER, press TAB, click the Enter button, or click in another cell.

Entering Data by Using Drag and Drop

You can also enter data by using drag and drop (unless you've deselected the Allow Cell Drag and Drop option on the Edit tab of the Options dialog box). Here's how drag and drop works:

- Move the mouse pointer over one of the borders of the selection to produce the drag and drop pointer. (Clicking in the selection will select the cell you click.)

- Drag and drop to move the selection. CTRL-drag and drop to copy the selection.

- Right-drag and drop to display a shortcut menu offering options such as Move Here, Copy Here, Copy Here as Values Only, Copy Here as Formats Only, Link Here, Create Hyperlink Here, Shift Down and Copy, Shift Right and Copy, Shift Down and Move, Shift Right and Move, and Cancel. Choose the appropriate option as needed. Copying values (rather than formulas) is often useful, as is copying formatting. (You can also use the Format Painter to copy formatting.)

Entering Data with Paste, Paste Options, and Paste Special

You can cut, copy, and paste data from the Windows Clipboard or the Clipboard task pane much as in the other Office applications but with the following variations:

- When you copy an item, Excel displays a flashing border around it. To paste a single time without using the Clipboard task pane, select the destination and press ENTER; Excel then removes the flashing border and clears the item from the Clipboard. To paste multiple times, issue a Paste command (for example, CTRL-V). Excel maintains the flashing border until you clear it by pressing ESC.

- When you paste the contents of multiple cells, Excel uses the active cell as the top-left corner of the destination range. So you don't need to select the whole of the destination range, just its top-left cell.

- When you paste data, Excel displays a Paste Smart Tag below and to the right of the destination cells. Click this Smart Tag to display a menu of paste options, as shown next. For example, you can choose between maintaining the formatting of the source cell and matching the formatting of the destination cell, apply formatting only, or paste a value rather than the formula that produces it. The options available depend on the type of data you've pasted.

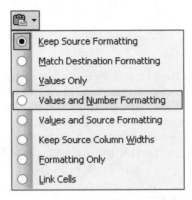

When the Smart Tag options don't give you the fine control you need, issue a Paste Special command from the Edit menu or the shortcut menu to display the Paste Special dialog box:

The Paste section of the Paste Special dialog box offers the following mutually exclusive options:

- **All**   Pastes everything copied: all values, formulas, formatting, and so on
- **Formulas**   Pastes all data—formulas, constants, and so on—without formatting
- **Values**   Pastes the values of formulas (rather than the formulas themselves) without formatting
- **Formats**   Pastes all formatting without any data or formulas
- **Comments**   Pastes all comments without other data
- **Validation**   Pastes the data-validation criteria

- **All Except Borders**   Pastes all data and formatting except cell borders
- **Column Widths**   Pastes the column widths without data and without other formatting
- **Formulas and Number Formats**   Pastes formulas and number formatting only
- **Values and Number Formats**   Pastes values and number formatting only

---

TIP   *The Paste Special dialog box limits you to a single operation at a time. But you can use multiple Paste Special operations with the same data range to transfer multiple items.*

The Operation section of the Paste Special dialog box offers mutually exclusive options for adding, subtracting, multiplying, dividing, or performing no operation (the default). To use these options:

1. Copy to the Clipboard the cell or range that contains the number or numbers you want to perform an operation on the other numbers. For example, if you want to multiply another cell by the contents of cell B5, select cell B5 and copy it to the Clipboard.

2. Select the cell or range on which you want to perform the operation. For example, if you want to multiply cell B6 by cell B5, select cell B6.

3. Display the Paste Special dialog box, choose the appropriate Operation option, and click OK.

The final section of the Paste Special dialog box contains the following options, which you can use with the Paste options and Operation options:

- **Skip Blanks**   Prevents Excel from pasting blank cells
- **Transpose**   Transposes rows to columns, and columns to rows

Linking Data Across Worksheets or Across Workbooks

=VLookup (Lookupvalue, tablerange

Chances are, your work in Excel involves a healthy variety of different worksheets or workbooks, some of which bear a relationship to one another. To avoid having to copy information manually from one worksheet or workbook to another each time it changes (let alone retype it), Excel lets you link data across worksheets or even across workbooks. For example, each departmental manager might maintain a separate workbook of productivity targets, with summaries from each of those workbooks linked to an executive-overview workbook used by the VPs.

To create a link:

1. Open the source workbook and the destination workbook. (If you're linking from one sheet of a workbook to another, open just that workbook.)

2. In the source workbook, copy the relevant cell or range.

3. Display the destination sheet of the destination workbook, issue a Paste Special command to display the Paste Special dialog box, and click Paste Link.

Excel updates links within the same workbook automatically and immediately when you change the data in the source. When you link from one workbook to another, here's what happens:

- If the source workbook is open and contains changes made since the destination workbook was last updated, Excel updates the links in the destination workbook when you open it.

- If the source workbook isn't open but contains changes made since the destination workbook was last updated, Excel's default behavior is to prompt you to update automatic links when you open the destination workbook. To make Excel update the links without prompting, deselect the Ask to Update Automatic Links option on the Edit tab of the Options dialog box.

You can also force updating manually by choosing Edit | Links and working in the Edit Links dialog box. This dialog box also lets you check the status of a link, change a link's source, or break a link (for example, if the source isn't available now and never will be again).

Improving Your View with Hiding, Splits, Extra Windows, Zooming, and Freezing

The next few sections discuss five features that can greatly help your ability to view your data and work effectively with it: hiding a window, splitting the window, using extra windows, zooming in and out, and freezing rows and columns.

Hiding a Window

You can hide the active window by choosing Window | Hide. Doing so can help you keep your Excel window uncluttered or protect against inquisitive coworkers.

To redisplay a hidden window, choose Window | Unhide, select the window in the Unhide dialog box, and click OK.

Splitting the Window

You can split a worksheet window into two or four panes so you can see two or four separate parts of the worksheet at once.

The easiest way to apply a two-pane split is to drag the appropriate split box (horizontal or vertical) to where you want the split to be. You can then drag the other split box (vertical or horizontal) to create a four-pane split. To split the window into four panes at once, position the active cell in the row above and column to the left of which you want to split the window. Then choose Window | Split to split the window both ways.

To adjust the horizontal or vertical split, drag the appropriate split bar. To adjust both at once, drag where they cross.

To remove a single split, double-click its split bar, or drag it out of the worksheet window. To remove all splitting, double-click the split bars where they cross, or choose Window | Remove Split.

Using Extra Windows

Another way of working more easily in two or more areas of a worksheet or workbook is to open two or more windows containing the same workbook. To open a new window, choose Window | New Window.

Excel names extra windows containing the same workbook by adding a colon and a number after the filename. For example, when you open a second window of Budget.xls, Excel renames the first window Budget.xls:1 and names the second window Budget.xls:2. You can easily switch from window to window by clicking a window (if it's visible) or by using the Window menu.

You can split each open window as needed. You can hide and unhide windows as usual.

Zooming In and Out

To make your worksheets easier to read on screen, you can zoom in and out either by using the Zoom box on the toolbar or by choosing View | Zoom and using the Zoom dialog box. These controls are largely self-explanatory, but you may benefit from knowing the following:

- Excel's zoom range is from 10 percent to 400 percent. For percentages other than 25, 50, 75, 100, and 200, type the percentage into the Zoom box or the Custom box in the Zoom dialog box.

- The Selection option in the Zoom drop-down list and the Fit Selection option in the Zoom dialog box zoom the worksheet to the largest size possible for the current selection. This option is great for concentrating on a group of key cells.

- Excel hides the cell grid lines at tiny magnifications to improve visibility.

Using Freezing to Keep Some Rows and Columns Visible

If you work on worksheets that contain more data than will fit on your monitor at a comfortable size, chances are you'll need to scroll up and down, or back and forth, to refer to labels and headings in the leftmost columns or topmost rows of the worksheet. Such frequent scrolling can be both frustrating and a waste of time.

To reduce scrolling, you can *freeze* specific rows and columns so that Excel keeps displaying them even though the other rows and columns scroll. For example, you could freeze column A and row 1 so that Excel would keep displaying them even when you navigated to cell IV65536.

To freeze rows and columns, select the cell to the right of the column and below the row you want to freeze, then choose Window | Freeze Panes. Excel displays a heavier line along the grid lines to show where the frozen section is. The frozen section then remains in place when you scroll the rest of the worksheet as usual.

To remove the freezing, choose Window | Unfreeze Panes.

Converting from Other Formats

Excel includes filters for converting data from other formats, such as Lotus 1-2-3, Quattro Pro, Microsoft Works, and dBASE, not to mention files in earlier Excel formats (for example, Excel 95 or Excel 97) and XML.

Excel can also open text files in widely used formats such as comma-separated values (CSV)—a format that uses commas to denote the divisions between data fields. To get data from applications such as address books or organizers into an Excel worksheet, you'll often need to export the data to a CSV file and then open that file in Excel. Similarly, if Excel doesn't have a converter for a spreadsheet file you need to open, use the application that created the file to save a copy in CSV format, and then open that copy in Excel.

To convert a file, open it via the Open dialog box as usual. Use the Files of Type drop-down list to specify the type of file you want to display in the main list box. If the type of file doesn't appear in the list, select the All Files option to display all files—but be warned that Excel probably won't be able to convert the file. If it can't, Excel displays a message claiming the file format is not valid.

***

NOTE *Excel also lets you save your workbook files in other formats (such as the formats used by various versions of Lotus 1-2-3) by using the options in the Save as Type drop-down list in the Save As dialog box. Use these formats only when you need to share your work with someone using these formats. Be warned that saving workbooks in non-Excel formats may lose some advanced features. Normally, however, plain data should transfer without problems.*

Printing Worksheets

When you've finished creating a worksheet, you may need to print it. The following sections discuss the steps you'll probably want to take before printing a worksheet— checking the page size and margins, adding headers and footers, and using Print Preview—and the process of printing.

Instant Printing with the Default Settings

For a small worksheet that you're sure occupies less than one sheet of paper, you can use the default print settings. To do so, click the Print button on the Standard toolbar. Excel prints the active worksheet without displaying the Print dialog box. If you haven't specified the area of the worksheet to print, Excel prints the worksheet up to the last cell that contains data.

In most cases, however, you'll want to use Print Preview (discussed next) to check how your worksheet will fit on the paper before you print it. You may also need to set the print area manually if you only want to print part of the worksheet, and you'll see how to do that shortly.

Using Print Preview

Use Print Preview to make sure your worksheet will fit on the paper and look as you want it to. You can display the active worksheet in Print Preview in any of the following ways:

- Click the Print Preview button on the toolbar.
- Choose File | Print Preview from the main menu.
- Click the Preview button in the Print dialog box.
- Click the Print Preview button on any tab of the Page Setup dialog box.

An example of Print Preview is shown in the following illustration. As you can see, it provides buttons for navigating to the next and previous pages of your workbook, zooming in and out (the one Zoom button), displaying the Print dialog box, displaying the Page Setup dialog box, toggling the display of the margins, displaying Page Break Preview, exiting Print Preview (the Close button), and displaying help. The bottom of the window shows the worksheet's footer, as well providing "Page X of X" information.

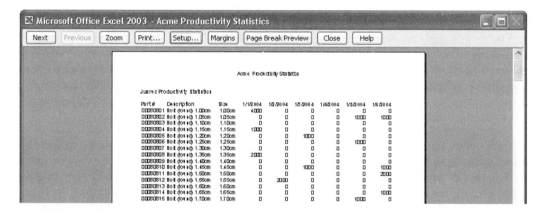

Setting the Print Area

To specify which cells of a worksheet to print, set the print area as follows:

1. Select the range of cells you want to print.

TIP *The print area doesn't have to be one range of contiguous cells—you can select multiple ranges by* CTRL-*clicking. When you issue the Set Print Area command, Excel creates a print area around each range of cells. Excel then prints each range of cells on a separate page.*

2. Choose File | Print Area | Set Print Area. Excel places a dotted line around the cells.

Note the following:

- Excel saves the print areas in the workbook, so you don't need to set the print area again until you need to print a different area of a worksheet.

- If you add or delete rows or columns within the print area, Excel adjusts the boundaries of the print area to compensate.

- However, if you add cells to the print area and use the Shift Cells Right option or the Shift Cells Down option rather than the Entire Row option or the Entire Column option, Excel doesn't adjust the boundaries of the print area. So data that was previously in the print area can move out of the print area.

- Likewise, if you delete cells (rather than entire rows or columns) within the print area, Excel doesn't adjust the boundaries of the print area. So data that was previously outside the print area may move inside the print area.

To change the print area, set the print area again. To clear the print area and return to default print settings, choose File | Print Area | Clear Print Area.

NOTE   You can also set the print area by clicking the Collapse Dialog button in the Print Area box on the Sheet tab of the Page Setup dialog box.

Setting Page Breaks

For a worksheet that prints on multiple pages, set page breaks manually to make sure the data is broken as sensibly as possible from one page to the next. Typically, you'll want to start by setting page breaks where they'll produce a suitably logical division in your spreadsheets. To do so, work in Normal view, select the cell above and to the left of which you want the new page break to fall. Then choose Insert | Page Break. Excel displays dotted lines down and across the screen to denote the page break. You can remove a manual page break by selecting the cell below and to the right of the page break's crossed dotted lines and choosing Insert | Remove Page Break.

Next, you may want to improve the positioning of any page breaks that your paper size and zoom percentage forces on your worksheets. To do so, use Page Break Preview by choosing View | Page Break Preview from the menu or clicking Page Break Preview from Print Preview. Excel shows the automatic page breaks as dotted blue lines (see the vertical lines by columns G and O in the illustration), which you can move to better positions by dragging with your mouse. Usually, it's best to start repagination at page 1 and to reduce pages rather than enlarging them.

Any manual page breaks you've set appear as solid lines. Once you've moved an automatic page break, Excel changes it to a solid line so that you can tell which page breaks are automatic and which you've placed manually. Excel changes the zoom to make the resulting pages fit on the paper size you're using.

NOTE   You can remove all page breaks from the active worksheet by clicking the Select All button and choosing Insert | Reset All Page Breaks.

Modifying Print Settings

The Page Setup dialog box provides a wide variety of options for configuring the layout of your worksheets on the page. You can change margins, choose to include extra items in the printout, scale your worksheets to better fit the paper size you're using, repeat row titles or column titles, and add headers and footers.

Checking and Changing Margins

Excel offers two ways of setting margins. Usually, it's best to start on the Margins tab of the Page Setup dialog box (shown here). This offers self-explanatory options for setting the top, bottom, left, and right margins, and for specifying the distance between the header and the top of the page and between the footer and the bottom of the page. You can also choose to center the printout on the page horizontally, vertically, both, or neither (the default).

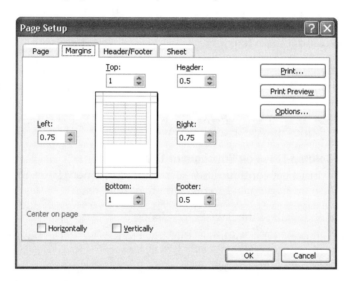

After setting margin distances on the Margins tab, click Print Preview, and then click Margins to make Excel display guidelines where the margins and the header and footer areas fall. You can change the margins and the header and footer areas by dragging these guidelines—for example, if you notice a deep header or footer is crashing into the worksheet. You can also drag the markers along the top border of the page to change column widths—for example, if you notice that a cell is too wide for its column.

After checking the margins, click Margins again to toggle off the guidelines.

Choosing Which Items to Include in the Printout

The Sheet tab of the Page Setup dialog box lets you include extra items not normally included in the printout and choose other options. You can

- Print grid lines, and row and column headings.
- Print colors as black and white (for a monochrome printer).
- Use draft quality for faster printing and lower ink use.

- Include comments. If you do, choose whether to print them at the end of the worksheet or in the positions in which they appear on the worksheet.

- Specify how to deal with cells that contain errors: display them, print blank cells, print two dashes (**--**), or print **#N/A** to indicate they're not applicable.

- Change the page order from Down, Then Over (the default) to Over, Then Down, to specify how Excel paginates and numbers multipage printouts.

Scaling Your Worksheets to Fit the Paper

The Scaling section of the Page tab lets you scale your worksheets up or down to the right size:

- Use the Adjust to *NN*% Normal Size option to specify an exact percentage.

- Use the Fit to *NN* Page(s) Wide by *NN* Tall options to tell Excel to resize a worksheet so it fits on the number of pages that suits you. These options can save you time and paper, but always use Print Preview to check that the results will look acceptable before you commit them to paper.

Choosing Print Options

To choose print options, click Options in the Page Setup dialog box, and work in the resulting dialog box. You can specify the orientation (portrait or landscape), the page order (front to back or back to front), the number of pages per sheet, and the paper source. Depending on your printer, other options may be available as well.

Repeating Row or Column Titles on Subsequent Pages

If the printout of a worksheet continues to a second or subsequent page, repeat the row or column titles (or both) on those pages to make them easy to read:

1. Display the Sheet tab of the Page Setup dialog box.

2. Click the Collapse Dialog button in the Rows to Repeat at Top box, and select the rows you want to repeat.

3. Click the Collapse Dialog button in the Columns to Repeat at Left box, and select the columns you want to repeat.

Adding Headers and Footers

Like Word, Excel provides good features for adding headers and footers to your worksheets to help you keep your printouts in order. Each worksheet in a workbook has its own header and footer, giving you fine control over the information included.

To create headers and footers:

1. Select the worksheet you want to affect.

2. Choose File | Page Setup, and click the Header/Footer tab.

3. Select a predefined header from the header drop-down list, or click Custom Header and work in the Header dialog box, shown in Figure 15-4. The controls are self-explanatory: click in Left Section, Center Section, or Right Section as appropriate; then use the buttons to insert the appropriate information and format it. Along with information on the filename and path, sheet name, date and time, page number, and

total pages, you can insert pictures and format them—for example, you might add a company logo.

4. Select a predefined footer from the Footer drop-down list, or click Custom Footer and work in the Footer dialog box. The Footer dialog box offers the same controls as the Header dialog box.

5. Click Print Preview to make sure the header and footer look right.

6. Click OK.

If you regularly need to add headers and footers to your worksheets, add the headers and footers to the templates on which the worksheets are based so that you don't have to enter them manually for each new workbook you create.

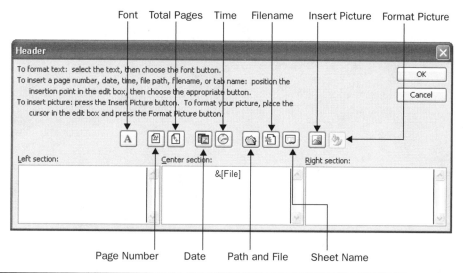

FIGURE 15-4   Use the Header dialog box to create custom headers when Excel's predefined headers don't meet your needs.

Formatting Worksheets and Restricting Data

A
s you saw in the previous chapter, Excel makes it easy to navigate in your worksheets, enter data in them, and print them. Excel also offers a wide variety of formatting options for presenting the data in your worksheets as effectively as possible. Formatting includes not only fonts and styles, but also the way numbers are presented, months are spelled, how cells and ranges display data, and the size of rows and columns.

This chapter also covers how to perform basic tasks such as adding, deleting, and renaming the worksheets in a workbook. You'll learn how to use Excel's features for validating the data that users enter and for protecting cells, worksheets, or even whole workbooks against being changed by the wrong users. You can further manipulate worksheets by using AutoFill to enter data quickly in ranges and Find and Replace features to search for and replace both data and formatting.

Adding, Deleting, and Manipulating Worksheets

Each Excel workbook contains 3 worksheets by default and can contain from 1 to 255 worksheets. In the following sections, we'll show you how to add, delete, hide, and redisplay worksheets; move and copy worksheets; rename worksheets; and change the formatting on default new worksheets that you create.

Adding, Deleting, Hiding, and Redisplaying Worksheets

You can add and delete worksheets to your workbooks as follows:

- To add a worksheet, select the worksheet before which you want to insert the new worksheet. Choose Insert | Worksheet or press either SHIFT-F11 or ALT-SHIFT-F1. Alternatively, right-click an existing worksheet, choose Insert, select Worksheet, and click OK. The new worksheet will be inserted before the existing one.

NOTE   *You can change the default number of worksheets in a new workbook by using the Sheets in New Workbook option on the General tab of the Options dialog box (Tools | Options).*

- To delete a worksheet, right-click it and choose Delete. Alternatively, select the worksheet and choose Edit | Delete Sheet. Excel deletes the worksheet without confirmation.

- To hide a worksheet from view, select it and choose Format | Sheet | Hide. To display the worksheet again, choose Format | Sheet | Unhide, select the sheet in the Unhide dialog box, and click OK.

Moving and Copying Worksheets

In a workbook that contains few worksheets, the easiest way to move a worksheet to a new position in the workbook is to drag its tab to the new position. You can copy the worksheet instead of moving it by holding down CTRL as you drag. The copy receives the same name as the original worksheet followed by (2).

In a workbook that contains many worksheets, it's easier to use the Move or Copy dialog box:

1. Select the worksheet or worksheets you want to move or copy.

2. Choose Edit | Move or Copy Sheet from the menu, or right-click a selected tab and choose Move or Copy. The Move or Copy dialog box appears:

3. Select the destination in the Before Sheet list box.

4. To copy the worksheet, select the Create a Copy option.

5. Click OK.

The Move or Copy dialog box also enables you to move or copy a worksheet to a different workbook. Open the workbook and follow the previous instructions. In the To Book drop-down list, select the destination workbook.

CAUTION   When you copy a worksheet, Excel copies only the first 255 characters of each cell. If any cell in the worksheet has contents longer than 255 characters, Excel warns you of this problem, but it doesn't specify the cells affected. To work around the problem, click the Select All button to select the source worksheet, issue a Copy command, and then paste the copies into the destination worksheet.

Renaming a Worksheet

You can rename a worksheet by double-clicking its tab, typing the new name (up to 31 characters long), and pressing ENTER or clicking elsewhere. Alternatively, right-click the tab and choose Rename.

TIP   To make a worksheet tab easier to identify among its siblings, you can change its color. Issue a Tab Color command from the Format | Sheet submenu or the tab's context menu, select the color, and click OK.

Changing the Formatting on New Default Worksheets and Workbooks

You can change the default formatting of the workbook and worksheets that Excel uses for the New Blank Workbook command by creating a template named Book.xlt in the *%userprofile%*\Application Data\Microsoft\Excel\XLSTART folder (for example, C:\Documents and Settings\Jane Phillips\Application Data\Microsoft\Excel\XLSTART). First, you'll need to display hidden files and folders (if you haven't already done so): choose Tools | Options in an Explorer window, select the Show Hidden Files and Folders option on the View tab of the Folder Options dialog box, and click OK.

Then open an Explorer window to the XLSTART folder, and take either of the following actions:

- If you have a workbook or template that contains the formatting you want to use for new default worksheets and workbooks, copy it to the XLSTART folder. Rename the copy Book.xlt. (If the file was a workbook, Windows will display a Rename dialog box warning you about the change of file extension. Click Yes.) Open Book.xlt and delete any contents you don't want to have in the new default worksheets and workbooks. Save and close the file.

- If you don't have a workbook or template that contains the formatting you want to use for new default worksheets and workbooks, create a new one. In the XLSTART folder, issue a New | Microsoft Excel Worksheet command from the File menu or context menu. Name the new workbook Book.xlt. Windows will display a Rename dialog box warning you about the change of file extension. Click Yes. Open Book.xlt, set it up with the formatting you want to use for new default worksheets and workbooks, save it, and close it.

Formatting Cells and Ranges

As you've seen, the cell is the basis of the Excel worksheet. A cell can contain any of various types of data—such as numbers (values that can be calculated), dates, times, formulas, and text—and can be formatted in a variety of ways. You can adjust everything from the formats in which different types of data are displayed, to alignment, to background color and grid lines.

The most basic type of formatting controls the way in which Excel displays the data contained in the cell. For some types of entries, Excel displays the literal contents of the cell by default, whereas for other types of entries, Excel displays the results of the contents of the cell. For example, when you enter a formula in a cell, Excel displays the results of the formula by default rather than the formula itself. So to be sure of the contents of a cell, you need to make it the active cell or edit it. Excel displays the literal contents of the active cell in the Formula bar; and when you edit a cell, Excel displays its literal contents in both the cell itself and in the Formula bar.

Even when Excel displays the contents of the cell, it may change the contents for display purposes. For example, when you enter a number too long to be displayed in a General-formatted cell, Excel converts it to scientific notation using six digits of precision. Similarly, Excel rounds display numbers when they won't fit in cells, but the underlying number remains unaffected.

Applying Number Formatting

The main way of applying formatting to cells and ranges is the Format Cells dialog box (Format | Cells). You can also apply basic formatting from the Formatting toolbar, shown here:

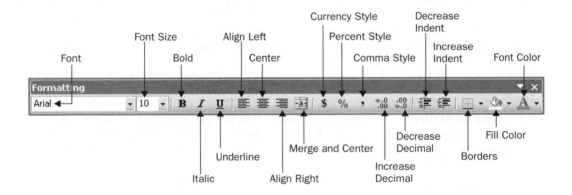

TIP   *If you find the Formatting toolbar a more convenient way to apply formatting than the Format Cells dialog box, customize the Formatting toolbar by adding to it buttons for the types of formatting you apply most frequently. You'll find a few extra buttons on the Add or Remove Buttons | Formatting submenu. You'll find all the formatting commands under the Format category on the Commands tab of the Customize dialog box. "Customizing Toolbars and Menus" in Chapter 2 explains how to customize toolbars.*

Excel's Format Cells dialog box (Format | Cells or press CTRL-1) offers a large number of options for formatting the active cell or selected range. We'll explore most of these options later in this chapter.

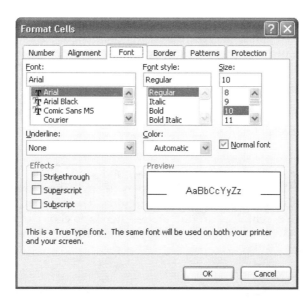

You can also apply some font formatting via Office-wide shortcuts (such as CTRL-B for boldface, CTRL-I for italic, and CTRL-U for single underline).

Understanding Excel's Number Formats

To make Excel display the contents of a cell in the way you intend, you apply the appropriate number format. You can apply number formats manually in several ways, but Excel also applies number formats automatically when you enter text that matches one of Excel's triggers for a number format. Because some of the triggers for automatic number formatting are less than intuitive, it's a good idea to know about them. That way, you can avoid having Excel apply the number formats unexpectedly.

General Number Format

The General number is the default format for all cells on a new worksheet (unless you've customized it). General displays up to 11 digits per cell and doesn't use thousands separators.

You can apply General format by pressing CTRL-SHIFT-~.

Number Format

The Number formats let you specify the number of decimal places to display (0–30, with a default of 2), whether to display a thousands separator (for example, a comma in U.S. English formats), and how to represent negative numbers.

You can make Excel apply the Number format with the thousands separator by including a comma to separate thousands or millions (for example, **1,000**, **1,000,000** or **1,000000**—only one appropriately placed comma is necessary).

Currency Format

The Currency formats let you specify the number of decimal places to display (0–30, with a default of 2), which currency symbol to display (if any), and how to represent negative numbers.

You can make Excel apply Currency format by entering the appropriate currency symbol before the number. For example, enter **$4** to make Excel display dollar formatting. If you enter one or more decimal places, Excel applies Currency format with two decimal places. For example, if you enter **$4.1**, Excel displays *$4.10*.

Accounting Format

The Accounting formats let you specify the number of decimal places to display (0–30, with a default of 2) and which currency symbol to display (if any). The currency symbol appears flush left with the cell border, separated from the figures. The Accounting formats represent negative numbers with parentheses around them—there's no choice of format.

You can apply the Accounting format quickly by clicking the Currency Style button on the Formatting toolbar.

Date Format

The Date formats offer a variety of date formats based on the locale you choose. These options are easy to understand. What's more important to grasp is how Excel stores dates and times.

Excel treats dates and times as serial numbers representing the number of days that have elapsed since 1/1/1900, which is given the serial number 1. For example, the serial date 37955 represents November 30, 2003.

For computers, serial dates (and times) are a snap to sort and manipulate: to find out how far apart two dates are, the computer merely subtracts one date from the other, without having to consider which months are shorter than others. For humans, serial dates are largely inscrutable, so Excel displays dates in your choice of formats.

If you want, you can enter dates by formatting cells with the Date format and entering the appropriate serial number, but most people find it far easier to enter the date in one of the conventional Windows formats that Excel recognizes. Excel automatically converts any entry that contains a hyphen (-) or a forward slash (/) to serial dates, and formats the entry with a Date format that matches a date and time format used by Windows. For example, if you enter 11/30/03, Excel assumes you mean November 30, 2003.

If you don't specify the year, Excel assumes you mean the current year.

Time Format

The Time formats offer a variety of formats based on 12-hour clocks and 24-hour clocks. These options are easy to understand. Excel treats times as subdivisions of days, with 24 hours making up one day and one serial number. So, given that 37987 is the serial date for January 1, 2004, 37987.5 is noon on that day, 37987.25 is 6:00 A.M., 37987.75 is 6:00 P.M., and so on.

You can make Excel automatically format an entry with a time format by entering a number that contains a colon (for example, 12:00) or a number followed by a space and "a" or "p" (uppercase or lowercase—for example, **1 p** or **11 a**).

Percentage Format

The Percentage format displays the value in the cell with a percent sign and with your choice of number of decimal places (the default is two). For example, if you enter **71** in the cell, Excel displays 71.00% by default.

You can make Excel automatically format an entry with the Percentage format by entering a percent sign after the number. If you enter no decimal places, Excel uses none. If you enter one or more decimal places, Excel uses two decimal places. You can change the number of decimal places displayed by formatting the cell manually.

Fraction Format

As you'd imagine, Excel stores fractions as their decimal equivalents—for example, it stores ¼ as 0.25. To display fractions (for example, ¼) and compound fractions (for example, 11¼) in Excel, you have to use the Fraction formats. Excel offers fraction formats of one digit (for example, ¾), two digits (for example, $^{16}/_{18}$), and three digits (for example, $^{303}/_{512}$); halves, quarters, eighths, sixteenths, tenths, and hundredths.

Before worrying about fractions being displayed as their decimal equivalents, however, you need to worry about entering many fractions in a way that Excel won't mistake for dates. For example, if you enter **1/4** in a General-formatted cell, Excel converts it to the date 4-Jan in the current year.

To enter a fraction in a General-formatted cell, type a zero, a space, and the fraction—for example, type **0 1/4** to enter ¼. To enter a compound fraction in a General-formatted cell, type the integer, a space, and the fraction—for example, type **11 1/4** to enter 11¼. Excel formats the cell with the appropriate Fraction format, so the fraction is displayed, and stores the corresponding decimal value.

If you need to enter simple fractions consistently in your worksheets, format the relevant cells, columns, or rows with the Fraction format ahead of time.

Scientific Format

Scientific format displays numbers in an exponential form—for example, 567890123245 is displayed as 5.6789E+11, indicating where the decimal place needs to go. You can change the number of decimal places displayed to anywhere from 0 to 30.

You can make Excel apply Scientific format by entering a number that contains an *e* in any position but the ends (for example, **3e4** or **12345E17**).

Text Format

For values that you want Excel to treat as text and not automatically apply another format, you use Text format. For example, if you keep a spreadsheet of telephone numbers, you might have some numbers that start with 0. To prevent Excel from dropping what appears to be a leading zero and converting the cell to a number format, you could format the cell as Text. Similarly, you might need to enter a value that Excel would take to be a date (for example, **1/2**), a time, a formula, or another format.

Excel left-aligns Text-formatted entries and omits them from range calculations—for example, SUM()—in which they would otherwise be included.

CAUTION   *For safety, force the Text format by typing a space before a numeric entry, or manually format the cell as Text before entering data in it. If you apply the Text format to numbers you've already entered, Excel will continue to treat them as numbers rather than as text. You'll need to edit each cell (double-click it, or press F2, and then press ENTER) to correct this error.*

Special Format

The Special formats provide a locale-specific range of formatting choices. For example, the English (United States) locale offers the choices Zip Code, Zip Code + 4, Phone Number, and Social Security Number.

As you'll quickly realize, these formats all have rigidly defined formats, most of which are separated by hyphens into groups of specific lengths. (Phone numbers are less rigid than the other formats, but Excel handles longer numbers—for example, international numbers—as well as could be expected.)

These Special formats enable you to quickly enter numbers of the given type and have Excel enter the hyphens automatically for you. For example, if you format a cell with the Social Security Number format and enter **623648267**, Excel automatically formats it as a social security number: 623-64-8267.

Custom Format

You can define your own custom formats for needs not covered by any of the built-in formats. Excel's variety of built-in formats cover general, numeric, currency, percentage, exponential, date, time, and custom numeric formats. You can base a custom format on one of the built-in formats.

To define a custom format:

1. Enter sample text for the format in a cell, and then select that cell. (Excel then displays the sample text in the format you're creating, which helps you see the effects of the changes you make.)

2. Display the Number tab of the Format Cells dialog box.

3. In the Category box, select the Custom item.

4. In the Type list box, select the custom format on which you want to base your new custom format. Excel displays the details for the type in the Type text box.

5. If the details for the type extend beyond the Type text box, double-click in the text box to select all its contents, issue a Copy command (for example, press CTRL-C), and then paste the copied text into a text editor such as Notepad. (For a shorter type, you can work effectively in the Type text box.)

6. Enter the details for the four parts of the type, separating the parts from each other with a semicolon. (See the detailed explanation that follows.)

7. If you're working in a text editor, copy what you typed and paste it into the Type text box. Check the sample text to make sure it seems to be correct.

8. Click OK.

As you can see in the Type list box, each custom format consists of format codes that specify how Excel should display the information. Each custom format can contain four formats. The first format specifies how to display positive numbers, the second format specifies how to display negative numbers, the third format specifies how to display zero values, and the fourth format specifies how to display text. The four formats are separated by semicolons. You can leave a section blank by entering nothing between the relevant semicolons (or before the first semicolon, or after the last semicolon).

Table 16-1 explains the codes you can use for defining custom formats and gives examples.

Code	Meaning	Example
[*color name*]	Display the specified color	Enter the appropriate color in brackets as the first item in the section: [Black], [Red], [Blue], [Green], [White], [Cyan], [Magenta], or [Yellow]. For example, **#,##0_);[Magenta](#,##0)** displays negative numbers in magenta.
Number Format Codes		
#	Display a significant digit	##.# displays two significant digits before the decimal point and one significant digit after it. (A *significant digit* is a nonzero figure.)
0	Display a zero if there would otherwise be no digit in this place	00000 displays a five-digit number, packing it with leading zeroes if necessary. For example, if you enter **4**, Excel displays *00004*.
%	Display a percentage	#% displays the number multiplied by 100 and with a percent sign. For example, **2** appears as *200%*.
?	Display as a fraction	# ????/???? displays a number and four-digit fractions—for example, 4 1234/4321.
.	Display a decimal point	##.## displays two significant digits on either side of the decimal point.
,	Two meanings: display the thousands separator *or* scale the number down by 1,000	Thousands separator example: $#,### displays the dollar sign, four significant digits, and the thousands separator. Scale by 1,000 example: €#.##,,, " billion" displays the euro symbol, one significant digit before the decimal point and two after, the number scaled down by a billion, and the word "billion" (after a space). For example, if you enter **9876543210**, Excel displays *€9.88 billion*.

TABLE 16-1   Codes for Creating Custom Formats

Code	Meaning	Example
Date and Time Format Codes		
d	Display the day in numeric format	d-mmm-yyyy displays 1/1/04 as *1-Jan-2004*.
dd	Display the day in numeric format with a leading zero	dd/mmm/yy displays 1/1/04 as *01/Jan/04*. Use leading zeroes to align dates.
ddd	Display the day as a three-letter abbreviation	ddd dd/mm/yyyy displays 1/1/04 as *Thu 01/01/2004*.
dddd	Display the day in full	dddd, dd/mm/yyyy displays 1/1/04 as *Thursday, 01/01/2004*.
m	Display the month in numeric format	d/m/yy displays 1/1/04 as *1/1/04*.
mm	Display the month in numeric format with a leading zero	dd/mm/yy displays 1/1/04 as *01/01/04*.
mmm	Display the month as a three-letter abbreviation	dd-mmm-yy displays 1/1/04 as *01-Jan-2004*.
mmmm	Display the month in full	d mmmm, yyyy displays 1/1/04 as *1 January, 2004*.
mmmmm	Display the month as a one-letter abbreviation	January, June, and July appear as *J*; April and August appear as *A*; and so on. This code is seldom useful because it tends to be visually confusing.
yy	Display the year as a two-digit number	d/m/yy displays 1/1/04 as *1/1/04*.
yyyy	Display the year in full	d-mmm-yyyy displays 1/1/04 as *1-Jan-2004*.
h	Display the hour	h:m displays 1:01 as *1:1*.
hh	Display the hour with a leading zero	hh:mm displays 1:01 as *01:01*.
m	Display the minute	h:m displays 1:01 as *1:1*.
mm	Display the minute with a leading zero	hh:mm displays 1:01 as *01:01*. To distinguish mm from the months code, you must enter it immediately after hh or immediately before ss.
s	Display the second	h:m:s displays 1:01:01 as *1:1:1*.
ss	Display the second with a leading zero	hh:mm:ss displays 1:01:01 as *1:01:01*.

TABLE 16-1   Codes for Creating Custom Formats *(continued)*

Code	Meaning	Example
.0, .00, .000	Display tenths, hundredths, or thousandths of seconds	h:mm:ss.00 displays 1:01:01.11 as *1:01:01.11*. Use further zeroes for greater precision.
A/P	Display A for A.M. and P for P.M.	h:mm A/P displays 1:01 as *1:01 A*. You can use uppercase A/P or lowercase a/p to specify which case to display.
AM/PM	Display AM for A.M. and PM for P.M.	h:mm am/pm displays 13:01 as *1:01 PM*. Excel uses uppercase whichever case you use.
[]	Display the elapsed time in the specified unit	[h]:mm:ss displays the elapsed time in hours, minutes, and seconds—for example, *33:22:01*.
Text Format Codes		
_	Display a space as wide as the specified character	_) makes Excel enter a space the width of a closing parenthesis—for example, to align positive numbers with negative numbers surrounded by parentheses.
*	Repeat the specified character to fill the cell	*A makes Excel fill the cell with A characters. This is sometimes useful for drawing attention to particular values—for example, zero values.
\	Display the following character	[Blue]$#,###.00 *;[Red]$#,###.00 \D displays positive numbers in blue and followed by an asterisk, and negative numbers in red and followed by a *D*.
"string"	Display the string of text	$#,##0.00" Advance" displays *Advance* after the entry. Note the leading space between the " and the word.
@	Concatenate the specified string with the user's text input	"Username: "@ enters **Username:** and a space before the user's text input. This works only in the fourth section (the text section) of a custom format.
N/A	Display the specified character	$ - + = / ( ) { } : ! ^ & ' ' ~ < > [space]

TABLE 16-1   Codes for Creating Custom Formats *(continued)*

Applying Visual Formatting

After specifying how Excel should represent the data you enter in the cells of your worksheets, you'll probably want to apply formatting to the worksheets to make them more readable. Excel offers a wide range of formatting options, most of which are easy to understand and which you can apply to a cell or range.

The following list outlines the main types of formatting that Excel offers. The primary way of applying these formatting options is the Format Cells dialog box.

- **Font formatting**   Change fonts, font size, font style (regular, bold, italic, or bold italic), underline, and color. When you change the formatting, Excel deselects the Normal Font option. Reselect this option to reapply the normal font—in other words, removing all font formatting you've applied to the selection.

- **Alignment formatting**   Change the horizontal and vertical alignment of the cells. Options include horizontal centering across the selection (which can be useful for centering a heading over several columns), vertical centering in a cell whose height you've increased, and indentation.

- **Orientation and text-direction formatting**   Specify the orientation of the text: for example, set text at a slant for special emphasis, or create a vertical heading to save space. Specify the direction of the text: Left-to-Right, Right-to-Left, or Context (Excel decides based on the context).

- **Text-control formatting**   Choose whether to wrap text in the cell, shrink it to fit the cell, or merge multiple cells into one cell. Wrapping text can greatly improve long entries, and you can break lines manually by pressing ALT-ENTER.

CAUTION   Be careful with the Shrink to Fit option. When it resizes the display of some cells to make their contents fit the column but leaves other cells at full size, it can produce the effect of formatting errors. For more control, resize your columns or fonts manually.

- **Border formatting**   Apply borders of assorted weights, styles, and colors around or across cells. For example, you might put a double line across the top of a cell containing a total. Select the style and color, and then click the Preview pane to apply a line. Click an applied line to remove it.

- **Pattern formatting**   Apply solid shades of color or colored patterns to add emphasis or create a design.

- **Protection formatting**   Choose whether to lock or hide particular cells. Locking and hiding take effect only when you protect the worksheet. "Protecting Cells, a Worksheet, or Workbook," later in this chapter, explains how to protect your work.

TIP   To copy formatting from one cell or a range or cells to another cell or range of cells, use the Format Painter button on the Standard toolbar. You can apply the formatting to multiple cells by double-clicking the Format Painter button first. After applying the formatting, press ESC or click the Format Painter button again.

Formatting Rows and Columns

In most worksheets you create, you'll need to change some columns from their standard widths to widths better suited to the data entered in their cells. Similarly, you may need to change row height—for example, to accommodate objects or taller text that you enter for headings.

The fastest and most effective way to change the width of a column or the height of a row is by using Excel's AutoFit feature. AutoFit resizes a column to just wider than its widest entry, and resizes a row to just high enough for its tallest character or object. To use AutoFit, double-click the right border bar of a column header or the bottom border bar of a row header. Alternatively, select the column and choose Format | Column | AutoFit Selection, or select a cell in the row and choose Format | Row | AutoFit. (You need to select either the whole column or its widest cell. Otherwise, Excel resizes the column to fit the selected cell.)

You can also change column width and row height manually by dragging the appropriate column border bar or row border bar. Excel displays a ScreenTip showing you the size to which you've currently dragged. The column-width ScreenTip shows the number of characters and the number of pixels. The row-height ScreenTip shows the number of points and the number of pixels.

The most formal way to change column width is to choose Format | Column | Width and enter the width in characters in the Column Width dialog box. Valid values are 0–255 characters. Similarly, you can change row height by choosing Format | Row | Height and entering the row height in points in the Row Height dialog box. Valid values are 0–409 points.

NOTE *You can change the standard column width for the active worksheet by choosing Format | Column | Standard Width, entering the width you want, and clicking OK. Excel doesn't apply this new standard width to any columns you've already adjusted.*

You can hide rows and columns by choosing Format | Row | Hide or Format | Column | Hide. Hidden rows and columns can be a great way of hiding the workings of your spreadsheets from inquisitive eyes, but you have to be aware of them when you copy data and paste it: unless you use Paste Special to limit the data pasted, Excel includes hidden rows and columns. This can produce some unpleasant surprises.

To redisplay hidden rows or columns, select the row headings or column headings around the hidden rows or columns, or select the whole worksheet to redisplay all hidden rows and columns. Then choose Format | Row | Unhide or Format | Column | Unhide.

TIP *Use the Column Widths option in the Paste Special dialog box to copy column widths to another worksheet without including their data.*

Conditional Formatting

The formatting we've examined so far is constant formatting—once you've applied it to a cell, range, column, or row, there it stays until you change it. But Excel also supports *conditional formatting*: formatting that Excel uses only when the specified conditions are met. Typical uses of conditional formatting include drawing attention to missing data or to figures that deviate significantly from expectations—for example, Stakhanovite productivity statistics or evidence of terminal idleness.

Conditional formatting is similar to the effect produced by some predefined number formats—for example, those that display negative numbers in a different color—but more subtle, in that you can set careful triggers for applying the formatting.

To apply conditional formatting:

1. Choose Format | Conditional Formatting. Excel displays the Conditional Formatting dialog box, shown here with two conditions entered:

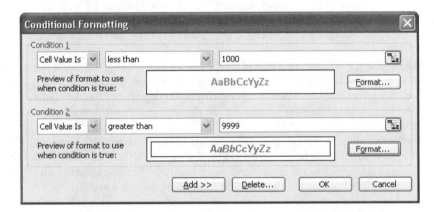

2. Use the options in the Condition 1 section to specify the condition:

   • Choose the Cell Value Is option or the Formula Is option as appropriate.

   • Choose the appropriate comparison: Between, Not Between, Equal To, Not Equal To, Greater Than, Less Than, Greater Than or Equal To, or Less Than or Equal To.

   • Specify the point or points of comparison. You can enter values or cell addresses.

3. Click Format and use the abbreviated version of the Format Cells dialog box to specify the formatting to use. This version of the dialog box offers only Font, Border, and Patterns tabs.

4. Click Add to add another condition, or click OK to finish.

NOTE   *If you use multiple conditions, Excel evaluates them in order and stops evaluating them after it finds one that's true.*

AutoFormat

Excel's AutoFormat feature provides a variety of canned formats for adding font formatting, borders, shading, and colors to your worksheets. To use AutoFormat:

1. Enter your data and arrange it to your satisfaction. (For example, sort the data into order.)

2. Select the range you want to affect.

NOTE   *If you don't select a range, AutoFormat uses the current region—the cells around the active cell up to the first empty row and empty column in each direction. In many cases, the current region will be larger than you want to affect, so usually, it's best to select the range manually when applying AutoFormat.*

3. Choose Format | AutoFormat. Excel displays the AutoFormat dialog box, shown here with its options displayed:

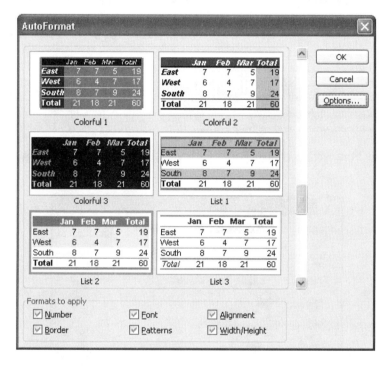

4. Select the automatic format you want.

5. To specify which elements of the automatic format are applied, click Options. Then select or deselect the Formats to Apply options as appropriate.

6. Click OK.

Using Styles in Excel

Like Word's documents and templates, Excel's workbooks and templates include a number of built-in styles that you can use to apply predefined sets of formatting quickly and easily. You can also create your own styles to meet your own formatting needs, and you can copy styles from one workbook or template to another workbook or template that you want to use them in.

Each default new workbook contains the styles Normal, Comma (for showing two decimal places), Comma [0] (for showing integers only), Currency (for showing two decimal places), Currency [0] (for showing integers only), Percent, Hyperlink (for links the user hasn't followed), and Followed Hyperlink.

Applying a Style

Normal style is applied to all cells in the default workbook format. You can apply the Comma style, the Percent style, and the Currency style from the corresponding buttons on the Formatting toolbar. Excel applies the Hyperlink style automatically to any cell in which you enter a recognizable URL or path, and changes the style to Followed Hyperlink when the link is clicked.

NOTE *You can turn off Excel's automatic creation of hyperlinks in two ways. Either display the AutoFormat as You Type tab of the AutoCorrect dialog box (Tools | AutoCorrect Options) and deselect the Internet and Network Paths with Hyperlinks option, or click the Smart Tag on a changed hyperlink and choose Stop Automatically Creating Hyperlinks from the menu.*

To apply the other styles, choose Format | Style, choose the style in the Style dialog box, and click OK.

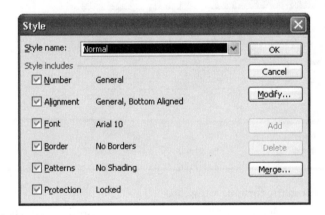

Creating Your Own Styles

To create your own styles:

1. Apply the formatting for the style to a cell.

2. Select that cell.

3. Choose Format | Style.

4. In the Style Name text box, enter the name for the new style. Excel changes the Style Includes area's name to Style Includes (By Example).

5. Deselect any check boxes for formatting that you don't want to include in the style.

6. Click OK.

Modifying a Style

To modify an existing style to better suit your needs:

1. Display the Style dialog box.

2. Select the style.

3. Click Modify. Excel displays the Format Cells dialog box.

4. Specify the new formatting for the style, and then click OK.

5. In the Style dialog box, click OK.

Merging Styles from Another Workbook

To copy styles from one workbook (or template) to another, you perform what Excel calls a *merge styles* operation. To do so:

1. Open the source workbook (or template) and the destination workbook (or template).

2. Activate the destination workbook (or template).

3. Choose Format | Style.

4. Click Merge. Excel displays the Merge Styles dialog box.

5. Select the source workbook (or template) and click OK.

6. In the Style dialog box, click OK.

Restricting Data and Protecting Workbooks

By default, Excel workbooks are open for editing: anyone who can access an Excel workbook in their computer's file system can open it and change it, or simply delete it. Such openness makes for easy work, but chances are that you won't want colleagues you barely know manipulating your valuable data or poking subtle alterations into your formulas. And you may want to restrict even your trusted colleagues from changing the design of your worksheets when they're only supposed to enter a few missing figures in particular cells.

Excel enables you to restrict other people's ability to change your workbooks in several different ways. You can restrict data entry in particular cells to make sure nobody enters invalid data. You can protect specific cells and protect a whole workbook against any change, or you can protect a worksheet but still allow users to edit certain ranges in it. Finally, you can password-protect a workbook either so that only people who know the password can open it or so that only people who know the password can modify it.

NOTE   *Your first line of defense for your Excel workbooks (and any other important files) should be to store them where people you don't want to access them can't get at them. Depending on your situation, such a location might be on your hard disk or in a network folder to which access is tightly controlled.*

Checking Data Entry for Invalid Entries

You can greatly reduce data-entry problems in your workbooks by making Excel check entries before entering them in specific cells. To do so, you define restrictions and data-validation rules for those cells. For example, often you'll need to make sure that a number the user enters is within a certain range, to prevent him or her from accidentally entering a different order of magnitude with a misplaced finger. Similarly, on an application form for permission to travel to an affiliate office, you could use a drop-down list of the possible destinations to prevent the user from typing in any other destination.

To check data entry for invalid entries:

1. Select the cell or range you want to affect.

2. Choose Data | Validation. Excel displays the Data Validation dialog box.

3. On the Settings tab (shown here), specify the validation criteria to use. Select the appropriate type (see the following list) in the Allow drop-down list, and then set parameters accordingly.

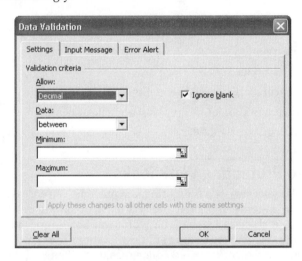

You have the following choices in the Allow drop-down box:

- **Any Value**   Accepts any input (Excel's default setting for cells). Use this to display an informational message for a cell or to remove validation.

- **Whole Number**   Lets you specify a comparison operator (see the following Note) and appropriate values. The user must not enter a decimal point.

NOTE   *The validation criteria use these comparison operators: Between, Not Between, Equal To, Not Equal To, Greater Than, Less Than, Greater Than or Equal To, and Less Than or Equal To.*

- **Decimal**   Lets you specify a comparison and appropriate values. The user must include a decimal point and at least one decimal place (even if it's .0).

- **List**   Lets you specify a list of valid entries for the cell. You can type in entries in the Source text box, separating them with commas, but the best form of source is a range on a worksheet in this workbook. If you hide the worksheet, the users won't trip over it. Usually, you'll want to select the In-Cell Dropdown option to produce a drop-down list in the cell. Otherwise, users have to know the entries (or enter them from the help message).

- **Date**   Lets you specify a comparison operator and appropriate dates (including formulas).

- **Time**   Lets you specify a comparison operator and appropriate times (including formulas).

- **Text Length**   Lets you specify a comparison operator and appropriate values (including formulas).

- **Custom**   Lets you specify a formula that returns a logical TRUE or a logical FALSE value.

4. Select or deselect the Ignore Blank option as appropriate.

5. On the Input Message tab (shown next), choose whether to have Excel display an input message when the cell is selected. If you leave this option selected (as it is by default), enter the title and input message.

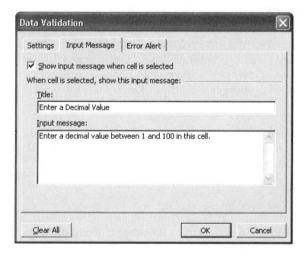

6. On the Error Alert tab, choose whether to have Excel display an error alert after the user enters invalid data in the cell. If you leave this option selected (as it is by default), choose the style (Stop, Warning, or Information), and enter the title and error message. Stop alerts prevent users from continuing until they enter a valid value for the cell. Warning alerts and Information alerts display the message but allow users to continue after entering an invalid value in the cell.

7. Click OK.

When a user selects a restricted cell, Excel displays the information message (unless you chose not to display one), as shown at the top of Figure 16-1. If the user enters an invalid value, Excel displays the appropriate alert message box. The bottom of Figure 16-1 shows an example of a Stop alert box.

CAUTION   *A user can bypass validation by pasting data into the cell instead of typing it in.*

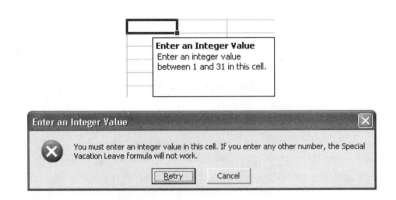

Protecting Cells, a Worksheet, or Workbook

The next stage in preventing users from mangling your workbooks is to prevent them from accessing cells they're not supposed to change. Excel offers several means of doing this: you can lock cells so that users can't change them; you can lock a workbook or a worksheet with a password to prevent changes; and you can password-protect a workbook against being opened or modified by people who don't know the password.

Locking a Cell or Range

To lock a cell or range, select it, choose Format | Cells, and select the Locked option on the Protection tab of the Format Cells dialog box. After locking one or more cells, you need to protect the workbook to make the locking take effect.

Protecting a Workbook

To prevent other users from changing a workbook, you protect it:

1. Choose Tools | Protection | Protect Workbook. Excel displays the Protect Workbook dialog box.

2. Choose whether to protect the structure of the workbook, the positions of its windows, or both. Protecting the structure prevents users from making changes to the worksheets—inserting or deleting them, hiding or displaying them, or renaming them.

3. Enter a password. The password is optional—but without one, the protection is worthless. With a weak password, the protection is worth little, so use a strong password—that is, a password that isn't a real word in any language; that contains at least six characters; and that includes letters, numbers, and symbols.

4. Click OK. If you used a password, confirm it in the Confirm Password dialog box and click OK.

To unprotect a workbook, choose Tools | Protection | Unprotect Workbook, enter your password, and click OK.

Protecting a Worksheet

Excel also enables you to protect one or more worksheets in a workbook:

1. Choose Tools | Protection | Protect Sheet. Excel displays the Protect Sheet dialog box:

2. Ensure that the Protect Worksheet and Contents of Locked Cells option is selected.

3. Enter a strong password.

4. Select or deselect the Allow All Users of This Worksheet To options to specify which actions all users may take with this worksheet.

5. Click OK.

6. Confirm the password in the Confirm Password dialog box and click OK.

To unprotect a worksheet, choose Tools | Protection | Unprotect Worksheet, enter your password, and click OK.

Allowing Users to Edit Ranges in a Protected Worksheet

When you protect a worksheet, you may want to allow users to edit specific ranges—for example, so they can fill in certain data (perhaps in validated cells) without changing other parts of the worksheet. Excel lets you do the following:

- Leave a range unprotected so that any user can edit it.

- Password-protect a range so that only users who can supply the password can edit the range.

- Password-protect a range (as above) but exempt specific users from having to supply the password. For example, you might exempt yourself from the password so you can edit the worksheet easily.

- Protect different ranges with different passwords to implement different levels of access to different groups of users with whom you share the passwords. For example, you might allow a group to edit most ranges but reserve other ranges for administrators.

To allow users to edit ranges in a protected worksheet:

1. Choose Tools | Protection | Allow Users to Edit Ranges. Excel displays the Allow Users to Edit Ranges dialog box, shown at the top of Figure 16-2 with some ranges created.

2. Create as many ranges as necessary by clicking the New button and working in the New Range dialog box (shown at the bottom of Figure 16-2):

   - Name each range (preferably descriptively), and specify which cells it refers to.

   - Enter a password if you want to use a password to restrict access to the range. You may want to leave the range open so anyone can edit it without a password.

   - If you use a password, click Permissions and use the Permissions dialog box to specify which users are permitted to edit the range without a password. Remember to add yourself if appropriate.

FIGURE 16-2
Using these two dialog boxes, you can allow named users to edit specific ranges in a protected worksheet.

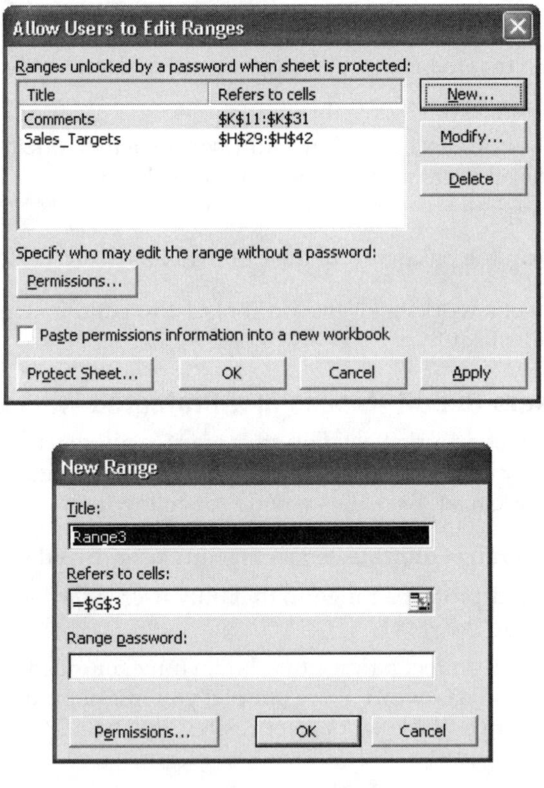

3. If necessary, click Modify to modify an existing range, or click Delete to delete an existing range. Select a range and click Permissions to change the permissions on it.

4. Click Protect Sheet to display the Protect Sheet dialog box, and then proceed as described in the previous section. (Alternatively, click OK to close the Allow Users to Edit Ranges dialog box, and protect your worksheet manually later.)

NOTE   To track the ranges, titles, password protection, and password-exempt users, select the option Paste Permissions Information into a New Workbook. When you close the Allow Users to Edit Ranges dialog box, Excel creates a new workbook with details of the ranges. Save this somewhere convenient for reference, or move the top worksheet to a workbook in which you store details of all your shared workbooks.

5. Save the workbook that contains the worksheet.

When a user tries to make an entry in a protected cell, Excel displays the Unlock Range dialog box demanding the password. If the user can't supply the password, Excel doesn't allow the entry in the cell.

Protecting a Workbook with Passwords

To keep users out of your workbooks without authorization, you can apply Open passwords and Modify passwords to them. An Open password requires the user to enter the password to open the workbook at all. A Modify password lets the user open the workbook in read-only format without a password. To open the workbook for editing, the user must supply the password.

To protect a workbook with a password:

1. Choose Tools | Options, and then click the Security tab.

2. To apply an Open password, enter it in the Password to Open box. If appropriate, click the Advanced button and specify an encryption type and appropriate details in the Encryption Type dialog box.

3. To apply a Modify password, enter it in the Password to Modify box.

4. Click OK.

5. Confirm the password in the Confirm Password dialog box and click OK.

6. Save your workbook.

The next time you open the workbook, you'll be prompted for the password. In the case of a Modify password, Excel will offer a Read Only button that you (or the user) can click to open the workbook in read-only mode. You can then change the workbook (depending on other forms of protection used) and save the results under a new name. You can't save changes to the original workbook.

To remove the password, delete the password from the Security tab of the Options dialog box and save the workbook again.

Using AutoFill

To enable you to fill in series of data quickly and easily in your worksheets, Excel provides the AutoFill feature. You select one, two, or more cells that contain the basis for a series, then drag the AutoFill handle to show AutoFill the range of cells you want to fill with the series of data. AutoFill analyzes the starting cells, determines what the contents of the other cells should be, and enters the information automatically.

The best way to get the hang of AutoFill is to play around with it for a few minutes. Open a new, blank workbook and try the following examples to see how AutoFill works and what it does:

- Enter **January** in cell A1 and drag the AutoFill handle to cell D1. As you drag, AutoFill displays a ScreenTip to show you the entry that the current cell will receive, as shown in the following illustration. When you release the mouse button, AutoFill enters the months February through April in the selected cells.

- Press CTRL-Z to undo the AutoFill operation, and then drag the AutoFill handle from cell A1 to cell M1 instead. AutoFill will start repeating the list and enter January in cell M1.

- Enter **0** in cell A2 and **5** in cell A3, select those cells, and then drag the AutoFill handle down column A. AutoFill continues the sequence by adding 5 to each number it enters in the successive cells.

NOTE   *The AutoFill series must be contained in a single row or a single column—it can't cover a range consisting of multiple rows and columns at once.*

- Drag the AutoFill handle from cell A3 to the right. AutoFill repeats the data in cell A3 (5), because there's no progression. You can use this behavior to extend a text label over a range of cells.

- Hold down CTRL and drag the AutoFill handle from cell A3 to the right. Holding down CTRL forces AutoFill to increment the number entered in the single cell over the AutoFill range rather than copy the number.

- Enter **Monday** in cell B2 and press CTRL-B to make it boldface. Then right-drag the AutoFill handle across to cell H2 and release the mouse button. AutoFill displays a context menu that includes options such as Copy Series, Fill Series, Fill Formatting Only, Fill Without Formatting, Fill Days, and Fill Weekdays. (For other content, the options Fill Months, Fill Years, Linear Trend, Growth Trend, and Series will be available as appropriate.) Select the appropriate item. For example, select Fill Formatting Only to fill the series with the formatting from cell B2 but skip filling the cells with the content.

You can change the item that AutoFill has entered by clicking the AutoFill Options Smart Tag that appears below and to the right of the last cell in an AutoFill series and choosing the appropriate option from the resulting menu.

Creating Custom AutoFill Lists

In addition to being able to extrapolate AutoFill sequences from data in cells, Excel includes several custom lists for frequently used data: months, three-letter months (Jan, Feb), days of the week, and three-letter days of the week (Sun, Mon). You can supplement these by defining your own lists.

To create a custom list:

1. Choose Tools | Options.

2. Display the Custom Lists tab:

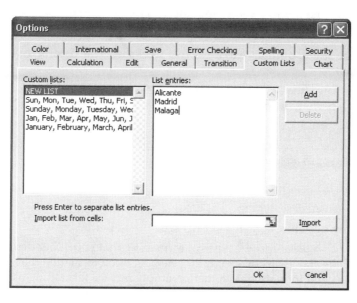

3. Select the NEW LIST item.

4. Enter the list items in the List Entries text box, one to a line.

5. Click Add.

NOTE   *You can also import an existing list from a range of cells in a worksheet. Click the button at the right end of the Import List from Cells box to minimize the Options dialog box, select the range in the worksheet, and then click Import. (Alternatively, select the range of cells before displaying the Options dialog box.)*

To delete a custom list, select it in the Custom Lists box and click Delete.

Find and Replace

Like the other Office applications, Excel includes find and replace functionality. Compared with the myriad options in Word's version of find and replace, Excel's version is refreshingly straightforward to use—but it offers plenty of power to make sweeping changes in your worksheets in moments.

To find items, choose Edit | Find from the menu, or press CTRL-F. To replace items, choose Edit | Replace, or press CTRL-H. Excel displays the Find tab or the Replace tab of the Find and Replace dialog box.

By default, Excel displays the reduced version of the Find and Replace dialog box. For a basic Find operation, enter the search text in the Find What text box, and click Find Next to find the next occurrence or Find All to find all occurrences. For a basic Replace operation, enter the search text and replacement text, and then use the Find Next, Find All, Replace, and Replace All buttons as appropriate.

For more options, click the Options button to reveal the rest of the dialog box. The top screen in Figure 16-3 shows the full Find tab of the Find and Replace dialog box. The bottom screen in Figure 16-3 shows the full Replace tab.

The extra options enable you to:

- Extend the search or replace to the active worksheet (the default) or the entire workbook.

- Search by rows (the default) or by columns. Searching by columns can be quicker, but search performance is rarely an issue unless you're working with colossal worksheets.

TIP   *To reverse the search direction, hold down* SHIFT *and click Find Next.*

- Search formulas, values, or comments.

- Use case-sensitive searching.

- Match only the entire contents of cells rather than partial contents.

- Search for or replace specific types of formatting that you either define using the Format Cells dialog box or specify by selecting a cell formatted that way. You can replace text and formatting together or simply replace formatting on its own. This allows you to make sweeping changes to the formatting of your workbooks.

FIGURE 16-3
The Find tab (top) and Replace tab (bottom) of the Find and Replace dialog box

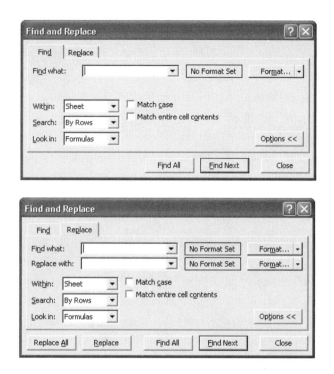

TIP   *If you can't find an item you're sure is in the worksheet, make sure that Find isn't set to use formatting. Click Format and choose Clear Find Format.*

Calculating with Formulas and Functions

To manipulate data and perform calculations with Excel, you use formulas and functions; so knowing the difference between the two and how to create formulas and use functions in your worksheets are key steps in using Excel. Once you know the basics (or if you already know them), you'll learn how to troubleshoot formulas when they go wrong, how to monitor calculations with the Watch window, use array formulas, and perform goal seeking and statistical analysis. The last part of the chapter covers the categories of functions in Excel and some sample functions.

Understanding What Formulas and Functions Are

A *formula* is a set of instructions for performing a calculation. Excel enables you to create a very wide range of formulas for performing whatever types of calculations you need.

Each formula begins with an equal sign, so the standard way of starting to enter a formula is to type an equal sign. However, Excel automatically enters the equal sign if you type + or – at the start of a formula, so you don't always need to type the equal sign.

Excel includes a large number of *functions*—built-in, predefined formulas for standard calculations. Excel's functions range from the everyday to the highly specialized. For example, the SUM() function adds two or more values together and displays the result, whereas the MINVERSE() function produces the inverse matrix for a specific matrix. SUM() is very widely used, MINVERSE() much less so.

A formula can contain up to seven nested functions—enough to enable you to perform highly complex calculations.

Components of a Formula

In a formula, you need to tell Excel which items to use and which operation or operations to perform on them. To do so, you use operands and operators.

Operands

The *operands* in a formula specify the data you want to calculate. An operand can be

- A constant value you enter in the formula itself (for example, **=8*12**) or in a cell (for example, **=B1*8**)
- A cell address, range address, or range name
- A worksheet function

Operators

Excel uses arithmetic operators, logical operators, reference operators, and one text operator. Table 17-1 explains these operators.

Operator	Explanation
Arithmetic Operators	
+	Addition
–	Subtraction
*	Multiplication
/	Division
%	Percent
^	Exponentiation
Logical Operators	
=	Equal to
<>	Not equal to
>	Greater than
>=	Greater than or equal to
<	Less than
<=	Less than or equal to
Reference Operators	
:	Range of contiguous cells (for example, A1:C16)
,	Range of noncontiguous cells (for example, A1, B2)
[space]	The cell or range shared by two references. For example, =SUM(B1:B10 A5:D6) adds the contents of cells B5 and B6, because these cells are at the intersection of the ranges B1:B10 and A5:D6.
Text Operator	
&	Concatenates (joins) the specified values. For example, if cell A1 contains 50 and cell A2 contains 50, the formula **=A1&A2** returns *5050*—the cell contents joined together rather than added together.

TABLE 17-1   Operators for Formulas

Understanding and Changing Operator Precedence

When a formula contains only one operator, you don't have to worry about the order in which Excel handles operators. But as soon as you create a formula that contains two or more different operators, you need to know the order in which they'll be evaluated. For example, consider the formula **=1000–100*5**. Does Excel subtract 100 from 1000 and multiply the result (900) by 5, giving 4500? Or does Excel multiply 100 by 5 and subtract the result (500) from 1000, giving 500? As you can see, the same calculation gives hugely different results depending on the order in which its operations are performed.

In fact, Excel multiplies 100 by 5 and subtracts 500 from 1000 using its default settings, so the result is 500. The following list shows the order of *operator precedence*—the order in which Excel evaluates the operators—in descending order. When a formula uses two operators that share a precedence, Excel evaluates the operators from left to right, in the same direction as you read.

Operator	Explanation
–	Negation (negative numbers)
%	Percentage
^	Exponentiation
*, /	Multiplication, division
+, –	Addition, subtraction
&	Concatenation
=, <>, <, <=, >, >=	Comparison operators

You can change operator precedence in a formula by using parentheses to indicate which items you want to calculate first. For example, to evaluate the formula **=1000–100*5** the other way, you would enter it **=(1000–100)*5**. Excel would subtract 100 from 1000 and then multiply the result (900) by 5.

When you nest multiple items, Excel evaluates the most deeply nested item first. For example, in the formula **=(100–(10*5))/20**, Excel evaluates 10*5 first, because that item is nested within two sets of parentheses. You can use many levels of nested parentheses if necessary.

TIP *If you find it hard to remember the order of operator precedence, you can use parentheses even when they're not strictly necessary.*

When you're editing a formula, Excel displays differently nested parentheses in different colors to help you keep track of which parenthesis is paired with which. When you use the LEFT ARROW and RIGHT ARROW keys to move through a formula that you're editing in the active cell or in the Formula bar, Excel flashes the paired parenthesis for each parenthesis you move over. If you omit a parenthesis in a formula, Excel does its best to warn you of the problem and identify where the missing parenthesis should go.

Even with Excel's help, however, formulas with many deeply nested items can be confusing to enter and difficult to troubleshoot when they don't produce the results you expect. If math isn't your forte, you may prefer to break a complex calculation down into a sequence of steps that you perform in separate cells. That way, you can trace the steps of the calculation more easily. And you can hide the rows or columns that contain the cells (or use a hidden worksheet) if you prefer not to let other people see them.

Controlling Excel's Automatic Calculation

As discussed in "Calculation Options" in Chapter 15, Excel's default setting is to automatically calculate all formulas all the time. If you're using a worksheet or workbook with enough data and complex calculations to slow your computer down while you're entering data in the workbook, you may prefer to turn off automatic calculation.

If you do turn off automatic calculation, Excel displays *Calculate* in the status bar when the workbook contains uncalculated calculations. You can force calculation manually for the active worksheet by pressing CTRL-F9 and for the entire active workbook by pressing F9.

How Excel Handles Numbers

Numbers in Excel aren't necessarily as precise as they appear to be. To avoid running into avoidable errors in your calculations, you should understand how Excel handles numbers.

The key limitation is that numbers in Excel can be up to 15 digits long. Those 15 digits can appear on either side of the decimal point—for example, 123456789012345, 1234567 .89012345, or .123456789012345. Excel changes all digits beyond the 15th to 0. So if you enter **1234567890123456**, Excel actually uses 1234567890123450. For very precise calculations, this truncation can cause problems.

You can format Excel to display up to 30 decimal places, but there's no reason to do so.

Referring to Cells and Ranges in Your Formulas

To refer to a cell or a range in a formula, enter its address either by typing or by using the mouse. When you use the mouse, Excel displays a flashing border to indicate the cell or range selected. When a formula includes two or more ranges, Excel uses different-colored borders to help you keep them straight.

To refer to a whole column, specify its letter as the beginning and end of the range. For example, to make column K reflect the contents of column C, click the column heading for column K, enter **=C:C**, and press CTRL-ENTER.

Similarly, to refer to a whole row, specify its number as the beginning and end of the range: for example, **4:4**. To refer to a set of columns, specify the beginning and ending letters: for example, **A:D**. To refer to a set of rows, specify the beginning and ending numbers: for example, **1:2**.

Referring to Other Worksheets in Your Formulas

To refer to another worksheet in a formula, enter the worksheet name (in single quotes if the name includes one or more spaces) and an exclamation point (!) before the cell address or range address. You can type the name if you choose, but most people find it easier to click the worksheet tab and select the cell or range. That way, Excel enters the details automatically for you, including single quotes if they're necessary.

If you rename a worksheet, Excel automatically changes the sheet name in all formulas that reference the worksheet.

Example of Entering a Formula

Here's an example of creating a simple formula:

1. Enter **2000** in cell A1, **4000** in cell A2, and **2** in cell B1.
2. Select cell B2.
3. Type **=(**.
4. Click cell A1. Excel enters it in the formula.
5. Type **+**.
6. Click cell A2. Excel enters it in the formula.
7. Type **)/**.
8. Click cell B1.
9. Press ENTER or click the Enter button to enter the formula.

Excel completes the formula and displays the result in cell B2.

TIP   *You can quickly copy a formula from one cell to other cells by using the Copy and Paste commands, by using CTRL-drag and drop, by using the options on the Edit | Fill submenu, or by dragging the AutoFill handle.*

Using Range Names and Labels in Formulas

An easy way of referring to a cell or a range is to define a name for it. ("Naming a Range" in Chapter 15 discusses how to define range names.) You can then use the range name in your formulas instead of specifying the cell address or range address. This technique is particularly useful for simplifying the process of referring to cells and ranges on other worksheets in a workbook.

CAUTION   *If you use range names in your formulas, be very careful when deleting range names. Otherwise, any formula that references the deleted range will display a #NAME? error.*

Another method of simplifying the process of entering formulas in worksheets that include row labels and column labels is to use labels to reference cell addresses. Using labels like this can save time and effort, but there are some potential problems you'll learn about in a minute. So by default this feature is turned off. To turn it on, choose Tools | Options, select the Accept Labels in Formulas option on the Calculations tab, and click OK.

To use labels to denote a reference, you specify the appropriate row label and column label with a space between the two. For example, the following worksheet contains the column labels Shanghai, Rangoon, and Hong Kong, and the row labels January, February, and March:

SQRT	▼	X ✓ fx	= Shanghai January + 'Hong Kong' January		
	A	B	C	D	E	F
1		**Shanghai**	**Rangoon**	**Hong Kong**		
2	**January**	90	65	204		
3	**February**	100	68	206		
4	**March**	110	71	202		
5		= Shanghai January + 'Hong Kong' January				

Cell B5 uses the formula **=Shanghai January + 'Hong Kong' January** to add cell B2 (the intersection of the Shanghai column and the January row) and cell D2 (the intersection of the Hong Kong column and the January row). Similarly, you could enter **=AVERAGE(Rangoon)** to average the contents of the Rangoon column.

As you can see in that example, you need to use single quotes around a label that contains one or more spaces so that Excel knows it should treat the label as a unit rather than as an intersection. Likewise, you need to use single quotes around any label that Excel would otherwise mistake for a cell address (for example, FY2003 or I80).

Labels can greatly simplify formulas, and Excel is designed to handle them intelligently. For example, AutoFill can extend formulas that contain labels, and Excel alters formulas appropriately when you use copy and paste to copy a formula that contains labels to a new location. Similarly, Excel updates all formulas that reference a label you alter.

However, you must watch out for the following problems:

- **Duplicate labels**   If you have two or more instances of a label, Excel can get confused as to which you mean.

- **Adding or deleting columns or rows**   If you add or delete columns or rows at the edge of a range referenced by a formula using a label, Excel may fail to change the formula accordingly. After adding or deleting columns or rows, it's best to edit each formula that might be affected and make sure the area it references is correct. Making this extra check can take more time than using labels saves you, so it can be a strong disincentive to using labels.

- **Merging cells**   When you merge cells, Excel stores their contents in the upper-left merged cell. If you merge row or column headings, you'll produce #NAME? errors in formulas that use labels referring to merged cells other than the upper-left cell.

Because of these potential problems, you may find it safer not to use labels in your formulas. To turn off the use of labels, clear the Accept Labels in Formulas option on the Calculation tab of the Options dialog box (Tools | Options). When you do this, Excel warns you that it will replace any labels used in formulas with cell references so that your formulas will continue to work. Click Yes to make this change.

Using Absolute, Relative, and Mixed References

Excel distinguishes between three kinds of references for cells and ranges: absolute references, relative references, and mixed references.

- An *absolute reference* always refers to the same cell, even when you move or copy it to another cell or range. For example, if you enter in cell A1 a formula that contains an absolute reference to cell B1, and then move the formula to cell C1, the reference will still be to cell B1.

- A *relative reference* refers to a cell's position relative to the cell that contains the formula. For example, if you enter in cell A1 a formula that contains a relative reference to cell B2, Excel notes that the reference is to one column over and one row down. If you move the formula to cell B1, Excel changes the relative reference to refer to cell C2, because C2 is one column over and one row down from the new location of the formula.

- A *mixed reference* is a mixture of an absolute reference and a relative reference. A mixed reference can be absolute in column and relative in row, or relative in column and absolute in row.

To tell Excel whether a reference is absolute, relative, or mixed, you use dollar signs ($). A dollar sign before a column designation means that the column is absolute; no dollar sign means that the column is relative. A dollar sign before a row number means that the row is absolute; no dollar sign means that the row is relative. For example:

- $A$1 is an absolute reference to cell A1.
- A1 is a relative reference to cell A1.
- $A1 is a mixed reference to cell A1 with the column absolute.
- A$1 is a mixed reference to cell A1 with the row absolute.

Excel's default setting is to use relative references, so if you need to use absolute references, you need to change them. The easiest way to change the reference type is by selecting the reference in a formula and pressing F4 to cycle through the options: absolute ($A$1), mixed with absolute row (A$1), mixed with absolute column ($A1), and relative. You can also type the necessary dollar signs manually.

CAUTION *If you move a formula by using cut and paste, Excel doesn't change any relative references that the formula contains.*

Displaying Formulas

When editing or troubleshooting formulas, you may benefit from displaying the formulas themselves rather than their results in the cells that contain them. To toggle the display between formula results and formulas, press CTRL-` or choose Tools | Options, select or deselect the Formulas option on the View tab, and click OK.

PART III

When displaying formulas, Excel automatically increases column width so that you can see more of each formula. Excel restores the previous column widths when you redisplay the formula results.

Hiding Your Formulas from Other Users

You can prevent other users from examining or editing your formulas by formatting the relevant cells as hidden and then protecting the worksheet or worksheets:

1. Select the cell or range of cells that contain the formulas.
2. Press CTRL-1 or choose Format | Cells.
3. Select the Hidden option on the Protection tab. Make sure the Locked option is selected as well (it should be selected by default).
4. Click OK to close the Format Cells dialog box.
5. Choose Tools | Protection | Protect Sheet.
6. Make sure the Protect Worksheet and Contents of Locked Cells option is selected.
7. Type the password for protecting the worksheet.
8. Click OK to close the Protect Sheet dialog box, type the password again in the Confirm Password dialog box, and click OK.

Troubleshooting Formulas

No matter how careful you are, many things can go wrong with formulas, and you need to know how to go about troubleshooting them. Eight common errors appear frequently in formulas, so we'll show you how to fix them. Some apparent errors are actually caused by formatting, whereas real errors tend to be caused by problems with operator precedence and range changes. Excel offers automatic error-checking features, such as the Formula AutoCorrect feature; you can supplement or replace this automatic checking with manual checking as needed.

Understanding and Fixing Basic Errors

Table 17-2 explains the eight errors you're most likely to see in your worksheets, in approximate order of popularity, and tells you what to do to fix them.

Fixing Formatting, Operator Precedence, and Range-Change Errors

Beyond the basic errors explained in the previous section, you may also run into apparent errors caused by formatting, real errors caused by Excel's default order of operator precedence, and real errors caused by the ranges referenced in formulas being changed.

Formatting Makes the Displayed Result Incorrect

If the result displayed in a cell is obviously incorrect but the underlying formula seems to be correct, check that the cell's formatting isn't forcing Excel to round the result for the display. For example, if you divide 2 by 3 and get the result 1, you might suspect a division error. But if the result cell is formatted to display no decimal places, Excel will round 0.6667 to 1.

Error	What's Wrong	How to Fix the Problem
####	The formula is fine, but the cell is too narrow to display the formula result.	Widen the column.
#NAME?	The formula contains a misspelled function name or the name of a range that doesn't exist.	If the problem is a function name or a misspelled range name, correct it. If you've deleted a range name, define it again.
#N/A	No valid value is available.	Enter a valid value if necessary.
#REF!	The formula contains an invalid cell reference or range reference. For example, you may have deleted a cell or range that the formula needs.	Change the formula to remove the invalid reference.
#DIV/0!	The formula is attempting to divide by zero.	If the divisor value is actually 0, change it. If a blank cell is producing the 0 value, add an IF() statement to supply the #N/A value or a usable value.
#VALUE!	The formula contains an invalid argument—for example, text instead of a number.	Correct the argument or change the formula.
#NULL!	The specified two ranges have no intersection.	Correct one or both ranges so that they intersect.
#NUM!	The number specified isn't valid for the function or formula. For example, using a POWER function has generated a number larger than Excel can handle, or SQRT (the square root function) has been fed a negative number.	Correct the number to suit the function.

TABLE 17-2   Common Errors in Excel Formulas

There's no error, even though there appears to be—but you may want to change the formatting to remove the apparent error.

Operator Precedence Causes an Incorrect Result

If a formula gives a result that's obviously incorrect, check the operator precedence for errors. Enter parentheses to specify which calculations need to be performed out of the normal order of operator precedence.

Range Changes Introduce Errors in a Formula

Another prime source of errors in a formula is changes to the ranges to which the formula refers. To check whether this has happened, select the formula and press F2 to edit it. Use the LEFT ARROW and RIGHT ARROW keys to move through the formula, and watch as Excel's Range Finder feature selects each range referenced. When you identify an error, correct the range involved by dragging its borders or by typing in the correct references.

Understanding Formula AutoCorrect

Excel's Formula AutoCorrect feature watches as you enter formulas and tries to identify errors as you create them. When it catches a mistake in a formula you're entering, Formula AutoCorrect suggests how to fix it. For example, if you type **A1;B2** in a formula instead of A1:B2, Formula AutoCorrect displays a message box alerting you to the error and suggesting how to fix it. You can accept the suggestion or return to the cell to edit the formula manually.

Configuring Error-Checking Options

You can configure how Excel handles errors in your worksheets by choosing Tools | Options and selecting and deselecting the options as appropriate on the Error Checking tab of the Options dialog box, shown here. Deselect the Enable Background Error Checking option if you want to disable error checking altogether. Otherwise, use the options in the Rules section of the tab to specify which rules to apply to your worksheets. (By default, Excel applies most of them.)

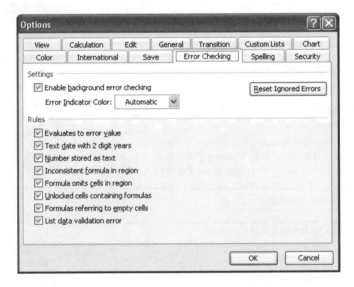

If you enter many formulas in your worksheets manually, you may well find the Inconsistent Formula in Region option useful for identifying inconsistencies in otherwise consistent ranges of formulas.

NOTE   *The Reset Ignored Errors button on the Error Checking tab of the Options dialog box lets you tell Excel that you want to see even those errors that you (or someone else) have specifically ignored. You may well want to use this option when you receive a workbook from someone else and need to make sure it doesn't contain any hidden errors.*

When Excel identifies an error that contravenes a rule that's selected, it displays a green triangle in the upper-left corner of the affected cell. Select the cell to display a Smart Tag, and then click the Smart Tag to display a menu that explains the problem and offers possible solutions. Here is an example of such a menu:

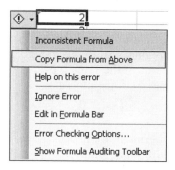

Checking for Errors Manually

If you turn off Excel's error checking, it's a good idea to check your worksheets manually for errors; if you use error checking, you may still want to check manually to make sure you haven't ignored any green triangle-flagged cells.

To check for errors, activate the worksheet you want to check, and choose Tools | Error Checking. If it finds an error, Excel displays the Error Checking dialog box (shown next) with an explanation of the error and buttons for taking action on the error, getting help on it, ignoring the error, and editing the error in the Formula bar while leaving the Error Checking dialog box open. After dealing with the error, click Next to move to the next error, or Previous to move to the previous error.

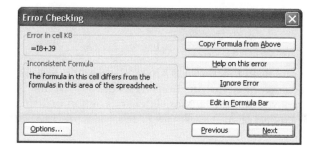

If the Error Checking dialog box contains the Show Calculation Steps button, you can click this button to display the Evaluate Formula dialog box, which provides options for stepping your way through the error to identify where it occurs. This option can be a considerable help in pinning down where an error occurs in the formula.

Entering Functions

As well as constructing your own formulas, you're likely to need to use some of Excel's many built-in functions in your worksheets. For example, you might use the =SUM function to add a range of numbers effortlessly or the =ROUNDUP function to round a number up to a specified number of digits.

Components of a Function

Each function has a name (for example, SUM). Almost all functions have one or more *arguments* that specify the elements and types of information you give them in order to get a valid result. (Some functions, such as =NOW(), =TODAY(), and =NA(), require no arguments at all.) The rules that govern the types of information a function needs are called its *syntax*. Excel shows required arguments in boldface, optional arguments in regular font, and an ellipsis to indicate where you can use further arguments of the same type.

For example, the syntax for the =SUM() function is

```
SUM(number1,number2,...)
```

Here, number1 is a required argument that specifies the first number to include in the sum: you can't have a SUM without a number. The number2 argument is an optional argument that specifies the second number, if there is one. The ellipsis indicates that you can use further arguments as necessary: number3, number4, and so on.

Entering a Function

Excel supports the following ways of entering functions in the active cell:

- Type the function and its arguments directly into the cell. Excel displays a ScreenTip that shows the syntax for the function and tracks your progress in entering the argument. The ScreenTip (see the example here) includes links that you can click to select an argument you've previously entered or to return to the argument you're currently entering.

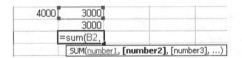

- Enter a frequently used function quickly by clicking the AutoSum button on the toolbar or choosing one of the functions on its drop-down list: Average, Count, Max, or Min (shown next). Choose the More Functions option to display the Insert Function dialog box, discussed next.

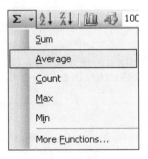

- Display the Insert Function dialog box by clicking the Insert Function button in the Formula bar, by choosing Insert | Function from the menu, or by clicking the More Functions option on the AutoSum drop-down list. The Insert Function dialog box walks you through the process of choosing a function and specifying its arguments correctly. This dialog box is the fastest and easiest method for entering all but the most basic functions.

Using the Insert Function Dialog Box

To enter a function by using the Insert Function dialog box:

1. Display the Insert Function dialog box. The illustration shows an example of the dialog box as it initially appears. The functions it displays at first depend on which functions you last used.

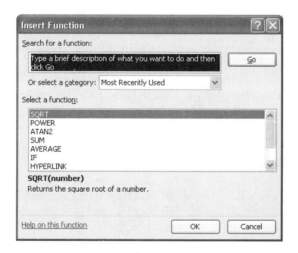

2. Select the function you want to enter in any of these ways:
   - If the Select a Function box already contains the function, click the function.
   - Select the appropriate category in the Or Select a Category drop-down list; then select the function in the Select a Function box.
   - Type keywords describing the function in the Search for a Function text box and click Go. Excel displays matching functions in the Select a Function box under the Recommended category. Select the function.

3. Check that the description of the function below the Select a Function box matches your expectations. (If necessary, click the Help on This Function link to display Excel's help entry on the function.)

4. Click OK. Excel displays the Function Arguments dialog box, shown here with data entered for the ROUNDDOWN function:

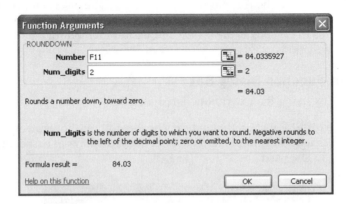

5. Enter the data in each argument box in turn, either by typing in the data or by using the Collapse Dialog buttons to specify the appropriate cell or range references. As you work, Excel displays information on the current argument and, as soon as appropriate, the result of the formula. Again, you can click the Help on This Function link to access help information.

6. Click OK. Excel enters the function in the cell.

Nesting One Function Inside Another Function

To achieve the calculations you need, you'll often use multiple functions in sequence. You can do this by entering a function in one cell, and then using another function in another cell to work on the result of that function. But you can also achieve the same effect in a single cell by nesting one function within another. Excel supports nesting up to seven levels of functions, so you can create highly involved calculations.

To nest one function within another, follow the procedure described in the previous section up to step 5. You'll have noticed that when the Insert Function dialog box or the Function Arguments dialog box is displayed, Excel replaces the Name box to the left of the Formula bar with a box that contains the name of the last function you used. As you might guess, this box is called the Function box.

In the Function Arguments dialog box, select the argument box in which you want to enter the nested function. Then click the drop-down list next to the Function box and choose either one of the listed functions (the last ten you've used) or the More Functions option to display the Insert Function dialog box again. Then select the function and specify its arguments as usual.

Editing a Function

To edit a function you've entered, select the cell that contains the formula and click the Insert Function button or choose Insert | Function. Excel displays the Function Arguments dialog box again.

Monitoring Calculations with the Watch Window

Excel's Watch window is a tool for monitoring the value of specific cells in a workbook as you work. The cells can be on any of the worksheets in the workbook or on a worksheet in a linked workbook.

The easiest way to display the Watch window is by adding a watch cell to it. To do so, right-click the cell and choose Add Watch from the shortcut menu. The following illustration shows the Watch window with several watch cells added. You can sort by any of the column headings, and you can double-click a watch cell to display its workbook and select the cell. Use the Add Watch button to add further watches and the Delete Watch button to delete existing watches.

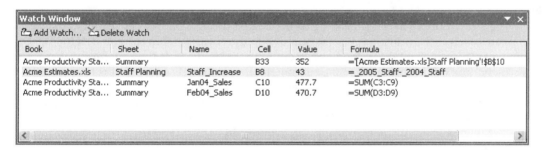

The Watch window is a toolbar, so you can also display it from the View | Toolbars submenu and from the context menu that Excel displays when you right-click a displayed toolbar. By default, Excel displays the Watch window in a floating configuration, but you can dock it like any other toolbar; usually the bottom of the screen is most convenient. The easiest way to close the Watch window is to click its Close button, but you can also hide it from the View | Toolbars submenu or from the toolbars context menu.

Working with Array Formulas

An *array formula* is a formula that works on an array (a range of cells) to perform multiple calculations that generate either a single result or multiple results.

To enter an array formula, create the formula as explained earlier in this chapter, but press CTRL-SHIFT-ENTER instead of ENTER to enter it. Excel displays braces—{ and }—around an array formula. Excel enters the braces automatically when you create an array formula. You can't achieve the same effect by typing the braces manually.

The example spreadsheet shown next tracks the vacation hours used by each employee. Each employee starts off (on an unseen area of the worksheet) with a number of vacation hours they've accrued. The worksheet contains details, in date order, of the vacation hours taken by each employee and a running total showing the number of vacation hours each employee has left.

	D8	▼	*fx* {=SUM(IF($B$2:B8=B8,$C$2:C8))}	
	A	B	C	D
1	Date	Employee	Hours Taken	Hours Remaining
8	5-Jan-04	Andrea Nemmanden	-8	52
9	6-Jan-04	Petra Gravis	-4	44
10	6-Jan-04	Andrea Nemmanden	-8	44
11	7-Jan-04	Andrea Nemmanden	-8	36
12	7-Jan-04	Anita Bichel	-4	40
13	7-Jan-04	Lol Ramirez	-8	88
14	8-Jan-04	Andrea Nemmanden	-8	28
15	8-Jan-04	John Mitchell	-8	32
16	9-Jan-04	Andrea Nemmanden	-4	24
17	10-Jan-04	Jane Truro	-8	24

The array formula in cell D8 is {=SUM(IF($B$2:B8=B8,$C$2:C8))}. The formula first compares each of the previous cells in column B to the current cell in column B. If the IF function returns TRUE, the second argument in the formula adds the contents of the corresponding cell in column C to the running total in column D. The effect is to keep a running total of the vacation hours available by employee.

You can edit an array formula that you've previously created by selecting the cell or the range of cells that contains it. If the array formula is entered in multiple cells, you need to select them all before you can edit the array formula.

Goal Seeking

If you ever find yourself trying to work backward from the result you want to achieve, you may well find Excel's Goal Seek feature valuable. For example, suppose you're using your current sales worksheet as the basis for next year's planning spreadsheets. The sales worksheet shows you how many units of each type of item have been sold and how much money that brings in—but you want to work out how many units of each type of item the company will need to sell in order to get sales up by another couple million dollars.

You could create a new copy of the worksheet and try increasing the numbers until you reached the level needed. Or you could build a new version of the worksheet with formulas that worked backward from your revenue target instead of forward to the revenue total. Or you could use Goal Seek, which can give you the information you need much more quickly.

To use Goal Seek:

1. Open the worksheet if it's not already open.

2. Select the cell that contains the formula you're interested in.

3. Choose Tools | Goal Seek. Excel displays the Goal Seek dialog box, shown here. The cell you selected in step 2 appears in the Set Cell box. (If you chose the wrong cell, type the reference for the correct cell, or click the Collapse Downloading button and select it.)

4. In the To Value box, enter the target value for the formula.

5. In the By Changing Cell box, type the reference for the cell whose value you want Goal Seek to manipulate. Alternatively, use the Collapse Dialog button to enter the cell reference.

6. Click OK. Goal Seek computes the problem and then displays the Goal Seek Status dialog box:

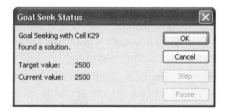

7. Goal Seek automatically enters the target value it achieved and the By Changing Cell value it found in the worksheet. Click OK to accept these values, or click Cancel to reject them.

Using the Solver

As you saw in the previous section, Goal Seek is a powerful tool for working backward from a conclusion by manipulating a single value. But if you need to work backward by manipulating two or more values, Goal Seek can't help you. Instead, you need to use the Solver, one of the add-ins that comes with Excel.

Load the Solver add-in by choosing Tools | Add-Ins, selecting the Solver Add-in option, and clicking OK. Then:

1. Open the worksheet if it's not already open.

2. Select the cell that contains the formula you're interested in.

3. Choose Tools | Solver. Excel displays the Solver Parameters dialog box, shown here with data entered. The cell you selected in step 2 appears in the Set Target Cell box. (If you chose the wrong cell, type the reference for the correct cell, or click the Collapse Dialog button and select it.)

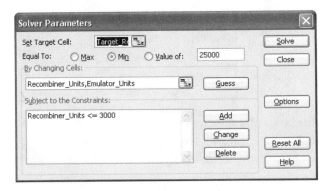

4. In the Equal To area, select the Max option, the Min option, or the Value Of option as appropriate, and type the value in the text box.

5. In the By Changing Cells box, type the references for the cells whose value you want the Solver to manipulate. Alternatively, use the Collapse Dialog button to enter the cell references. In most cases, you won't want to use the Guess button unless you're seeking entertainment rather than answers.

6. If you want to apply constraints to the Solver, use the controls by the Subject to the Constraints box to add, edit, and delete constraints. The basic procedure is to click the Add button, use the controls in the Add Constraint dialog box (shown next) to specify the cell reference, the operator, and the constraint, and click OK. Use the other controls to change or delete any constraints you've already applied.

7. Click Solve to start computing the solution. When the Solver has finished, it displays the Solver Results dialog box:

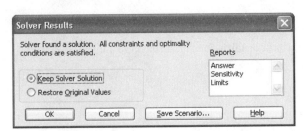

8. Select the Keep Solver Solution option or the Restore Original Values option as appropriate.

9. To see one or more reports, select them in the Reports list either by clicking (to select one), SHIFT-clicking (to select a range of contiguous items), or CTRL-clicking (to select noncontiguous items). The Solver inserts each report on a fresh worksheet.

10. Click OK.

> **NOTE**   *If you find the Solver useful, you may also want to examine Excel's Scenarios feature (Tools | Scenarios), which enables you to examine different scenarios for the same data set in a workbook. From the Solver Results dialog box, you can save a scenario.*

Examples of Functions in Action

Excel offers nine categories of functions, including database, logical, statistical, and text functions. Some categories contain too many functions to list all of them here, but all nine categories are discussed, with examples of some functions in each category.

Database Functions

Excel's 12 database functions are for identifying which values in an Excel database or list match certain criteria. For example:

- DCOUNT returns the number of records that match the criteria.
- DSUM adds the numbers in the specified column of the records that match the criteria.
- DSTDEVP returns the standard deviation based on the entire population of entries that match the criteria.

Chapter 19 discusses how to create databases in Excel.

Date and Time Functions

Excel's date and time functions are widely useful in worksheets for a variety of operations. Table 17-3 explains the date and time functions.

Function	What It Returns
DATE	Serial number of the specified date
TIME	Serial number of the specified time
DATEVALUE	Serial number of the specified text-formatted date
TIMEVALUE	Serial number of the specified text-formatted time
DAY	Day of the month for the specified serial date, as a serial number between 1 and 31

TABLE 17-3   Excel's Date and Time Functions

Function	What It Returns
MONTH	Month of the year for the specified serial date, as a serial number between 1 and 12
YEAR	Year for the specified serial date (for example, 2007)
DAYS360	Number of days between the two specified dates, based on a 360-day year (used for some accounting purposes)
HOUR	Hour for the specified serial time, as a serial number between 0 and 23
MINUTE	Minute for the specified serial time, as a serial number between 0 and 59
SECOND	Second for the specified serial time, as a serial number between 0 and 59
TODAY	Current date, formatted as a date
NOW	Current date and time, formatted as a date and time
WEEKDAY	Weekday for the specified day, as a serial number between 1 (Sunday) and 7 (Saturday)

TABLE 17-3   Excel's Date and Time Functions *(continued)*

Here are three examples of using the date and time functions:

- Use **=TODAY()** to enter the current date in a cell, or **=NOW()** to enter the current date and time, in an automatically updating form.

- **=DATEVALUE("2004-4-1")** converts the text string "2004-4-1" to its corresponding serial date. By default, Excel displays the result with Date formatting, but you can apply other cell formatting. For example, you might choose to display the serial number for the date.

- **=HOUR("11:45 PM")** returns 23, the hour derived from 11:45 P.M.

Financial Functions

Excel includes 16 financial functions for common calculations, and the Analysis ToolPak adds about three dozen extra financial functions for more arcane calculations. Table 17-4 explains the built-in financial functions.

Here are two examples of using the financial functions:

- **=PMT(7.25%/12,24,-20000)** calculates the payment required to pay off a $20,000 loan at 7.25% APR over 24 payments.

- **=DB(15000,3000,6,3)** calculates the depreciation over the third year of an asset with an initial cost of $15,000, a salvage value of $3,000 at the end of its life, and a life of six years.

Function	What It Returns
DB	Depreciation using the fixed-declining balance method
DDB	Depreciation using the double-declining balance method or other method
FV	Future value of an investment
IPMT	Interest payments for an investment for a specified period
IRR	Internal rate of return for cash flows
MIRR	Modified internal rate of return for cash flows
ISPMT	Interest paid for an investment over a specified period
NPER	Number of periods for an investment
NPV	Net present value of an investment
PMT	Payment for a loan
PPMT	Payment on the principal for an investment
PV	Present value of an investment
RATE	Interest rate per period of an investment
SLN	Straight-line depreciation for an asset
SYD	Sum-of-years' digits depreciation for an asset
VDB	Depreciation for an asset using the double-declining balance method or a variable declining balance

TABLE 17-4   Excel's Financial Functions

Logical Functions

Excel's six logical functions, explained in Table 17-5, enable you to test logical conditions. By combining these logical functions with other functions, you can make Excel take action appropriate to how the condition evaluates.

Function	What It Returns
AND	TRUE if all the specified arguments are TRUE, otherwise FALSE
FALSE	FALSE (always—use to generate a FALSE value)
IF	The specified value if the condition is TRUE and the other specified value if the condition is FALSE
NOT	FALSE from TRUE, and TRUE from FALSE
OR	TRUE if any of the specified arguments is TRUE; FALSE if all arguments are FALSE
TRUE	TRUE (always—use to generate a TRUE value)

TABLE 17-5   Excel's Logical Functions

Here are two examples of using the logical functions:

- =IF(C21>4000,"More than $4,000","Less than $4,000") returns *More than $4,000* if C21 contains a number greater than 4000. Otherwise, the function returns *Less than $4,000*.

- =AND(INFO("system")="pcdos",INFO("osversion")="Windows (32-bit) NT 5.01",INFO("release")="11.0") returns TRUE if the user is running Excel 2003 (version 11.0) on Windows XP (aka Windows (32-bit) NT 5.01) on a PC.

IF is often used with the information functions discussed in the next section. See the next section for further examples.

Information Functions

Excel offers 16 information functions for returning information about the contents and formatting of the current cell or range. Some of these information functions (explained in Table 17-6) are widely useful, whereas others are more specialized.

Function	What It Returns
CELL	Specified details of the contents, location, or formatting of the first cell in the specified range
COUNTBLANK	Number of empty cells in the specified range
ERROR.TYPE	A number representing the error value in the cell: 1 for #NULL!, 2 for #DIV/0!, 3 for #VALUE!, 4 for #REF!, 5 for #NAME?, 6 for #NUM!, and 7 for #N/A
INFO	Information about Excel, the operating system, or the computer
ISBLANK	TRUE if the cell is blank, FALSE if it has contents
ISERR	TRUE if the cell contains any error except #N/A, otherwise FALSE
ISERROR	TRUE if the cell contains any error, otherwise FALSE
ISLOGICAL	TRUE if the cell contains a logical value, otherwise FALSE
ISNA	TRUE if the cell contains #N/A, otherwise FALSE
ISNONTEXT	TRUE if the cell contains anything but text—even if it's a blank cell; otherwise FALSE
ISNUMBER	TRUE if the cell contains a number, otherwise FALSE
ISREF	TRUE if the cell contains a reference, otherwise FALSE
ISTEXT	TRUE if the cell contains text, otherwise FALSE
N	A number derived from the specified value: A number returns that number. A date returns the associated serial date. TRUE returns 1 and FALSE returns 0. An error returns its error value (see the ERROR.TYPE entry, earlier in this table). Anything else returns 0.
NA	#N/A (used to enter the error value deliberately in the cell)
TYPE	A number representing the data type in the cell: 1 for a number, 2 for text, 4 for a logical value, 16 for an error value, and 64 for an array

TABLE 17-6   Excel's Information Functions

Here are three examples of using the information functions:

- **=INFO("osversion")** returns Windows' internal description of the operating system version—for example, *Windows (32-bit) NT 5.01* for Windows XP. **=INFO("directory")** returns the current working directory. **=INFO("numfile")** returns the number of active worksheets in all open workbooks.

- **=IF(ISERROR(Revenue/Price), "Units not available", Revenue/Price)** checks to see whether dividing the cell referenced by the name Revenue by the cell referenced by the name Price will result in an error before it performs the calculation. If the calculation will result in an error, the formula displays a label in the cell instead. If the calculation won't result in an error, the formula performs the calculation and displays its result.

- **=IF(ISBLANK('Amortization Estimates.xls'!Amortization_Rate), "Warning: Base rate not entered","")** displays a warning message if the Amortization_Rate cell in the Amortization Estimates workbook is blank. Otherwise, the formula displays nothing.

NOTE   *The Analysis ToolPak also contains the ISEVEN function, which returns TRUE if the specified number is even, and the ISODD function, which returns TRUE if the specified number is odd.*

Lookup and Reference Functions

Excel includes 18 lookup and reference functions for returning information from lists. You'll see some of these functions in action in Chapter 19, which discusses how to create databases in Excel.

Mathematical and Trigonometric Functions

Excel offers 50 mathematical and trigonometric functions. (The Analysis ToolPak offers about 10 further mathematical and trigonometric functions.) Many of these functions are self-explanatory to anyone who needs to use them in their work. For example, COS returns the cosine of an angle, COSH returns the hyperbolic cosine, ACOS returns the arccosine, and ACOSH returns the inverse hyperbolic cosine.

Table 17-7 explains the mathematical and trigonometric functions you might use occasionally for more general purposes.

Function	What It Returns
ABS	Absolute value (without the sign) of the specified number
EVEN	Specified positive number rounded up to the next even integer, or the specified negative number rounded down to the next even integer
ODD	Specified positive number rounded up to the next odd integer, or the specified negative number rounded down to the next odd integer

TABLE 17-7   General-Purpose Mathematical and Trigonometric Functions

Function	What It Returns
INT	Specified number rounded down to the nearest integer
MOD	Remainder left over after a division operation
RAND	Random number (greater than or equal to 0 and less than 1)
ROMAN	Roman equivalent of the specified Arabic numeral
ROUND	Specified number rounded to the specified number of digits
ROUNDDOWN	Specified number rounded down to the specified number of digits
ROUNDUP	Specified number rounded up to the specified number of digits
SIGN	1 for a positive number, 0 for 0, and −1 for a negative number
SUM	Total of the numbers in the specified range
SUMIF	Total of the numbers in the cells in the specified range that meet the criteria given
TRUNC	Specified number truncated to the specified number of decimal places

TABLE 17-7   General-Purpose Mathematical and Trigonometric Functions *(continued)*

Here are three examples of using the general-purpose mathematical and trigonometric functions:

- **=SUM(A1:A24)** adds the values in the range A1:A24.
- **=RAND()** enters a random value that changes each time the worksheet is recalculated. (Unless you turn off automatic calculation, Excel recalculates the worksheet each time you enter a change.)
- **=ROMAN(1998)** returns *MCMXCVIII*.

Statistical Functions

Excel includes a large number of statistical functions that fall into categories such as calculating deviation (including AVEDEV, STDEVA, STDEV, and STDEVP); distributions (BETADIST, CHIDIST, BINOMDIST, EXPONDIST, KURT, POISSON, WEIBULL); and transformations (FISHER, FISHERINV).

Unless you're working with statistics, you're unlikely to need most of the statistical functions. However, you may need to use some of the statistical functions for more general business purposes. Table 17-8 lists the main contenders for general usage.

Here are three examples of using the general-purpose statistical functions:

- **=AVERAGE(Q1Sales)** returns the average value of the entries in the range named Q1Sales.
- **=COUNTBLANK(BA1:BZ256)** returns the number of blank cells in the specified range.

Function	What It Returns
AVERAGE	Average of the specified cells, ranges, or arrays
MEDIAN	Median (the number in the middle of the given set) of the numbers in the specified cells
MODE	Value that occurs most frequently in the specified range of cells
COUNT	Number of cells in the specified range that either contain numbers or include numbers in their list of arguments
COUNTBLANK	Number of empty cells in the specified range
COUNTIF	Number of cells in the specified range that meet the specified criteria
MAX	Largest value in the specified range
MIN	Lowest value in the specified range

TABLE 17-8   General-Purpose Statistical Functions

- **=COUNTIF(Q2Sales,0)** returns the number of cells with a zero value in the range named Q2Sales.

Text Functions

Excel contains 24 functions for manipulating text. One of them (BAHTTEXT) is highly esoteric, and another (CONCATENATE) is seldom worth using because the & operator is usually easier for concatenating text strings. You may find the other text functions useful when you need to return a specific part (for example, the first five characters) of a text string, change the case of a text string, or find one string within another string.

Table 17-9 explains the text functions.

Function	What It Returns
BAHTTEXT	Number converted to Thai text and with the *Baht* suffix
CHAR	Character represented by the specified character code
CODE	Character code for the first character in the specified string
CLEAN	Specified text string with all nonprintable characters stripped out (sometimes useful when importing files in other formats)
CONCATENATE	Text string consisting of the specified text strings joined together
DOLLAR	Specified number converted to text in the Currency format
EXACT	TRUE if the specified two text strings contain the same characters in the same case, otherwise FALSE

TABLE 17-9   Excel's Text Functions

PART III

Function	What It Returns
FIND	Starting position of one specified text string within another text string—case sensitive
FIXED	Specified number rounded to the specified number of decimals, with commas or without
LEN	Number of characters in the specified text string
LEFT	Specified number of characters from the beginning of the specified text string
RIGHT	Specified number of characters from the end of the specified text string
MID	Specified number of characters after the specified starting point in the specified text string
LOWER	Text string converted to lowercase
UPPER	Text string converted to uppercase
PROPER	Text string converted to "proper case"—first letter capitalized, the rest lowercase
REPLACE	Specified text string with the specified replacement string inserted in a specified location
REPT	Specified text string repeated the specified number of times
SEARCH	Character position at which the specified character is located in the specified string
SUBSTITUTE	Specified text string with the specified new text string substituted for the specified old text string
T	Text string for a text value, empty double quotation marks (a blank string) for a nontext value
TEXT	Text string containing the specified value converted to the specified format
TRIM	Specified text string with spaces removed from the beginning and ends, and extra spaces between words removed to leave one space between words
VALUE	Value contained in the specified text string

TABLE 17-9   Excel's Text Functions *(continued)*

Here are three examples of using the text functions:

- **=EXACT(A1,A2)** compares the text in cells A1 and A2, returning TRUE if they're exactly alike (including case) and FALSE if they're not.
- **=IF(LEN(H2)>=5, LEFT(H2,5),H2)** returns the first five characters of cell H2 if the length of the cell's contents is five characters or more. If the length is less than five, the formula returns the full contents of the cell.
- **=TRIM(CLEAN(C2))** strips nonprintable characters from the text string in cell C2, removes extra spaces, and returns the resulting text string.

Viewing and Manipulating Data with Charts and PivotTables

After entering data, formulas, and functions in your worksheets, you'll probably want to put the resulting information to use, either by using it to create charts that convey a particular message or by manipulating it to make it deliver up the secrets that lie buried within it. This chapter shows you how to do both.

First, you'll see how to use Excel's chart features to create charts that illustrate the points you're trying to make. Then we'll explain what PivotTables are, what they're for, and how to work with them, before going on to do the same for PivotCharts.

Working with Charts

Excel can create both *embedded* charts (charts positioned on a worksheet page alongside other data) and charts that appear on their own worksheet page. Embedded charts are useful for charting small amounts of data and for experimenting with the best ways to chart data that you need to edit while creating the chart. But for maximum effect, you'll generally want to create each chart on its own worksheet page.

Components of an Excel Chart

Typical charts consist of the following components:

Component	Explanation
X-axis	The category axis of the chart—usually horizontal, but some charts have a vertical X-axis
Y-axis	The series axis—the vertical axis on which the categories are plotted
Z-axis	The value axis—the depth axis of the chart (3-D charts only)

Component	Explanation
Axis titles	A title (name) for each of the axes used
Chart title	The name of the chart
Data series	The set or sets of data from which the chart is created. Some charts, such as pie charts, use only one data series. Other charts use two or more data series. The chart represents the data series as data markers.
Data marker	The chart's representation of a point in a data series. You may want to display data markers in different data series as differently shaped points to distinguish them from one another.
Data labels	Text that appears on or near points in the data series to identify them
Legend	Notes on the color, pattern, or other identification used to distinguish each data series
Grid lines	Reference lines drawn across the chart from the axes so that you can see the values of the data series
Categories	The distinct items in the data series. For example, in a chart showing the sales performance for each of a company's regions, each region would be a category.
Chart area	The area occupied by the entire chart, including legend, labels, and so on
Plot area	The area occupied by the data plotted in the chart (not including legend, labels, and so on)

Figure 18-1 shows a straightforward chart with its components labeled.

Using the Chart Wizard

The Chart wizard is the fastest and easiest way of creating a chart. Use the Chart wizard as follows:

1. Select the range of data from which you want to create the chart, including any headings you want to use as labels. You can select either a contiguous range or a noncontiguous range.

NOTE *You can adjust any of the parameters for the chart after finishing the Chart wizard, so mistakes matter little. (Alternatively, you can delete the botched chart and run the wizard again.)*

2. Click the Chart Wizard button on the Standard toolbar, or choose Insert | Chart from the menu. The Chart wizard displays the Chart Type screen. The left screen

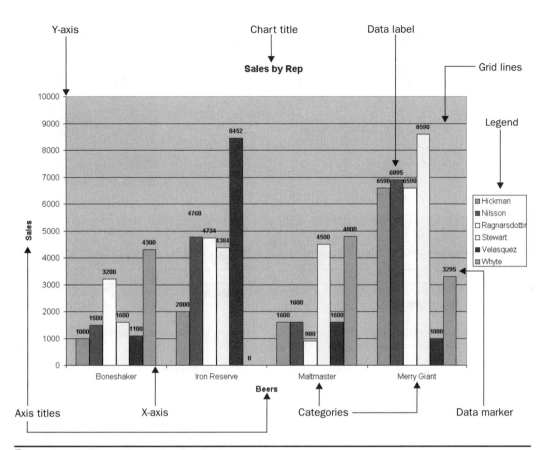

FIGURE 18-1   The components of a chart

in Figure 18-2 shows the Standard Types tab. The right screen in Figure 18-2 shows the Custom Types tab with the Built-In option selected to display Excel's built-in custom chart types. (The User-Defined option displays custom chart types you add.)

3. Choose the type of chart you want to create, and then choose the subtype (for one of the standard types). On the Standard Types tab, you can click the Press and Hold to View Sample button to have Excel build a preview of the chart type using the data you've selected.

4. Click Next to display the Chart Source Data screen. The left screen in Figure 18-3 shows the Data Range tab. The right screen in Figure 18-3 shows the Series tab.

5. On the Data Range tab, check that the wizard has identified the data range correctly. If not, click the Collapse Dialog button (at the end of the Data Range field) and

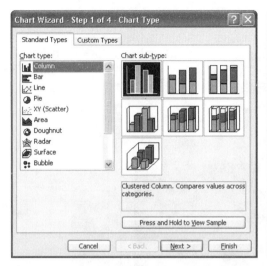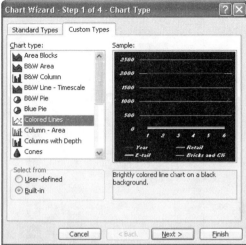

FIGURE 18-2   Choose the chart type on the Standard Types tab (left) or the Custom Types tab of the Chart Type screen.

select the correct range. If necessary, change from the Rows option to the Columns option to make Excel recognize the series.

6. On the Series tab, use the controls in the Series area to add and remove series and adjust their names and values. Use the Category (X) Axis Labels box to specify the range that will provide the labels for the X-axis.

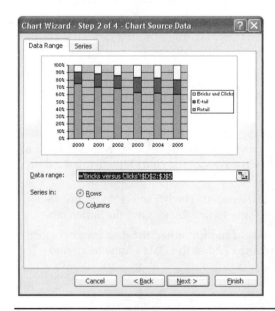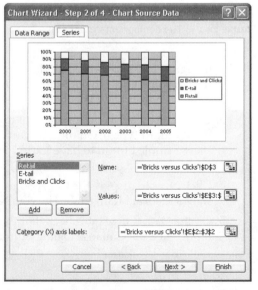

FIGURE 18-3   Use the two tabs of the Chart Source Data screen to adjust the range used as source data for the chart.

7. Click Next to display the Chart Options screen, and then choose options on its six tabs:

- **Titles**   Enter the chart title and the title for each axis that needs one.

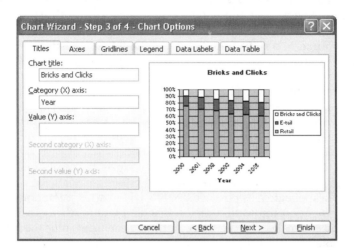

- **Axes**   Choose which axes are displayed. (In most cases, you'll want all the axes used by the chart type.)

- **Gridlines**   Choose whether to display major grid lines, minor grid lines, or both for each axis in the chart. Apply grid lines when they'll help the viewer see the value of a data marker more easily.

- **Legend**   Choose whether to display the legend and (if so) where to place it.

- **Data Labels**   Choose whether to display data labels and (if so) what data to display for them: for example, the data markers' values or the category name.

- **Data Table**   Choose whether Excel displays the data from which the chart was drawn and (if so) whether it includes the legend. Showing the data table is usually useful only for charts drawn from small amounts of data—otherwise, the data detracts from the chart.

8. Click Next to display the Chart Location screen.

9. Choose whether to place the chart on a new chart sheet (by selecting the As New Sheet option and specifying the name for the new sheet) or as an embedded chart (by selecting the As Object In option and using the drop-down list to designate the worksheet).

10. Click Finish. Excel creates the chart with the options you chose.

Choosing the Right Type of Chart for Your Data

As you saw in the Chart Type dialog box, Excel offers an extremely generous range of charts—14 standard types, each with two or more subtypes, and 20 built-in custom types. You can also add your own custom chart types if Excel's built-in chart types don't meet your needs. ("Creating Custom Chart Types," later in this chapter, discusses how to do this.)

Such a wide choice of chart types can make it difficult to decide which type to use: should you use a conventional bar chart or line chart; go for an area chart, a doughnut, or radar; experiment with a Pie Explosion; or visit the Outdoor Bars? But in general, you should use the simplest type of chart that can present your data satisfactorily. Don't feel you have to use an unusual type of chart just because Excel makes doing so easy or because the standard chart type seems boring. As a rule of thumb, if you don't know what a chart type is for, take a quick look at the example in the Chart Type box and see if it's easy to understand. If not, leave that chart type alone.

Many of the more esoteric chart types are designed for highly specific needs. For example, stock charts are designed for tracking the opening, closing, and high and low prices of a stock over a given time period. If you use a stock chart for your sales results or your staffing forecasts, the result will be of little use. Similarly, the Stack of Colors custom chart type is designed for showing the contribution of constituent parts over time. If you use Stack of Colors to chart your company's output of widgets, the results will be meaningless.

Beyond using the simplest type of chart that can present the data satisfactorily, keep the chart itself as simple and legible as possible. Excel's wide variety of options may tempt you to indulge in unnecessary complications; resist this temptation. Always ask yourself: Is the chart as clear as you can make it? Does it need titles on each axis, plus the legend, *and* its underlying data table? Are those frills you've added necessary, or are they distractions?

In business (and occasionally at home, if you have a complicated home life), you may sometimes need to use a chart to obscure the facts rather than highlight them. For example, you might need to use a chart creatively to mask deficient sales results or to put the best possible spin on a drastic budget overrun. In such a situation, an esoteric chart type might seem a good idea—but it's not.

If you need to con your audience with a chart, choosing an unusual or complex chart type is almost always a bad move. An unusual or incomprehensible chart type will make your audience scrutinize it much more closely than an apparently straightforward chart on which you've subtly manipulated the axis values. For example, you might be able to change the timescale on a chart to obscure a decline in sales. Such sleight of mouse is much more likely to pass unnoticed because the chart itself is unremarkable. If you can't produce a suitable chart from the data you have, you'll need to find better data to chart.

Creating a Chart Instantly Using the Keyboard

For times when you choose not to use the Chart wizard, you can create a chart instantly from selected data by pressing F11 or ALT-F1. Excel creates a chart of the default chart type on its own page in the workbook. You can then change the chart type and details by using the options on the Chart toolbar.

TIP   *If you frequently need to create charts of the same type, customize the default chart setting by choosing Chart | Chart Type, selecting the chart type in the Chart Type dialog box, clicking the Set As Default Chart button, and clicking Yes in the confirmation dialog box.*

Editing Charts

If you make all the right choices in the Chart wizard, the wizard will deliver the perfect chart. You may need to apply a little formatting to the chart to emphasize its subtleties or play down data markers you'd rather pretend were elsewhere; this type of formatting is discussed in "Formatting Charts," a little later in the chapter.

What's more likely is that you'll need to edit the chart produced by the Chart wizard to make it show the data you want in the way you want it.

Using the Chart Toolbar

Excel's prime tools for working with charts are the Chart menu, which contains a handful of commands for manipulating charts, and the Chart toolbar, shown here. Excel automatically displays the Chart menu and the Chart toolbar when you select an embedded chart or display a chart page in a workbook.

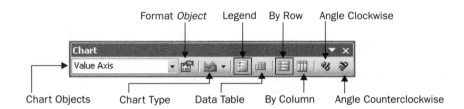

Here's what the controls on the Chart toolbar are for:

- **Chart Objects**   Use the drop-down list to select an object in the chart by name.
- **Format *Object***   Display the Format dialog box for the currently selected object. The name changes to reflect the currently selected object. For example, when the legend is selected, the button is named Format Legend, and it displays the Format Legend dialog box.
- **Chart Type**   Display a menu of chart types that you can apply quickly.
- **Legend**   Toggle the display of the legend.
- **Data Table**   Toggle the display of the data table (the cells from which the chart data is drawn).
- **By Row and By Column**   Switch the data series to being drawn by row and by column, respectively. The current button appears pushed in.
- **Angle Clockwise and Angle Counterclockwise**   Apply a 45-degree angle in the specified direction to the selected object.

Selecting Objects in a Chart

You can select objects in a chart in any of the following ways:

- Click with the mouse. This technique is easiest for large objects and those that aren't obscured by other objects.
- Use the Chart Objects drop-down list on the toolbar. This technique is useful for selecting small objects or objects that are obscured by other objects.
- Use the arrow keys to select the next element in the appropriate direction.

Configuring Chart Options

The options on the Chart tab of the Options dialog box (Tools | Options) give you control over the following:

- Decide how Excel should handle empty cells in the range from which the chart is drawn. The default setting is not to plot the empty cells, leaving gaps. You can choose to plot the empty cells as zero (for example, to highlight their omission) or to interpolate data points (for example, to indicate a trend from incomplete data).

- Choose whether Excel plots only visible cells or includes hidden cells in the range.

- Choose whether Excel resizes chart sheets when you resize the window, so that the chart sheet fills the whole window. This setting applies only to chart sheets, not to embedded charts.

- Choose whether Excel displays the names and values of chart tips when you hover the insertion point over a chart item.

Changing the Chart Type

You can change the chart type in either of the following ways:

- Select the chart, click the Chart Type button on the Chart toolbar, and choose the new chart type from the menu.

- Choose Chart | Chart Type to display the Chart Type dialog box, select the chart type and subtype, and click OK.

Changing a Chart's Source Data

To change the source data a chart is drawn from, choose Chart | Source Data, and then use the tabs of the Source Data dialog box (shown in Figure 18-3, earlier in this chapter) to specify the new source data.

Changing the Plotting Order of the Data Series

Sometimes, you may need to change the order in which the data series in a chart are plotted. You can do this by changing the data source for the chart, but in some cases making such a change may cause more problems in the worksheet than it solves in the chart. You can also change the plotting order of the data series just for the chart by selecting the data series you want to move, displaying the Format Data Series dialog box, and using the options on the Series Order tab, shown in the following illustration. The preview shows you how changing the plotting order affects the chart, so you can see whether the change is correct before you commit it.

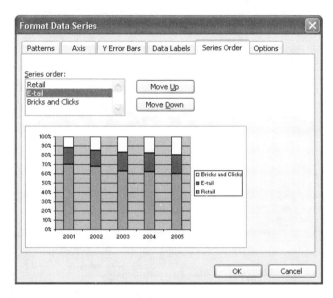

Toggling a Chart Between Embedded and Chart Sheet

You can change a chart from embedded to being on its own chart sheet by making the appropriate choice in the Chart Location dialog box. To display the Chart Location dialog box, issue the Location command from either the Chart menu or the context menu for the chart.

Changing the Scale of an Axis

One trick that can be very effective is changing the scale of an axis from its default settings. You can change the minimum value, maximum value, the major units and minor units used for grid lines, and where another axis crosses this axis (for example, where the X-axis crosses the Y-axis). You can also apply a logarithmic scale and reverse the order of the values on the axis.

To change the scale of the axis, right-click the axis and choose Format Axis to display the Format Axis dialog box. Work on the Scale tab, shown here:

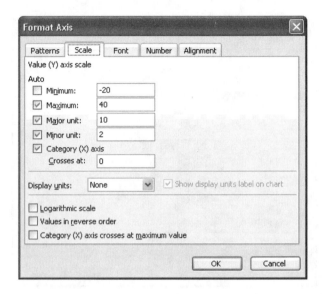

Formatting Charts

Excel gives you fine control over how your charts behave and how they look. You can resize embedded charts, zoom chart sheets, and apply formatting to either the entire chart area or just about any item in the chart.

TIP   *Before formatting an embedded chart, you may want to display it in its own window so that you can see it at a larger size. To do so, right-click the chart and choose Chart Window from the shortcut menu.*

Resizing a Chart

To resize an embedded chart, select it and drag one of the sizing handles to the size you want.

You shouldn't need to resize a chart on a chart sheet, because Excel automatically expands the chart to fill the size of paper you're using. However, you can zoom the chart in and out to see it at different sizes.

Formatting the Chart Area

When formatting a chart, typically you'll want to start by formatting the chart area, because the chart area exercises the greatest influence over how the chart looks as a whole. For example, you can set a background color or pattern for the chart area, specify a border for it, and set overall font formatting for the chart. You can then apply further formatting to the elements of the chart as necessary to pick them out.

To format the chart area, select it so that its handles appear, right-click, and choose Format Chart Area from the shortcut menu to display the Format Chart Area dialog box:

- Use the Patterns tab to apply a border and a background color. You can also apply round corners to the chart. (This option is surprisingly popular.)

- Use the Font tab to apply font formatting. Select the Auto Scale option if you want the fonts to rescale automatically when the chart is resized.

- For an embedded chart, use the Properties tab to control whether the chart moves and resizes with cells, whether it prints with the worksheet, and whether it's locked.

Formatting Individual Chart Elements

After formatting the chart area, apply formatting to individual chart elements as necessary to create the effects you want. Select the chart element either by clicking it or by using the Chart Objects drop-down list on the Chart toolbar; then click the Format *Object* button to display the Format dialog box for the object.

Most of the formatting options are straightforward, but the following points are worth mentioning:

- To format the numbers displayed on an axis, or to format the values or percentages displayed for data points, select the appropriate axis or the data labels and issue a Format command. In the Format Axis dialog box or the Format Data Labels dialog box, use the options on the Number tab to format the numbers. For example, you might reduce the number of decimal places displayed on the chart to fewer than in the source cells. Clear the Linked to Source check box to break the formatting link between the values and their source cells.

- Click the Legend button on the toolbar to toggle the display of the legend.

- To apply or remove grid lines, use the options on the Gridlines tab of the Chart Options dialog box. You can also remove displayed grid lines by selecting one of them and pressing DELETE.

- To rotate a 3-D chart, select it and choose Chart | 3-D View; then use the controls in the 3-D View dialog box (shown next) to rotate the chart to the angle you want. Click the Apply button to see the effect of the change without closing the dialog box.

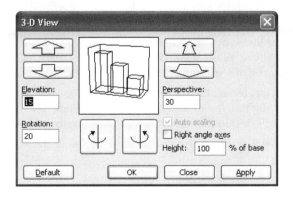

TIP   *Where Excel's chart tools don't meet your needs, consider using arrows, callouts, and text boxes (or other AutoShapes) from the Drawing toolbar to draw viewers' attention to particular items. "Working with Shapes, AutoShapes, and WordArt" in Chapter 5 discusses how to add AutoShapes to your documents.*

Copying Formatting from One Chart to Another

Once you've applied custom formatting to a chart, you can quickly copy it to another chart:

1. Select the chart area of the source chart.
2. Issue a Copy command (for example, press CTRL-C).
3. Select the destination chart.
4. Choose Edit | Paste Special to display the Paste Special dialog box.
5. Select the Formats option and click OK.

Unlinking a Chart from Its Data Source

By default, Excel automatically updates your charts when you edit the data sources they're drawn from, so your charts remain accurate without your needing to update them manually. Usually, this updating is convenient, because it prevents the potential embarrassment of showing a chart that doesn't represent its current data.

Sometimes, though, you may want to generate several charts from the same data source without having each linked to the data source, so that the charts can show different values in the data series. For example, you might want to create multiple charts showing sales projections without keeping multiple sets of projection figures in your worksheet.

You can do so by following this somewhat awkward procedure:

1. Create a new workbook for temporary use during this procedure.
2. Copy or move the chart from the existing workbook to the new workbook:
   - For an embedded chart: Select the chart, issue a Copy command or Move command, activate the new workbook, and issue a Paste command.
   - For a chart sheet: Select the chart sheet, and choose Edit | Move or Copy Sheet to display the Move or Copy dialog box. Specify the appropriate worksheet in the new workbook as the destination, select the Create a Copy option (if you want to preserve the original chart), and click OK.
3. Remove the link created by the Copy operation by choosing Edit | Links in the new workbook, selecting the link in the Edit Links dialog box, and clicking the Break Link button in the confirmation dialog box. Click Close to close the Edit Links dialog box.
4. Move the chart back to the original workbook by using the same techniques described in step 2.
5. Delete the new workbook without saving changes.

Perhaps an easier method is to copy the data series you used for the original chart, paste it into another location in the same workbook, alter the values as appropriate, and create another chart linked to those values. Remember to remove the extra copy of the data and its associated chart when you no longer need it.

Printing Your Charts

To print a chart, select it and issue a Print command as usual. Bear the following considerations in mind:

- Before printing a chart, use Print Preview to check how it will look. If you're using a color printer, you shouldn't need to worry about how the colors will look. But if you're using a black-and-white printer, check how the chart will look in grayscale.

- If necessary, use the controls on the Patterns tab of the Format Data Series dialog box or the Format Data Point dialog box to apply distinct markings to the data markers.

- To constrain the size of a chart on a chart sheet to less than the entire page that Excel allots it by default, use the options in the Printed Chart Size section of the Chart tab of the Page Setup dialog box (File | Page Setup).

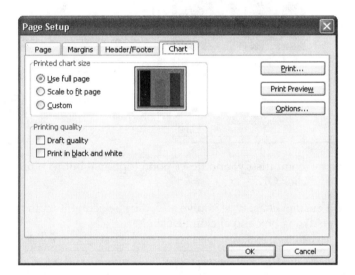

- To print a chart in draft quality (saving ink) or black and white (rather than color), use the options in the Printing Quality section of the Chart tab of the Page Setup dialog box (File | Page Setup).

Creating Custom Chart Types

You can add custom chart types that you create to the Custom Types list in the Chart Type dialog box. By doing so, you can reuse the chart type quickly and easily.

To add a custom chart type:

1. Create the chart and apply formatting as needed.

2. Select the chart.

3. Choose Chart | Chart Type to display the Chart Type dialog box.

4. Click the Custom Types tab to display it if it's not already displayed, and then select the User-Defined option in the Select From area. Excel displays the list of user-defined

charts, as shown on the left in the next illustration. If you haven't added any, you'll only see the default chart type.

5. Click Add to display the Add Custom Chart Type dialog box, shown on the right here:

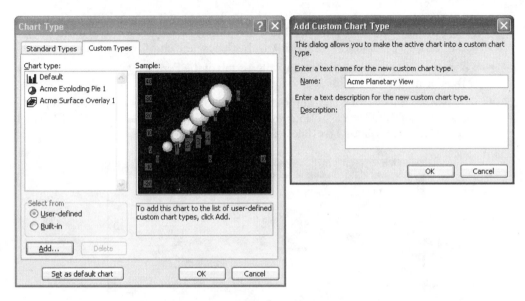

6. Type the name (compulsory) and description (optional but recommended) for the chart type, and click OK.

You can delete a custom chart type you've added by selecting it on the Custom Types tab of the Chart Type dialog box and clicking Delete.

TIP   *You can edit Excel's built-in custom chart types by opening the file XL8GALRY.XLS, which you'll find in the Program Files\Microsoft Office\Office 11\locale_ID folder—for example, the Program Files\Microsoft Office\Office 11\1033 folder for a U.S. English installation of Office.*

Working with PivotTables

If you've never heard of a PivotTable and your boss has asked you to create one, or if you've used them but maybe not to their fullest advantage, you'll find everything you need in this discussion. You'll learn what PivotTables are, what they're for, how to create them, and how to manipulate them. Then in the last part of the chapter, we'll show you how to create PivotCharts and standard charts from PivotTables.

NOTE   *To create a PivotTable, you'll need a database of some kind—either an Excel database or an external database. Chapter 19 discusses how to create databases in Excel.*

What Is a PivotTable?

A PivotTable is a form of report that works by rearranging the fields and records in a database into a different format. You can rotate (*pivot*) the columns in the PivotTable to display data summarized in different ways; you can sort the database easily in various ways; and you can collapse and expand the level of information displayed.

The PivotTable creates a PivotTable field from each field in the database (each column, in the default orientation). Each PivotTable field contains items that summarize the rows of information that contain a particular entry.

Creating and manipulating the PivotTable doesn't change the contents or layout of the database, so you can safely use a PivotTable to experiment with your data without worrying about corrupting the data or needing to restore the database's layout afterwards. A PivotTable also enables you to perform what would otherwise be relatively complex calculations by using its built-in features.

TIP *If PivotTables seem mysterious—don't worry, that's a normal reaction. The best way to come to grips with PivotTables is by using them to experiment with practice data over which you have control, or with a spare copy of real data that you can reduce to an easily manageable quantity, when you're not under pressure to deliver results.*

Until you start using data in a PivotTable, the features and benefits tend to be woolly. The following illustration shows a section of a database that we'll use for examples in the rest of this discussion. The database tracks sales of a microbrewery's products by category (strong ales, standard ales, health products, animal feedstuffs, and so on); item; date (year and month, in separate columns); the rep who made the sale; the sales amount; the customer; and so on. The illustration shows only the most interesting fields for our present purposes, leaving out various other fields (such as when the order was posted, when it was fulfilled, and when it was paid).

	A	B	C	D	E	F	G	H
6	Order #	Year	Month	Rep	Category	Item	Sales	Customer
7	20040045	2004	August	Hickman	Health	Brewer's Yeast	$800	Goods4U
8	20040044	2004	August	Hickman	Feedstuffs	Protein Mix	$400	Winners
9	20040043	2004	August	Velasquez	Str Ale	Boneshaker	$300	Countrywide
10	20040042	2004	August	Hickman	Feedstuffs	Protein Mix	$900	Winners
11	20040041	2004	September	Nilsson	Str Lager	Iron Reserve	$2,384	Extra Continental
12	20040040	2004	July	Hickman	Std Ale	Merry Giant	$3,295	Extra Continental
13	20040039	2004	June	Velasquez	Str Ale	Boneshaker	$400	Countrywide
14	20040038	2004	April	Hickman	Health	Brewer's Yeast	$995	Goods4U
15	20040037	2004	March	Stewart	Std Ale	Corn Circle	$2,500	Moose Pubs

You can use a PivotTable to ask questions of the data, such as the following:

- Which of our categories of product are waxing and which are waning?

- Which are the key customers we should concentrate on?

- How do our sales this year compare to our sales in another year?

- Which rep sells most of which product? (Or, perhaps more pertinently: should we refocus any particular rep on another product?)

We'll look at examples of manipulating the sample database to deliver answers to such questions after setting up the PivotTable.

Running the PivotTable and PivotChart Wizard

To create a PivotTable:

1. Open the workbook that contains the database you want to manipulate.

2. Display the worksheet that contains the database, and click a cell in the database. To use just part of the database, select the particular part.

3. Choose Data | PivotTable and PivotChart Report. Excel displays the first screen of the PivotTable and PivotChart wizard:

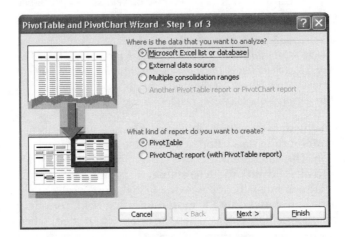

4. Make sure the Microsoft Excel List or Database option and the PivotTable option are selected, and click Next. The wizard displays its second screen:

TIP *You can also use the PivotTable and PivotChart wizard to create PivotTable reports (and PivotCharts) from data sources external to Excel—for example, by using Microsoft Query to return data from a database. See "Customizing a Query with MS Query" in Chapter 19 for a brief discussion of returning data from a database with MS Query.*

5. Enter the database range in the Range text box:

• If you selected a cell in the database in step 2, the wizard should have identified the range that contains the database. (See Chapter 19 for a discussion of what constitutes a database. Briefly, Excel understands a blank row or column to denote the end of the database, so your database can't contain any blank rows or columns.)

- If the wizard selected the wrong range, click the Collapse Dialog button and select the range manually.

6. Click Next. The wizard displays its third screen.

7. Select the New Worksheet option or the Existing Worksheet option to specify where to place the PivotTable. In most cases, the New Worksheet option (the default) is the better choice. If you choose the Existing Worksheet option, you can use the Collapse Dialog button to specify the location.

8. At this point, you can also specify the layout of the PivotTable (by clicking Layout and working in the Layout dialog box) or options for the PivotTable (by clicking Options and working in the PivotTable Options dialog box). Using the Layout dialog box was the standard way of creating a PivotTable in earlier versions of Excel, and it is useful when you're working with so much data that the report is slow to display when working directly with the PivotTable. The newer way, which is easier, is to lay out the fields directly on the blank PivotTable, as discussed in the following section. "Choosing PivotTable Options" (later in this chapter) discusses how to choose options.

9. Click Finish. The wizard creates the new worksheet or selects the specified existing worksheet (depending on your choice), creates a blank PivotTable, and displays the PivotTable toolbar and the PivotTable Field List, as shown next. As you can see, you are presented with a page area, a row area, a column area, and a data area.

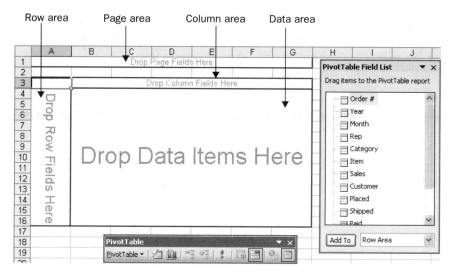

Work in your PivotTable as described in the following sections.

NOTE When you create a second PivotTable that uses the same source data as an existing PivotTable, Excel displays a message box offering to base the new PivotTable on the data in the existing PivotTable. By doing so, you can save memory (which can improve performance when you're working with large amounts of data) and reduce file size.

Creating Your PivotTable

Now create your PivotTable by dragging the appropriate field buttons from the PivotTable Field List window to the appropriate areas of the blank PivotTable. Here's an illustrated example using the sample database:

1. Drag the Year field to the page area. Excel adds the field, displays a drop-down list next to it for selecting the years, and selects the (All) entry, as shown here:

2. Drag the Rep field to the row area. Excel adds the field with a drop-down list button for selecting the rep name, enters the rep names in the cells (again, displaying all items), and adds a Grand Total entry under them:

3. Drag the Category field to the column area. Excel adds the field with a drop-down list button for selecting the category, enters the categories in the cells across the columns, and adds a Grand Total entry immediately to their right, as shown next.

	A	B	C	D	E	F	G	H
1	Year	(All) ▼						
2								
3		Category ▼						
4	Rep ▼	Feedstuffs	Health	Std Ale	Std Lager	Str Ale	Str Lager	Grand Total
5	Hickman							
6	Nilsson							
7	Ragnarsdottir		Drop Data Items Here					
8	Stewart							
9	Velasquez							
10	Whyte							
11	Grand Total							

4. Drag the Sales field to the data area. Excel snaps the data into place and displays a Sum of Sales button at the intersection of the rows and columns, as shown in the next illustration. Now you can see which rep has sold how much of each category of product.

	A	B	C	D	E	F	G	H
1	Year	(All) ▼						
2								
3	Sum of Sales	Category ▼						
4	Rep ▼	Feedstuffs	Health	Std Ale	Std Lager	Str Ale	Str Lager	Grand Total
5	Hickman	12600	23030	30490	1600	1000	2000	70720
6	Nilsson			7595	1600	1500	4768	15463
7	Ragnarsdottir			20090	900	3200	4734	28924
8	Stewart			29590	4500	1600	4384	40074
9	Velasquez			11500	1600	1100	8452	22652
10	Whyte			34833	4800	4300		43933
11	Grand Total	12600	23030	134098	15000	12700	24338	221766

5. To see the reps' results for a specific year (as the next illustration shows), instead of for all years, choose the year from the Year drop-down list.

	A	B	C	D	E	F	G	H
1	Year	2004 ▼						
2								
3	Sum of Sales	Category ▼						
4	Rep ▼	Feedstuffs	Health	Std Ale	Std Lager	Str Ale	Str Lager	Grand Total
5	Hickman	4300	7820	27195	1600			40915
6	Nilsson				1600	300	4768	6668
7	Ragnarsdottir			11295		800		12095
8	Stewart			12295		800	2000	15095
9	Velasquez			2500		700	2384	5584
10	Whyte			5795	3200	3900		12895
11	Grand Total	4300	7820	59080	6400	6500	9152	93252

Changing the PivotTable

You can change a PivotTable by dragging the fields you've already placed to different locations, by removing one or more of those fields, or by adding other fields. Here are quick examples of manipulating the PivotTable created in the previous section:

- Drag the Item field to the column area. Excel breaks down each category by its components, as shown here. (The illustration only shows some of the categories.)

Year	2004 [▼]						
Sum of Sales	Category [▼]	Item [▼]					
	Feedstuffs	Feedstuffs Total	Health	Health Total	Std Ale		Std Ale Total
Rep [▼]	Protein Mix		Brewer's Yeast		Corn Circle	Merry Giant	
Hickman	4300	4300	7820	7820	23900	3295	27195
Nilsson							
Ragnarsdottir					8000	3295	11295
Stewart					9000	3295	12295
Velasquez					2500		2500
Whyte					2500	3295	5795
Grand Total	4300	4300	7820	7820	45900	13180	59080

- Drag the Category field off the PivotTable area to remove it. (Either drop the field in limbo anywhere outside the PivotTable or drop it back on the PivotTable Field List window.) The PivotTable then shows how much of each item each rep sold in the specified year, as you can see in the next illustration, which shows very clearly which rep is selling most of which item.

Year	(All) [▼]							
Sum of Sales	Item [▼]							
Rep [▼]	Boneshaker	Brewer's Yeast	Corn Circle	Iron Reserve	Maltmaster	Merry Giant	Protein Mix	Grand Total
Hickman	1000	23030	23900	2000	1600	6590	12600	70720
Nilsson	1500		700	4768	1600	6895		15463
Ragnarsdottir	3200		13500	4734	900	6590		28924
Stewart	1600		21000	4384	4500	8590		40074
Velasquez	1100		10500	8452	1600	1000		22652
Whyte	4300		31538		4800	3295		43933
Grand Total	12700	23030	101138	24338	15000	32960	12600	221766

- Drag the Customer field to the row area to produce a PivotTable showing which rep sold how much of which item to which customer. Drag the Rep field off the PivotTable to display a breakdown of which items each customer purchased:

Year	(All) [▼]							
Sum of Sales	Item [▼]							
Customer [▼]	Boneshaker	Brewer's Yeast	Corn Circle	Iron Reserve	Maltmaster	Merry Giant	Protein Mix	Grand Total
Countrywide	12700							12700
Extra Continental				24338		32960		57298
Goods4U		23030						23030
IntraBrew			76938					76938
Moose Pubs			24200		15000			39200
Winners							12600	12600
Grand Total	12700	23030	101138	24338	15000	32960	12600	221766

Using the PivotTable Toolbar

When you're working in a PivotTable, Excel displays the PivotTable toolbar by default. Here it is, with the buttons labeled:

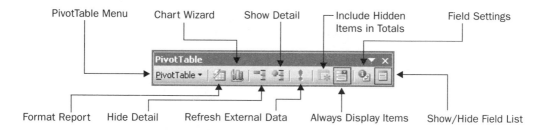

Here's what the controls on the PivotTable toolbar do:

- **PivotTable Menu**   Display commands for working with PivotTables.

- **Format Report**   Display the AutoFormat dialog box, from which you can quickly apply any of a wide selection of canned formats to the PivotTable.

- **Chart Wizard**   Launch the Chart wizard.

- **Hide Detail** and **Show Detail**   Toggle the display of detail in the PivotTable.

- **Refresh External Data**   Force Excel to refresh the data contained in the PivotTable. Click this button to update the PivotTable after changing data in the cells from which the PivotTable is drawn.

- **Include Hidden Items in Totals**   Control whether Excel includes hidden items in the totals displayed in the PivotTable.

- **Always Display Items**   Control whether Excel always displays the items in the table.

- **Field Settings**   Display the PivotTable Field dialog box for configuring settings for the selected field.

- **Show/Hide Field List**   Toggle the display of the PivotTable Field List window.

Formatting a PivotTable

The standard method of formatting a PivotTable is to apply an AutoFormat by clicking the Format Report button on the PivotTable toolbar, selecting the most suitable AutoFormat in the AutoFormat dialog box, and clicking OK. Excel maintains the AutoFormat's properties on the relevant cells when you rearrange the PivotTable—no mean feat, given how drastically a PivotTable can change when you add, remove, or move a field.

You can also apply formatting manually to the data area of the PivotTable, but be warned that visual elements will disappear when Excel reapplies the current AutoFormat to the PivotTable unless the Preserve Formatting option in the PivotTable Options dialog box is selected (see "Choosing PivotTable Options," later in this chapter). What you're most likely to benefit from changing is number formatting—for example, to display the data in currency format or with thousands separators. Number formatting isn't affected by the reapplication of AutoFormats.

Changing a Field to a Different Function

To change the function used for summarizing the data area, select the Field button on the PivotTable, and click the Field Settings button on the PivotTable toolbar. Use the options in the PivotTable Field dialog box, shown here, to specify the function you want.

To apply number formatting from here, click the Number button and work on the Number tab of the Format Cells dialog box. To show the data in a different way than normal, click Options and use the Show Data As drop-down list, the Base Field list, and the Base Item list to specify the format you want. (For example, you might choose Difference From in the Show Data As drop-down list to show how the data differs from the specified base field.)

Choosing PivotTable Options

You can choose PivotTable options either when creating the PivotTable (by clicking Options on the third screen of the wizard) or by choosing PivotTable | Table Options from the PivotTable toolbar. Most of the options in the PivotTable Options dialog box, shown in Figure 18-4, are easy to understand: you can turn off the grand totals for columns and rows, turn off AutoFormat, control page layout, and specify how often Excel refreshes the PivotTable from its data.

TIP   *Two useful options in the PivotTable Options dialog box are the For Error Values, Show option and the For Empty Cells, Show option. These let you control what's displayed in cells that would otherwise be empty or contain error values.*

Working with PivotCharts

As you'd guess from the name, a PivotChart is a chart related to a PivotTable. The advantage of a PivotChart over a regular chart is that you can drag items about the chart layout to display different levels of detail or different views of the data. This flexibility makes PivotCharts great for analyzing data.

You can create a PivotChart in either of the following ways:

- Create a PivotTable as described earlier in this chapter (in "Running the PivotTable and PivotChart Wizard"), and then click the Chart Wizard button on the PivotTable toolbar.

- Run the PivotTable and PivotChart wizard, and select the PivotChart Report (with PivotTable Report) option on the first screen of the wizard. This option creates the

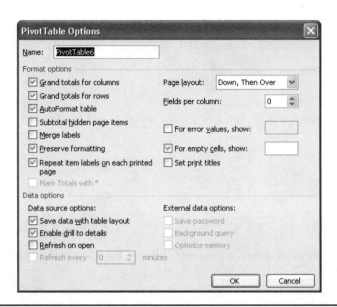

FIGURE 18-4   Choose formatting options and data options in the PivotTable Options dialog box.

PivotTable for you (on your choice of a new worksheet or an existing worksheet, as before), creates a new chart page named Chart*n* (where *n* is the lowest unused number), and places the skeleton of a PivotChart on it.

Drag the fields to the appropriate places in the chart to pivot it and display the data you want. Figure 18-5 shows a PivotChart that shows sales by the Customer field.

You can use any of the drop-down lists on the chart to change the data displayed. In the preceding example, you can change the year, the customer, and the item. Similarly, you can add or remove fields to pivot the chart. Figure 18-6 shows reps added to the mix so that the chart shows each rep's sales to each customer.

TIP   *You can create a PivotChart instantly with the default settings by selecting a PivotTable and pressing* F11. *If you customize the default settings to the type of PivotChart you usually need to create, you may find this option useful.*

Creating a Conventional Chart from PivotTable Data

Sometimes, you may also want to create a conventional chart from data in a PivotTable rather than an interactive PivotChart. To create a conventional chart, you need to extract the values from the data in the PivotTable and then use the Chart wizard. Follow these steps:

1. Select the data in the PivotTable. If you need to include field buttons and any data contained in the first column and row of the report, drag upward and across from the lower-right corner of the data range rather than dragging down and across from the upper-left corner.

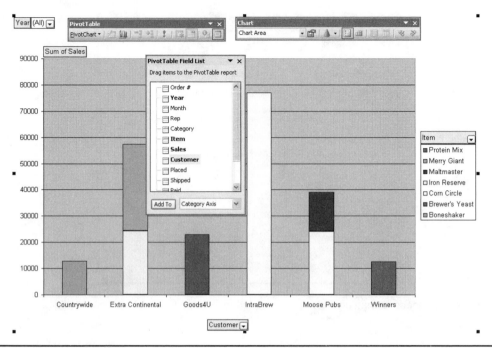

FIGURE 18-5 This PivotChart displays sales by the Customer field.

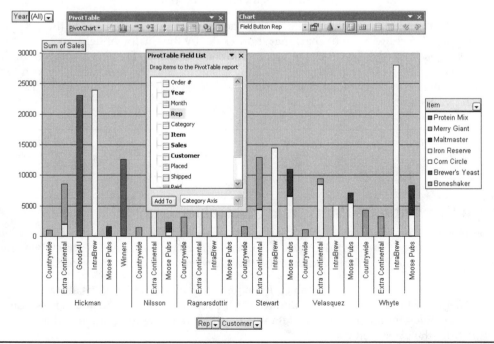

FIGURE 18-6 This PivotChart breaks down the sales by rep, showing each rep's sales to each customer.

2. Issue a Copy command (for example, press CTRL-C).

3. Select a cell in a blank area of the same worksheet or a different worksheet that will contain the data values.

4. Choose Edit | Paste Special to display the Paste Special dialog box.

5. Select the Values option.

6. Click OK. Excel pastes the values from the PivotTable data into the range that starts with the cell you selected.

7. Click the Chart wizard, and use its options to create the chart as usual.

Creating Excel Databases

As you saw in Chapter 10, Word's table features enable you to create and sort lists in Word; and as you saw in Chapter 14, you can use Word tables as databases for mail-merge operations. But if you want to create simple databases, Excel is a much better bet than Word, because it provides better tools for sorting, checking, and locating data. (If you want to create large or complex databases, or databases that contain nontext data such as sounds or pictures, you should use Access rather than Excel. See Part VI of this book.)

Creating a Database

Before we get into the considerations for creating a database, a word on terminology.

A *database* is an organized collection of data. Just about any organized collection of data can qualify for the term, be it stored in a paper address book, a PDA, a computer, or a server farm. We use *database* to mean a collection of data stored either in Excel or in a full-fledged database application such as Access, SQL Server, or Oracle. Microsoft prefers the term *list* for a database stored in Excel, but we'll use *database* in this chapter, because it's clearer and less potentially confusing than *list*.

You enter data in the cells in the database using the techniques described earlier in this part of the book, and you can use Excel's database functions to find and manipulate data.

A database is a block of data stored on an Excel worksheet without any blank rows or columns in the block. Blank *cells* in a database are fine—for example, if you don't have the data for a cell. But make sure your database doesn't include any blank rows or columns, because to Excel these denote the boundary of the current database.

In a database, each row represents a data *record*—for example, the details of an invoice, or the name, address, and contact information for a customer. Each column represents a *field* in the record. In the case of an invoice, one column might contain the field for the invoice number, another the field for the date, another the field for the purchaser's name, and so on; in the case of a customer, separate fields would typically contain the last name, first name, middle initial, title, and so on.

NOTE *You can use databases to create PivotTable and PivotChart reports (discussed in "Working with PivotTables" and "Working with PivotCharts" in the previous chapter).*

For your Excel database to work properly, you have to lay it out and enter your data in the way Excel expects it. These are the essential rules:

- Create each database on a separate worksheet. If you have just one database, this is no problem. If you have multiple databases, either create each database on its own worksheet or finesse the problem by combining the databases and using an extra field in the database to distinguish them.

- Enter the names of the database's fields in the header row. Technically, your database doesn't *have to* have a header row. But if you want to use AutoFilter (discussed in "Performing Quick Filtering with AutoFilter," later in this chapter), or if you want to use forms to simplify data entry, your database needs a header row. So in practice, your database must have a header row.

- Make each label in the header row unique so that Excel (and you) can distinguish each field from the other fields. This requirement may seem a no-brainer—but if you extend an existing database by incorporating new fields, you may have to rename existing fields to give each a unique label. For example, if your database contains a field named E-mail for the record's e-mail address, and you need to add another e-mail address, you might need to rename the E-mail field to E-mail 1 for uniqueness and clarity.

- Keep the column labels reasonably concise, because Excel displays them on data entry forms you use for the database. One long label produces an awkwardly wide form and wide gaps between shorter labels and their fields, which can make them slower to read.

- Format the header row differently from the data area. Doing so has twin benefits: it makes Excel recognize the row as a header row, and it helps you to distinguish it.

- Make sure your database area doesn't contain any blank rows or columns, because these will interfere with Excel's sorting and searching.

The following illustration shows a section of an example database in Excel. We used a Window | Freeze Panes command to make the column headings stay on screen no matter how far down the worksheet is scrolled.

	A	B	C	D	E	F	G	H	I Horiz. Res.	J Vert. Res.	K Weight (lb)	L
1	Quantity	Stock #	Brand	Manufacturer #	Category	Description	Color	Price ($)				More Info
16	0	SDK848	SkullDam	000348392E	Other	SkullBand monitor decor	Many	$24.99	#N/A	#N/A	2.0	
17	4	LCD001	Elcidee	ED-440-1500J	LCD Monitor	Elcidee 15 inch LCD	Jet	$199.99	1024	768	7.5	Contrast ra
18	2	LCD002	Elcidee	ED-440-1500B	LCD Monitor	Elcidee 15 inch LCD	Beige	$199.99	1024	768	7.5	Contrast ra
19	2 on 4/14/04	LCD003	Elcidee	ED-440-1700J	LCD Monitor	Elcidee 17 inch LCD	Jet	$299.99	1280	1024	10.9	Contrast ra
20	1	LCD004	Elcidee	ED-440-1700B	LCD Monitor	Elcidee 17 inch LCD	Beige	$299.99	1280	1024	10.9	Contrast ra
21	1	LCD005	Elcidee	ED-440-1800J	LCD Monitor	Elcidee 18 inch LCD	Jet	$499.99	1280	1024	15.3	Contrast ra
22	1	LCD006	Elcidee	ED-440-1800B	LCD Monitor	Elcidee 18 inch LCD	Beige	$499.99	1280	1024	15.3	Contrast ra
23	Special order	LCD007	Elcidee	ED-440-2000J	LCD Monitor	Elcidee 20 inch LCD	Jet	$999.99	1600	1200	25.0	Contrast ra
24	Special order	LCD008	Elcidee	ED-440-2000B	LCD Monitor	Elcidee 20 inch LCD	Beige	$999.99	1600	1200	25.0	Contrast ra
25	Special order	LCD009	Elcidee	ED-440-2200J	LCD Monitor	Elcidee 22 inch LCD	Jet	$1,299.99	2048	1536	33.6	Contrast ra
26	Special order	LCD010	Elcidee	ED-440-2200B	LCD Monitor	Elcidee 22 inch LCD	Beige	$1,299.99	2048	1536	33.6	Contrast ra
27	5	MCB121	Elcidee	ED-370-0001	Cable Monito	Elcidee VGA cable 1m	Gray	$9.99	#N/A	#N/A	1.0	
28	4	MCB122	Elcidee	ED-370-0002	Cable Monito	Elcidee DVI cable 1m	Gray	$12.99	#N/A	#N/A	1.0	
29	1	MCB123	Elcidee	ED-370-0003	Cable Monito	Elcidee VGA cable 2m	Gray	$12.99	#N/A	#N/A	1.0	
30	2	MCB124	Elcidee	ED-370-0004	Cable Monito	Elcidee DVI cable 2m	Gray	$14.99	#N/A	#N/A	1.0	

Entering Data in Your Database

You can enter data in your database either by using standard data entry techniques or by using a custom data entry form (discussed in the upcoming sections). Most likely, you'll choose to work with standard techniques while laying out your database and entering the first records. After the database contains more than a few records, a data entry form becomes invaluable.

Entering Data by Using Standard Techniques

You can enter data in your database by using standard Excel techniques:

- Type directly into a cell.

- Select a range of cells, type, and press CTRL-ENTER to enter the same item in each cell.

- Use copy and paste or CTRL-drag and drop to reuse existing data.

- Use AutoFill to repeat the contents of the current cell or to extend the current database. Depending on the types of data your database contains, you may find it helpful to create custom AutoFill lists. "Creating Custom AutoFill Lists" in Chapter 16 explains how to do so.

- If a column contains repetitive entries (such as product names or town names), AutoComplete will suggest a matching entry as soon as you type enough letters to distinguish it from all other entries.

- You can also reuse an existing entry by right-clicking the cell, choosing Pick from List, and selecting the entry from the list that Excel displays. Because of the amount of clicking and scrolling this technique entails, it's usually slower and clumsier than other methods—especially if the column contains a large number of different entries (rather than fewer repeated entries). However, it may be useful for complex entries that are awkward to type.

All these techniques work fine on a long list, but entering data in your database by moving around a huge worksheet gets old fast. If the columns in your database contain long entries, you'll either need to scroll sideways frequently or display only part of each column's contents. As soon as your database grows beyond a few screens of data, you'll probably want to use forms to make data entry faster and easier.

TIP   When you enter a new record in your database manually, it's usually easier to enter the new record at the end of the database and then sort the database (if necessary) rather than locating the place where the new record should appear and inserting a row there.

Entering and Editing Data with Data Entry Forms

The most effective way of entering data in a database of any size or complexity is to use Excel's data form feature. A *data form* is a custom dialog box (technically, a userform like those you can create with Visual Basic for Applications) that Excel creates and populates with fields that reflect the column headings in your database. The following illustration shows a data form derived from the sample database shown earlier in this chapter.

PART III

Excel enters the worksheet's name in the title bar of the form, so you can easily see which database you're working on.

To use a data form, activate a cell within the database and choose Data | Form. Excel generates the data form from your database's column headings and displays the data from the first record in the database in it.

Data forms are straightforward to use:

- Use the Find Prev button and Find Next button to navigate to other records in the database.

- To change a record, navigate to it, make the changes, and press ENTER. To undo changes you've made to the record, click Restore. This works until you commit the changes by pressing ENTER.

- To add a new record to the database, click New. Enter the data for the new record in the form, then press ENTER. Excel adds the new record at the end of the database.

- To delete the current record, click Delete. Excel displays a message box warning you that the record will be permanently deleted. Click OK to delete the record. Note that you won't be able to recover the record (you can't undo the deletion) unless you close the workbook without saving changes; if you do that, you'll lose any other changes you've made to the database since you last saved it.

- To search for records that match only specific criteria, click the Criteria button. Excel clears the data form and displays *Criteria* above the New button. Specify the criteria in the appropriate boxes and click Find Next or Find Previous.

- To leave the criteria view, click Form to return to the regular form view.

TIP   *To find a particular blank field in a criteria search, enter = and nothing else in that field.*

Sorting

After entering data in your database, you'll probably need to sort it so that you can view related records together. For example, you might need to sort a product database by product category, or a mailing database by last name.

Excel offers tools for quick sorting, for performing a multifield sort, and for defining custom criteria for sorting. However, before you sort your database at all, you may need to tag the records with the existing sort order.

Preparing to Sort Your Database

If for any reason you need to be able to return your database to the order in which you created it, there's an additional step you need to perform *before* you sort the database at all. (Or you might need to sort the database at first to get it into the preferred order that you want to be able to return to when necessary.) Add another column to the database and give it an appropriate name, such as Sort Order. Then enter the appropriate number in each cell: for example, enter **1** in the first cell, and then use AutoFill to enter the incremented series of numbers in the other cells. Once you've done this, you'll be able to sort the database by this column to restore its records to the original order.

Performing a Quick Sort

The easiest type of sort to perform is a quick sort, which sorts data by a single field in ascending order (A to Z, lowest numbers to highest) or descending order (Z to A, highest numbers to lowest). To perform a quick sort:

1. Activate a cell in the column that contains the field you want to sort.
2. Click the Sort Ascending button (shown on the left here) or the Sort Descending button (shown on the right) on the Standard toolbar, as appropriate.

NOTE   *In a default configuration of Excel, the Sort Descending button usually appears on the hidden area of the Standard toolbar until you use it, so you'll need to click the Toolbar Options button, and then choose the Sort Descending button on the resulting panel.*

If necessary, you can then perform a further sort by another column, and then another, to sort by other fields. But in most cases, you'll do better to follow the procedure described next.

Performing a Multifield Sort

To sort by multiple fields at once, use the Sort dialog box:

1. Choose Data | Sort. Excel displays the Sort dialog box, shown here with fields specified:

2. Use the controls in the Sort By section and the two Then By sections to specify one, two, or three fields to sort by. For each, specify ascending or descending order as appropriate.

3. In the My List Has section, check that Excel has selected the Header Row option if your database has a header row. (If you're sorting part of the database without a header row, or if you're sorting rows in a worksheet that isn't a database, make sure Excel has selected the No Header Row option.)

4. Click OK. Excel closes the Sort dialog box and performs the sort.

Sorting by a Custom Sort Order

From the Sort dialog box, you can also specify a custom sort order for the first sort key. To do so, click Options to display the Sort Options dialog box, and choose the sort order in the First Key Sort Order drop-down list.

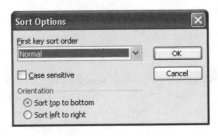

The First Key Sort Order drop-down list contains a Normal entry for the default sort order, together with Excel's four built-in AutoFill lists (Sun through Sat, Sunday through Saturday, Jan through Dec, and January through December), and any custom AutoFill lists you've defined (see "Creating Custom AutoFill Lists" in Chapter 16 for instructions). For example, you might want to sort a set of month entries by months rather than alphabetically. Or you might need to sort your company's locations in their order of importance rather than alphabetically.

The Sort Options dialog box also contains options for performing case-sensitive sorting instead of case-insensitive sorting (Excel's default) and for sorting from left to right instead of from top to bottom (in other words, sorting by column instead of by row).

Finding and Replacing Data in Databases

You can use Excel's Find functionality to find data in your database as you would in any other worksheet. Likewise, you can use Replace to replace particular entries—but you need to be careful. This is because in a large database that contains many entries, distinguishing one data record from another similar record can be difficult, and any mistakes made can be hard to track down later. In particular, performing a Replace All operation on a database is fraught with danger.

More often, what you'll need to do in a database is identify all the records that match one or more specified criteria. To do so, you use filtering.

Filtering

To find all the records that match one or more specified criteria, you apply logical filters. Filters work by hiding all the records that don't match the criteria, so you see only the records that do match.

You can apply filtering by using Excel's AutoFilter feature or by creating filters manually. AutoFilter is much easier than creating filters manually, so it's best to use AutoFilter unless you actually need the extra control that manual filters can deliver.

Performing Quick Filtering with AutoFilter

AutoFilter lets you quickly apply filters by choosing filter values from drop-down lists. AutoFilter is great for quickly filtering down a database by specific criteria so you can see the matching records, but you can't store the results: when you turn off AutoFilter, your full database is displayed again. So AutoFilter is primarily useful for looking up entries on the fly—for example, in response to a customer inquiry.

To use AutoFilter, activate the worksheet that contains the database you want to filter. (If the worksheet contains more than one database, make a cell in the appropriate database active; otherwise, AutoFilter won't know which database to filter.) Then choose Data |

Filter | AutoFilter. Excel displays a drop-down arrow at the right side of each column heading. Here is an example with an AutoFilter list displayed:

	A	B	C	D	E	F	G	H	I
1	Quantity ▾	Stock ▾	Brand ▾	Manufacturer ▾	Category ▾	Description ▾	Color ▾	Price ($ ▾	Horiz. Res. ▾
2	0	SDK848	SkullDam	000348392E	Other	(All)	Many	$24.99	#N/A
3	4	LCD001	Elcidee	ED-440-1500J	LCD Monitor	(Top 10...)	Jet	$199.99	1024
4	2	LCD002	Elcidee	ED-440-1500B	LCD Monitor	(Custom...)	Beige	$199.99	1024
5	2 on 4/14/04	LCD003	Elcidee	ED-440-1700J	LCD Monitor	Barebones P4 2.4GHz	Jet	$299.99	1280
6	1	LCD004	Elcidee	ED-440-1700B	LCD Monitor	Barebones P4 2.8GHz	Beige	$299.99	1280
7	1	LCD005	Elcidee	ED-440-1800J	LCD Monitor	Barebones P4 3.0GHz	Jet	$499.99	1280
8	1	LCD006	Elcidee	ED-440-1800B	LCD Monitor	Elcidee 15 inch LCD	Beige	$499.99	1280
9	Special order	LCD007	Elcidee	ED-440-2000J	LCD Monitor	Elcidee 17 inch LCD	Jet	$999.99	1600
						Elcidee 18 inch LCD			
10	Special order	LCD008	Elcidee	ED-440-2000B	LCD Monitor	Elcidee 20 inch LCD	Beige	$999.99	1600
11	Special order	LCD009	Elcidee	ED-440-2200J	LCD Monitor	Elcidee 22 inch LCD	Jet	$1,299.99	2048
12	Special order	LCD010	Elcidee	ED-440-2200B	LCD Monitor	Elcidee DVI cable 1m	Beige	$1,299.99	2048
13	5	MCB121	Elcidee	ED-370-0001	Cable Monito	Elcidee DVI cable 2m	Gray	$9.99	#N/A
						Elcidee DVI cable 3m			
14	4	MCB122	Elcidee	ED-370-0002	Cable Monito	Elcidee DVI cable 5m	Gray	$12.99	#N/A
15	1	MCB123	Elcidee	ED-370-0003	Cable Monito	Elcidee VGA cable 1m	Gray	$12.99	#N/A
16	2	MCB124	Elcidee	ED-370-0004	Cable Monito	Elcidee VGA cable 2m	Gray	$14.99	#N/A
						Elcidee VGA cable 3m			
						Elcidee VGA cable 5m			
17	0	MCB125	Elcidee	ED-370-0005	Cable Monito	Monitor shield	Gray	$14.99	#N/A
						Elcidee VGA cable 3m			

From the drop-down list for a column, select the item by which you want to filter the list, or choose Top 10, Custom, Blanks, or NonBlanks as appropriate:

- **(Top 10)**   Displays the Top 10 AutoFilter dialog box, in which you can choose Top or Bottom, specify the number of entries (10 is the default), and choose Items or Percent. Top 10 works only for numbers; if you try to use it on a column that contains no numbers, Excel doesn't apply the AutoFilter.

- **(Custom)**   Displays the Custom AutoFilter dialog box (shown next), in which you can create custom filtering criteria. For example, you could create a custom filter that displayed all entries in the column that contained a particular keyword and were below a certain price. The comparison operators are easy to understand, and you can create either AND filters (both conditions must be met for inclusion in the results) or OR conditions (either condition can be met).

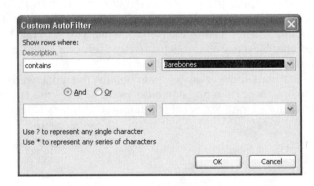

- **(Blanks)**   Displays all records that have blank cells in this column.
- **(NonBlanks)**   Displays all records whose cells in this column are not blank (they have some form of entry).

To display all entries in a column again, choose the (All) item.

After you apply an AutoFilter, Excel displays the resulting set of records. You can then apply further AutoFilters as necessary to narrow down the display to the records you're interested in.

To show you that AutoFiltering is applied, Excel displays the row numbers of matching fields and the drop-down list button on filtered columns in blue rather than black.

Choose Data | Filter | AutoFilter again to turn off AutoFilter and restore the display of your database to normal.

Creating Custom Filters Manually

For finer control over filtering than AutoFilter can deliver, create custom filters:

1. Activate the worksheet that contains the database you want to filter.

2. Select cells in the top five rows. (For example, drag from cell A1 to cell A5 to select those cells, or drag through the row headings.)

3. Choose Insert | Rows to insert five new blank rows above the selected rows. These rows will contain the criteria for filtering and are known as the *criteria range*.

4. Click the row heading for your column headings to select the row, and issue a Copy command to copy the headings to the Clipboard.

5. Click the row heading for row 1, and issue a Paste command to paste the headings in there, thus creating headings for the criteria range.

6. In row 2, enter the criteria for the first condition you want to implement:

   - Excel treats your entries in the same row as an AND condition: all of the entries must be met for the condition to be true and for a row to be included in the results.

   - If you make multiple entries in different rows of the same column, Excel treats them as OR conditions.

   - To match fields that begin with specific text, enter that text in the cell. For example, enter **Elcid** to find all the Elcidee entries.

   - To specify exact text matching, enter an equal sign, opening double quotes, another equal sign, the text, and closing quotes. For example, to find records that have the text *LCD monitor* in a field, enter **="=LCD monitor"**.

7. Use rows 3 through 5 to specify further conditions if necessary. If you use row 5, insert another blank row below it so that Excel can distinguish the criteria range from the database. The next illustration shows two filters applied: one to catch items whose entry in the Category column starts with *LCD*, whose price is less than $1000, and whose horizontal resolution is greater than or equal to 1280; and the other to catch

items whose Category entry starts with *CRT*, whose price is less than $500, and whose horizontal resolution is greater than or equal to 1600.

	A	B	C	D	E	F	G	H	I	J
									Horiz.	Vert.
1	Quantity	Stock #	Brand	Manufacturer #	Category	Description	Color	Price ($)	Res.	Res.
2					LCD			<1000	>=1280	
3					CRT			<500	>=1600	
4										
5										
									Horiz.	Vert.
6	Quantity	Stock #	Brand	Manufacturer #	Category	Description	Color	Price ($)	Res.	Res.
7		2	SDK848	SkullDam	000348392E	Other	SkullBand monitor decor	Many	$24.99	#N/A	#N/A
8		4	LCD001	Elcidee	ED-440-1500J	LCD Monitor	Elcidee 15 inch LCD	Jet	$199.99	1024	768
9		2	LCD002	Elcidee	ED-440-1500B	LCD Monitor	Elcidee 15 inch LCD	Beige	$199.99	1024	768
10	2 on 4/14/04	LCD003	Elcidee	ED-440-1700J	LCD Monitor	Elcidee 17 inch LCD	Jet	$299.99	1280	1024

8. After entering your criteria, select the criteria range (including the criteria headers) up to the last row you've used—in other words, don't include any blank rows in the criteria range. Then choose Insert | Name | Define, and create an easy name for the criteria range. (This step isn't essential, but it's helpful.)

9. Select a cell in the database again (so that the criteria range is no longer selected) and choose Data | Filter | Advanced Filter. Excel displays the Advanced Filter dialog box:

10. Excel's default setting in the Action section of the Advanced Filter dialog box is to filter the database in-place. Select the Copy to Another Location option if you want to export the matching records to another location, and enter the destination in the Copy To box.

11. Check that the List Range box contains the correct range for your database. If necessary, correct it by using the Collapse Dialog button. Include the database's header row in the range.

12. Enter your criteria range in the Criteria Range box. If you defined a name for the range, type the name. Otherwise, click the Collapse Dialog button and select the range manually, including the headers for the criteria range but excluding any blank rows in the criteria range.

13. Select the Unique Records Only option if you want Excel to suppress any duplicate entries in the results.

14. Click OK. Excel applies the filter and displays the results.

To remove filtering from your database, choose Data | Filter | Show All.

Linking to an External Database

If you (or your company) store information in a relational database rather than in an Excel database, you may want to be able to manipulate a subset of that information in Excel. You can do so by performing a query on that database and importing the resulting set of information.

Excel offers two options for querying an external database:

- Use the Query wizard to construct a simple query that enters a reference in your worksheet to the appropriate range in the external database.

- Use MS Query to create more complex queries to extract data from the external database.

Linking to a Database with the Query Wizard

Excel's Query wizard represents the easiest way to access an external database. To use the Query wizard:

1. Choose Data | Import External Data | New Database Query. Excel displays the Choose Data Source dialog box:

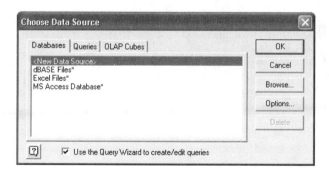

NOTE *If MS Query isn't installed on your computer, Excel prompts you to install it. Click Yes and provide the installation source (for example, supply the Office System CD or provide the path to a network share containing the files) if your computer doesn't have the installation files cached.*

2. Verify that the Use the Query Wizard to Create/Edit Queries option is selected.

3. Choose the data source you want to use:

- Choose the dBASE Files option, the Excel Files option, or the Microsoft Access Database option (as appropriate) on the Databases tab. (You might use the Excel

Files option to pull some data from your main Excel database into another worksheet so you could experiment with it.) Click OK.

- To use an ODBC data source, choose the <New Data Source> option and click OK. In the Create New Data Source dialog box that Excel displays, enter the name you want to use for the data source, specify the driver to use for accessing the data source, and click Connect. In the resulting dialog box, specify information as required—for example, the server name, your login ID and password, and whether to use a trusted (secure) connection.

4. Use the options in the Select Database dialog box to specify which database to open:

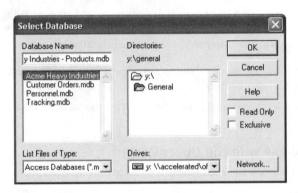

5. Click OK. Excel attempts the connection to the database and, if successful, launches the Query wizard. The following illustration shows the Choose Columns screen, the first Query wizard screen displayed when you're connecting to an Access database.

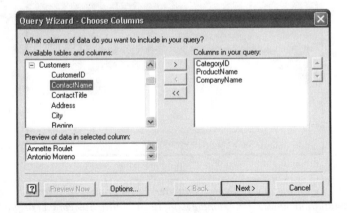

6. Follow the steps of the Query wizard, choosing data and options relevant to your needs. The Filter Data screen lets you set one or more filters for specifying which records you want. The Sort Order screen lets you choose sorting by one or more fields.

NOTE   *Depending on the options you choose, you may need to join fields together in MS Query before you can import the data into Excel.*

7. On the Query Wizard – Finish screen, make sure the Return Data to Microsoft Excel option is selected. (For coverage of the View Data or Edit Query in Microsoft Query option, see the next section.)

8. If you want to be able to use this query in future, click Save Query and specify the name in the resulting Save As dialog box. Excel's default location for saving queries is your *%userprofile%*\Application Data\Microsoft\Queries folder. You may want to save the query elsewhere so your colleagues can use it as well.

TIP   *Once you've saved a query, you can reuse it by choosing Choose Data | Import External Data | New Database Query, selecting the query on the Queries tab of the Choose Data Source dialog box, and clicking OK.*

9. Click Finish. Excel displays the Import Data dialog box:

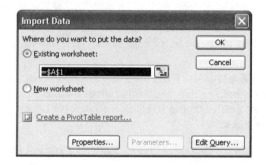

10. Specify whether to import the data into the current worksheet, into a new worksheet, or to create a PivotTable with it. Then click OK. Excel imports the data in the way you specified and displays the External Data toolbar:

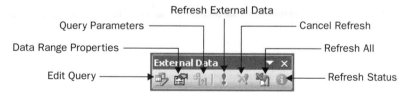

The External Data toolbar offers the following buttons for working with the data you've imported:

- **Edit Query**   Relaunches the Query wizard for editing the query.
- **Data Range Properties**   Displays the External Data Range Properties dialog box, shown in Figure 19-1, which contains options for saving the query definition, protecting it with a password, controlling how and when Excel refreshes the query,

and specifying formatting and layout options for the external data. These options are largely self-explanatory once you know where to find them.

- **Query Parameters** Displays the Parameters dialog box in which you can check or change the parameters for the query:

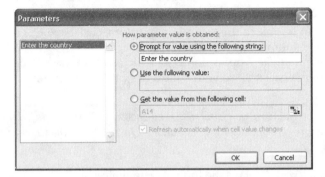

- **Refresh External Data** Forces an immediate refresh of the active external range.

- **Cancel Refresh** Cancels an ongoing refresh (for example, if it's taking too long).

- **Refresh All** Forces immediate refreshes of all external ranges in the active workbook.

- **Refresh Status** Displays the External Data Refresh Status dialog box, which shows you which query is being refreshed and enables you to stop the refresh. This dialog box is useful when you're trying to refresh all external ranges and need to see which refresh is getting stuck.

You can also refresh the data by choosing Data | Refresh External Data.

FIGURE 19-1
The External Data Range Properties dialog box

Customizing a Query with MS Query

By using MS Query, you can create a custom query that contains only the data you need, or a parameter query that enables you to specify values for given parameters each time you refresh the data.

To create either kind of query:

1. Follow steps 1 to 6 of the list in the previous section to run the Query wizard and define your query.

2. On the Query Wizard – Finish screen, select the View Data or Edit Query in Microsoft Query option.

3. Click Finish. The Query wizard displays MS Query.

4. If the Criteria fields aren't displayed, click the Show/Hide Criteria or choose View | Criteria to display them.

5. Define criteria for the query (see the following sections).

6. Save the query by choosing File | Save and specifying the name and location in the Save As dialog box.

7. Choose File | Return Data to Microsoft Excel to return the data from the query to Excel.

Creating a Custom Query

To create a custom query, proceed to step 5 in the previous list, and then define criteria as follows:

1. Click in the first Criteria Field box and select the field you want to use for the criteria from the resulting drop-down list.

2. In the first Value field, enter the value for the field. The following illustration shows a query under construction.

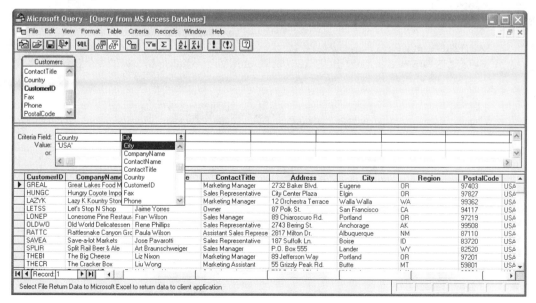

3. Add further criteria as necessary. When you move the focus from the first Value field, MS Query displays the Enter Parameter Value dialog box with the prompt you set.

4. If necessary, choose Criteria | Remove All Criteria to remove all criteria, and then start again.

Creating a Parameter Query

To create a parameter query, proceed to step 5 in the "Customizing a Query with MS Query" list, earlier in this chapter, and then:

1. Click in the first Criteria Field box and select the field you want to use for the criteria from the resulting drop-down list.

2. In the Value field below the Criteria Field box, type an opening bracket ([), the prompt MS Query should display to elicit the information from you, and a closing bracket (]). For example:

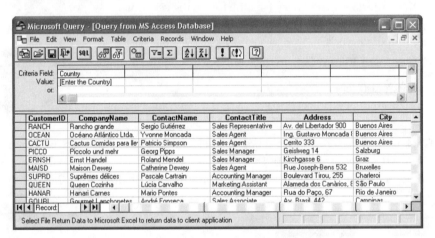

3. Add further criteria as necessary. When you move the focus from the first Value field, MS Query displays the Enter Parameter Value dialog box with the prompt you set, as shown here:

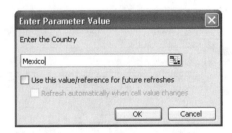

After creating a parameter query and returning to Excel, you can change the criteria for the query by clicking the Refresh button (or choosing Data | Refresh External Data Source). Excel displays an Enter Parameter Value dialog box for each criterion you defined. When you've specified your criteria, Excel returns the records that match them.

Performing Web Queries

Excel can also extract data from tables in web pages by using its built-in Web Query feature:

1. Open Internet Explorer and browse to the page that contains the table you're interested in.

2. Select a table or a cell, right-click, and choose Copy from the shortcut menu to copy it to the Clipboard.

3. Activate Excel, and activate the worksheet in which you want the data to appear.

4. Right-click the cell in which the upper-left corner of the data should appear, and choose Paste from the shortcut menu.

5. Click the Paste Options Smart Tag that results from the Paste operation, and choose the Create Refreshable Web Query option. Excel displays the New Web Query dialog box, shown in Figure 19-2, with a black-on-yellow arrow next to each available table on the page.

FIGURE 19-2
In the New Web Query dialog box, select the check box for each table you want to include.

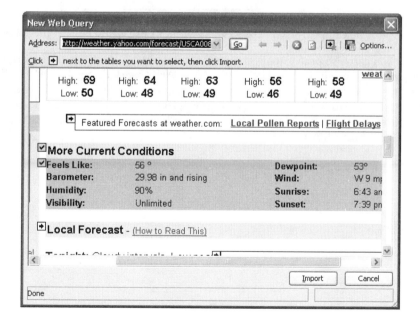

6. Click the arrow for each table or cell you want to add. Excel changes the arrow to a black-on-green check mark.

7. Click Options to display the Web Query Options dialog box, shown next, and specify the import settings you want to use for the table. The most important settings are the options in the Formatting section, which enable you to choose among full HTML formatting, rich text formatting, and no formatting (plain text). You can also specify import settings for preformatted blocks, disable date recognition, and disable web query redirections. Click OK.

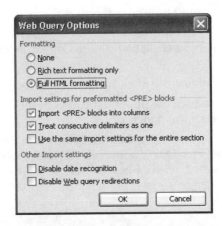

8. Click Import. Excel creates a live link in the worksheet to the table on the web page.

You can also perform a web query by choosing Data | Import External Data | New Web Query and specifying the URL in the New Web Query dialog box manually. In most cases, using copy and paste as described in the previous list is faster and easier.

After creating the link, you can refresh the data in the link by selecting it and clicking the Refresh button on the External Data toolbar. To refresh all links on the active worksheet, click the Refresh All button.

Presentations

PART IV

CHAPTER 20
PowerPoint

CHAPTER 21
Creating and Editing Slides

CHAPTER 22
Adding Graphics,
Multimedia, and Special
Effects to Slides

CHAPTER 23
Showing Your PowerPoint
Presentations

PowerPoint

PowerPoint 2003 is a complete presentation program that allows you to generate interesting and exciting content. This content can be displayed on an overhead projector during a sales talk, a team meeting, a civic meeting, a church event, or just about anywhere else that you might stand in front a group of people and discuss a topic. PowerPoint makes it easy for you to organize your ideas and get them across to your audience. However, PowerPoint also provides you with easy ways to publish presentations on the Internet. Using PowerPoint, you can create a presentation and publish it on an Internet site so that Internet users can access your presentation and view it.

In this chapter, we'll get started with PowerPoint. You'll see how to create presentations, how to use design templates, how to work with layout as well as AutoContent. By the time you finish this chapter, you'll be able to put together a basic presentation in Microsoft PowerPoint.

Exploring the PowerPoint Interface

To start PowerPoint, you simply need to launch the program. Once you have installed Microsoft Office, PowerPoint is installed on your computer, and you'll find it under the Programs portion of your Start menu. To start PowerPoint, click Start | All Programs | Microsoft Office | Microsoft Office PowerPoint. The empty PowerPoint interface, as shown in Figure 20-1, appears on your computer screen.

The PowerPoint interface is basically a collection of different toolbars and work areas that allow you to create stunning presentations. As you can see, the interface is similar to other Office applications, making it easier to find your way around. Just as the dashboard of your car contains a number of different controls that work different parts of the car, the PowerPoint interface also contains different controls that you use to create and view presentations.

Menus in PowerPoint

The menus appear at the top of the PowerPoint interface. They give you access to a number of options and controls within the application. The following list summarizes what you'll find on each menu:

- **File**   The File menu helps you manage PowerPoint files and printing from within PowerPoint, and you can exit the program here as well. Use the New or Open command to create a new presentation or open an existing one. Use the Save options to save your presentation. You can also generate a print preview of a presentation and print it from the File menu, along with other related features.

- **Edit**   The Edit menu gives you standard editing tools such as cut, copy, and paste, and you can also work with hyperlinks from this menu. You can select slides, delete slides, and even find and replace words or phrases within slides and speaker notes.

- **View**   The View menu helps you manage PowerPoint views and toolbars. You can toggle between Normal, Slide Sorter, Slide Show, and Notes Page views. You can also manage toolbars, Master Documents, and use a ruler and several other features here.

- **Insert**   The Insert menu gives you a way to insert items into your presentations. You can insert all kinds of items, including slides, the date/time, comments, pictures, diagrams, text boxes, movies, sound files, charts, and other objects.

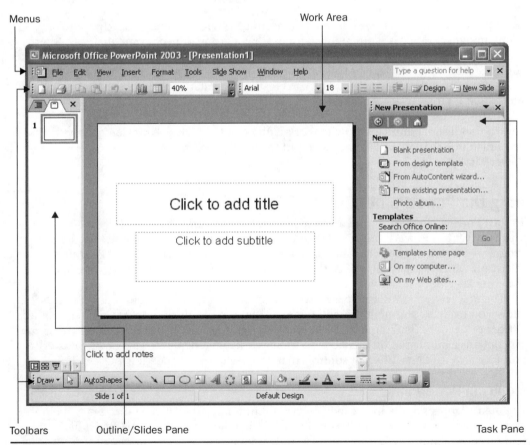

FIGURE 20-1   Standard parts of the PowerPoint interface

- **Format**   The Format menu allows you to choose fonts, configure bullets and numbering, line spacing, and alignment. You can also manage slide design and layout here, and you can format a slide's background.

- **Tools**   The Tools menu gives you access to a number of PowerPoint tools that can help you with your presentations. You can access spelling, language, and speech features, and you can use a research feature if you have an Internet connection. You can also use online collaboration, use macros and add-ins, and you can access customization and options features here.

- **Slide Show**   The Slide Show menu gives you can easy way to view a slide show, set one up, time your rehearsals, record narration, and even broadcast your slide show online. You can manage action buttons, animation, and slide transitions from here as well.

- **Window**   The Window menu allows you to manage multiple windows within PowerPoint. You can arrange windows, cascade them, and move between panes.

- **Help**   Access PowerPoint's Help files locally and on the Internet using the Help menu.

PowerPoint's Toolbars

Like all Microsoft Office applications, PowerPoint offers toolbars to make your work easier. Toolbars contain commonly accessed features and components so you can simply click what you need on the toolbar without having to wade around in menus. There are a number of toolbars available in PowerPoint, but when you first start, you are given the four most commonly used toolbars. The following sections give you a brief overview of them.

Standard Toolbar

The Standard toolbar, shown here, provides a collection of buttons for basic functions. You can open and save presentations with this toolbar, print, e-mail a presentation, cut, copy, paste, insert a chart or table, as well as other commands. Just click the desired button on the toolbar to access the feature you need.

TIP   *Not sure what function a button on a toolbar stands for? No problem, just point to the button with your mouse, and a little note appears telling you what the button represents.*

Formatting Toolbar

The Formatting toolbar gives you a quick way to format text and create new slides. Adjust the font, size, bold, italic, underline, and superscript properties. You can also manage paragraphs, bullets, and numbering, as well as font colors. You can use this toolbar to access slide design templates, which we'll talk about later in the chapter.

Drawing Toolbar

Drawing tools and related functions are located on the Drawing toolbar. This toolbar, which appears at the bottom of the PowerPoint interface by default, allows you to add and manage shapes and graphics, insert symbols, photos, and clip art, and perform related graphics functions.

NOTE *The default locations of the toolbars you see are just suggested locations. You can move them around to wherever you want. Notice at the beginning of each toolbar, you see a series of vertical dots. Just grab those with your mouse, and you can drag the toolbar to any location!*

Task Pane

The task pane is a specialized toolbar that changes according to what you are doing. Its job is to provide common task options so you can easily click and use them. In the task pane shown here, you can create a new slide by clicking the New Slide button on the Formatting toolbar. The task pane changes to the slide layout options so you can easily select the layout you want.

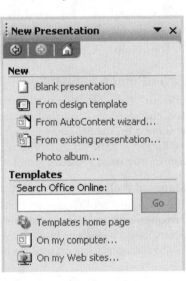

As mentioned earlier, the task pane changes according to what you are doing in PowerPoint. As such, there are a number of different "faces" the task pane may wear. If you click the down-arrow on the top bar of the task pane, a submenu appears showing all of the different task collections the pane can display.

Other Toolbars in PowerPoint

The three toolbars you see are just suggestions—you don't have to use them, or you can add a number of other toolbars that PowerPoint makes available to you. You can access the toolbar options by clicking View | Toolbars. A list of toolbars appears and the ones you are currently using have a check box next to them. To use additional toolbars, just click them. To stop using a toolbar, just click it on the menu and it will disappear from the interface.

In addition to the current toolbars you are already using, here's a sampling of some additional toolbars you might like to use:

- **Control Toolbox** This toolbar gives you an easy way to add control button options to a slide that you would use for web input. Common examples are push buttons, radio buttons, text boxes, and so forth.

- **Outlining** The Outlining toolbar gives you a few controls that make outline creation easier. You can use promote and demote buttons, move up and move down, collapse and expand, and so forth.

- **Picture** The Picture toolbar gives you buttons for working with pictures on a slide. You can insert a picture or manage the picture's brightness/contrast, color, and rotation. You can even crop the picture. You can also compress pictures to reduce transmission time when e-mailing presentations or posting them on the Web. If you work with a lot of photos in your presentations, this is definitely a toolbar you'll want to use.

- **Reviewing**   If several people are reviewing and editing your presentation, use the Reviewing toolbar to manage reviewers, see viewer comments, add comments, and so forth.

- **Revisions Pane**   This toolbar gives you a slide-by-slide view showing slide changes and presentation changes when other people have reviewed and edited your presentation.

- **Tables and Borders**   This toolbar provides common tools and functions you use when adding tables and borders to slides.

- **Visual Basic**   This small toolbar is used when programming macros for use in PowerPoint.

- **Web**   The Web toolbar gives you basic browser functions to navigate the Web in PowerPoint. You get back and forward buttons, home buttons, favorites, and an address bar.

- **WordArt**   The WordArt toolbar allows you to apply WordArt styles to text on your slides.

NOTE   *You can even get crazy with toolbars by creating your own. Click View | Toolbars | Customize to rename existing toolbars and create your own. You can create custom toolbars that hold the features and functions from other toolbars that you most commonly use. You can also set basic toolbar options on the Options tab of the Customize dialog box.*

Outline/Slides Pane

The Outline/Slides pane appears on the left side of the PowerPoint interface. This pane allows you to toggle between Slides view, shown here, or Outline view, where you see the titles of the slides and any text you have on them. You can also use the Normal view, Slide Sorter view, or Slide Show buttons at the bottom of the pane to toggle between these different views. In short, the Outline/Slides pane gives you a quick and easy way to move around in your presentation and find the slide you need. That may not seem like much help, but once your presentations have a number of slides, you'll find this pane very helpful!

Work Area

The main area of the PowerPoint interface, which we'll call the "work area," gives you a place where you can create slides and speaker notes, manage the order of slides, apply transitions, and most anything else you might want to do with your slides. You can use the

Outline/Slides pane to toggle between Normal view, where you work on a single slide, or Slide Sorter view, where you can see all of your slides, reorganize them, apply transitions, and perform other tasks. Either in Normal view or Slide Sorter view, the work area is where you'll spend most of your time working on your presentation.

Starting a Presentation

Now that you are familiar with the basic interface of PowerPoint, you are ready to start a presentation. A presentation is just a file that you create and save. The presentation contains all of your slides, the transitions, graphics, and movie files on those slides, your speaker notes, and practically everything else you put in your presentation. When you save the presentation, you get a single file containing everything.

When you first start PowerPoint, the program automatically starts a new presentation for you and calls it "Presentation 1." You can see the name of the presentation at the very top of the PowerPoint interface. At this point, you are free to start creating your slides. If you use the default "Presentation 1" as your presentation, don't worry, you can rename it when you save it. (See "Saving a Presentation," later in this chapter.)

However, there a few other ways you can start a presentation. First, if you want to create a new presentation, you can do so at any time by clicking File | New. The task pane changes to give you some options you can click:

- Blank Presentation
- From Design Template
- From AutoContent Wizard
- From Existing Presentation

Using Blank Presentation

If you choose the Blank Presentation option, PowerPoint creates a blank presentation with no formatting, as you can see in Figure 20-2. There are no color themes used, and you'll need to choose slide layouts and contents. Use the Blank Presentation option when you want the most control over how your presentation will look and how you will format it. You'll learn how to create and format presentations throughout the rest of this part of the book.

Essentially, this "blank" presentation bypasses the option to use design templates. The cool thing, however, is that you are not locked into a blank presentation without templates. At any time during your presentation, you can simply click the Design button on the Formatting toolbar to open the design templates and apply them to your once "blank" slides. So, as you can see, the line between using a blank presentation and a design template is rather blurry, since you can always return to design templates and apply them anyway.

For some PowerPoint users, the Blank Presentation option gives them more flexibility without a design template getting in the way. And of course if you want to use a design template on certain slides later (or all of them for that matter), you can go to the Slide Design pane and use the templates—even in the once blank presentation.

From Design Template

If you choose the From Design Template option, the Slide Design options appear on the task pane, where you can choose the template you want. When you choose a template, all of your

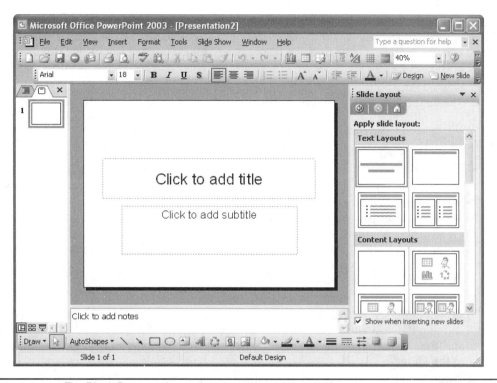

FIGURE 20-2 The Blank Presentation option gives you a clean slate.

slides get some standard formatting provided by the template, along with standardized fonts and colors. The design templates give you an easy way to create a flashy, uniform presentation without having to format background colors, graphics, and fonts on individual slides.

To use a design template, click File | New. In the New Presentation task pane, click the From Design Template link. This action changes the task pane to show slide designs, where you can choose from a list of design templates. Follow these steps to choose a design template:

1. On the Slide Design task pane, shown here, scroll through the list of templates to locate the one you want to use. Notice that you can also click the Color Schemes link to look at a different collection of more basic slides that use color schemes.

2. Once you have located the template you want to use, point to it with your mouse. Notice the drop-down arrow control that appears on the right side of the slide. Click the arrow. A menu appears,

which gives you the option to apply the template to all slides or only to a selection of slides. It also gives you the option to see a large preview of the slide. If you want your presentation to be uniform throughout, choose the Apply to All Slides option. Each new slide that you create in your presentation will then have this design. If not, choose the Apply to Selected Slides.

3. The template is applied to your current slide, which is your title slide by default.

4. Notice that you now have a presentation with only one slide. This method of creating presentations doesn't give you a preconfigured list of slides and outline suggestions, so you must continue to create your presentation.

5. On the Formatting toolbar, click the New Slide button. This creates a new slide in your presentation. In step 2, if you chose to apply the template to all slides, the new slide automatically appears with the template. If not, you can choose a template for the new slide.

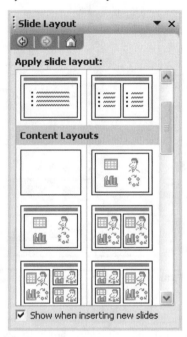

6. The task pane now changes to Slide Layout, shown here. Scroll through the list to find the slide layout you want to apply to this slide, and then click the desired layout to apply it to the slide.

7. Continue this process to create additional slides and layout choices. You can stop and edit your slides at any time, then add more later if you like.

AutoContent Wizard

PowerPoint gives you an AutoContent wizard that can help you create a presentation. It allows you to choose the kind of presentation you are going to give and how you will give that presentation (on screen, the Web, etc.). The AutoContent wizard helps you generate automatic content for your presentation. Basically, it helps you create the slide structure you need and the outline you might need for your presentation. If you are suddenly faced with the task of creating a presentation and you're not sure how to start, the AutoContent wizard can be a big help.

You can access the AutoContent wizard on the New Presentation task pane. In PowerPoint, just click File | New. The New Presentation task pane appears. You see the link option From AutoContent Wizard listed there. To use the AutoContent wizard, just follow these steps:

1. On the New Presentation task pane, click the From AutoContent Wizard link. The AutoContent wizard appears.

2. On the first screen, you see that the wizard is designed to help you get started by suggesting ideas and an organization for your presentation. Click Next to continue.

3. The second page of the AutoContent wizard, shown here, allows you to select the kind of presentation you are going to give. The push buttons on the left side of the window allow you to see all presentations, or narrow them down by selecting a category, such as General, Corporate, and so forth. Choose a presentation type by selecting it in the dialog box, and click the Next button.

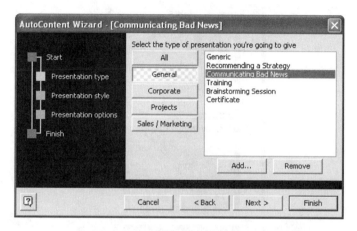

4. The next page asks you to select an output type. Here, you need to tell the program how you will use the presentation, such as on screen, a Web site, and so on. Make a selection by clicking the desired radio button and click Next.

5. In the next window, enter a title for your presentation. Also, if you want to include a footer on each slide, enter the text you want in the dialog box. You can also choose to include the date the slide was last updated on the slide and the slide number if you want. Just clear the check boxes if you do not want to use these features. Click Next.

6. Click Finish. The presentation is created and now appears on the work area along with Outline view, shown here:

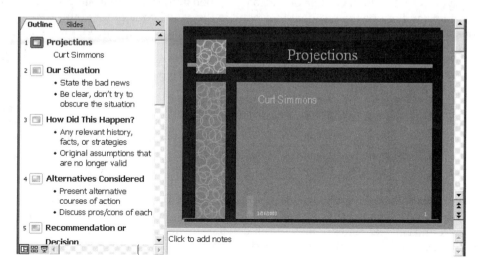

Notice that the AutoContent wizard has chosen a design template for you and created an outline that you can use. In the Outline view, the bullet points simply tell you what to enter to create your presentation. Click the Slide Sorter view to see all of the slides that have been created.

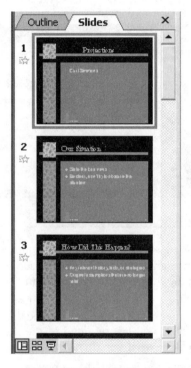

You are now ready to begin customizing the content. Return to Normal view and select the slide you want to edit in Outline or Slides view; then in the work area, simply click on the titles and text and retype them so that they contain the actual content for your presentation. Use the AutoContent's suggested outline to help you create an organized, professional-looking presentation in no time.

Browsing a Presentation

Once you have created your presentation using one of the three methods PowerPoint provides, you may begin to wonder how you move around through the presentation. Keep in mind that a presentation is just a collection of slides, and PowerPoint gives you a few ways to move around and see individual slides, collections of slides, and even a preview of your presentation. The good news is that you can easily move around in your presentation in a number of ways.

The PowerPoint Outline/Slides pane shows your outline or slides in the Outline/Slides viewer while also allowing you to view slides individually in the work area. Use the scroll bars to move around between slides or move around in the Outline/Slides viewer. You can click any slide in the Outline/Slides viewer, and the slide will magically appear in the work area.

There are also two other ways to browse through your presentation. The first is the Slide Sorter view. You can access the Slide Sorter view by clicking the Slide Sorter View button at the bottom of the Outline/Slides view. Or, you can click View | Slide Sorter. Either way, you end up at the Slide Sorter view, which lists all of your slides in order. So, what is the advantage of using the Slide Sorter view over the Outline/Slides view? You can see more of your slides on the screen this way, and you can reorganize them in the Slide Sorter view with more ease.

Finally, you can also browse your presentation by taking a look at a preview of it. On the Outline/Slides view, just click the Slide Show button at the bottom of the view to start the slide show. This action will display your slides in full-screen mode so you can see how they look. You can click View | Slide Show to start the slide show as well.

Saving a Presentation

When you are ready to stop working, you need to save the presentation. This process saves your presentation as a file so you can open it later and continue editing it, or use it when you are ready. To save your presentation, just click File | Save, or you can click File | Save As. Either method opens the Save As dialog box, where you can enter a desired name for the file and decide where on your computer you want to save it.

Notice that by default, your presentation is saved as a PowerPoint presentation. However, if you click the Save as Type drop-down menu, you see that you also have a number of options. Here are some of the more commonly used ones:

- **Single File Web Page**   This action saves your presentation with all photos and text embedded on the page. You can then upload your single page to a web site or send it through e-mail to other users. Any web browser can open and display the presentation.

- **Web Page**   This action saves your presentation as a web page with the photo and graphics files in a separate folder. This option is best to use when you will be uploading your presentation to a web server.

- **PowerPoint 97 & 95**   This option saves your presentation so that previous versions of PowerPoint can open and display it. Use this option if you need to send your presentation to someone who is not using PowerPoint 2002 or PowerPoint 2003.

- **Presentation for Review**   This option saves your presentation so that it can be opened in PowerPoint and reviewed. However, it cannot be edited.

- **PowerPoint Show**   This option saves your presentation so that users with PowerPoint Viewer can open the presentation and view it.

- **File Formats**   These options allow you to save each slide of your presentation in a common graphics file format, such as GIF or JPEG. The slides are saved in a folder, where you can share them or post them on the Internet.

Creating and Editing Slides

In Microsoft PowerPoint, slides hold all of your content. From text, to photos, to graphics, to charts, and even multimedia such as movies, you work with slides when you create presentations. As such, the presentations depend on the power and flexibility of slides. You don't have anything to worry about though. From the standard layout design to custom slides that you can create, slides in PowerPoint presentations are versatile and can be manipulated to meet your needs.

In this chapter, you'll explore slides in Microsoft PowerPoint. You'll see how to put information on slides and how to edit slides so that your presentation can look exactly the way you want it to.

Working with Slides

Most of your work with a presentation is going to involve working on individual slides. The slides, after all, make up your entire presentation. Here, we'll explore the common tasks you need to master in order to work with slides in your presentation. After just a little practice, you'll be moving around in your presentation and working with your slides with ease.

Add a Slide

You can add a slide to a presentation at any time by simply clicking the New Slide button on the Formatting toolbar. You can also click Insert | New Slide. This action creates a new slide and opens the Slide Layout task pane so you can choose a layout for the slide. Once you have chosen the slide layout, you can then edit your slide to add content (see the "Editing Slides" section later in this chapter for details).

What if you spend a lot of time formatting a particular slide, and then you discover that you need another slide that is very similar to it. Do you have to start all over with a new slide? No, not at all—you can just duplicate it. Select the slide you want to duplicate and click Insert | Duplicate Slide. This creates a copy of the slide you have selected, which you can then edit and customize as needed. You can also do the same thing by selecting a slide in the Slides view, clicking Edit | Copy, then Edit | Paste.

Remove a Slide

At any time when you are working on a presentation, you may decide that you want to get rid of a particular slide. That's no crime, and you can easily delete individual slides from your presentation. Just select the slide you want to remove in either the Slides view or the Slide Sorter view, then click Edit | Cut. The slide will disappear from your presentation.

Reorganize Slides

Let's say your presentation has ten slides. After working on your presentation, you determine that slide 8 and slide 9 should swap places. No problem, in PowerPoint, you can easily reorganize slides at any time should the need arise. Even if your presentation was created using the AutoContent wizard, you still have the freedom to reorganize the slides in any way you want.

You can reorganize slides in either the Slides view or the Slide Sorter. In either location, all you have to do is drag the slides around to reorder them. Use your mouse button to click and hold down the slide, and then drag it to its new location, shown in Figure 21-1. You don't have to worry about your slide numbers—PowerPoint will automatically renumber the slides for you when you reorganize them. In Figure 21-1, slide 7 is being dragged to a new position. Once a slide is moved, PowerPoint will automatically renumber the remaining slides.

NOTE *You can also move slides around between two presentations using the Slide Sorter. Simply open the two presentations in PowerPoint; then in Slide Sorter view, click Windows | Arrange All. You can then move slides around between the two presentations.*

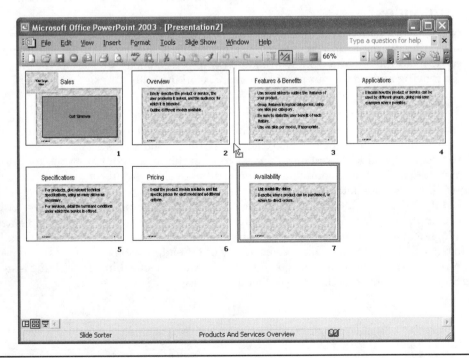

FIGURE 21-1   Drag slides to reorganize them.

Editing Slides

Aside from working with your slides, you'll also spend a lot of time editing the content on those slides. In fact, this is the crux of what you'll do in PowerPoint. After all, the look of your slides and what they actually say are the meat of your presentation.

Changing Text

Slides are designed to hold text, graphics, charts, movies, and just about anything else of a multimedia nature that you want to put on them. When you use the AutoContent wizard, the wizard suggests content for the slides and organizes them for you. When you create a presentation using either the Design template option or the Blank presentation option, you choose the slide layout that you want. That layout can include text only, text and graphics, text and movies, charts and graphics—you name it. To see a full list of available options, click the title bar of the task pane, and choose Slide Layout. You can then scroll through a long list of layout designs that you can apply to any slide.

To change the text on a slide, click on the area that you want to change, and then type your new text. Notice that because PowerPoint uses slide layouts, you may be limited to how much text you can apply. Since you are using templates here, the basic format of the template is maintained by PowerPoint. So, you can't type your life story, and after all, you don't want to. Remember that text on a slide should be succinct and to the point. If you will be using your PowerPoint presentation during a live presentation, you want your audience members to be able to quickly look at the slide and grasp its contents. They should not have to read more than necessary because this takes their attention from you, the speaker.

Most slides use some kind of bulleted list for text information on the slide, as shown in Figure 21-2. This works best and is easier for your audience to read. You can add more bullets than your slide has by default. Just keep typing and pressing ENTER to create new bullets.

Changing Design

In some cases, you'll apply a design to your presentation, then decide later that you want to change to a different design template. That's no problem; you can change templates for your whole presentation at one time, or you can apply different templates to individual

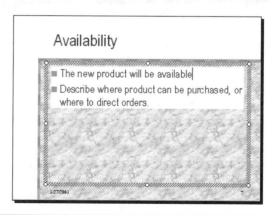

FIGURE 21-2   Type your new text.

slides. Keep in mind that your layout on the slide will stay the same, and some templates lend themselves naturally to certain layouts due to the colors and graphics used. To change the template design, follow these steps:

1. Choose the desired slide in the Slides view, then click the Design button on the Formatting toolbar.

2. On the Slide Design task pane, locate the design you want to use and point to it.

3. Click the arrow on the right of the design card and choose Apply to All Slides or Apply to Selected Slides. The template will change on your selected slide, or all slides, depending on the option you click.

TIP   You can change the design of any presentation, including those generated by the AutoContent wizard.

Changing Layout

Just as you can change the design template of a page or all pages in your presentation, you can also change the layout of a slide. To change the layout of a slide, select the slide in the Slides view so that you see it in the work area, and then click Format | Slide Layout. This action causes the task pane to display Slide Layout. You can then scroll through the list of layouts and simply click a new layout to apply it to your slide.

Keep in mind that if you have already edited the text on the slide or inserted graphics, the new layout will change the appearance of the slide. In fact, some of the material you previously put on the slide may no longer fit or look right. You'll need to choose a layout that will accommodate the material on your slide, or split the content between two different slides.

NOTE   Keep in mind that slides should be simple. The audience should be able to glance at a slide and grasp its meaning. If your slides seem to have a lot of material on them, this is a good sign that you need to use additional slides, rather than crowding content onto a single slide.

Formatting Text

The cool thing about Microsoft Office is that all applications are integrated and similar. The way you format text in Microsoft Word is basically the same way you format text in Microsoft FrontPage, and yes, Microsoft PowerPoint.

After you choose the design and page layout of a slide, your next step is to click in the text boxes and retype the sample text you see there. Some text boxes may not contain sample text, in which case you just click your mouse inside of the text box and start typing. Once you type your text, you can then change the formatting of it in any way you want. In other words, you don't have to accept the default fonts, sizes, and colors on the slide text— you can simply change them.

You have two ways to change the format of text on a slide. First of all, using your mouse, select the text by swiping over it while holding down your left mouse button. This highlights the text. Then, use the Formatting toolbar to change the text as desired. Here is the Formatting toolbar, followed by an explanation of the options, from left to right.

- **Font** Click the Font drop-down menu and select the desired font for your text. When you click a font, the selected text on your slide automatically changes to that font.
- **Font Size** Click the Font Size drop-down menu to choose a size for your font.

NOTE   You can also click inside the Font Size box and type the font size you want to use instead of choosing the size from the drop-down menu.

- **Bold** This option bolds any selected text.
- **Italic** This option italicizes any selected text.
- **Underline** This option underlines any selected text.
- **Shadow** This option creates a shadow effect on any selected text.

TIP   You can use combinations of bold, italic, underline, and shadow on the same text.

- **Alignment** Use the paragraph buttons to justify your text to the left, centered, or right on your slide. You can learn more about formatting paragraphs in the next section of this chapter.
- **Numbers and Bullets** Click the Numbers or Bullets button to convert text to a numbered list or bulleted format. You can learn more about formatting bullets and numbering in the "Formatting Bullets and Numbering" section later in this chapter.
- **Increase/Decrease Font Size** This is the same thing as using the Font Size drop-down menu, but you can more easily test different sizes using the Increase/Decrease Font Size buttons.
- **Decrease/Increase Indent** For text that is indented, you can increase or decrease the indent spacing using these buttons.
- **Font Color** Click the Font Color button, and a color menu appears where you can choose a different color for your text.

Aside from using the Formatting toolbar, you can access the Font dialog box by clicking Format | Font. The dialog box that appears also allows you to choose the font, font style, size, and color, but you have some additional effects not available to you on the Formatting toolbar, such as emboss, superscript, and subscript. Just make any selections you want and click OK.

NOTE *You can also type and format text in the Outline Viewer. Use the Formatting toolbar or the Font dialog box to choose your font, size, and style selections, and then type your text in the Outline Viewer. Your text automatically appears on the slide with the correct formatting!*

Formatting Paragraphs

You are free to create paragraphs on your slides, rather than bulleted or numbered lists. This PowerPoint freedom makes it easy for you to customize your slides as you wish. If you are thinking about using a paragraph format, however, keep two important points in mind:

- *Keep your paragraphs short.* As a general rule, keep paragraphs short and to the point. This is especially true if you will be using your presentation in an on-screen format before a live audience. You want your audience to spend most of their time listening to you—not trying to read too much text on the screen.

- *Bulleted and numbered points are easier to read.* Although paragraphs can be useful, keep in mind that bulleted and numbered lists are easier to read. They also convey your presentation points in quick meaningful bursts that are easier for your audience to remember.

To create a paragraph, simply choose a slide layout option that provides space to type a paragraph. You can also reformat an existing bulleted list on a slide layout by pressing BACKSPACE to remove the first bullet, then typing your paragraph. You can also create custom slide layout designs using text boxes, if needed.

Once you have typed your paragraph, you can select it and make any font, size, style, color, or paragraph alignment changes you need using the Formatting toolbar. Remember to use a font and size (as well as a color) that is easy to read, such as Times New Roman or Arial at 10 or 12 points. Generally, darker text is easier to read than lighter text.

If you want to adjust the line spacing of the paragraph, click Format | Line Spacing. This action opens the Line Spacing dialog box, shown in Figure 21-3, where you can configure the line spacing of the paragraph itself, along with the spacing before and after the paragraph.

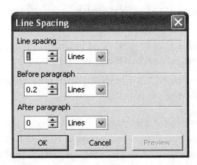

FIGURE 21-3   Format line spacing as desired.

Formatting Bullets and Numbering

Bullets and numbering are mainstays of PowerPoint presentations. Lists help you convey your message in quick bursts of information that your audience can remember. Also, the natural format of a bulleted or numbered list easily lends itself to a presentation, so the odds are quite good that you'll use bullets and numbered lists often.

The good news is PowerPoint knows that bullets and numbering are important, and it gives you some cool options to format and customize your lists. The following steps show you how to configure a bulleted or numbered list:

1. Choose a slide layout that provides bullets or numbers.

2. Click in the bulleted or numbered area of the slide, and then choose Format | Bullets and Numbering.

3. In the Bullets and Numbering dialog box, choose the Bulleted tab. You can choose from any of the available bullet formats provided. Simply click the desired box and click OK to use one of the formats. As you can see, you have standard bullet options, boxes, and also check marks.

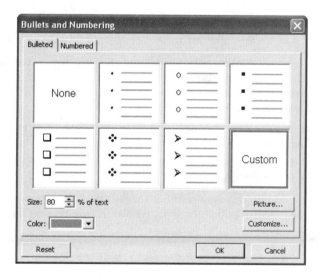

4. In the Size selection box, you can adjust the size of the bullets in relation to the text. By default, the setting is 100%, but you can raise or lower this value as needed.

5. In the Color drop-down menu, you can choose a different color for your bullets. Simply click the menu option and make a selection. You can also click the More Colors option to choose the color from a color palette.

6. On the lower-right corner of the Bulleted tab, you see a Picture button. If you click the button, a Picture Bullet window appears with several selections. You can use any of the Picture Bullets you see here by clicking the bullet and clicking OK. You

can also import any existing bullet collections you have into PowerPoint by clicking the Import button.

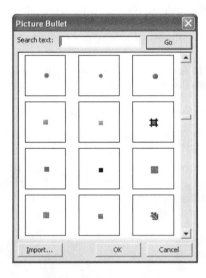

7. Also on the lower-right corner of the Bulleted tab, you see a Customize button. If you click this button, the Symbol dialog box appears. From this dialog box, you can choose any symbol to use as your bullets. Simply select the symbol and click OK, and your bulleted list will be formatted using the symbol.

8. When you are done selecting your bullet style, just click OK on the Bulleted tab. Your bullet formatting now appears on your slide.

9. In order to configure numbered lists, click Format | Bullets and Numbering once again, then choose the Numbered tab.

10. On the Numbered tab, choose a number format, the size percentage, and color. Notice that you can also adjust the Start At box in case you do not want your numbered list to start at 1.

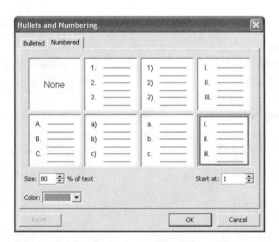

11. Once you have made your selections, click OK, and your numbered format will be applied.

TIP   You can toggle between bullets and numbers on the same slide if you like. Just place your mouse cursor in the desired position on the slide, and click the Bullets and Numbering dialog box to select a format. This will change the formatting to your selection.

As you are working with bullets and numbering, keep in mind also that you can create subbullets and subnumbers. For example, let's say you have a bullet titled "policies," and under that bullet, you have three additional subbullets you want to use. No problem—just press the SPACEBAR on your keyboard and then press TAB. This will indent the bullet so that it is a subbullet.

Adjusting a Placeholder Box

As you have noticed, PowerPoint gives you a number of different slide layouts. The layouts are designed to keep your slides looking nice and neat, and they provide you an easy way to create presentations without having to do a lot of manual slide formatting.

However, in some cases, the default layout can give you some problems. Maybe you need to put more text on a placeholder than there is room, or maybe you just want to customize them a bit. We should mention that PowerPoint can help you manage text that is running out of room on a placeholder—see the next section for details—but if you just need a quick fix, you can also adjust the placeholder's size to meet your needs.

In the work area, you see a placeholder box around your text. Notice the circle dots around each edge and in the middle. If you click and drag one of the dots, you can increase or decrease the size of the placeholder in order to meet your needs, as shown in Figure 21-4.

NOTE   The only problem with this practice is "slide continuity." Here's what we mean. If you manually change the placeholder size of one slide, it will not match up with the placeholder positions on the next slide. This will cause your slides to have a "jumpy" effect as you move through them, rather than a smooth movement to each slide. This is particularly true if you are using the same layout on a number of slides. If you manually change the size of the placeholders as needed on each slide, the continuity between slides will be lost. That might not be such a big deal, but it can affect the overall look of your presentation.

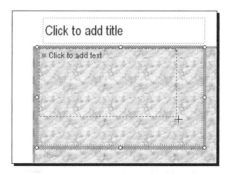

FIGURE 21-4   Drag to increase or decrease the size of the placeholder.

PART IV

Managing Placeholder Layout

Sometimes you need to type more text than a placeholder can hold. That's no crime, and the good news is PowerPoint can automatically help you fix the problem. When you are typing your text, a little AutoFit Options box appears in the work area as you begin to run out of room in the placeholder, shown in Figure 21-5.

If you click the little down arrow that appears when you point to the AutoFit Options box, a context menu appears where you can choose some different options:

- **AutoFit Text to Placeholder**   This option automatically begins shrinking your text to make it all fit to the placeholder. This is selected by default and can be helpful, but be careful that the text doesn't become too small to read.

- **Stop Fitting Text to This Placeholder**   This option stops AutoFitting text to the placeholder, in which case your text will run off the slide. If you use this option, you need to make some adjustments to your text or layout in order to fit all of your text on the actual slide.

- **Split Text Between Two Slides**   This option automatically creates an additional slide, and then PowerPoint logically splits your text between the two or more slides.

- **Continue on a New Slide**   This option doesn't split your text, but it basically moves the text that is running over the placeholder to the next slide. This keeps your basic format as you have typed it, but the run-over text simply moves to the next slide.

- **Change to Two-Column Layout**   This option creates a two-column layout on the same slide so that all of your text fits on the same slide. This option works great, unless of course you do not want to use a two-column layout.

- **Control AutoCorrect Options**   This option opens the AutoCorrect properties dialog box where you can control how AutoCorrect works. As a general rule, the default options work well, so don't change anything here unless you have a specific reason for doing so.

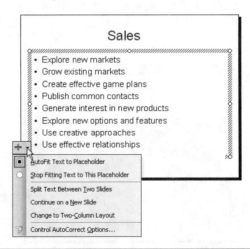

FIGURE 21-5   AutoFit Options

Checking Spelling and AutoCorrect Options

Spelling in a presentation is critical. No matter how hard you work on your presentation, misspelled words make you look unprepared and uncaring, so make sure you get your spelling right! The good news is PowerPoint contains Microsoft Office's spelling checker, so you can easily check your spelling and make sure everything is correct.

First things first—although you may not know it, PowerPoint is probably checking your spelling for you automatically. As you type text on a slide, you may notice a red underline appear under a word. If you right-click the word, a context menu appears where PowerPoint suggests the correct spelling for you. If the word is spelled correctly on the context menu, just click it to correct your text. Of course, you may have some words that the dictionary doesn't recognize. This is especially true of acronyms, technical or medical words, and other business jargon. In this case, you can make sure the word is spelled correctly, then right-click the word and click Add to Dictionary so that PowerPoint recognizes it and doesn't flag it as misspelled.

Even though AutoCorrect is at work to catch those misspelled words, you can check the spelling in your entire presentation by clicking Tools | Spelling. PowerPoint will check the spelling on all slides and in your speaker notes. It will prompt you for a correction when it finds misspelled words.

There are a few spelling rules PowerPoint follows, and you can change those rules if necessary. Click Tools | Options, then click the Spelling and Style tab. By default, PowerPoint checks spelling as you type, suggests corrections, ignores words in uppercase type (PowerPoint assumes these are acronyms), and ignores words that have numbers. If you want to change any of these default rules, just click or clear the check boxes next to them as needed.

If you click the Style Options button, you see the Style Options dialog box, where the basic rules for case, end punctuation, and visual clarity are followed. The rules you see here are self-explanatory, so feel free to edit them as needed for your presentation.

Finally, PowerPoint also uses some "AutoCorrect" options by default. If you have noticed that PowerPoint is subtly changing your text, such as capitalizing the names of days or correcting Caps Lock mistakes, you're right—these functions are part of AutoCorrect. If you click Tools | AutoCorrect Options, you get a properties dialog box with three tabs that shows you what PowerPoint will automatically correct as you type. You should look through these tabs and get familiar with the AutoCorrect features, since some may be a nuisance, depending on what you are typing. A helpful feature on the AutoCorrect tab is the Replace feature. As you can see, AutoCorrect will replace certain text with the correct symbols, and you can even add your own to this list.

Inserting a Table

Tables present information in a logical manner so that it is easy to read and understand. For this reason, tables are very effective in presentations, and PowerPoint gives you a way to insert and format a table.

First of all, if you choose a slide layout that supports content, you can easily create a table. To do so, just follow these steps:

1. Click the Insert Table icon on the slide placeholder.

PART IV

2. In the Insert Table dialog box, choose the number of rows and columns you want for your table.

3. Click OK. The new table now appears on your slide, as you can see here:

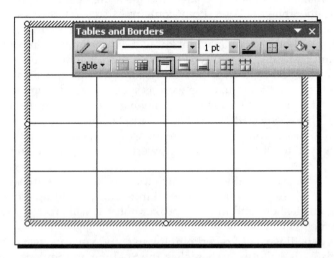

You can also insert a table by clicking the Insert Table icon on the General toolbar. When you click the icon, a table drop-down grid appears where you can choose the size of table you want. Just use your mouse to select the squares to create your table. Once you have your table, you can format it and enter data.

Entering Data

Once you have created your table, you can enter the text you want in the table's cells. Just click inside a cell with your mouse and type the desired text. You can move from cell to cell using the TAB key or mouse. Keep in mind that you can format text in a table's cell to use any desired font, size, or style.

Formatting Tables

When it comes to tables, you have a number of formatting options—more than you'll need most of the time—and you have a few different methods for formatting tables, depending on what you need to do.

First of all, you can right-click a table to insert and delete existing rows. For example, you can double-click a row with your mouse, then right-click it and click Delete Rows to remove it. You can also select a number of cells, right-click them, and click Merge Cells to make them into one cell.

You can right-click the table and click Borders and Fill. This opens the Format Table dialog box, shown in Figure 21-6. As you can see, you can adjust the borders, fill color, and text box alignment. These options are self-explanatory.

You can also edit tables using the Tables and Borders toolbar, which you can access by clicking View | Toolbars | Tables and Borders. Using this toolbar, you can format borders,

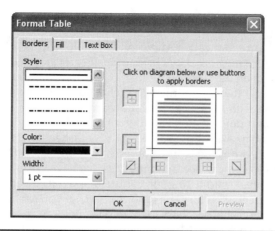

FIGURE 21-6   Borders tab of Format Table dialog box

sizes, colors, as well as alignment. Just click the button you want to use. A cool and helpful feature is the pencil option. You can use the pencil to draw new tabs or split an existing cell, just by drawing on the table. Likewise, use the Eraser button to erase cells and other portions of the table.

Insert Microsoft Word Table

If you prefer to create tables using Microsoft Word, no problem, you can do just that. Follow these steps:

1. Choose the desired slide, then click Insert | Object.
2. On the Insert Object window that appears, choose the Create New button, and choose Microsoft Word Document. Click OK.
3. A Word document appears on your slide, and your PowerPoint toolbars and menus have now changed to Word menus and toolbars. Create your table as desired.
4. When you are done, click anywhere outside of the slide area, and your PowerPoint interface will return as normal with your new Word table on the slide.

NOTE   *If you already have a table in Word, or any other content for that matter, you can easily cut and paste between Microsoft Office applications. Just select the table in Word and click Edit | Copy. Then, in PowerPoint, click Edit | Paste to paste the table onto the slide.*

Inserting a Chart

You can insert a chart onto a slide by directly creating the chart on the slide, cutting and pasting the chart from an existing source, such as Word or Excel, or you can also directly create a new chart from Microsoft Excel. The following two sections show you how.

Creating a PowerPoint Chart

PowerPoint uses a little program called Microsoft Graph to help you create charts quickly and easily. You can create a new chart by clicking the Insert Chart icon on the placeholder, by clicking the Chart icon on the General toolbar, or by clicking Insert | Chart.

No matter how you get there, your menu bar changes to the charting options and you see a default chart, along with a datasheet, as shown in Figure 21-7.

Now, this default chart doesn't mean anything to you, but you can edit it using the datasheet and the menu bar. Adjust the values in the datasheet to create your own chart. Note that you can delete entries, lines, and columns, as well as add them, until you end up with a chart you want. As you can see in Figure 21-8, we have created a completely different chart in a matter of minutes by adjusting the values on the datasheet.

Obviously, the default chart is just one kind of chart, so you can use the Chart menu to create something new. If you choose Chart | Chart Type, you can choose from standard types of charts and even create your own. Choosing a new chart type automatically converts your data on the datasheet to the new chart format. Use the Data menu to adjust how chart data is displayed.

Tip *We've given you enough to get you started here. You can do all kinds of things with your charts. Right-click them to format colors and borders and even add data labels. All the tools you need are at your fingertips, so start exploring!*

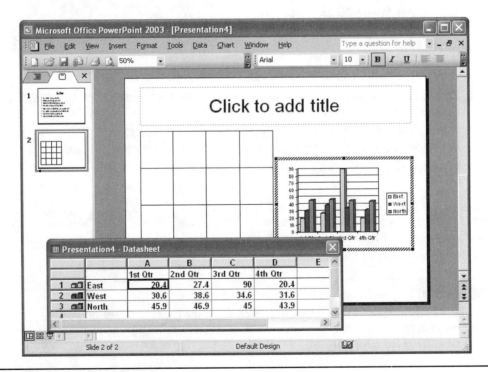

Figure 21-7 Formatting a chart

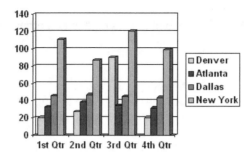

FIGURE 21-8   Use the datasheet to chart as needed.

Use a Microsoft Excel Chart

Microsoft Excel is obviously a much better program for creating charts, so PowerPoint gives you a quick and easy way to do just that. Follow these steps:

1. On the desired slide, click Insert | Object.

2. In the Insert Object dialog box, click Microsoft Excel Chart and click OK.

3. A chart appears on your slide, and your menus and toolbars change to Excel. You can now create your chart directly in PowerPoint using Excel.

Inserting an Organization Chart

PowerPoint also supports an automatic organization chart feature. Organization charts are helpful with any kind of slide where you need to show an organizational data flow or hierarchy. To create an organization chart, just follow these steps:

1. On a new slide, access the Slide Layout pane.

2. Scroll to the bottom of the slide layout selection, and you'll see an organization chart option. Click the option to apply it to your current slide.

3. On your slide placeholder you see instructions to double-click the icon to create an organization chart. Double-click the icon.

4. The Diagram Gallery appears. Choose a desired diagram or chart format and click OK.

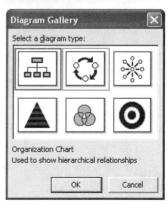

5. Your chart selection now appears on the slide. Click the titles and retype the text to customize them. Also, use the toolbar provided to add other elements to your diagram.

Inserting a Text Box

A text box is just that—it is a box where you can type text. Text boxes are helpful when you are creating slides from scratch without the help of slide layout, and they can be helpful when you want to add a little blurb of text somewhere on a slide where previously you couldn't add text.

To insert a text box on a slide, click Insert | Text Box. The text box appears on your slide. You can move it around and use the rotation handle to rotate it as you like, as shown here. Note that you can format the text in the box just as you would any other text.

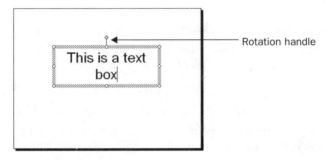

In case you're wondering how useful text boxes are, here's a little blurb of text that was added to a standard slide layout. Since the box can be resized and rotated, there are more text options that are useful in a number of ways.

Inserting an Object

You can insert a number of items from other Office programs directly into a PowerPoint slide. If you click Insert | Object, you see the Insert Object dialog box. Note that you can use the items you see listed here to create objects, or you can insert a file directly in a slide. You can insert everything from charts to media clips. Basically, the object feature is simply a link to these different programs so you can use them directly within PowerPoint to create slide content. Depending on how you use slides, you'll find the insert content feature especially helpful if you generate information and content using several of Office's applications.

Inserting a Hyperlink

You can easily insert a hyperlink in your slides using the Insert | Hyperlink option. This hyperlinks the content so that you can jump from your presentation slide to a web site during a live presentation, or your viewers can do the same if they are viewing your presentation online.

First things first—PowerPoint automatically hyperlinks URLs. For example, if you type **http://www.curtsimmons.com** into a slide, PowerPoint will hyperlink it. If you want to jump to the web site during a live presentation, you can simply click the link. The same is true if you share the presentation online.

So, why would you need the Insert | Hyperlink feature? Simple—you can also hyperlink other items, including non-URL text and images. When you want to create a hyperlink, you can simply choose Insert | Hyperlink and enter the text you want displayed and the link to the existing slide or web page. If you want to hyperlink some existing text or an image, just select it first and click Insert | Hyperlink; then enter the link location for the text or image.

Adding Graphics, Multimedia, and Special Effects to Slides

One of the great things about Microsoft PowerPoint is that you are free to use all kinds of photos, clip art, graphics, multimedia, and even animation and transition effects on your slides. This robust assortment of features allows your presentations to have that extra "snap" that makes them look great in front of an audience, or displayed on the Web. The graphics and multimedia features help keep your audience interested, and they help communicate your meaning.

In this chapter, you'll see how to insert these objects, how to control them, and how to make them work in the best way for you.

Insert Clip Art and Photos

Office has a vast collection of clip art at your disposal. From a "clip art" point of view, clip art includes cartoon characters, photos, borders, icons, and a number of other features. When you use PowerPoint to insert clip art, PowerPoint will try to locate any existing photo files and GIF images on your computer, and it will show you its arsenal of clip art files as well.

Insert Clip Art

You can insert clip art in two different ways, and each one has its own options and benefits. The following steps show you how to use the slide layout feature to insert clip art.

1. The content Slide Layout option that you choose creates a collection of icons on the placeholder that you can click. To insert clip art, click the Insert Clip Art button (which looks like a cartoon head) on the Drawing toolbar.

   The Select Picture dialog box opens. You'll see some photos from your My Pictures folder, and you'll see a collection of Office's photos and clip art as well.

2. Obviously, thinning the clip art down to the images you may actually want can be difficult, so use the Search Text drop-down box to locate the kind of images you want. As you can see here, we have searched only for images of dogs.

3. Finally, notice the Import button at the bottom of the Select Picture dialog box. If you click the Import button, a standard browse window appears, where you can locate images that you want to add to the Office Organizer. This feature allows you to download all kinds of clip art from the Internet or use clip art programs to insert clip art into your slides.

4. When you have decided which clip art to use, just select it and click the OK button on the Select Picture window.

5. The clip art is inserted in your PowerPoint slide, and the Picture toolbar automatically appears, as you can see in the next illustration. See the "Edit a Clip Art Image" section to find out how to adjust the clip art's size and colors.

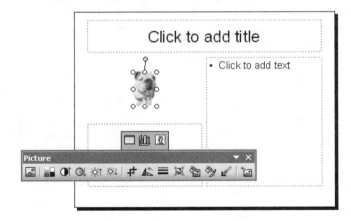

TIP *If you make a mistake, remember that you can always click Edit | Undo.*

Another way to insert clip art into a slide is to use the Insert | Picture | Clip Art command. This action allows you to insert clip art at any location on a slide (assuming it will fit) instead of using the Slide Layout option. However, even if you have chosen a Slide Layout option that supports content, you can still use the Insert command, and the clip art will be inserted into the correct placeholder on the slide.

So, what's the advantage? When you use Insert | Picture | Clip Art, the Clip Art task pane appears, which you may find a bit friendlier than the Select Picture window. The Clip Art pane allows you to search for clip art and import it as well, but you can use the Search In drop-down menu to limit your search to certain kinds of clip art, such as photos. You can also access additional clip art on microsoft.com using the Clip Art pane. Other than these features, however, the process for insertion on a slide works the same. Just locate the clip art you want to use and click it, and it will appear on your slide.

NOTE   *In truth, the Clip Art pane appears whenever you choose to insert any kind of clip art. Even if you use the Placeholder button and get the Select Picture window, you can just click the X in the upper-right corner of the Select Picture window and close it, then use the Clip Art pane if you like. Either way, you can easily choose the clip art you want.*

Edit a Clip Art Image

When you insert a clip art image into a slide, the image is inserted with control handles, and the Picture toolbar appears. Using the control handles and the Picture toolbar, you can make just about any change to the clip art you want. Let's explore what you can do.

Position Clip Art

The control handles that appear around the image, as you can see in the adjacent illustration, allow you to control the position of the clip art as well as the size. To control the position of the clip art, notice the green rotation handle. If you grab the green handle with your mouse and begin moving it, you'll see that your image rotates. This feature allows you to tilt the image slightly (or a lot) and positions it exactly as you like.

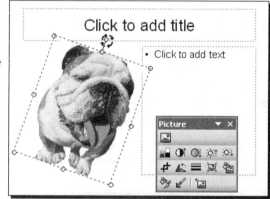

Resize Clip Art

The default size of the clip art may not work for you when it is inserted on your slide. That's no problem, because the remaining control handles allow you to resize it as you wish. Notice the handle on each corner of the image. If you drag one of these handles, you'll notice the image is enlarged or made smaller, depending on your dragging motion. However, the image perspective is kept intact. In other words, using a corner handle to resize the image doesn't distort it, as you can see here.

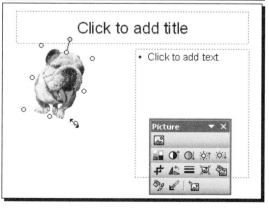

You also have handle controls in the middle of each horizontal and vertical side of the image. You can resize the image using these, but you get perspective distortion if you do, as shown here. Of course, in some circumstances, the distortion may be desirable.

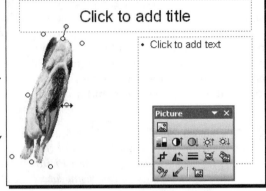

Move Clip Art

You can move a clip around on a slide by simply pointing to the clip with your mouse, then holding down your left mouse button and dragging the image around. Obviously, if you are using text and other images, you'll need to take care so that other placeholders do not get distorted, but with the freedom to move clip art around, you have the freedom to customize your slides if you like.

Recolor Clip Art

On the Picture toolbar, you have a Color button and a Recolor Picture button. If the Picture toolbar has disappeared or you have closed it, just click View | Toolbars | Picture to get the toolbar back.

First, click your clip art image on the slide to make sure it is selected. Then, click the Color button on the Picture toolbar. You see a menu appear with four options. Leave the color as Automatic, which is whatever color it came to you from the Clip Art Organizer, or you can choose Grayscale, or Black & White. You also have a Washout option that dims the photo, which may be effective on some slides.

You also have a Recolor Picture button on the Picture toolbar. If you click this option, you see a listing of colors in the photo. You can then choose to change some of the colors to give your photo a new look.

Adjust Contrast and Brightness

The contrast setting in photos affects how sharply the colors contrast with each other. Thus, a high-contrast photo will seem more "loud" than a lower-contrast image. You can use the Picture toolbar to adjust the contrast of an image. Just click the More Contrast or Less Contrast buttons to adjust your photo as desired.

You can also use the Picture toolbar to adjust the brightness of an object. You see a More Brightness and Less Brightness button. Use the buttons to adjust the brightness of the clip art as needed.

Crop an Image

When you import clip art or photos from the Organizer or directly from your computer, you may need to crop those images to get what you want. When you *crop* an image, you trim away excess portions that are not desirable. For example, we have used a photo of a dog from clip art as an example. What if you only wanted to show the dog's face? You can simply crop the rest away, and here's how you do it:

1. On your slide, select the image you want to crop, and on the Picture toolbar, click the Crop button. A box appears around the image, as you can see here:

2. Drag the crop box around to reposition it as you like. You can drag the crop box by positing your mouse in the box and simply dragging. Anything outside of the crop box is cut away, as you can see in the next illustration. When you're done, just click outside of the image to remove the crop box.

Rotate Clip Art

You can easily rotate a photo using the Rotate button on the Picture toolbar. You can use this button to rotate a photo 90 degrees around to different positions as needed.

Apply a Line Style

Line style refers to the box that surrounds an image. You can click the Line Style button on the Picture toolbar and choose a desired style—you have everything from a small, barely noticeable line to a large line that resembles a border. Simply click the Line Style button and make your selection from the menu list that appears.

Compress Pictures

If you use photos in your slides, you may need to think about photo compression. Since photos are often large in terms of file size, they can present some problems when you choose to post them on the Internet or e-mail them for others to see. If you are using the presentation on screen or you are printing it, you don't need to worry about compressing photos in your presentation, but when you take your presentation online, you'll certainly want to think about file size and download time.

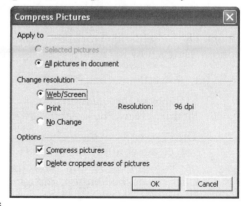

The good news is the Picture toolbar allows you to compress photos as you insert them. Just click the Compress Pictures button, and you'll see the Compress Pictures dialog box. As you can see, you can apply your settings to selected pictures or all pictures in the presentation. You can then choose a resolution setting for your photos.

Format Picture

The Format Picture button on the Picture toolbar opens the Format Picture properties dialog box. Basically, the tabs you see here give you the same features as the Picture toolbar. You can adjust colors and lines, the picture's size and position, make cropping changes, and so forth. The options you find are self-explanatory, so feel free to explore. However, we think you'll find the Picture toolbar easier to use.

Set Transparent Color

The final option you see on the Picture toolbar is the Set Transparent Color option. If you click the button, your mouse will turn to a paintbrush, and you can click on areas of the photo that you want to make transparent, or "wash out." This feature can be helpful if you want to blot away a portion of a picture or deemphasize it.

Insert a Photo

In PowerPoint, actual photos work just like clip art—they are all picture content—and you can insert them using the Placeholder button or the Insert menu. You can then edit them using the same Picture toolbar explored in the previous sections in this chapter.

The primary difference, though, is that you can use Insert | Picture to insert photos directly from a file on your computer, a CD, or even a network share; or you can choose the From Scanner or Camera option to directly import photos from a scanner or camera.

Another and perhaps much easier option is to drag photos directly from a folder on your computer, a CD, network share, or other location to PowerPoint and drop them. PowerPoint will automatically insert the photo on the current slide. At this point, you can use the Picture toolbar to do any necessary editing.

Create a Photo Album

Aside from inserting photos into a presentation, PowerPoint also gives you a cool option to create a photo album. You can then use the album as a way to store photos, as a slide show, to share on the Internet, or anything else you might like.

It is important to realize that the photo album feature is simply a PowerPoint presentation—it is just a way to help you get photos onto the presentation, then use the presentation as an album. The presentation works the same as all others, and you have the same saving options. Here's how to create a photo album:

1. In PowerPoint, click File | New.

2. In the New Presentation pane, click the Photo Album options, or click Insert | Picture | New Photo Album.

3. The Photo Album dialog box appears, as shown in Figure 22-1. This is the area where you create your photo album. First, you'll need to choose the photos you want to use in the photo album. You can get them from a file or disk or a scanner/camera. Click the desired button, and a browse dialog box appears where you can select the

pictures to import. Select them and click the Insert button. The new photos now appear on the Photo Album dialog box.

NOTE   *You can insert text boxes into the album as well. This feature allows you to enter text in the box that will appear in the presentation.*

4. Under Picture Options, notice that you can choose to use captions under all photos. This will allow you to enter the captions you want once you create the photo album. Also, you see a check box option to make all photos black and white if you like.

   The selected photo appears in the Preview window. Notice that you also have editing commands, such as rotate, contrast, and brightness controls, so you can adjust the photo as necessary. If you need to do more editing to a photo, keep in mind that once the album is created you can use the Picture toolbar to make additional edits.

5. Under Album Layout, you can choose Picture Layout, which determines how many photos appear on each slide and whether or not you use titles. You can also adjust the frame shape. As you can see in Figure 22-1, we chose the Rounded Rectangle option. These shape features will make your photos look nicer on the slides. Finally, you can also choose a design template by clicking the Browse button. We selected the Curtain Call template.

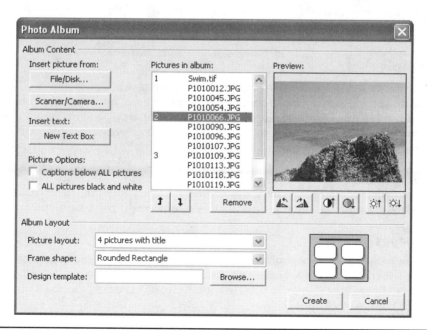

FIGURE 22-1   The Photo Album dialog box

PART IV

6. When you are done, click the Create button. Your photo album is now created—an example is shown in the following illustration. You can work through the photo album and add any text you like. You can also reedit slides as needed.

TIP *Don't forget that you have several Save As options available on the File menu. You can save your presentation as a PowerPoint show so anyone can view it with PowerPoint Viewer, or you can save it as a web page.*

Using Draw Tools

You can use the Drawing toolbar to insert a number of preconfigured shapes into your presentations, such as arrows, basic shapes, flowchart shapes, and so forth. In truth, you can insert these shapes, change them in any number of ways, and even create your own. The more you use PowerPoint, and the more you create presentations, the more you will discover the usefulness of shapes in your presentations. Drawing skills give you all kinds of ways to highlight or call attention to information, make your presentation more interesting and easier to understand. The more you work with PowerPoint's drawing tools, the more you will see how shapes have a great visual impact on your audience and how they can help communicate your message. Let's explore the drawing tools and options.

Modify Shapes

The Drawing toolbar provides a number of predesigned shapes on the AutoShapes menu. The toolbar, which resides at the bottom of your PowerPoint interface by default, gives you quick access to these AutoShapes. If you click the AutoShapes button on the toolbar, a menu appears with these AutoShapes options:

- **Lines** These shapes provide you with basic lines. Use them to connect items on a slide or add emphasis.

- **Connectors** These shapes provide dynamic connectors that you can use to connect other objects or AutoShapes. They are typically used in flowcharts.
- **Basic Shapes** These include squares, rectangles, circles, brackets, and so forth. You'll even find a smiley face here.
- **Block Arrows** Blocked drawings of arrows using different styles can be used as pointers or to indicate direction in a graphical way.
- **Flowchart** These are the typical triangles, ovals, and boxes used when creating a flowchart.
- **Stars and Banners** As the name describes, you can access several different styles of stars and banners here.
- **Callouts** Callouts are boxes you use to draw attention to some item by providing additional text. Callouts include "balloon" shapes for captions as well as other boxed options.
- **Action Buttons** Use these buttons to put navigational elements in your presentation. See the "Configure Action Buttons" section later in this chapter for additional information.
- **More AutoShapes** This option takes you to clip art where you can access more AutoShapes.

The good news is AutoShapes are easy to insert and modify, and you have a number of modification options that we'll explore in the upcoming sections.

A shape works like any object inserted into a PowerPoint slide. You can modify the shape by using the resize handles available on each corner of the object and positioned on each side, as you can see here:

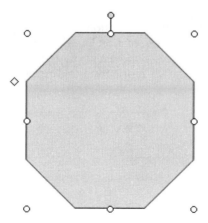

To resize the object and keep the object's perspective correct (which doesn't distort the object), use one of the resize handles on a corner of the object. Click and hold down the handle, and then move your mouse in or out to resize the object.

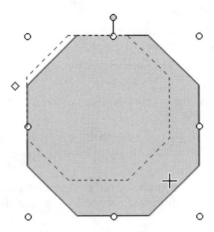

If you don't want to keep the shape's original perspective, you can use the handles on the sides of the shape to resize it any way you want. This action will distort the shape, depending on how you resize it.

TIP   *If you want to move an AutoShape to a different location on the slide, just grab it anywhere with your mouse (but not using the resize handles) and drag it to the new location.*

Modify Orientation

As with any object, you can modify the orientation of a shape by using the green handle. If you position your mouse over the green rotation handle, your mouse cursor changes to the rotation symbol. Simply grab the green handle and drag your mouse to change the object's orientation. As you can see here, we are reorienting this arrow so that it is pointing down.

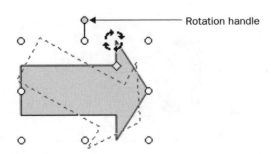

Rotation handle

Adjust an AutoShape

Some shapes have an adjustment handle that allows you to adjust the shape. The adjustment handle is a yellow triangle that appears somewhere on the shape. If you grab the adjustment handle and drag your mouse, you'll see some alternative shapes that you can use. For example, in the illustration here, we are dragging the handle backwards, and you can see an alternative arrow shape forming in the background. This quick fix allows you to try different variations of a single shape so you can find the one that meets your needs.

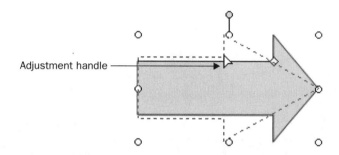

Some adjustment handles simply give the shape a different look. Here, you see an original action button shape on the left. On the right, you see its adjusted shape after using the adjustment handle. Notice how the change has given the action button a 3-D look.

Tip   *Don't be alarmed if you don't see an adjustment handle on an AutoShape—they do not appear on all of them, but only those that have some practical adjustment properties.*

Make a Shape 3-D

The Drawing toolbar gives you an option to make AutoShapes that you insert on a slide appear in a 3-D format. Select the shape that you want to make 3-D on your slide, and then on the Drawing toolbar, click the 3-D button in Figure 22-2. Click a 3-D shape you want to apply to the AutoShape, and it is applied. If you don't like what you see, just click a different 3-D shape to change it.

One thing you should definitely note is the 3-D Settings options that appear when you click the 3-D button on the Draw toolbar. If you click 3-D Settings, the 3-D Settings toolbar

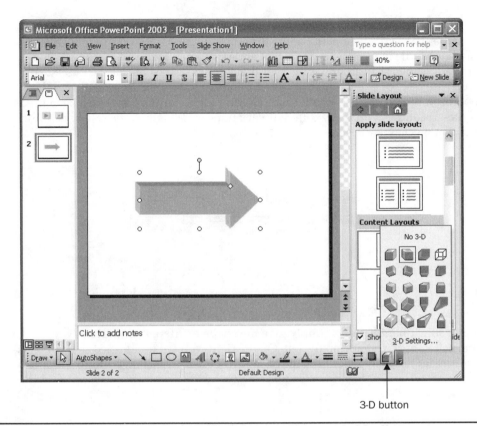

3-D button

FIGURE 22-2   Use the 3-D Shapes button on the Drawing toolbar to apply 3-D effects.

appears in your work area. This little toolbar packs a lot of power, and you'll use it time and time again when you are working with 3-D effects.

Using the 3-D Settings toolbar, you can adjust the tilt angles, 3-D depth, direction, lighting, surface appearance, and color. This illustration shows the 3-D Settings toolbar, and you can see the shape made from the arrow image used earlier, except we have tilted it and changed the 3-D color with the toolbar. As you can imagine, using the 3-D Settings toolbar, you can customize your 3-D shapes so they appear exactly as you want them to.

Change a Shape's Fill Color

The fill color used on AutoShapes can have a significant impact on the overall look of your presentation, so you'll want to take a hard look at color and decide how to fill your AutoShapes. As a general rule, err on the conservative side—AutoShapes that are too loudly colored will distract from the other elements of your slide and your overall presentation. So, as you think about color, consider the function of the shape on the slide and decide how much color emphasis it should get in relation to the other slide elements.

To change a shape's fill color, simply select the shape on the slide and click the Fill Color menu on the Drawing toolbar. You can choose a standard color, or choose More Fill Colors from the menu to select or configure your own. Also, you can choose the Fill Effects option, which will open the Fill Effects dialog box. Here, you can apply a gradient pattern to the fill effect, a texture, a pattern, or even a picture. This illustration shows an AutoShape with a standard fill color, one with a gradient, a texture, a pattern, and a picture as the fill. As you can imagine, you have a number of creative options for your presentations!

Change an AutoShape

Consider this scenario: You choose an AutoShape for a presentation. You change the size and orientation, add 3-D effects, then use a custom photo for the fill color. The shape looks great. However, once you have finished, you discover a different AutoShape that would work a lot better. So, do you have to throw out your former AutoShape and start from scratch? No, PowerPoint allows you simply to change it to a different AutoShape, keeping your edits intact. Here's how:

1. On the slide, select the AutoShape that you want to change.

2. On the Drawing toolbar, click the Draw button. From the menu that appears, choose Change AutoShape.

3. A submenu appears, listing all the categories of AutoShapes and the actual shapes in additional submenus. Browse and locate the shape you want to use to replace your existing shape; then just click it.

4. The new shape replaces your old shape, but all of your edits remain intact. It's a quick and easy way to change shapes or try out different ones.

Edit Line Properties

Naturally, each shape has a boundary that defines the shape. However, you can further manipulate that boundary using the Drawing toolbar. Notice that you have button options for Line Color, Line Style, and Dash Style. You can select the AutoShape you want to edit, then use one of these tools on the Drawing toolbar to change the line color, the basic line style, or dash style. You can even define a pattern for the line if you want. This illustration shows an object with two different line effects.

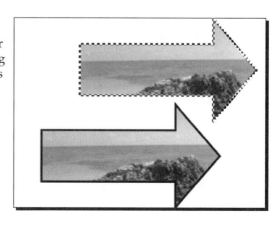

Copy and Paste Shapes

You insert an AutoShape onto a slide by selecting the shape you want from the AutoShape menu on the Drawing toolbar. You then click your mouse or click and drag your mouse on the slide to insert the shape. Once you resize and position the shape as necessary, change its fill color, make it 3-D, or anything else you might want to do, you can simply copy and paste the shape over and over again on the same slide or between slides in your presentation. Here's how you do it:

1. On your slide, select the shape that you want to copy; then click Edit | Copy.

2. If you want to paste the copied selection on the same slide, simply click Edit | Paste.

3. If you want to paste the copied selection to a different slide, use the Slides pane to move to the desired slide; then click Edit | Paste.

4. The copy is pasted to the slide. You can now move the copy around, resize it, and customize it as you like.

TIP   *For faster use, try the keyboard shortcuts. Select the object and press* CTRL-C *to copy it and* CTRL-V *to paste it.*

Align a Shape

Let's say you have four AutoShapes on a particular slide, and you want those four objects to line up exactly. Sure, you can move them around and hope for the best, but PowerPoint gives you two tools for making sure your objects are positioned exactly.

The first is the Align or Distribute option found on the Draw menu of the Drawing toolbar. Just select the objects on your slide (CTRL-click them to select multiple objects); then click the Draw button and point to Align or Distribute. From the submenu choose an alignment or distribution option that meets your needs, such as Align left, Align top, or Distribute horizontally.

Another feature you can use to manually help you get objects in just the right position is Grid and Guide view. You can access the Grid and Guides dialog box by clicking View | Grid and Guides. In the Grid and Guides dialog box, shown in Figure 22-3, you can choose to have objects snap to the invisible grid that resides on each slide. You can also have objects snap to other objects, which typically you will not want to do.

You can adjust the size of the grid and choose to display the grid and display the drawing guides on the screen, as shown here. These items will help you place objects in accurate locations as needed.

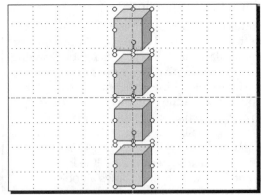

Manage Stack Order

You may often want to use AutoShapes so that they slightly "stack," or overlap each other. This feature can be helpful if you want to use shapes to convey a process. For example, consider the items shown in the

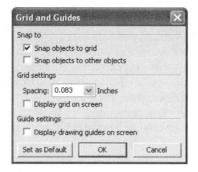

FIGURE 22-3   Grid and Guides

following slide. The order of the stacked items was determined as we added and placed items on top of each other. However, what if you wanted to reorder them so that the first step is not overlapped by the second, and so forth?

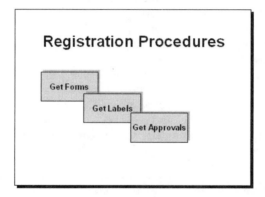

To reorder the objects, select the one you want to reorder, and then click the Draw button on the Drawing toolbar. From the menu, point to Order and click the desired order option. In this case, we've chosen Bring to Front. Repeat this process with any remaining slides, and as you can see here, we have quickly and easily reordered the stack.

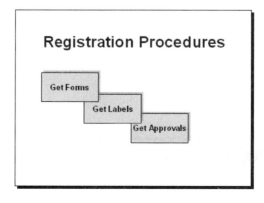

PART IV

Create Shapes

Aside from working with AutoShapes, you can also draw some of your own. Your drawing features in PowerPoint are not as flexible as they would be in a program such as Paint. Of course, you should keep in mind that you can draw an object in any other program, save it as a JPEG file, and then import the object as a picture into PowerPoint and use the drawing that way. However, PowerPoint does give you a few quick and easy draw options. In the following sections, we'll take a look at those, and we'll also put some of your skills to work by creating a flowchart, connected objects, and text, which we'll add to shapes. We'll also look at using action buttons.

Draw Basic Shapes

PowerPoint gives you a few automatic shapes that you can draw on a slide with your mouse. Those shapes are a straight line, an arrow line, an oval, and a square. You can draw them at any size, and position them just as you would an AutoShape. In fact, you can adjust the line and fill colors, 3-D effects—anything described in the previous sections.

To draw a basic shape, click the shape you want to draw on the Drawing toolbar. Then, position the mouse at the place on the slide where you want to create the shape. Your mouse cursor appears as crosshairs. Hold down your left mouse button and begin dragging to create the shape, as shown in this illustration.

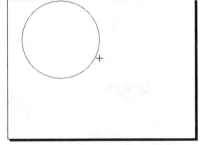

When you have about the correct size, release the mouse button, and the shape will appear. If the shape is an oval or square, the default fill color will be applied. At this point, you can select the object and resize it, adjust it, change its fill color, or anything else you might want. Figure 22-4 shows you the basic shapes you can draw.

NOTE   *If you draw an arrow using the Arrow button on the Drawing toolbar, you can select the arrow and click the Arrow Style button on the toolbar to change the style of the arrow.*

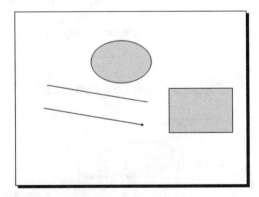

FIGURE 22-4   Basic shapes you can draw with the mouse

Draw an Arc and Other Standard Shapes

Aside from basic shapes on the Drawing toolbar, you can also draw an arc and some other standard shapes that appear when you click the AutoShapes menu, and point to and click one of the line shapes at the bottom of the menu. The difference with these AutoShapes is that they don't appear automatically on the slide when you select them and click the slide area. Instead, you have to use your mouse to draw the object in the position you want. Like all other objects, though, you can always resize and move them around after you draw them.

The process for drawing an arc or other standard shape is the same. Just select the shape from the Basic Shapes menu by clicking it. Then, position your mouse where you want to start drawing the shape (your mouse cursor becomes crosshairs). Click and drag your mouse to create the shape. As you can see here, we are creating an arc to connect the two shapes.

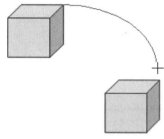

Group Shapes

Let's say you have five small shapes on a slide. You want to move the shapes around as a group and even change their positioning as a group. No problem. With PowerPoint, you can group the objects and move them around as a group, yet still perform individual editing changes to single objects just by selecting them. Here's how:

1. On the slide, make sure none of the shapes are selected.

2. Position your mouse and drag to create a selection box around them. When you release your mouse, all of the items will become selected, as you can see here. (You can also select them by holding down the CTRL key and clicking each shape.)

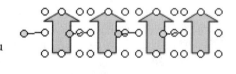

3. On the Drawing toolbar, click Draw | Group. The objects are grouped together. You can now drag them around and reposition them as a group, as shown here:

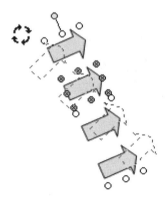

NOTE   *Although you can individually edit members of the group, you can no longer individually drag them around. If you want to take a shape out of the group, select it and click Draw | Ungroup on the Drawing toolbar.*

Insert Text on Shapes

You can easily insert text on any shape that you place on a slide. You can use the Formatting toolbar to format the text font, size, and style as needed, just as you would when you work with text on any other portion of the slide.

Adding text to a shape is easy, and the following steps show you how.

1. First, add the shape to your slide and adjust it so that it is the desired size. Here we have added a callout from the AutoShapes menu to a cartoon clip art character.

2. On the Drawing toolbar, click the Insert Text Box icon, and then click on your shape.

3. Type your text and use the text box to center it, stretch it, or whatever you need. Then, use the Formatting toolbar to format the text as desired. You can even use WordArt if you like (available on the Drawing toolbar as well), as you can see in the caption we added here.

Use Connectors

The AutoShapes menu provides a Connectors option with a list of available connectors. Connectors are just that—lines you can use to connect other objects, and they work great for flowchart or work flow kinds of graphics. The connectors range from hard lines to movable lines and even free-form lines.

To use a connector, select it from the Connectors menu; then click and drag your mouse to create the connector on the slide. Basically, using a connector works like drawing anything else, but there is one helpful feature you should note. Some of the connectors have a yellow adjustment handle in the middle that allows you to adjust the line as you like. For example, the following shows the same connector, but we have simply changed the shape of the connector using the yellow handle.

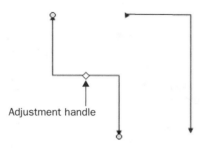

Adjustment handle

Create a Flowchart

Flowcharts are great ways to organize and display information on a slide. They are particularly helpful in cases where you want to show some kind of information flow, process, organizational model, or the like. You can create a flowchart from scratch using the skills you have learned in this chapter, and the following steps give you a guide. Try this out yourself!

1. First, determine the slide background, slide title, and anything else you want displayed on the slide besides the flowchart. We have a basic slide ready to go:

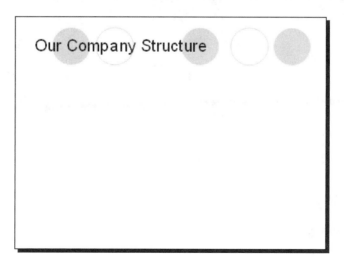

Our Company Structure

2. Using the Draw menu, access AutoShapes | Flowchart. Choose the shapes you want and arrange them on the slide as desired.

3. Next, apply any slide formatting you want and insert the text. As you can see in the next illustration, we are showing the company's departmental "chain of command."

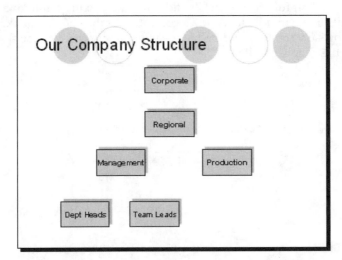

4. Finally, use the AutoShapes | Connectors menu to choose the connectors for the blocks on the flowchart. The following completed flowchart took only a few minutes to create!

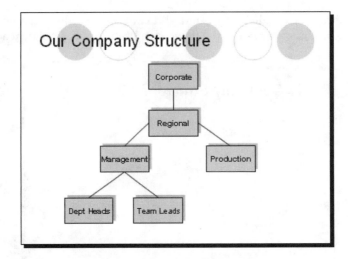

Configure Action Buttons

PowerPoint contains some cool action buttons that you can add to your presentation. Action buttons are just that—they can be clicked with a mouse and some action will happen. You can insert direction buttons that someone can click to look through your slide show, or you can create a button that hyperlinks to another presentation or web location. You can also create buttons for help, information, home, sound control, and for starting a movie file. You'll use these buttons a lot when you create presentations for the Web, and the good news is they are easy to configure.

To insert an action button on a slide, use the AutoShapes menu to select the action button you want, and then click and drag to create it on your slide. Once the action button is drawn, an Action Settings dialog box appears. As you can see in Figure 22-5, we have inserted a navigation button for a web slide show. The Action Settings dialog box has already guessed that we will want to hyperlink to the next slide when someone clicks the button. Of course, you could choose other options, such as running a program or macro, or playing a sound, depending on what you want the button to do. If you insert a Movie button from the Action Buttons list, you would configure this dialog box to run a program, then link to the movie program you want to run.

An action button is just a shape with an underlying clickable link. As such, you can format it just like any other shape and change it as needed for your presentation.

Inserting Multimedia Content

Multimedia content loosely refers to movies and sound files. It is content that provides some movement, rather than simple photos or graphics. When you work with a slide, PowerPoint refers to multimedia as "media clips," and this includes movie files and sound files. You can use media clips from your clip art collection, or you can insert your own.

For the most part, inserting multimedia content into a slide works just like inserting any other content. On the Slide Layout icon, click the Insert Media Clip icon (looks like a camera), or you can click Insert | Movies and Sound, and choose from one of the submenu options. From this menu, you can even choose to record sound and play a CD audio track.

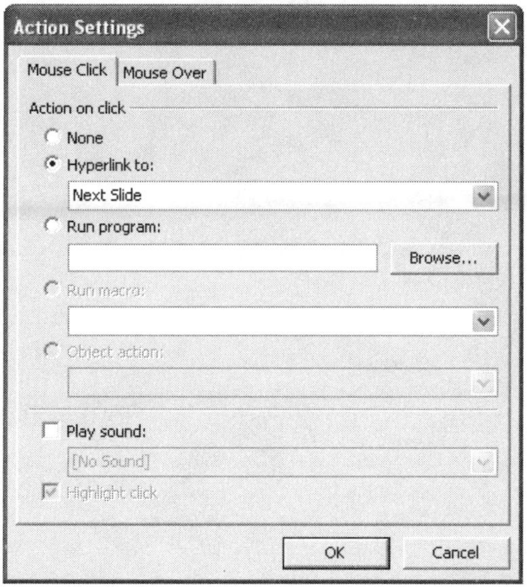

FIGURE 22-5   Action Settings

The multimedia content appears on the slide. All animation for the content is used when you actually play the slide (it is not animated in the work area.) When you insert a movie or sound clip, you can choose to have it play automatically, or when you click it, as you can see here, which shows you a video clip of a newborn waking up after a short nap.

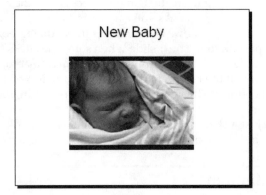

Showing Your PowerPoint Presentations

The main task you perform when designing and creating presentations is working with individual slides. After all, it's the slides that communicate your message to the audience, and it is the slides that make the content of your message more interesting and easier to understand.

As you finish up the slides for your presentation, you'll get ready to use them in whatever way you choose to communicate your message. You may choose to use the slides on screen during a live presentation, or you may publish the presentation to a web site where people can view it on the Internet. Regardless of how you plan on using your presentation, there are a few last-minute features you should look into, and we'll cover those concepts in this chapter. So, in this chapter, we'll take a look at using transitions, animation effects, and techniques for presenting your slide show, and then we'll see how to generate speaker notes and audience handouts.

Transitions and Animation

Slide transitions and animation give your presentations that extra "pop" that makes them look smooth and attractive. A *transition* is a visual effect that occurs when you are changing from one slide to the next. The transition may blend into the next slide or "box out/box in" (the screen seems to close down or open in a box) into the next slide. Animation features allow you to animate the text on your slides: bulleted points jump onto the slide when you are ready for them, or fade in one by one, for example.

Setting Up Transitions

You use transitions to move your presentation, thus your audience, from one slide to the next. Overall, transitions make your presentation more professional and more pleasing to the audience. You have a number of different transition effects to choose from, and you can control the speed at which those transitions take place. However, keep in mind that transitions are there to give an extra boost to your presentation, but wild transitions can be more distracting than helpful, so make sure you err on the side of being conservative when using them. You can use a different transition effect on each slide, although many presenters prefer to use the same transition effect on all slides in order to give the presentation more continuity and better flow.

The good news is that applying transitions is easy. You can click Slide Show | Slide Transition, or you can just right-click any slide and click Slide Transition. Either way, this opens the Slide Transition pane. As you can see, you have a few different transition options:

First of all, click the down arrow at the top of the pane to choose the transition you want from the list (there are over 50 of them to choose from). Just scroll through the list and locate the transition. When you click a transition, it is enacted on the current slide so you can see if you like the transition.

Once you choose a transition, it is automatically applied to the slide. If you look in the slide view, shown here, you see a star next to the slide. This tells you the transition has been applied to your slide.

On the Slide Transition pane, you can then adjust the speed of the transition. Use the Speed drop-down menu to choose a speed, and if you want a sound played on the transition, choose one from the drop-down menu, or choose Other Sound to use one of our own.

Under the Advance Slide option, you can choose to advance on mouse click or automatically after a certain period of time that you specify. Finally, at the bottom of the pane, you can apply the transition to all slides by clicking the provided button option, and you can also play the transition and view the entire slide show so you can see how the transition looks.

TIP   *If you later decide that you want to remove a transition from a slide, just open the slide and go back to the transition pane. In the transition list, choose No Transition. The transition will be removed from that particular slide. If you want to remove the transition from all slides, choose No Transition, and then click the Apply to All Slides button on the Slide Transition pane.*

Using Animation

You can animate the text on your slides to liven up an otherwise dry presentation. This feature allows the title to fly in or appear in any number of effects, or you can have bulleted points appear one at a time. The latter works particularly well because you can animate bulleted point slides and only have the point you are discussing appear. Animation can be a great delivery aid, but like transitions, a little goes a long way. Be sure not to overanimate your slides, or they tend to become distracting to audience members.

To use slide animation, open the desired slide, and click Slide Show | Animation Schemes. The task pane turns to Slide Design with Animation Schemes selected:

You can then choose the desired animation from the list. The animation is applied to the slide, and if you want the same animation to appear on all slides, click the Apply to All Slides button.

One problem with the animation schemes is that they animate the entire slide. What if you have a title on a slide, then two different text boxes, but you only want to animate the content in one of the text boxes? In this case, you must set up a custom animation scheme for that text box. Right-click the text box on the slide and click Custom Animation. The Custom Animation pane appears:

Click the Add Effect button to choose an effect from the different categories that appear. Then, use the Modify section of the pane to choose how you want to use the animation, such as no mouse click, the direction, and how fast you want the effect to work. You can experiment with these settings to find the one you want, and you can always use the Remove button on the Custom Animation pane to remove any animation you have previously applied.

Getting Ready for Your Presentation

Once you have applied any transition and/or animation effects you want, you are ready to begin using your presentation for rehearsal. Before doing so, play your slide show on your computer and take an overall look at it. Check for general slide order, and also read everything carefully. Make sure your sentences and phrases mean what they intend, and it's a good idea to have someone else read through your presentation for possible errors. Keep in mind that if you find something you want to change, you can always go back and edit your presentation and use the Slide Sorter View to rearrange slides if necessary.

To see your slide show full screen, click Slide Show | View Show, or press F5 on your keyboard. You can then walk through your presentation by clicking your mouse. Press the ESC key at any time to exit the presentation.

Rehearsing Your Presentation

If you are using your slide show as a live presentation, you can rehearse your timing to see how long the presentation takes and how long each slide is displayed. This feature helps you get an overall timing for the presentation, but it also helps you see how long you are spending on each slide. This can help you identify areas where you need to cut some information to shorten, or perhaps add some information to a particular slide.

When you rehearse your presentation, it's a good idea to use the same computer you'll use when showing your presentation, if possible. This way, you get a feel for the computer and you know what to expect. When you are ready to rehearse your timing, simply click Slide Show | Rehearse Timings, or you can click Slide Sorter View and click Rehearse Timings on the toolbar. Either way, the slide show begins. A rehearsal box appears, as shown in Figure 23-1. You also see some slide navigation buttons in the lower-left corner of the screen.

The first timing dialog box shows you the time on the individual slide, while the second one shows you the time for the entire presentation. As you click through the slides, the first dialog box will be reset to record the time you spend on the next slide. This way, you can see an overall timing and individual slide timing. When you are done, a message appears giving you a total time. You can then keep the new slide timings so you can see how long you spent on each slide (they appear in the Slide Sorter View). You can run the Slide Timings feature again and again until you get your timing just as you want it.

Using Hidden Slides

Let's say you are giving a presentation and you run five minutes short. Sure, you can ad lib and ask for questions, but five minutes of extra time can seem like an eternity. In order to prevent such a problem, you can create a few extra hidden slides. The hidden slides contain

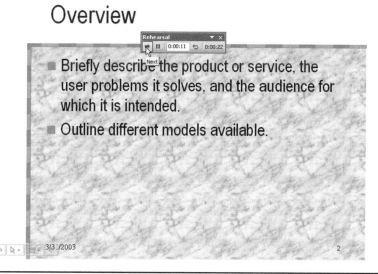

FIGURE 23-1   Checking your slide timings

extra information that you don't need for your presentation, but they are available if you need them to fill up some time. When you run your presentation, the slides remain hidden and are never shown unless you specifically tell PowerPoint to show them.

To hide a slide or multiple slides, switch to Slide Sorter View, and select the slide you want to hide. If you want to hide multiple slides, CTRL-click them to select them all. Click Slide Show | Hide Slide. The slide(s) is now hidden and will not be displayed during the presentation.

TIP   It is a good idea to put your hidden slides at the end of the presentation. This way, you'll always know where they are. Use the Slide Sorter View to reorganize the slides, if necessary.

So now that you have hidden slides, you know that you will not see them during your presentation. What do you do should the need arise to use them? Since you'll be in the actual slide show, you use your mouse and right-click any area on the current slide, then choose Go to Slide. The list of slides appears, and the hidden slides are numbered with parenthesis around the number. For example, if your first hidden slide is the 3rd slide in the show, it will be displayed as (3), as you can see here. Just click the hidden slide to display it.

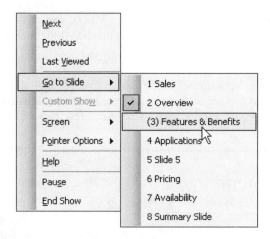

Using a Pen/Highlighter

During a presentation, it would certainly be helpful if you could use an on-screen pen or a highlighter to emphasize particular points or phrases. Relax, you can with no problem. When you are showing the presentation, just right-click anywhere on the screen, and choose Pointer Options. You can choose from an arrow, ballpoint pen, felt-tip pen, or highlighter (see Figure 23-2). You can use the Ink Color option to change the color of ink and the eraser to erase your ink. Using these features, you can highlight options on the screen as you discuss them.

TIP   When you are presenting your slides, there may be times when you would like the screen to go black so your audience will focus on you, rather than the slide. No problem—just right-click anywhere on the screen during a presentation, and click Screen | Black Screen.

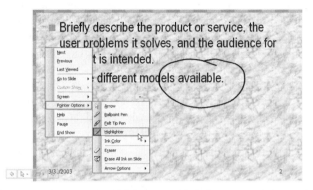

FIGURE 23-2 Use a pen or the Highlighter option to emphasize words or phrases.

Set Up Show Options

If you are going to use your presentation live (you presenting it), you have nothing more to set up. But what if your show will be browsed by people at terminals or run automatically at a kiosk, such as you might see at a trade show? PowerPoint gives you some setup options for choosing how to use your show.

Click Slide Show | Set Up Show. In the dialog box that appears, shown in Figure 23-3, you see the option to choose a show type. Once you choose that show type, you can choose from additional options and even choose a performance level. The options here are self-explanatory, so look through them and choose what will be right for your show.

FIGURE 23-3
Set Up Show
options

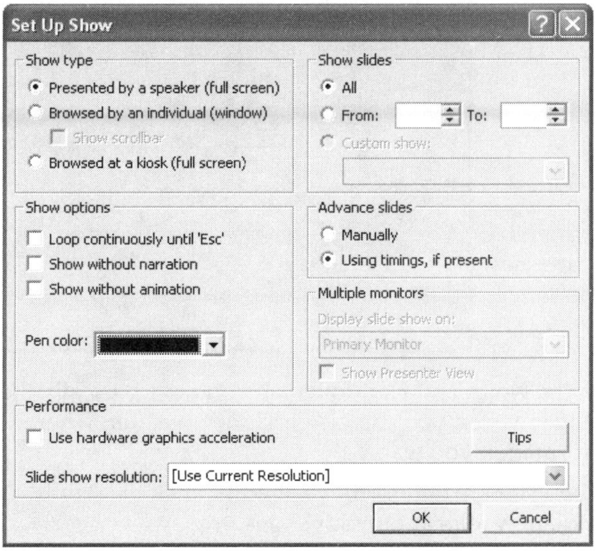

Printing Speaker Notes and Audience Handouts

Printing a presentation may not seem like a big deal, but PowerPoint gives you several print options that you'll want to explore and get familiar with. PowerPoint gives you the flexibility to print slides, handouts, speaker notes, and an outline view, and there are a few options concerning each of these printing features that you should know about. In the following sections, we'll take a look at some different printing features available to you.

Add a Header and Footer

When you use your presentation on screen or on the Web, you probably don't want to use headers and footers, since they can be difficult to read. However, when you print a presentation, headers and footers can be helpful, and PowerPoint gives you the ability to add them.

Follow these steps to add a header and footer to a presentation:

1. In PowerPoint, open the desired presentation using the File | Open command.

2. Choose View | Header and Footer.

3. In the Header and Footer dialog box, choose the Slide tab, shown next. This tab allows you to configure headers and footers that will display on each slide. Note that you can include the date and time and have them updated automatically, or include a fixed date and time. You can also include the slide number and a footer. If you don't want this information to appear on the title slide, click the Don't Show on Title Slide check box.

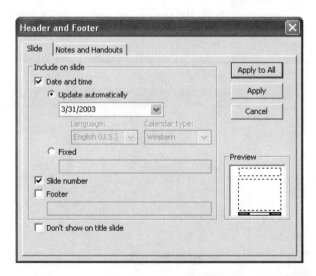

4. On the Notes and Handouts tab you have basically the same options as the Slide tab. However, you can also include a header, where you can type whatever information you want.

5. When you are done with your edits, click the Apply to All button. The edits you made now appear on your slides.

Configure Print Settings

Before you print a slide show, notes, or any other print option, you should take a look at your printer settings to make sure those settings will work for you. You can access the print settings on the Page Setup dialog box, which is found in File | Page Setup.

In the Page Setup dialog box, shown next, you have the option to choose what size paper you will print to, which is typically going to be letter paper (8.5×11). When you choose your paper option, PowerPoint scales the slides in order to accommodate the paper size so that your printouts will look attractive. Notice also that you can adjust the orientation of the slides, as well as the notes, handouts, and outline prints, from portrait to landscape. Make any selections you want here, and click OK to save your Page Setup settings.

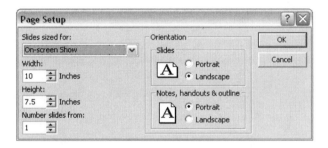

Use Print Preview

I'll tell you a secret—Print Preview is your friend—big time! This little feature, which you can access by choosing File | Print Preview, allows you to quickly get exactly the kind of printout that you want.

When you choose Print Preview from the File menu, a preview window appears. In this window, you are shown a preview of your print job, and you are given a number of helpful controls. Figure 23-4 shows you print preview and points out the controls available to you.

Let's take a quick look at what you can do in Print Preview:

- **View your print job**   The Print Preview window shows you exactly how your printout will look on the printed page. Keep in mind that your paper size shown here is the size you choose in Page Setup (see the previous section).

- **Preview/Next Page**   Use these buttons to move between pages in your presentation to see how they will look when printed.

- **Print**   This option prints your presentation.

- **Print Options**   If you click the Print What drop-down menu, you can choose from slides, handouts, notes pages, or outline view. Notice that if you choose a handouts page, you can choose how many slides you want printed per page. This feature saves paper and prints a nice handout of all of your slides that you can distribute to your audience. The Outline view is another alternative to handouts, since it condenses your presentation to text only, neatly fitting on a page or two (depending on the length of your presentation). This kind of printout makes useful speaker notes as well.

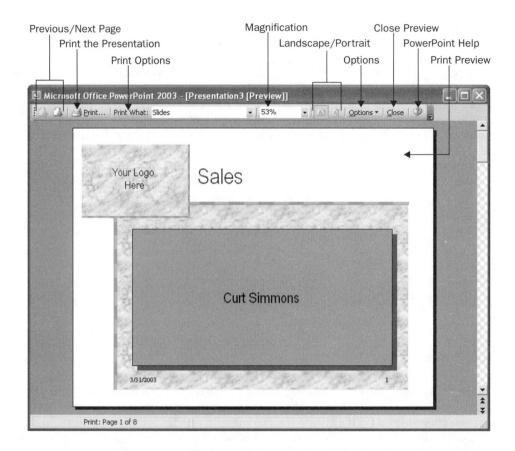

FIGURE 23-4 Print Preview

- **Magnification** Use the Magnification buttons to zoom in and out of your preview pages so you can see them more clearly. You can also zoom in and out by simply clicking on the page in the Preview window.

- **Landscape/Portrait** Use these buttons to toggle between landscape and portrait views in order to make a final orientation decision before you print.

- **Options** The Options button contains a drop-down menu that gives you these helpful printing choices:

  - **Header and Footer** This opens the Header and Footer dialog box that we explored previously in this chapter.

  - **Color/Grayscale** This pop-out menu allows you to print your slides in color, grayscale, or in pure black and white.

  - **Scale to Fit Paper** This option enlarges your slides so that they will fit to your paper.

- **Frame Slides** This option puts a thin frame around your slides so that they actually look like slides on the printout. This works well when you are printing handouts with several slides on a page.

- **Print Hidden Slides** In PowerPoint, you can hide slides so that they do not appear in the presentation. Hidden slides can contain speaker content or other information you do not want to show your audience. This option prints all hidden slides.

- **Print Comments** You can also insert comments into slides that do not appear on the actual slide. Comments help you stay organized or can function as reminders, and this option prints all comments as well.

- **Printing Order** This option allows you to adjust the printing order of your slides.

- **Close** This button closes the Print Preview window.
- **Help** Get PowerPoint help by clicking the Help button.

Print a Presentation

When you are ready to print your presentation, you can do so by clicking the Print button in the Print Preview window, or by clicking File | Print. Either way, you see a standard Print dialog box, shown in Figure 23-5. Notice the Print Range options, where you choose what slides to print and how many copies. At the bottom of the window, you see the same options that are available in Print Preview—you can choose what to print, the color, scaling, and so forth. When you are ready, just click the Print button to print your presentation!

FIGURE 23-5
Print dialog box

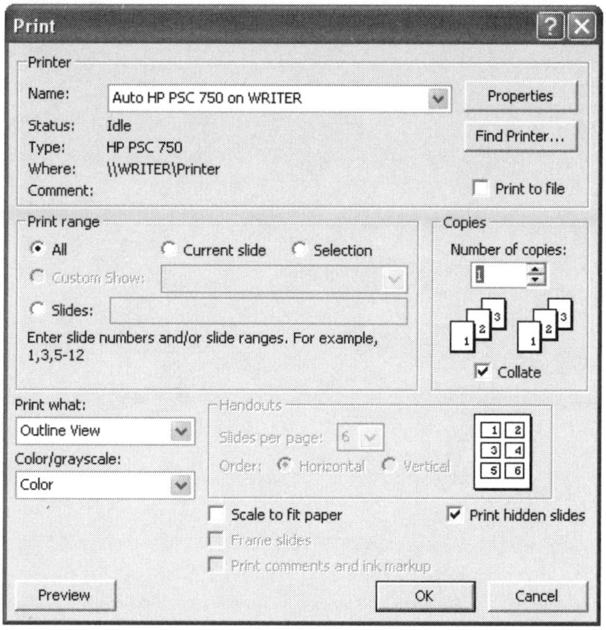

V PART

Schedule and Contact Management

CHAPTER 24
Outlook

CHAPTER 25
Outlook E-mail

CHAPTER 26
Outlook Calendar and
Task Lists

CHAPTER 27
Managing Contacts and
Taking Notes

CHAPTER 28
Scheduling and Planning
with Others

Outlook

Managing personal information is a major need in today's work environments. From e-mail, to scheduling, to calendars and tasks, to managing contacts, personal information management is a necessary part of offices today, and Microsoft Office provides Outlook as the software you need for personal information management. Generally thought of as "e-mail software," Microsoft Outlook is actually much more. You can manage e-mail, but you can also manage your own calendar, tasks list, contacts, as well as scheduling and planning with others. In short, Outlook is designed to help you manage information, and as you'll find out in the coming chapters, it is powerful software.

This chapter will get your feet wet with Outlook. You'll see how to use the interface and use some standard Outlook options. In other chapters in this part of the book, we'll take a detailed look at Outlook's different features.

A First Look at Outlook

When you start out, you see a few different panes and the Outlook Today window, shown in Figure 24-1. This is Outlook's default interface. As you can see, the Outlook Today portion of the interface provides you with calendar information, tasks, and mail message information. Of course, since you haven't configured Outlook to use any of these features, they will all be blank at first.

In the left side of the interface, you see a Navigation pane, where you can choose the feature that you want to use, such as Mail, Calendar, Contacts, and Tasks. If you click a selection, the Outlook interface changes. Let's take a quick look at each portion of the interface.

Mail

The Mail interface, shown in Figure 24-2, provides mail folders and the ability to read mail in the Reading pane. This feature allows you to click through your mail and read the entire mail message without opening it in a different window. As you can see in Figure 24-2, you have a list of personal folders, such as Deleted Items, Drafts, Inbox, Junk E-mail, and so forth. Personal folders allow you to easily manage your mail, and you can create new folders as well.

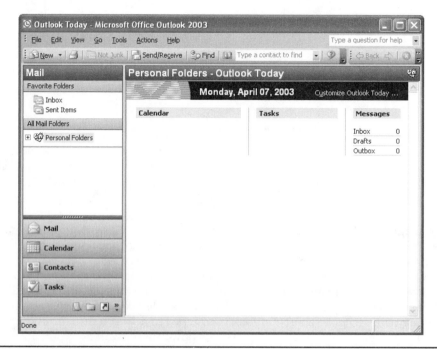

FIGURE 24-1 Outlook's initial window

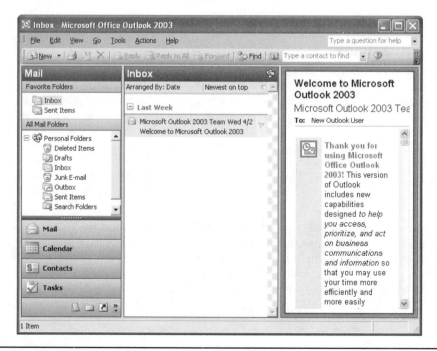

FIGURE 24-2 Use the Mail interface to manage and read e-mail.

TIP   *If you have used previous versions of Outlook, you may prefer that the Reading pane be displayed on the bottom instead of on the side as it now is in Outlook 2003. No problem—just click View | Reading Pane, and choose the Bottom option (or Off if you don't want to use the Reading pane at all.*

Calendar

If you click the Calendar button on the left pane, the Outlook interface changes to Calendar view, shown in Figure 24-3. Notice that the toolbar also changes to provide you with different calendar functions. Using this view, you can configure appointments and even set up Outlook to alert you when new meetings are nearing. You can share calendars with other people so that a group of workers can use the same calendar. You can learn all about Outlook's calendar feature in Chapter 26.

Contacts

The Contacts view is opened by clicking Contacts in the left pane. Your interface changes to a view where you can enter contact information and keep it neatly stored and organized—ready to use when you need it. You can view contact information by address cards, phone lists, categories, companies, locations, and a number of other view features. See Chapter 27 to learn more about using the contacts feature.

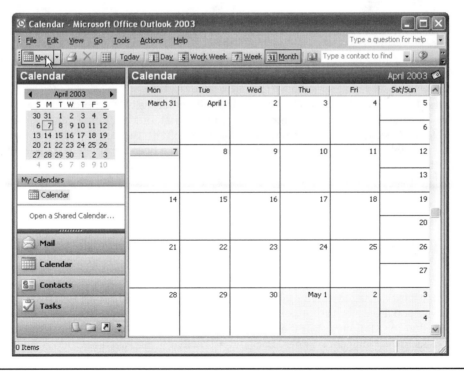

FIGURE 24-3   Calendar view

FIGURE 24-4   Use Tasks to create tasks and reminders.

Tasks

You use the Tasks view, shown in Figure 24-4 above, to enter tasks that need to be completed by you or a group. That may not sound too exciting at first, but you can actually do a lot with this feature because you can have Outlook keep up with the tasks, when they are due, who is responsible for them, and whether or not they have been completed. As with the other Outlook features, your interface changes in order to give you the tools you need to configure and use the tasks feature.

Using Outlook's Toolbars

Unlike other Office applications, Outlook's toolbars are rather simple, due to the basic design of Outlook. If you click View | Toolbars, you'll see three toolbars that you can use within Outlook:

- **Standard**   The Standard toolbar, shown here, provides standard functions for the view you are using in Outlook. For example, this illustration shows you the Standard toolbar for Mail view, but the toolbar changes if you choose Calendar, Contacts, or Tasks in the Navigation pane. The Standard toolbar is displayed in Outlook by default.

- **Advanced**   The Advanced toolbar, shown next, has some specific buttons depending on what Outlook feature you have selected in the Navigation pane, but it also has some standard buttons, such as Outlook Today, Back/Forward, Reading Pane selection, Print Preview, and so forth. By default, the Advanced toolbar is not shown.

- **Web**   The Web toolbar, shown here, gives you just a few options so that you can use web features within Outlook. You can use Back/Forward buttons, Stop, Refresh, Home, and search the Web. By default, the Web toolbar is not shown.

Aside from the three toolbars Outlook gives you, you can also customize the toolbars, or you can create your own. This customization feature allows you to add features to toolbars that you most often use. To customize a toolbar, click View | Toolbars | Customize. In the Customize window, use the Toolbars pane to choose which toolbars you want to use. If you want to create a custom toolbar, click New and give the toolbar a name. Then, click the Commands tab to locate the command category and the commands you want to use, and simply drag the desired commands to the toolbar, as shown in Figure 24-5. You can also use the Options tab to configure some basic toolbar options, which you'll find self-explanatory.

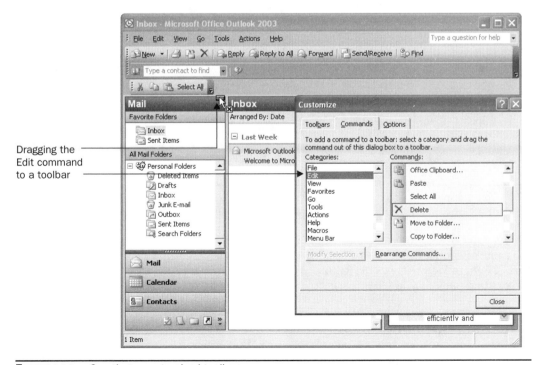

FIGURE 24-5   Creating a customized toolbar

Using Categories

Outlook 2003 provides you with a feature called "categories." Categories are simply labels that you can assign to different entries in Outlook. You can then search on a category and locate all of the entries for that category. For example, let's say you have 100 e-mail messages. You label five of them "personal." Then, you simply need to search on "personal" to find the desired messages.

Like most things in Outlook, categories are only as good as your application of them, so if you want to use categories, make sure you apply them judiciously as needed. You can assign categories to such items as e-mail messages, calendar appointments, as well as tasks. This feature allows you to identify different entries in Outlook.

As you might imagine, categories can be as simple or complex as you make them. If you use Outlook at work and at home, for example, you may simply have a "business" category and a "home" category to keep different items straight and easily searchable.

If you select an item in Outlook, such as an e-mail message, you can click Edit | Categories to apply the desired categories. Simply make your selections from the list and click OK. If you want to add a category item, just type it in the dialog box and click Add to List, as shown here:

Tip *You can remove categories from an item at any time by simply selecting the item, clicking Edit | Categories, then clearing the desired check boxes in the Categories dialog box.*

As you can see, you can create categories on the fly as needed, but you can also manage the entire categories master list by clicking Edit | Categories, then clicking the Master Category List, shown in Figure 24-6. This feature allows you to add new categories or remove any of the existing ones, as you like.

Data File Management

Your Outlook data is stored in a data file. Since Outlook is designed to function in a multiuser environment, several different people can log on to the same computer and use Outlook for

FIGURE 24-6
Master
Categories
List

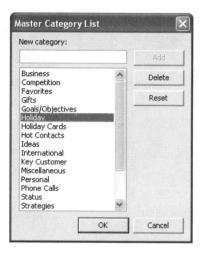

personal information management. Outlook can keep these different people's files and e-mail separate because it stores each user's information in a specific data file. This feature allows each user to keep his or her files private, but still allows Outlook to be used by several different people.

By default on Windows XP, your data file is stored in C:\Documents and Settings\ *username*\Local Settings\Application Data\Microsoft\Outlook. Using Data File Management, you can change this location, but you can also change the password that allows you to access the personal file folder, and you can choose to compact your personal file folder in order to save space.

Click File | Data File Management. The Data Files dialog box appears, shown in Figure 24-7. You can click Open Folder to see the actual data file folder, or you can click Add to add a new data file, such as a personal file folder compatible with earlier versions of Outlook. However, the item you'll probably need most is the Settings option, so click the Settings button.

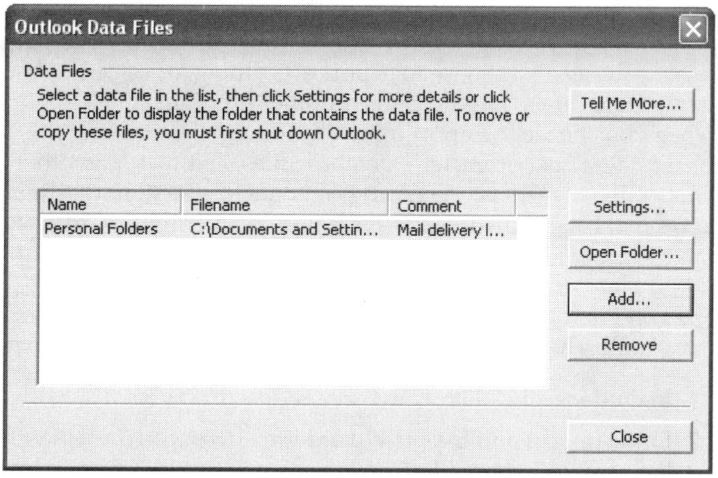

FIGURE 24-7
Outlook data files

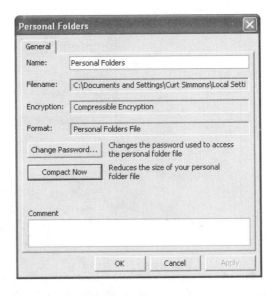

FIGURE 24-8
The Personal Folders dialog box is where you do most of your "housekeeping" in Outlook.

The Settings button opens the Personal Folders dialog box, shown in Figure 24-8 above. If you click the Change Password button, you can enter your old password, then create a new one. If you want to reduce the size of your Outlook folder, click the Compact Now button, and Outlook will compress the folder. From time to time as your Outlook folder grows, it is a good idea to return to the Personal Folders dialog box and click the Compact Now button to keep the data files compact.

Importing and Exporting Data

Without a doubt, Outlook is not the only mail client that exists in the world. As such, you may need to import data into Outlook or export it so that it can be used in another mail program. Either way, Outlook 2003 provides a standard Import and Export wizard. Using the wizard, you can import vcards, calendars, mail, or data from another program or file, or you can import Internet mail account settings as well as Internet mail and addresses. Likewise, you can also choose to export everything, or selected Outlook items, to a file so that the data can be imported into another program.

When you choose to import from another program or file, you can import data from personal folders (.pst extension), database files, text files, and other support files, or you can import directly from certain programs, such as Act!, Lotus Organizer, Microsoft Access, Microsoft Excel, and Schedule+. When you choose to import Internet mail settings or Internet mail and addresses, Outlook is referring to importing mail and settings from Outlook Express or Eudora Light or Pro, not mail from web servers themselves.

The good news is that importing or exporting data is easy, thanks to the Import and Export wizard. The following steps show you how to import or export data:

1. In Outlook, click File | Import and Export Data.

2. In the Import and Export Wizard screen, choose the action that you want to take. We want to Export all of our data to a file so that we can import it into another

program, so we're going to choose Export to a File. Click Next once you have made your selection.

3. In the next window, you'll choose the kind of file type you want to create (comma or tab separated values), or if you are importing, you'll choose what kind of file or program you are importing from (Acess, Excel, or Personal Folder file). Make a selection and click Next.

4. The next window may ask for additional information, or prompt you to select the folders you want to export, if you are exporting. Make a selection and click Next.

5. If you are exporting, you'll be asked where you want to save the file and the export name. You also have the option to replace any duplicates, if necessary. Click Finish to complete the wizard.

Archiving Data

Archiving data is the process of removing older items from your file folders and storing them in an archive file, thus reducing clutter in your personal folders in Outlook. By default, Outlook automatically archives data every 15 days (but prompts you before doing so). However, you can change the AutoArchive settings, and you can manually archive data as you like.

First of all, if you want to manage AutoArchiving, click Tools | Options, and then click the Other tab. Click the AutoArchive button. As you can see in Figure 24-9, you can adjust the interval for AutoArchive, and you can stop Outlook from prompting you when AutoArchive runs. You also see a number of additional settings concerning what Outlook should do with old items. Note that by default, old items are moved to an archive.pst file. However, you can change this as desired.

FIGURE 24-9
AutoArchive options

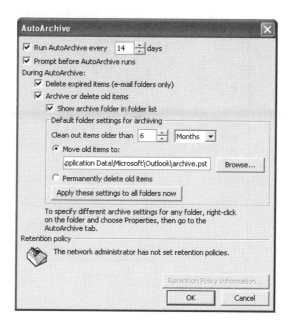

PART V

Aside from using AutoArchive, you can also manually archive data using File | Archive. In the Archive window (Figure 24-10), you can choose to archive specific folders with items that are older than a certain date. If you have AutoArchive settings configured, you do not need to manually run the archive, but the option is available should you need it.

If you decide to manually run an archive by choosing File | Archive, you'll see a simple Archive dialog box where you can select the folder you want to archive. Note, however, that the name for the archive file is archive.pst by default. Each time you choose to manually archive a folder, the same name is applied. So, you'll need to change the default archive.pst file to a unique name with the .pst extension. In fact, you can also adjust the archive file path so that it is saved in the location of your choice, or just click the Browse button and browse to the desired location.

Finally, once you create an archive file, what can you do with it? Because the folder or items have been archived, you'll need to bring them out of their archived state in order to use them. You can choose to bring the items in an archive file back to their original folders in Outlook, you can copy archived items from an archived file into a new Outlook folder, or you can move individual items from an archived file back to their original folder or a new one. You can perform these actions in one of two ways:

- You can use the File | Import and Export option. Simply follow the wizard steps and choose to import the archived .pst folder. You can choose to import the folder back to its original position, or create a new location.

- You can also click Go | Folder List. Click the archived file that appears in your folder list, then click the archived folder. Locate the desired item in the folder, then drag the item to its original location in the Folder List. Repeat this process as necessary.

FIGURE 24-10
Options for manually archiving data

CHAPTER 25

Outlook E-mail

Without a doubt, composing, sending, and managing e-mail is one of the major tasks that you will do with Outlook. In fact, it is the task that people spend most of their time doing. Outlook users expect the program to provide solid, yet flexible e-mail capabilities, and they expect the program to help them manage the mail they receive. The good news is Outlook can do just that. Using Outlook, you can compose messages and format them as you like, send attachments to recipients, receive mail and attachments, and manage the mail you get using personal folders.

In this chapter, you'll not only see how to work with all of the e-mail features, but also how to configure Outlook's mail options so that they meet your specific needs.

Setting Up a Mail Account

Before you can send and receive e-mail, you must configure an account on Outlook. An account simply tells Outlook where to check for mail. The account includes the mail servers from your ISP along with your e-mail username and password. If Outlook is used in a corporate environment, your network administrator has probably already configured Outlook to check mail with the network's mail server, such as Microsoft Exchange, that handles all incoming and outgoing mail. But if you are getting mail directly from an ISP over a dial-up connection or a broadband connection, you'll need to set up Outlook to check for mail at your ISP.

The good news is that setting up a mail account is rather easy and straightforward. Before you begin, make sure you have the e-mail documentation that your ISP provided to you so you'll have the correct settings to enter; then simply follow these steps:

1. In Outlook, click Tools | E-mail Accounts.

2. In the E-mail Accounts window that appears, choose the Add a New E-mail Account radio button and click Next.

3. In the Server Type window, choose the type of server you are connecting to: Microsoft Exchange Server, POP3, IMAP, HTTP, or additional server types. Generally, if you are connecting to an ISP server, you will probably be connecting to a POP3 server. Check your ISP documentation for details. Note that you can also connect to an HTTP server, such as Hotmail or MSN, so that you can manage web-based mail through Outlook. Make your selection and click Next.

4. The settings window appears, which varies according to your selection in step 3. In the following illustration, we are using a POP3 server. Check your documentation to determine what information to enter in the incoming and outgoing mail servers text boxes, as well as password information. Note the Log on Using SPA check box—see your ISP documentation to determine whether you need to use this option. When you are done, click the Test Account Settings button (you'll need an active Internet connection) to see if Outlook can connect. Click Next.

5. Click Finish.

NOTE   *E-mail accounts sometimes change, or you may switch to a different provider. Keep in mind that you can configure additional e-mail accounts or edit existing ones at any time by simply clicking Tools | E-mail Accounts.*

Sending and Receiving E-mail

Once you have configured an e-mail account, Outlook can send and receive mail, assuming you have an active Internet connection. Outlook is configured to send and receive automatically by default, but you can change that setting (see the "Configuring E-mail Options" section later in the chapter). You can also send and receive mail at any time by clicking Tools | Send/Receive | Send/Receive All, or, more simply, by pressing F9. This action checks your mail server for mail and sends any mail you have created.

When mail is downloaded, it appears in your Inbox. Click the Inbox on the Navigation pane, and you'll see any mail that has downloaded appear in the main window. If you have the Reading pane configured (on the right), you see the subject of the selected message as well, as shown in Figure 25-1.

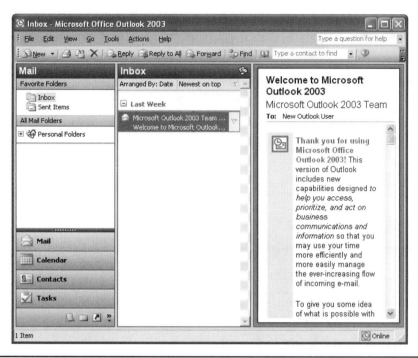

FIGURE 25-1   Received mail

Any mail that you create is stored in your Outbox, found in your Personal Folders on the Navigation pane, until it is sent. Once the mail message is sent, a copy of it is stored in the Sent Items folder so you can go back at any time and review it.

Reading E-mail

You can read and respond to mail messages directly from the main Outlook interface, assuming you have the Reading pane open (see Chapter 24 for more information). Simply select a message you want to read, and the text of the message appears in the Reading pane. If you want to respond to the message, you can click the Reply, Reply to All, or Forward buttons on the toolbar. Here's what each button does:

- **Reply**   This option replies directly to the sender.
- **Reply to All**   This option replies to everyone the message was sent to, including the sender and any other recipients that were included.
- **Forward**   This option allows you to forward the message to someone else.

You can also double-click a message to open it in its own window. As you can see in Figure 25-2, you have the same reply options, but you can also more easily see who the message is from, when it was sent, and who it was sent to.

PART V

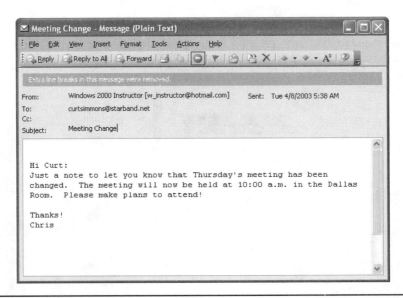

FIGURE 25-2   Mail message window

Composing and Responding to E-mail

You can easily compose new e-mail messages and reply to e-mail that you receive. To compose a new e-mail message, click the New button on the Outlook toolbar, or choose File | New | Mail Message. Either way, an untitled message appears, shown in Figure 25-3. You can then type the e-mail address of the person you want to send the message to, the subject, and the text of your message.

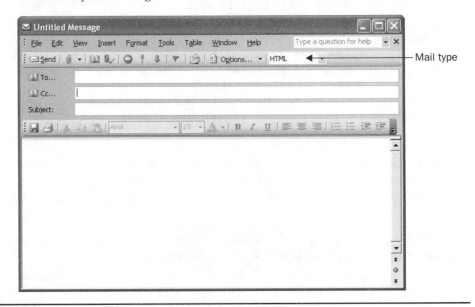

FIGURE 25-3   Untitled message

Outlook supports three different kinds of mail, which you can choose from the drop-down menu on the toolbar. The options are

- **HTML**   Using HTML, the mail message is formatted with the same language used on web browsers. This feature allows you to use formatting options that can be read by most e-mail clients and web browsers.
- **Rich Text**   This option allows you to use text formatting and other features, but they may not be interpreted correctly by some e-mail systems. Also, rich text can cause problems with attachments if you are not sending mail to other Outlook or Outlook Express clients.
- **Plain Text**   Only plain text is used. You cannot format the text, but it ensures the most compatibility between e-mail clients.

If you choose to use HTML or Rich Text, you can use the Formatting toolbar on your message to format text as you type:

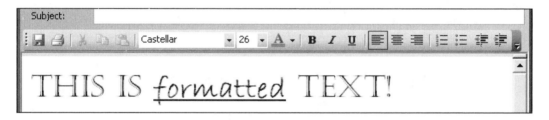

In order to send the e-mail message to recipients, simply type their e-mail addresses in the To or Cc fields. You can type multiple e-mail addresses in a field—simply separate them with a semicolon. Also, if you have addresses in your address book, simply click the To or Cc book icon on the message to open the address book. You can then choose the e-mail addresses you want to send the message to. See Chapter 27 for more information about the address book.

TIP   *If you are writing a message and you decide that you want to complete it later, just click File | Save. This action will put the message in your Drafts folder. You can then return to the message at any time, finish it, and send it.*

As with sending new messages, you have the same options when replying to or forwarding a message. You can type your new message, format it as you like, and determine who should get the message by entering their e-mail addresses. You can also add attachments when you compose or respond to the message.

Managing Attachments

An attachment is any file that you send with an e-mail. Attachments can include documents, photos, movies, programs—you name it. When you send an attachment, the file is attached to the e-mail message so that your recipient can open and read or see the attachment. For most of us, sending attachments means sending documents or photos of some kind.

CAUTION   *Keep in mind that some attachments, particularly photos, can be quite large. The larger the attachment, the longer it will take for your recipient to download if he or she is using a modem connection instead of a broadband connection. So, just use common sense and remember that no one wants to wait half an hour for mail to download due to an attachment.*

Sending an Attachment

Sending an attachment is easy. Open a new e-mail message and click the Attach button on the toolbar (looks like a paper clip), or click Insert and choose the kind of attachment you want to send. You'll get a standard browse window where you can locate your attachment and click the Insert button. Your attachment then appears on your message, as shown in Figure 25-4. You can double-click it to open it, or right-click it and click Clear if you decide you don't want to send it. Keep in mind that you can add multiple attachments to a message if you like, but do take into account their size. If you need to send several files that are near or over one megabyte, it is best to send each of them in individual messages.

TIP   *You can also just drag and drop files to a new e-mail message in order to attach them to the message. This action does not move the file from its original location on your computer—it simply attaches a copy to the e-mail message.*

FIGURE 25-4   Message attachment

Opening a Received Attachment

If you get a mail message that has an attachment, the attachment will show up as a paper clip in your Inbox, and if you have the Reading pane turned on, you can see the attachment file in the Reading pane, as shown in Figure 25-5. If you open the mail message in its own window, you can see the attached file as well.

To open the attached file, just double-click it. Assuming your computer has a program that can read the attachment, the program will come to life and open the attachment for you. You can then save the attachment to a different location on your computer if you like.

TIP *If you want the attachment out of Outlook, you can simply drag it from the mail message to your desktop or another folder.*

When you first open an attachment, you'll see a message telling you that you should only open attachments from trustworthy sources, and then you have the option to go ahead and open the attachment or save it.

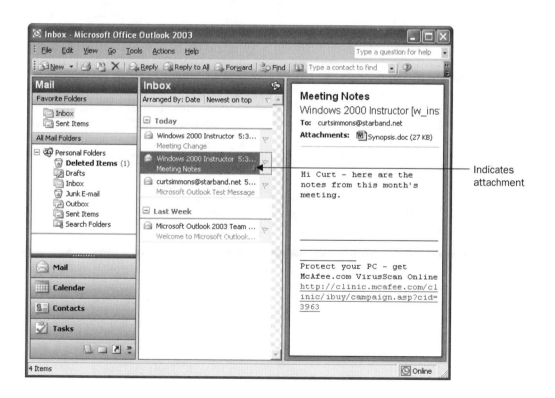

Indicates attachment

FIGURE 25-5   Received attachment

CAUTION *Attachments can carry computer viruses, so do not open attachments from unknown sources. Even when you open them from known sources, you should make certain that you have up-to-date antivirus software running. It is much better to be safe than sorry!*

Configuring E-mail Options

Outlook 2003 works out of the box just as it is—you really don't have to configure anything else once your e-mail account is configured within Outlook. However, Outlook provides a number of important options and features that you should get to know. These features can make your work with Outlook better and give you an e-mail management experience that you really want. Just check out the following sections for details.

Standard E-mail Options

If you click Tools | Options, you see an Options dialog box. On the Preferences tab, you see an E-mail category with an E-mail Options button. If you click the E-mail Options button, you arrive at a standard E-mail Options dialog box where you can choose a number of Outlook behaviors. As you can see in Figure 25-6, this self-explanatory tab allows you to determine how messages are saved and sent. You can also configure advanced e-mail and tracking options that allow you to automatically save messages, play sounds when new messages arrive, configure desktop alerts, as well as manage tracking options. Note that you can also determine whether or not to include the original message when replying or forwarding a message. As a general rule, the preselected options are probably all you need, but it is a good idea to read through them and determine whether there are any changes that you want to make. Once you make any changes, just click OK to apply them.

FIGURE 25-6
Standard E-mail options

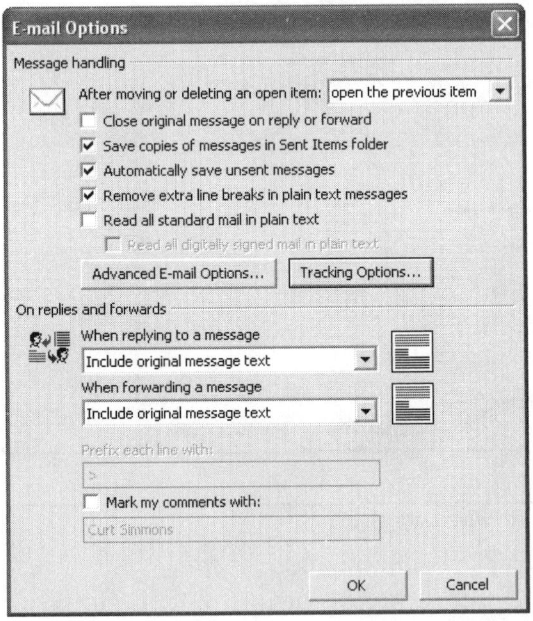

Using a Signature

You can configure a signature that automatically appears each time you compose a new e-mail message. This feature is really helpful to business users who do not want to type their name, e-mail address, phone number, web address, and other common business info into each e-mail message—you can simply configure a signature to appear each time and do it for you. To create a signature, follow these steps:

1. Click Tools | Options.
2. On the Options dialog box, click the Mail Format tab. At the bottom of the Mail Format tab, you see that no current signatures are selected, since you haven't configured one. Click the Signatures button.
3. On the Create Signature window, click the New button.
4. On the Create New Signature dialog box, shown next, enter a name for the signature. Then choose to start with either a blank signature or a template if you have an existing signature template. Click Next.

5. On the Edit Signature window, enter the signature you want. Notice that you can edit the font and even use advanced editing with a program such as FrontPage. Create your signature and click OK.

TIP   *You can edit the signature and add more signatures at any time by returning to the Mail Format tab of the Options dialog box.*

Using Stationery

If you send a message using HTML, you can apply stationery to the message. Stationery is just as it sounds—it is a background file that your message is typed on. You can choose from such stationery as leaves, ivy, jungle, and so on, or you can import your own. Stationery just adds more pizzazz to your e-mail, but keep in mind that not all e-mail clients can display it, and it does increase the amount of download time required to display your messages.

If you want to use stationery, click Tools | Options. On the Options dialog box, click the Mail Format tab, then click the Stationery Picker button. This opens a dialog box, shown in Figure 25-7, where you can choose the stationery you want, create new stationery, or get more from the Internet.

Managing Automatic Send/Receive

We noted earlier in the chapter that Outlook can be configured to automatically check for mail periodically. This feature works great if you have an "always on" broadband connection such as DSL or cable. Outlook can also check for mail if you have a dial-up connection. It will cause the dial-up launcher to dial the number automatically, then hang up when mail is finished. However, dialing out automatically may get frustrating since the feature will interrupt anything else you are using the phone line for.

No matter what your needs are, you can manage how Outlook automatically sends and receives mail, and if it does so at all. Click Tools | Options. On the Mail Setup tab, click the Send/Receive button. This action opens the Send/Receive Groups dialog box, shown in Figure 25-8. Using Outlook, you can create groups and specify how mail is delivered to anyone in that group. Note that the default group is "All Accounts," and you have options for what Outlook should do when sending and receiving mail either online or offline. Notice on Figure 25-8 that you can schedule automatic sending and receiving (or not). Make any desired selections and simply click OK.

FIGURE 25-7
Stationery Picker

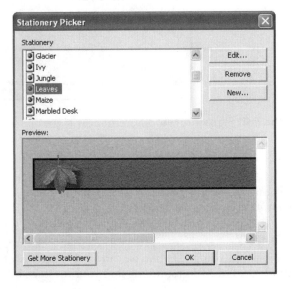

FIGURE 25-8
Send/Receive
Groups

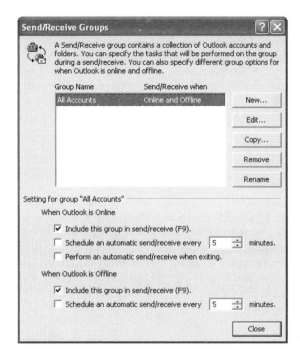

Flagging Messages

When you are creating mail messages, you may wish to use a message flag. A *flag* is simply additional information that is sent with the message telling the recipient that some action is necessary. For example, you can flag a message as needing follow-up, for information only, needing a return call, and so on. These flags just give the recipient some additional instructions.

Applying a flag is easy. When you are composing a new mail message, just click the Flag icon on the toolbar. This will open the Flag dialog box. Choose the kind of flag you want from the drop-down menu and assign any due date if necessary.

PART V

TIP   *If you want to send the message as "high importance," click the exclamation point on the Mail Message toolbar. You can also send messages with a "low importance" using the low importance button as well.*

Managing Mail

Outlook not only allows you to send and receive mail, but it also allows you to manage all that mail once you get it. There are a few items you need to know about mail management, and the following sections tell you about them.

Using Personal Folders

Outlook manages your mail using personal folders. Personal folders include such items as Deleted Items, Drafts, Inbox, Junk E-mail, Outbox, and so forth, as shown in Figure 25-9.

Items that you send are automatically placed in the Sent Items folder so you can return to them and review them as needed. Any mail that you delete is placed in the Deleted Items folder. Mail that you are working on currently and have saved is stored in the Drafts folder. At any time, you can simply click a folder in the Navigation pane to see its contents in Outlook. Use the Find button on the toolbar to search for mail items or recipients in your personal folders.

FIGURE 25-9
Personal folders

You can also create new folders. Simply right-click Personal Folders and click New Folder. You can then type a name for the new folder and click OK. You can also add subfolders to existing folders by right-clicking the folder name and clicking New Folder. As you can see here, we have added a new folder called Projects, which contains a subfolder called Current. You can drag and drop mail between folders as needed. Mail that is currently in your Inbox can simply be dragged to the folder of your choice. Over all, personal folders are very flexible and a great way to keep your mail organized.

TIP   *If you want to lose all of your deleted items, right-click the Deleted Items folder and click Empty Deleted Items Folder. This will permanently delete all mail in the Deleted Items folder from your computer's hard drive.*

Managing Junk E-mail

Junk e-mail is a major problem these days. In the past, junk e-mail was merely an annoyance, but in today's e-mail happy society, you may get many, many junk e-mail messages in a single day. Outlook can help you manage junk e-mail by looking at subject headers, content, as well as senders that you specify, and automatically placing suspected junk e-mail into the Junk E-mail folder. Of course, Outlook doesn't actually read the e-mail, so you should get in the habit of inspecting the Junk E-mail folder and making sure none of your regular mail ends up there.

You can configure how junk e-mail behaves, however. Click Tools | Options. On the Preferences tab, click the Junk E-mail button. On the Junk E-mail Options dialog box, shown in Figure 25-10, choose the level of filtering you want on the Options tab. You can choose from no protection to high protection. Also, click the Trusted Senders and Trusted Recipients tabs and add the people you commonly communicate with to ensure that messages from those individuals never get put in the Junk E-mail folder. You can also create a list of junk senders' e-mail addresses in order to identify those people as junk e-mail.

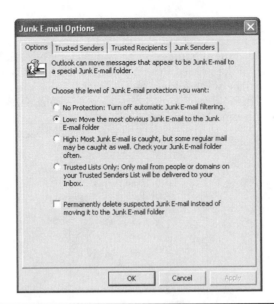

FIGURE 25-10   Junk E-mail Options

About Message Rules

Along with junk e-mail, you can also create message rules that determine how certain mail is handled. For example, you can create a rule so that messages with certain keywords are automatically sent to the Deleted Items folder, or you could create a rule that places all mail from a certain person into a certain personal folder. You have a number of different options, and they are easy to configure. First determine what rules you need and how they can benefit your use of e-mail. To configure a message rule, simply click Tools | Rules and Alerts, and then click the New Rule button. Follow the instructions that appear to create a new message rule.

Outlook Calendar and Task Lists

Being the personal information management software it is, Outlook gives you a way to manage your personal calendar and the tasks that you must complete on schedule. Using Outlook, you can keep track of what is coming up, what tasks need to be completed, who needs to complete them and when; and Outlook can even help you keep track of all your appointments and tasks through different kinds of alerts. Using Outlook, you can also set up meetings by e-mailing invitations to other users, and once they accept the meeting, it is automatically put on their Outlook calendars. Overall, these features are very beneficial for office personnel, and they can be quite helpful for the home user with a busy schedule.

In this chapter, you'll see how to use and configure and how to make the most of Outlook's calendar and task lists features.

Outlook Calendar

Outlook's calendar feature gives you a handy way to track appointments, meetings, events, and even configure reminders so that Outlook will alert you to an appointment, meeting, or event that is coming up. In short, the Outlook calendar works just like a paper calendar, except Outlook helps you keep track of your calendar.

First things first—when you click Calendar in the Navigation pane, you see the default Month calendar appear in Outlook. Notice that your toolbar has changed as well to reflect calendar options. You can choose to continue to view your calendar by month, shown in Figure 26-1, or you can switch between week, work week, and daily calendars as needed.

Outlook supports four basic kinds of calendar entries:

- **Appointments** These activities consume a certain portion of time on the calendar. They could be meetings with clients, phone calls, doctor's visits, or any type of appointment you want to put on the calendar.

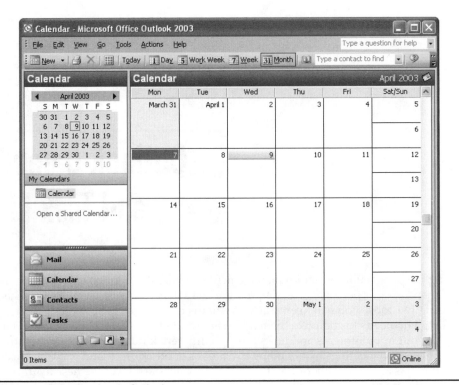

FIGURE 26-1   Calendar view in Outlook

- **Meetings**   Meetings are like appointments in that they consume a certain period of time, but they involve other people. Using Outlook, you can e-mail a meeting invitation to other Outlook users.

- **Events**   An event lasts all day, and could be things such as company picnics, trade shows, and birthdays.

- **Reminders**   When you have set a reminder for one of the three previous entries, it appears on the calendar.

Configuring Appointments

Appointments are entries that essentially concern you. Perhaps you have to meet a client, or maybe you have a hair appointment—you could even configure an appointment to remind you to pay bills if you like. The choice is completely up to you, but the distinction to remember is that Outlook considers appointments to belong primarily to you instead of other people in your organization. Appointments can also be one-time appointments or recurring appointments. For example, if you meet with a certain client at 10:00 A.M. every Tuesday, you need only configure one appointment that recurs each Tuesday.

Configuring One-Time Appointments

Follow these steps to create a one-time appointment:

1. In Outlook, click Calendar in the Navigation pane.
2. On the toolbar, click the New button, or click Actions | New Appointment.
3. In the Appointment tab of the Appointment dialog box, enter the subject, location, label if desired, start date and time, and end date and time.

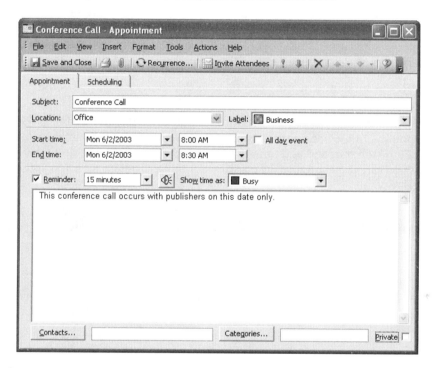

4. If you want a reminder to pop up onscreen, click the check box and determine when it should appear (such as 15 minutes before the meeting). If you would like a sound to accompany the reminder, click the Sound button and a Reminder Sound dialog box appears. By default, the reminder.wav file is selected as the sound but you can use any other WAV file you want by clicking the Browse button.

5. You can also choose a time color (such as Busy) from the Show Time As drop-down menu. The time color is shown on the calendar and gives you an easy way to look at your busy times. Calendar colors can indicate free, busy, tentative, and out of the office.

6. You can type any additional notes you want in the large text box. You can also configure the category if you like (see Chapter 24), and you can make the appointment private. Click the Save and Close button when you are done.

TIP *Since you are configuring only a single appointment for yourself, you don't need to do anything on the Scheduling tab.*

Once you configure the appointment, it appears on your calendar. In Figure 26-2, you can see three events on a calendar (in Day view), two of which are business and one of which is personal.

Configuring Recurring Appointments

The recurring appointment feature is useful if you have the same appointment occur at the same time on the same day each week. Using this feature, you can simply create the appointment one time, and it will recur on your calendar for as long as you want. To configure a recurring appointment, follow these steps:

1. Create the appointment and schedule it as desired. See the steps in the previous section for details.

2. Before saving and closing the appointment, click the Recurrence button on the Appointment toolbar. In the Appointment Recurrence window that appears, configure the start and end times and the recurrence pattern as desired. Note that you can also configure the end date for the recurrence pattern if you like, as shown here:

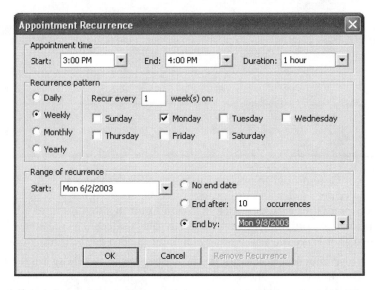

3. Click OK when you are done, and click Save and Close to save the appointment.

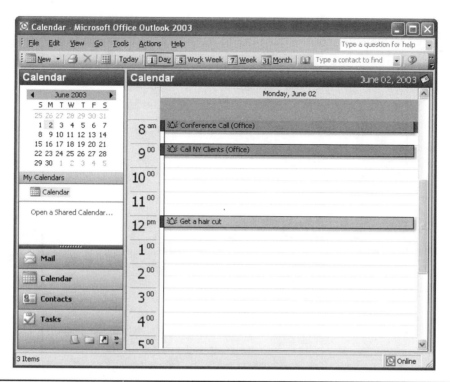

FIGURE 26-2   Appointments appear on your calendar.

TIP   *Recurring appointments appear on your calendar in Day view with a recurring symbol (as on the Recurrence button). They can be seen in the Work Week and Week views as well.*

Configuring Meetings

In truth, configuring meetings is just like configuring appointments, and appointments can even turn into meetings if you invite others. The major difference with meetings is that other Outlook users receive a meeting request, which can then be automatically added to their calendars. To configure a meeting, follow these steps:

1. In Calendar view, click the New drop-down menu item and click Meeting Request, or click Actions | New Meeting Request.

2. In the Meeting request window, enter the e-mail addresses in the To line (you can click To in order to access your address book), a subject, and then configure the meeting as you would an appointment. An example is shown in the following illustration. Notice that you can also configure an online meeting using a meeting

workspace or NetMeeting, Microsoft Exchange Conferencing, or Windows Media Services, for environments that have these services configured.

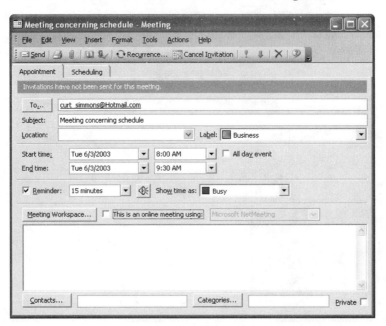

3. You can click the Scheduling tab to see other meetings or appointments that are scheduled. Depending on your environment, you may be able to see other users' schedules here as well.

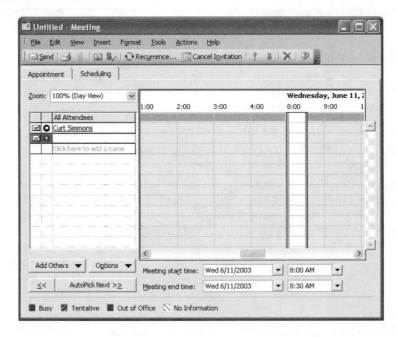

4. Once the recipient has received the meeting notice, he or she can accept the meeting, mark it as tentative, or decline the meeting, as you can see in the next illustration. If the recipient accepts the meeting, it is added to his or her calendar.

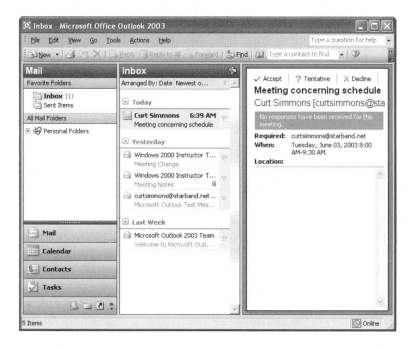

Scheduling an Event

An event is something that lasts all day. You configure an event in the same way you configure an appointment. However, on the Appointment tab, you simply click the All Day Event check box. You can then enter your subject, location, label, reminder, and anything else you might want as well. Click Save and Close when you're done.

Working with Reminders

Once you configure a reminder for a meeting, an appointment, or an event, you'll hear a sound played and you'll see a dialog box, shown in Figure 26-3, appear on your screen. Notice that you can then dismiss the reminder, open the item from your calendar and view it, or use a Snooze option, which will cause the reminder to appear again in the amount of time you choose.

Calendar Management

Obviously, life is not a static calendar and things change, so you should know about a few management tasks that let you make changes to your appointments, meetings, and events as needed. Keep the following points in mind:

- Double-click a calendar item to open and change it. This provides you with the same appointment or meeting dialog box you first used to create the event.

PART V

FIGURE 26-3
Reminder
dialog box

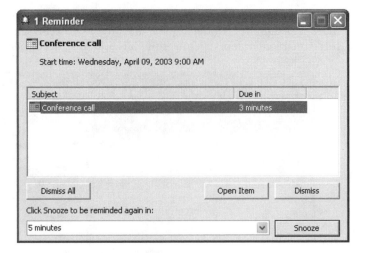

- You can change an appointment's private status by right-clicking the appointment and either enabling or clearing the Private check box. Once the meeting is "private," it doesn't show up on your public calendar for others to see.

- You can change the show time and label features of an appointment.

- You can delete an appointment, meeting, or event by right-clicking the item on the calendar and clicking Delete. If you choose to delete a recurring appointment, you can choose to delete the individual appointment or the entire series of appointments.

Using Tasks

Tasks are simply jobs that must be completed, either by you or someone else. Outlook can track tasks for you, their deadline dates, and give you status information about when a task is completed. This feature is useful for home users who need to keep up with a bunch of tasks at the same time and is, of course, helpful to office personnel who need to manage office tasks and assign tasks to others using Outlook.

Creating a Task

If you click the Tasks option on the Navigation pane, you see a listing grid with nothing in it, since you have not yet configured any tasks.

Adding tasks works a lot like adding appointments. Simply click the New button on the toolbar, or click Actions | New Task. In the Task dialog box that appears, shown in Figure 26-4, enter the subject, due dates, and reminders if desired. Then click Save and Close. Notice the Details tab as well. You can return to the task once it is completed and enter completion information on the Details tab if needed.

Once you have added tasks, they appear in your tasks list, as shown in Figure 26-5. Notice that you can choose from a variety of different views on the Navigation pane.

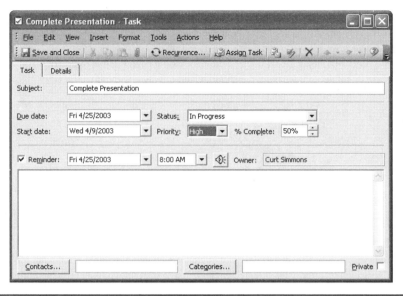

FIGURE 26-4   Task dialog box

FIGURE 26-5   Tasks appear in the task list.

By default, you can view a simple list of tasks, but you see that you can also view them based on details, overdue tasks, categories, and so forth.

When tasks are completed, you can simply click the check box next to them, and the task will be marked out, as shown here. You can also right-click a task and mark it as complete, delete it, or assign it to someone else, which we'll explore in the next section.

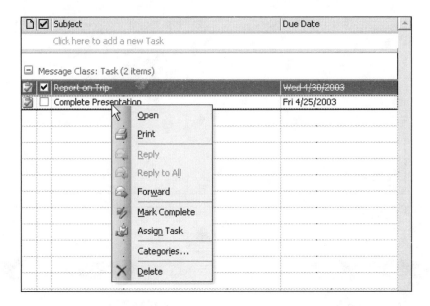

TIP   *If you want to change the date on a task, click the date in the Task view, and a drop-down menu will appear where you can change the date.*

Assigning a Task

You can choose to assign tasks to other users of Outlook. Basically, this feature is like sending a meeting request. Users will receive a task request e-mail, which they will either accept or decline. If you click Actions | New Task Request, you can enter the subject's e-mail address, or click the To button to access your address book, and then enter task information, due dates, and general data that you want to convey by typing it in the dialog box. Note that you can also choose to keep an updated copy of the task on your task list, and you can be sent a status report when the task is complete, as shown in Figure 26-6.

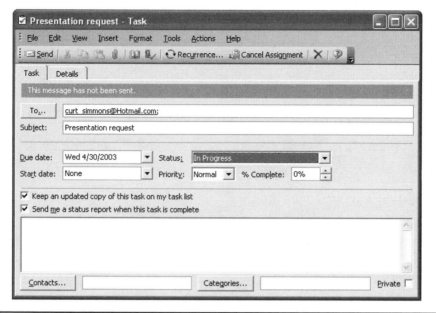

FIGURE 26-6   Assign a task to another person.

NOTE   *As with meetings or appointments, you can assign a recurring task as well. Just click the Recurrence button to set it up.*

Managing Contacts and Taking Notes

Personal information management software wouldn't be much help if it didn't let you keep track of people. After all, in your daily management of people and office management of work contacts, you'll have a number of e-mail addresses, phone numbers, business addresses, and the like that you must keep up with. In the past, you might use a paper address book, but with the constant changes in contact information, paper address books aren't too practical. For this reason, Outlook gives you a handy contacts feature. You can record contacts, keep up with the information you need, and directly use that contact information with other Outlook processes. Outlook also gives you a quick and handy way to take notes and keep track of them; we'll explore this feature in this chapter as well.

Outlook Contacts

Outlook's contacts feature allows you to keep up with people. You can record all kinds of information about them, including e-mail addresses, phone numbers, physical addresses, and related information. Once you have created a contact, you can then use it with e-mails that you send, tasks, meeting requests, and so forth.

Creating a Contact

To create a contact, you basically open a Contacts window and fill in the desired information. Before doing so, however, you need to switch to Contacts in the Navigation pane. Just click the Contacts button and Outlook will change to a Contacts focus. As you can see in Figure 27-1, the contacts list is empty since we have not created any contacts yet.

FIGURE 27-1 Contacts view in Outlook

To create a new contact, follow these steps:

1. Click the New button on the toolbar, or just double-click the area of open space in the address book, as you can see in Figure 27-1. You can also click Actions | New Contact.

2. On the General tab of the new Contact dialog box, enter the desired information, as shown in the following illustration. Note that you can choose to enter or leave blank any information you want. Click the drop-down arrows to change the dialog box options. For example, under Phone Numbers, you can click the drop-down menus and change the default Business, Home, Business Fax, and Mobile values to different options.

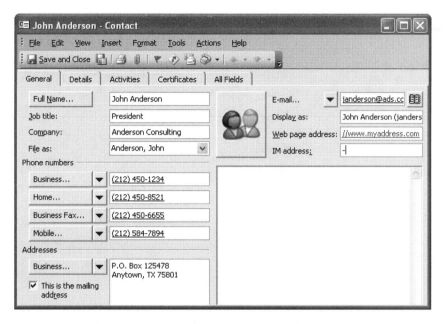

3. Click the Details tab to enter additional information. You can include department, office, profession, manager's name, and so on. You can also include more personal information (such as birthday and anniversary day) and online NetMeeting settings as well. Again, you can enter any information you want here, and leave any blank that you do not want to include.

4. On the Activities tab, you can view all current activities that are in progress with the contact, such as e-mails, contacts, journal entries, notes, upcoming tasks or appointments, and so on. This is a good tab to come back to at a later time to see all communication with the contact.

5. The Certificates tab includes any digital certificates that Outlook can use to send encrypted e-mail to the contact. You can import a certificate to use for receiving digitally signed mail from this contact or by importing a certificate for the contact.

6. The All Fields tab allows you to choose different fields and get a quick look at the information for those fields. For example, the following illustration contains address

fields only. This feature basically allows you to customize the format of the contact's information.

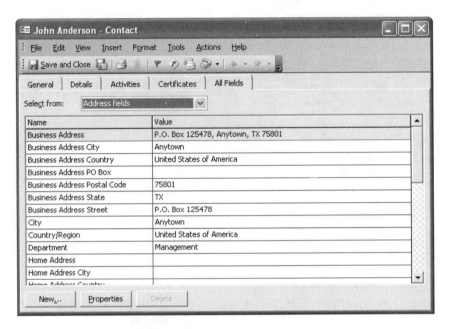

7. When you have finished creating the contact, click Save and Close.

TIP   *Notice the Save and New button on the toolbar. This feature allows you to save the contact and get a new blank contact dialog box so you can create another contact. This feature saves you a step when you are creating several contacts in a row.*

Viewing Contacts

Once you enter contacts, you can view them in the main Outlook interface when you choose Contacts in the Navigation pane. Notice, as shown in Figure 27-2, that you can view contacts information by choosing a desired view, such as Address Cards, Phone List, By Company, and so on. Also notice that you can click through your contacts in alphabetical order by clicking the button with the appropriate letters in the right-hand column.

NOTE   *Birthdays that you enter for contacts will automatically show up on your Outlook calendar as all-day events.*

Editing Contact Information

Naturally, contact information changes from time to time. A contact may get a different e-mail address or phone numbers. As you would expect, you can easily change contact

FIGURE 27-2   Choose a contact view

information within Outlook at any time. In Contacts view, just double-click any entry. Or, you can right-click the Contacts entry and click Open. This will open the same Contact window you used to create the contact originally. Just make any changes that you want and click Save and Close.

Working with Contacts

The contacts feature in Outlook wouldn't be too exciting if you couldn't use the contacts directly with other Outlook features. The good news is you can, and with these features, contacts become much more than a simple electronic version of a paper address book. At any time, you can access an entry in the address book.

To use a contact, just right-click it in the Contacts view, or you can open a contact and click the Actions menu to access the same options.

You have the following options:

- **New Message to Contact**   This option opens an e-mail message with the recipient's contact information, ready to e-mail. You can also simply type the recipient's name in any e-mail message, and Outlook will resolve that name to the e-mail address you have entered for the contact.

- **New Appointment with Contact**   This option creates a new appointment with the contact that can then be e-mailed to her or him.

- **New Meeting Request to Contact**   This option creates a new meeting request with the contact that can then be e-mailed.

- **New Task for Contact**   This option creates a new task for the contact. You can then e-mail the new task to the contact.

- **New Journal Entry for Contact**   This option creates a new journal entry for the contact. Journal entries can be any kind of additional information about the contact that you want to keep a record of.

- **Call Contact**   If your computer is connected to your phone, this feature allows Outlook to dial the desired phone number you have entered for the contact. You simply pick up the phone receiver and Outlook will dial the number for you!

Taking Notes

Do you constantly write down little pieces of information or reminders that you want to keep up with? Rather than having them all over your desk or stuck to your computer screen, you can use Outlook to jot down notes and keep up with them easily.

Creating a Note

To create a note, you'll need to open Notes view on the Navigation pane. The Notes view may not appear as a button option, like Mail, Calendar, Contacts, and Tasks. If it is not listed, the Notes option is available as an icon at the bottom of the Navigation pane. Just click the Notes icon to switch to Notes view.

To create a new note, follow these steps:

1. Click the New button on the toolbar, or click Actions | New Note.

2. In the note dialog box that appears, type the note:

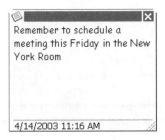

3. When you're done, click the X to close the note dialog box. The new note now appears in Notes view, as shown here:

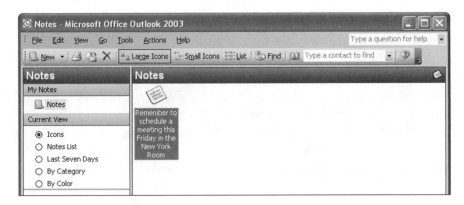

Viewing Notes

Once you create notes, they appear in the Notes pane, as you just saw. You can use the Current View option in the Navigation pane to view notes in a few different ways: as icons, as a notes list, for the last seven days, by category, or by color (see the next section to change a note's color). Notice also that you can use the Notes toolbar to choose between large icons, small icons, or a list. Naturally, you can search for notes if necessary using the Find option on the toolbar.

Changing a Note's Color

You can assign different colors to notes in order to make certain notes stand out. By default, notes are yellow, but if you right-click a note, you can choose a different color from the color menu. There is not an exact system here; you can make up color codes according to whatever you need. For example, you might color code urgent notes green while standard notes remain yellow. The choice is yours.

TIP   *You can also e-mail a note to someone quickly and easily. Just right-click the note and click Forward.*

Changing Note Preferences

By default, notes are yellow and they use a Comic Sans MS font. You can change the default behavior quickly and easily, and here's how you do it:

1. Click Tools | Options.

2. On the Options Preferences tab, click the Note Options under Notes.

3. In the Notes Options dialog box, change the color, size, and font as desired. Click OK when you're done.

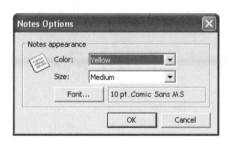

Scheduling and Planning with Others

One of the benefits of using Outlook is that you can share calendars and schedule meetings and appointments with others. As we have looked at Outlook's options in the past few chapters, we have mentioned these features, but this chapter focuses on scheduling and planning with others. In network environments, Office users can easily share information and schedule meetings and tasks with other Outlook users. You can do the same from a home computer, assuming you are scheduling and planning with other users of Microsoft Outlook.

Sharing Your Calendar

You can share your Outlook calendar so that other people can access it and see your schedule if your network is a Microsoft Exchange network. This feature is particularly helpful in corporate environments because several people can use the same calendar, see each other's daily list of events, and update them as necessary. In order to share your calendar in Outlook, follow these steps:

1. Click Calendar in the Navigation pane.

2. In the Navigation pane, click Share My Calendar. Or, right-click your Calendar icon in the Navigation pane and click Sharing.

3. You can choose to allow anyone to access your calendar, or you can specify who can access it. Under Permissions, select Default to allow anyone to access the calendar. If you only want certain people to access the calendar, click the Add button and type the name or select the name from the list box that you want to grant permission to. Click Add, and then click OK.

Accessing a Shared Calendar

If you need to access a shared calendar, you'll see a link for Open a Shared Calendar on the Navigation pane. Click the link and a dialog box appears. Enter the name of the calendar, or click the Name button and choose from a list of users in order to access their shared calendars.

TIP   *Of course, if the user's calendar has not been shared, you can't access it using the shared calendar feature.*

Hiding Personal Calendar Data

With shared calendars, the only problem you are likely to encounter is privacy. After all, there may be events on your calendar that are private and you do not want shared. In this case, all you need to do is make the appointment private. When you make an appointment private, you can see it on your calendar with a small key icon noting the appointment is private. When others access your calendar, they can see that you are booked, but they cannot see the event. To make an event private or to make a private event public, just right-click the event on the calendar and click Private.

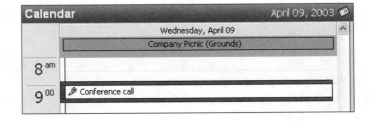

Working with Free/Busy Times

There may be people in your environment who do not have access to your calendar. In this case, you can use the Microsoft Office Internet Free/Busy Service or another Internet/intranet location to publish times when you are free or busy. This feature basically provides users with static calendar information so they can see your schedule on a daily basis and know when you are available. Your organization will need to be using the Microsoft Office Internet Free/Busy Service for this feature to work, so contact your network administrator for details.

To configure Outlook to use the free/busy feature, follow these steps:

1. In Outlook, click Tools | Options.

2. On the Preferences tab, click the Calendar Options button.

3. On the Calendar Options window, click the Free/Busy Options button.

4. As shown in the next illustration, you can configure how many months of calendar data you want to publish and how often it is updated on the free/busy information server. At the bottom of the window, notice that you can choose alternative publishing locations, such as a web server. Again, contact your network administrator for details. Click OK and OK again when you are done.

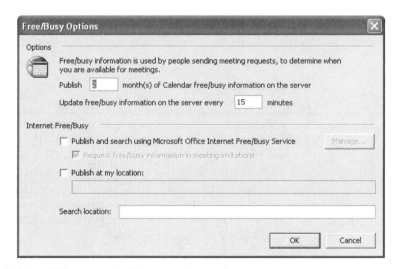

Working with Scheduled Meetings and Appointments

In Chapter 26, you took a look at working with meetings and appointments, and we noted that you can send meeting notices and appointments to other users with Outlook. Refer to Chapter 26 for standard information, but we want to point out a few additional options and features to keep in mind when you are working with scheduled meetings and appointments involving other Outlook users.

When you choose to create an appointment or meeting, you can simply choose to invite attendees, as you can see in Figure 28-1. This allows you to enter attendees' e-mail addresses and send them an invitation.

Once you send the invitation, the recipient receives a standard e-mail message. However, the e-mail message allows the recipient to accept, tentatively accept, decline, or reply with proposed new times for the appointment or meeting.

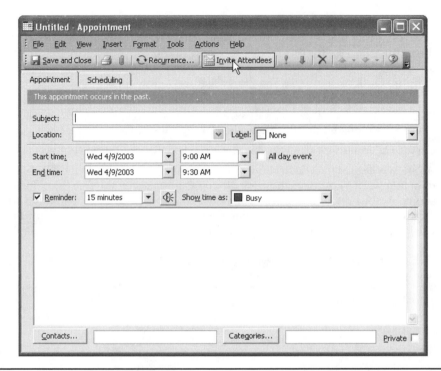

FIGURE 28-1   Choose to invite attendees

So, what happens if something changes? Maybe you need to invite more attendees or un-invite some. How can you send an e-mail to the meeting or appointment organizer? How can you delete a shared meeting or appointment? The good news is these management tasks are easy, and the following sections show you how to manage them.

NOTE   *Keep in mind that as you schedule shared meetings or appointments, attendees can use the reminder features. You simply configure the reminder on the standard meeting or appointment dialog box, then when your recipients accept the meeting or appointment, the reminder will be configured on their calendars.*

Rescheduling a Shared Appointment or Meeting

Meetings and appointments often change, so in the event that a shared meeting or appointment changes, you'll simply need to double-click the meeting or appointment on your calendar, then adjust the dates on the start and end time. Then, click Save and Close. You'll see a message asking if you want to send the updated meeting to your attendees. Click Yes. Your meeting recipients will receive another e-mail with an updated meeting time. They can then choose to accept, tentatively accept, decline, and so forth.

Changing Meeting Attendees

Just as you can change a meeting or appointment time, you can also change a meeting's attendees. Right-click the event on the calendar and click Add/Remove Attendees. In the Select Attendees and Resources dialog box that appears, shown in Figure 28-2, click the Required or Optional buttons to add or remove current attendees. Click OK when you are done. Once again, this will take you back to the standard meeting or appointment window where you can Save and Close the change. Attendees will then be notified by e-mail of the change.

Send an E-mail to the Meeting or Appointment Organizer

You may need to communicate with a meeting or appointment organizer before the event occurs. You can simply use Outlook's standard e-mail feature to send an e-mail. However, you can also right-click the event on your calendar and reply, reply to all, or forward. This will allow you to easily send an e-mail directly to the sender or to all appointment or meeting recipients. You can also forward the meeting request to another user.

Delete a Meeting or Appointment

You can delete any meeting or appointment by right-clicking the event on your calendar and clicking Delete. Concerning shared meetings or appointments, you'll see a dialog box that will allow you to send a cancellation notice to attendees of the meeting or not. Of course, as a general rule, you should choose to send the cancellation notice. This will open a standard

FIGURE 28-2   Select Attendees and Resources

meeting or appointment window noting that the meeting has been canceled. Just click Send to send the cancellation notice to the attendees.

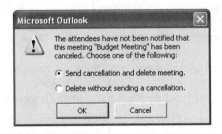

TIP   *Keep in mind that if this is a recurring meeting, you'll have the option to cancel the specific meeting on the specific date, or the entire recurrence of the meetings. Either way, attendees will be notified of the change.*

VI

PART

Databases

CHAPTER 29
Databases in Access

CHAPTER 30
Defining and
Developing Tables

CHAPTER 31
Creating Queries

CHAPTER 32
Forms and Reports

CHAPTER 33
Building a Database
Application

Databases in Access

Access, the database component in Office, isn't as well understood as other Office applications. Most people know that Access can be used for creating small relational databases and therefore is an alternative to Microsoft's large enterprise-level database product, Microsoft SQL Server. But Access goes well beyond creating small databases. Although it certainly can be used as a tool for entering and retrieving data in its own file format, that's not all. Access can also act as a powerful front end for manipulating data stored in SQL Server. It can share data from other manufacturers' databases. It can be used to generate detailed reports from any of its possible data sources. Access can even be used to create data-driven applications, either standalone using forms, or web based. It can be said that Access truly lives up to its name—it gives you access to your data no matter what its shape or size.

Unlike the other workhorse Office applications like Word and Excel, Access isn't conceptually limited to a single task, such as creating documents or crunching numbers. Instead, it is more of a general-purpose tool for building applications that deal with data. Using Access in this manner is more akin to programming than it is to document creation. It is this very flexibility that makes it harder to approach and use than other Office programs.

Access Components

Access consists of two distinct components that together add up to the whole—the Access application and the database engine. These components are fully independent of each other, for a very good reason: Access isn't a one-size-fits-all application. Access can connect to databases using one of several different engines. Likewise, the database engine is designed to be used by other applications, without having to involve Access.

Although most of the Access chapters in this book are concerned with how to use the Access program itself (an application of which is shown in Figure 29-1), understanding the various supported database engines and the role they play goes a long way to mastering Access.

The Database Engine

The database engine is the component that works behind the scenes to connect you to your data. A variety of database engines are available for use by Access depending on the needs of the database, which can range from an Access database file on up through various flavors

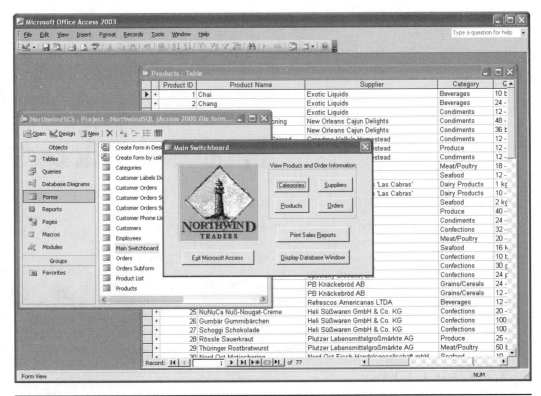

FIGURE 29-1 Access isn't just a tool for creating databases. It's also used as a client for running forms, reports, and database applications.

of SQL Server databases operating either on the same computer or remotely. Data is always accessed through the engine, either by the Access application itself or by the applications and web pages it generates. The database engine can also be used independently of Access, such as by ActiveX Data Object (ADO) web or client-server applications.

- **Jet engine**   The Jet engine is the standard engine used by Access for creating database files with the familiar .mdb extension. Because it is file based, the Jet engine allows for a lot of flexibility. It's easy, for example, to use standard Windows file management tools to make a backup of an MDB file, or copy it onto a laptop so that you can take it with you. However, Jet is really designed for databases that only an individual or a small group of users need to access.

- **SQL Server 2000 Desktop Engine**   The Microsoft SQL Server 2000 Desktop Engine (MSDE) is also included with Access. It is a scaled-down version of Microsoft SQL Server 2000 designed to run on a workstation—scaled down in that it doesn't support huge databases or provide the SQL Server management tools that the full SQL Server product includes. The limitations mean that it really can't handle much more of a workload than a Jet database; however, its compatibility with SQL Server makes it ideal for development with SQL Server in mind, or as a portable data store for taking a subset of a SQL Server database for offline use.

- **SQL Server**   Along with MSDE, Access can also use the full SQL Server product. This gives you the maximum combination of database power along with Access's application development capabilities to quickly build powerful data-driven applications.

- **ODBC**   If that isn't enough, Access has the capability to use many different ODBC-enabled data sources as well. This lets you create Access projects that work with Oracle databases.

Databases and Projects

Access can be used to work with two different application types. As mentioned earlier, traditional Access database files have the familiar .mdb extension. These files by themselves are a self-contained database. They contain all of the database objects, including tables, queries, and more, along with the data itself.

By contrast, Access *projects* contain only the objects used to work with data forms, reports, pages, and modules. The data itself, along with the information defining how the data is organized and the queries used to retrieve and update it, is located in a separate database.

Creating a Database

The first step in building an Access database is to create it. As with other Office applications, there are two approaches you take with this. The first is to create a blank database and create all of the database objects you need yourself. Alternatively, you can use one of the database template wizards to get you started.

Before you create your database, give some thought to how you plan to use it, what information it needs to store, and how that information should be organized. Think about how the tables in your database will relate to each other. This can minimize duplication of fields in tables, as you'll be able to draw information from various tables and combine them into the same query, form, or report.

Building a Blank Database

The quickest way to get started, especially if you know one of the template wizards will not meet your needs, is to create a blank database. Follow these steps to do so:

1. Choose File | New from the main menu. This will open the New File task pane.

2. Choose Blank Database on the task pane.

3. In the File New Database dialog, choose a location and a filename for your database.

That's it! You've just created a blank database, ready for you to populate with tables, queries, forms, and (of course) data. We'll cover these basic database objects later in the chapter, and the chapters following this one show you how to work with them.

Using a Template Wizard

Access includes templates for many different common databases, including Asset Tracking, Contact Management, Inventory, Time and Billing (see Figure 29-2), and many others. You aren't limited to using the included templates, either. The New File task pane includes a search box and a link to the Templates home page on microsoft.com to download more.

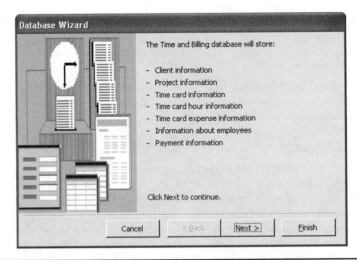

FIGURE 29-2   Database template wizards let you get started quickly with a full-featured database application.

To create a database using a template, follow these steps:

1. Choose File | New from the menu.

2. In the New File task pane, choose one of the following:
    - Templates home page, to browse for templates on the Web.
    - Search term to find an appropriate template.
    - On My Computer to select an existing template.

3. In the Templates dialog box, click the Databases tab and choose a template.

4. Choose a filename and location in the File New Database dialog.

5. In the Database wizard, select each of the tables and check any optional fields if you want them. Click Next.

6. Continue through the wizard, choosing the display backgrounds and styles, as well as any custom form information that is requested. At any time during this process, you can click the Finish button to select the defaults for the remainder of the wizard.

The wizard will create all of the required database objects, including tables, forms, and the switchboard used for a complete database application, which can be enhanced or modified to suit your needs. Database objects are discussed in the "Database Objects" section later in this chapter.

Choosing a File Format

One important decision you have to make when you create an Access database is the file format to use. Each version of Access adds new features and objects that can only be used by the version of Access that created it or later. For example, Access 2000 and earlier versions only supported SQL queries written using the ANSI 89 syntax, but later versions support the more up-to-date ANSI 92 syntax for better compatibility and an easier upgrade path to SQL Server. (Please see Chapter 31 for more information about SQL queries.)

If you are creating a database that is going to be used by a large organization, or distributed publicly to people who may be using older versions of Access, you should choose the lowest version that you want to support.

TIP   *By default, Access creates databases using the Access 2000 format. If you want to take advantage of the newest features of Access, and you know that your database will only need to be opened with Access 2002 or later, you can change the default database format. Select Tools | Options menu, and click the Advanced tab. Select Access 2002 from the Default File Format drop-down list.*

Converting a Database

Access provides the ability to update an older database to the latest Access formats or to SQL Server. Although being able to easily convert a database to SQL Server is quite useful, you may just need to convert a database to a different version of Access so that someone with an older version can read it.

Converting a database to a different version of Access is easy. Simply choose the Tools | Database Utilities | Convert Database menu, and choose the format you wish to use. Access can convert databases in versions all the way back to Access 2.0 to the most recent formats, but it can only convert newer versions back to the Access 97 format. If you really need to make data viewable in a version of Access earlier than 97, you can export the data instead.

CAUTION   *Converting an Access database is irreversible. Later versions of Access support features not recognized by earlier versions, so be sure to back up your database first using the File | Back Up Database menu item.*

Creating a Project

At first glance, an Access project may look like a database, but it's really a completely different ballgame. Unlike Jet database files, which are self-contained files that include the database definitions as well as the data, projects really only provide an Access face to a SQL Server database. The tables, queries, and data all live in a Microsoft SQL Server database, while the project file contains the information necessary to access the database as well as Access-specific objects such as forms and reports. Access projects are a great way to combine the ease and power of Access database applications with the power of the enterprise-level SQL Server engine.

If you're creating a project instead of a database, there are a few additional steps involved.

1. Choose File | New from the menu.

2. On the New File task pane, choose Project Using New Data to create an empty project.

3. In the Microsoft SQL Server Database Wizard dialog, enter the database connection information for the database that you want to associate with the project. This includes the SQL Server host and the login ID and password for the connection. Add the database.

NOTE *To make use of a SQL Server database, you need the proper permissions to connect to the database. If you are using an existing database, you must have CREATE TABLE and CREATE DEFAULT permissions. If you are creating a new database, you must also have CREATE DATABASE privileges. If you are using MSDE or SQL Server running locally, consult the documentation for those products. If you are using a remote SQL Server database, you can obtain this information from a database administrator.*

Upsizing a Database

At first glance you may wonder what the term *upsizing* means when it comes to a database. No, it does not make the database bigger. Rather, upsizing lets you convert some or all database objects in an Access database to a SQL Server database. This lets you take advantage of the extra benefits of SQL Server databases, including availability, scalability, security, and server-based processing. Although Access is a powerful desktop-level database solution, here are some of the ways in which SQL Server may be a better fit:

- **Availability** SQL Server has built-in database logging and backup features that Access lacks. A SQL Server database can be rolled back to a known good condition, but Access databases must be backed up by archiving the MDB file somewhere. SQL Server also supports *clustering*—providing for automatic rollover to a backup if the primary server goes down.

- **Scalability** Access databases are limited to 2GB files, while SQL Server supports many times more than that. SQL Server also includes built-in database locking, making it much speedier than Access databases, which depend on file system locks in multiuser environments.

- **Security** SQL Server has integrated security and database access, while Access is limited to a simple password and file system permissions. SQL Server databases can only be accessed through the server, while Access files, like any files, can be copied directly using the OS or any other file tool.

- **Server-based processing** SQL Server can execute compiled queries as stored procedures directly on the database server, whereas Access queries must always be run on the client machine, requiring the data to be read from the file first.

Fortunately, if your Access database has outgrown its original requirements and requires the robustness of SQL Server, you can use the Upsizing wizard to convert it to an Access project.

TIP   *If you use a template to create your database, you are restricted to creating an MDB file. Creating a project isn't an option. However, with the Upsizing wizard, you can later upsize a database created from a template just as easily as you can any other database.*

Running the Upsizing Wizard

To use the Upsizing wizard, do the following:

1. Open your Access database (MDB file) in Access.

2. Choose Tools | Database Utilities | Upsizing Wizard from the menu. This will open the Upsizing Wizard dialog box.

3. If the database you want to use already exists, choose Use Existing Database. If you want to create a new database, choose the Create New Database option, and click Next.

4. Enter the database connection information that you want to use for the project. This includes the SQL Server host and the login ID and password for the connection. You must have CREATE TABLE and CREATE DEFAULT permissions to use the login information if you are using an existing database. If you are creating a new database, you must also have CREATE DATABASE privileges. If you are using MSDE or SQL Server running locally, consult the documentation for those products. If you are using a remote SQL Server database, you can obtain this information from a database administrator.

5. Choose the tables to export to SQL Server. You can choose any or all of the tables in the database, but if there are table dependencies, you must choose those. Click Next.

6. Choose the table attributes to upsize. By default, Indexes, Validation Rules, Defaults, and Table Relationships are all checked. You should generally stick to the defaults. Here, you can also choose to create the table structure without importing any data if you so desire. Click Next.

7. Choose how you want your existing database to be modified. You can choose a new project application, continue to use the existing database application with references to the SQL Server tables, or leave the existing application unchanged. Click Finish to upsize the database.

When the upsizing process is complete, the Upsizing wizard report details the results of the database conversion along with any errors encountered.

Importing and Exporting Data

Although Access tries hard to be the one application you need for accessing all of your data, there will inevitably come a time when you will need to import data from some foreign application, or provide it in a form that is readable by another application. Fortunately, Access is well versed in other file formats. Access allows you to import data from everything from simple comma-separated value (CSV) files, XML, other Office applications, and even other small and large databases. Supported file formats are shown in Table 29-1.

Importing Data

Importing data allows you to quickly fill a database table from another source, whether from another Access database, an XML file, or some other source. Once imported, however, the data is copied and no longer tied to the original source data. Any changes made to the data in Access must be exported back to the original file format if you wish to view it using that application. To get around this, use linking, as described in the next section.

To import data into a database or project, choose File | Get External Data | Import from the main menu to open the Import dialog box. Choose the file type you want to import, and browse to the file. Depending on the type of data you want to import, you may be presented with a choice of tables or a wizard to help you tell Access about the format of your data. Generally, Access will ask you to choose a subset of data from the chosen source, and then ask if you want to create a new table or use an existing table for the data.

CAUTION   *Inevitably, Access may have a hard time converting the data you import. In these cases, an additional table is created with the same name and a "$_ImportErrors" suffix. This table consists of a list of the errors encountered and their location in your imported table.*

Data File or Source	Supported Versions
Microsoft Access database	2.0, 95, 97, 2000, Access 2002, and Access 11 MDP files.
Microsoft Access project	2000, 2002, or Access 11 ADP files.
Microsoft Excel spreadsheet	3.0, 4.0, 5.0, 95, 97, 2000, 2002, and Excel 11.
Microsoft Exchange	All versions supported.
Paradox	Versions 3, 4, 5.0, and 8.0 are supported for importing. Drivers are available from Microsoft to enable linking.
Lotus 1-2-3 spreadsheets	All formats are supported up to .wk4. Lotus spreadsheets can be linked, but writing isn't supported.
dBASE	Versions III, IV, 5, and 7. Linking can be enabled by obtaining updated ISAM drivers from Microsoft.
Text files	You can import from delimited or fixed-width text files.
HTML	You can import from tables or lists embedded in an HTML document.
XML	XML and XSD files are supported.
ODBC data sources	Some ODBC data sources are supported for import and linking. You can use ODBC drivers for SQL Server, Oracle, Visual FoxPro, and others.

TABLE 29-1   Supported Import/Link Data Sources

Linking Data

Linking is similar to importing in that you read data created by another application into your Access database. However, linking is much more efficient than importing because it doesn't change the original data and, in fact, lets you modify the original data with Access. Linked data can therefore be managed both by Access and the source application without having to do further conversions or imports/exports.

With some creativity, this powerful feature allows you to combine data from other databases, whether Access, SQL Server, those from other manufacturers, such as Paradox, or even any database with an ODBC driver. You can change data in either the original application or Access and have the changes automatically available in the other.

Exporting Data

The counterpart to importing and linking external data is exporting. Access allows you to export database objects. Just as with importing and linking, Access supports a large number of data source and file formats, as shown in Table 29-2.

Data File or Source	Supported Versions
Microsoft Access database	2.0, 95, 97, 2000, Access 2002, and Access 11 MDP files.
Microsoft Access project	2000, 2002, or Access 11 ADP files.
Microsoft Excel spreadsheet	5.0, 95, 97, 2000, 2002.
Paradox	Versions 3, 4, 5.0, and 8.0 are supported. Requires the Borland Database Engine 4.x or later. Drivers are available from Microsoft.
Lotus 1-2-3 spreadsheets	.wj2, .wk1, and .wk3 formats.
dBASE	Versions III, IV, 5, and 7. Requires the Borland Database Engine 4.x or later. Drivers are available from Microsoft.
Text files	You can export to delimited or fixed-width text files.
HTML files	You can import from tables or lists embedded in an HTML document.
IDC/HTX files	Microsoft's Internet Information Server web server uses IDC and HTX files to display data from an ODBC data source as HTML.
Active Server Pages (ASP) files	All versions.
XML documents	You can export to XML documents, formatted to match your table structure.
ODBC data sources	Some ODBC data sources are supported for export. You can use ODBC drivers for SQL Server, Oracle, Visual FoxPro, and others.

TABLE 29-2   Supported Export File Formats

PART VI

Database Objects

Whether using a Jet file or a project connected to SQL Server, an Access database application consists of a collection of objects that define how the database is arranged and used. Think of the database objects as the building blocks of an Access database application, with the database or project acting as the container for the objects.

When you open an Access database, the database window is displayed. This window gives you a way to create and edit all of the objects in the database. Most of the object types have the same general options for creating and editing objects. The next few sections give an overview of the different types of objects used in Access databases. More information about using these objects to build complete Access applications can be found in the following chapters. Chapter 30 covers tables and relationships. Chapter 31 explains how to create queries. Chapter 32 shows how to design and use forms and reports. Finally, Chapter 33 explains how to create a complete database application.

Tables

The most important database objects are tables because they define the kinds of data that the database will store and how they relate to each other. The tables may exist in a Jet file or in a SQL Server database project.

A table is a collection of related data, such as a list of employees or a product inventory. The table also defines the format for this data. A *table definition* consists of a list of fields. A field is a single piece of data with a specific data type, such as text, number, date/time, currency, yes/no, and so on. For example, for a product inventory table, you might have fields for the product name, the quantity in stock, and a unit price, among others.

Data is entered into a table in units called records. Each record consists of its own values for each field.

Access presents data in tables in a grid (called, obviously enough, a *datagrid*), with the individual records in rows and the fields that make up the records as columns. Thus, records are often referred to as rows, and fields as columns. For more details about creating and working with tables, see Chapter 30.

Queries

Whereas tables provide the means for storing data, queries provide the means to get at the data. Queries can be used to retrieve and update information in tables, and are used as a source of data for forms and reports.

Access supports several different types of queries:

- **Select queries**   These are used to retrieve data from one or more tables and display it in a datasheet based on some criteria. You can choose which fields to display from the tables, the criteria to determine which records to retrieve, as well as the sort order.

- **Crosstab queries**   You use these queries to display records differently from the datagrid display of a select query. Crosstab queries are useful if you need to display a field based on two different criteria. The first field is displayed down the left side of the grid, and the second across the top.

- **Parameter queries**   This special type of select or crosstab query can prompt for one or more pieces of information to use as parameters to the query, rather than always returning data matching the same criteria. Parameter queries are typically used in forms and reports.

- **Action queries**   These are used to update, delete, or append data from a table, or to create new tables based on data obtained from another query.

- **SQL queries**   Written directly using Structured Query Language (SQL), these queries can be used to perform all of the same functions as the other query types. In fact, behind the scenes, Access creates SQL equivalents for queries created in Design mode.

Refer to Chapter 31 for more information about creating and working with queries.

Forms

Although tables and queries are the foundation for a database, forms make the data accessible to the user. Forms allow you to provide an interface that can guide users and simplify the tasks of data entry and retrieval. Forms can also link to other forms, and this becomes the basis for complete Access database applications. For more information about creating and using forms, see Chapter 32.

Reports

Reports are used to present data in a custom format and style in order to make reading and understanding the data easier. Reports allow you to display a specific range of data, organize it into groups, perform calculations, and display charts.

A report is typically bound to one or more tables or queries in a database, although you can choose to display only certain fields from those tables and queries. In addition to the data provided by the tables and queries that you associate with the form, a report can contain static information such as title and column headings, or descriptive text giving an explanation of what the presented data represents. Reports are described in more detail in Chapter 32.

Data Access Pages

Data access pages, shown simply as Pages in the database window, are an alternative to form and report objects and can be used similarly to build data-driven applications. The difference is that data access pages do not require Access to run once completed. Rather, they can be added to web sites using FrontPage or another web development tool. They can then be used by anyone with a web browser.

Data access pages are in reality HTML web pages, and can be placed on a corporate intranet or even on the World Wide Web.

Macros

With macros, you define a sequence of operations to automate common tasks. They have a variety of uses in an Access database. Macros can be attached to buttons in forms to perform a sequence of operations at the touch of a button; for instance, opening a new form with data displayed based on the value of fields for a current form.

You can also use macros for data validation. Although forms allow you to specify basic validation rules for data entry, you can use macros if your validation rules are more complex. Say, for instance, the allowed values for one field change depending on the value of another field; or you want to display custom error messages for the field.

Modules

The last of the database objects, modules, are collections of Visual Basic for Applications (VBA) statements and procedures, giving you a powerful means of working with your data. VBA is explained in Chapters 42 and 43. Although the capabilities provided by Access are quite powerful, writing VBA functions can give you an additional level of control. Use VBA modules to create functions that perform complex calculations and handle errors.

The Database Window

A convenient place to start working with all of the objects in a database is the database window. The Time and Billing database window is shown here. The actions that you can perform from this window are similar for all of the database objects, so once you understand the concepts of creating one object type, you'll be pretty comfortable with the others.

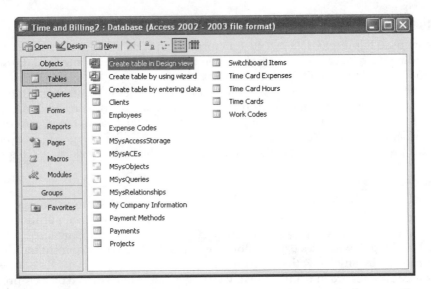

The left side of the database window contains a list of database object types that your database either has or can have. To see a list of objects of a specific type, simply choose that type from the list. If your database is empty, there won't be any objects to start with. All you will see are the icons for creating an object using Design view or the wizard. (Tables have an additional option—to create a table by entering data.) We'll give you an overview of those actions that work with all objects.

Creating Objects

The steps for creating objects are similar to the steps you take to create tables, queries, forms, reports, and data access pages.

1. Open the database window. If you have another window open, you can quickly return to the database window by pressing F11.

2. Choose the object type from the list on the left side of the database window.

3. Finally, create the object in one of the following ways. Note that both methods are similar, with the New button providing more choices and the shortcut icons providing a somewhat faster way of creating an object.

   - Click the New button on the object toolbar. This will open a dialog box giving you a choice of options for creating this type of object, including Design view and a variety of wizards. When you are just starting out, this is probably the best way to create objects because you may not realize that some of the wizards are available otherwise.

   - Double-click one of the shortcut icons at the top of the object list, or select one of the objects and click the Open button on the toolbar. These icons present the various ways to create an object, either by using a wizard or the Design view. Note that the Wizard icon will start the most common wizard for that object, while the New object dialog box (like the one shown in the following illustration) lists all available wizards for an object. If you don't see shortcut icons, they may not be enabled. You can enable them by choosing the Tools | Options menu item, and checking New Object Shortcuts in the View tab.

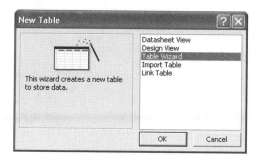

TIP *The object list doesn't show all of the options available to create objects. For example, the Query list gives you the option to create queries using Design view or the Simple Query wizard. And the New button presents additional options: the Crosstab Query wizard, Find Duplicates Query wizard, and Find Unmatched Query wizard.*

Editing in Design View

Use the Design view when you create objects or edit existing ones. Although each type of object has a unique design view, you access them all the same way. An example is shown in Figure 29-3.

PART VI

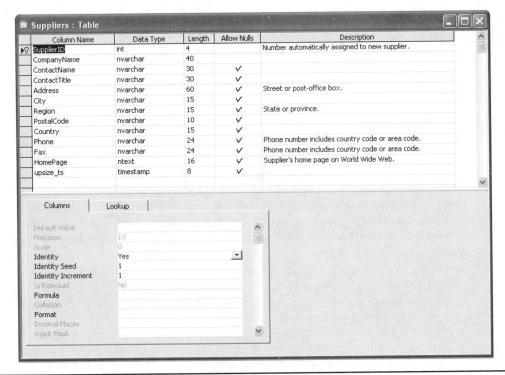

FIGURE 29-3   Design view is used to create and edit database objects.

To open a design view window for an object, do the following:

1. Open the database window.

2. From the list on the left side of the database window, choose the object type you want to create.

3. Select an object to edit on the left.

4. To open Design view, do one of the following:
   - Click the Design button on the object toolbar.
   - Right-click on the object and choose Design View.

Design view features for the various object types are discussed in the chapters on each object type.

Customizing Access

Like other Office applications, Access allows you to set options to suit your needs and desires. Many of the settings Access allows you to change, such as international and spelling options, are similar to those in other Office applications. Access has a number of options specific to it, such as those covered in the following sections.

Most of the customization that Access allows you to make takes place in the Options dialog box, shown in Figure 29-4 with the View tab open. Choose Tools | Options from the main menu to open it. Note that this menu item isn't enabled unless you have a database open in Access.

View Tab

You can show or hide various items in Access by using the View tab. As you can see in Figure 29-4, among these items are the status bar, startup task pane, and new object shortcuts.

- **Show**   Choose various options to show or hide by default. The items you can choose are the status bar, the startup task pane, new object shortcuts in the database window, hidden objects, and system objects. You can also choose to show open database object windows in the Windows taskbar.

- **Show in Macro Design**   These options let you specify optional columns to display in the Macro Design view. You can choose the Names and Conditions columns. Showing these items will make it easier to see at a glance what a macro does when you are in Design view.

- **Click Options in Database Window**   By default, this setting is set to double-click, which requires you to double-click on an object icon to open it. Change this if you want to open an object with a single-click, like a web link.

General Tab

Although many of the settings on the General tab, such as margins, sound, and default folder, are common to other Office applications, there are still a number of features that are unique to Access.

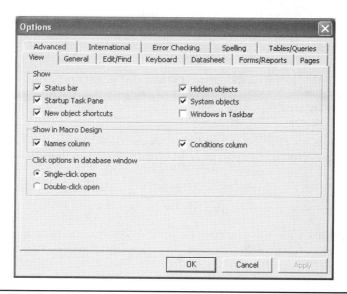

FIGURE 29-4   The Options dialog box allows considerable customization of the Access application.

PART VI

- **Use Four-Digit Year Formatting** You can choose whether dates are displayed with two or four digits. Select This Database if you want to make this change for the current database, or All Databases if you want to make four-digit year formatting the norm.
- **Remove Personal Information from This File** Check this to remove your name and other personal information from the database properties.
- **Compact on Close** You can improve the performance of your database by choosing to compact it when you close Access.

Edit/Find Tab

The Edit/Find tab lets you set some of the data editing features. You have three options for the default find and replace behavior in a datasheet: Fast Search will only search the current selected field, General Search searches all fields and matches any part of the field, and Start of Field searches all fields, but only matches the beginning characters. This behavior can be overridden in the Find/Replace dialog box.

Datasheet Tab

The Datasheet tab allows you to choose display options for datasheet windows, including colors, fonts, and how cells and gridlines are displayed. You can also choose to show animations and smart tags. Changes made on this tab won't apply to any currently open datasheets, but will apply to any subsequently opened sheets.

Forms/Reports Tab

The Forms/Reports tab allows you to set the default settings to use for forms and reports. The most important option here is choosing a default template to use for forms and reports. In addition, you can choose how selections work, whether events should always be handled by VBA procedures, and whether to show smart tags and windows themed controls on forms.

Pages Tab

The Pages tab is used to set some defaults for creating data access pages.

- **Default Designer Properties** Set the default fonts and color styles to use in your data access pages.
- **Default Database/Project Properties** Specify the locations for data access pages, as well as a default database connection file that pages will use to retrieve data.

Advanced Tab

Some of the more esoteric Access settings can be set under the Advanced tab.

- **DDE Options** You can set how you want Access to behave in the face of dynamic data exchange (DDE) requests from other applications. You can choose to ignore DDE requests altogether, specify a refresh interval, or specify custom command line arguments to pass to Access when it is launched.

- **Default File Format**   As described earlier in this chapter, you can choose to change the default database format that Access uses from Access 2000 to newer formats.

Tables/Queries Tab

The Tables/Queries tab allows you to set some defaults for creating table and query objects.

- **Default Field Sizes**   Set the size to use for text fields when creating a table.
- **Default Field Type**   Set this to any type to save time if you find yourself using one type significantly more than others.
- **Query Design Font**   Choose the font to use in the Query Design view. It's a good idea to leave this at the default setting or you may find the Design view more difficult to use.

Defining and Developing Tables

At the heart of any database is the data, and in most databases, including Access, that data is stored in tables. In Access, a table is one of the database objects you can add in the database window. It is the first type of object listed because it is the most important object in the database. Tables tell the database what kind of data the database contains, what type of information the data consists of, and how data in other tables relates to it. All of the other database objects (queries, forms, reports, and data access pages) eventually work with data stored in a table.

Data is organized in tables because they are a logical way to represent related information. Tables are represented in a row-column format, as shown in Figure 30-1. The related bits of information, known as fields, are displayed across the top of a table as columns. A collection of fields is called a record, and because they are displayed vertically from the top of the table, they are also called rows.

Most databases have more than one table, with each table containing fields that are specific to that record type. For example, a contact management database could have a table for contacts, a table for types of contacts, a table for calls, and a table for types of calls. An expense database might have a table for employee information, a table for expense reports, and a table for individual expense details.

The interrelationship among all of the tables that make up a database is what makes databases like Access *relational databases*. Most of the work in designing and creating databases is in determining what data to include in a particular table, and how all of the tables relate to each other. While this chapter isn't intended as a database design tutorial, it will show you how to use Access to create tables and table relationships.

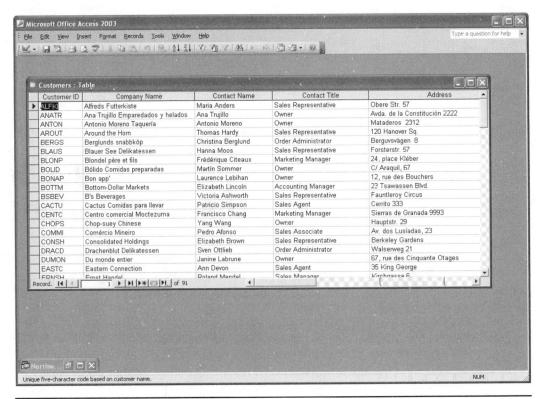

FIGURE 30-1   Tables are used to organize your data.

Creating Tables

Tables can be created in a number of ways. The Table wizard and the new Table Design view are used to create tables from scratch. You can also create a table from data imported from another database or file.

Using the Table Wizard

The Table wizard provides a good starting point for creating a table. As you can see in the following illustration, the wizard lets you choose from a list of premade tables, along with the fields that a table of that type would typically contain. You can pick and choose which fields to include, and then how the table relates to other tables already in your database.

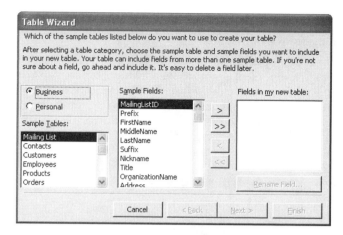

These steps show how to go about using the Table wizard to create a table:

1. Open the database window.

2. Select the Tables category from the list on the left side of the screen.

3. You can start the Table wizard in one of two ways:

   • Click the New button on the toolbar and choose Table Wizard from the dialog that pops up.

   • Double-click the Create Table by Using the Wizard shortcut in the object list. (Single-click if you have set single-click to open objects in the Access options.)

4. In the Table Wizard dialog, choose a table category to start with. The Business category shows tables often used in business-related databases, while Personal shows tables with more of a hobbyist, small business, or personal finance bent.

5. Choose a table from the Sample Tables list. Each table you select will show a list of possible fields in the Sample Fields list.

6. Choose the fields to include in the table from the Sample Fields list.

TIP   *Although it might be tempting to select all the fields shown in a Table wizard, just in case you might need them, that is not the most efficient way to make a table. Choose only the fields that you know you will need. You can always customize the table later in the Design view.*

7. Once fields are in the selected fields list, you can choose to rename them.

8. Click the Next button.

9. Enter a name for your table, and choose whether you want the wizard to select a primary key for you. The *primary key*, discussed later in this chapter, provides a unique identifier for each record. These are important when setting up relationships between tables. Click Next.

10. If you chose to select the primary key yourself, the wizard will prompt you to select a field and the format of that field.

11. Next, you have an opportunity to show how your table relates to other tables in your database. If you select a table to set a relationship to, you will be able to specify how the new table relates to the selected table. (Your options are shown in the following illustration.) Once you have set up your preliminary relationships, if any, click Next. Don't worry if you're not sure about the relationships you set up: you can always change them later. (We'll discuss this in more detail later in this chapter, in the "Table Relationships" section.)

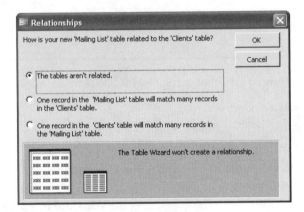

12. You need to tell Access how to open the table for you once it is created. You can choose to go straight to Design mode, open the table for data entry, or have Access automatically generate a data entry form for the table. Click Finish when you have made a selection.

Table Design View

Whether you create a table using the Table wizard, create one without fields or relationships, or edit an existing table, the Table Design view, shown in Figure 30-2, is the place to go to create or make changes to your data fields. Enter the Design view in either of two ways:

- Select the table you want to edit in the database window object list, and click the Design button on the toolbar.

- Right-click on the table in the database window list and choose Design View.

Table Design view is divided into three sections. At the top, across the entire width of the window, is the list of fields and their data types, along with an optional description you can add for more information in this window as well as on forms.

Below the field list and to the left of the window is where you set field properties. The properties you can set depend on the data type of the selected field.

At the lower right of the Design view is contextual information about the currently selected input box. Pay attention to this text if you are unsure about a setting.

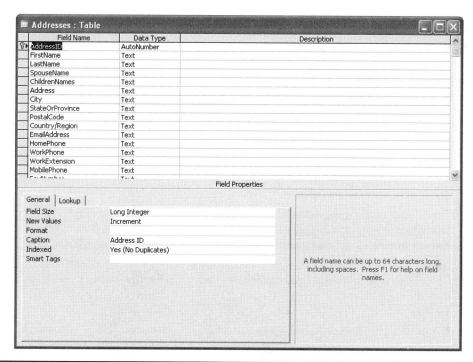

FIGURE 30-2   Table Design view is where you build a table, adding data fields and setting their properties.

Entering Fields

Adding a new field to a table is simple—click in one of the blank spaces in the field list and type in the name. Then click in the adjacent space in the Data Type column and choose a data type. (If you skip selecting a data type, it will be created using the default value set in the Access Options dialog. This is initially Text).

TIP   *If you leave blank fields between your existing fields and the new one, don't worry too much about it. Access is smart enough to remove these blank fields when it updates your table.*

When you have chosen a data type (more on this later), go down to the Field Properties section and fill in the properties unique to that field and type.

If you want to add a field between two existing fields, right-click on the field that you want to insert the new field before, and choose Insert Row.

To remove a field from your table, right-click on that field and choose Delete Row.

Finally, to move a field to a new position in the table, you can cut and paste it. Right-click on it and select Cut; then position the pointer where you want the field to be, right-click and select Paste. The cut field will be inserted before the field that you selected. Another way to move a field is to click on the box in front of the field, and then click again and drag the field where you want it to go.

Choosing Data Types

One of the most important decisions to make when creating a table is deciding what fields to include and what data type to make them. Each field data type has a specific use and also allows you to specify default values and validation rules specific to that data type to help ensure that your data is complete. Here is a list of the field data types supported in Access:

- **Yes/no (boolean)** Also referred to as the true/false data type, the boolean value is used for fields that have only two possible values. Boolean types are the simplest data type and are often used for searching. As an example, if you are building a list of customers and want to get a list of those who want you to send e-mail notices, a search on a boolean field will quickly retrieve those addresses. Format options allow you to use True/False or On/Off values as well as Yes/No.

- **Text** Text fields are general-purpose containers for a variety of information. You can put any alphanumeric data into a text field up to the defined field size. The default field size is 50 characters, but it can be set as high as 255.

- **Memo** When 255 characters isn't enough, use the memo data type to allow up to 65,536 characters. Memo fields aren't as efficient as Text fields, so they should be used with caution. Use them for storing large blocks of text, but not text that you want to index.

- **Number** This data type is used to store numeric characters, along with the symbols specifically used with numbers, the minus sign, and the period. You can choose from a variety of field sizes for numbers, ranging from byte (8 bits) to integer (16 bit), to long integer (32 bits). Nonintegers are also supported, with the single, double, and decimal field sizes.

- **Date/Time** You store a value as a date/time using this data type. The Format property allows you to specify a variety of date/time formats, including time only, date only, general time and date times, long date strings with the words, or shorter strings with only numbers.

- **Currency** Currency values are specialized number values for displaying and calculating values using monetary units up to four decimal places. Currency values are accurate to 15 digits on the left side of the decimal point and 4 digits on the right.

- **AutoNumber** Access automatically sets this value, which is a guaranteed unique number, when a new record is inserted into the table. The value can be determined incrementally or randomly based on the New Values setting. The Increment setting starts at 1 and adds 1 for each new record. Random creates a unique random number within the range of the data size. (Either a 32 long integer or a 16-bit referential ID are supported.) Because they are guaranteed to be unique, AutoNumber fields are often used for primary keys.

- **OLE Object** This is an object linked from another application, such as a Word document, an Excel spreadsheet, or some other object that conforms to the Object Linking and Embedding protocol.

- **Hyperlink**   This specialized text field contains information for displaying an HTML hyperlink. These links can be used to provide links to the web in forms and data access pages.

- **Lookup Wizard**   This field will allow you to choose a value from another table or from several values using a list box or a combo box. When you add a field of this type, the Lookup wizard is started, which takes you through the process of choosing the data for this field.

Setting Field Properties

When adding or modifying fields in a table in Design view, the lower portion of the window shows a list of properties that can be set for that field. These properties allow you to give more information about a field that can be used to improve searching efficiency, specify the data size and how it is formatted when presented, and give validation rules to help prevent data entry errors. Many of the most useful properties are discussed in the following sections.

Primary Keys

As mentioned earlier in the chapter, primary key fields are important when you are setting up relationships between tables. They provide a unique identifier for each record in a table and make looking up data in the relational database fast and efficient. Each table you create should have one or more fields designated as a primary key.

Primary keys are often AutoNumber fields. AutoNumber fields are automatically incremented numeric fields, and because of this they are guaranteed to be a unique value. This gives the ideal situation of a single field, numeric primary key.

Other data types can be used as primary keys as well, but there are some things you need to keep in mind. Numeric data types generally allow for faster searching than string data types, and it's easier to guarantee a unique value for them, so numeric fields such as an ID number are a good choice. Any field you choose for a single primary key cannot have null or duplicate values.

If you import a huge table and are having trouble coming up with a single field to use as the primary key, you also have the option of designating more than one field as primary keys. A database that tracks workshop registrations might have the same person signing up for multiple workshops and each workshop being booked by several people. Each person can only sign up once for an individual workshop, however, so a table with multiple primary keys—the CustomerID and the WorkshopID—would ensure that each record is unique. In the case of multiple primary keys, the combination of the chosen fields must be unique, which means that either one of the fields could conceivably contain duplicate data as long as the other one differs.

To make a field a primary key, select it in the Table Design view and choose Edit | Primary Key from the main menu. To set more than one field as the primary key, hold the CTRL key while you select the fields to use, and the primary key status will be applied to all selected fields.

Indexes

In order to make it easier to search a table, you can create an index for a field. An index allows the database engine to find information quickly, much like the index of a book. The database essentially "pre-searches" the data, and creates a behind-the-scenes list based on the indexed field that allows retrieval of records without scanning the entire table for them. Like a primary key field, an indexed field must contain unique values. If the field you want to index doesn't have unique values, you can index based on multiple fields instead.

Indexing makes sense for most tables, but you should still take care when deciding which fields to use. Primary key fields are indexed automatically, so you don't have to worry about them. For other fields, consider indexing them when the following situations apply:

- The field contains unique or mostly unique data values.
- You are going to sort based on the field.
- You are going to search the table based on the field.

TIP   *Be careful about adding a lot of indexes to a single table that is updated frequently. Indexes have an impact on inserting and updating records in the table, because the indexes have to be updated as well. The cost of this update is usually well offset by the benefit of using indexes for queries, but you should avoid creating indexes that you won't use.*

Input Masks

When entering formatted text data into a table, or providing a means for others to do so, you want to be able to enforce the formatting. Social security numbers, phone numbers, and account numbers all have a predictable format, and these numbers are frequently entered into a database. An *input mask* allows you to specify the format of the data that goes into a text or date field, and it not only enforces the required information (such as the nine digits of a social security number) but also makes the data entry easier (by automatically entering the dash character between the three sections.) With input masks you wind up with more consistent data and less wear and tear on your data entry person.

When you choose to add an input mask to a text field, the Input Mask wizard first allows you to choose the input mask you want to apply (along with a handy text box to test the mask).

If one of the provided masks doesn't quite work for your needs (say, for a non-U.S. telephone number field), don't worry. Click Next in the wizard, and you will have the opportunity to customize the input mask to your liking. You can also specify a *placeholder* value—that is, a value that is shown in place of the numbers that will be typed in the field.

Next, you choose how you want the data stored. You can choose to store data with the symbols in the mask, or with just the characters that are entered. Click Finish and the mask is created.

Creating a Mask

The wizard is the easiest way to create an input mask, but if you want, you can create one by hand just by typing into the Input Mask property of a text or date field. The Input Mask property consists of up to three sections separated by semicolons (;).

- The first section specifies the input mask itself; for example, !(999) 999-9999. For a list of characters you can use to define the input mask, see Table 30-1.

- The second section tells Access how to store the characters in the table. If you put a 0 in this section, all of the characters in the mask including the literals (for example, the parentheses in a phone number input mask) are stored with the value. If you enter a 1 or leave the second section blank, only the characters that are typed in are stored.

- The third section specifies the placeholder character. That is, the character that Access displays for the space where you should type a character in the input mask. You can use any character in this spot, including a space if it's enclosed between double primes (" ").

Table 30-1 shows the characters that have special meaning in an input mask.

Character	Meaning
0	Digit (0 to 9) with required entry.
9	Digit or space with optional entry.
#	Digit or space (entry not required; spaces are displayed as blanks while in Edit mode, but blanks are removed when data is saved; plus and minus signs allowed).
L	A required letter (A to Z).
?	An optional letter (A to Z).
A	Alphanumeric digit (letter or number, entry required).
a	Alphanumeric digit (letter or number, entry optional).
&	Any character or a space, entry required.
C	Any character or a space, entry optional.

TABLE 30-1 Characters Used to Define an Input Mask

Character	Meaning
. , : ; - /	Separators and placeholders for decimal point, thousands separator, and date and time separators. The actual character used depends on the settings in regional settings in the Windows Control Panel.
<	Converts all characters to lowercase.
>	Converts all characters to uppercase.
!	Causes the input mask to display from right to left, rather than from left to right. Characters typed into the mask always fill it from left to right. You can include the exclamation point anywhere in the input mask.
\	An escape character that causes the character that follows to be displayed as the literal character (for example, \A is displayed as just A).

TABLE 30-1   Characters Used to Define an Input Mask *(continued)*

The sample input masks in Table 30-2 illustrate how these mask characters can be used.

Format Properties

While the Input Mask property controls the format of data as it is input to a field, the Format property can be used to customize the way most fields are displayed and printed. The different data types have their own predefined formats and can also have custom formats created for them.

Input Mask	Description and Example
000-00-0000	U.S. social security number Example: 123-45-6789
00000-9999	U.S. zip + 4 code, five required digits followed by four optional digits Example: 45231-8910
>L0L 0L0	Canadian postal code Example: B1Y 3X6
>L<?????????????	A proper name—this mask forces the first letter to be required and uppercase, with remaining letters optional and lowercase

TABLE 30-2   Input Mask Examples

Text and Memo Formatting

Text and memo fields do not have predefined formatting options, but they do have a way to create custom formatting. The following table shows the special characters you can use in a text or memo formatting string.

Character	Meaning
@	A required text character
&	An optional text character
<	Force all characters following to uppercase
>	Force all characters following to lowercase

Text and memo formatting strings have up to two semicolon-separated sections. The first section provides the formatting to be used when the field contains data. The second, optional section, provides text to be displayed when the field is null or empty. For example, this formatting string will allow the field's value to be displayed unless it is empty or null, in which case the word *None* is displayed instead:

```
@;"None"
```

Yes/No Formatting

The different formatting possibilities provided for the boolean data type are Yes/No, True/False, and On/Off. However, you can use a custom format string to define your own values for the true and false conditions.

The boolean formatting string consists of three sections separated by semicolons (;). The first section is not used for this data type, but a semicolon is required. The second section describes the text to display in place of the Yes value. The third section describes the text to display in place of the No value. The following example shows a formatting string for a custom Yes/No data type value:

```
;"Up";"Down"
```

Date/Time Formatting

The Date/Time data type has some of the richest formatting options of any data type. Not only does Access provide a wide variety of predefined date and time formats, but also the means to create custom formats.

The standard date/time formatting options are good enough for almost all cases. They are as follows:

Format	Example
General Date	Displays a combination of the Short Date and Long Time formats. If the Date field only contains a date or a time value, only that value will be displayed. Example: 2/24/03 06:25:00 PM

Format	Example
Long Date	Displays a date in the same manner as the regional settings in the Windows Control Panel. Example: Monday, February 24th, 2003
Medium Date	Displays the day, three-letter abbreviation for a month, and a year. Example: 24-Feb-03
Short Date	Displays a short date using the regional settings in Windows. Example: 2/24/03
Long Time	Displays the time according to the setting of the Time tab in the regional setting of Windows. Example: 6:25:00 PM
Medium Time	Displays the time without the seconds. Example: 6:25 PM
Short Time	Displays the time in 24-hour format. Example: 18:25

Custom formatting options are available too. For example, this string shows formatting for a combination of the Long Date and Long Time formats, which would produce a date/time value of Monday, February 24th, 2003, 6:25:00 PM:

```
dddddd, ttttt
```

Number and Currency Formatting

Number and Currency data formats also have a variety of predefined formats to choose from, such as those shown in the table that follows.

TIP *Setting a format property only affects how fields are displayed, not how they are stored. For example, if you set a date field format to display the time only, all of the date information is still stored in the field and can be retrieved using a different format.*

Format	Example
General Number	The default setting; this does not apply any formatting to the number, but displays it as entered.
Currency	Displays a number as currency with the symbol specified in the current regional settings in Windows. Example: $10.00
Euro	Uses the Euro symbol (€) regardless of the currency symbol specified in the regional settings of Windows. Example: €10.00
Fixed	Displays a short date using the regional settings in Windows. Example: 2/24/03

Format	Example
Standard	Uses the thousands separator specified by the regional settings of Windows for negative numbers, decimal point symbols, and currency. Example: 1,234.56
Percent	Multiplies the number by 100 and adds a percent sign to the end. Example: 45%
Scientific	Uses scientific notation. Example: 3.14E+03

Default Values

Default value properties for table fields are pretty self-explanatory. With a default value, you can set an initial value for a field when a record is inserted without specifying a value for this field. The type of data that can be chosen for a default value is, of course, limited to data of the same type as the field.

Default values are not limited to a static value, however. You can also use expressions that call built-in Access functions to generate the default value. Access provides a dialog box called the Expression Builder that you can activate by clicking on the button that is visible to the right of the Default Value property when it is selected.

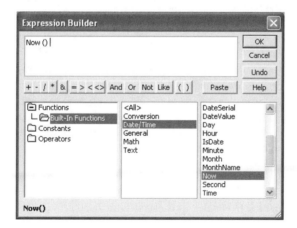

One very convenient default value can be used for Date/Time fields. Use the expression Now() to fill a data field with the time that the record was created, and you automatically have a time stamp for your records.

NOTE   *The Default Value property is available for all data types, with the exception of OLE Object and AutoNumber. The reasons should be pretty obvious—AutoNumbers generate their own default value.*

Validation Rules

The Validation Rule property lets you set requirements for the data that is entered into a field. When data is entered that violates the validation rule, the text in the Validation Text property can be used to show a custom message to the user.

A validation rule is a valid expression, although there are some limitations to the valid expressions that you can use for field validation. In general, though, most built-in functions and operators can be used to ensure that data entered falls within your prescribed limits. As with setting default values, you can use the Expression Builder to create your expression by clicking the button visible to the right of the Validation Rule field when it is selected.

This table shows some samples of validation rules to give you an idea of the possibilities available:

Validation Rule	Validation Text
>= 18	Please enter a value of 18 or higher.
<> 0	This item cannot be 0.
>= #1/1/01#	Please enter a date on or after January 1st, 2001.

NOTE   *If you set the Validation Rule property without setting a value for the Validation Text, Access displays a generic error message when invalid data is entered. If you set the Validation Text property, your text will be used as the error message.*

Data Normalization

If you are a spreadsheet user, you may know what it's like to have a huge, single spreadsheet filled with every piece of data imaginable. After a while, this data gets harder and harder to maintain, to the point that you lose much of the benefit of storing your data electronically at all. It becomes difficult to find related information because it is spread out all over the sheet, and it's hard to get a subset of the information. Not to mention, there is a lot of wasted space for cells that may only be used infrequently in a row.

For example, a spreadsheet organized in rows and columns that contains a list of employees and their dependents would need to have a column for every possible dependent. If an employee showed up with more dependents than the spreadsheet allowed, you would need to add a column just for that case. In these situations, a relational database like Access is better suited for the job.

So, what is data normalization, and what does it have to do with managing your data in a better way? Basically, *normalization* is the process of breaking data down into the chunks necessary to create an efficient relational database. It's the process you follow when deciding which fields to place in one table as opposed to another, and how many tables overall you need to organize your data for efficient retrieval.

NOTE   *This not only means that Access can search faster, it means that it's easier for you to get only the data you need when you make a query.*

There are two goals to keep in mind when you are designing your database tables: eliminate redundant data, and only store those fields in a table that make sense. Database gurus have come up with a set of rules to ensure that a database design is normalized. These rules are referred to as the *normal forms*. Typically, the first three normal forms are discussed when talking about database design, and this section will be no exception. We won't advocate that you stick to the rules at all costs—in some cases, it might make sense to violate the rules in order to have tables make logical sense or to meet some business goal. However, when you do stray from the normalization rules it is important to realize it and understand what effect it might have on your database. So, what are the normal form rules?

- **First normal form**   Eliminate duplicate columns from the same table, and create separate tables for each group of related data. Each table should have a unique identifier (the primary key) as one of its fields.

- **Second normal form**   Remove subsets of data that apply to multiple rows of a table, and create new tables. Create relationships between these tables and their predecessors with foreign keys.

- **Third normal form**   Remove any field from a table that is not dependent upon the primary key.

Non-Normalized Example

To explain how to go about normalizing data, we'll start with an example of data that has been organized poorly. This may be because it grew from a simple spreadsheet and was later imported into Access, or designed that way from the start. Either way, it is an example of poor table design that can be optimized in Access.

The table in the following illustration shows a list of employees along with their dependents. Because employees might have more than one child, multiple columns have been added. At first glance, this might seem like a straightforward way of organizing the data, but there are two problems with it—it doesn't provide room for growth, and it includes data that isn't related directly to the employee.

Employee ID	Name	Title	Spouse_name	Child1_name	Child1_age	Child2_name	Child2_age	Child3_name	Child3_age
1	George Smith	Manager	Linda	George Jr.	12	Georgette	5		
2	Harold Brown	Salesman	Sarah		0		0		0
3	Gilda Jones	Accountant	Steven	Mike	8	Jackie	6	Linda	3
(AutoNumber)					0		0		0

Record: 14 ◄ 1 ► ►I ►✱ of 3

The first indication that something in here does not belong is the fact that we have numbered fields for each child. While something like this might be common in a spreadsheet, it's a big no-no in relational database design, for a number of reasons. The biggest one is that there is no room to grow—if an employee comes along with four children, this table can't cope. We also see a violation of the first rule of normalization mentioned earlier, that a table shouldn't contain duplicate columns.

Normalized Example

In this normalized example, shown next, we've broken the table into two tables and created a relationship between the tables.

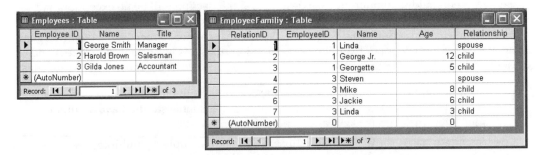

These tables are much better than the original one. You can see that the Employees table isn't burdened with information that isn't necessarily relevant to the employee, and that the EmployeeFamily table can grow if Gilda Jones decides to have another child.

Table Relationships

You may notice that while the Employee ID is the primary key for the Employees table, it is also used as a non-unique value in the EmployeeFamily table. This is known as a *one-to-many relationship* between the two tables, and is an important aspect of relational database design.

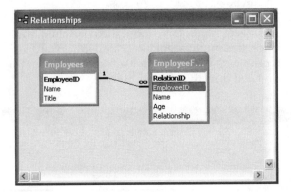

Here is a description of the various types of table relationships and how they might be used:

- **One-to-many relationships** A *one-to-many relationship* is the most common type of relationship. In a one-to-many relationship, a record in one table can have multiple matching records in another table. However, a record in the "many" table can only have one match in the first table. In this case, each employee can have many children, but each child only belongs to one employee.

- **One-to-one relationships**   In a *one-to-one relationship*, each record in the first table can only have one corresponding record in the second table. This type of relationship isn't used very often, because this information is usually contained in a single table. One example of where it might be useful is when a table contains fields that are rarely used, or fields that relate to more than one table. It can sometimes make more efficient use of database storage to create a separate table for this information using a one-to-one relationship.

- **Many-to-many relationships**   A relationship in which a record in the first table can have many related records in the second table, and where a record in the second table can likewise have many related records in the first table is called a *many-to-many relationship*. When a relationship of this type is desired, it is necessary to create a third table known as a *junction table*. A junction table consists of two columns, matching the primary keys in each of the two original tables. A many-to-many relationship is really two one-to-many relationships. An example of this type of relationship might be a video rental store database. The relationship between a table of videos for rent and a table of customers is many-to-many: customers can rent more than one video, and a video may have been rented by many customers.

To set a table relationship in Access, open the Relationships window. Use the Tools | Relationships menu, or right-click in the database window and choose Relationships.

The Relationships window, shown in Figure 30-3, shows a visual representation of all the tables in the database, along with their relationships. Tables with related fields are shown with a line drawn between them. This line might also display symbols at either ends of the line, a 1 if the field may only exist once in the relationship, or an infinity symbol for fields that have a many relationship. A table may have exactly one relationship with any other table, but a field in a table may be involved in relating a table to more than one other table. You can reorganize this window by simply dragging a table to a new location. This is useful when your relationships get complicated and you want to keep from having lines zigzagging across the window.

To set a relationship between two tables, you can simply drag the field to relate from one table to another. This opens the Edit Relationships dialog, where you can change the fields in the relationship (if you happened to have dropped it on the wrong field), or add fields to the relationship. Access automatically determines the type of relationship based on whether

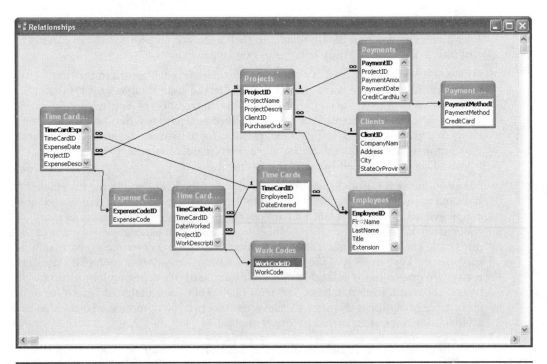

FIGURE 30-3 The Relationships window shows you how tables relate to one another.

the chosen field is a primary key in either of the tables. As you can see, there are three check boxes below the field list:

Check the box for Enforce Referential Integrity if you want Access to prevent you from adding records to a table when the related field doesn't have a match in the other table. When you check this box, two other options appear: Cascade Update Related Fields and Cascade Delete Related Records. Checking these will make Access automatically update or delete a record in a table if a field that it refers to in another table changes.

CHAPTER

Creating Queries

After defining tables and entering data, the next most important aspect in database design is providing a way to retrieve and update your data. Access uses database objects called queries for this purpose. Queries are not only used by themselves to retrieve and modify data, but they are also the workhorse objects used to populate forms, reports, and data access pages with data, and once records are added or changed, queries restore data in the appropriate table.

Queries are very versatile, and you can use them to manipulate data in a lot of different ways. Fields in a table can be displayed as is, or they can be used in calculations to generate new fields. Records from multiple tables can even be combined and returned as if they came from a single table.

Access provides several different types of queries and three different ways to create them ranging from an easy-to-use wizard, to the Design view, to creating your own SQL statements. This flexibility makes it possible to create powerful Access queries no matter what your level of expertise.

Query Types

Access has two types of queries—those that retrieve data from tables and those that modify data and tables. The most common types of queries are select queries. After all, the purpose of a database is to make it easy to find the information you are looking for. Access provides three types of select queries: select, parameter, and crosstab. The other type of query, the action query, is often used by forms at data entry time to input new records. Action queries include delete, update, append, and make-table queries.

Select Queries

By far the most common type of query is the select query. You use them to pick and choose the data that you want to retrieve for a particular function and present it to the user in a form or a datasheet. In some cases, data presented in a datasheet from a select query can be changed and resaved in the database.

Select queries can contain any of the following:

- Fields from one or more tables or existing queries

- Calculated fields, using functions to calculate sum, average, counts, minimum, maximum, and other statistical operations

- Hidden fields, useful for sorting and filtering selected data, but not actually displayed in the results

Select queries are the basis for all other queries. Therefore, the basic steps you go through in Design view, using the datagrid to create select queries, will also apply to other queries. To create a select query using the Design view, do the following:

1. Create a query by clicking the Create Query in Design View item in the query list of the Database window. You can also click the New button in the Database window toolbar and choose Design View from the list in the New Query dialog box.

2. Choose one or more tables and queries in the Show Table dialog box. If necessary, use the Table, Query, and Both tabs to change the list of available objects. Double-click on the table or query, or select it and click the Add button to add it to the query. Click the Close button when you are finished.

3. Choose fields you want to use for the query from the field list. Double-click them or drag them to add them to the design grid in the lower part of the window.

4. Enter criteria (expressions used to limit the records that are included in the query) to specify the records you want to retrieve, as shown here.

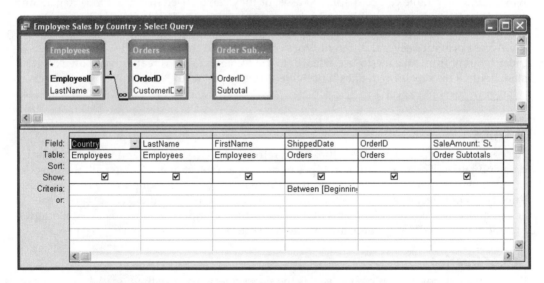

5. Click the View button on the main window toolbar to see the results of the query. Click the View button again to return to Design view.

6. Close the Design view when you are finished with your query in order to save it. You may now run the query at any time by double-clicking on it in the Database

window. (Single-click if you happen to have Single-Click Open selected in the Access View options.)

Updating Queries

In some cases, the datasheet you view as the result of a select query can be used to change and save updated data back to the database as well. Figure 31-1 shows a datagrid with editable values in the datasheet. Simply highlight the value you want to change and type in a new value. The following are some scenarios where you can and sometimes cannot update data. You can update data from a query when it meets one of these conditions:

- The query is of a single table
- The query is based on tables with a one-to-one relationship

Queries of tables with one-to-many relationships can be updated in certain cases as well:

- Join fields from the "one" side of the relationship can be updated if cascading updates are enabled between the two tables.
- New records can only be added if all of the primary key fields are present in the query.

Country	Last Name	First Name	Shipped Date	Order ID	Sale Amount
USA	Peacock	Margaret	06-Jun-1997	10551	$1,677.30
USA	Fuller	Andrew	05-Jun-1997	10552	$880.50
USA	Fuller	Andrew	03-Jun-1997	10553	$1,546.30
USA	Peacock	Margaret	05-Jun-1997	10554	$1,728.52
UK	Suyama	Michael	04-Jun-1997	10555	$2,944.40
USA	Fuller	Andrew	13-Jun-1997	10556	$835.20
UK	Dodsworth	Anne	06-Jun-1997	10557	$1,152.50
USA	Davolio	Nancy	10-Jun-1997	10558	$2,142.90
UK	Suyama	Michael	13-Jun-1997	10559	$520.41
USA	Callahan	Laura	09-Jun-1997	10560	$1,072.42
USA	Fuller	Andrew	09-Jun-1997	10561	$2,844.50
USA	Davolio	Nancy	12-Jun-1997	10562	$488.70
USA	Fuller	Andrew	24-Jun-1997	10563	$965.00
USA	Peacock	Margaret	16-Jun-1997	10564	$1,234.05
USA	Callahan	Laura	18-Jun-1997	10565	$639.90
UK	Dodsworth	Anne	18-Jun-1997	10566	$1,761.00
USA	Davolio	Nancy	17-Jun-1997	10567	$2,519.00
USA	Leverling	Janet	09-Jul-1997	10568	$155.00
UK	Buchanan	Steven	11-Jul-1997	10569	$890.00
USA	Leverling	Janet	19-Jun-1997	10570	$2,465.25
USA	Callahan	Laura	04-Jul-1997	10571	$550.59
USA	Leverling	Janet	25-Jun-1997	10572	$1,501.08

FIGURE 31-1   The result data of a select query can often be edited directly in the datasheet and saved back to the database.

In the following cases, data cannot be updated in the select query's datasheet:

- The query is a crosstab query.
- The query is a SQL pass-through query.
- The query is a union query.
- The field is a calculated field.

Crosstab Queries

Crosstab queries are a special type of select query that present the data for easy analysis. Crosstab queries display some sort of statistical or total value for data that is grouped by two fields. One field is used for the row and the other for the columns. The result is a PivotTable, so named because some of the data is turned so it can be viewed from a different perspective.

To create a crosstab query using the Design view, follow these steps:

1. Create a query by clicking the Create Query in Design View item in the query list of the Database window.

2. Choose one or more tables and queries in the Show Table dialog box. If necessary, use the Table, Query, and Both tabs to change the list of available objects. Double-click on the table or query, or select it and click the Add button to add it to the query. Click the Close button when you are finished.

3. Drag fields from the field list onto the design grid to select the fields to include in the query.

4. Enter any criteria to use for selecting the fields.

5. In the Query Design view, click the Query Type button on the toolbar, and then select Crosstab Query. Or, you can choose Query | Crosstab Query from the main menu.

6. Choose the field or fields to use as row headings. Do this by clicking in the Crosstab cell in the design grid and choosing Row Heading.

7. Choose a field to use as the column heading. Do this by clicking in the Crosstab cell in the design grid and choosing Column Heading. Because the column heading is used as select criteria for the cross-referenced data, you can only choose one field for the column heading.

8. Choose a field to use as the cross-tabulation value by clicking the Crosstab cell and choosing Value.

9. Click in the Total cell for the field you selected for the value in step 8, and choose an aggregate function to calculate the total value. The Query Design view window will now look something like what's shown next.

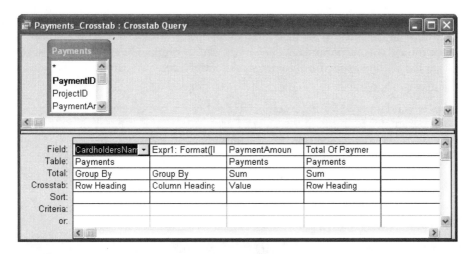

10. Click the View button to preview the query, and again to return to Design view.

Parameter Queries

Select queries are useful when you want to select data based on the same criteria every time. But often, you need more flexibility. For example, you may want to select sales for a particular month. You could create individual select queries for each month, but you would soon have too many query objects to manage easily. If you wanted to query on even more specific criteria, such as sales for a particular month by an individual salesperson, you would be hard pressed to come up with individual queries. An easier and more flexible option is to create a parameter query.

Parameter queries allow you to specify one or more values as parameters to search. When you run a parameter query, a dialog box opens to prompt for the information. Parameter queries are also quite useful as the basis for forms, reports, and data access pages, as you will see in the next chapter. To create a parameter query, you start with a select or crosstab query, and specify the parameter information in the criteria rows for the appropriate fields, as shown in the following steps.

1. Create a query using the basic steps for a select query. Choose a table or tables for the source of the query.

2. Enter an expression followed by text in square brackets; this will be used as a prompt. For example, to prompt for a minimum value to use as a selection criteria, you might enter the following:

```
>=[Maximum number of purchases:]
```

When the query is run, the user will be prompted to enter a value using the provided prompt, and the value the user enters will be substituted in the expression. You can use more than one parameter, even in the same criteria. For example, to select records that fall within a specific date range, you might enter an expression such as this:

```
Between [Enter starting date:] And [Enter the ending date:]
```

3. Specify a data type for parameters. To do this, choose Query | Parameters and enter the parameter prompts in the Query Parameters dialog box. Click on the Data Type field, and choose a data type for the fields. You must specify a data type if any of the following conditions is true:

- The query is a crosstab query.
- The query is used as the source for a chart.
- The parameter is a Yes/No data type.

Action Queries

Along with the select queries used to retrieve data from tables come the action queries. You use these to make changes to existing records in the database, or move data into a new table. Access provides four different action queries—delete queries, update queries, make-table queries, and append queries.

TIP   *Action queries are indispensable for maintaining your database, but run the wrong query and your precious data could be history. This is especially a possibility when you are making changes to an action query. Be wary of this possibility, and take steps to prevent it. Making a backup copy of your database file or copying the data you are working with to another table for safekeeping are both good ideas.*

Delete Queries

Use delete queries to remove records from one or more tables. They are often used to remove obsolete information from a database, such as products that are no longer being sold or event calendar entries that are in the past. Follow these steps to create a delete query:

1. Create a query using the basic steps for a select query. Choose a table or tables for the source of the query.

2. In the Query Design view, click the Query Type button on the toolbar, and then select Delete Query. Or, choose Query | Delete Query from the main menu.

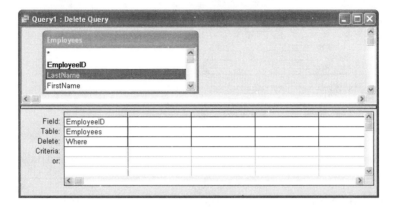

3. Drag the asterisk from the field list of the table you want to delete records from to the design grid, or double-click on it to select all the fields of that table.

4. Drag additional fields to the design grid to set criteria for selecting those records.

5. In the design grid, enter the criteria to use for deleting records.

TIP   *Before actually deleting records, click the View button on the toolbar to preview the records that will be deleted. This will help ensure that your selection criteria is valid and you aren't about to accidentally delete the wrong data. Click the View button a second time to return to Design view.*

6. Click Run on the toolbar to execute the query and delete the records.

Update Queries

There are two steps involved in designing an update query. The first step is to choose the criteria for selecting records to update. Second is to provide replacement data or an expression to generate that data. Although you can modify data in a select query, an update query is more flexible and more powerful. While you are limited to updating a single field at a time in a select query datasheet, an update query can update many fields of many records across multiple tables. Follow these steps to create an update query:

1. Create a query using the basic steps for a select query. Choose a table or tables for the source of the query.

2. In the Query Design view, click the Query Type button on the toolbar, and then select Update Query. Alternatively, you can choose Query | Update Query from the main menu.

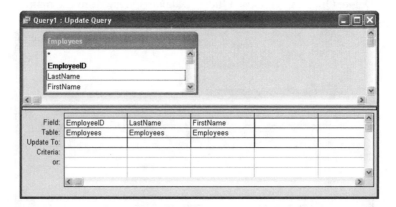

3. Drag the fields that you want to update or provide selection criteria for from the field list to the design grid.

4. Enter any criteria into the criteria fields.

5. Enter the value or an expression in the Update To row of the design grid. If a value is entered, all records that are updated will have the same value. If an expression is entered, the expression will be performed on each record individually.

6. Click the View button on the toolbar to preview the changes.

7. Once you are satisfied that the update query is correct, click Run to execute the query and update the database.

Make-Table Queries

To create new tables from the data obtained as a result of a select query, you use a make-table query. While at first, the idea of copying data into a new table may seem to violate the cardinal database design rule of only storing information in a single place, there are valid reasons for being able to copy data to a new table. For example, you may want to export selected portions of your data to another application for external processing, without having to export an entire table that includes unrelated fields. Another use for make-table queries is to create a snapshot of data as it exists at the time, or create an archive of old data from an active table before deleting it, as shown in Figure 31-2. Create a make-table query by doing the following:

1. Create a query using the basic steps for a select query. Choose a table or tables for the source of the query.

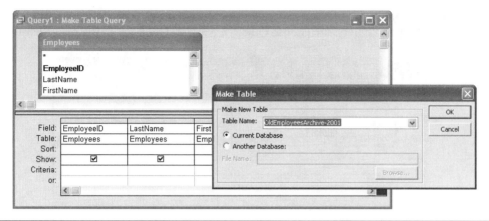

FIGURE 31-2   Make-table queries are used for saving the results of the query to another table.

2. In the Query Design view, click the Query Type button on the toolbar, and then select Make-Table Query. Or, choose Query | Make-Table Query from the main menu.

3. Enter a table name for the new table to create, and choose whether this table will go into the current database or a different existing database. Click OK.

4. Drag the fields from the field list that you want to include in the new table.

5. Enter any selection criteria you want to use in the Criteria row.

6. Click View on the toolbar to preview the data that will be selected, to avoid any surprises. Click View again to return to Design view.

7. Click Run to execute the make-table query once you are sure that the data you are selecting is the correct data.

Append Queries

Use append queries to add new records to a table from the results of another query. Append queries are often used to combine imported data into an existing table. Data can be selected from the source table using normal selection criteria, and it is appended to the existing table of your choice, in either the current or another database. Append queries can be used similarly to the make-table query example—to create an archive of older data—with the difference being that the data is appended to an existing table instead of always put in a new table. To create an append query, perform the following steps:

1. Create a query using the basic steps for a select query. Choose a table or tables for the source of the query.

2. In the Query Design view, click the Query Type button on the toolbar, and then select Append Query. Or, choose Query | Append Query from the main menu.

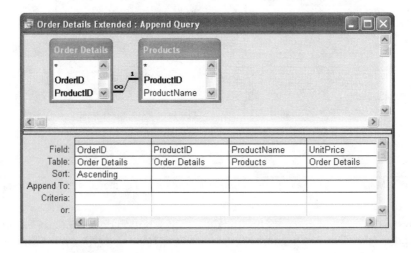

3. Choose a table to append to, either by selecting a table from the list or entering the table name.

4. Choose whether the table is in the current database or in a different one. This database can be an Access database, an ODBC database such as FoxPro, or even a connection string to a SQL Server database. Click OK.

5. Drag fields from the field list to the design grid. If the table you are appending to has all of the same fields, you can drag the asterisk instead.

6. If you have an autonumber data type, you have two choices. Either don't drag the autonumber field to the design grid, and Access will automatically add new numbers for appended records; or drag it, to have Access use the existing autonumber values.

7. Enter any criteria you want to use for selecting data in the design grid.

8. If the fields you are appending to have different names than the fields in the query, enter the names of the destination fields in the Append To row.

9. Click View to preview the query. Click View again to return to Design view.

10. Click Run when you are satisfied that the query fields and criteria are correct.

Query Wizards

The query wizards in Access are a great way to get started creating basic select or crosstab queries. While a little limiting, considering there are only four basic query wizards, they provide a good way to get started, especially for those unfamiliar with the Query Design view. Design view can be used to modify a query created by a query wizard.

Simple Query Wizard

The Simple Query wizard is the easiest way to get started creating a select query, and is the wizard that is used the most. The Simple Query wizard allows you to choose fields from one or more tables and queries. You can also choose to return all of the data, or a summary based on sum, average, minimum, maximum, or a count of records.

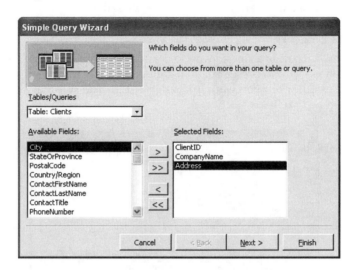

Follow these steps to create a select query using the Simple Query wizard:

1. In the Database window, select the Queries category from the list at the left, and click the New button on the Database window toolbar.

2. Select Simple Query Wizard from the list of options, and click OK.

3. From the Tables/Queries list, choose the first data source in the query.

4. Choose fields to include in the query from the Available Fields list. Click on fields and use the arrow buttons between the lists to move highlighted fields into the Selected Fields list.

5. If you want to use more than one table for the query, repeat steps 3 and 4. The tables you choose must be related in some way. When you are finished choosing fields, click Next.

6. Choose whether to show a detail or summary query. A detail query shows all records for all selected fields. A summary query returns a single row with the result of some calculation based on the data. Note that this option will only be presented if you choose a numeric field type.

7. If you choose a summary query, click the Summary Options button, and choose the summary criteria for each appropriate field. You can choose one or more of the following: sum, average, minimum, and maximum. You can also choose to display a count of the total number of records retrieved. Click OK when done.

8. If you have chosen a summary query, and you have included a date field, you can choose to group data based on date. Choose one of the following: Unique date/ time, Day, Month, Quarter, or Year. Then click Next.

9. Choose a name for the query, and choose whether you want to run the query now or go directly to Design view to make further changes to the query design.

10. Click Finish to create the query and exit the wizard.

Crosstab Query Wizard

The Crosstab Query wizard is a simple way to create a crosstab query. As described earlier, a crosstab query allows you to present data in a more compact form than a standard select query, but is only useful when you want to display a statistical summary of data that can be cross-referenced by two fields.

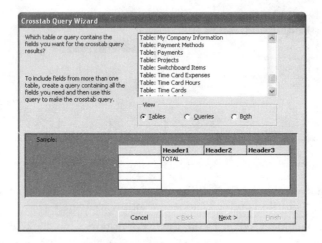

Follow these steps to create a crosstab query using the wizard:

1. In the Database window, select the Queries category from the list at the left, and click the New button on the Database window toolbar.

2. Select Crosstab Query Wizard from the list of options, and click OK.

3. Choose a table or query to use as the data source from the list. You can set the View options to filter the display list by tables, queries, or both.

4. Choose the field(s) to use for row headings. You can choose up to three fields for the display. When finished, click Next.

5. Choose a field to use for the column headings. Click Next.

6. If you chose a Date field for the columns in step 5, you now must select a date interval. Choose one of date/time, date, month, quarter, or year. Click Next.

7. Choose a field to use as a basis for the value to display at the junction between the rows and columns. You can then choose a function to perform on the data. The functions shown depend on the data type of the selected field. For numeric fields, you can

choose from average, count, first record, last record, max value, min value, standard deviation, summation, or variance. Click Next.

8. Choose a name for the query, and choose whether you want to run the query now or go directly to Design view to make further changes to the query design.

9. Click Finish to create the query and exit the wizard.

Find Duplicates Query Wizard

The Find Duplicates Query wizard is used to find records in a single table or query with duplicate entries. A useful example of this might be to find customers who have made multiple purchases, or to find students enrolled in more than one class.

Follow these steps to create a query to find duplicate records:

1. In the Database window, select the Queries category from the list at the left, and click the New button on the Database window toolbar.

2. Select Find Duplicates Query Wizard from the list of options, and click OK.

3. Choose a table or query from the list. This is the table or existing query that contains the duplicate records. You can use the View selection to choose to show tables, queries, or both in the list of choices. When finished, click Next.

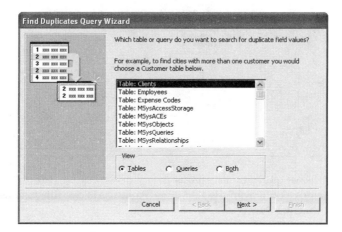

4. Choose a field to use for the duplicate record comparison. For example, if you are trying to get a list of customers who have made multiple purchases, you might choose the customer ID. You can choose more than one field. When you are done, click Next.

5. Choose one or more additional fields to display in the result datasheet field. When you are finished, click Next.

6. Choose the fields that you want to have displayed in the query results, and click Next.

7. Finally, enter a name for the query, and choose to view it (the default) or go directly to design mode by making the appropriate selection, and click Finish.

Find Unmatched Query Wizard

The Find Unmatched Query wizard is used to create a query that compares the records in one table with those in another. It returns all of the records in the first table that don't have a match in the second table. This could be used, for example, to provide a list of employees who haven't signed up for a particular benefit program by comparing the table of employees with that of the benefit.

Follow these steps to run the Find Unmatched Query wizard:

1. In the Database window, select the Queries category from the list at the left, and click the New button on the Database window toolbar.

2. Select Find Unmatched Query Wizard from the list of options, and click OK.

3. Choose a table or query to show. This is the table that is used as the source data for the query. Under the View options, you can decide whether to include tables, queries, or both in the list of options. When you have chosen a table or query, click Next.

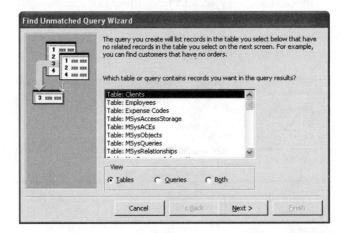

4. Choose a table or query that contains the related records. This is the data source that is used to remove data from the first table. Again, you can filter the list by table, query, or show both. Click Next.

5. Choose a field that both databases have in common. For example, for an employee table, the employee ID may be used as a field in the benefit table. The fields do not have to be the same name, but they do have to contain related data. When you are finished, click Next.

6. Choose the fields that you want to have displayed in the query results, and click Next.

7. Finally, enter a name for the query, and choose to view it (the default), or go directly to design mode by making the appropriate selection, and click Finish.

Working in Query Design View

Now that you know what type of queries you can create in Design view or by using a wizard, it's time to go into a little more detail on how to use the design grid to get the most out of your queries. Whether you create a query with a wizard, create one directly in the Design view, or edit a query generated by an Access database wizard, you will eventually want to customize a query.

In the Design view, the query is represented by two panes. The top pane shows the tables and queries chosen as the data source objects for the query. The lower pane shows a design grid with the fields selected from the tables to include in the query, along with several properties that are dependent on the type of query you are creating.

Choosing Tables

If you are creating a query from scratch, or are editing a query and wish to include data from a table that isn't shown in the table view at the top of the page, you must start by adding a table. A table or query must be visible here in order to include fields in the query.

To add a table, either choose Query | Show Table from the main menu, or right-click in the window and choose Show Table. Choose a table (or query) from the list in the Show Table dialog box, using the tabs to filter the presented list to show only tables, queries, or both. Select the table you want to add, and either double-click on it or click the Add button. When you are done choosing tables and queries, click Close.

Removing a table is just as straightforward. Select the table to remove, and either choose Query | Remove Table from the menu, or right-click on the table and choose Remove Table. Once removed, any fields from that table in the query design grid will be removed as well.

Choosing Fields

You have three options for adding a field to the query from the list of tables:

- Drag the field from the table to the design grid. If you drag it on top of an existing column, the field will be inserted before it.

- Double-click on the field to add it to the next available column on the design grid.

- Click in the field row, and choose a field from the drop-down list. All available fields from the chosen tables are shown. You can insert a blank column into the query using the Insert | Columns menu item.

You may, in fact, choose a field more than once—say, once for a calculation and once for display.

There are frequently times when you want to display all of the data in a table. Instead of dragging each individual field into the Design view to accomplish this, drag the special asterisk field at the top of the table fields. This special field is a shortcut that means you want all fields from the table to be included in the query.

Moving and Deleting Fields

Deleting a field is accomplished by clicking on the bar above the field name and choosing Edit | Delete Columns, or by simply pressing the DELETE key.

Moving a field is accomplished by dragging it to a new position. Select the bar above the field name in the column, and drag it to a new position.

Sorting Fields

You can choose to sort the query results based on any field by choosing a sort order in the Sort row. You can choose from ascending, descending, or unsorted. Sorting can be applied to more than one column in the query. Columns to the left have sorting priority over columns farther to the right when multiple sorting fields are chosen.

Showing and Hiding Fields

By default, fields added to a query are shown in the resulting datasheet. It is possible, however, to include fields in the query that are only used for selection criteria or sorting. To hide a field that you don't need to see in the query results datasheet, uncheck the box in the Show cell for that field.

Defining Query Criteria

A query performed on the fields added to the query will return every single record in the table if you do not use some method to filter the data. In Access, criteria are used to filter fields so that you will only get the records that you want in the query. Criteria consist of one or more expressions entered into the criteria field. Because a record is either included in a query or it isn't, all criteria expressions must evaluate to a True or False value.

You can enter criteria by either typing an expression in directly, or by using the Expression Builder. To enter criteria directly, simply click on a field's criteria cell and type it in. To open the Expression Builder, right-click on the criteria cell and choose Build.

Multiple expressions can be used in a query. If the expressions are added on the same row, they are treated as an And case, where all of the criteria must be met for a record to be included in the query results. Expressions added on another row are treated as an Or case— a record only has to satisfy the criteria specified in one row to be returned. In addition to these automatic logical operators, you can use additional logical operators (And, Or, and Not) to join multiple expressions in a single criteria cell.

The following table lists some common examples of expressions that can be used as query criteria.

Expression	Meaning
> 100	Greater than 100
< 100	Less than 100
<= 100 and >=50	Less than or equal to 100, and greater than or equal to 50
Between #5/15/1992# and #11/11/1995#	A date falling within this range (using ANSI 89 syntax)
Between '5/15/1992' and '11/11/1995'	A date falling within this range (using ANSI 92 syntax)
Not "AZ"	For a state field, may be used to determine whether sales tax should be applied to orders going out of state

Expression	Meaning
"Kettell"	For a text field, returns all fields containing the exact string. The Like operator is implied here.
Like "K*"	Wildcard search on a text field, matches all fields that start with K (ANSI 89 syntax)
Like 'K%'	Wildcard search on a text field, ANSI 92 syntax
Date()	For a date field, fields that match the current date
Is Null	The field is null.

Performing Calculations

Not all data displayed in query fields has to come from a table or an existing query. Calculated columns use expressions to calculate a value for the data shown in the field, and the value is recalculated on the fly every time the query is run.

To define a calculated column, enter the expression directly into the Field cell of the column. You can also use the Expression Builder to create the expression and make sure the syntax is valid by right-clicking on the field name and choosing Build.

SQL Queries

Like many modern relational databases, Access uses Structured Query Language (SQL) to query and manage data. Even when you create a query using the wizard or the Design view, Access creates SQL statements that actually do the job behind the scenes (Figure 31-3). A tutorial on SQL is beyond the scope of this book, however. If you are already familiar with SQL or wish to learn it, it is important to know how SQL is used in Access.

Because the queries you create use SQL behind the scenes, you can edit existing queries by modifying their SQL statements directly. You do this by choosing the View | SQL View menu item when in the datasheet or Design view. View | Design View returns you to that view.

Using SQL as a Record Source

A common use for SQL statements is in place of a table or query as the record source for a form or a table. This is useful when creating a special one-off report that needs some slight modifications to an existing query, or when the desired SQL statements are too simple to bother with creating a query object.

In fact, there are times when Access does this for you. For example, when you use a wizard to create a form or report that combines data from a source more complex than a single table, such as a combination of tables and existing queries, Access creates a SQL statement to place in the form or report's RecordSource property. SQL statements are also generated for the RowSource property when you create a list box or a combo box using a form wizard. You can also use SQL statements as the source for a subquery. A subquery statement can be used in the Field row of a select query to define a field, or in the Criteria row to define selection criteria for a field.

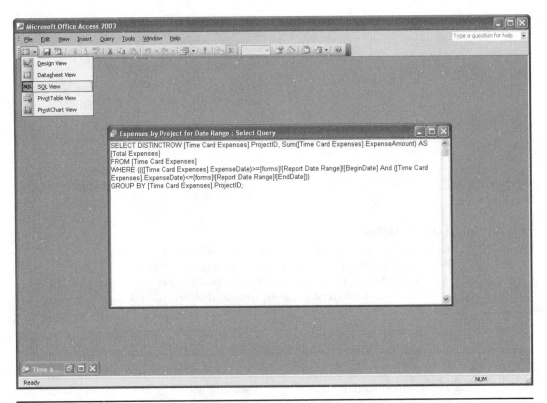

FIGURE 31-3   All queries use SQL behind the scenes to talk to the database engine.

ANSI SQL Query Modes

In Access 2000 and earlier, SQL queries could only be made using the Jet engine's ANSI 89 query syntax. Although this syntax conforms fairly closely to the American National Standards Institute's ANSI 89 SQL specification, there are a few differences, especially with the wildcard syntax, that keep it from being fully ANSI 89 compatible. Access 2002 and later provide a new ANSI SQL mode based on the ANSI 92 specification. This mode provides close compatibility with the ANSI 92 standard used by SQL Server, and updates the wildcard syntax to conform to SQL standards.

By default, Access databases are created using ANSI 89 mode. You may want to consider changing to the new syntax if you want to take advantage of features specific to ANSI 92. These include the ability to use the LIMIT TO clause to limit the number of rows returned by a query, or to use wildcard syntax that is the same as that used by MS SQL Server if you think you may need to upgrade your database to an Access project. If you do change to ANSI 92, however, your queries may not be able to run correctly if you change the database type to Access 2000 or Access 97. It is best to make a decision on which mode to use before creating any queries, because changing in the middle of database development is sure to lead to errors.

> To change the ANSI SQL mode to ANSI 92 for a database, choose the Tools | Options menu, and click on the Tables/Queries tab. Then check one or both of the SQL Server Compatible Syntax check boxes to set the compatibility mode for the current database and for new databases.

SQL-Specific Queries

Some queries can't be created in the design grid. These queries, called SQL-specific queries, can only be created by entering the SQL code directly.

Union Queries

A union query combines the fields from two or more tables into a single field of the query's result. Union queries are useful as a source for a make-table query, when you want to generate a new table based on information in similar but different tables. For example, the following union query

```
SELECT Name, City, State from Customers
UNION
SELECT Name, City, State from Suppliers
```

results in a list of all customers and suppliers, along with their locations.

Data Definition Queries

Data definition queries are useful for performing operations on tables directly. You can create, delete (drop), or alter tables using SQL syntax as an alternative to using the objects in the Database window. For example, you could use a DROP TABLE command to delete an old archive table programmatically or from a form.

```
DROP TABLE Archive_1996
```

Forms and Reports

Tables and queries, discussed in the previous two chapters, are the building blocks of a database. There are, however, other objects that help you get the most out of it. Access provides two additional objects—forms and reports—that can be used to make a database more accessible. When used together, these objects turn a plain database into a database application.

While it is possible to run queries directly in Access, forms make things a lot easier on the end user. For instance, instead of having to run a data entry query over and over to insert records into a table, a form can prompt for all of the necessary information, validate the entered data and prompt for corrections, create or update a record in the table when data entry is complete, and then automatically start over, prompting the user for the next record.

Reports, on the other hand, are used simply for data presentation. Reports produce data in a form suitable for printing. Reports often display statistical information from a query, such as the sum of all values in a column, or the number of records in a table.

Although forms and reports may be quite different in terms of purpose, they function in much the same way in Access. They both bind to a table or a query as a data source, they both utilize layout elements for presentation, and they both use the same Design view editor.

NOTE   *There is actually a third object that can be used for data entry and display—the data access page. Data access pages are web pages that are bound to an Access data source that can be used across an intranet or even the Internet. More information about generating data access pages as well as web pages from other Office applications can be found in Chapter 39.*

Forms

Access forms are database objects used to enter or display data. Unlike queries, forms include a visual component as well: they display data in a formatted dialog box on the screen in a manner convenient for data entry or retrieval, along with other relevant information and instructions if the form designer wants to add them.

Most forms have a record source—that is, a table or query used as the source of data. Depending on the type of form, a single record or multiple records may be used to populate data field controls. In addition to the data from the source, forms often contain titles, descriptive text, labels, and graphical elements such as lines and rectangles. If it will make it easier for users to understand the form, you can make them as fancy as you want.

Although most forms are bound to a data source, there are other types as well. Switchboard forms are used to provide menus that direct users to the form that they want to use. As such, they are the glue that holds a database application together. Switchboard forms and database application design are described in more detail in Chapter 33. Custom dialog forms can also be created. These forms are also not data bound, but instead pop up to prompt the user for input—say, to prompt for criteria to use for generating a query or report.

Anatomy of a Form

Forms serve two roles in Access—an interactive role as well as a printed role. When used in Form view, a form allows a record or group of records to be inserted into a database or modified. However, forms are also useful for printing formatted data. A form can be used to print a table or a collection of formatted records with headers and footers.

Forms may contain from one to five sections. Each form has a Detail section, which is where the data from the record or query is presented. In addition, a form may have header and footer sections for the page as well as a header and footer section for the form. While text and controls can appear in any of the sections, they become important for formatting when you print a form. These sections are added to the form in header/footer pairs, by checking the Page Header/Footer and Form Header/Footer menu items on the Insert menu. Each of these sections is displayed in order from top to bottom when enabled, as shown in Figure 32-1.

Forms may contain as many as five sections:

- **Form Header**   This section displays information that remains the same for every record. For this reason, it is often used to display column headings on a tabular form. The form header appears at the top of a page in Form view. When a multipage form is printed, the form header will only be printed at the top of the first page.

- **Page Header**   This section differs from the form header in two significant ways. It isn't visible at all in Form view. However, when the form is printed, the page header is displayed at the top of every page.

- **Detail**   The Detail section contains the controls that display data and allow data entry. Depending on the type of form, the detail section may display fields for one record, or for many.

- **Page Footer**   Like page headers, page footers only appear in printed forms, at the bottom of each page. This section typically contains date/time stamps, or page numbers.

- **Form Footer**   This section displays information that is the same for every page; this is a good place to put instructions for using the form, or command buttons linking to other forms. A form footer appears at the bottom of the page in Form view and after the last Detail section when it is printed.

Creating Forms

As with the other Access database objects, forms can be created in several ways. They can be created directly in Design view, or, more likely, with one of the wizards.

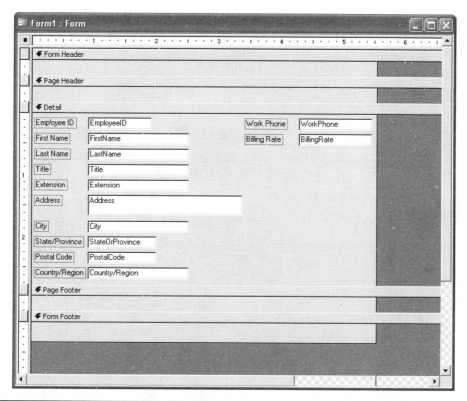

FIGURE 32-1   Each form has a Detail section, and may also contain page and form headers and footers.

Using the Form Wizard

The most common way to generate a form in Access is by using the Form wizard. If you are making a form that will be used to update records in a single table, or in more than one related table, the Form wizard can generate forms and subforms that can either be used right away or customized further in Design view. Follow these steps to create a form using the Form wizard. You can click Finish any time it is enabled in the wizard to accept the defaults for the remaining options.

1. Open the database window, and select the Form category from the object list on the left.

2. Click the New button on the toolbar, and choose Form Wizard from the New Form dialog. If you like, you can also choose a table or query to use as the data source in this dialog. Click OK when you are done.

3. In the Form Wizard dialog box, choose a table or query for a data source (if you didn't already choose one in step 2).

4. From the table or query in the Available Fields column, choose the fields that you want to include in the form, and use the arrow buttons to move them to the Selected Fields column.

5. Repeat steps 3 and 4 if you want to add data from additional tables. Click Next when all the fields you want on the form are shown in the Selected Fields column.

6. If you have chosen more than one table or query for the form, choose one to use as the main data source in the table. Then choose whether to display the other data sources as subforms or as linked forms (more on this in "Linked Forms and Subforms," later in the chapter). Click Next.

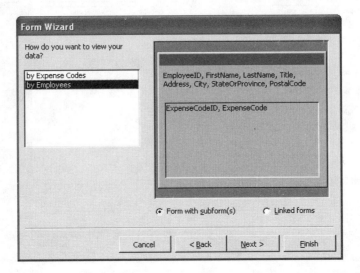

7. Choose a style for the form. You can choose from several included styles, each with its own look for the background image, fonts, and colors. Click Next.

8. Choose a title for the form (and linked forms and subforms, if any).

9. Choose whether to open the form immediately after it is created, or go directly to Design view for further editing. Then click Finish to generate the form.

TIP *If you don't like any of the form styles provided with Access, you aren't stuck with them. After you change the style to suit your tastes in the Design view, choose Format | AutoFormat from the menu. You can then click the Customize button and choose either to create a new AutoFormat based on the changes or update the selected AutoFormat.*

Using an AutoForm Wizard

The AutoForm wizards are sometimes useful as a shortcut to the more general Form wizard. If you know the format of the form, and want to use all of the fields of a query or table, you can use the AutoForm wizard to automatically generate a form.

To create a form using an AutoForm wizard, open the New Form dialog as described in steps 1 and 2 for the Form wizard. Choose one of the following AutoForm wizards. As you select them, the image on the left side of the New Form dialog box shows a small representation of what the form will look like.

- **AutoForm: Columnar**   In this type of form, all of the fields are displayed on a separate line, with a label on the left. This type of form is appropriate when the form is to update or display a single record at a time.

- **AutoForm: Tabular**   The tabular form lists each field on the same horizontal line, with a label displayed above the field. This type of form is useful for displaying multiple records at a time.

- **AutoForm: Datasheet**   This type of form is very similar to a tabular form. The biggest difference is that the default view is the datasheet view (much like when opening a query or table directly), along with fewer display property settings.

- **AutoForm: PivotTable**   This opens the form in PivotTable view—convenient when the source of data is a PivotTable. Drag the fields that you want from the list to use as rows and columns in the PivotTable.

- **AutoForm: PivotChart**   Opens the form in PivotChart view. Choose the fields that you want to use in the PivotChart by dragging them to one of the labeled spots on the form.

NOTE   *When you create a form using an AutoForm wizard, Access automatically uses the last format chosen, either in the Form wizard or the AutoFormat dialog box.*

Creating Forms in Design View

Creating a form from scratch using Design view can be time consuming, especially when you haven't created many before. For this reason, you are usually better off starting with one of the wizards and then customizing it in Design view. However, if none of the wizard form styles appeals to you, Design view can be used from the start.

To create the form, start off in the same way as you would in a wizard. Open the database window, select the Forms category, and click the New button on the toolbar. In the New Form dialog box, choose a table or query to use for the data source, and make sure Design view is selected in the list. Then click OK.

If you forget to choose a data source in the New Form dialog box when creating a Design view form, you can still set it. Use the form selector—the box in the upper-left corner, at the junction of the two rulers—either by double-clicking it or by selecting it and choosing Properties from the View menu. Click the Data tab, and choose the table or query you want for the Record Source property, as shown in Figure 32-2.

While you are in the Form properties dialog, there are a number of other important properties that you can set:

- **Filter**   You can specify a SQL filter to limit the number of records displayed in the form. For example, you may want to limit the form to editing records in a date range. However, a better way to apply filters is to create a query and then use it as the record source for the form. See Chapter 31 for more information about queries.

- **Order By**   Enter a field to sort the records by. Again, this could also be part of a query used as a record source.

- **Caption**   Ordinarily, the name of the form is displayed at the top of the window in Form view. You can set a custom title to display at the top of the form window instead by setting this field.

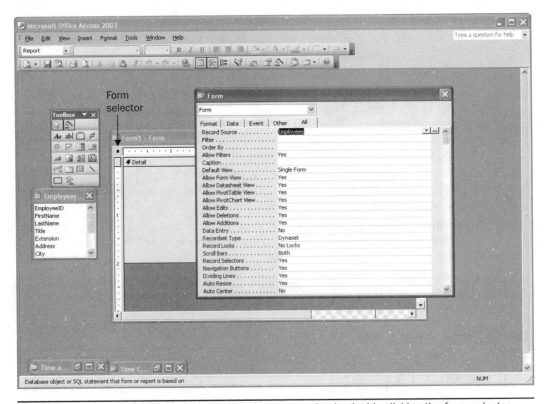

FIGURE 32-2   Set the record source and other form properties by double-clicking the form selector.

- **Default View**   You can set the default way that records are displayed. Choices are Single Form, Continuous Forms, Datasheet, PivotTable, and PivotChart. The two most important choices here are Single Form, to display one record at a time, or Continuous Forms, to display all records retrieved from the record source in the details view. When you create a form in the wizard, columnar format uses Single Form view and tabular uses the Continuous Forms view.

- **Data Entry**   Set this property to Yes, which restricts the form to only entering new data. When you do this, the form will not display any existing records, but only ones that are entered on the form.

- **Allow Edits, Allow Deletions, and Allow Additions**   These options allow you to restrict the usage of the form. Set all of these to No to make the form read only, making it usable for data retrieval but not data entry.

Adding fields to the Details window in Design view is a snap. When you define a record source for a form, a Field List window is displayed that lists the fields returned by the table or query. (If it is not visible, you can show it using the View | Field List menu.)

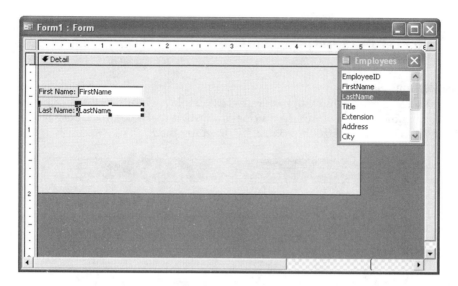

The easiest way to add a field to the form is to drag it from the field list. When you do this, Access automatically adds a text box and a label for the field.

TIP   *When you select a control other than a text box in the toolbox, that type of control will be created when you drag a field from the field list into the form, rather than a text box.*

Customizing Forms

As with most Access objects, creating a form is only the first step. Access provides a wide array of customization options in Design view that can help you make the form more powerful and easier to use.

The individual elements that are added to a form are called *controls*. Controls include labels, text boxes, command buttons, images, tab controls, and more, but they can be divided into two basic types—bound and unbound.

Bound controls are tied to a specific field in the database. This means that the data in that field is displayed in the control, and when the data is entered, it is saved back to that field in the database. When you drag a control from the field list, it is automatically bound to that particular field. However, it is possible to bind a control to a different field by selecting it in Design view and choosing Properties from the View menu. Click on the Data tab and choose a field to use for the Control Source property. Controls that can be bound to a field include text boxes, toggle buttons, option buttons, check boxes, combo boxes, and list boxes.

Unbound controls are the static elements on a form. They include labels, images, option groups, command buttons, tab controls, and others. Unbound controls cannot be associated with a field, and as such they don't change.

The toolbox is indispensable when it comes to working with controls. This box, which can also be docked as a toolbar, contains buttons for each of the controls that you can add to a form. Controls can be created from the toolbox in two different ways. The first way is to select a control and then click in the form where you want it. When you add a control using this method, you must set the control source yourself in the control property sheet.

The second way to add a control using the toolbox is to select the button for the control that you want and drag a field from the field list. Controls added this way are automatically bound to the field.

Positioning Controls

When you select a control in Design view, Access displays eight handles around the outside of it. These handles not only provide a visual indication that a control is selected, but can also be used to move or resize the control by dragging them.

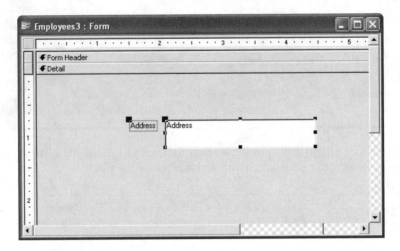

The handle on the upper-left corner of the control is larger than the rest. This handle can be used to reposition the control in the form. When you drag this handle, the mouse pointer, shown as a hand with a pointing finger, allows you to position the control where you want.

TIP *If the control has a label, as most do by default, dragging the control or the label using the upper-left corner handle will move it independently. If you want to move both together, you can move the mouse pointer over the border of either the control or the label instead of over a handle. When the mouse pointer changes to a hand, you can drag both the control and its label at the same time.*

Along with simple positioning, Access allows you to group controls together and align them relative to one another. This makes it much easier to get precise alignment of controls than you can get just by dragging.

To align controls relative to one another, you need to select them. You can select multiple controls by dragging a rectangle around them. Another way to select exactly the controls you want is to click on each one while holding the SHIFT key.

When you have selected the controls you wish to align, use the Format | Align menu to set their alignment. Controls will be aligned relative to the control farthest in that direction. For instance, if you are aligning controls to the right, the control that is already farthest to the right is used as the baseline control to move all of the others.

If controls are arranged in a column or row, you may want to make sure that they are spaced evenly. The Format menu contains Horizontal and Vertical spacing options for this purpose. The Make Equal option will force all of the controls to be spaced evenly in that direction. You can also use the Increase and Decrease options to tweak the spacing.

Once you have controls aligned, you may want to make sure they stay that way. Grouping allows controls to be moved as a group, maintaining any alignment relative to each other. Choose Format | Group to do this. The Ungroup menu item can be used to split the group into its component controls if you later need to position them independently.

Setting Control Properties

As mentioned in the previous section, controls have their own property sheets that allow you to set properties unique to each one. To open the property sheet for the control, select it and choose Properties from the View menu. Click the All tab to see all properties, or use one of the other tabs to organize properties by category. While the properties available vary depending on the control type, the following options are useful for many data bound controls:

- **Control Source**   Specify the field to use as the data source for the control.
- **Format**   Specify a format for appropriate fields, such as dates and numeric fields.
- **Display When**   You can choose whether a control should be displayed in Screen only, Print only, or Always.
- **Locked**   When this is set to Yes, the field may not be edited.

TIP   *The Format tab of the control property sheet contains many properties pertaining to the style of the control, including the foreground color, background color, border styles, and fonts. These properties are useful for giving controls and text a distinctive look to draw attention to them.*

Linked Forms and Subforms

When you create a form using the wizard, you can choose more than one related table or query to use in the form. When a table has a one-to-many relationship with the second table, there may be more than one record in the second table that matches the query. Access forms allow you to deal with this in two ways—with a linked form or a subform.

Linked forms are tied to the main form using a command button. When you generate a linked form using the wizard, Access creates a VBA procedure to link it to a command button on the parent form. When you click the command button, the form is automatically launched filled with records that match the primary key. For example, a table of employees may have a one-to-many relationship with an expense account table, with each employee having many possible expenses. You can create a main form that shows data from the employee table, with a linked form for expenses. When running the form, clicking the Command button opens the subform in another window, as shown in this example:

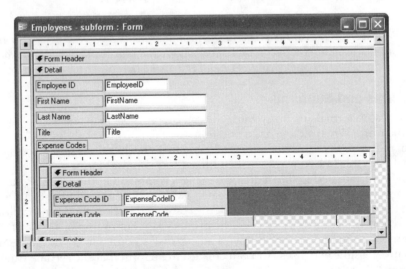

The other way multiple tables are used in a form is with a *subform*. A subform is nested directly on a main form. Subforms are very useful when it comes to displaying data with a one-to-many relationship. The main form contains the data from the "one" side of the relationship, and the subform contains data from the "many" side. Using a subform or a linked form is mostly a matter of choice, but there are some guidelines you may want to keep in mind. If a secondary table contains a lot of fields, or contains information that will not be accessed frequently, using a linked form may leave your main form less cluttered and easier to understand.

Access allows any number of subforms linked directly from the main form. In addition, subforms themselves may have their own subforms. Access allows subforms to be nested up to seven levels deep.

When you create a form and subform using the Form wizard, Access automatically generates the control source SQL statement that is necessary to populate the control based on the parent form. You can also create a subform in Design view, by clicking the Subform/Subreport button in the toolbox and clicking where you want to position the subform. Access helps out when you add a subform in this manner as well. It activates a wizard that walks you through choosing a data source for the subform, and also lets you choose how to link it to the main form.

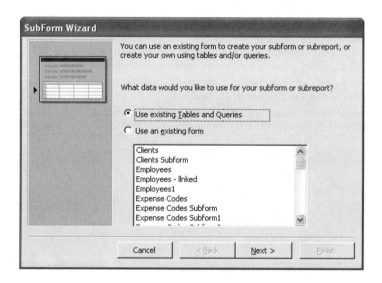

Reports

In a lot of respects, reports and forms are very similar. Both allow you to set layout for bound and unbound controls, add descriptive text, and set formatting styles, and both use a record source of either a table or a query as the source of data to display.

Even with these similarities, they serve different roles. Although forms can be used for printing records, they are usually used as a means for data entry and retrieval, and to link to other forms and reports when building a database application. Reports, on the other hand, are strictly for presentation. Reports can be used for a variety of printed needs, including mailing labels, charts, and data totals and summaries.

Report Layout

Like forms, reports are laid out in horizontal sections, with the sections always appearing in the same order, as shown in Figure 32-3. Like forms, there are header and footer sections that display at different times, as well as a Detail section to display the data from the record source. If the record source returns multiple records, the Detail section is repeated for each of them.

The following is a list of the report headers and what they are used for.

- **Report Header/Footer**   These sections are displayed once on the report. The report header appears at the top of the first page of the report, while the report footer appears after the last record displayed. Use these sections to display titles, logos, and dates.

- **Page Header/Footer** These sections appear on every page in the report. The page header appears at the top of the page and the footer at the bottom. Use these fields to display such things as column headings, page numbers, or dates.

- **Detail** The Detail section is the main body of the report. This section is repeated once for each record displayed in the report.

- **Group Header/Footer** These sections are unique to reports. They allow you to organize records in a report into groups. For instance, you could have a report listing employee records grouped by department, or a sales report grouped by region. The group header and footer sections are shown in design mode according to the field name. For instance, a report grouped by a field named *ProductID* could have a header labeled *ProductID Header* and a footer labeled *ProductID Footer*. These headers and footers allow you to add titles or other descriptive information for a group.

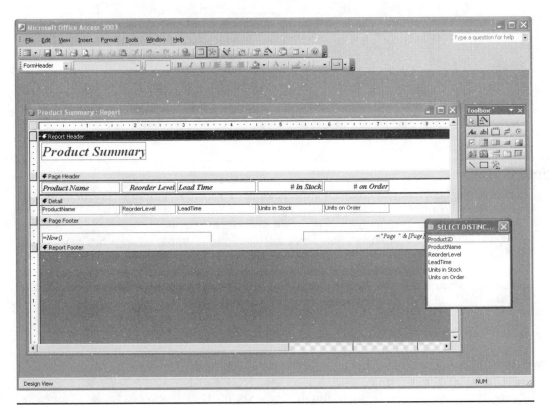

FIGURE 32-3 Reports, like forms, can contain header and footer sections, as well as data displayed in the Detail section.

Creating Reports

Reports, like forms, can be created in several different ways depending on your needs. Access provides a Report wizard, two AutoFormat Report wizards, and wizards for creating chart reports and mailing labels.

Using the Report Wizard

As with the Form wizard, the Report wizard is the quickest and easiest way to create reports. Follow these steps to create a report using this wizard. You can click Finish any time it is enabled in the wizard to accept the defaults for the remaining options.

1. Open the database window, and select the Reports category from the object list on the left.

2. Click the New button on the toolbar, and choose Report Wizard from the New Report dialog box. If you like, you can also choose a table or query to use as the record source in this dialog box. Click OK when you are done.

3. In the Report Wizard dialog box, choose a table or query for a data source (if you didn't already choose one in step 2).

4. Choose the fields from the table or query in the Available Fields column that you want to include in the report, and use the arrow buttons to move them to the Selected Fields column.

5. Repeat steps 3 and 4 if you want to add fields from more than one table or query. Click Next when you are done choosing fields.

6. If you have chosen more than one table or query, choose one as the main section. This is typically the table on the "one" side of a one-to-many relationship. Click Next when ready.

7. If you want to add a grouping field, choose one or more to add. Use the up and down arrows to adjust priority of the group nesting. (There is more information about grouping fields in the later section "Grouping and Sorting Records.") Click Next.

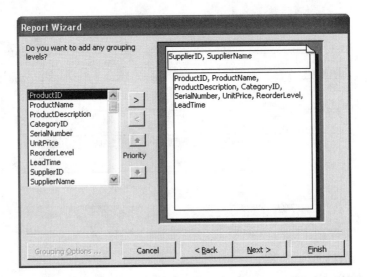

8. If you have chosen a second table, choose a sort order for detail records.

9. Choose a layout for the report. Layouts include Stepped, Block, Outline, and Align. A representation of the layout is displayed on the left side of the dialog. You can also choose Portrait or Landscape layout on this page. Click Next.

10. Choose a style for the report. The provided styles give you several options that generate professional-looking reports.

11. Finally, choose a name for the report, and select whether to edit it right away in Design view, or run it. Click Finish to exit the wizard.

Other Report Wizards

While the Report wizard is a general-purpose report generator, there are several other wizard options available that can quickly generate reports that meet a specific predefined format. However, because of the large amount of customization that reports typically require, they are generally not quite as useful as their form counterparts.

To create a report using one of the other wizards, open the New Report dialog box as described in steps 1 and 2 for the Report wizard. As you select them, the image on the left side of the New Report dialog box shows a small representation of what the report will look like. Choose one of the following options.

- **AutoReport: Columnar** Each field of a record appears on a separate line, with a label to the left.

- **AutoReport: Tabular** A record is displayed on a single line, with a header used to display column titles.

- **Chart Wizard**   This option creates a report with a chart. Because reports often contain summary or statistical information, charts are useful for conveying that information.

- **Label Wizard**   This wizard generates pages of mailing labels. A wide variety of label products from many manufacturers are included.

Grouping and Sorting Records

One of the most useful capabilities when building Access reports is the ability to group records. You may group records by the values in one (or more) fields of the record source. For example, if you are generating a sales report, you might want to group records according to some measure of time, say a week or a month. When grouping fields, Access adds header and footer sections to the report for the group. This gives you the opportunity to specify custom titles for the group to make your report more readable.

Access also allows you to specify fields to sort by. Sorting fields is similar to grouping fields. However, there is no header or footer section for them. Use grouping fields for major categories that you want to see broken out in the report, and sorting fields for those inside a group.

You can have up to ten nested sorting and grouping levels in a report, which is plenty for almost any conceivable circumstance. Most reports will contain no more than three. To specify grouping and sorting fields in a report, follow these steps:

1. Open the report in Design view.

2. Click the Sorting and Grouping button on the toolbar to open the Sorting and Grouping dialog box.

3. In the first available Field/Expression entry, choose a field to group or sort by.

4. Under the Sort Order column, choose whether to sort this field Ascending or Descending.

5. If this is a grouping field, set either the Group Header, Group Footer, or both properties to Yes. The grouping icon will show to the left of the field in the Field/ Expression column.

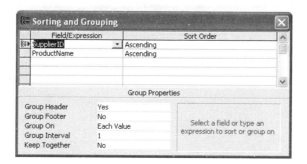

6. Choose a value for the Group On field. If it is a numeric or date field, you can choose to group based on each unique value, or an interval. If it is a text field, you can choose to group by unique values as well as by a prefix.

7. Choose an interval, if grouping by an interval or a prefix. For a prefix, enter the number of characters to use to obtain the substring for grouping.

8. In the Keep Together field, you can choose to keep all of the records in a group on the same page. Set this to No if you don't want a new page generated for each group.

Calculating Running Sums

It is often useful to be able to have a report perform some calculation on a data field that it is reporting. You can use expressions in the Control Source property for a field, but Access also provides a built-in way to have a text box field provide a calculation unique to reports— a running sum over the course of a report or a report group.

To set a text box field to calculate a running sum, follow these steps in Design view:

1. Click the Text Box button on the toolbox.

2. Click in the report where you want to place the field. If you put it in the Detail section, it will calculate a running sum that increases with every record. You can also put it in a group header or footer section to have the sum displayed only with each group of records.

3. Open the property sheet for the text box by selecting it and clicking the Properties button on the toolbar.

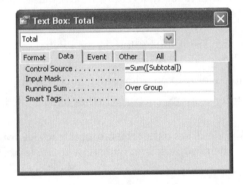

4. In the Control Source property, enter an expression or choose a field that contains the value that you want to keep a running sum.

5. In the Running Sum property, choose how the sum should behave. Over All will increase the sum over the course of the entire report. Over Group will cause the sum to reset to zero at the start of each new group, allowing summations to be done at a group level.

Building a Database Application

The database objects discussed in the previous chapters—tables, queries, forms, and reports—really start to shine when you put them all together. In Access parlance, this is known as a database application.

An Access database application may contain some or all of the types of database objects discussed so far, including tables and data, queries for accessing the data, and forms and reports for presenting information to the user. In addition to those objects, an application usually contains one or more switchboard forms that tie everything together, allowing you to navigate to the various forms and reports without the need to run them directly from the database window.

Planning an application can take some thought. One of your goals should be to make sure that all of the objects that you include in the application relate to a common purpose. While you may at first be tempted to create a single database application to serve your small business, that application is likely to grow unwieldy as you add to it if it has many unrelated components. It is often better to build a database around a single need, such as inventory management, and then build the application to support it.

Using a Database Application Wizard

Access provides database application wizards that take a lot of the guesswork out of designing an application. Assuming that your database falls into one of the application categories, these wizards are without a doubt the easiest way to get started creating an application. Even when the wizard isn't an exact fit for the type of application you want, it's still often easier to modify one of the existing ones to suit your purposes than it is to start from nothing.

In keeping with Access's role as a small solutions database, the prepackaged templates are geared primarily for creating applications for small business use. Many of the common small business database needs are covered, including asset tracking, inventory control, contact management, and time and billing.

To create an application from a template, choose File | New to open the New File task pane. Choose the On My Computer link to open the Templates dialog box, shown in Figure 33-1. Click the Databases tab to show a list of templates on your computer.

After you choose a wizard, Access prompts you for a filename and then walks through a series of windows prompting you for information to customize and personalize the application.

Templates Home Page

If the application templates provided with Access aren't quite what you want, don't automatically resign yourself to creating a database application from scratch. Microsoft's Templates home page is another source for templates that you can use as a starting point for your application. You can find templates for applications dealing with inventory management, resource scheduling, or even personal use applications for such tasks as managing your workout or maintaining your DVD collection.

You can access the Templates home page by browsing to http://office.microsoft.com and choosing Template Gallery. Entering **Access** in the search box will limit the templates displayed to those for Access.

You can navigate directly to the Templates home page from the New File task pane as well. Open the task pane by choosing New from the File menu. From here, you can search

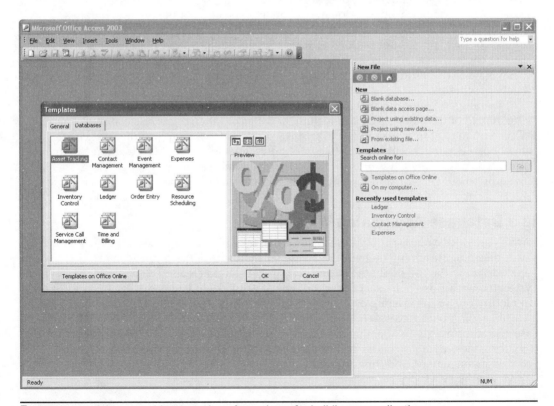

FIGURE 33-1   Access provides a number of templates for building an application.

for a template by entering your criteria in the Search Office Online box, or click the Templates home page link to open the home page in your browser.

Building Applications from Scratch

If you don't want to use any of the existing templates as a starting point for your application, it's perfectly possible to build your own. Building a database application is simply a matter of creating the various tables, queries, forms, and reports, and then linking them all together using switchboards. Information about creating the various building block objects is discussed in more detail in the following chapters: Chapter 30 for tables, Chapter 31 for queries, and Chapter 32 for forms and reports.

Switchboards

In Chapter 32 we presented an overview of the Form object and mentioned that there was another type of form supported in Access that makes it possible to build an application. This form type is called a *switchboard*, so named because like an old-fashioned telephone switchboard, it links one form to another form or a report. The switchboard also serves as the entry point menu for your application, providing links to other switchboards, forms, and reports.

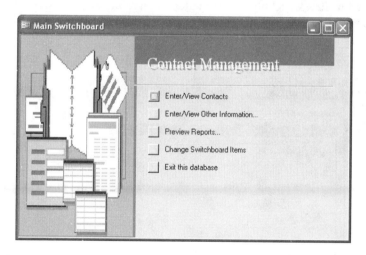

No matter how many separate menus your application needs, you really only need one switchboard form object. An Access utility called the Switchboard Manager allows you to create additional switchboards, specify the menu items on each switchboard, and choose a default switchboard.

TIP   *When a database is created using a database wizard, Main Switchboard is set as the default switchboard. The default switchboard is the one that is run by Access when you first load the database, which makes it the entry point for your application. If you'd rather use a different form for the default switchboard, select it in the Switchboard Manager and click the Make Default button.*

The Switchboard Manager

Although a switchboard is a form object, it isn't built in the Form design view. The menu items on a switchboard serve as the record source for a switchboard form, just as a table or query serve as the record source for other forms. In fact, switchboard menu items are stored in a table. Access creates a special table named Switchboard Items that contains a record for every switchboard item. The switchboard form queries this table to display the proper menu items for the current switchboard.

You don't even have to create the form itself in Design view or by using a wizard. In fact, it's preferable not to. Access automatically creates a switchboard for every database wizard. All you have to do is modify it to suit your needs. In the case of databases built from scratch, the switchboard form is automatically generated by Access whenever you create a switchboard in the Switchboard Manager.

Follow these steps to create a switchboard in the Switchboard Manager, whether or not the database contains existing switchboards.

1. Open the database.

2. Open the Switchboard Manager by choosing Tool | Database Utilities | Switchboard Manager. If no switchboard form exists in the database, Access will prompt you to create one. You must choose Yes to continue.

3. If this is the first switchboard, the Switchboard Manager shows the Main Switchboard entry, with (Default) specified after it. Click Edit to continue. If the database has existing switchboards, click New and enter a descriptive name for the new switchboard. Then click OK.

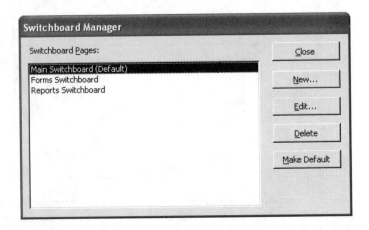

CAUTION   *Once Access creates a switchboard, it will never allow you to delete the default switchboard. However, it does let you delete the switchboard form itself. Be careful not to do this! Once the form is deleted, it won't automatically be re-created when you run the Switchboard Manager. Your best bet in this circumstance is to create a new blank database, build a switchboard form in it, and copy and paste it to your application to ensure that it is wired properly to run as a switchboard.*

Once your database has a switchboard form and at least one switchboard in the manager, the next step is to add items to the switchboard to make it functional:

1. Open the database.
2. Open the Switchboard Manager by choosing Tools | Database Utilities | Switchboard Manager.
3. Choose the switchboard that you want to add items to, and then click the Edit button to open the Edit Switchboard Page dialog box.
4. Click New to add a new item to the switchboard.
5. Enter the text for the item. This is the text that will be displayed for the form item when the switchboard is run.
6. Choose a command for the item using the Command drop-down list. You can choose from the following.

   - **Go to Switchboard**   Make another switchboard the destination.
   - **Open Form in Add Mode**   Open a form in data entry mode so that new records can be added.
   - **Open Form in Edit Mode**   Open a form for editing existing records.
   - **Open Report**   Run a report.
   - **Design Application**   Run the Switchboard Manager.
   - **Exit Application**   Close the current database.
   - **Run Macro/Run Code**   Execute a macro or VBA code. See Part IX for information on creating macros and VBA code.

7. Depending on the command you choose, the Edit Switchboard dialog box may show another combo box where you can choose the item to open. For example, if you choose Go to Switchboard for your command, this box will let you choose from a list of switchboards in the application. Choose the item you want and click OK.
8. Repeat steps 4 through 7 to add the rest of the items to your database.

The Edit Switchboard Page is useful for more than just creating new switchboard items. You can use the Move Up, Move Down, Edit, and Delete buttons with an existing switchboard to further customize it.

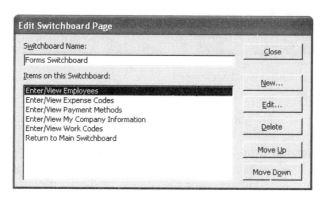

A switchboard form may be edited in Design view, just like any other form. You do, however, need to use some caution. Because the switchboard form is autogenerated, Access assumes that the controls for making the form work are going to be there. When you customize the switchboard form, it is a good idea to limit your modifications of the controls to changing their styles and rearranging them on the screen (such as to create two columns). Adding other design elements such as labels and graphical style elements to the form is perfectly acceptable as well.

Customizing the User Interface

One of the hallmarks of a good database application is an uncluttered, easy-to-follow user interface. To this end, Access allows additional customization of your forms and reports to make your application easier to use and more secure by preventing users from doing things you don't want them to do. You can add custom menus and toolbars, show or hide title bar buttons, and more.

Adding Custom Menus and Toolbars

Like other Office applications, Access allows you to create custom menus and toolbars. Because Access is also an application development environment, you can harness this power for use in your applications by creating menus and toolbars that display when the application is run, or even when a specific form or report is open.

Setting Startup Options

Access gives you the ability to lock down your application so that users can't get to aspects of Access that you don't want them to get to. The Startup dialog box lets you decide how much of a customized environment you want application users to see.

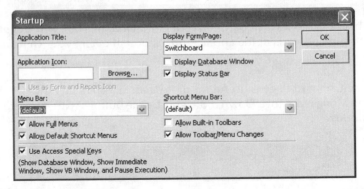

Open the Startup dialog box by choosing Tools | Startup. The following settings are available:

- **Application Title**   Choose a title for your application. This will replace Microsoft Office in the application title bar.
- **Application Icon**   This option lets you choose a custom icon for the application. This icon will be displayed instead of the Access icon. Check the Use as Form and Report Icon to use this icon when displaying open or minimized forms and reports.

- **Menu Bar**   If you create a custom menu bar (using Tools | Customize), you can choose it as the menu bar to display when your application runs.

- **Allow Full Menus**   Uncheck this option to prevent the standard Access menus from appearing when the application is run.

- **Allow Default Shortcut Menus**   Uncheck this to prevent the default Access shortcut menu from displaying. You can add custom shortcut menus instead.

- **Use Access Special Keys**   Uncheck to prevent users from using the special keys to open various database design windows.

- **Display Form/Page**   Choose a default form to display when the application opens. In most cases this will be a switchboard, but you could use it to display a splash screen style form before going to the switchboard.

- **Display Database Window**   Uncheck this option to keep the database window from showing, ensuring that the only way to access objects is through your interface.

- **Display Status Bar**   Uncheck to hide the status bar.

- **Shortcut Menu Bar**   You can choose a custom shortcut menu if you like.

- **Allow Built-in Toolbars**   Uncheck to prevent standard Access toolbars from being displayed.

- **Allow Tool/Menu Changes**   Uncheck to prevent changes to the menus.

In order to provide the most customized environment, clear all of the check boxes in this dialog box and add custom menus and toolbars. Most of these settings don't take effect right away, so be sure to close and reopen your database to see the changes.

Locking a Database

Even with all of the customization options and the ability to hide the Access menus and toolbars, savvy Access users will still be able to get into your database. Holding the SHIFT key down when opening a database bypasses the startup options and allows full access to all of the customization options. If you need to prevent all user-level access, your best bet is to set user-level security.

User-level security allows you to create different levels of access for your database and objects. When the database is opened, users must enter their username and password. Access then compares this to information stored in its workgroup information file, and opens the database with the appropriate permissions.

Creating user-level security for a database can be difficult to understand at first, but the User-Level Security Wizard (shown in Figure 33-2) helps by allowing you to create a workgroup information file with the initial database groups and users, and what they are able to do. Follow these steps to run the wizard:

1. Open the User-Level Security wizard (shown in Figure 33-2) by choosing that option from the Tools | Security menu.

2. If you already have a workgroup information file for the database, you can choose to modify it. Otherwise, create a new one and click Next.

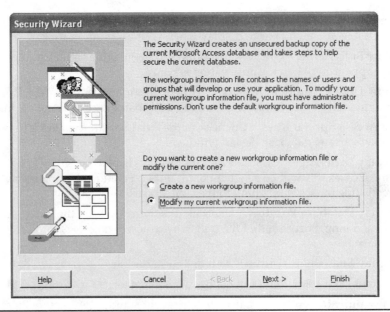

FIGURE 33-2   The User-Level Security wizard greatly simplifies the task of securing your database.

3. A page with a tabbed list of all your database objects is displayed. By default, all objects are checked. If there are any objects you don't want to secure, uncheck them. For the most part, you will leave all of these checked. Click Next to continue.

4. Choose the security groups that you want to include in the database. An Admin group and a Users group are always created. You can check one or more of these options if you want to be able to set multiple levels of security. Click Next when you are ready.

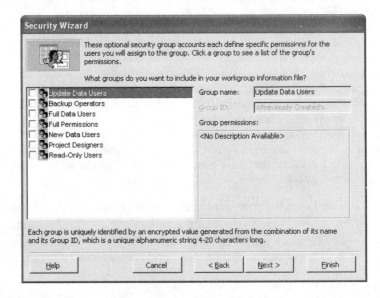

5. On the next page, you can assign some or all permissions to the Users group. For instance, if you want users to be able to modify queries or add data directly to a table, you can first choose the Yes option and then set the specific object permissions you want them to have. Click Next when you are finished setting permissions.

6. The next step is to add or modify users. Click Add New User and enter username and password information for the user. By default, your Windows username is displayed in the list. Set a password for yourself as well. Click Next.

7. Now you can assign users to the appropriate groups, or groups to the appropriate users. In many cases you will have a small number of groups and a large number of users. In this case it's easier to choose Select a Group and assign users to the group, because you can see at a glance which users belong to the group. Click Next.

8. Finally, choose a name for the database backup. Access creates an unsecured backup of your database so that you can get back into it if you run into any problems with the security. Click Finish.

When the wizard completes, it generates a report listing all users and protected objects, groups, and users, as shown in Figure 33-3. Access will prompt you to save this report in a snapshot (.snp) file that you can refer to later if you need to re-create the workgroup

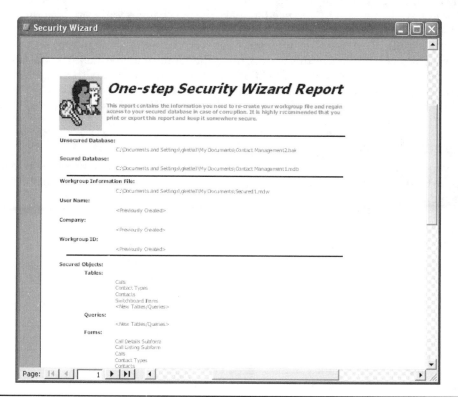

FIGURE 33-3   The Security wizard generates a report containing information that you can use to re-create your workgroup information file if necessary.

information file. The report only shows changes made during the current run through the wizard, so make a new snapshot whenever you make changes.

After you have created a security information file with the wizard, you can create additional groups and assign or remove permissions without having to run the wizard again. You can also change the default permissions that are assigned to any new objects that may be created. Use the User and Group Permissions dialog box to set the permissions each group has. Use the User and Group Accounts dialog box to add new users and assign them to groups. Both dialog boxes are accessible from the Tools | Security menu.

Making an MDE File

Another step you can take to protect your database, as well as make it run faster, is to save it as an MDE file. Saving a database as an MDE file compiles all VBA code and removes editable source code to prevent users from viewing or editing your code. An MDE file also prevents users from modifying forms and reports without the requirement that users log on to the database and without the need for setting and managing user-level security. All other aspects of the database function normally. Saving your Access database as an MDE file prevents database users from using Design view to view or modify forms and reports, and prevents them from importing and creating references to external data.

If you decide to save your database as an MDE file, be sure to keep a copy of your original MDB file as well. That way, if you need to make design changes to the application, you can load the MDB file, make the changes, and save again as an MDE file.

It can be difficult to reconcile differences between data stored in tables when you save a database as an MDE file. For this reason, MDE files are usually best used as the front-end portion of a front-end/back-end application—that is, an application with the tables and data stored in a separate "back-end" database file. The next section describes the process of splitting a database into separate front-end and back-end databases.

Making Data Available

Once you've created the perfect Access application, the next step is to distribute it to the people who need to use it. Access gives you two ways to make a database available to a wide audience: splitting the database into separate front-end and back-end components, and replicating the database.

Linking to External Data

In many cases, a database needs to be used by more than one person simultaneously. One way that Access allows this to be done is to split a database into two parts, a back-end component containing tables and data, and a front-end component containing the forms, reports, and other objects.

In Chapter 29, we discussed the difference between Access projects and databases. Access projects are applications that use a Microsoft SQL Server database as a back end, with the project containing the forms, reports, and other application objects. MDB databases using the Jet engine can make use of a similar capability.

While you could use the File | Get External Data command to open tables stored in another copy of the database, it can become quite messy trying to get this method to work with an existing database. Access comes to the rescue with the Database Splitter.

The Database Splitter is a utility that greatly simplifies the task of splitting a database into separate components. After first making a backup copy of your database, choose the Tools | Database Utilities | Database Splitter menu and follow the instructions. When you are prompted for a location for the back-end database, choose a network location accessible to all of the database's users.

Replicating a Database

It is often not practical to have a single location for a database that all users connect to. If your database users work disconnected from the corporate network, they may need to have their own copy of the database. Replication allows users to add and modify database records and then incrementally update the main database when they connect back to the network.

The items on the Tools | Replication submenu are used to create replicated databases, otherwise known as replicas. When you create one or more replicas, the original copy of the database becomes the Design Master. The Design Master is the only copy of the database that can have design-level changes made to it. Replicas can only add, modify, and delete existing records.

VII PART

Web and Print Layout

CHAPTER 34
Designing Pages and Sites
in FrontPage

CHAPTER 35
Advanced Management
Features and Web Site
Publishing

CHAPTER 36
Creating Publications
in Publisher

CHAPTER 37
Publishing Documents
in Publisher

Designing Pages and Sites in FrontPage

Microsoft FrontPage is a popular program for designing web sites and web pages. Using FrontPage, you are free of having to know HTML and other web languages. You can design an effective web site with a number of interactive features using the graphical interface without any programming. However, if you are into programming, you are free to work directly with HTML in FrontPage as well.

FrontPage 2003 is easier to use and more flexible than previous versions, on both the design and publishing side of things. In this chapter, we'll take a look at designing sites and pages in FrontPage, and in the next chapter, we'll take a look at publishing and management issues.

Creating a New FrontPage Site

A web site is a collection of web pages. When you visit a web site, you click through hyperlinks in order to view different pages on that web site. When you are designing a new web site using FrontPage, you have many decisions to make. You'll need to determine the site's content, how many pages the site will contain, how the pages will lay out and look, and so forth. All of the pages you create and all of the content you use are found in a *site*, and when you publish your new web site, you will publish it as a site.

You can easily create a new web site in FrontPage. FrontPage will set the site up, and if you like, you can use a template to apply certain settings. The following steps show you how to create your site:

1. In FrontPage, click File | New.

2. In the New task pane that appears, you can choose to create a blank, one-page web site, a SharePoint-based team web site (for environments using SharePoint Team Services), or you can choose from web site templates by clicking either Web Package Solutions or More Web Site Templates.

3. For these steps, we are going to create a web site from a template. In the Web Site Templates dialog box, you can choose to create the kind of site you want. Note that you can also choose Empty Web Site. In this case, the template does not apply any formatting—that will all be up to you. Note the location where the new web site will be saved, make changes as necessary, and click OK.

4. Once the web site has been created, it is displayed in FrontPage, as shown here. Notice the folders FrontPage has created for the web site and the default web site pages (if you choose a design template). Also note that the web site is stored on your local computer since it has not been published yet. At this point, you are ready to start working on your web site.

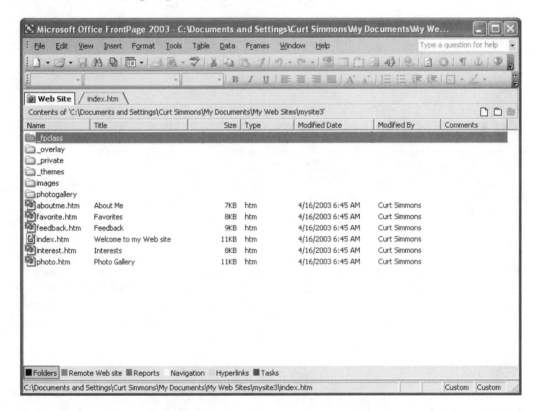

So, those are the basics of creating a web site. The following sections give you some details about setting up that site.

Choosing a Design Template

When you create a new site, you can choose from several site design templates. This is FrontPage's way of helping you create the site. As you noticed in the steps in the previous section, you have the option to choose a design template. So, what are the options available to you? The following bullets give you a quick summary.

- **One Page Web Site**   A new web with a single blank page.
- **Corporate Presence Wizard**   A complex web with dozens of pages that can be converted into a web site for a corporation.
- **Customer Support Web Site**   A web site that includes input forms for customer questions and feedback.
- **Database Interface Wizard**   An online database with input forms to collect data, queries to present data, and forms to enable visitors to edit the database content.
- **Discussion Web Site Wizard**   A wizard that leads you step by step through the process of creating a web site in which visitors can post questions and get answers.
- **Empty Web Site**   A web site without pages.
- **Import Web Site Wizard**   A wizard that leads you through the process of assembling a web site from pages created outside of FrontPage.
- **Personal Web Site**   A four-page web site that works well for sharing your interests.
- **Project Web Site**   A specialized web site template for project managers only.
- **SharePoint Team Site**   An intranet portal with a schedule, a documents library, links, and other office intranet features.

Obviously, some of the template options are specialized for specific purposes. Others, such as the Empty Web or One Page Web, give you a basic web site that you can then customize to meet your needs. As an experiment, you might try creating several web sites for testing purposes in order to get more familiar with the options available to you.

Deciding on a Structure for Your Site

Web sites are designed so that users can navigate between different pages within a site. As a web site designer, you'll mostly focus on creating pages of content. However, your visitors will need to be able to move in a logical and easy manner from page to page. As a general rule, web sites are designed using either a linear page design or a hierarchical page design. Most web sites are organized in some version of a hierarchical structure, but both design strategies can be useful, depending on the kind of presentation you are preparing for visitors. Most often, a linear approach works best only in situations where you want visitors to "tour" your site, such as in the case of showing visitors products and services that you offer. In all other cases, the hierarchical approach works best. When you use a hierarchical approach, you use one or more main pages, with additional subpages linked from those main pages, like the example in Figure 34-1.

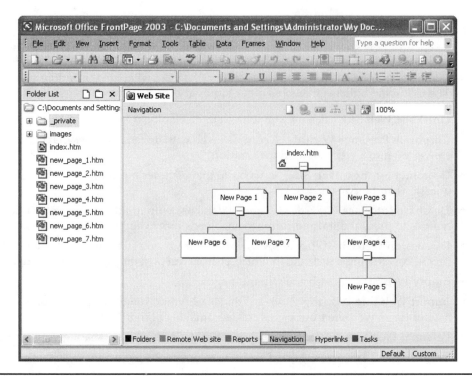

FIGURE 34-1 A hierarchical view

The point to keep in mind here is that you should have some idea about how your site will be structured before you start creating pages within the site. As with most projects, you may wish to sit down with a pencil and paper and sketch the structure of your site before you start the site creation process.

Importing an Existing Web Site

What if you already have a web site that you want to import from the Web so that you can work with it in FrontPage? No problem—FrontPage can help you import the site with a wizard. Using the wizard, you can import an existing web site from the Web, an intranet, or even a folder on your local hard drive or the network. Once you import the site, you can work with it as you would any FrontPage web, organizing it in Navigation view, and adding themes, shared borders, link bars, and so on.

To import files into a new web, follow these steps:

1. Select File | Import. The Import dialog box appears.

2. Click the Add File button to add a file (or selected files) to your site, or the Add Folder button to add one or more folders.

3. In the Open File dialog box, navigate to the file(s) or folder(s) you wish to import. Use SHIFT-click to select more than one file or CTRL-click to select more than one folder. Click the Open button to add selected file(s) or folder(s) to the Import list.

4. Click OK in the Import dialog box to add the files to your site.

To import an existing web site into a FrontPage web, follow these steps:

1. Select File | Import.

2. Click the From Web button. The Import Web Site wizard opens:

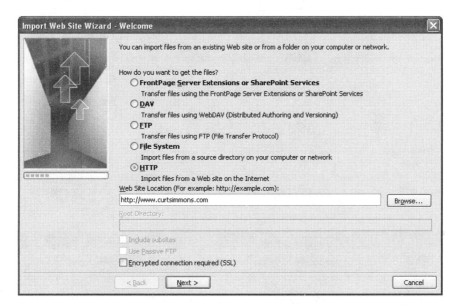

As you can see, you have the option to:

- Transfer from FrontPage Server Extensions or SharePoint Team Services
- Transfer using WebDAV
- Transfer using File Transfer Protocol (FTP)
- Transfer files from a source directory or computer
- Import files from an Internet site

Make a selection, complete the requested information, and click Next.

3. The next screen lets you choose the destination web site (where you will import the files). You can also choose to use Secure Sockets Layer (SSL) if necessary. Click Next.

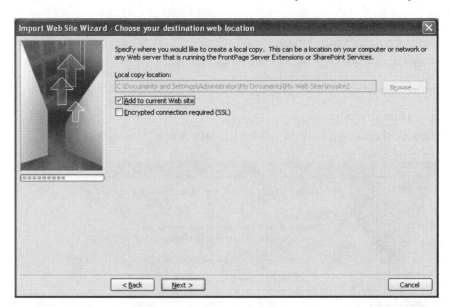

4. In the Set Import Limits window, shown next, choose to import a specified number of home page plus link pages, a maximum number of kilobytes, or only HTML and image files. Click Next.

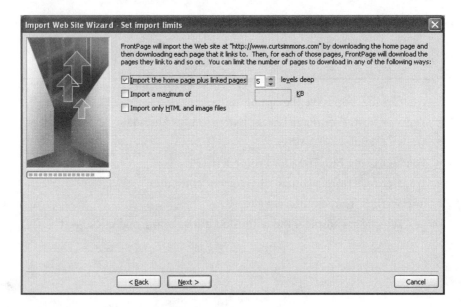

5. Click Finish to start the import.

Saving Your Web Site

When you create a web site, you can choose to create it on a web server that will host your site, or you can choose to save the site to a folder on your computer. Webs saved to your hard drive do not always have the advanced features available in FrontPage, such as the ability to collect data from input forms. Nor can they, of course, be visited by anyone else. You can, however, use your local drive to design a web, and then publish it to a web server when one becomes available.

When you create the site, you can choose to enter a drive and folder location in the drop-down box labeled Specify the Location of the New Web Site on the right side of the Web Site Templates dialog box, shown in Figure 34-2.

If you have access to an Internet or intranet web server, you can publish your web there. You need a URL (site address) from your web administrator, and you need to be connected to the Internet or your intranet. Establishing these connections is the job of your Internet Service Provider (ISP) or your local intranet administrator. They should provide you with the URL address to which you are publishing, and a password. If you have a web server, enter the URL of the web address in the drop-down box labeled Specify the Location of the New Web Site in the Web Site Templates dialog box. After you select a template and click OK, you'll be connected to your web server and prompted to enter a username and password.

Of course, in many cases, you may want to create your web site and save it on your computer, then publish the web site to a web server of your choice later. We'll explore publishing in more detail in Chapter 35.

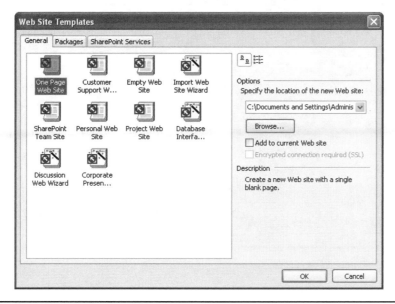

FIGURE 34-2   Save the web site to a folder.

Getting Around in FrontPage

Before you start working on individual pages in your web site, it is a good idea to make sure you understand the interface. For the most part, FrontPage looks like most other Office applications, which is a good thing. However, there are a few differences you should note before you get too involved creating pages.

First of all, take a look at the View options on the View menu. In Figure 34-3, we are using the View | Folder List option. In this view, you can click on a page and see the actual page content on the right side of the window. This feature lets you see the folder list and pages, and work on individual pages at the same time.

If you are using the Folder List option, notice that you can switch between Folder List and Navigation in the Navigation pane. Likewise, if you choose to view the web site in the right pane, you can toggle between several different views:

- **Folders**   This view displays a list of folders and pages.
- **Remote Web Site**   If your site is stored on a remote web site, you can view the site by clicking this button.

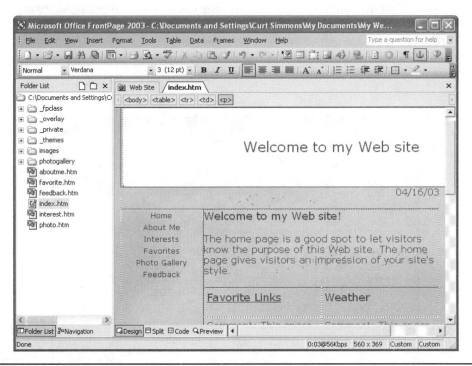

FIGURE 34-3   View options in FrontPage

- **Reports**   FrontPage can generate a number of reports about your web site. Click the Reports button to view reports.

- **Navigation**   Use this option to see a graphical view of the navigation structure of your site.

- **Hyperlinks**   Use this to see the hyperlinks in your site, as shown here:

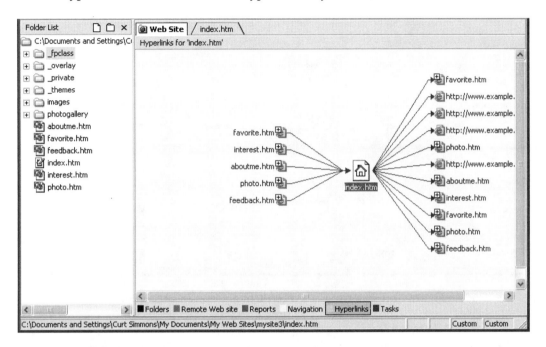

- **Tasks**   In this view, you can see any tasks associated with the web site. Tasks are simply that—task assignments that you build into the web site for developers and administrators to handle, a feature often used in larger web sites that require the work of several people.

In the same manner, if you are working on an individual page, you can choose a few different view options:

- **Design**   This option displays your page in Design mode, where you can edit and work with it in a graphical way. In Design mode, FrontPage basically works like an advanced word processor. You get a "what you see is what you get" environment.

- **Split**   This option, shown in the following illustration, shows you both Design and Code views, allowing you to work on your page in either mode. This feature is ideal if you are having problems getting the results you want in Design mode. You can use the split view to see the code, manipulate it, then see the results in the Design mode.

- **Code** This option shows you the HTML of a page. You can directly edit the HTML here. Use this feature if you prefer to create web pages by directly editing the HTML, rather than using the graphical interface.

- **Preview** This option shows you how the page will look when it is published. Note that some features will not work under this view until the page is actually saved and published on a web server.

NOTE *Like all Office 2003 applications, FrontPage 2003 uses the task pane, where you can access many different features as you work on pages. Just click View | Task Pane to make the task pane appear at any time.*

As with other Office applications, you notice two main toolbars that are available at the top of FrontPage by default: the Standard and Formatting toolbars. These toolbars are very similar to other Office applications, but you need to know the options available on the toolbars in order to get around in FrontPage.

These toolbars are detachable, and can be moved off the top of the window by clicking and dragging on the toolbar (but not on a button). Detached toolbars can be re-anchored at the top of the window by dragging them back to the top of the screen.

Although the Standard toolbar includes some buttons that you already know from other Office applications, many other buttons are unique to FrontPage. The following list explains what each tool does.

- **Create New**   Toggles between creating a new (blank) page, web site, blank page, text file, Sharepoint List, or Folder.
- **Open**   Toggles between opening a new file or site.
- **Save**   Saves the open, selected web page file and all embedded image files within that page.
- **Find**   Searches your computer (not your web site) for files.
- **Publish Site**   Uploads web files to a server.
- **Toggle Pane**   Switches back and forth between displaying navigational structure (Navigation pane) or file folder structure (Folder) to the left of the open web page.
- **Print**   Prints the open page (and only the web page) without allowing you to make selections in the Print dialog box.
- **Preview in Browser**   Displays the page in your default browser, which is the only way to know how the page will look in a web site.
- **Spelling**   Checks the current page.
- **Cut**   Cuts selected material from a page.
- **Copy**   Copies any selected item(s) on a page.
- **Paste**   Allows you to paste items copied from other pages or sources onto the page.
- **Format Painter**   Transforms the cursor into a brush temporarily, to "paint" formatting onto existing text. You activate it by selecting text whose formatting you want to copy.
- **Undo**   Undoes your last action (which can help if you have accidentally deleted something).
- **Redo**   Undoes undo.
- **Web Component**   Opens a dialog box full of FrontPage components such as Hover buttons and tables of contents.
- **Insert Table**   Generates tables for displaying data or page layout.
- **Insert Picture from File**   Embeds an image file.
- **Drawing**   Opens the Drawing toolbar, which among other features, allows you to use simple drawing tools right in FrontPage to generate vector markup language (VML) images.
- **Insert Hyperlink**   Assigns a hyperlink to the selected text or image.
- **Refresh**   Restores the last saved version of a page file.
- **Stop**   Stops uploading to the server.
- **Show All**   Displays invisible formatting elements such as paragraph marks, forced line breaks, and image anchors.
- **Show Layer Anchors**   Displays the anchor marks for any layers you have used on the page.

- **Microsoft FrontPage Help** Opens a window to the right of the FrontPage window, with many options for online help.
- **Add or Remove Buttons** Enables you to customize the Formatting toolbar.

Most of your web page text formatting is controlled from the Formatting toolbar in Page view. You'll recognize many of the Formatting toolbar buttons, but it also includes some unique buttons that are not on other Office application formatting toolbars.

- **Style** Assigns styles from a list. The styles are HTML styles, which are not customizable in the same way that styles are defined in word processors or desktop publishing applications.
- **Font** Assigns fonts to selected text. How fonts display in a browser depends on whether the fonts are installed on a visitor's computer.
- **Font Size** Assigns font size to selected text. The limited selection of sizes reflects the limitations of HTML.
- **Bold** Assigns boldface to selected text.
- **Italic** Assigns italics to selected text.
- **Underline** Lets you underline text as well as deselect underlining for links.
- **Align Left** Left-aligns selected paragraph(s).
- **Center** Centers selected paragraph(s).
- **Align Right** Right-aligns selected paragraph(s).
- **Justify** Aligns text evenly between the margins. Justification is supported by Netscape 4.5+ and Internet Explorer 4.0+, so you are constrained only by the odd spacing you might get between letters and words.
- **Increase/Decrease Font Size** Increases or decreases the selected font size.
- **Numbering** Assigns sequential numbering to selected paragraphs
- **Bullets** Assigns indenting and bullets to selected paragraphs
- **Decrease Indent** Moves selected paragraphs to the left (undoes indenting)
- **Increase Indent** Indents entire selected paragraph(s)
- **Highlight** Adds a background highlight to selected text
- **Font Color** Assigns colors to selected text
- **Add or Remove Buttons** Enables you to customize the Formatting toolbar

Working with Pages in FrontPage

Once you have created your web site in FrontPage, you are ready to begin working with the individual pages. After all, it is the pages that make up the web site anyway—the pages are what your viewers will see. There are a lot of formatting options, and in the following sections we'll take a look at the major formatting features you are likely to use.

Creating New Pages

If you have used a template to create your site, FrontPage has already created some default pages for you. For example, if you choose to create a personal web site, FrontPage creates an index.htm page (which you need for every web site), an aboutme.htm page, a photo.htm page, and so forth. You can use the default pages, delete them (just right-click the page and click Delete), or you can add more pages to your web site at any time. To add pages, follow these steps:

1. Click File | New, or click the New button on the toolbar.

2. In the New task pane, click either Blank Page or More Page Templates to create a page using a template.

3. If you choose to use a template, the Page Templates dialog box appears, as shown in the following illustration. Choose the kind of page template you want to use, and click OK. Note that you can also use the Form Page wizard to customize a form page if needed.

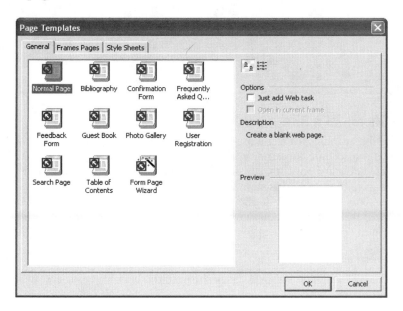

4. The new page appears in the FrontPage interface, shown next. By default, your new page is simply named new_page_x.htm, where x is the number of the new page. You can rename this page to whatever you want by clicking File | Save As. Keep in

mind that the name you give the page will be used in your site navigation, so try to keep the name descriptive and short if possible.

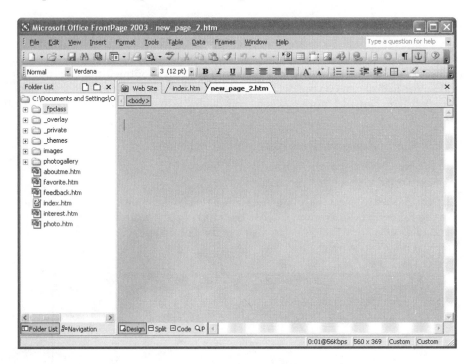

Applying a Theme to a Site

Creating all of the graphics for a site may sound like a fun and creative process, but let's face the facts, it is also time consuming. As such, FrontPage can do it for you using themes. A theme is a collection of borders, colors, and styles that you can apply to all pages on a web site. This gives the site a consistent look and feel without any formatting work on your part. Of course, you are restricted to the theme, and making changes to themes can be a little challenging, but overall, if you want to quickly create a site that looks great, a theme can be your friend. You can easily apply a theme to a site by following these steps:

1. Click Format | Theme.

2. The Theme task pane appears. Look through the list of themes and locate one that you like.

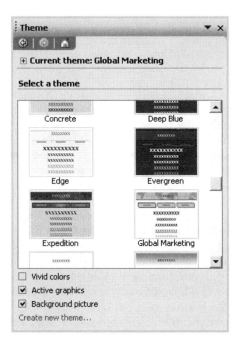

3. Click the desired theme one time. A menu arrow appears. If you click the arrow, you see that you can apply the theme to a selected page or an entire web site. Click the desired option.

4. The new theme is applied to the page or the entire site, according to your specifications. The following illustration shows you an example of a theme.

Working with Text

FrontPage is designed to work just like Microsoft Word in terms of formatted text, bullets, and numbering. Simply type your text, or edit existing text, and then use the Formatting toolbar to change fonts, sizes, styles, paragraph formatting, bullets and numbering, and so forth. You can also use the Format menu to access styles for these same options.

For the most part, formatting text in FrontPage works just like formatting text in a Word document. Of course, you are working with HTML, which can be a bit more aggravating to manage in terms of a What You See Is What You Get interface. Once you type text, you can assign basic font attribute(s) to selected text by using the Formatting toolbar. First, select the text, and then click a toolbar button. For example, you can assign fonts from the Font drop-down menu, assign font size from the Font Size drop-down menu, and assign boldface by clicking the Bold button, and so forth, just as you would do in Word. You can also assign colors to selected text by clicking the down arrow next to the Font Color button. This opens the (detachable) Font Color palette, shown in Figure 34-4.

Aside from basic selected text formatting, you can also format other standard page items using the options on the Format menu, such as Paragraph, Bullets and Numbering, or Borders and Shading. These menu options control the basic look of text.

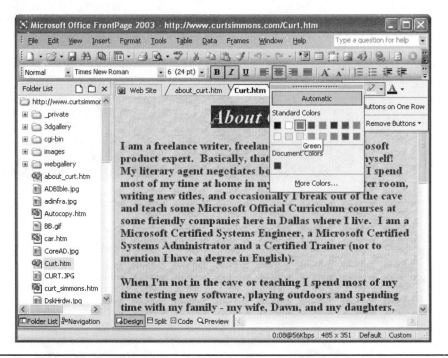

FIGURE 34-4   Use the Color Palette to assign color to selected text.

NOTE   *Generally speaking, most web browsers can display basic text styles. However, note that some older browsers will not accurately display the configurations you apply to paragraph alignment, bullets, borders, shading, and so forth. If you know that many of your visitors are using older browsers, you may want to avoid some of the following formatting options and stick to a basic text look. Internet Explorer versions 5.0 and later can accurately display these options, however.*

The great thing about additional formatting options that FrontPage gives you is they can make your page look more like a printed, published document, rather than a web page. That's good news to those of you who want a very professional looking site without having to know anything about HTML programming.

To apply paragraph formatting to selected text, choose Format | Paragraph. In addition to alignment options, you can assign indentation before text (on the left), after text (on the right), or to the first line only.

You can also assign vertical spacing by entering values in the Before or After spin boxes, and define word spacing by entering values in the Word spin box. You can choose between single spacing, 1.5 spacing, or double-spacing in the Line Spacing drop-down menu, as shown in Figure 34-5.

Normal bullets and numbering can be quickly assigned from the Formatting toolbar. Detailed control over bullets and numbering is available for selected text by choosing Format | Bullets and Numbering. The Picture Bullets tab, shown in Figure 34-6, enables you to choose an image for your bullets by clicking the Browse button and navigating to an image file. Of course, you will first need to design, or get and save, a small image to use as a bullet. The Plain Bullets tab and Numbers tab provide bullet and numbering options similar to those in Word—you can assign automatic numbering as Roman numerals or

FIGURE 34-5
Paragraph
formatting options

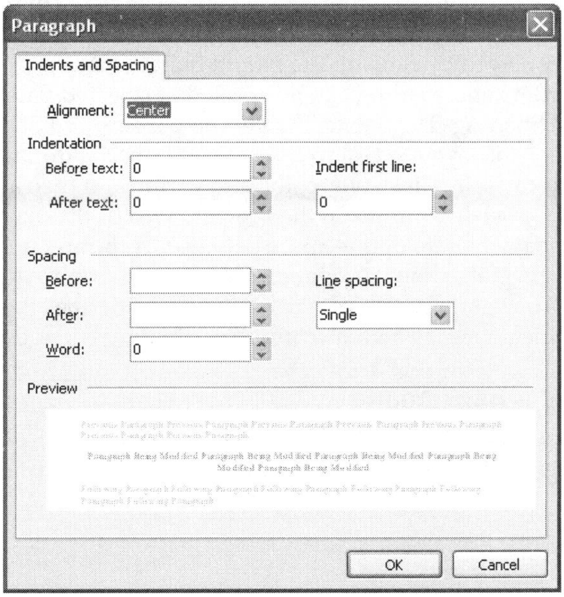

FIGURE 34-6
Use the bullets
and numbering
options to
customize
your page.

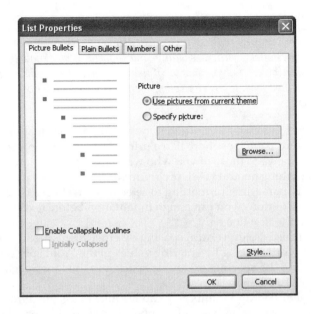

letters, and define a starting number for a list. The Enable Collapsible Outlines check box in
each tab generates Dynamic HTML (DHTML) code that enables visitors in supported browsers
to expand or collapse multilevel outlines. This feature is not supported in Netscape 4+
browsers.

If you select the Enable Collapsible Outlines option, you can indent lower-level bullets
or numbering by selecting paragraphs in a bulleted (or numbered) list and clicking the
Increase Indent button in the Formatting toolbar twice. This assigns lower-level status to
a bulleted (or numbered) list item. When viewed in Internet Explorer, these items can be
hidden or displayed by clicking the parent bulleted item.

Both borders and shading can be applied to selected paragraphs by choosing Format |
Borders and Shading. The Borders tab in the Borders and Shading dialog box, shown in
Figure 34-7, enables you to assign a variety of borders around paragraphs, just as you can
in Word. You can select line style, color, and width, and then apply these attributes by clicking
one of the four border buttons in the Preview area of the dialog box. The four Padding area
spin boxes enable you to define space between the border and the text.

The Shading tab, shown in Figure 34-8, enables you to define a background color for a
paragraph. The Foreground Color drop-down list defines the color of text. Again, keep in
mind that older browsers may not interpret shading correctly.

Formatting a Background

You can format the background of a web page so that it displays a color, or you can even
use a picture file or clip art file if you like. This flexibility is great when you design pages

FIGURE 34-7
Use borders and
shading options
to make pages
visually appealing.

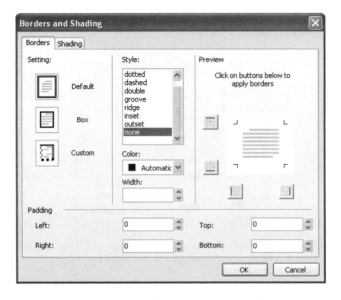

because it allows you to control the overall look and feel of the page. To format the
background, just follow these steps:

1. Open the page you want to edit, and click Format | Background.

2. The Formatting tab of Page Properties opens, as shown next. Note that you
   can choose to use a background picture, watermark the page, and then browse
   for the background picture you want to use. Background pictures can include
   actual JPEG photos, or JPEG clip art. Notice under the Colors option that you

FIGURE 34-8
Use the Shading
tab to choose
foreground and
background colors.

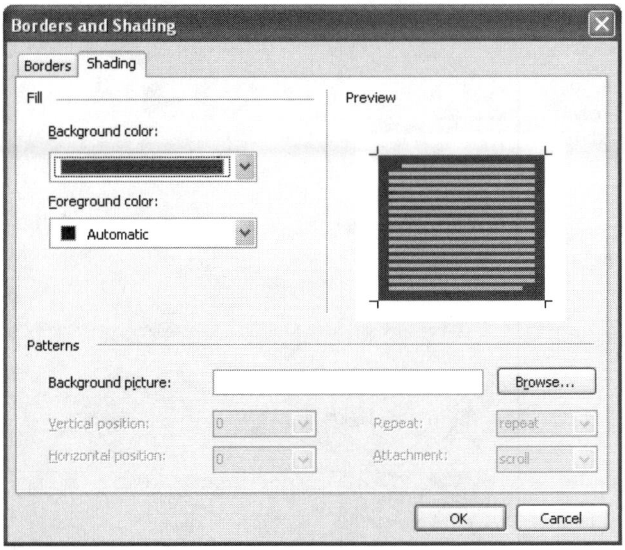

can choose a background color, text color, and hyperlink colors as well. Click OK when you're done.

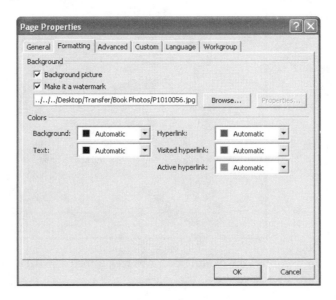

As you are working with background options, one thing you need to carefully consider is how your text will look on the background. For example, in Figure 34-9, we used a photo of the ocean for the background. Notice how hard it is to read the text on the page. In order to make this text stand out, we need to format it with a different color, and perhaps even font. You have probably visited web sites where the background overpowered the text and made the site difficult to read. Make sure you do not do this! Carefully consider your background images and colors, and experiment with text to make sure it is easy to read.

FIGURE 34-9
You can barely read the text on this ocean background; make sure the background and text work together.

TIP   *If you access the Formatting tab to change the background and all of your options are grayed out, you are using a theme, which will not allow you to manually edit the background.*

The Formatting tab lets you define both the page background and default text colors. Defining both simultaneously is helpful. For example, if you create a dark-blue page background, you'll probably want to change your default text color to white, yellow, or another bright, light color that can be read against a dark background. Here are some additional details about the options on the Formatting tab.

- **Background Picture check box**   Enables you to define a graphic image to tile in the background of your web page. Tiled images repeat horizontally and vertically, as necessary, to fill all the space behind your web page.

- **Browse button**   Lets you locate a background image on your local computer or web site by navigating to the image file.

- **Watermark check box**   Freezes a background image on the browser screen; as visitors scroll up and down your web page, the background image stays in the same place.

- **Background drop-down list**   Enables you to select a color from a color palette to assign to your web page background. Background images override background colors, so if you want the selected background color to work, deselect the Background Image check box.

- **Text drop-down menu**   Opens a color palette from which you can assign a default text color for your page.

- **Hyperlink drop-down palettes**   Enables you to define colors for links on your page

The Formatting tab controls important page design options. You can assign default colors for page text, and the three states of page links, as well as a page background color or image.

Using Background Sounds

Just as you can configure a background picture, you can also configure background sounds or music that plays when a visitor opens the page. This is done by associating a background sound with the page itself. Sounds, however, can be overdone, and there are some common problems with background sounds. First, visitors get no warning that a sound is coming, which can be disruptive in some work environments or simply annoying in general. Also, for slow Internet connections, sounds slow down page download time considerably. Most Netscape browsers don't work with sound, and users also can't turn the sound off on the page. Generally, we recommend avoiding background sounds unless they have a specific purpose on the page. If they are nothing more than entertainment, it is better to skip them.

If you decide to add background sounds, FrontPage lets you include sound files in many audio file formats: .wav, .mid, .ram, .ra, .aif, .au, and .snd. These formats enable you to assign sound files created in all popular Windows and Macintosh audio software. Both page titles and background sounds are defined in the General tab of the Page Properties dialog box, shown in Figure 34-10.

The Loop spin box in the General tab of the Page Properties dialog box defines how many times the sound will play. The Forever check box plays a background sound repeatedly,

FIGURE 34-10
Use the General
tab to assign
background
sounds.

as long as the page is open. When you save a web page, FrontPage will prompt you to
save all embedded files, including a background sound file if you have assigned one.

Assigning Page Titles

The page title displays in the title bar of a visitor's web browser. Your web page may be
called index.htm or default.htm (these filenames designate home pages that open first when
a visitor comes to your web site). Alternatively, your page's filename may be newpage4.htm.
Regardless of what the filename is, you can create a *title*, such as "Welcome to My Site," and
that page title will display when visitors come to your web page.

   To enter a title for your page, right-click on the page and choose Page Properties. Enter
a page title in the Title area of the General tab. Titles can break rules that apply to page
filenames. Therefore, you can assign the same title to more than one page, and you can
include any combination of uppercase and lowercase, numbers, symbols, and spaces in
a page title.

Using Photos and Clip Art

Photos and clip art add a lot of interest to a web site, and FrontPage allows you to easily
insert them. If you click the Insert | Picture option, you can insert a picture from clip art,
a file, a scanner, or camera, create a new photo gallery, or create other drawings and shapes.
You'll find that the features here work in a similar way as inserting photos and clip art on
Word or PowerPoint documents. Once the photo or clip art is on the page, you can use the
handles at each corner to resize as necessary, as shown next:

If you right-click the photo and click Picture Properties, you can manage the wrapping style of the photo (how it falls on the page), the layout, size specifications, and other general properties. You can also open the Pictures toolbar by clicking View | Toolbars | Pictures. The Pictures toolbar, discussed in the upcoming section, allows you to make a number of editorial changes to the photo directly within FrontPage. For example, you can use it to rotate photos, increase or decrease brightness, crop a photo, and other related editing features.

TIP   *You can easily create a photo gallery on your web site by clicking Insert | Pictures | New Photo Gallery. This feature lets you choose the photos you want to include and then arrange them on a template for easy viewing. See "Photo Gallery" later in this chapter for details.*

So, what exactly can you do with these features? Let's face it, modern web pages are visual in nature, so pictures and clip art are major considerations when you create pages. Carefully consider how photos and clip art will make your pages look, generally speaking. Just as visual attraction is important, it is also important not to go overboard. Plan your pages carefully so that they not only look attractive but are easy to read. Once you decide to use images, including photos and clip art, you'll need to manage them on the page. The following sections show you how to do that.

Working with the Pictures Toolbar

When you select an image in Page view, the Pictures toolbar at the bottom of the window becomes active, shown in Figure 34-11. The tools in the Pictures toolbar let you adjust the appearance of your graphic image right in FrontPage. If you don't see the Pictures toolbar, right-click the picture and choose Show Pictures Toolbar.

The buttons on the Pictures toolbar include the following:

- **Insert Picture from File**   Opens the Image dialog box, so that you can insert a new image.
- **Text**   Creates a text box in which you can enter caption text for the selected image.
- **Auto Thumbnail**   Generates a small version of your image. Thumbnails are often used as links to larger pictures, and their small size saves file space and speeds up page downloading.
- **Position Absolutely**   Locks the position of your image to any spot on your page.
- **Bring Forward**   Moves selected images in front of other objects on the page.
- **Send Backwards**   Moves selected images behind other objects on the page.

- **Rotate Left 90°, Rotate Right 90°, Flip Horizontal, and Flip Vertical**   Rotates your selected image.

- **More Contrast, Less Contrast, More Brightness, and Less Brightness**   Adjusts the brightness and contrast of your image.

- **Crop**   Crops material based on your crop marks. Click and drag these handles to define crop marks for your picture, and then click the Crop button again to finalize your cut.

- **Line Style**   Sets line thickness in various point sizes, creates colored lines, and offers various line styles, such as dashed lines or arrows.

- **Format Picture**   Sets brightness and contrast, recolors your image, and lets you specify cropping in inches from Left, Right, Top, or Bottom.

- **Set Transparent Color**   Displays an eraser tool. Point at and click any one color in your image to make that color disappear, allowing the page background to show through.

- **Color**   Allows you to choose grayscale, black and white, or washout.

- **Bevel**   Adds a 3-D frame around an image, suitable for navigation buttons.

- **Resample**   Saves your image as a smaller file if you've reduced the size of your image. Once the file size is decreased, your web page will open faster in a browser.

- **Select**   Deselects other tools.

- **Rectangular Hotspot, Circular Hotspot, and Polygonal Hotspot**   Creates clickable links called image maps, which are discussed in detail later in this chapter.

- **Highlight Hotspots**   Helps identify hotspots.

- **Restore**   Undoes editing changes to your picture, as long as you haven't saved the changes.

Importing Images

When you embed an image in a web page, FrontPage automatically adds the graphic file to your web. This means the file is saved as a part of your web site, whether your web site is stored locally on your computer or on a remote web server. In most cases, the easiest way to import images is simply to add them to your web pages as needed, then save the pages. FrontPage will prompt you to make sure you want to save the embedded images in your web site. However, sometimes it will be faster and easier to import graphic files into your web first, and then insert them in web pages. For example, if you have dozens of photos that you want to use in your web site, you can first import them, and then assign them to pages directly from the current web site. You may have noticed when you created your web that FrontPage created an empty folder called "images," which is a convenient place to store your images.

To import images directly into your web site before placing them on a web page, follow these steps:

1. Select File | Import to open the Import dialog box.

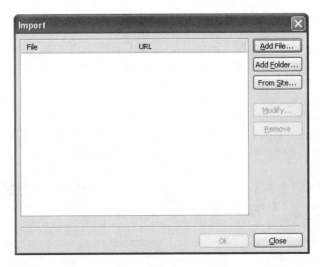

2. Click the Add File button to add a file from your local computer or network, or click the From Site button to add a file from a location on the Web or an intranet.

3. Navigate to and select the image file that you want to add to your web site.

4. Add more files, if you want to, by clicking the Add File or From Site buttons.

5. After you add all the files that you want to the list, click all of those that you want to import (use SHIFT-click to select more than one). Then, click the OK button in the dialog box, and wait while the image files are imported into your web site.

After you import images, they appear in the list of image files in your web site when you click the Insert Picture button on the Standard toolbar.

Managing Images

As mentioned before, you can make editorial changes to images once they are embedded on the desired page in your web site. Even though the image is part of the page, you retain control over the image and can work with it individually in a few different ways. The following sections describe what you can do.

Resizing Images   You can make images smaller or larger, as needed, by resizing them. Select the image by clicking it. Notice the little black rectangles that appear around it—these are its handles, as we mentioned earlier. You can resize the graphic any way you like by dragging these handles, shown here. If you drag from one of the corners, you can resize the graphic in two directions simultaneously, maintaining the height-to-width ratio of the graphic.

Resizing by clicking and dragging is quick and easy, and graphical. But keep in mind that you can easily distort the dimensions of an image if you drag on a *side* (as opposed to a corner) resizing handle. Notice the box, called Picture Actions, that appears below the photo. The Picture Actions box is a small white box with an inward-pointing arrow. If you click the box, you can choose to modify the size attributes as you resize, or you can have FrontPage resample the picture to match the size you choose.

Positioning Images   When you position an image, you determine where the image fits on the page. You have two basic choices in positioning your image. First, you can choose to align it in relation to a paragraph, which enables you to flow text around an image, and to have the image move with the associated text. See the "Alignment Options" section, coming up shortly, for more details. Secondly, you can position your image at an exact spot on your web page, which means you drag your image to the exact point on the page where you want it to display. If you display an image on top of text or other page elements, you have the option of moving the image behind or on top of the other page elements.

The good news is that the positioning feature puts you in the driver's seat so you can get images onto your pages and looking exactly the way you want. To assign an absolute position to an image, select it and click the Position Absolutely button in the Pictures toolbar. Then, click the image and move it to a desired location.

Working with the Appearance Tab

Once an image is embedded in a web page, you can right-click the image and click Picture Properties, which opens an Appearance tab, shown in Figure 34-12, where you can configure several important image-related settings. The Appearance tab contains image properties that directly affect the way the selected image is displayed. The options in the Layout section of the Appearance tab are described in the following sections.

FIGURE 34-12
Use the
Appearance tab
to change image
properties.

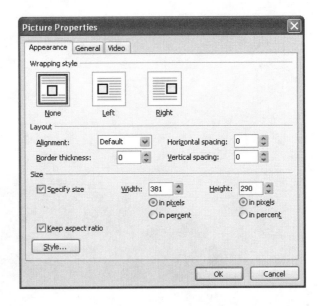

Alignment Options   The alignment options affect how an image is aligned in relation to the text around it. The most powerful alignment options are left and right alignment. Left or right alignment allows you to wrap text around a picture. The small arrow to the left of the paragraph indicates where the picture is anchored, and the picture can be moved by clicking and dragging that anchor arrow. Images can also be centered. However, text will break on either side of the image, which makes reading difficult. The other alignment options control how images are positioned in relation to a line of text. These options are somewhat esoteric, and are used for fine-tuning the exact alignment of tiny graphics inserted into text. These alignment features are used when an inserted image is smaller (shorter in height) than the line of text in which it is inserted.

Horizontal and Vertical Spacing   Use the Vertical Spacing and Horizontal Spacing options to determine how much white space appears between an image and the surrounding text. These options are particularly useful when used in conjunction with the left- and right-alignment options to control how text wraps around an image.

Border Thickness   If you associate an image with a hyperlink (we'll explore hyperlinking later in this chapter), by default, the hyperlink displays with a thin border that is the color of the other hyperlinks on the page. You can use the Border option to hide this border or control its width. In addition, you can use the Border option to add a border to nonhyperlinked images. To add a border to an image, simply designate its thickness, measured in screen pixels. The border displays in the color of the default text on the web page.

Size Options   The Size section of the Appearance tab indicates the width and height of the current image, designated in screen pixels. By default, these values are grayed out. You can alter them directly by first checking the Specify Size check box. This is the equivalent of resizing the image. Values for the size property can be given either in pixels or in percentages. If you select percentages, the size of an image changes in relation to the size of the web browser window. To maintain the same proportions between height and width as you resize, click the Keep Aspect Ratio check box. Then, when you change either the height or width, the other dimension will be reset automatically to keep the same aspect ratio.

Working with the Drawing Toolbar

FrontPage has a Drawing toolbar that allows you to create basic line art images. You may find this feature useful for illustration purposes and for adding quick and easy graphics to your page. I don't mind telling you up front that the Drawing toolbar is a basic feature that doesn't provide you with a lot of options; it is designed for simple graphics, nothing of a custom nature. For that, you may consider creating line art graphics in another image editing program, such as Adobe's Photoshop, then save the image as a JPEG and import it as you would any other photo.

However, if you want access to simple line art tools, FrontPage does give you the basics. You can open the Drawing toolbar, shown in Figure 34-13, by choosing View | Toolbars | Drawing.

The drawing tools that generate graphic objects are AutoShapes, Line, Arrow, Rectangle, Oval, Text Box, and Insert WordArt. The Insert ClipArt and Insert Picture from File buttons duplicate features on the Pictures toolbar. The Fill Color, Line Color, Font Color, Line Style, Dash Style, Arrow Style, Shadow Style, and 3-D Style tools apply effects to existing text or graphic objects.

The AutoShapes tools include palettes of preset shapes, which are

- **Line**   Use this tool for freehand drawing. Double-click to complete a shape.

- **Basic Shapes**   Use this tool to draw a heart, trapezoid, happy face, and other shapes. Click and drag to define the size of the shape. (See Figure 34-13.)

FIGURE 34-13
Drawing toolbar

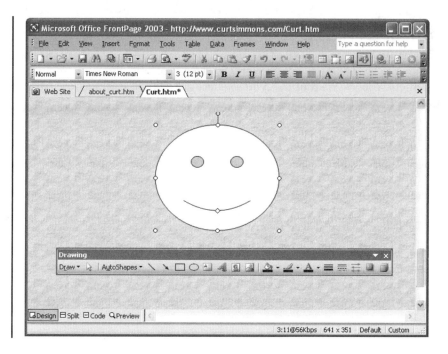

- **Block Arrows**   This tool provides a selection of different arrows.
- **Flowchart**   This is a palette of shapes used in drawing flowcharts.
- **Stars and Banners**   Use this to insert stars and banners.
- **Callouts**   Cartoon or bubble callouts are available here.
- **More AutoShapes**   Additional shapes are offered here.

Aside from basic AutoShapes, you can also draw a line by clicking on the Line tool, and then clicking and dragging on your page to create the line. In the case of both lines and arrows, you can force the angle of the line to 15-degree increments (for example, 15 degrees, 30 degrees, 45 degrees, and so on) by holding down the SHIFT key as you draw. Draw an arrow by selecting the Arrow tool, then clicking and dragging on the page. The direction you click and drag determines the direction in which the arrow is pointing. You can use this same process to create an oval or rectangle by clicking those tool options on the toolbar and clicking/dragging.

You can also apply shading, color, and other attributes to selected shapes. First, use the Select Objects tool (the white arrow in the Drawing toolbar) to select the object to which you are applying effects. Click on a shape with the Select Objects tool, and then use the Line Style, Dash Style (works only with lines), Arrow Style (works only with lines), Shadow Style, or 3-D Style tool to choose various effects from the pop-up palettes. To apply a fill or line color, or attribute, to a selected object, click on the Fill Color, Line Color, Line Style, Dash Style, Arrow Style, Shadow Style, or 3-D Style tool, and choose a color or style from the palette associated with that tool.

You can also use the Drawing toolbar to create text boxes and WordArt. Text boxes are similar to the shapes created with FrontPage drawing tools except that they cannot be rotated. To create a text box, choose the Text Box tool, and click and drag on the page to generate the box. A text cursor appears inside the box when it is selected, and you can insert and edit text within the box. You can format text in the text box by using the tools in the Formatting toolbar.

WordArt is a feature that allows you to apply an entertaining set of effects to text. To generate WordArt, click the Insert WordArt tool, and choose a style from the WordArt Gallery. The WordArt option you see here is exactly the same WordArt feature found in Word and PowerPoint.

As with any other object, you can resize, move, or rotate a selected line shape. Text boxes can be moved and resized, but not rotated. Use the Select Objects tool to select the shape first. A selected shape displays with six handles (a selected line or arrow displays with two handles). Move selected objects by clicking and dragging on them. Shapes, text boxes, and lines can be resized by clicking and dragging on either side or on the corner handles. (Lines have only two handles—one on each end.) Clicking and dragging on corner handles maintains the original height-to-width ratio, while clicking and dragging on a side handle can stretch or compress a shape.

You can *group* (temporarily combine) objects by holding down the SHIFT key while using the Select Objects tool to select more than one object, and then choose Group from the Draw tool menu in the Drawing toolbar, as shown in Figure 34-14. Grouped objects can be moved, resized, or rotated together. You can also apply fill and line properties to a group of selected objects all at once. To ungroup a selected group, click on the Draw tool and choose Ungroup.

FIGURE 34-14
Group objects
for greater
management
control.

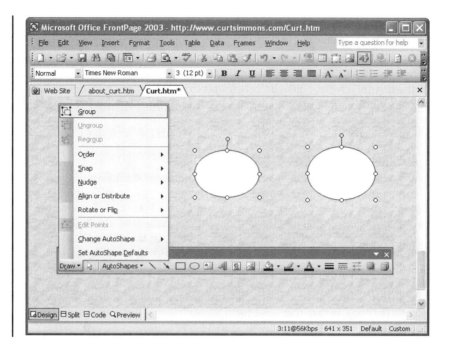

The Draw tool has features to align, locate, and flip selected objects. Align selected objects by clicking on the Draw tool in the Drawing toolbar and choosing Align and Distribute. The options allow you to distribute (evenly space) or align objects. The Snap option in the Draw tool menu allows you to set objects to snap to either another object or a grid. The Nudge option allows you to move any selected object(s) in small increments; and the Rotate option in the Draw tool menu allows you to flip objects horizontally or vertically.

Inserting Web Components

Web components are a collection of different features that you can add to your web sites. Essentially, these features are different scripts that perform when users access your site or interact with the component. Using FrontPage, you can simply insert these components without having to do any script writing. The following sections give you a quick overview of your options.

Dynamic Effects

The Dynamic Effects option in the Insert Web Component dialog box offers two options for presenting *active* page elements: interactive buttons and scrolling text marquees. These elements are active, as opposed to *static* text and images that just sit there.

The dynamic effects web components rely on HTML and Java to generate small programs right in your web site to produce interactivity. Therefore, these web components are compatible with Netscape 4.7. And they do *not* require FrontPage server extensions, or even a web server, to work.

Web Search

The Web Search component creates a form that allows visitors to search all or part of your web for pages containing one or more text strings. Results of a search are displayed by listing the titles of matching pages, with each title hyperlinked to the actual page. Details of the results page can also be controlled via the Search Form component. If you have a content-rich site and are looking for a relatively simple way to enhance the usability, the Search Form component could be just the thing. Your site must be published to a server running FrontPage server extensions in order for the web search feature to work.

Spreadsheets and Charts

You can create spreadsheets and charts manually within FrontPage, but by using this web component, you can insert Office spreadsheets, charts, and PivotTables into your web pages. This feature allows you to more easily integrate Office data into FrontPage webs. These can be static spreadsheets and charts that you create, or you can link the spreadsheet to the page using the Insert | Web Component option. You can then edit the spreadsheet or chart directly in FrontPage, just as you would within another Office application.

Hit Counters

The Hit Counter component displays the number of times that a particular page has been accessed, or *hit*. You can choose from a variety of styles and features when you insert a hit counter. The site must be published to a server running FrontPage server extensions in order for the hit counter to work.

When you choose to insert a hit counter, you can choose the style, reset the counter, and you can even choose a fixed number of digits. Once inserted, you can double-click the hit counter in Design view and change the style or reset the numbers at any time.

Photo Gallery

The Photo Gallery web component generates a JavaScript element that allows you to display photos in tables. You can choose one of the photo gallery options that display on the right side of the Insert Web Component dialog box. When you click Finish, the Photo Gallery Properties dialog box opens, allowing you to define your photo display. Overall, it is a fast and easy way to share photos without having to know programming.

You can quickly create the gallery, then put it on the Web for others to see, or you can print the gallery. The following steps show you how photo gallery works.

1. Click Insert | Web Component.

2. In the Insert Web Component dialog box, choose Photo Gallery. In the right side of the page, choose a Photo Gallery layout option, and then click Finish.

3. In the Photo Gallery Properties dialog box, shown next, use the Add button to add the desired photos from your computer to the gallery. You can then use the Thumbnail Size option to adjust the thumbnails and rearrange the photos using the Move Up and Move Down buttons. Depending on the layout selection, you may be able to add captions and descriptions. If you want to change the layout option you selected, just click the Layout tab and choose again.

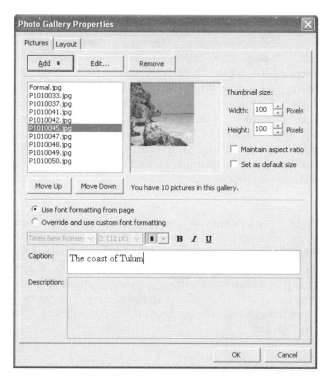

4. When you're done, click OK. The photo gallery is created. In FrontPage, click the Preview button to save your gallery and see how it will look on the Web.

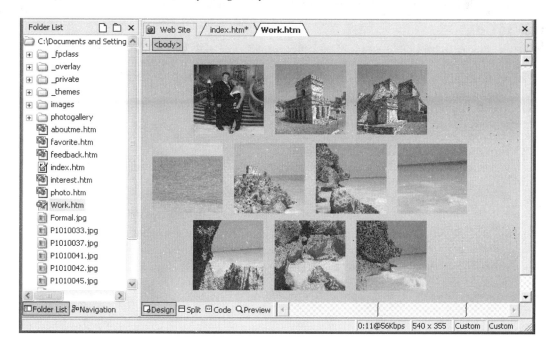

Included Content

The Included Content category of web components has five helpful ways to embed content from your web site in a web page. The options vary from embedding the content of one page in a second page, to embedding a picture based on a schedule. All the Included Content web components are tools for automating site content. For example, you can use the Page option to create an "updatable" page that is embedded in other pages. Every time you update the embedded page, the content changes on all pages in which this page is embedded.

In many cases, the included content feature is used when you have a section of a page that changes frequently, such as news or stock quotes. The content might actually be coming from a different server, but you can use the included content feature to subdivide the page, yet keep the desired content all in one place.

Link Bars

Link Bar components provide a variety of generated links on a page. Link bars can be based on a defined set of pages, or they can be generated by a site's navigational structure. Using the web component feature, you can determine the links that are used, you can use "Next" and "Back" links, and you can use a link bar based on your site's navigation structure.

In many cases, FrontPage templates will automatically create link bars for you. You can manage the link bar by using the Navigation view of the Web Site view feature, as shown in Figure 34-15. You can then change the navigation structure and add new pages to the navigation flow of the link bar.

Table of Contents

FrontPage provides options for generating tables of contents. You can create a table based on the entire web site, or based only on a selected category of web pages. A table of contents can be an effective tool for embedding automatically updated site maps in a page. You can create a table of contents based on the web site itself on a particular page.

Top 10 Lists

Top 10 lists work for pages saved to web sites on servers with FrontPage extensions. They generate lists based on data collected by the server when visitors come to your site. Top 10 lists are a way of sharing with your visitors information similar to what you see internally when you view usage reports. For example, the information shown in the Browsers Usage Report tells you how many people visited your site using what browser. That same information can be shared with visitors in a Top 10 browsers list.

List View and Document Library Components

List views and document libraries are interactive ways for visitors to upload documents and contribute to online discussions. These components require that a site is published to a server with SharePoint extension files. SharePoint is a Microsoft technology used in larger networking environments where users can manage files and documents through a SharePoint server.

FIGURE 34-15
Use the Navigation view of the Web Site to manage items such as link bars.

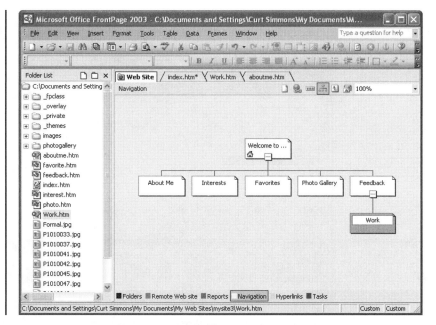

Commercial and Additional Components

FrontPage offers a number of embedded commercial content options. These options are generally self-explanatory content that is provided by other companies (or Microsoft). When you embed this content in your page, the trade-off is that you advertise their product, provide a link to their site, and facilitate their sales. In return, you get their content.

Advanced Controls

Advanced controls include HTML content, Java applets, plug-ins, ActiveX controls, and related features. You can use the Advanced Controls options to insert one of these features, then programmatically manage the control in a way that is useful on your web site.

Inserting a Web Component

Web components can be easily inserted on a FrontPage page, and depending on what you decide to insert, the steps will vary a bit. Each component will require different input information from you, so simply follow the prompts on your screen. As an example, the following steps show you how to insert an MSN Component.

1. Click your cursor on the page where you want to insert the component.
2. Click Insert | Web Component.

3. In the Insert Web Component dialog box, shown in the following illustration, choose a component type and a component or effect, as shown.

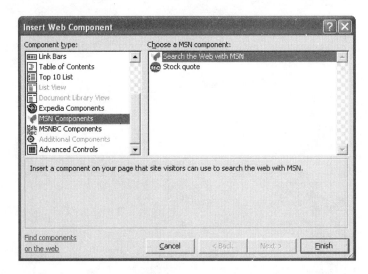

4. Click Finish. Additional instructions may appear in order to insert your component.

Inserting Tables

No matter what kind of table you need to create, the process of defining a table is the same. To use tables as design tools or to display data, first define the location of your table, and then define how many rows and columns you need. These attributes are easy to edit. Three ways exist to create a table in FrontPage—using the Insert Table button or Insert Table dialog box, or drawing a table. All three options are explored in the following sections.

Insert Table Button

In many cases, you can use the Insert Table button in the Standard toolbar to create a quick sketch of your table. Because you graphically create your table all in one step, the Insert Table button is probably the most efficient way to add a table to your web page.

With a web page open in Page view, you can insert a table by following these steps:

1. Click to place your insertion point at the spot where you want the table to appear in your web page.

2. Click the Insert Table button on the Standard toolbar.

3. Click and drag to the right in the Grid palette to add columns; click and drag down to add rows. The following illustration defines a table that is three rows long and four columns wide. Then, just click and your table will appear on the page.

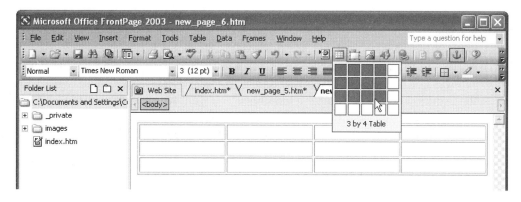

Inserting and Defining a Table

Inserting a table by using the Insert Table dialog box provides greater initial control over the appearance of your table. Although not every table option is available in this dialog box, enough options are there to make setting up your table easier, as you can see in Figure 34-16.

The main options of initial concern are located in the Size and Specify Width sections of the dialog box. These options enable you to specify how many rows and columns your table has, and its overall width.

FIGURE 34-16
Insert Table

To insert a table, follow these steps:

1. Select Table | Insert Table to open the Insert Table dialog box.

2. Set the size, layout, and width options. If you deselect the Specify Width check box, FrontPage will generate a table just wide enough to display the content of cells. Use the Borders and the Background features if you want to dress up your table.

3. If you want to assign in-line styles, click the Style button, and use the Format button in the Modify Style dialog box to define local font, paragraph, border, or number styles for your table.

4. Click OK to insert the table.

Drawing a Table

The Insert Table dialog box enables you to define many table properties digitally, by entering numbers in fields. The Table toolbar enables you to format your table in a graphical form, using the tools on the toolbar, which you can access by clicking View | Toolbars | Tables.

The Table toolbar provides much of the table formatting power you find in Word or Excel, such as cell background shading and alignment control. You get a nice selection of table autoformatting features as well. Other table features are a bit odd or disappointing compared with formatting available in Word or Excel. Fill Down and Fill Right speed up data entry, though not in the intuitive way you would expect. They simply *copy* the content of the top (or left) cell into cell(s) below or to the right of the selected cell(s).

For the purposes of defining a new table, the important tool is the Draw Table tool. Appropriately named, this tool enables you to create a table simply by drawing its structure in your page. Use the following steps to create a table by using the Draw Table tool:

1. Select the Draw Table tool from the Table toolbar; if the Table toolbar isn't visible, select Table | Draw Table. The cursor changes to a pencil, and the Table toolbar opens.

2. Click and drag the cursor to define the overall rectangular shape of the table that you want to create. When the table is the size that you want, release the mouse button.

3. Add rows and columns to your table simply by drawing them.

4. After you finish creating your table, click the Draw Table tool in the toolbar again to deselect it. The cursor returns to normal.

Importing a Table

As noted earlier in this chapter, you can format tables nicely in FrontPage, but your ability to create them is limited by disappointing data-fill features and a lack of calculation or sorting power. Therefore, you're likely to create larger tables in Word or Excel and then copy and paste them into FrontPage. The good news is that this works seamlessly, and most of your formatting is imported into FrontPage intact.

To copy spreadsheet cells into FrontPage:

1. Start Microsoft Excel, or another program with a table (such as Microsoft Access or Word), and open the file containing your table.

2. Highlight the cells that you want to include in your page, and copy the selection either by selecting Edit | Copy or by using the command-key shortcut CTRL-C.

3. Place the cursor where you want the table to be placed, and either select Edit | Paste or press CTRL-V to paste the table into FrontPage.

Creating Hyperlinks

Hyperlinks allow visitors to move around in your site to different pages, or even outside of your site to other resources on the Internet. The good news is hyperlinks are easy to configure and very flexible. Virtually anything in your site can be a hyperlink, including text, photos, clip art, borders, you name it. To create a hyperlink, follow these steps:

1. Select the text, photo, or other object that you want to become a hyperlink.

2. Click the Hyperlink button on the toolbar, or click Insert | Hyperlink.

3. In the Insert Hyperlink dialog box, shown in the following illustration, choose the page you want to link to. If you want to link to a site outside of yours, just enter the URL in the Address bar. You can also create a hyperlink to an e-mail address. Click the E-mail Address option in the Link To box, and enter the requested information.

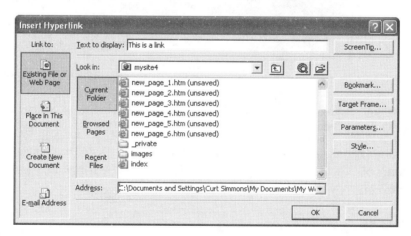

4. When you're done, click OK.

Assigning Hyperlinks to an Image

The easiest way to assign a link to an image is to click the image and then click the Hyperlinks button in the Standard toolbar. The Create Hyperlink dialog box opens, and you can assign a link to a page in your web site from the list at the top of the dialog box. Or, you can enter a URL. After you define your target, click OK in the Create Hyperlink dialog box. When you test your link in a browser, the target displays in the status bar of the browser, not in the alternative text caption that appears when you point to the linked graphic. Keep that in mind when you decide what alternative text to assign to a graphic.

Defining an Image Map

An *image map* allows you to define a hotspot within an image for hyperlinking. For example, you could have an image of a boat on an ocean. By using an image map, you can hyperlink only the boat area in the image so that users can click on it. Defining an image map is as

FIGURE 34-17
Create a hotspot using the Pictures toolbar.

easy as drawing a rectangle, an oval, or a shape. First, click the image to which you are assigning links. Then, choose either the Rectangular Hotspot, Circular Hotspot, or Polygonal Hotspot tool from the Pictures toolbar and (using the pencil cursor) draw an area on the picture that you want to associate with a link, as shown in Figure 34-17 above. After you complete your hotspot, the Create Hyperlink dialog box will open, in which you can define the target for the hotspot link.

Creating a New Theme

When you create a FrontPage site, you can use built-in page theme options to easily create a streamlined look for your site. Essentially, the theme handles all of the page design issues, from basic graphics, link bars, and fonts, to background colors and images. The good news, however, is that you can modify any of the existing themes to meet your needs, or create your own theme. The advantage of creating your own theme is that you can completely customize your site, and using the theme, make sure each page has the same basic look for consistency's sake.

If you click Format | Theme, you see a Create New Theme link at the bottom of the Theme menu that appears on the right side of the FrontPage interface. Click the Create New Theme link and the Customize Theme window appears, as shown in Figure 34-18. The Customize Theme window gives you a basic template for creating a new theme, including options to modify colors, graphics, and text. Note that you can also use Vivid Colors, Active Graphics, and Background Picture. You can modify these options to create your custom theme.

FIGURE 34-18
Customize Theme

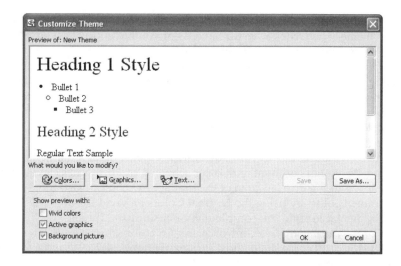

Configuring Theme Colors

Theme colors can be defined in two basic ways. You can choose a color scheme, or you can assign colors to different elements of your pages individually. Preset color schemes are faster and easier to configure. However, assigning specific colors to page elements provides much more control over how pages look.

You can replace a theme color with one of many predefined color schemes by clicking the Colors button on the Customize Theme window. The Color Schemes tab of the Customize Theme dialog box, shown in Figure 34-19, illustrates each theme—although it doesn't tell you exactly how the color scheme will be applied. You can click on a scheme that you like, then choose either the Normal Colors or Vivid Colors radio button—as you do, the Preview area of the dialog box illustrates how the theme will look. It shows you exactly how colors

FIGURE 34-19
Color Schemes

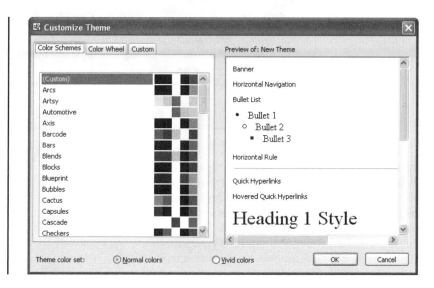

will be applied to text and page background. Click OK to apply your new color scheme to your theme. Then, click Save (or Save As, if you haven't yet saved your theme) to save the new color scheme as part of your theme.

For even more color scheme options, click the Color Wheel tab in the Customize Theme dialog box. The Color Wheel tab enables you to generate an aesthetically matched five-color color scheme to apply to your theme. (It's kind of like having an interior decorator for your home or office and telling him or her, for example, that you want a color scheme built around the color blue.) To generate a color scheme, click the Color Wheel tab in the Customize Theme dialog box. You'll see the color wheel, as shown in Figure 34-20.

To adjust the colors in your customized color scheme, change the Brightness slider's setting. As you experiment with color schemes and brightness levels, you'll see the results previewed in the Preview area of the dialog box. You can also toggle between intense colors and muted colors by using the Normal Colors or Vivid Colors radio buttons. Both options will be available after you complete your customized theme.

For the most complete control over your color scheme, you can use the Custom tab in the Customize Theme dialog box, shown in Figure 34-21. With the Custom tab selected, pull down the Item drop-down list and select the page element (Background, for example) or the type of text to which you want to assign a color. Then, click the Color drop-down list and select a color to assign to that text element.

When you open the color palette in the Custom tab, you'll see a More Colors option in addition to the 16 preset colors. Click the More Colors option to open the More Colors dialog box:

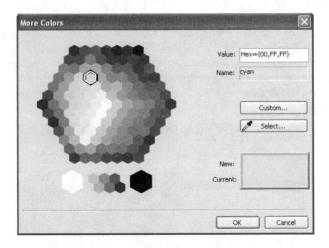

The color template displays colors that can be accurately interpreted by major web browsers. You can assign a color by clicking a color in the palette. If you are an experienced, professional web designer working from your own palette of hexadecimal color values, you can select a color by entering a hexadecimal (six-character) color code in the Value field. To create a custom color, click the Custom button, and use either the color grid or the two alternate color definition options (Hue, Saturation, Value; or Red, Green, Blue) to define a color. Finally, you can use the Select button to turn your cursor into an eyedropper. With the eyedropper cursor, point and click anywhere on your screen to load a color into the palette. After you

FIGURE 34-20
The Color Wheel
tab gives you
more options.

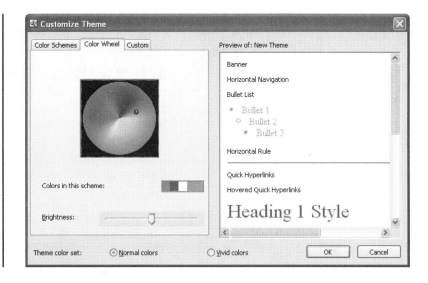

assign colors to your theme elements, click OK in the dialog box. You'll return to the main Theme dialog box, where you can now define custom font styles and graphics for your theme. After you modify your customized theme's color scheme, click the OK button in the Customize Theme dialog box.

Working with Custom Font Styles

Just as you can work with custom color, you can also configure custom font styles for your new theme. Click the Text button on the Customize Theme dialog box to define text fonts for any HTML style. You can define a font for a standard HTML style by first selecting that style from the Item drop-down menu shown in Figure 34-22. Then click one of the fonts in the Font list. You can use the vertical scroll bar to see more fonts, if necessary.

FIGURE 34-21
The Custom tab
allows you to
modify specific
colors.

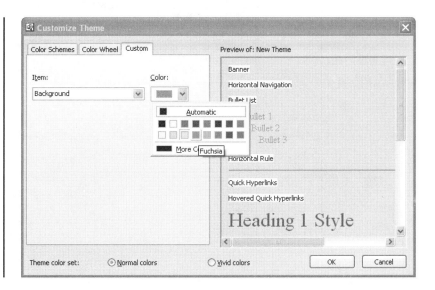

FIGURE 34-22
Choose an item
and font style.

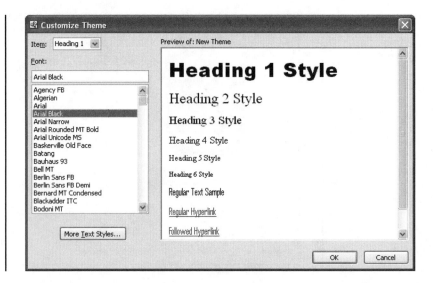

You can only choose a font for various style elements on this dialog box. To define additional text attributes for a style, click the More Text Styles button. Then select your style from the list in the Style dialog box, as shown in Figure 34-23.

With the style selected, click the Modify button. Then use the Format button in the Modify Style dialog box to define a new style and assign font type, size, color, and even paragraph formatting. Choose from four categories of formatting: Font, Paragraph, Border, or Numbering. Use the dialog boxes that open to define different attributes for your style. These formatting attributes will be displayed in the Preview window of the dialog box.

FIGURE 34-23
Style options

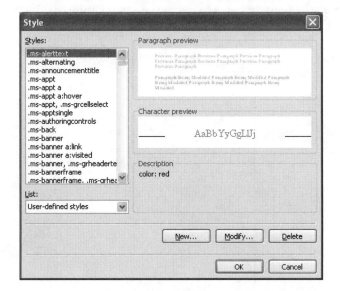

After you define your additional style attributes, click the OK button in the Modify Style dialog box. Your new, custom-defined style will be available in the list of styles to edit in the Style dialog box. After you assign custom fonts to different styles, click the OK button to close this dialog box and return to the Customize Theme dialog box.

Creating Theme Graphics

Theme graphics applies to such items as the background image, banner, bulleted list graphics, navigational buttons, and other standard components that are used on pages within your site. Each element you can configure may also have a maximum number of different theme designs used in a theme. Navigation buttons have a maximum of three different images— for each button's up, hovered-over, and selected states. There are three bullet images for three sizes of buttons, and so forth.

When you apply an existing theme, a full set of graphic files is added to the theme folder in your web site. These files provide images that become the background for navigational buttons and banners, as well as bullets (of different sizes), horizontal rules, and page background tiles.

If you want to create a unique theme, you need to create a full set of theme graphics. The text that is placed over these graphics (banners at the top of pages, and horizontal and vertical navigation buttons) is generated in either your web pages or your navigation bars. You can assign custom images for each of these elements in your theme. You can also change the font of the text that is added to these images. Therefore, when you create your own custom graphics for a FrontPage theme, do not include text in these images. Simply create the background buttons (and banner) and let FrontPage overlay text on them.

To customize theme graphics, click the Graphics button in the Theme dialog box. A Customize Theme dialog box opens, as shown in Figure 34-24.

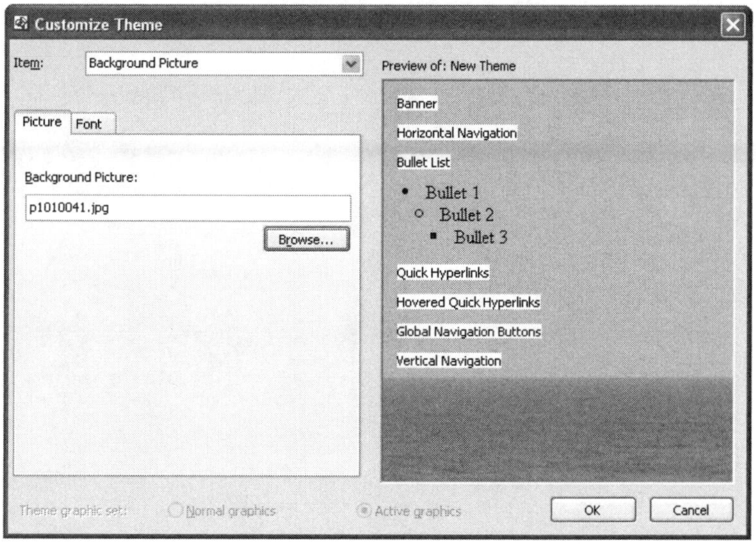

FIGURE 34-24
Customizing graphics for a theme

Many graphic elements (navigation buttons and banners) include both images and text. Navigation buttons, for instance, consist of a graphical button and button text. Some graphic elements, such as the background page color, don't have text, so you don't need to define text fonts for them.

To define text for a graphic element, select the Font tab of the dialog box, shown in Figure 34-25. Font sizes and types for navigation buttons are controlled in the Graphics Theme dialog box, but font colors are assigned in the Colors tab. When you have made your selections, simply click OK and choose to save your theme. You will now be able to select your custom theme, just as you would any other theme in FrontPage.

FIGURE 34-25
Choose the
Font tab.

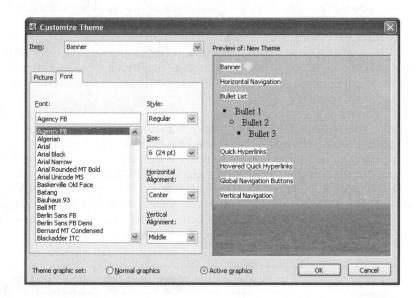

Advanced Management Features and Web Site Publishing

FrontPage is a tool that works great for the beginning web site developer, or one that can be used by more advanced developers who need to work with custom features. Using FrontPage, you can develop basic web sites quickly and easily using the features explored in Chapter 34, but you can also use some advanced features, such as HTML editing and database inclusion, in your web sites.

In addition to advanced management features, FrontPage provides the tools and options to publish sites to web servers in order for the world to see them. FrontPage 2003 supports more flexible publishing features than we have seen in earlier versions of Office, which means you have more options concerning how a site is published and where it is published. In this chapter, we'll explore some of FrontPage's advanced features, and you'll see how to publish a web site.

Working with HTML in FrontPage

We should tell you up front that this is not a how-to section on using HTML. Like all computer languages, HTML requires time and patience to learn, and you'll need a book on HTML or perhaps even a class to master HTML. However, many web developers prefer to use HTML over the graphical interface when they work on web pages. Why? (You might ask.) The answer is simply that HTML is more flexible and provides more page development options, when you really understand how to use the language. Let me again say that knowledge of HTML is not required to produce outstanding web pages in FrontPage. But if you already know how to use HTML, you will certainly want to take advantage of the HTML options and features provided by FrontPage 2003. The following sections explore those features.

Code and Split-Pane View

FrontPage 2003 allows you to easily toggle between three different views: Code, Design, and Split-Pane, where you can see both code and design. As you are working in FrontPage, you can toggle between the three views to see the HTML, the design of the page, or both at the same time. When you click the Code view option, you can easily type and correct HTML because this view works much like a basic text editor. Figure 35-1 shows HTML in Code view. You can use it to insert or edit HTML tags and text directly or to make adjustments to the HTML that can't be made in Design view. If you insert the cursor at a given location or select text in Normal view and then switch to Code view, the cursor remains at the same location or the text remains selected.

Working with Tags

A helpful improvement to FrontPage is the ability to insert HTML tags by using the menu commands, even when you are in Code view. This means that you can insert HTML without knowing the correct syntax and see the results instantly. You can insert tags for the majority of the commands under the Insert menu, but there are some exceptions. However, you may have noticed that when you are in HTML view, you can't use the formatting menu commands. Instead, you can access formatting properties by accessing Tag properties. In Code view, right-click the beginning paragraph (<p>) tag. (Alternatively, you can select the tag and then right-click anywhere on the page.) Select Tag Properties in the Option menu.

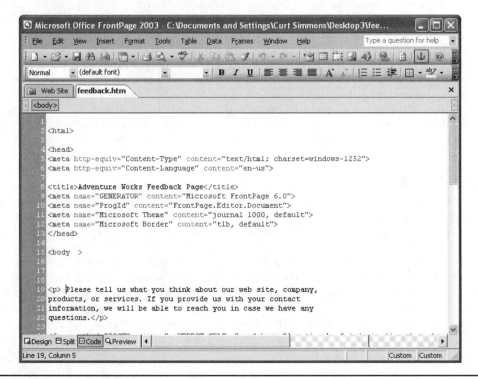

FIGURE 35-1   HTML in Code view

FrontPage displays the normal Paragraph Properties dialog box, enabling you to format the paragraph as you wish. For example, you might change the alignment from its default status to right alignment. Click OK to close the dialog box, and FrontPage updates the paragraph tag. This same technique works for all HTML tags.

Controlling Color Coding

By default, Code view color codes various HTML elements so you can tell what element you are working with simply by color. By default, FrontPage uses the following color coding:

- Normal text – Black
- Tags – Purple
- Tag attribute names – Red
- Tag attribute values – Blue
- Comments – Gray
- Scripts – Dark Red

Color coding is a simple, helpful feature, but you can turn it off or change it as you like. To turn off color coding, go to Code view, right-click anywhere on the page, and select the Show Color Coding option to uncheck it. This will turn all color coding text to black and white.

If you want to change the default color coding, select Tools | Page Options and click the Color Coding tab, shown in Figure 35-2. Use the color-picker to adjust the display colors for any of the elements previously indicated. You can also use this tab to check or uncheck the Show Color Coding option.

Finding and Replacing Text and Finding Line Numbers

In addition to the other regular editing features, the find and replace features are active in Code view to help you quickly find or replace HTML code in your pages. These features work just as they do in Normal view. To use the Find dialog box, select Edit | Find or press CTRL-F, enter the text that you're looking for in the Find What text box, and then click the Find Next button. The text (if it exists on your page) will be highlighted.

To use the Replace dialog box, select Edit | Replace or press CTRL-H, enter the text that you want to replace in the Find What text box, and then enter the text to replace it with in the Replace With text box. To review each change before it's made, click the Find Next button to highlight the text you're looking for, and then, if you want to change it, click the Replace button. The Replace button changes the text and then highlights the next instance of the text. To replace all instances of the text at once, click the Replace All button.

You can also jump to a certain line number when you are working with HTML. Access this feature by right-clicking the page in Code view and selecting Go To Line from the options menu, which displays the Go To Line dialog box. Type the number of the line in the dialog box, and then click OK.

Using Custom HTML

If you are editing web pages that contain elements from other programming environments, such as XML or JSP, FrontPage allows you to use the custom HTML without trying to correct

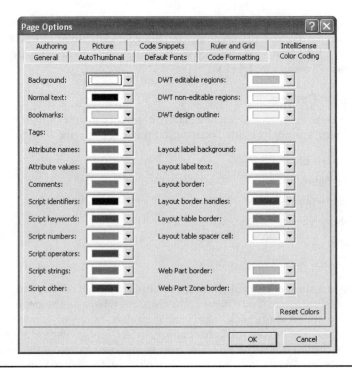

FIGURE 35-2   Adjusting the color coding

or change it in any way. Obviously, this trick is for advanced web developers who want to include programming code in their web sites that is not natively supported by FrontPage. If you use this feature, make sure any code you paste into FrontPage is correct, as FrontPage provides no checking or support.

Working with Reveal Tags

HTML reveal tags can be a great way to see how your FrontPage is laid out, even when you are working in Design mode. This feature is called "reveal tags," which is roughly equivalent to the Show All icon that reveals other "hidden" symbols, such as line and paragraph breaks. With reveal tags, FrontPage turns on icons that represent the beginning and ending tags in your HTML document, as shown in Figure 35-3. To show reveal tags, select View | Reveal Tags. To hide the codes, select View | Reveal Tags again. From a practical standpoint, reveal tags does have some limited value in that it provides a shortcut to the tag properties dialog boxes. If you double-click a Reveal Codes tag, for example, you bring up the properties dialog box that corresponds to that tag set, just as you do when you select Tag Properties (described earlier in the chapter) in the HTML tab.

Managing HTML Preferences

Most people who use HTML have a few tricks up their sleeves to make the writing of HTML easier. For example, you may use capital letters for all tags and attributes to distinguish

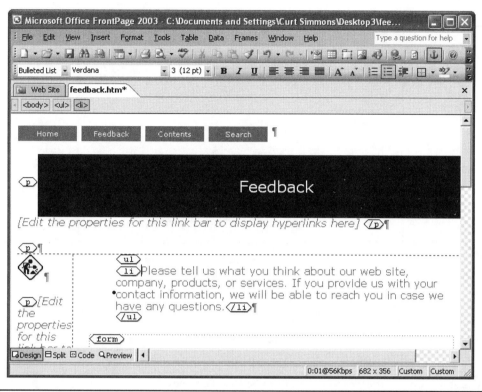

FIGURE 35-3 Reveal tags

them from the actual page content. Or, you may divide the lines of HTML and perhaps indent them to make them easy to read. You may add comments internally to help you identify major sections of more complex pages.

The good news is FrontPage 2003 will allow you to format your HTML as you want, within some reasonable parameters. You set your HTML formatting preferences by using the Code Formatting tab. To access this tab, select Tools | Page Options and click the Code Formatting tab in the Page Options dialog box, shown in Figure 35-4.

The Code Formatting tab contains two main sections: Formatting and Tags. In the Formatting section, decide whether you want FrontPage to reformat your HTML to rules that you define, or simply to preserve the existing HTML. Here are some of the common items you can choose:

- **Tag Names Are Lowercase**   Uncheck this option if you want HTML tags written in uppercase.

- **Attribute Names Are Lowercase**   Uncheck this option if you want HTML attributes within tags to be uppercase.

- **Allow Line Breaks Within Tags**   Uncheck this option to prevent tags from wrapping around to a second line. (Splitting a tag into multiple lines is perfectly valid in HTML.)

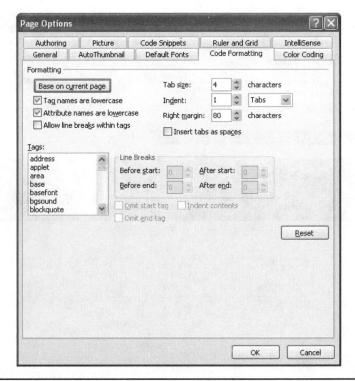

FIGURE 35-4   Code Formatting tab of the Page Options dialog box

- **Indent**   Select a quantity and a unit (spaces or tabs) to indicate how much to indent tags (in the Tags list at the bottom of the HTML Source tab) that have the Indent Contents check box selected.

The remaining formatting options pertain to individual tags. To set these options for a specific tag, first select the tag by clicking it in the scrolling Tags list. Then, configure the listed formatting options.

NOTE   *One other important option in the Code Formatting tab is the Base on Current Page button. When you select this option, FrontPage analyzes the current page to determine how you would like your HTML to appear.*

Working with Forms and Form Input

In Chapter 34, you learned how to design a standard web page that includes text and pictures or other common content. However, you'll notice that standard web pages are great for providing information, but not so great for gathering input from viewers. With the exception of links to e-mail addresses, viewers have no way to communicate with you, and you have no way to gather information from them. The good news is FrontPage provides the features you need to create forms and gather input from viewers using those forms. Forms can be used as a way to collect information from users, request feedback, initiate a database query, or facilitate a discussion. All of this is possible without any programming by using built-in form handling components in FrontPage. In the following sections, you'll see how to create forms, manage them, and gather the input that users enter into the forms.

Creating Forms

The most basic form contains an input field, a button to submit the results, and a results message. To create a form in FrontPage, first create a new blank page by selecting Insert | Form, and then select a form element to add to your form from the pop-up menu that appears. The most basic of all forms is the text box, which places a box on your page where users can input data. The text box form element is inserted, complete with Submit and Reset buttons.

Along with your text box, you can add other boxes as well as other descriptive text that will create your form, as you can see in Figure 35-5.

Notice that if you click on the field box to select it, you can drag the corners to make it longer or shorter but not taller. If you double-click the field box, it opens the Text Box

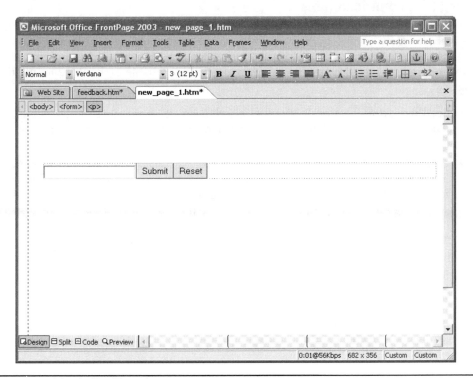

FIGURE 35-5   A basic FrontPage form

Properties dialog box, shown here. You can give the text box a name, manage its width, and use a password field if you like.

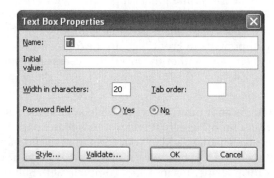

As you noticed, when you insert a text box, FrontPage provides you with a Submit button. However, FrontPage has to know what to do with the information in the text. Don't worry, you'll see how to configure those options later in this chapter.

Working with Form Templates

FrontPage includes several templates that contain predesigned forms. If you are looking for a relatively standard form type, starting with one of these templates is likely to save you some time. A Form wizard is also available, which can help you create the form you need quickly and easily. The following are the form templates available in the Page Templates dialog box:

- **Feedback form** A simple form designed to solicit comments from users on a variety of company-related topics. It uses the Save Results component to send input to a text file.

- **Guest book** A basic text-input form that enables site visitors to record a comment, much like the guest register of a small hotel or bed-and-breakfast inn. Although this form is a relatively simplistic way to encourage user involvement on your web, a surprising number of people actually take the time to sign your guest book (especially if you let them read what they and others have written). The Guest Book form uses the Save Results component to send comments to an HTML page that can be viewed by visitors to your web site.

- **Search page** A simple one-field text-string search form used in conjunction with FrontPage's built-in text search engine.

- **User registration** A form that allows users to enter a username and password for accessing a designated access-controlled web. This component is restricted to certain web servers and must be saved in a root web. Results are processed by the Web Registration component.

Exploring Form Elements

At the beginning of this section, you took a look at some quick steps for creating and managing a simple text box in a form. As you can see, FrontPage provides you with several different kinds of form elements, one of them being the text box. You can see your other options if you click Insert | Form. Here is an overview of the other elements available on the Insert | Form menu and how you can use them.

Textbox

The one-line text box is the staple of most online forms. It is suitable for short input and is commonly used in forms. To resize the input box, select it and drag either side handle of the box. A one-line text box can't be resized vertically (in other words, it can be made wider or narrower, but not taller). You can define font attributes, paragraph formatting, and borders for text fields. These formatting features are available through the Style button in the Form Field Properties dialog boxes. Font attributes can be applied to any input form field that displays text.

Text Area

A Text Area is a dialog box that allows for multiple lines of text, as you can see in Figure 35-6. Typically, a scrolling text box is used when a paragraph of text is called for, such as comments

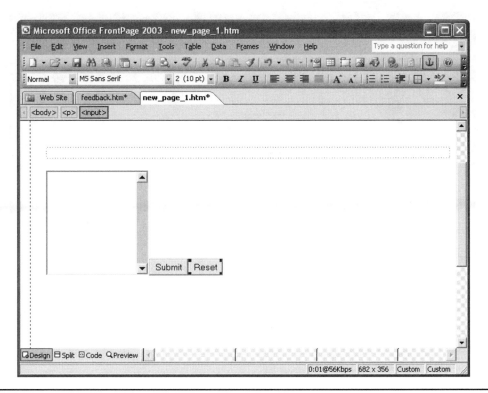

FIGURE 35-6   Select Text Area to create a scrolling text box.

or messages. To create a scrolling text box, select Insert | Form | Text Area. You can resize a text area element both horizontally (make it wider or narrower) and vertically (make it taller or shorter) by dragging any of the eight corner or side handles that appear when the box is selected. To edit the text area properties, either double-click the input box or right-click the box and select Form Field Properties to open the Text Area Box Properties dialog box. You have the same basic properties options as the text box.

File Upload

The File Upload option allows you to insert a form option so that users can upload a file to you. The option prompts you to choose a folder on your web site where the file uploads will be stored. Users see a simple text box option, but in addition to the Submit and Reset buttons, they also see a Browse button so they can browse for the desired file on their computer. The simple properties dialog box for this form element simply allows you to name the form and manage form width.

Checkbox

Check boxes are just that—small square boxes that when clicked with a mouse, note some selection, such as those shown in Figure 35-7. Basically, check boxes are used for selection input or for yes/no input. Although check boxes are often used for a group of

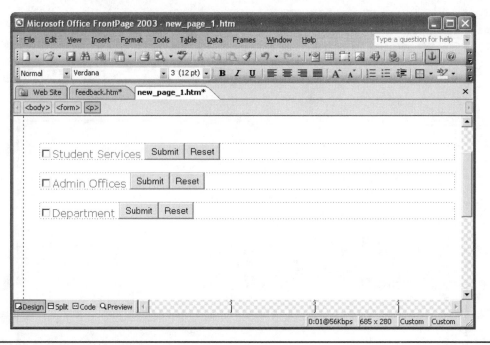

FIGURE 35-7   Check box option

options, they are nonexclusive, which means that checking one box does not restrict the user from checking another box in the same grouping. This is the chief difference between check boxes and option buttons. Option buttons are exclusive, which means a user can select only one option button in a group.

To create a check box, select Insert | Form | Checkbox. To edit the check box properties, double-click the check box or right-click the box and select Form Field Properties. The Check Box Properties dialog box, shown here, is displayed.

Option Button

Option buttons, also called radio buttons, are like check boxes, but they are best used in a list where users can select only one item. For example, if you have a site where you are shipping a product to a customer, an option button list would work well since the customer can only select one shipping option. Keep in mind that a check box is nonexclusive—users can select multiple check boxes. An option button, however, only allows the user to select one option. To create an option button, select Insert | Form | Option Button.

To edit the option button properties, either double-click the option button or right-click the button and select Form Field Properties. The Option Button Properties dialog box allows you to assign a group name, initial state, and tab order.

Group Box

The Group Box element is a visual border you can use to organize form elements into labeled boxes. It has no functionality of its own. A group box is especially handy if you have a long form that would benefit from breaking the input elements into sections of related items. To add a group box, select Insert | Form | Group Box from the menu to open the Group Box Properties dialog box.

Drop-Down Box

Drop-down boxes, which allow users to select an item from a list, are similar to check boxes or groups of option buttons in that they enable a visitor to make selections from a group of options. The difference is mainly in the appearance of the form field. Most often, drop-down boxes enable a visitor to choose one option from a list. To create a drop-down box, select Insert | Form | Drop-Down Box. This creates an empty drop-down box. To add items to the menu list, edit the drop-down box properties either by double-clicking the drop-down box or right-clicking and selecting Form Field Properties. The Drop-Down Box Properties dialog box, shown here, is displayed.

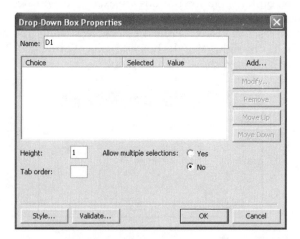

Use the Choice option by clicking the Add button to create the list of items that appears in the drop-down menu. To add an item, select Add. This opens the Add Choice dialog box:

Type the list item into the Choice input field. Optionally, check the Specify Value field and type a value to be sent when the form is submitted. This feature allows you to specify a different text option when the form is sent. If you do not specify a value, the form uses the Choice text, so you don't need to specify a value unless you want the information to be different from the Choice text. Select the Selected option button to have this item selected by default.

Push Button

In order to receive any input from any kind of form that you create, you'll need some kind of Submit button, which is called a push button. Push buttons are special-purpose buttons that automatically instruct the web browser to send back the form input. All you have to do is add the button to the page. If you create a form element by selecting Insert | Form, FrontPage automatically adds both a Submit and a Reset button.

You can change the name and the label of the Submit button by double-clicking the button in Normal view, or by right-clicking it and selecting Form Field Properties from the Option menu. This opens the Push Button Properties dialog box, where you make your changes.

Advanced Button

An advanced button is just a normal button that you can resize and then type in the name directly rather than using a properties box. Essentially, the button doesn't do anything that is "advanced," but it's easier to modify than a standard button. To create a new advanced button, select Insert | Form | Advanced Button. Click on the button's label to change the text. Drag the corners of the button to change its width or height. Or, if you prefer, double-click the button and edit these elements directly in the Advanced Button Properties dialog box.

Picture

A picture button, once again, does the same thing as any other kind of button, but you can use a picture or clip art for the button itself. The only negative aspect of this option is that the picture button will not "push" when you click it, but other than that, the functionality is the same. You can use any standard picture as a button, although users are more likely to click on pictures that resemble buttons. To create a picture button, select Insert | Form | Picture, and select the image you want using the regular Picture dialog box. Although it appears that you are simply adding a picture to your page, you are in fact adding a button. Clicking on this picture causes the page to submit, much as it would if you had used a Submit button.

Label

Typically, when you create an HTML form, you label fields using standard HTML text. The Label element enables you to link a label specifically to another form element. As mentioned when describing option buttons, the Label element may bring with it some additional functionality for your page. To add a label, first create another form field. Then type the label you want to use. Select both the label and the form and, from the menu, select Insert | Form | Label. Notice that FrontPage puts gray dashed lines around the label.

Confirmation Page

When you create a form in FrontPage, FrontPage automatically uses a default confirmation message. In other words, when users click Submit, the data is uploaded to the server, and they see a confirmation message telling them so. You can see the default confirmation message by clicking the Options button in the Form Properties dialog box and then selecting the Confirmation Page tab from the Saving Results dialog box. This tab, shown in Figure 35-8, allows you to define your own custom confirmation page. In the absence of one, it returns a default page.

Using the Form Page Wizard

In addition to the form templates described in the previous sections, FrontPage includes a Form Page wizard that can help you construct a sophisticated form quickly. To create a form

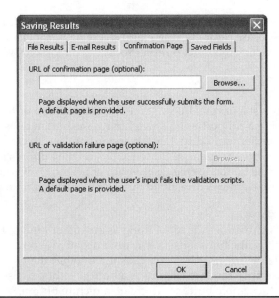

FIGURE 35-8   A default confirmation page is used.

using the Form Page wizard, select File | New and choose Form Page Wizard from the Page Template dialog box. The following steps show you how to use the wizard.

1. The initial wizard page gives you an introduction to creating the form. Read the information here and click Next.

2. In the next dialog box, you select the questions you plan to include in your form. Click Add to add a new question. Select the type of input to include from the drop-down list, shown in the following illustration, and customize the prompt question to your liking. You have the following options:

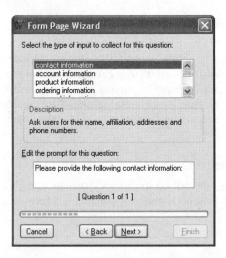

- **Contact Information**   Builds form fields to capture name, affiliation, address, and phone number
- **Account Information**   Prompts for username and password
- **Product Information**   Asks for a product name, model, version, and serial number
- **Ordering Information**   Produces a form to take a sales order, including a list of products to order, billing details, and shipping information
- **Personal Information**   Collects information such as username, age, and other personal characteristics
- **One of Several Options**   Requires users to pick exactly one option
- **Any of Several Options**   Enables users to pick zero or more options
- **Boolean**   Prompts to input a yes/no or true/false question
- **Date**   Prompts to input a date format
- **Time**   Prompts to input a time format
- **Range**   Creates a rating scale from 1 to 5
- **Number**   Creates an input box for a number
- **String**   Creates a one-line text box
- **Paragraph**   Creates a scrolling text box

3. After you select the input type for your form, click the Next button in the dialog box. You are prompted for details about the specific form data that you want to include in this form. For example, if you ask for contact information, you can use the check boxes in the dialog box, shown in the following illustration, to define exactly what contact information you want to collect. Click Next.

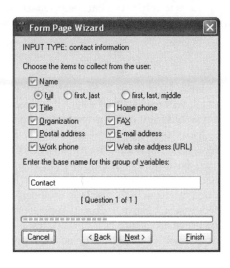

4. The Presentation Options dialog box, shown in the following illustration, enables you to define the look of your form page. The group of four option buttons at the

top of the Presentation Options dialog box enables you to lay out your questions as normal paragraphs, as a numbered list, as a bulleted list, or as a definition list. Select one of these options for organizing your form questions. The Yes and No option buttons under Would You Like a Table of Contents for This Page? enable you to place a table of contents on your form page. The table of contents generates links within the page to each question, allowing a visitor to jump directly to a selected question. Make your selections and click Next.

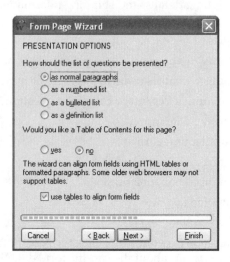

5. In the Output Options dialog box, you determine what happens to the data submitted in a form. Select the Save Results to Web Page option button to send the input to a page that can be viewed in your browser. Or, select the Save Results to a Text File option button to send the results to a file that can be opened with a word processor. Make your selections, and then click Next and Finish. Your form now appears on the page.

Gathering Form Input

One of the most important aspects of any form is the actual gathering of information once the user clicks the Submit button. After all, where does that data go and how can you access it? Fortunately, FrontPage gives you a few different options for gathering form input data.

Once again, you configure your form to handle input results by using the Form Properties dialog box. To access this dialog box, you first need a form. As you can see in Figure 35-9, we are using a standard form created with the Form Page wizard.

To configure your form's properties, right-click anywhere inside the form and select the Form Properties item from the options menu, which displays the Form Properties dialog box, shown in Figure 35-10. You can select Insert | Form | Form Properties to get the same results.

The Form Properties dialog box consists of two principal parts: a section to designate where to send the form results and a section to designate basic form properties. The following sections review the options you have for sending form contents.

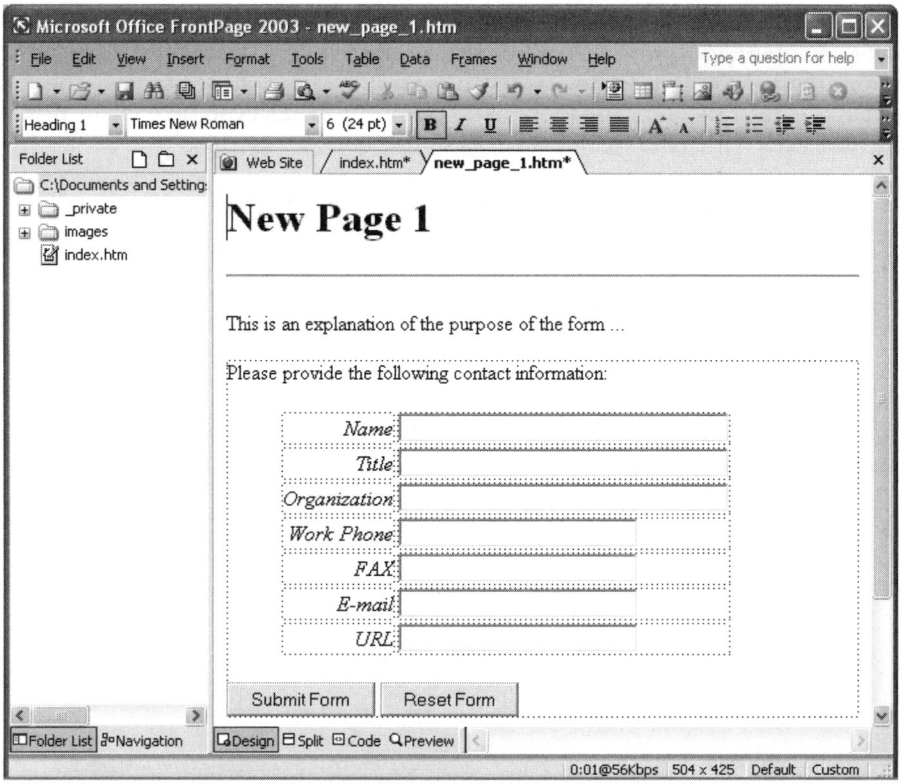

FIGURE 35-9   Standard form

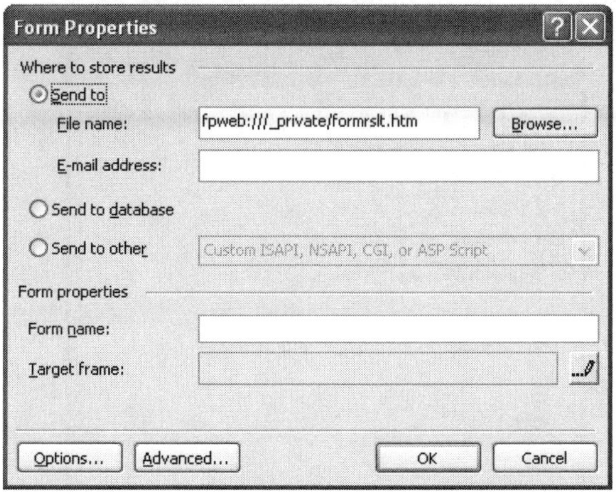

FIGURE 35-10   Setting form properties

Send to File

By default, all FrontPage forms are configured to send results to a simple web page. Using the Form Properties Options button, you can control the type of file to which the data is output, and the quantity of information that is output. You can even save the results to two separate files, each with a different format, as shown here.

Send to E-mail Address

You may want the form data sent to you by e-mail. This is especially true for smaller sites, or when form data requires a quick response. If you want to be alerted to form input, simply enter your e-mail address in the E-mail Results tab of the Saving Results dialog box, shown here (click the Options button on the Form Properties dialog box).

As with the results file, you can specify the format of the e-mail message that is sent. All the file formats previously listed for the results file apply here as well. The chief difference is that an e-mail message always contains data for one record. In addition, remember that your e-mail reader must support HTML formatting if you want to receive the file in one of the HTML formats.

Adding Results to a Database

If you are using a database with your site, you can also send form results directly to a database. Obviously, this kind of approach is used with larger sites and e-commerce sites. A discussion of database usage with FrontPage is beyond the scope of this book, but do keep in mind that FrontPage can easily send form results to a database, if a database is configured for use. Just select the option on the Form Properties dialog box and use the Options button to configure database results on the Database Results tab.

Managing Browser Compatibility

If you have ever wondered how different web browsers, such as Internet Explorer, Netscape, and Opera, use the same HTML code and interpret it the same way, the issue all comes down to standards. After all, one of the major goals of the Web is standard compatibility, whereby people can access information without having to use one specific browser or brand of software. Of course, that lofty goal can be difficult to accomplish. As you probably know, many different technologies, protocols, and languages are used on the Web these days, and the primary problem now comes down to compatibility with older browsers. In fact, industry competition and changes over time to the HTML standards have resulted in many small, but sometimes debilitating, differences in browser behavior.

FrontPage tries to help you with browser compatibility problems by letting you choose your compatibility preferences, using the Authoring tab in the Page Options dialog box. To access the Authoring tab, shown in Figure 35-11, select Tools | Page Options and switch to the Authoring tab.

Use the Authoring tab to select the browsers you want to support. The Authoring tab offers the following options:

- **Browsers**   You can specify the browsers you want to support. If you select one of the available options, you must also select a browser version option before FrontPage makes any adjustments.

- **Browser Versions**   You can select options for browser versions 3.0, 4.0, 5.0, and later. If you select a browser version level, you must also select browser options before FrontPage makes any adjustments.

- **Schema Versions**   Options include Internet Explorer versions 3.0 and later and Apache. If you select Apache, FrontPage disables Active Server Pages (ASP) support.

***

NOTE   *Notice that when you specify the browser or schema versions you need to support, FrontPage automatically checks and unchecks the available technologies for your configuration. This results in FrontPage disabling particular menu items so that you do not inadvertently create browser problems.*

FIGURE 35-11   Authoring tab in Page Options

If you leave the Authoring tab's browser and schema options set to their default—Custom—you can select the particular technologies you want to support, regardless of which browsers happen to support those features. Your options include the following:

- **ActiveX Controls**   Microsoft-based components that can be embedded in web pages. Unchecking this option disables the ActiveX Advanced Control in the Web Components dialog box.

- **VBScript**   A compact version of Visual Basic designed for use as a client-side scripting language. Only Internet Explorer supports it. Unchecking this option disables VBScript support.

- **JavaScript**   A client-side scripting language used to provide user interaction. Unchecking this option disables all FrontPage features that require JavaScript.

- **Java Applets**   Small Java-based applications designed to run inside a web page. Unchecking this option disables the Java applet Advanced Control.

- **Frames**   A feature that enables you to create "embedded" HTML pages. Unchecking this option removes the Frames templates from the Page Templates dialog box and disables the Frames menu command and the Inline Frame command.

- **Active Server Pages**   A Microsoft server-side programming environment that uses VBScript. Unchecking this option disables FrontPage support for ASP scripting elements. Because this is a server-side programming environment, it is server dependent, not browser dependent as most of the other options are.

- **CSS 1.0 (Formatting)**   The standard used by FrontPage when you create styles. CSS stands for cascading style sheets. Unchecking this option disables the Styles menu command and removes the Style Sheet templates from the New Page Templates dialog box.

- **CSS 2.0 (Positioning)**   An option that you can select if you enable CSS 1.0 support, giving you CSS 2.0 support, or at least the positioning aspects that FrontPage supports.

- **PNG Graphics**   A newer graphics file format supported by newer browsers. Checking this option allows your site to provide PNG graphics.

Publishing Sites and Pages

In FrontPage, the term "publishing" refers specifically to the process you use to copy one or more web pages from one location to another. This generally means publishing the web page from a development area that is off-limits to the general public to a production web server. In general, think of publishing in FrontPage as "copying"—when you publish pages in FrontPage, you are copying files from one location to another in a manner that enables FrontPage to do several things: keep track of the changes you are making, make any necessary adjustments to links and other features, and ensure that your web site works correctly in its new location.

There are a few different ways you can use FrontPage to publish your pages to a web server:

- *Develop locally, publish remotely*. If you are creating your own site, and have sole responsibility for creating and approving the content, the best scenario is to maintain a local, "development" version of your site. From here, you can make changes and test and preview them before you publish to your "live" server, which in most cases will be hosted. This approach is especially useful if you are operating over a relatively slow dial-up connection, as it enables you to make changes offline and then dial up to publish your changes all at once. As a general rule, this is the method that most people use to publish their sites.

- *Use multiple workgroups and publish to a single server*. If you are creating a site with a team of developers, you need to give some thought to how you will divide the task of updating pages without accidentally overwriting someone else's changes. One approach is to use the check-in/check-out functionality of FrontPage to ensure that only one person at a time edits a file. However, this model requires that you check out a fresh copy of a page from a central location each time you want to edit it. You may also consider dividing the web site into subwebs that different people manage.

- *Publish live on a server*. If you have a small web site that isn't critical to your business, you can also just edit directly on the web server. Once your site is initially published to the server, you can simply choose File | Open Site and open your site directly from the web server. Changes you make are saved directly to the web server and are available for the world to see immediately.

Choosing a Web Provider

Once you have created a web site using FrontPage, it doesn't do much good if it is not on the Internet so people can actually see it. In order to publish your web site, you'll need a web provider, which essentially is going to provide you with the web server space for your site so that it can be accessed by the world.

In the beginning, the only Internet connectivity providers were Internet access providers (IAPs), more commonly known as Internet service providers (ISPs). An ISP primarily offers their customers connectivity to the Internet. Most ISP accounts come with e-mail, including some amount of online storage space for e-mail messages. Increasingly, ISPs also offer their customers other kinds of space, principally web site space (and sometimes storage for anonymous FTP, as well). Typically, however, ISPs (with notable exceptions) are primarily in the connectivity business. They aren't as strong in the area of providing support and development services for business-oriented customers.

So, a new kind of provider emerged—the web hosting company (sometimes called web presence providers, WPPs). These folks don't deal in providing Internet access for you. Instead, they focus on providing a safe and easily accessible home for your web site on the Internet. In principle, this focus means that they can provide more expertise in the area of web development, but they assume that you can find your own access to the Internet elsewhere.

Of course, the divisions are not always clear-cut. Many ISPs offer web hosting services. Some companies that focus on web hosting also offer various forms of access, although frequently they have simply partnered with a traditional ISP to provide this access. In general, you are likely to get a better deal by combining your dial-up service and web hosting with the same company, but support may not be equally strong in both connectivity issues and web site hosting.

Microsoft maintains a list of web hosting providers who support FrontPage. To access their list of providers, select File | Publish Site and click the Click Here to Learn More link in the Remote Web Site Properties dialog box. This opens the Microsoft web page entitled "Locate a Web Presence Provider," which enables you to search for FrontPage-friendly providers, as you can see in Figure 35-12.

Aside from using Microsoft's site to find a provider, it is also a good idea to talk to other people and even do a few web searches on your own. Microsoft's list is not comprehensive, and you may find better deals by searching on your own.

If you already have an ISP that provides you with a dial-up account to the Internet, you might want to find out whether it provides web site presence as part of that account and, if so, whether it supports FrontPage. An increasing number of ISPs do, although they may not have made it onto Microsoft's list.

A wide range of services and prices is available, so be sure to check out your options carefully. Once you have a short list of possibilities, ask any WPP you are considering to provide you with a list of references you can check directly, and ask those references how satisfied they are with the service. Here are some additional considerations:

- **Features and pricing**   Do you need dial-up access in addition to web hosting? Do you need e-mail? Programming and/or database support? Do you plan to use streaming multimedia in your site? Do you have specific requirements regarding usage reporting? All of these are available, but compare packages carefully—prices and services vary considerably. These days, you can get a fairly decent hosting package for under $20 a month, and you can even find some reasonably good free hosting sites.

- **Support** If you plan to use FrontPage exclusively, one of your main considerations is the level of FrontPage support provided. Options in the support category range from no support (the FrontPage extension is installed for you, but you are on your own) to extensive (and expensive) on-site training options. Many providers have added FrontPage Server Extensions because of customer demand, but they are not providing technical support for FrontPage. The list of providers with qualified, experienced support and technical staff to assist you with FrontPage questions is much smaller. Make certain the site specifies that they are running the FrontPage Server Extensions, and be clear about which versions are available.

- **Reliability** Ideally, you want to know two things: does the provider keep their servers up and running, and do they keep them running efficiently (as opposed to bogging them down by overloading too many customers on the same server). This is sometimes difficult to judge until it's too late, but providers should be able to supply statistics showing their uptimes, which should be well over 99 percent, and also share with you their policies concerning server loads.

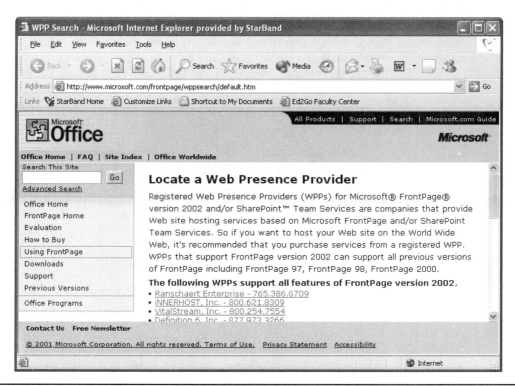

FIGURE 35-12 Web presence providers at microsoft.com

Publishing Your Site

Once you have selected a web provider, you'll sign up, and the provider will give you a username and password that you'll need in order to publish your site to the web server. Now you are ready to go through the actual process of publishing your web site for the first time. The good news is the process is generally easy and trouble free.

First of all, you have four different options when publishing to a remote server:

- **FrontPage or SharePoint Services**   You select this option when you are publishing to a server that supports FrontPage or SharePoint Services.

- **DAV**   FrontPage can also publish to sites that support DAV, or Distributed Authoring and Versioning. Although FrontPage sites will function on DAV servers, any elements that require FrontPage server extensions will not work.

- **FTP**   You can publish your site to servers using the File Transfer Protocol, for which FrontPage 2003 provides better support.

- **File System**   This option allows you to save your site to a folder on your computer or on a network instead of a remote web site. This is an effective way to create a backup copy of your site.

When you are ready to publish your site, just follow these steps:

1. Click File | Publish Site.

2. In the Remote Web Site Properties dialog box that appears, shown in the following illustration, choose the kind of remote server that you want to use in order to publish your site. Enter the site location, such as the URL, or click Browse if necessary. Click OK.

3. The web site is contacted, and you may be prompted to log in. Next, you see a window in FrontPage showing the pages that will be copied to the remote web site. If you do not want to publish a particular page, just right-click it in the Local Web Site window, and click Don't Publish. Otherwise, click the Publish Web Site button when you are ready.

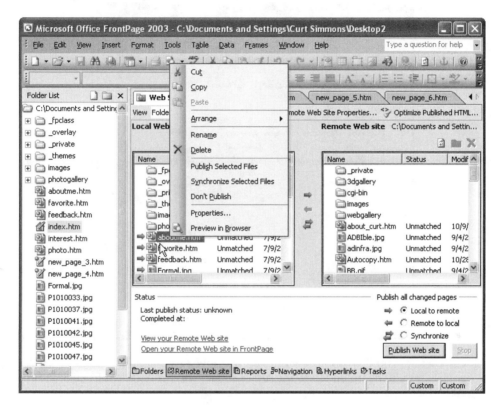

4. When publication is successful, you'll see a message telling you so in the Status area of the publish window. You can choose to view the publish log file, the remote web site, and even open the remote web site in FrontPage by simply clicking the provided links.

Updating Your Site

Once you publish your site, you access it with any browser and see your new creation on the Web. However, what happens when you need to add some new content to your site, or fix some problems you have discovered? No problem, FrontPage lets you make those editorial changes and upload the changes to the web server as well. When you make changes to your site and you need to update it on the server, just follow these steps:

1. Click File | Publish Site.

2. In the Remote Web Site Properties dialog box that appears, again choose your type of web site and location. This page will default to your last published site, so you probably will not have to do anything here.

3. Click the Publishing tab. This tab, shown in the following illustration, dictates how publishing occurs. As you can see under Publish, Changed Pages Only is selected. This means that FrontPage does not have to re-upload all of the pages in your site every time you republish it. Just click OK.

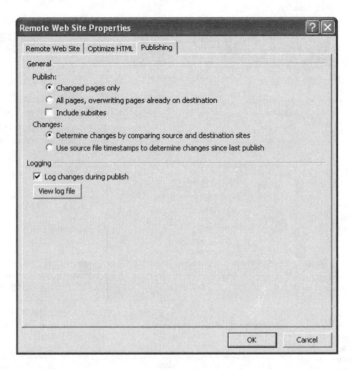

4. Once again, you'll return to the publish window. FrontPage will show you the pages that will be uploaded to the remote site. When you are ready, click Publish Web Site.

Using Reports to Manage Your Web Site

Web reports provide ready access to a wide variety of useful information about your web site. Both before and after you publish changes to your site, you can use web reports to help you keep track of your web pages, to identify and help you correct problems, and to manage the maintenance process.

You can navigate through the reports in several ways. Click View | Reports to see a listing of report options. The following sections give you an overview of what is available and how to use the reports.

Site Summary

The Site Summary report, shown in Figure 35-13, gives you a high-level overview of the health and status of your web. For each summary item, this report indicates the report name, a count of the number of items included in the report, a file size total where relevant,

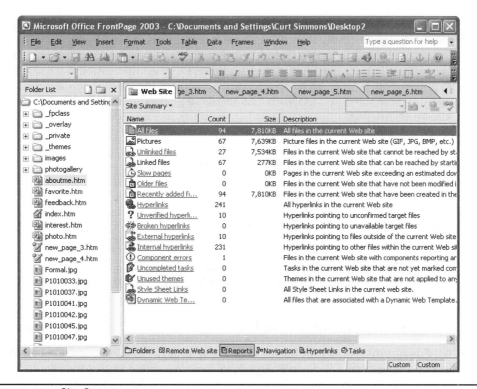

FIGURE 35-13   Site Summary

and a description. Many, but not all, items have a detail page. To see the details for an item in the Site Summary report, click the hyperlinked line in question. However, note that not all of the available reports have links from Site Summary. To access these, you must use the View | Reports listing.

All of the reports have some basic features in common. Although some functionality varies depending on the context, in most, you can do all of the following tasks:

- Double-click a filename to open it. You can also usually access all of the normal file property options by right-clicking on the filename in the list.

- Click on any column header in a report to re-sort the report on the information in that column; clicking a second time reverses the order of the sort.

- Drag the edge of a column to expand or shrink it.

- Drag the column header to reorder the columns.

- Filter report results using the pull-down menus in each column. Click the downward arrow in the column header to reveal a drop-down menu containing the options: All (the default), Custom, and a list of the specific items currently in the list. In cases where blank values are allowed, you will also see Blank and Non-blank as filter options.

- You can right-click the title bar of a report to call up an options menu, with the following options: New Page, Copy Report, Paste (if relevant), Remove Filters (assuming filters are in effect), and Web Settings, a link to the dialog box of that name (found under the Tools menu). Of these, the most interesting is the Copy Report option. Selecting this option creates a copy of the current report, which you can paste into another Office document (such as Word or Excel) or even into an HTML page.

Detailed Reports

FrontPage 2003 includes over a dozen detailed reports that you can use to view information about the contents of your web. In most cases, you can sort reports and even make changes to report items from within the report itself. Thus, the report serves as a powerful Find feature for problems when you are first preparing to publish or when you are doing periodic maintenance reviews of your site. Reports are available on files, shared content, problems, workflow, and usage.

NOTE   *The reports you read about here are available on the View | Reports menu.*

Reports on Files

The following report options are available to you:

- **All Files**   Provides details for the All Files summary item. For each file it includes the following: Name, Title, In Folder, Size, Type, Modified Date, Modified By, and Comments. You can change the filename and its title, and add comments from this list. This is a great place to check your page titles for consistency, by the way, because you can see all of your titles simultaneously.

- **Recently Added Files**   Lists all files added within a definable date range. For each file it includes the following: Name, Title, Created Date, Modified By, Size, Type, and In Folder. You can edit Name and Title. Use the Report Settings menu to define the date range. You can also configure the date that defines recent files in the Reports View tab of the Options menu or in the Reports toolbar.

- **Recently Changed Files**   Lists all files added within a definable date range. It includes the following: Name, Title, Modified Date, Modified By, Size, Type, and In Folder. You can edit Name and Title. Use the Report Settings menu to define the date range. You can also configure the date that defines recent files in the Reports View tab of the Options menu. Figure 35-14 shows an example report of recently changed files.

- **Older Files**   Provides details for the Older Files summary item. It includes the following: Name, Title, Modified Date, Modified By, Size, Type, and In Folder. You can edit Name and Title. Use the Report Settings menu to define the date range. You can also configure the date that defines recent files in the Reports View tab of the Options menu or in the Reports toolbar.

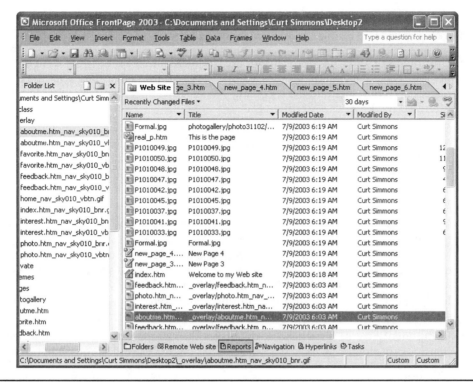

FIGURE 35-14   List of recently changed files in Reports view

Shared Content

The following shared content items are available to you:

- **Dynamic Web Templates**   Provides details about dynamic web templates that are in use on the web site. This report includes Name, Title, Dynamic Web Template, In Folder, Size, Type, Modified Date, and Modified By.

- **Shared Borders**   Shows a listing of files and pages used in shared borders on the site. This report includes Name, Title, Shared Borders, In Folder, Size, Type, Modified Date, and Modified By.

- **Style Sheet Links**   Lets you view style sheet links. The report includes data for Name, Title, Style Sheet Links, In Folder, Size, Type, Modified Date, and Modified By.

- **Themes**   Gives you information about the theme in use. The report includes Name, Title, Theme, Vivid Colors, Active Graphics, Background Picture, In Folder, Size, Type, Modified Date, and Modified By.

Reports on Problems

The following reports on problems are available to you:

- **Unlinked Files**   Provides details for the Unlinked Files summary item. An unlinked file is any file that cannot be accessed by following links beginning with the home page. This report includes the following: Name, Title, In Folder, Links To, Links From, Modified By, Type, and Modified Date.

- **Slow Pages**   Provides details for the Slow Pages summary item. It includes the following: Name, Title, Download Time, Size, Type, In Folder, Modified Date, and Modified By. You can edit Name and Title. You can define a slow page in the Reports View tab of the Options menu or in the Reports toolbar. Note that download times are calculated based on the Assume Connection Speed Of option in the Reports View tab of the Options dialog box.

- **Hyperlinks**   Provides file details for the Broken Link summary item. It includes the following: Status, Hyperlink, In Page, Page Title, Destination, Type, and Modified By. You cannot edit fields. Double-click a file to open the Edit Hyperlink dialog box. Right-clicking on a file in this report brings up a set of options specific to fixing the hyperlinks: Edit Hyperlink, Edit Page, Verify Hyperlink (the selected link), and Show All Hyperlinks (including nonbroken ones), in addition to the standard options: Copy Report, Remove Filter, and Web Settings.

- **Component Errors**   Provides file details for the Component Errors summary item. It includes the following: Name, Title, Errors, Type, and In Folder. You cannot edit fields.

Workflow Reports

The following workflow reports are available to you:

- **Review Status**   Lists review information for each file in the web. You can also use this report to modify review information. It includes the following: Name, Title, Review Status, Assigned To, Review Date, Reviewed By, Expiration Date, Type, and In Folder. You can edit Name, Title, Review Status, Expiration Date, and Assigned To.

- **Assigned To**   Lists details about page assignments for each file in the web. You can also use this report to modify assignment information. It includes the following: Name, Title, Assigned To, Assigned Date, Assigned By, Comments, Type, and In Folder. You can edit Name, Title, Assigned To, and Comments. Double-click a file to open it.

- **Categories**   Lists category details about each file in the web. It includes the following: Name, Title, Category, Type, and In Folder. You can't edit Category information in this report. You can use the Reports toolbar to filter the report on a specific category.

- **Publish Status**   Lists publishing details for each file in the web. It also lets you enable or disable publishing for a file. It includes the following: Name, Title, Publish, Modified Date, Review Status, Size, Type, and In Folder. You can edit Name, Title, Review Status, and Publish.

- **Checkout Status**   Available only if you have enabled source control for the current web. It includes the following: Name, Title, Checked Out By, Version, Locked Date, Type, and In Folder. You can edit Name and Title only.

Usage Reports

In FrontPage, the usage reports provide instant information about who is visiting your site, when they visit, and which pages they view. The reports also provide useful information about your visitors, such as the browsers they are using, where they are coming from, and what, if any, search engine terms they typed to locate your site. All of this information is helpful in planning both the marketing and further development of your site.

Because there are so many usage reports, we are not going to list them all here, but note that you can access such items as monthly summary, monthly page hits, daily page hits, and browsers. In short, these reports can give you a lot of information about how your site is used, which can help you make changes to the site that are effective and helpful to your visitors.

Setting Reports View Options

To configure various Reports view options, select Tools | Options and choose the Reports View tab (see Figure 35-15). Options you can configure include the following:

- **Recent files**   Indicate how many days a file should be considered recent.
- **Older files**   Indicate how many days before a file should be considered old.
- **Slow pages**   Indicate download time to define a slow page.
- **Connection speed**   Select a download connection speed for use in calculating download times.

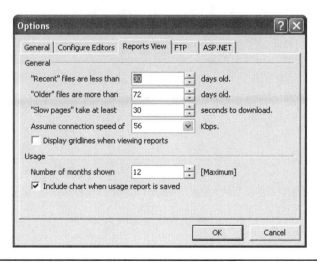

FIGURE 35-15   Reports View options

- **Display gridlines**   You can show or hide lines in your reports—for the design-conscious report reader.

- **Usage**   Set the number of months of usage you want to view.

- **Usage charts**   You can elect to include these in saved usage reports or not, as you prefer.

Creating Publications in Publisher

Microsoft Publisher is just that—a program that allows you to create print and web documents. You may be thinking, "Sure, but I can use Word to do that." The difference is that Publisher is specifically designed to be a program that creates documents for printing and online viewing. It gives you more control of layout and design than Word, and it provides you with more production options. In Publisher, all objects and text are placed in boxes and frames, so the program does not work like Word either. The good news is the flexibility Publisher gives you can help you get the kind of publication you want so that when you print it, the publication you made will look just like it did on the screen.

This chapter shows you how to create a publisher document. You'll see how to create publications from templates and how to make your own from scratch.

Creating Publications with Templates

Microsoft Publisher looks and works in a similar way to other Office 2003 applications. If you have used Word or FrontPage, you'll find that the interface works in the same basic manner: you have toolbars, a task pane, and a work area in which you can create your publications.

The other piece of good news is that Publisher, like PowerPoint, contains a series of design templates that you can use to quickly create a presentation. When you first open Publisher, you see the Start option that allows you to choose a template and start working right away, shown in Figure 36-1.

Design templates are easy to use and rather intuitive. The following steps walk you through a sample.

1. In the New Publication task pane, choose a desired category, such as Publications for Print, for the Web, and so forth.

2. Once you click a category, it expands to reveal subcategories. Some subcategories have additional subcategories. Browse through the option and select a category that you want.

3. In the right side of the window, locate the desired template that you want to use and double-click it.

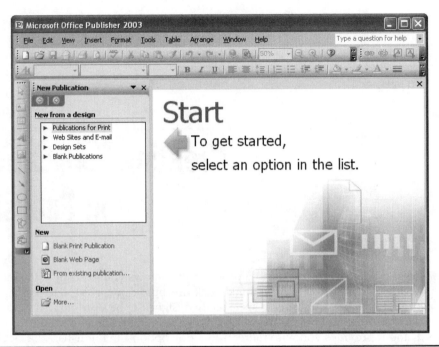

FIGURE 36-1 Publisher design options

4. The template appears in the work area, shown next. Now you can simply click in the text boxes and change the text as desired.

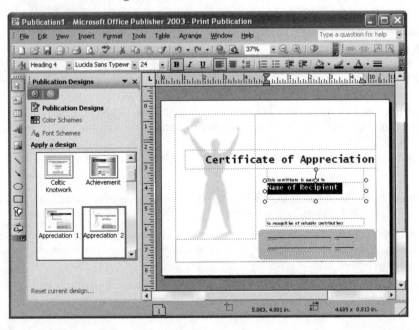

5. Notice in the task pane, now labeled Publication Designs, that you can change the design by simply clicking another design option, or you can change the color scheme of the certificate or the font scheme by clicking those options and making the desired changes.

6. Once you are done, click File | Save As to save your publication, or you can choose File | Print to print it.

TIP   *If your publication will be printed in black and white, it is a good idea to use the Color Schemes option to change the publication to black and white so you can see exactly how the presentation will look on your screen before you print it.*

Creating Custom Publications

The presentation templates that Publisher gives you work great for a number of different publications, and if you peruse the listings, you see that you have a number of options. However, what if the templates do not meet your needs? What if you need to create a corporate document using specifications someone else has provided you with? In this case, you can create a custom publication, and Publisher gives you all the tools you need to do just that.

First of all, if you want to create a custom presentation, you'll start out with a blank page. Click File | New. In the New Publication task pane, click the Blank Publications option in the New from a Design box. As you can see in Figure 36-2, this option gives you everything from single blank pages to web pages, to folding cards, and so forth. Simply double-click the option you want.

Once you make a selection, the blank page appears, and the Publication Designs task pane appears automatically. Even though you have chosen to use a blank publication, you may still want to apply a design. As you can see in Figure 36-3, we have applied a background to the blank page. You can still customize everything on this page, but using the design templates makes some of the work easier. Also note in the Publication Designs task pane that you can choose Quick Publication Options, which will allow you to choose some basic template designs, typically creating text and picture boxes so you don't have to create them yourself, and you can also apply different color schemes and font schemes as you like.

Even though the quick publication options, designs, and other features of Publisher will generally enable you to make the publications you need, you can design the actual pages from scratch without much difficulty. This flexibility allows you to create documents exactly to your specification (or the specifications of someone else). The following sections explore how to create custom publications.

Setting Up Publication Pages

When you design pages from scratch, you should first think about a few setup options that will determine how your pages look and how certain functions within those pages are uniformly applied. In other words, before you start constructing your own Publisher pages, think first about overall publication formatting and make some decisions. The following sections take a look at your options.

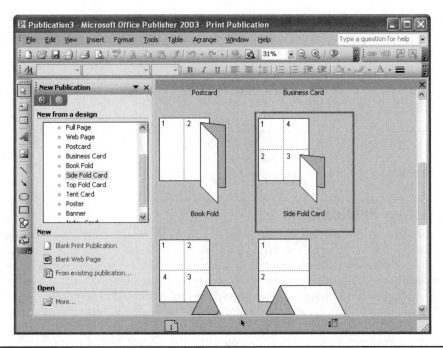

FIGURE 36-2   Choose a blank publication type.

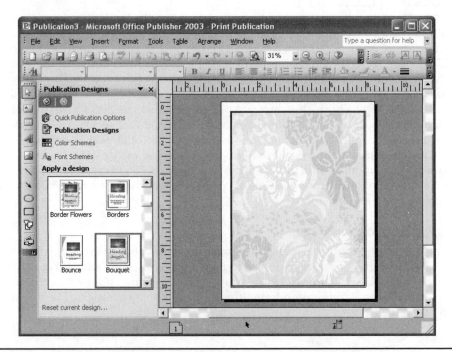

FIGURE 36-3   You can apply designs and other features directly to blank presentations.

Managing Layout Guides

Layout guides determine how objects are placed on your pages. They keep everything aligned and determine how margins look in your printed publication. You can easily configure the layout guides for a publication by clicking Arrange | Layout Guides. This action opens the Layout Guides dialog box. As you can see here, you can adjust the margins for your publication by simply entering the desired values. By default, the margins are 1 inch.

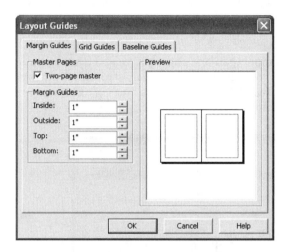

In setting the Grid Guides options, you should think carefully about the layout of your document. When you create your text boxes, you can have them snap to the grids so that each page of your presentation is consistent. Just adjust the Columns and Rows boxes to adjust the grid guides. As you can see, we have made a grid consisting of four parts. When you work on the page, you can work within the individual grids in order to format pages and make sure each page looks consistent.

Under Baseline Guides, you can determine the horizontal spacing and offset, which is 12 points by default. These settings change the number of spacing points between each line of text in your document. The more you increase this value, the more space that appears between each line. As a general rule, the 12 point setting works well for most font types and is easy to read, but if you are using an unusual font or font size, you may need to make adjustments to the Baseline Guides so that your text will layout in a pleasing manner. When you make a change on this tab, the Preview window shows you how the changes will look in your document. Make any desired changes and click OK.

Inserting Page Numbers

If your publication has more than one page, you may wish to include page numbers. You can configure Publisher to place them on the pages automatically, ensuring proper layout on each page. Just click Insert | Page Numbers. In the Page Numbers dialog box, you can determine the position of the page number and alignment.

Managing Hyphenation

You can have Publisher automatically hyphenate words at the end of lines in a text box, or not. To manage hyphenation, click Tools | Options, and then click the Edit tab. If you choose the Automatically Hyphenate in New Text Boxes option, you can also manage the hyphenation *zone*, which tells Publisher how often it can hyphenate words. The default hyphenation zone is .25 inch. Increasing this value tells Publisher that it can hyphenate more words, while decreasing the value means fewer words will be hyphenated.

Entering Personal Information

If you use Publisher to create business cards and related business or even personal documents, you may benefit from entering additional information into Publisher so that it can provide information about you directly to documents. To enter your personal information, just click Edit | Personal Information. For example, you can enter your name, address, business tag line/motto, organization name, address, phone, fax, and e-mail information so that Publisher automatically includes it in publications that use personal information. Of course, you can always edit the information after it is automatically placed on Publisher documents that use personal information, but the idea is that you don't have to type it over and over again when you create different publications.

Using Custom Colors

As you have noticed, Publisher allows you to use any number of design templates and color options to make the colors on your publication look great. But what if your company uses a certain color that you want to use in several publications? In this case, you can create a custom color to match your company's color. The same feature is used to create any custom color; just follow these steps:

1. Open a publication for which you want to create the custom color.

2. Click Format | Color Schemes to display the Color Schemes task pane. At the bottom of the window, click the Custom Color Scheme link.

3. On the Custom tab, shown next, use the New drop-down boxes to select the new colors for the custom scheme. Click the Save Scheme button, enter a new name for your scheme, and click OK. Your scheme will now appear in the list of color schemes for future use.

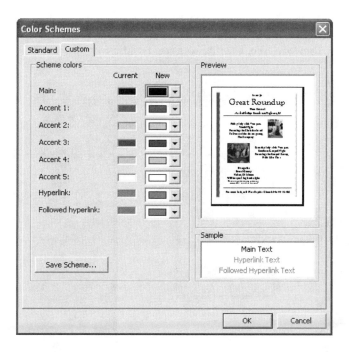

Working with Content

Once you have your basic publication set up the way you want it, you are ready to begin adding content. Working with content is easy, and for the most part, you can use the Objects toolbar, which appears on the left side of Publisher by default, shown in Figure 36-4.

Before you start inserting content, you should first get familiar with the concept of boxes in Publisher. Boxes are used to manage all kinds of Publisher content, including text, clip art, photos, and just about anything else you might want to put in your publication. As such, you'll work with boxes a lot, and at first, they can seem a bit confusing. Don't worry—this section is here to help you get a handle on boxes and how to use them.

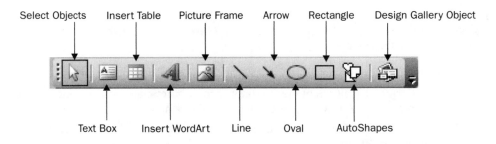

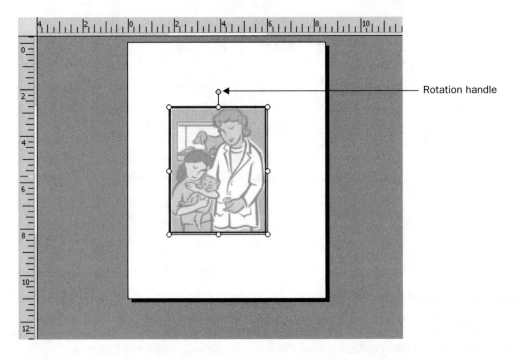

FIGURE 36-4   Objects toolbar

A box is used to hold some content in Publisher. As you can see here, this box contains clip art. Notice the circles on the border. You can use these to resize the box (and thus the clip art) in any way that you like. Use the rotation handle to rotate the box in any direction.

As you are working with boxes in Publisher, another item to notice is the resize and magnification options on the Standard toolbar. These options allow you to make the document larger so you can work with different portions of it. Keep these features in mind as you move forward.

TIP   *You can move a box by placing your mouse cursor inside the box, then dragging.*

Text Boxes

To create a text box in a Publisher file, just click the Text Box button on the Objects toolbar. Position your mouse on the document (the mouse pointer will turn to crosshairs), hold down the mouse button, and draw the box, as you can see here.

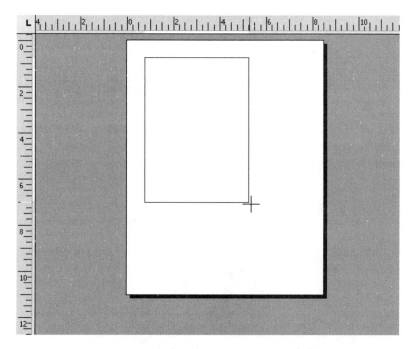

You can now type your text in the box and use the Formatting toolbar to change the fonts, styles, sizes, and so on. You can resize the text box and rotate it as well.

If you have already created your text in Word or in any text file format, you can import that text into your text box(es). The following steps show you how.

1. Select the text box in which you want to insert the text.

2. Click Insert ! Text File.

3. In the Insert Text dialog box that appears, browse and locate the text file you want to import.

4. If the text file contains more text than can fit in one box, you'll be asked if you want to use AutoFlow. AutoFlow will automatically create additional text boxes to hold the content. You can then arrange those text boxes on the page or pages as you desire.

5. Depending on your selections, AutoFlow will create additional boxes as needed. Just follow any additional prompts that appear on your screen.

Finally, you can also create connected text boxes. Let's say you are creating a newsletter. You have a vertical text column on the left side, a photo in the middle, and a vertical text column on the right side. As you type your text on the left side, you want it to overflow to the column on the right side. This way, you end up with two columns of your story that are connected and easily edited. No problem—in Publisher you can just connect the text boxes, and the text will automatically flow between the boxes. Here's how you do it:

1. Create the desired boxes. Note that they do not have to be on the same page of your publication.

2. Select the box containing the text you want to flow into the second box.

3. Click the Create Text Box Link button on the Connect Text Boxes toolbar. If you don't see the toolbar, click View | Toolbars | Connect Text Boxes.

4. As you can see in the following illustration, text will now flow from one box to the next seamlessly.

Tables

You can create tables directly within Publisher, or you can import them from another Office application using copy and paste. To create a table directly within Publisher, just click the Insert Table button on the Objects toolbar. You draw a box, and then the Create Table dialog box appears:

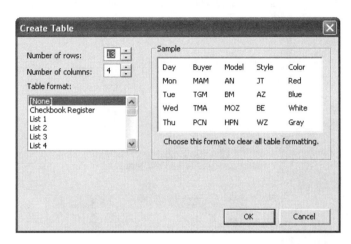

Choose the rows and columns you want, and the format, and click OK. The table appears on your publication. At this point, you can enter data and resize it just as you would any text box. You can also right-click the table to access a number of standard table formatting options.

WordArt

WordArt is a graphics feature that appears in most Office programs. Using WordArt, you can quickly create titles and other text features that show your text in 3-D, with shadow effects, and so forth. WordArt functions the same in Publisher as in any other Office program. Just click the WordArt button on the Objects toolbar, and follow the instructions that appear.

Pictures

You can insert pictures and clip art in basically the same way that you insert text. If you have used PowerPoint to create presentations, you'll find the photo and clip art insertion features similar in Publisher. To insert a photo or clip art, just click the Picture Frame button on the Objects toolbar. In the drop-down menu that appears, choose Clip Art, Picture from File, Empty Picture Frame, or From Scanner and Camera. Then, you'll just draw your picture frame, and Publisher will automatically lead you to the next step.

For example, if you want to insert a photo, draw the picture frame, and Publisher will prompt you to browse for the photo. Once the photo or clip art is inserted, you can then resize and rotate it as desired. If you are inserting a photo, the Picture toolbar automatically appears, where you can adjust the photo as needed, shown next. The features here work the same as they do when you create presentations in PowerPoint; see Chapter 22 for more information about managing photos.

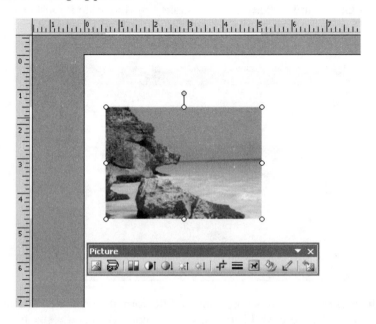

Shapes

In addition to photos and clip art, you can add a number of shapes to your publications, such as lines, arrows, and many predefined shapes. Click the option you want on the Options toolbar, hold down your mouse button, and simply swipe to draw the object on the publication. You can then resize and rotate the object, as well as use fill colors and other effects as desired by right-clicking the object. The objects here work the same as they do when creating presentations in PowerPoint; see Chapter 23 for more information.

Design Gallery Objects

Publisher contains a design gallery of many different templates that you can use to insert into your publications. Click the Design Gallery button on the Objects toolbar to open the design gallery. You can also access design gallery objects from the Insert menu. As you can see in Figure 36-5, you can choose from a variety of categories and designs. Then you can insert the object, and edit it to meet your specific needs. Overall, using design gallery objects is easy; they can save you a lot of time, and they can help you personalize your publication.

FIGURE 36-5 A sample from design gallery

Layering Objects

As you are working with text boxes, clip art, design gallery objects, and other objects that you insert in your publication, keep in mind that boxes are individual units of information. Keeping that thought in mind, you can layer objects on top of each other as needed. For example, you may have a photo and a piece of clip art on the same page. You can drag one so that it slightly overlaps the other, or even greatly overlaps it, depending on the effect you want. Keep in mind that you can create boxes and adjust the fill color and line color to create any effect that you might want.

The trick with layering and with your design is not to think in symmetrical terms. Many times, publications look better if some portions of the page do not fall in a symmetrical pattern, but rather overlap. Check out the Quick Publication Options on the Publication Designs task pane, which contains a bunch of templates, and study how the different designs are created. You'll discover overlapping elements and features that make the page stand out, and you can mirror this design in your own publication!

Publishing Documents in Publisher

Microsoft Publisher is designed for hard copy or web output. After all, the purpose of using Publisher is to create documents that can be printed or produced electronically. The good news is that publishing documents with Publisher is rather easy, and you have the option to print them locally, prepare them for a professional printer, or save them as web documents and publish them on the Internet. This chapter explores your three publishing options.

Printing on Your Home or Office Printer

Once your Publisher document is ready to be printed, the printing process basically works like any other print job that you send to your local printer. Before printing, make sure that the printer has enough ink or that laser toner is sufficient. Also, you should consider the paper that you will use. If your publication has a lot of photos and you want photo-quality printing, you may need to use photo-quality paper or at least paper that is designed to handle photo printing. So, just think about your needs, and there is certainly nothing wrong with experimenting with different kinds of paper.

Once you are ready to print, simply click File | Print, or you can click File | Print Preview in order to view your document as it will look in printed form and access a few additional options (see Figure 37-1). You can choose to click through various pages of your file and view them. You can also change the view so that you can see multiple pages at the same time. You can change a photo to grayscale and choose some different printing options if applicable to your publication. When you are ready, click the Print button to print your publication.

Working with Professional Printers

Publisher was designed for use in home printing and small office printing; as such, many professional printing companies will not work directly with Publisher files. Some will, some won't, so before you do anything, it is a good idea to talk to the printer to determine whether

FIGURE 37-1 Viewing your document in Print Preview

they will work with Publisher files. If they will not, they will probably give you some instructions on how to save the Publisher documents in a different file format so that they can print them.

If the printers will work with Publisher files, there may be some different settings that they will want you to configure before bringing or sending them the publication files. The following sections explore these options so you know what they mean. Whenever you work with a printing company, make sure you follow the instructions that they give you. You'll find all of these options in Tools | Commercial Printing Tools.

Color Printing

If you click Tools | Commercial Printing Tools | Color Printing, you see a Color Printing dialog box:

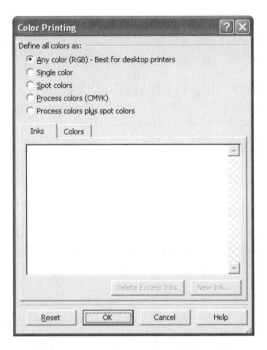

As you can see, this option allows you to choose various color definitions, based on the settings your printers need. You can choose between RGB, which works best for desktop printers and is the default selection; a single color; spot colors; CMYK process colors; or you can use process colors plus spot colors. These different color options are designed to work with different kinds of professional printing processes. Again, the issue with color options is that they need to be set according to your printing company's specifications. Once you choose a color, Publisher will convert the color in your file according to your selection, at which point you can save the file and deliver it to your printer.

Registration Settings

Called *overprinting settings* in Publisher, registration settings can be applied per publication as well as per object. You can configure overprinting for the entire publication by clicking Tools | Commercial Printing Tools | Registration Settings | Publication. As you can see in the dialog box that appears, you can set a Text Below setting and an Overprint Threshold. You can apply these settings to lines, fills, and imported pictures. In the same manner, you can set registration settings per object for border, fill, and text by choosing Tools | Commercial Printing Tools | Registration Settings | Per Object.

These settings are not useful to you unless you are sending your file to a commercial printer, so the printer will need to instruct you as to which settings you need.

Fonts

The Fonts option, available by clicking Tools | Commercial Printing Tools | Fonts, allows you to embed system fonts into the Publisher file. This ensures that you actually get the same fonts from the printer, even without those fonts being installed on their system. Some fonts have licensing issues you'll need to consider, and again, you'll need to work with your printing company to determine the settings you need here.

Using Pack and Go

Pack and Go is a feature that allows you to bundle all of the files in your publication into one file so that you can then move the presentation to another computer or a commercial printer. When you use the Pack and Go wizard to prepare your publication for commercial printing, the wizard will split large publications across multiple disks, embed fonts, include any linked graphics, create links for embedded graphics, and print composite and separation proofs.

To use Pack and Go, follow these steps:

1. Click Start | Pack and Go | Take to a Commercial Printing Service.

2. The Pack and Go wizard appears. Click Next.

3. Choose where you would like to save your publication, as shown in the following illustration. Note that by default, the publication is saved to your floppy disk drive. Of course, you can save it to your desktop or another folder for later network transfer or to be placed on a CD-ROM.

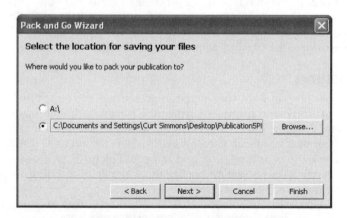

4. In the Fonts and Graphics window, shown in the following illustration, you can choose to embed TrueType fonts, include linked graphics, and create linked graphics for embedded graphics. Make your selections and click Next.

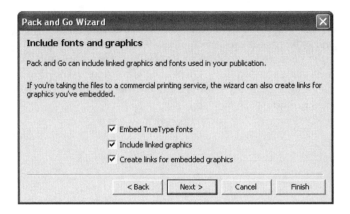

5. Click Finish to pack up the publication.

NOTE   *When you pack your presentation, the wizard will also copy Unpack.exe to the desired location on your computer. Use Unpack.exe to unpack the publication on the remote computer.*

Publishing to the Web

Technically, Publisher doesn't allow you to publish documents to the Web. What it can do is save your Publisher files as web documents, which you can then upload to a web server using a web authoring or transfer program, such as FrontPage.

To save your document as a web page, click File | Save As, and choose the Web Page option. Publisher will convert your publication to an HTML format and save it. You can also click File | Preview as a Web Page to see how the publication will actually look on the Web. If you click File | Preview as a Web Page, and the page has not been saved as a web page, you'll be prompted to allow Publisher to convert the publication to an HTML format. Once the conversion takes place, you can then view the page using any browser.

As you can imagine, there are many applications of using Publisher files as HTML files. You can post them on web sites, send them through e-mail, and you can view them with any program that can read HTML files.

Web Publishing and Photos

If you are planning on publishing to the Web and you are using photos in your Publisher document, you'll need to strike a balance between photo quality and download time. As you are probably aware, photos with high resolution also come with a larger file size, which translates into longer download times for users. For this reason, many publishers of web material adjust photos so that they are low JPEG quality, and also generally a smaller size. This reduces the quality of the photo, but also reduces the download time.   *(continued on the next page)*

Unless you want web users to be able to print your photos at high quality, it's a good idea to reduce the file size as much as possible. You can do this through editing with a photo editor, such as PhotoShop or PhotoShop Elements, and even through freeware programs such as Irfanview. The main point to keep in mind is that most web users will not wait a long time for your Publisher document to download, so keep the file size as small as possible.

VIII

PART

Integration and Collaboration

CHAPTER 38:
Using Office Applications Together

CHAPTER 39:
Using Office on the Web

CHAPTER 40:
Collaboration Using Office Tools and SharePoint Team Services

Using Office
Applications Together

By renaming each of the Office applications to include the word "Office"—Office Word 2003, Office Excel 2003, and so on—Microsoft is seeking to emphasize how thoroughly the Office applications are integrated and the extent to which they work together. While users who work mainly with one or two applications may perceive the Office applications as being entirely different from each other (having different looks, being used for different purposes, and creating different types of files), you'll know from working with the applications that you can pass information between the applications in several ways.

The primary tools for passing information from one application to another are ones you've already used extensively in this book—the Windows Clipboard and the Office Clipboard. For example, you can copy data from a table in a Word document and paste it into the appropriate number of cells in an Excel spreadsheet, or onto a slide in a PowerPoint presentation.

You can also use the Clipboard and the Office Clipboard to embed or link data from a file created in one application in a file created in another application. For greater control over the objects you embed and link, you can use the Object dialog box.

For heavier-duty data sharing in a corporate environment, you can use Word's and Excel's XML features to manipulate XML data files and to save data in a machine-readable format.

Using the Clipboard

As you saw in Chapter 4, the Windows Clipboard and the Office Clipboard provide an easy means of copying and moving data between applications: from the source application, you issue a Copy command or a Cut command to place the appropriate data on the Windows Clipboard or the Office Clipboard, then switch to the destination file in the destination application and issue a Paste command or Paste Special command to insert the information.

These are the main points you need to remember:

- The Windows Clipboard can hold several different types of data, including text and graphics, but it can hold only one item of each type at once. When you issue another Cut command or Copy command, Windows overwrites the contents of the Clipboard for that data type with the new information.

- The Office Clipboard can contain up to 24 items of the same type or of different types.

- You can use the Paste Special dialog box to control the format in which the object is pasted.

- You can also simply go ahead and issue a Paste command to paste the object in the default format. (The default format varies depending on the type of object you're pasting and the destination application into which you're pasting it.) If you don't get the result you want, you can use the Paste Options Smart Tag to change the format in which the object was pasted. (Alternatively, you can undo the Paste operation and then use the Paste Special dialog box instead.)

Embedding and Linking Objects

The Office applications support three different ways of including an object created in one application in a file created in another application: embedding, linking, and inserting. An *object* is a component of a file that can be handled separately. Examples of objects include tables in Word, charts and ranges in Excel, and slides in PowerPoint.

You'll read about embedding and linking at some length in this section. Inserting is relatively straightforward, and you've probably inserted various objects already if you've worked your way through this book. When you insert an object in a file, the file contains neither the information for editing the object in place nor a link to the source file that contains the object: the object simply appears in the file in the place you specify. Graphics are typically inserted in another file (for example, a document, workbook, or presentation) rather than being embedded or linked.

It's worth knowing the terminology used for embedding and linking, even if you choose not to use the terminology yourself:

- **Compound document**   A document that contains data of two or more different types. For example, a Word document that contains an Excel chart is a compound document.

- **ActiveX object or COM object**   An object that can be embedded in or linked to a file in another application. Unless you're programming, it's usually easier to describe each embedded or linked item simply as an "object" rather than worrying about exactly which type of object it is.

- **ActiveX container or COM container**   A document that can contain objects such as ActiveX objects or COM objects.

Before using embedding or linking, you should understand the differences between the two, the effects they produce, and know when to use which technique.

Understanding the Differences Between Embedding and Linking

Embedding is the basic means of inserting an object created in another application into a file. For example, if you need to create slides that contain charts or WordArt objects, you use embedding. When you embed an object in a file, the file contains a full copy of that object. For example, if you embed an Excel chart in a Word document, that document contains a full copy of the chart. Depending on the type of object involved, embedding can greatly increase the file size.

The copy is independent of the original chart in the Excel workbook, and you can edit it separately. You can't update the copy directly from the original chart. Instead, you can replace the copy with a new copy of the updated original. Manual updating like this is too slow and clumsy to make sense in most cases, but for some purposes (for example, version control of documentation) it can sometimes prove a better option than linking.

NOTE   *Embedding is so deeply ingrained in PowerPoint that almost any slide that contains anything except plain text or graphics contains embedded objects: charts, Word tables, Excel ranges, WordArt objects, and so on, are all embedded. So in PowerPoint, you tend to use embedding without really thinking about it. By contrast, in the other Office applications, you'll usually be more aware of when you embed an object. For example, when you embed a PowerPoint slide in a Word document, you'll usually be well aware of what you're doing.*

Linking is the more complex method of inserting an object created in another application into a file. When you link an object to a file, the file displays the current information for that object but stores only a link that describes the object, where it's located, and other relevant information. Storing the information about the link is much more compact than storing the actual data for even the smallest object, so the size of the file that contains the link hardly changes.

Linking can be a great help when you need to keep down the size of a document. For example, if you create a Word document that consists of a hundred pages of text, that document will be relatively compact—probably considerably less than a megabyte altogether. If you then add a couple dozen large graphics to the document, and save the graphics in the document, the file size will balloon to many megabytes. By contrast, if you link the graphics to the document, its file size will remain small, even though it displays the graphics in the positions you placed them.

When you link an object, you can update the link by issuing an Update command. The application reads the latest data from the source of the link and displays it in the file. However, the application can't update the link if either the source or the destination is offline relative to the other or if the source file has moved or been renamed so that the application and Windows can't identify it. (The applications and Windows are now better at identifying renamed files successfully, but you may still be able to confuse them.)

Choosing When to Embed and When to Link

To decide when to embed objects and when to link objects, consider the following:

- Will you need to edit the object in the destination file? If so, embed it.
- Do you need to keep file size down? If so, link the objects (especially any large graphics).
- Will the destination file and the source files stay in the same place as when you create the destination file, or do the files need to be able to move independently of each other? If you need to be able to move the destination file to another computer that won't be able to access the source files, embed the objects rather than linking them.

- Will different people need to work on different components of the same project at the same time? Even with Office 2003's improved support for a single file to be opened for editing by multiple people at the same time, it's best to keep shared editing to a minimum (or avoid it altogether). By linking objects rather than embedding them, you can enable different people to work on different components without the possibility of confusion or corruption. For example, you might continue to hack at the Word report while Annie polished the slides linked to it and Bill hammered the latest data in the Excel spreadsheet that provides the linked charts.

Depending on the type of file you need to produce, the decision between embedding and linking can be tricky. To help you escape this decision, Word and Outlook include a command called Insert and Link that offers the best aspects of both embedding and linking. This command embeds a copy of the picture in the file but also creates a link to the source file. When commanded to update the linked object, the application tries to use the link to retrieve the current version of the object. If the source file isn't available (for example, because your computer is offline), Word or Outlook falls back to the embedded version of the object instead. The object isn't up-to-date as it would be if the source had been available, but neither does it appear as a placeholder that creates a potentially embarrassing gap in a document or message.

Verifying Whether an Object Is Linked or Embedded

By looking at an object in a document, you can't immediately tell whether it's linked or embedded. These are the easiest ways to find out:

- In Word, PowerPoint, and Outlook, right-click the object and see whether the shortcut menu contains an Update Link command. If so, the object is linked; if not, the object is embedded.

- In Excel, select the object and check the readout in the reference area. If the readout starts with "=EMBED" (for example, =EMBED("Word.Document.8","")), the object is embedded. If the readout contains a reference to a file by name (for example, =Word.Document.8 | 'C:\Temp\Doc1.doc'!!OLE_LINK1'), the object is linked.

In Word, you can also verify whether an object is linked or embedded by checking whether its field code starts with the word "EMBED" or the word "LINK." Here's how to display field codes:

- To check the field code for a single object, right-click the field and choose Toggle Field Codes. (Alternatively, place the insertion point in the field and press SHIFT-F9.)

- To view the field codes for all objects, choose Tools | Options, select the Field Codes option on the View tab, and click OK. Repeat the procedure but deselect the Field Codes option to display the field results again.

Embedding or Linking an Object

This is the easiest way to embed or link an existing object:

1. In the object's source application, select the object and issue a Copy command (for example, press CTRL-C).

2. Activate the destination application and select the location in which you want to embed or link the object.

3. Choose Edit | Paste Special to display the Paste Special dialog box. This illustration shows the Paste Special dialog box for Excel with a Word table on the Clipboard:

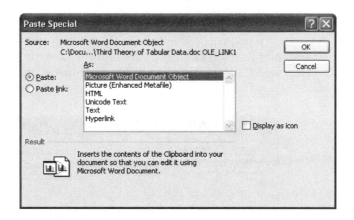

4. Choose the format in which you want to embed or link the object. The choices available depend on the type of object you copied and the destination application.

5. Select the Paste option button to embed the object. Select the Paste Link option button to link the object.

6. Click OK.

You can also embed a new object that you create and embed in the same process:

1. In the destination application, choose Insert | Object to display the Object dialog box. (In PowerPoint, the dialog box is called Insert Object and is configured a little differently.)

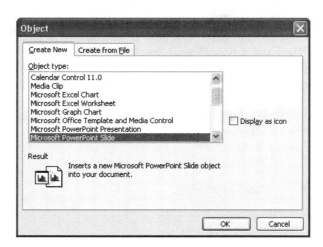

2. On the Create New tab, select the type of object you want to create and embed.

3. Click OK.

By using the Create from File tab of the Object dialog box, you can embed or link an object that consists of the entire contents of an already existing file:

1. In the destination application, choose Insert | Object to display the Object dialog box.

2. On the Create from File tab, enter the path and filename in the File Name text box. (The easiest way to enter this is to click Browse and use the Browse dialog box.)

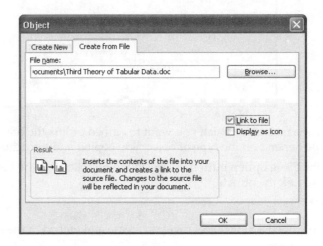

3. Select the Link to File option if you want to link the object rather than embed it.

4. Click OK.

Editing an Embedded Object

When you've embedded an object, you edit it "in place"—in its location in the destination file. The easiest way to start the editing is to double-click the object, but you can also right-click the object and issue an Edit command from the object's submenu. For example, right-click an embedded PowerPoint slide and choose Slide Object | Edit from the shortcut menu.

When you issue an Edit command in either of these ways, the application displays a thick shaded border around the object and replaces its own menus and toolbars with those of the application that created the object. For example, the following illustration shows an embedded PowerPoint slide being edited in a Word document. Word is displaying the PowerPoint menus and toolbars. You can then edit the object as if you were working in the other application (which, in effect, you are).

CAUTION   *For you to be able to edit an embedded object, the application that created the object must be installed on the computer you're using. This can cause problems when you move a document to a different computer. For example, say you create a Word document that contains a couple of Excel objects on your work computer. If you take this document home and open it on your home computer, which has Word and Microsoft Works installed, you'll be able to edit the Word parts of the document but not the embedded Excel objects.*

Editing a Linked Object

You edit a linked object in its source application rather than in place in the destination application. Right-click the object and issue an Edit command (for example, Document Object | Edit for a Word document object) from the shortcut menu to open the object for editing in the source application. You can then edit the object as usual. When you close the object in the source application, the linked object in the destination application is updated.

Editing, Updating, and Breaking Links

To work with links in a file, choose Edit | Links and work in the Edit Links dialog box:

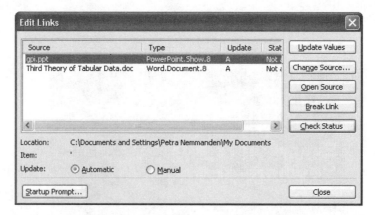

From here, you can take the following actions to a selected link:

- Click the Update Values button to update the link.
- Click the Change Source button and use the resulting Change Links dialog box to change the link to a different file.
- Click the Open Source button to open the source file for the link in the source application.
- Click the Break Link button to break the link. Click the Break Links button in the warning dialog box that the application displays.
- Click the Check Status button to check the status of the link.
- Switch the link between automatic updating and manual updating by selecting the Automatic option button or the Manual option button as appropriate. For example, you might switch to manual updating before taking a file offline from the sources of its linked objects.
- In Word, lock the updating method for the link.
- In Excel, click the Startup Prompt button to control whether Excel offers the user the choice of updating the link when the file is opened.

Using Office's XML Capabilities

The versions of Word and Excel included in Office Professional 2003, and the standalone versions of Word 2003 and Excel 2003, contain powerful features for creating and working with XML files. The versions of Word and Excel included in versions of Office 2003 other than Office Professional have much more limited XML capabilities: Excel can save files in the XML Spreadsheet format, and Word can save documents in the XML Document format, but the applications don't have the other XML capabilities discussed in this section.

Refer to Appendix B for an explanation of what XML is, what it's for, why it's important, and how it works. But here's an executive summary for the meantime:

- Saving files in XML format makes their contents easier to index, search, and access than saving them in their native formats (for example, in the Word document format or the Excel workbook format).

- Most companies have large amounts of potentially valuable information stored in native formats (such as Word documents, Excel workbooks, PowerPoint presentations, Outlook messages) that are difficult to search effectively. By using XML, they can make that information more easily available.

- Most Office users have extensive experience in using Word and Excel. Now that Word and Excel can open, manipulate, and save XML files, users can create and work with XML without needing to learn a new application.

- You're unlikely to need XML capabilities for home or SOHO use of Office, which is why only Office Professional provides XML capabilities. At this writing, XML is used mostly by corporations, government departments, and other large organizations.

PART VIII

NOTE *At the other end of the scale, XML is also used by some bloggers for creating weblogs enabled with Rich Site Summary (RSS). Arguably, this area of XML use is growing faster than the corporate area.*

What You're Likely to Do with XML Files

Depending on the type of work you do, you're likely to work with XML documents in one of two very different ways:

- **As a user** Most people who use XML documents will fill in documents, and create new documents, by using existing schemas created by developers in their company or organization. To fill in existing XML documents, and to create new XML documents based on existing schemas, you need only add a few skills to the core Word and Excel skills you probably already possess.

- **As a developer** Someone needs to develop the XML documents and related schemas that the other users will work with. If you're a developer of XML documents and schemas, you'll need a much wider set of skills than if you just need to fill in the documents.

The following sections discuss these separate possibilities, first for Word and then for Excel.

Working with XML Documents in Word

For opening, editing, and saving XML documents, you use many of the same commands as for working with regular Word documents. The following sections discuss the particulars you need to know.

Opening an XML Document

You can open an existing XML document by using standard Word commands:

- Choose File | Open to display the Open dialog box, navigate to and select the XML document, and click Open.

- Click File and choose an XML document from the recently used area at the bottom of the File menu.

- Right-click an XML document in a Windows Explorer window (or on your desktop), and choose Open With | Microsoft Word from the shortcut menu.

Editing an XML Document

An XML document attached to an external schema contains tags that mark the areas occupied by each XML element. Tags are used in pairs: each element has a starting tag and an ending tag. Word represents these tags as pink outlines with the barely describable outline shapes shown here:

first_name Gabrielle first_name

Tags nested inside other tags appear in a more compact format, as shown next. Notice how the end tags are collapsed to a thick parenthesis without any text:

employee first_name Gabrielle middle_initial P last_name Engel employee

You can toggle the display of XML tags in a Word document by pressing CTRL-SHIFT-X or by displaying the XML Structure task pane (View | Task Pane, then choose XML Structure from the drop-down list) and selecting the option Show XML Tags in This Document. By default, Word hides the tags in an XML document except when you're using the XML Structure task pane to place or manipulate tags in the document.

So normally, when you're editing an XML document, its tags will be hidden: to all appearances, you'll be editing a "normal" document and using normal editing commands. When the tags are hidden like this, you can easily delete them without noticing. To prevent this, developers are likely to protect an XML document as a form so that you can fill in those areas you're permitted to access without having to worry about inadvertently deleting tags or other vital elements you can't see.

NOTE *You can print XML tags with a document by selecting the XML Tags option on the Print tab of the Options dialog box (Tools | Options) or the Print tab of the Print dialog box (choose File | Print, and then click Options in the Print dialog box).*

Saving a Word Document in XML Format

If you open an XML document in Word, Word keeps the document in XML format when you issue a Save command.

NOTE *You can also save a Word document originally created in a non-XML format (for example, a document in the regular Word Document format) in the XML Document format. Saving a document from Word in the XML Document format saves the document in WordML, an XML format that can express both the content and the formatting of a Word document in pure XML.*

To save a Word document in the XML Document format:

1. Choose File | Save As to display the Save As dialog box.

2. In the Save As Type drop-down list, choose XML Document. The Save As dialog box displays extra options when you make this choice:

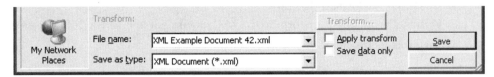

3. If necessary, choose XML-related options:

- To apply a transform, select the Apply Transform option and click the Transform button to display the Choose an XML Transform dialog box (which is a renamed common Open dialog box). Navigate to and select the transform, and then click Open.

NOTE *Applying a transform is an advanced maneuver that we don't discuss in detail in this book. See "Saving Only the Data from an XML Document," later in this chapter, for a discussion of the implications of saving only the data from a Word document.*

- To save only the XML data from the document (rather than saving its formatting as well), select the Save Data Only option. You'll almost never want to use this option when saving a document in XML format for the first time.

4. Click Save to save the document. If you chose to apply a transform or to save data only, Word displays a dialog box warning you that the save operation may lose document features such as formatting, pictures, and objects. Click Continue to proceed, or click Keep WordML to keep the formatting.

Creating XML Documents in Word

As you saw in the previous section, Word can save a document in the XML Document format using WordML by writing the details of the contents and the formatting of the document to a text file formatted with XML tags. Doing so creates a standalone XML file—one without an external schema or document type definition attached to it.

However, if your company needs you to create XML documents in Word, chances are that you'll need to create documents that conform to an external XML schema—either a proprietary XML schema developed by your company or an XML schema published by an organization such as the World Wide Web Consortium (W3C; www.w3.org). You and your colleagues can then create XML documents that conform to the schema and validate them to ensure that they contain the required information in the formats specified by the schema.

To create your own XML documents in Word, you'll need to take the following steps:

1. Create or obtain an XML schema for the documents.

- If your company can provide the schema for you (for example, because someone else has developed it), you're all set.

- If not, you'll probably need to create the XML schema yourself, which can take a considerable amount of work.

2. Attach the XML schema to a new document or an existing document.

3. Use the XML Structure task pane to add XML tags to the appropriate parts of the document.

4. If necessary, choose XML options.

5. Optionally, apply a transform to the XML document to create a different view of it.

6. Save the document or the appropriate parts of it.

Appendix B discusses what an XML schema is and what its components are. The following sections discuss how to attach a schema, add tags, and choose XML options. This chapter doesn't cover applying XML transforms.

Creating a New XML Document

To create a new XML document:

1. Choose File | New to display the New Document task pane.

2. Click the XML Document link. Word creates a new blank document based on the Normal template and displays the XML Structure task pane.

3. Attach an XML schema to the document as described in the next section.

Instead of creating a new XML document from scratch, you can create an XML document by attaching an XML schema to a document, as described next.

Attaching an XML Schema to a Document

To attach an XML schema to a document:

1. Click the Templates and Add-Ins link in the XML Structure task pane to display the XML Schema tab of the Templates and Add-Ins dialog box. (Alternatively, choose Tools | Templates and Add-Ins to display the Templates and Add-Ins dialog box, and then click the XML Schema tab.)

2. Specify the schema or schemas you want to add to the document:

- If the schema is listed in the Checked Schemas Are Currently Attached list box, select the check box.

- To add a schema to the Checked Schemas Are Currently Attached list box, click Add Schema, and follow the steps in the next section to add the schema. After adding the schema, select its check box.

- You can also add a schema to the schema library by working in the Schema Library dialog box. To do so, click the Schema Library button, and work as described in the next section.

3. Click OK to close the Templates and Add-Ins dialog box. Word attaches the XML schema to the document and displays the XML Structure task pane.

Adding a Schema to the Schema Library

To add a schema to the list of schemas available, you add it to the schema library. You can do this in either of two ways:

- By working from the Schema Library dialog box (shown here). To display this dialog box, click the Schema Library button on the XML Schema tab of the Templates and Add-Ins dialog box.

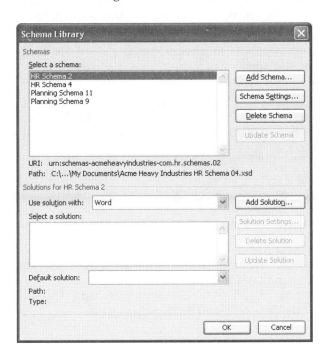

- By working from the XML Schema tab of the Templates and Add-Ins dialog box.

To add a schema from either of these locations:

1. Click the Add Schema button to display the Add Schema dialog box (which is a renamed common Open dialog box).

2. Navigate to the schema and select it.

3. Click the Open button. Word displays the Edit Schema Properties dialog box:

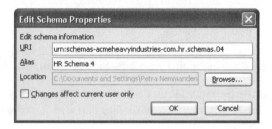

4. Specify the details for the schema:

   - Enter the uniform resource indicator in the URI text box.

   - Enter the alias for the schema in the Alias text box. The alias provides an easier means of referring to the schema than the URI—the friendly name, as it were.

   - To restrict the scope of the changes you're making so they affect only yourself, select the Changes Affect Current User Only option. Normally, when you're developing XML documents for other people to use, you'll want to leave this option deselected, as it is by default.

5. Click OK. Word closes the Edit Schema Properties dialog box and adds the schema to the list in the Schema Library dialog box or in the Checked Schemas Are Currently Attached list on the XML Schema tab of the Templates and Add-Ins dialog box.

Removing a Schema from the Schema Library

To remove a schema from the schema library, select the schema in the Select a Schema list box, and then click the Delete Schema button. Word displays a message warning you that removing the schema and all its associated files may affect any application that uses the schema. Click the Yes button if you're sure you want to proceed.

Removing an XML Schema from a Document

To remove an XML schema from the active document, choose Tools | Templates and Add-Ins to display the Templates and Add-Ins dialog box, and then clear the appropriate check boxes in the Checked Schemas Are Currently Attached list box on the XML Schema tab. Click OK to close the Templates and Add-Ins dialog box.

Adding XML Tags to a Document

To add XML tags to a document to which you've attached a schema:

1. Display the XML Structure task pane if it's not already displayed. For example, choose View | Task Pane, and choose XML Structure from the task pane's drop-down menu. At this point, the Elements in the Document list box will be empty except for placeholder text, the Show XML Tags in the Document option will be selected, and the XML elements will appear in the Choose an Element to Apply to Your Current Selection list box, as shown here:

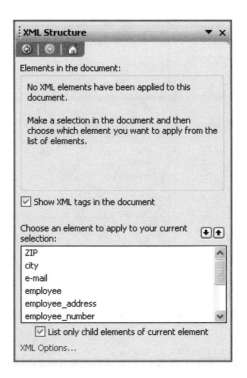

2. Select the object you want to tag. The object can be a collapsed selection (a point in the document), one or more words, a paragraph, or a field; a cell, column, or row in a table; a picture, or another object.

3. In the XML Structure task pane, select the XML element you want to add. Word adds the appropriate tags around the selection in the document and updates the

Elements in the Document list box to show the elements you've added, flagging any that are incomplete or incorrectly used. Here's an example with several elements:

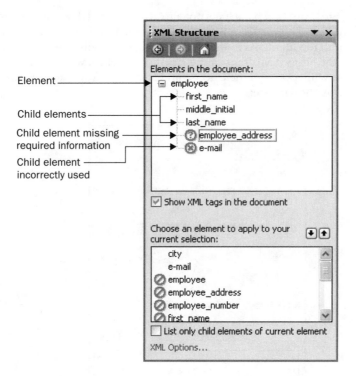

- Right-click a missing-information icon or an error icon to display information on the problem.
- If you're adding the root element from the XML schema to the document, add it first.
- When you add the first element to the document, Word displays the Apply to Entire Document? dialog box, asking whether you want to apply the element to the entire document or just to the selection. Click the appropriate button.
- When adding the tags for child elements, you can select the List Only Child Elements of Current Element option to restrict the display to the child elements available for the current element. This restriction makes it easier to find the elements you need and to avoid putting elements in the wrong places.

4. If necessary, specify an attribute for the element:

- Right-click the element and choose Attributes from the shortcut menu to display the Attributes dialog box, shown next.

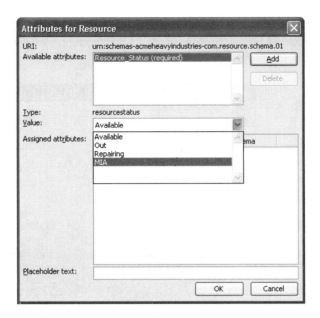

- Select the attribute in the Available Attributes list.
- Choose or enter the value for the attribute.
- Click OK to close the Attributes dialog box.

5. Add further tags by repeating steps 2 through 4.

Removing XML Tags from a Document

To remove XML tags from a document:

1. Display the XML Structure task pane if it's not already displayed.

2. Display the XML tags in the document by selecting the Show XML Tags in the Document option in the XML Structure task pane or pressing CTRL-SHIFT-X.

3. Remove a tag in either of the following ways:
   - Right-click the element in the Elements in the Document box and choose Remove *Element* from the shortcut menu (where *Element* is the element's name).
   - Right-click the start or end tag for the XML tag you want to remove and choose Remove Tag from the shortcut menu.

Choosing XML Options

To make Word's XML behavior suit your needs, you can set XML options as follows:

1. Display the XML Structure task pane if it's not already displayed.

2. Click the XML Options link to display the XML Options dialog box. (Alternatively, click the XML Options button on the XML Schema tab of the Templates and Add-Ins dialog box.)

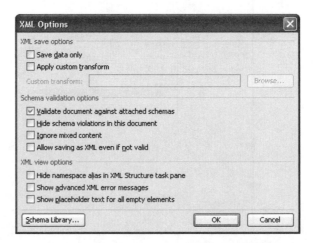

3. Choose the appropriate options. These are the choices available:

- **Save Data Only**   This option makes Word save only the data in the XML document, not the formatting. Selecting this option is the equivalent of selecting the Save Data Only option in the Save As dialog box. Select this option if you need to save data only for all or most of your XML documents.

- **Apply Custom Transform**   This option makes Word apply the specified transform by default to XML documents you save. Selecting this option is the equivalent of selecting the Apply Transform option in the Save As dialog box. Select this option if you need to apply the same custom transform to all or most of your XML documents.

- **Validate Document Against Attached Schemas**   This option controls whether Word compares the document's data and structure to the schemas attached to it. This option is selected by default. Usually, you'll want to use this option to make sure your XML documents don't contain schema violations, but you may sometimes want to turn this option off for testing purposes.

- **Hide Schema Violations in This Document**   This option controls whether Word flags schema violations with wavy purple lines in the document. You may want to turn off the flagging of violations when experimenting with XML schemas.

- **Ignore Mixed Content**   This option controls whether Word strictly enforces the data types specified for elements. By default, this option is deselected, so enforcement is strict.

- **Allow Saving as XML Even if Not Valid**   This option enables you to save a document as XML even if it's not structurally valid. You may occasionally need to use this option when experimenting with XML documents. However, for real work with XML documents, make sure this option is deselected.

- **Hide Namespace Alias in XML Structure Task Pane**   This option controls whether the XML Structure task pane displays the alias assigned to the namespace or the namespace itself. The default is to display the alias, which is much easier to read.

- **Show Advanced XML Error Messages**   This option controls whether Word displays detailed error messages (for example, for missing elements or incorrectly used elements) or more compact and generic error messages (the default).

- **Show Placeholder Text for All Empty Elements**   This option controls whether Word displays placeholder text consisting of the element's name (for example, Word displays *Resource* as a placeholder for an element named Resource). The placeholder text makes it easier to see which element appears where, especially when tags are not displayed in the document. Word uses a different font for the placeholders to distinguish them from "real" contents.

Saving Only the Data from an XML Document

If you're using an XML document attached to an external schema to gather data, you may want to save only the data the user has entered in the XML element—the contents of the form fields, as it were—rather than the whole document, including its layout and formatting. The Save Data Only option in the Save As dialog box and in the XML Options dialog box lets you do just this.

What's important to understand is that using this option with an XML document that's not attached to an external schema causes severe problems: essentially, such a save discards all the data in the document because no data is extracted. To help you avoid losing the document's content like this, Word displays severe warnings before letting you perform this maneuver.

Validating an XML Document

After creating or working with an XML document, you should validate the XML to make sure the document doesn't contain any schema violations—data that doesn't match the schema's requirements.

To validate an XML document:

1. Display the XML Schema tab of the Templates and Add-Ins dialog box (Tools | Templates and Add-Ins).

2. Select the Validate Document Against Attached Schemas option, and make sure the Allow Saving as XML Even if Not Valid option is deselected.

3. Click OK to close the Templates and Add-Ins dialog box.

4. Display the XML Structure task pane if it's not already displayed.

5. Verify the readouts in the XML Structure task pane to see which elements are invalid and what Word thinks the problem is.

6. Correct any problems you find. For example, an element may be missing a required child element, or text may be entered in a location in which it's not permitted.

PART VIII

Protecting XML Tags from Being Deleted

To prevent users from accidentally deleting XML tags as they enter data in XML documents, protect the tags as follows after laying out the document:

1. Display the XML tags by pressing CTRL-SHIFT-X or selecting the Show XML Tags in the Document option in the XML Structure task pane.

2. Choose Tools | Protect Document to display the Protect Document task pane.

3. Select the Allow Only This Type of Editing in the Document option, and make sure No Changes (Read Only) is selected in the drop-down list.

4. For each XML element you want users to be able to edit, select the contents of the element, and then select the Everyone option in the Exceptions list box in the Protect Document task pane.

5. Click the Yes, Start Enforcing Protection button to display the Start Enforcing Protection dialog box.

6. Select either the Prevent Accidental Changes option button and enter a password or the Prevent Intentional or Malicious Changes option button to use authentication to protect the document.

7. Click OK.

Inserting an XML File into a Word Document

You can insert an existing XML file into a Word document in either of two ways. The first way also lets you insert only a specific part of the XML file rather than the entire file:

1. Move the insertion point to where you want the XML data to appear.

2. Choose Insert | Field to display the Field dialog box. The following illustration shows the Field dialog box with options for inserting an XML file already chosen.

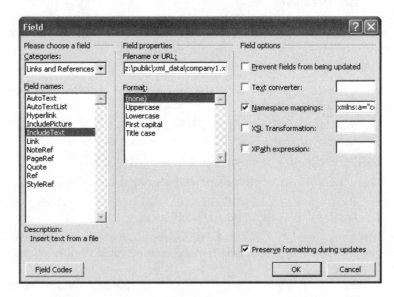

3. In the Categories drop-down list, choose Links and References.

4. In the Field Names list, select IncludeText.

5. In the Field Properties section, enter the full path and filename, or the URL, in the Filename or URL box.

6. Select the Namespace Mappings option, and enter the appropriate namespace in the text box. Enter **xmlns**, a colon, the appropriate variable, an equal sign, and the namespace in double quotation marks—for example, **xmlns:a="corpschema1"**.

7. To insert only a specific part of the XML file rather than the entire file, select the XPath Expression option and type the XPath in the text box. Use the format a:*root_element*/ a:*element*. For example, to insert the Location1 element from the root element Buildings, you'd use **a:Buildings/a:Location1**.

8. Click OK to insert the data.

The other way to insert an entire XML file is as follows:

1. Choose Insert | Insert File to display the Insert File dialog box.

2. Choose XML Files in the Files of Type drop-down list.

3. Navigate to and select the file.

4. Click Insert to insert the data.

This technique doesn't let you insert only a part of the file.

Working with XML Files in Excel

For opening, editing, and saving XML files, you use many of the same commands as for working with regular Excel worksheets and workbooks. The following sections discuss the particulars you need to know.

First, we should mention the distinction between files in the XML Spreadsheet format and XML data files. XML Spreadsheet, or XMLSS, is a schema that enables Excel to save Excel workbooks (minus a few elements, such as AutoShapes, charts, and other objects, and VBA projects) in XML-encoded files. XML Spreadsheet files are Excel files encoded in XML rather than in the native Excel workbook format, so you open them, work with them, and save them in the same ways as regular Excel workbooks. By contrast, XML data files contain XML data, typically including references to external schemas. When you open an XML data file, you get to decide whether to import all of its data into an Excel worksheet, whether to open the file as a read-only list, or whether to perform a custom mapping of elements in the file's attached schema to specify exactly which data you want to extract from the file.

Opening an XML Spreadsheet File in Excel

You can open an XML spreadsheet in Excel by using standard Excel commands:

- Choose File | Open to display the Open dialog box, navigate to and select the XML file, and click Open. (If necessary, choose the appropriate item in the Files of Type drop-down list to display the file type.)

- Click File and choose an XML file from the recently used area at the bottom of the File menu.

- Right-click an XML file in a Windows Explorer window (or on your desktop), and choose Open With | Microsoft Excel from the shortcut menu. (The first time you do this, you may have to choose Open With | Choose Program and use the Open With dialog box to specify Excel. Thereafter, Excel will appear on the Open With shortcut menu.)

Opening an XML Data File in Excel

You can open an existing XML data file in Excel by using the standard Excel commands mentioned in the previous section. What's different is that when you take any of these actions, Excel displays the Open XML dialog box, with the following options:

- **As an XML List**   Excel imports the data from the XML file into a new workbook containing one worksheet and displays the schema for the XML file in the XML Source task pane.

- **As a Read-Only Workbook**   Excel opens the XML file as a spreadsheet under its own name and doesn't create a schema. The file is read-only, so you can't save changes to it under its own name, but you can save changes to it under a different name.

- **Use the XML Source Task Pane**   Excel displays the schema for the XML file in the XML Source task pane. From here, you can map the elements contained in the schema to cells or ranges in the worksheet.

Choose the appropriate option for your needs, and then click OK.

If you open the file as an XML list or using the XML Source task pane, and the XML file doesn't contain a reference to a schema, Excel displays a message box informing you that it will create a schema based on the XML source data. Click OK to dismiss this message box (there's no other choice but OK). You can suppress the display of this message box in the future if you want.

Saving Excel Files in XML Formats

Excel can save your data either as an XML spreadsheet (retaining all data and most objects) or in XML data format (retaining just the data mapped to the elements in the XML schema attached to the workbook).

To save a workbook in XML:

1. Click the Save button or choose File | Save to display the Save As dialog box. (If the file has already been saved in a different format, choose File | Save As.)

2. In the Save As Type drop-down list, select the XML Spreadsheet item or the XML Data item as appropriate.

3. Click Save.

Creating XML Files in Excel

The second and more difficult stage of using XML with Excel is creating your own XML files attached to an external schema and mapping the appropriate elements so that you can extract the relevant pieces of information from the files.

First, you attach an XML schema to a workbook. This creates what's called an *XML map*— a relationship between the schema and the workbook. You use this map to map elements in the schema to cells and ranges in worksheets in the workbook to define which element in the schema is represented by which cell. For example, you could map cells in a schema to specify which output from your manufacturing database you wanted to analyze in a worksheet containing custom calculations.

NOTE *A workbook contains a single XML map or multiple XML maps. When a workbook contains multiple XML maps, each can refer to a different schema, or two or more maps can refer to the same schema.*

Once you've performed the mapping, you can export data from the mapped cells and ranges—for example, so you can use the data with another application. You can also import an XML data file into an existing XML mapping, so that the relevant parts of the data file snap into place. For example, you could import different months' output from your manufacturing database so that you could analyze them.

You can also use an XML mapping to import XML-formatted data from a web source into a worksheet.

Attaching an XML Schema to a Workbook

To attach an XML schema to a workbook:

1. Choose Data | XML | XML Source to display the XML Source task pane.

2. Click the Workbook Maps button to display the XML Maps dialog box:

3. Click the Add button to display the Select XML Source dialog box (which is a renamed Open dialog box).

4. Navigate to and select the XML schema you want to use.

5. Click Open. If the schema you specified contains more than one root element, Excel displays the Multiple Roots dialog box so that you can choose which root element to use for the XML map. Select the root element and click OK.

6. Excel adds the XML map to the XML Maps dialog box:

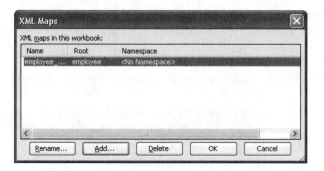

7. If necessary, rename the map from its default name by clicking the Rename button (or clicking the Name entry for the map twice in slow succession), typing the new name, and pressing ENTER.

8. Click OK to close the XML Maps dialog box. The XML Source task pane, shown next, displays the XML map you've added, showing the elements in the schema (or partial schema) as a hierarchical list.

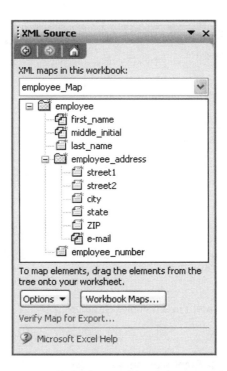

You can now map elements to cells in the workbook by using the XML Source task pane.

Understanding the Icons in the XML Source Task Pane

The XML Source task pane uses different icons to represent the different elements in an XML schema. The following table explains what the icons mean.

Icon	Meaning
	Parent element
	Repeating parent element
	Required parent element
	Required repeating parent element

Icon	Meaning
	Child element
	Repeating child element
	Required child element
	Required repeating child element
	Attribute
	Required attribute
	Simple content in a complex structure

Mapping XML Elements to an Excel Worksheet

To map XML elements from a schema to a worksheet:

1. If the XML Source task pane isn't displayed, display it in either of the following ways:
   - Choose Data | XML | XML Source.
   - Choose View | Task Pane (or press CTRL-F1), and then choose XML Source from the task pane menu.
2. If you've added multiple maps to the workbook, select the appropriate map in the XML Maps in This Workbook drop-down list.
3. Select one or more elements in the schema:
   - Click a parent element to select it and all its child elements.
   - Click to select a single element.
   - CTRL-click to select multiple elements.
4. Drag the element or elements to the appropriate cell or range in the worksheet and drop it there. Excel adds the element and displays a blue border around the mapped cell to indicate that there's a mapping. (This blue border doesn't print.)

- In the example spreadsheet shown here, the first_name and middle_initial elements have been added to the cells below their corresponding headings, and the employee_number element is being dropped on cell A2.

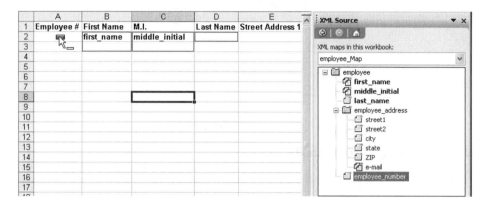

- You can also map an element to a cell by right-clicking it in the XML Maps in This Workbook list and choosing Map Element from the shortcut menu, using the Insert XML List dialog box to specify the cell or range, and clicking OK.

- The XML Source task pane displays mapped elements in boldface and unmapped elements in regular font.

- If Excel displays a Smart Tag when you map the field, you can choose the appropriate heading option from the Smart Tag's menu. The choices are My Data Already Has a Heading, Place XML Heading to the Left, and Place XML Heading Above.

- When you map an element declared as having two or more values, Excel creates a drop-down list named after the element, as shown next. The drop-down list offers the Sort Ascending, Sort Descending, (All), (Top 10), and (Custom) choices that you'll recognize from using AutoFilter (see "Performing Quick Filtering with AutoFilter" in Chapter 19).

To remove an element you've mapped, right-click it in the XML Source task pane and choose Remove Element from the shortcut menu.

Configuring Properties for an XML Map

To configure properties for an XML map, you use the options in the XML Map Properties dialog box:

You can display this dialog box in either of two ways:

- In the XML Source task pane, activate the appropriate map by selecting it in the XML Maps in This Workbook drop-down list. (If the workbook contains only one XML map, that map will already be selected.) Then choose Data | XML | XML Map Properties.

- In the worksheet, right-click a cell to which one of the elements from the appropriate map is mapped, and choose XML | XML Map Properties from the shortcut menu.

The options that you can set in the XML Map Properties dialog box are as follows.

- **Name**   You can change the name assigned to the mapping. However, changing the name via the XML Maps dialog box is usually easier.

- **XML Schema Validation section**   Select or deselect the Validate Data Against Schema for Import and Export option to control whether Excel validates the data in this mapping against the schema when you import or export data.

- **Data Source section**   The Save Data Source Definition in Workbook option, which is selected by default, saves the XML binding in the workbook. Deselect this option to remove the XML binding from the workbook. This option is sometimes unavailable.

- **Date Formatting and Layout section**   Select or clear the options to specify whether or not to adjust column width; preserve column sorting, filtering, and layout; and preserve number formatting.

- **If the Number of Rows in the Data Range Changes upon Refresh/Import section**   Choose between the Insert Cells for New Data, Delete Unused Cells option (the default setting) and the Overwrite Existing Cells with New Data, Clear Unused Cells option.

- **When Refreshing/Importing Data section**   Choose between the Overwrite Existing Data with New Data option (the default setting) and the Append New Data to Existing Data option. In most cases, you'll want to overwrite the existing data with the new data.

Choosing XML Options

To configure how XML behaves in Excel, click the Options button at the bottom of the XML Source task pane and choose the appropriate item from the menu:

- **Preview Data in Task Pane**   This option controls whether the XML Source task pane displays sample data next to each mapped element in the element list. By default, this option is deselected. Previewing the data can help you identify problems in the mappings.

- **Hide Help Text in the Task Pane**   This option controls whether Excel hides the help text that it normally displays below the element list in the XML Source task pane.

- **Automatically Merge Elements When Mapping**   This option controls whether Excel automatically expands an XML list when you drop an element in the cell adjacent to the list.

- **My Data Has Headings**   This option controls whether Excel uses your existing data as column headings when you map repeating elements to a worksheet.

- **Hide Border of Inactive Lists**   This option controls whether Excel hides the borders of a list or cell when you select a cell outside the list.

Importing an XML Data File into an Existing XML Mapping

Once you've mapped the appropriate XML elements to cells or ranges in a workbook, you can import an XML data file into the mapping you've created. This creates what's called an *XML data binding* between the XML data file and the XML map. Each XML map can have only a single XML data binding, which is bound to each mapping created from the XML map.

Importing XML data in this way enables you to use Excel as a front end for manipulating data saved in XML format using the schema you've mapped to the workbook. This XML data can come from any XML-compliant source using the same schema. Using Excel like this helps companies avoid having to retrain users in XML applications, instead leveraging their existing Excel skills and keeping them within their comfort zone.

To import an XML data file into an existing XML mapping:

1. Select a cell in the mapped range into which you want to import the data from the XML data file.

2. Click the Import button on the List and XML toolbar, or choose Data | XML | Import, to display the Import XML dialog box.

3. Navigate to and select the file you want to import; then click the Import button.

4. Excel checks the data and raises any issues:

   • If the XML data file doesn't refer to a schema, Excel displays a dialog box to notify you that it will create a schema based on the source data. As before, you can choose to suppress this warning in the future by selecting the In the Future, Do Not Show This Message option before dismissing the dialog box.

   • If Excel encounters a problem with the XML data file you're trying to import, Excel displays the XML Import Error dialog box, which lists the errors encountered. You can select an error and click Details to display a dialog box giving more information on the error and where it occurred. This information may help you fix problems in the XML data file so that you can subsequently import it without errors.

5. Excel displays the Import Data dialog box to let you specify where to import the data:

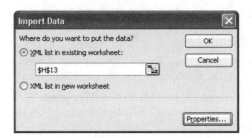

6. Choose whether to import the list to the active worksheet (and if so, specify a location) or to a new worksheet. You can also set properties for the XML map by clicking Properties and working in the XML Map Properties dialog box.

7. Click OK in the Import Data dialog box to import the data.

NOTE   *If Excel discovers noncritical errors that allow it to import some or all of the data, it imports the data and displays the XML Import Error dialog box to notify you of the errors. For example, Excel may need to truncate data that's too long for worksheet cells.*

Refreshing an XML Data Binding

To refresh the data in an XML data binding by importing the latest data available in the data source, issue a Refresh command in either of these ways:

- Click the Refresh button on the List and XML toolbar.
- Choose Data | XML | Refresh XML Data from the main menu.

Verifying a Map for Export

To verify an XML map for export before exporting it, click the Verify Map for Export link in the XML Source task pane. Excel checks the map and displays a message box telling whether all is well or you need to make changes.

Exporting XML Data

To export XML data from a workbook:

1. Choose Data | XML | Export, or click the Export button on the List and XML toolbar, to display the Export XML dialog box.
2. Specify the filename and location for the file to which you want to export the data.
3. Click Export. Excel exports the data.
4. If there's a problem with the schema, Excel displays a dialog box such as that shown here. Click Details to learn what the problem was.

Using Office on the Web

As you saw in Part VII of this book, FrontPage provides powerful features both for developing web sites and creating content for them. As you also saw, you can publish your Publisher documents to the web as well.

In this chapter, you'll learn how to create web content from the files you create in the other main Office applications—Word documents, Excel worksheets, PowerPoint presentations, and Access data access pages. You'll also learn about HTML and round tripping, the different web file formats the applications offer, and how to create links to Office documents.

HTML and Round Tripping

For creating web content, the Office applications use Hypertext Markup Language (HTML), a formatting language that's extensively used and understood more or less perfectly by all modern web browsers. HTML uses tags (codes) to specify how an item should be displayed. For example, if you apply an <H2> tag to indicate that some text is a level-two heading, any browser should recognize the tag and apply the appropriate formatting to the heading.

The Office applications automatically apply all necessary tags when you save a file in one of the HTML formats. (See the next section for a discussion of these formats.) Roughly speaking, the tags break down into two separate categories:

- Standard HTML tags for coding those parts of the file—the text and its formatting—that will be displayed by a web browser.

- Custom, Office-specific HTML tags for storing document information and application information. For example, when you save a Word document in the Single File Web Page format or the Web Page format, Word saves items such as the revision number, creation date, and VBA projects using custom HTML tags.

Office's custom tags should be ignored by web browsers, which don't care about document items such as whether the spelling state of the document is "clean" (contains no errors) or "dirty" (contains errors), the name of the person who last modified the document, or the application that created the file. These tags are used for *round tripping*: saving a file with all its contents, formatting, and extra items (such as VBA code) so that the application that created the file can reopen the file with exactly the same information and formatting as when it saved the file.

If that's a frown on your forehead, you're perhaps thinking that round tripping is technobabble for what every worthwhile application should be able to do anyway—save files without losing the information they contain. That's so, but in most cases, applications that create rich content (as opposed to, say, basic text) have used proprietary formats for saving their contents rather than HTML. For example, Word used to be able to save entire Word documents only in its Word Document format; Excel its workbooks in the Excel Spreadsheet format; and PowerPoint its presentations in the PowerPoint Presentation format. At first, when these applications created HTML files, they weren't able to round trip: the HTML files contained only a subset of the data saved in the native file format, and if you reopened such an HTML file in the application that created it, most of the noncontent items would be missing.

But in Office 2003 (and in Office XP), the applications support HTML as a native format alongside their previous native formats. This means that, should you need to, you can save files in HTML instead of the native format, without losing any parts of those files.

Understanding the File Formats Available

Word, Excel, and PowerPoint each offer two or more HTML formats to choose from. So before you save a file in HTML, you should understand the basics of the formats available.

Each of these three applications offers the Single File Web Page format and the Web Page format. Word offers the Web Page, Filtered format as well.

Single File Web Page Format

The Single File Web Page format creates a web archive file that contains all the information required for the web page. Again, this doesn't seem like much of an innovation until you know that the Web Page format (discussed next) creates a separate folder to contain graphics. Use the Single File Web Page format to create files that you can easily distribute.

Files in the Single File Web Page format use the .mht and .mhtml file extensions. These files use Office-specific tags to preserve all of the information the file contains in an HTML format.

Web Page Format

The Web Page format creates an HTML file that contains the text contents of the document, together with a separate folder that contains the graphics for the document. This makes the web page's HTML file itself smaller, but the page as a whole is more awkward to distribute, because you need to distribute the graphics folder as well. The folder is created automatically and assigned the web page's name followed by _files. For example, a web page named My Web Page.htm has a folder named My Web Page_files.

Files in the Web Page format use the .htm and .html file extensions. These files also use Office-specific tags to preserve all of the information the file contains in an HTML format.

Web Page, Filtered Format

The Web Page, Filtered format is available only in Word. Like the Web Page format, this format creates an HTML file that contains the text contents of the document, together with a separate, automatically named folder that contains the graphics for the document. However, this format removes Office-specific tags from the document. Removing these features reduces the size of the file, but the file loses items such as document properties and VBA code, so it's not useful for round tripping complex documents.

Files in the Web Page, Filtered format use the .htm and .html file extensions.

> **NOTE**   *In addition to the HTML formats just mentioned, Word offers the XML Document format and Excel offers the XML Spreadsheet format. See the previous chapter for a discussion of these formats.*

Publishing Documents on the Web

As discussed in "Using Office over the Internet" in Chapter 3, the Office applications can store files directly on a web server, an FTP server, or a SharePoint server. (Chapter 40 discusses SharePoint.) This capability can be very useful for working with intranet sites, because you can open a page on an intranet server directly in an Office application, edit or update the page, and then save it. To open a file from a server, you need *read permission*; to save a file to a server, you need *write permission*.

You can also work directly with files on Internet servers (as opposed to intranet servers) by using Web Digital Authoring and Versioning (usually shortened to WebDAV, and also sometimes called Web Sharing). But unless your Internet connection is fast and reliable, you may experience problems with saving the data. Because such problems can lead to your losing or corrupting your file, it's best not to work directly with files on Internet servers but instead download a copy of the file, modify it locally, and then upload the modified copy to the Internet server. This way, you keep a copy of the file on your local disk at all times and can avoid losing any data.

You can download and upload files from Internet servers by using Windows' Network Places, Internet Explorer, a third-party graphical FTP client, or even the command-line FTP client built into Windows XP and Windows 2000.

Using Hyperlinks in Office Documents

You can insert a hyperlink in an Office file by choosing Insert | Hyperlink (or pressing CTRL-K) and using the options in the Insert Hyperlink dialog box (Figure 39-1).

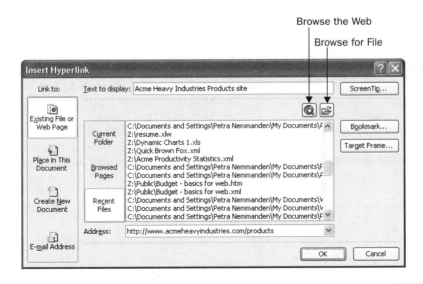

FIGURE 39-1   Use the Insert Hyperlink dialog box to insert hyperlinks to web pages, files, or local folders.

You can create the following types of hyperlinks by using the buttons in the left panel of the Insert Hyperlink dialog box:

- **Existing File or Web Page**   Creates a standard hyperlink to the file or the web page specified. The file can be stored on a local drive or a network drive, as necessary. The web page can be stored on a local drive, a network drive, an intranet server, or an Internet server. Use the Browse the Web button to locate a web page, or use the Browse for File button to locate a file.

- **Place in This Document**   Creates a hyperlink to a specified place in the document. In Word, you can choose an item such as the top of the document, a specific heading, a bookmark, or frames. In Excel, you can type a cell reference, select a worksheet name, or select a defined name. In PowerPoint, you can choose the first slide, last slide, next slide, or previous slide; a particular slide by name; or a custom show. In Access, this tab of the Insert Hyperlink dialog box is called Page in This Database, and it lets you choose one of the pages in the database.

- **Create New Document**   Lets you create a new document for the hyperlink to lead to, and lets you choose whether to edit the new document now or later. This may seem an awkward time to create a new document, but it ensures that the hyperlink contains the correct path and name to the document. (By contrast, if you create the document manually later, you may inadvertently enter the wrong name or save the document in a different folder.) In Access, this tab of the Insert Hyperlink dialog box is called Create New Page but fulfills a similar function.

- **E-mail Address**   Creates a hyperlink using the mailto command. You specify the destination e-mail address and the subject line for the message.

For any hyperlink, enter the text you want displayed for the hyperlink in the Text to Display box. To specify a ScreenTip for the browser to display when the user hovers the mouse pointer over the hyperlink, click ScreenTip and enter the text in the Set Hyperlink ScreenTip dialog box. For example, the ScreenTip might contain a fuller explanation of the page or other location to which the hyperlink leads.

Choosing Web Options

To control how one of the Office applications creates web pages, you can choose options in the Web Options dialog box. Choose Tools | Options, and then click the Web Options button on the General tab of the Options dialog box to display the Web Options dialog box. The options available in this dialog box depend on the application.

The Web Options dialog box for Word contains five tabs: Browsers, Files, Pictures, Encoding, and Fonts. The Web Options dialog boxes for Excel and PowerPoint contain those five tabs and a sixth tab, General. The Web Options dialog box for Access contains only a single tab, General.

You can set the web options separately for each application: changes you make in one application don't affect the other applications.

General Tab Options

The contents of the General tab of the Web Options dialog box vary depending on the application, as explained in the following list.

- Excel lets you choose whether to save additional hidden data needed to maintain formulas (almost always a good idea, and selected by default) and whether to load pictures from web pages not created by Excel (also selected by default).

- PowerPoint lets you control whether the web page includes slide navigation controls (this is selected by default) and, if so, which colors to use; whether to show slide animation while browsing (deselected by default); and whether to resize graphics to fit the browser window (a good idea, and selected by default).

- Access lets you specify the color of followed hyperlinks, the color of unfollowed hyperlinks, and choose whether to underline hyperlinks.

Browsers Tab Options

The Browsers tab of the Web Options dialog box (Figure 39-2) lets you specify the types of browsers for which you want your web page to work properly.

Select the lowest expected version of browser in the People Who View This Web Page Will Be Using drop-down list. (The default setting is Microsoft Internet Explorer 4.0 or later, which plays safe.) The application automatically selects and deselects the options in the Options box to match that browser's needs. You can also select and deselect options manually to suit your needs:

- Choose whether to allow web pages to use the Portable Network Graphics (PNG) format.

- In Word, choose whether to disable features not supported by browsers of the specified type. Doing so is almost always a good idea.

- Choose whether to use cascading style sheets (CSS) for font formatting.

- Choose whether to rely on Vector Markup Language (VML; a text-based format for vector graphics) for displaying graphics.

- Choose whether to save new web pages using the Single File Web Page format by default.

FIGURE 39-2
On the Browsers tab of the Web Options dialog box, specify the types of browsers for which you want the web page to work.

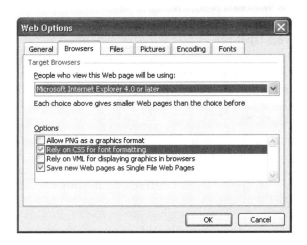

Files Tab Options

The Files tab of the Web Options dialog box varies a little between Word, Excel, and PowerPoint. These are the options you can set:

- Whether to organize supporting files in a subfolder of the folder that contains the page rather than in the same folder. Using a subfolder tends to be neater and easier. This option is selected by default.

- Choose whether to use long filenames if possible when saving files to a web server. This option is selected by default. You may want to deselect this option to force the application to use short (eight-character) names.

- Choose whether to automatically update hyperlinks in the page when you save it. Updating the links helps prevent the page from containing broken links. This option is selected by default.

- Choose whether the application should check if an Office application is the default editor for web pages created by Office applications. This option is selected by default but is a matter of preference. If you prefer to use a non-Office web editor, deselect this option to prevent the Office applications from constantly warning you about a choice you know you've made.

NOTE   *Word also offers the option of checking if Word is the default editor for web pages not created by the Office applications. Again, if you use another web editor rather than Word, you'll probably want to deselect this option, which is selected by default.*

- Choose whether Office should download Office Web Components when they're available. If so, specify the location in the text box.

Pictures Tab Options

On the Pictures tab of the Web Options dialog box, you can select the screen resolution of the monitor on which your web pages will be viewed. The default is 800×600 resolution. In Word and Excel, you can also specify the number of pixels per inch on that monitor. The default is 96 pixels per inch.

Encoding Tab Options

On the Encoding tab of the Web Options dialog box, you can select the type of encoding to use for the web page—for example, Western European (Windows) or Unicode (UTF-8)—and whether to always save web pages in the default encoding.

Fonts Tab Options

On the Fonts tab of the Web Options dialog box, you can choose the character set, proportional font, and fixed-width font for your web pages. The default character set is English/Western European/Other Latin Script, and you'll seldom need to change it unless you need to create (say) Arabic or Japanese pages. The fonts, on the other hand, you may well want to change for visual effect.

Saving a File as a Web Page

To create a web page from a file, follow the procedures outlined in the following section for the application you're using. The procedures vary enough from application to application to make it difficult to discuss them all together.

First, though, we'll briefly discuss using Web Page Preview and setting the title for the web page.

Using Web Page Preview to Check How Your File Looks

First, before saving the file as a web page, use Web Page Preview to make sure the page will look okay. To do so, choose File | Web Page Preview.

The application creates a temporary file in your *%userprofile%*\Local Settings\Temporary Internet Files\Content.MSO*Application*WebPagePreview\ folder, where *Application* is the application name—for example, WordWebPagePreview or ExcelWebPagePreview. The application then displays the page in your default browser (for example, Internet Explorer). Figure 39-3 shows an example of Web Page Preview.

Check the web page, and then close the browser window. If the page needs changing, make the changes, and then use Web Page Preview again to verify them.

Setting the Page Title

Each web page has a page title—the text that's displayed in the browser's title bar when the page is loaded. You can set the title in either of two ways:

- When you issue the Save as Web Page command to display the Save As dialog box, the Office applications suggest a default page title of the first paragraph in the file (or part of it, if the paragraph is long). You can change the title by clicking Change Title in the Save As dialog box, entering the text in the Set Page Title dialog box, and clicking OK.

- To change the title at any other time, choose File | Properties, change the Title entry on the Summary tab of the Properties dialog box, and click OK.

Saving a Word Document as a Web Page

To save a Word document as a web page:

1. Choose File | Save as Web Page to display the Save As dialog box with controls added for creating web pages. Shown here is the relevant section of the Save As dialog box for Word:

2. Specify the folder (or network place) and the file as usual.

3. Choose the appropriate file type in the Save as Type drop-down list. For example, use the Web Page, Filtered format to reduce the file size by stripping out information that won't be required to produce a satisfactory web page.

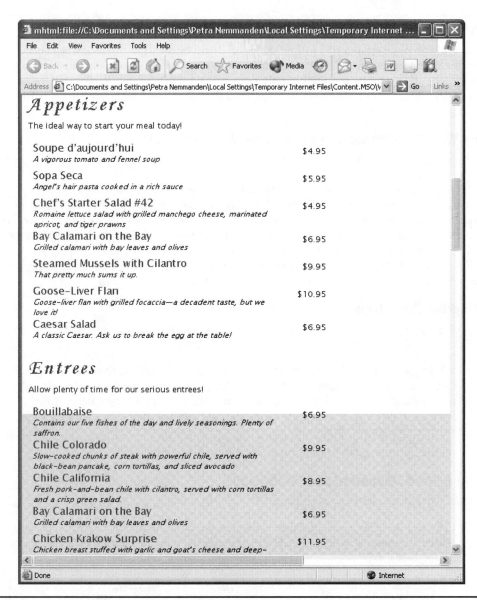

FIGURE 39-3   Use Web Page Preview to check how a page will look before you save it.

4. Check the title that Word has assigned to the web page. If necessary, click Change Title and use the Set Page Title dialog box to change it.

5. Click Save.

Saving an Excel Worksheet or Workbook as a Web Page

While Word creates only static web pages (pages that don't change), Excel offers you the choice of creating a static web page or an interactive worksheet that users can manipulate. To manipulate the interactive worksheet, users need to be using Internet Explorer rather than any other browser; but given that Internet Explorer currently enjoys more than 90 percent of the browser market, the chance that any given user has it is high.

Excel also offers you the choice between merely saving the workbook (or part of it) as a web page and *publishing* a copy of the workbook (or the specified part of it). When you publish a copy of the workbook (or part of it), Excel creates a copy of the workbook or part and saves it under the specified filename, but doesn't save the workbook itself. So you can publish a copy of an unsaved workbook if you choose.

To save an Excel workbook, worksheet, or part of a worksheet as a web page:

1. If you want to save a worksheet rather than a workbook, select the worksheet. If you want to save a range from a worksheet, select that range.

2. Choose File | Save as Web Page to display the Save As dialog box with controls added for creating web pages. Here's the relevant section of the Save As dialog box for Excel:

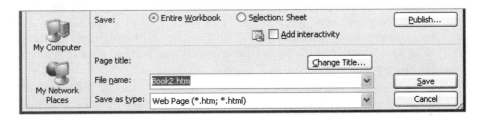

3. In the Save section, select the Entire Workbook option or the Selection option to specify whether to save the whole workbook or just the active worksheet.

4. If you want to make the web page interactive for Internet Explorer users, select the Add Interactivity option.

5. Check the title (if any) assigned to the web page. If necessary, click Change Title and use the Set Page Title dialog box to change it.

6. If you're saving the workbook for the first time:
   - Enter the filename in the File Name text box.
   - In the Save as Type drop-down list, choose the Single File Web Page item or the Web Page item as appropriate. (See "Understanding the File Formats Available," earlier in this chapter, for an explanation of the differences.)
   - Click Save to save the workbook.
   - Choose File | Save as Web Page again to display the Save As dialog box once more so that you can publish it.

7. Click Publish to display the Publish as Web Page dialog box (Figure 39-4).

FIGURE 39-4
Choose
publication options
for an Excel
workbook,
worksheet, or
range in the
Publish as Web
Page dialog box.

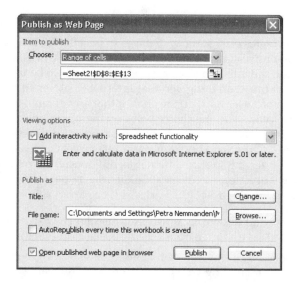

8. Check the choices in the Items to Publish section. If necessary, change the item selected in the Choose drop-down list. (If you selected the appropriate worksheet or range in step 1, the selection here should be correct.) If you select the Range of Cells item, Excel displays a Collapse Dialog button that you can click to select a range in the appropriate worksheet.

9. In the Viewing Options section, verify the setting of the Add Interactivity With option. If necessary, change the drop-down list between Spreadsheet Functionality and PivotTable Functionality.

10. In the Publish As section, check and change the page title, filename, and location as necessary.

11. Select the AutoRepublish Every Time This Workbook Is Saved option if you want Excel to automatically publish this web page again each time you save the file. This option is convenient for making sure the web page is always up-to-date, but use it only if you have a permanent and fast connection to the site on which you're publishing the web page.

12. Select the Open Published Web Page in Browser option if you want Excel to display the web page in your browser so that you can check it.

13. Click Publish. Excel publishes the page and (if appropriate) displays it in your browser.

Saving a PowerPoint Presentation as a Web Page

To save a PowerPoint presentation as a web page:

1. Choose File | Save as Web Page to display the Save As dialog box with controls added for creating web pages. The following illustration shows the relevant section of the Save As dialog box for PowerPoint.

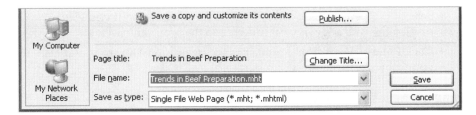

2. Check the title (if any) assigned to the web page. If necessary, click Change Title and use the Set Page Title dialog box to change it.

3. If you're saving the presentation for the first time:

   • Enter the filename in the File Name text box.

   • In the Save as Type drop-down list, choose the Single File Web Page item or the Web Page item as appropriate. (See "Understanding the File Formats Available," earlier in this chapter, for an explanation of the differences.)

   • Click Save to save the presentation.

   • Choose File | Save as Web Page again to display the Save As dialog box once more so that you can publish it.

4. Click Publish to display the Publish as Web Page dialog box (Figure 39-5).

5. In the Publish What? section, choose which part of the presentation to publish: the complete presentation, a range of slides, or a custom show (if available). Select the Display Speaker Notes option if you want to include the speaker notes with the slides.

6. In the Browser Support section, select the option for the browsers for which you want the web page to be viewable.

7. In the Publish a Copy As section, check or change the page title and filename as appropriate.

FIGURE 39-5
In the Publish As Web Page dialog box, choose which parts of the PowerPoint presentation to publish and which browsers to support.

8. Select the Open Published Web Page in Browser option if you want PowerPoint to display the web page in your browser so that you can check it.

9. Click Publish. PowerPoint publishes the page and (if appropriate) displays it in your browser.

Saving an Access Data Access Page as a Web Page

To create web content from Access, you use a data access page—a live page bound to a database. When you publish a data access page to the Web, users of Internet Explorer version 5 or later can access and manipulate the database through the web page. Users of other browsers can view the web page but can't manipulate the data on it.

To save a data access page to a web server:

1. Display the Database window, select the Pages item, and then double-click the data access page to open it.

2. Choose File | Save As to display the small Save As dialog box shown here:

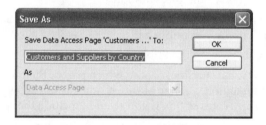

3. Enter the name for the data access page and click OK. Access displays the Save As Data Access Page dialog box, which is a common Save As dialog box.

4. Specify where to save the file (for example, click the My Network Places link in the Places bar, and then select the appropriate place), and then click Save.

NOTE   *If you enter an absolute path (for example, Z:\Public\DAPS\) for the data access page, Access warns you that the absolute path may cause problems and suggests that you specify a UNC path instead so that computers connecting through the network can connect to the data access page. Enter the UNC path (for example, \\acmeheavysv404\public\daps\) if users will need to connect through the network.*

Collaboration Using Office Tools and SharePoint Team Services

Y ou can get a long way by working on your own—especially if you use all the features of the Office applications described in the previous chapters. But if you're working in a business environment, chances are that you'll need to collaborate with your colleagues on some, many, or most documents. The Office applications can help you here too.

In this chapter, you'll learn about the Office applications' powerful tools for collaborating with your colleagues, beginning with the review tools that lurk within Word, Excel, and PowerPoint. After that, you'll learn how to protect a document, how to send documents via e-mail, and how to use SharePoint Team Services to facilitate teamwork.

Review Tools

To streamline the process of collaborating with your colleagues on the production of documents, Word and Excel offer features for tracking the changes made to a document. You can then work through the document with the changes highlighted on screen, deciding which changes to keep and which to reject.

Word and PowerPoint include features for comparing two versions of the same document and merging the changes from one document into another document. For example, if you send a copy of a Word document to several colleagues, and they return the copies with changes, you can merge their changes back into your master document.

Tracking Changes in Word Documents

For many purposes, the easiest method of soliciting, reviewing, and analyzing input from your colleagues on a Word document is to use the Track Changes feature. Ideally, you circulate the same copy of the document among your colleagues in series, so that each person adds his or her input and moves the document along toward completion, and you don't need to merge multiple documents together. But at other times, you may need to have your colleagues review the document in parallel, which means they'll each need a copy. After receiving all the copies back, you'll need to merge those edits that you want to keep into a single document, either manually or by using the Compare and Merge command (discussed in "Comparing and Merging Documents in Word," later in this chapter).

Depending on your work circumstances, you may find it best to circulate the document in ascending order of decision making (lower orders first, upper echelons last, so that each reviewer effectively signs off on the changes made so far) or in descending order of the amount of input each reviewer is likely to contribute (verbose first, laconic last, so that each reviewer sees as much of the completed document as possible). The least satisfactory method tends to be making the document available on the network for people to review at their leisure. Either you wind up with half-completed changes from the few moments that people found to work on the document, or everyone forgets (or "forgets") about reviewing the document until the last moment, at which point they pile on it like wolves on a kill—but only one person can edit the document at a time.

The Basics of Change Tracking in Word

Here's the gist of how change tracking works:

- Before having a colleague review a document, you turn on change tracking. Word then tracks all insertions, deletions, formatting changes, and comments added or deleted.

- Optionally, you can protect the document so that your colleague can't turn off Track Changes. If your company has a formal review process, protecting the document is likely to be a good idea. See "Securing Documents," later in this chapter.

NOTE   *Track Changes does a good job of catching most changes to a Word document, but there are a few types of changes that it doesn't catch, including changes of case by using the Change Case command (SHIFT-F3 or Format | Change Case).*

- When change tracking is on, you (or the user) can control how changes are displayed on screen. If you turn off the display of tracked changes, you can edit the document almost as if changes weren't being tracked. (Even with the display of tracked changes turned off, there are some minor differences in the editing process that may remind you that changes are being tracked. For example, sometimes when you've selected a space, you're unable to delete it by pressing DELETE but you can delete it by pressing BACKSPACE.)

- When you get the review document back from your colleagues, you can easily review the edits they've made by using the tools on the Reviewing toolbar. You can set Word to display each reviewer's set of revisions in a different color, make Word display only one reviewer's revisions, and so forth. You can accept any revision, reject it, delete it, or type something else over it.

You'll learn the details in the following sections.

Turning Change Tracking On and Off in Word

You can toggle change tracking on and off in any of the following ways:

- Double-click the TRK indicator in the status bar, or right-click the indicator and choose Track Changes from the shortcut menu.
- Choose Tools | Track Changes.
- Press CTRL-SHIFT-E.
- Click the Track Changes button on the Reviewing toolbar.

When you turn change tracking on, Word displays the Reviewing toolbar if it's not already displayed.

Controlling How Word Displays Tracked Changes

In Print Layout view, Web Layout view, and Reading Layout view, Word displays balloons containing details of changes that may not immediately be visible, together with arrows linking the balloons to the parts of the document they refer to (Figure 40-1). Word doesn't show deleted text in these views, which makes the edited text easy to read.

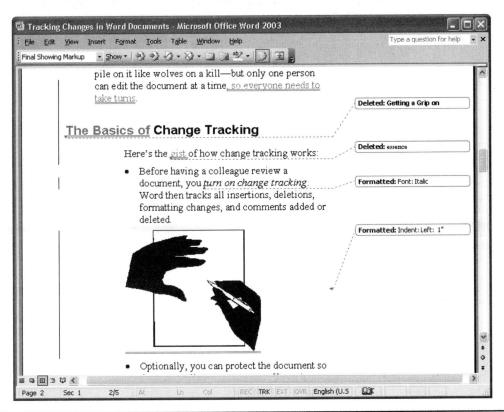

FIGURE 40-1   In Print Layout view and Web Layout view, Word displays balloons containing the details of changes you can't immediately see.

In Normal view and Outline view, Word displays deleted text in place along with inserted text. These views let you see the details of edits more clearly than the results of the edits:

~~Getting a Grip on~~ <u>The Basics of</u> Change Tracking

Here's the ~~essence~~ <u>gist</u> of how change tracking works:

To control how Word displays tracked changes, right-click the TRK indicator in the status bar and choose Options. Word displays the Track Changes dialog box (Figure 40-2), which contains only one tab: Track Changes. This tab also appears as the Track Changes tab in the Options dialog box, so you can also access it by choosing Tools | Options and clicking the Track Changes tab.

On the Track Changes tab, you can choose the following:

- How to display insertions: with no marking, with a color only, in bold, in italic, underlined, double underlined, or with strikethrough. The default setting is underlined, but if your documents contain underlines anyway, you may find double underline more useful. Use the top Color drop-down list to choose whether to display a different color for each author (the default setting) or to use a specific color for all insertions.

- How to display deletions: with no marking, with a color only, in bold, in italic, underlined, double underlined, with strikethrough, hidden, with carets (^), or with pound signs (#). Displaying deletions as hidden makes them disappear as if they

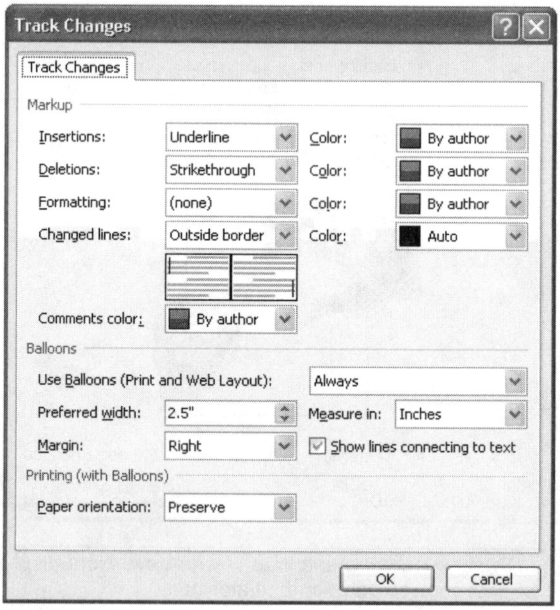

FIGURE 40-2
Use the Track Changes dialog box (or the Track Changes tab of the Options dialog box) to control how Word displays tracked changes.

were actually deleted. This can be a useful setting when you're editing (as opposed to reviewing edits). Use the second Color list to choose the color for deletions. Again, the default is to use a different color for each author.

- How to display formatting changes: with no marking (the default setting), with a color only, in bold, in italic, underlined, double underlined, or with strikethrough. If you need to be able to identify formatting changes by eye, choose a type of formatting that doesn't normally appear in your documents. Use the third Color list to choose the color for formatting changes if necessary. Again, the default is to use a different color for each author.

- Whether and where to display a line in the margin beside a line of text that contains a change. These lines help you quickly identify individual formatting changes or small insertions or deletions. (Large insertions or deletions tend to catch the eye.) You can display these lines (which Word calls *changed lines*) in the left border, in the right border, in the outside border (in the left border for left pages, in the right border for right pages), or not display them at all. Yet again, choose the color for the lines. The default setting is Auto, which is black for a white background. You may prefer a more lively color to draw your attention.

- Which color to use for comments. The default setting is to use a different color for each author.

- How to display revision balloons in Print Layout view and Web Layout view: always, never, or only for comments and formatting (which tend to be harder to see than most insertions and deletions). You can choose the preferred width for the balloons, which margin to place them in, whether to measure them in inches or as a percentage of the space available, and whether to display lines connecting them to the text they refer to (this is usually helpful).

- Whether to preserve the paper orientation when printing with revision balloons, print in landscape instead (giving more space for the balloons), or use automatic settings.

Click OK to close the Track Changes dialog box (or the Options dialog box) and apply your choices. You can then choose View | Markup to toggle the display of tracked changes in your document.

TIP   *The Privacy Options section of the Security tab of the Options dialog box also contains a couple of options that affect how Word handles revision marks. The option Make Hidden Markup Visible When Opening or Saving forces Word to display markup in documents you're opening, even if the previous user has hidden the markup. This option is selected by default and helps prevent you remaining unaware of hidden markup. You may want to check the option Warn Before Printing, Saving, or Sending a File That Contains Tracked Changes or Comments, which is cleared by default. It can help you avoid unpleasant surprises in documents that you print or circulate.*

Using Word's Reviewing Toolbar

The Reviewing toolbar (Figure 40-3) is the nerve center for viewing and reviewing edits. Most of the buttons are straightforward to use, but three items deserve brief explanation.

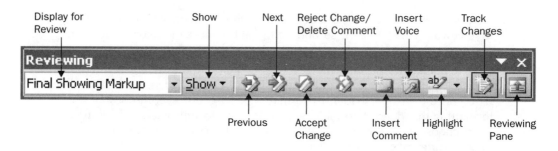

- Use the Display for Review drop-down list to switch between the different versions available: Final Showing Markup, Final, Original Showing Markup, or Original. As you'd guess, Original shows what the document contained before you turned on Track Changes, and Final shows what the document contains now.

- Use the Show drop-down list to toggle the display of individual elements: comments, ink annotations, insertions and deletions, and formatting changes. You can also toggle the display of changes by particular reviewers on and off by using the Reviewers submenu; this enables you to focus on the changes that one reviewer made. You can change the display of balloons (the options are the same as in the Track Changes dialog box), toggle the Reviewing pane on and off, and display the Track Changes dialog box (by choosing Options).

- To insert a voice annotation, click the Insert Voice button. Word launches Sound Recorder. Click the Record button to start recording. Obviously, you need a functional microphone for this to work.

Using the Reviewing Pane to Get an Overview of Changes

When a Word document has been reviewed by more than a handful of people, or has been brutally edited by even a couple of people, the morass of changes in the text and the weight of balloons in the margin can make it hard to see who has done what. To the rescue comes the Reviewing pane (Figure 40-4; click the Reviewing Pane button on the Reviewing toolbar), which gives you an overview of the changes made to the different parts of the document (the main document, the header and footer, text boxes, endnotes, and so on) and lets you access any given change by double-clicking its heading in the Reviewing pane.

To remove the Reviewing pane from the screen, click the Reviewing Pane button on the Reviewing toolbar, double-click the split bar that separates the Reviewing pane from the main document, or drag the split bar to the bottom of the Word window.

Tracking Changes in Excel Workbooks

Excel lets you track changes made to a workbook so that you can see who changed what when. Normally, people use change tracking on shared workbooks; so to streamline this process, Excel automatically shares a workbook when you turn on change tracking.

FIGURE 40-4
Use Word's
Reviewing pane to
get an overview of
the changes in the
different parts of a
document.

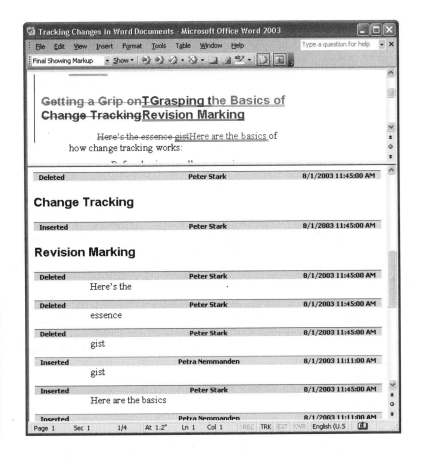

Turning On and Configuring Change Tracking in Excel

To turn on and configure change tracking:

1. Choose Tools | Track Changes | Highlight Changes to display the Highlight Changes dialog box:

2. Select the option "Track Changes While Editing. This Also Shares Your Workbook". Excel makes all the other controls in the dialog box available.

3. In the Highlight Which Changes section, specify which changes you want to track by selecting the appropriate check boxes and choosing suitable options:

   • The When drop-down list offers the choices Since I Last Saved, All, Not Yet Reviewed (changes you haven't reviewed yet), and Since Date (you specify the date).

   • The Who drop-down list offers the choices Everyone, Everyone but Me, and each user by name (including you). For example, you might choose to see only the changes that your supervisor makes.

   • The Where text box lets you restrict change tracking to a specific range (or multiple ranges) instead of the whole workbook.

4. Leave the Highlight Changes on Screen option selected (as it is by default) if you want to see the tracked changes on screen. Deselect this option if you want the tracked changes to be hidden. Hiding the tracked changes can help keep your worksheets easy to read.

5. Select the List Changes on a New Sheet option if you want Excel to create a list of the tracked changes on a separate worksheet called History. This overview lets you quickly scan the list of changes without having to examine each worksheet separately, but it includes only the changes made in the current editing session.

NOTE *Excel reserves the name History for change tracking and prevents you from changing a worksheet's name to History.*

6. Click OK to close the Highlight Changes dialog box. If the workbook wasn't already shared, Excel shares it now and displays a message box warning you that it will save the workbook. Click the OK button.

Working in Excel with Change Tracking On

When change tracking is on, you can perform basic editing, apply formatting, and work with formulas, but you can't make major changes to the design or layout of the workbook.

If Excel is set to display changes on screen, any cell that you change is marked with a border and with a triangle in its upper-left corner. Hover the mouse pointer over the cell to display a comment box containing details of the change:

| Montreal | 8 | 44 | **Paul Ryman, 7/27/2003 12:09 PM:** |
| Quebec | 10 | 95 | Changed cell C8 from '??' to '95'. |

If Excel is set not to display changes on screen, you won't see any visual indication of the tracking of the changes you make.

If Excel is set to list changes on a new worksheet, you'll notice that a worksheet named History appears at the end of your workbook.

Reviewing Tracked Changes in Excel

If Excel is set to display changes on screen, you can use the technique of hovering the mouse pointer over a cell to see the change made. This technique tends to be useful only when you've tracked changes to just a handful of cells.

To work your way through the tracked changes in a workbook:

1. Choose Tools | Track Changes | Accept or Reject Changes. Excel displays the Select Changes to Accept or Reject dialog box:

2. Select or clear the When, Who, and Where options as appropriate, and use their options to specify which changes you want to review.

3. Click OK. Excel displays the Accept or Reject Changes dialog box and selects the first cell that contains a change matching the details you specified:

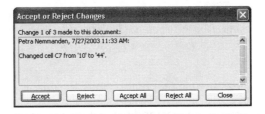

4. Click Accept to accept this change, or click Reject to reject this change, and move on to the next change. Alternatively, click Accept All to accept all the remaining changes, or click Reject All to reject all the remaining changes, without reviewing them further.

5. After reviewing the changes, click Close.

If you set Excel to log the changes on a separate worksheet, display the History worksheet to get an overview of the changes to the workbook in the current editing session. Figure 40-5 shows an example of the History worksheet, which you can filter by using the column headings.

Comparing and Merging Documents in Word

Word's Compare and Merge feature can save a lot of time when you need to put your colleagues' input from multiple copies of a document into a single copy. Provided that

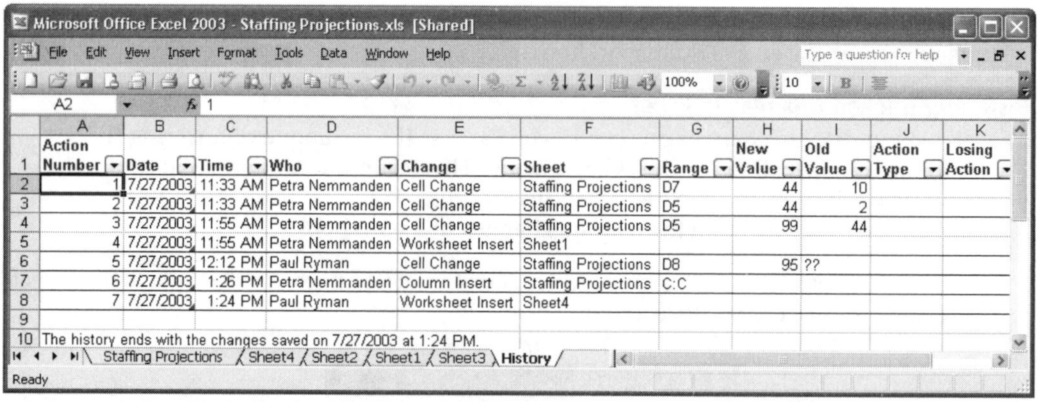

Action Number	Date	Time	Who	Change	Sheet	Range	New Value	Old Value	Action Type	Losing Action
1	7/27/2003	11:33 AM	Petra Nemmanden	Cell Change	Staffing Projections	D7	44	10		
2	7/27/2003	11:33 AM	Petra Nemmanden	Cell Change	Staffing Projections	D5	44	2		
3	7/27/2003	11:55 AM	Petra Nemmanden	Cell Change	Staffing Projections	D5	99	44		
4	7/27/2003	11:55 AM	Petra Nemmanden	Worksheet Insert	Sheet1					
5	7/27/2003	12:12 PM	Paul Ryman	Cell Change	Staffing Projections	D8	95	??		
6	7/27/2003	1:26 PM	Petra Nemmanden	Column Insert	Staffing Projections	C:C				
7	7/27/2003	1:24 PM	Paul Ryman	Worksheet Insert	Sheet4					

The history ends with the changes saved on 7/27/2003 at 1:24 PM.

FIGURE 40-5 Display the History worksheet to get an overview of the changes to the workbook in the current editing session.

the changes from one copy to another are relatively straightforward, the Compare and Merge feature can merge the input very competently. But if one of your colleagues has changed the document beyond all recognition, all bets are off: you may need to integrate that person's changes manually in order to make sense of them. So it's generally simpler to circulate a single copy of a document for review and force your colleagues to use revision tracking than to use Compare and Merge. If you forgot to turn revision tracking on when you circulated the document, you can use the Compare and Merge feature as a fallback.

TIP *You can also compare different versions of the same document that you've saved by using the File | Versions command. However, you need to save the earlier version of the file under a different filename (in other words, as a separate file rather than as a component of the current file) to make this work.*

To compare and merge different copies of the same document in Word:

1. Open your copy of the document, and make it the active window. If you were the originator of the document, this will be the master copy. This document is called the *baseline document*.
2. Choose Tools | Compare and Merge Documents to display the Compare and Merge Documents dialog box. This is a common Open dialog box with a few tweaks.
3. Select the document that you want to merge with the active document.
4. Select the Legal Blackline option if you want to merge the documents into a new document, accept all changes in the baseline document, and display only the differences between the baseline document and the other document. The Legal Blackline option is deselected by default. When you select this option, Word changes the Merge button in the Compare and Merge Documents dialog box to a Compare button.
5. Select the Find Formatting option if you want to include changes to formatting (as opposed to changes to text) in the Compare and Merge operation.

6. Choose the appropriate option from the Merge button:

- Click the Merge button itself to merge the changes from your baseline document (the document you opened in step 1) into the document selected in the Compare and Merge Documents dialog box.

- Click the Merge into Current Document item on the Merge button's drop-down list to merge the changes from the document selected in the Compare and Merge Documents dialog box into the baseline document.

- Click the Merge into New Document item on the Merge button's drop-down list to make Word create a new document and merge the text from the documents into it. This option is useful for evaluating the extent of changes without changing your copy of the document.

- Click Compare if you've selected the Legal Blackline option. Word creates a new document and merges the text from the documents into it, marking the changes with revision marks.

TIP   *To help ensure that Word can merge documents effectively, leave the option Store Random Number to Improve Merge Accuracy selected in the Privacy Options section of the Security tab of the Options dialog box (Tools | Options). This random number is a potential privacy concern because it can tie a particular document to a particular computer.*

Comparing and Merging Changes in PowerPoint

PowerPoint's Compare and Merge features work in a similar way to Word's but have fewer wrinkles:

1. Open your copy of the presentation and make it the active window. This is the baseline document.

2. Choose Tools | Compare and Merge Presentations to display the Choose Files to Merge with Current Presentation dialog box. This is a common Open dialog box.

3. Select the presentation or presentations that you want to merge with the active presentation.

4. Click Merge to close the dialog box and perform the merge operation. PowerPoint merges the changes and displays the Revisions task pane.

Here's how to work with the Revisions task pane:

- Use the Gallery tab (Figure 40-6) to get an overview of the different versions of the slide. Click one of those versions to display it, or hover the mouse pointer over a version and choose a command from the drop-down menu. The menu lets you apply and unapply changes by this reviewer, show only this reviewer's changes on the main slide, preview the animation on the slide, or indicate that you're done with this reviewer. You can also use the Reviewers drop-down list to restrict the display to one particular reviewer.

- Use the List tab to get an overview of the changes to the active slide and to the presentation as a whole (for example, details of slides added or deleted). Again, you

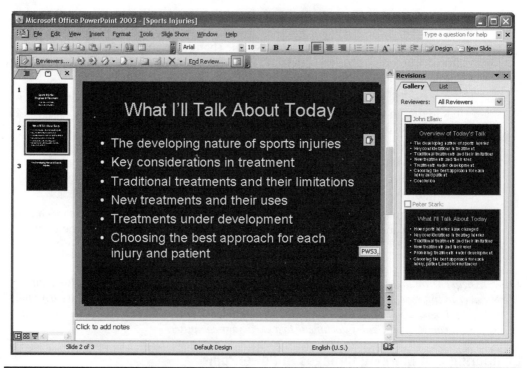

FIGURE 40-6   The Gallery tab of the Revisions task pane enables you to navigate between the different versions of the slide.

can use the Reviewers drop-down list to restrict the display to one particular reviewer.

- Click a Smart Tag on the presentation to see the details of the changes made to a particular element. You can turn each change on or off to see the difference it makes.

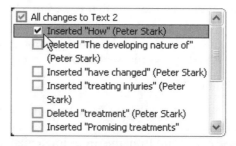

Securing Documents

Word, Excel, and PowerPoint offer several options for securing your documents against intrusion and unwanted modification. To use these options, choose Tools | Options, and then display the Security tab of the Options dialog box. The left screen in Figure 40-7 shows the Security tab of the Options dialog box for Word, while the right screen shows the Security tab of the Options dialog box for PowerPoint.

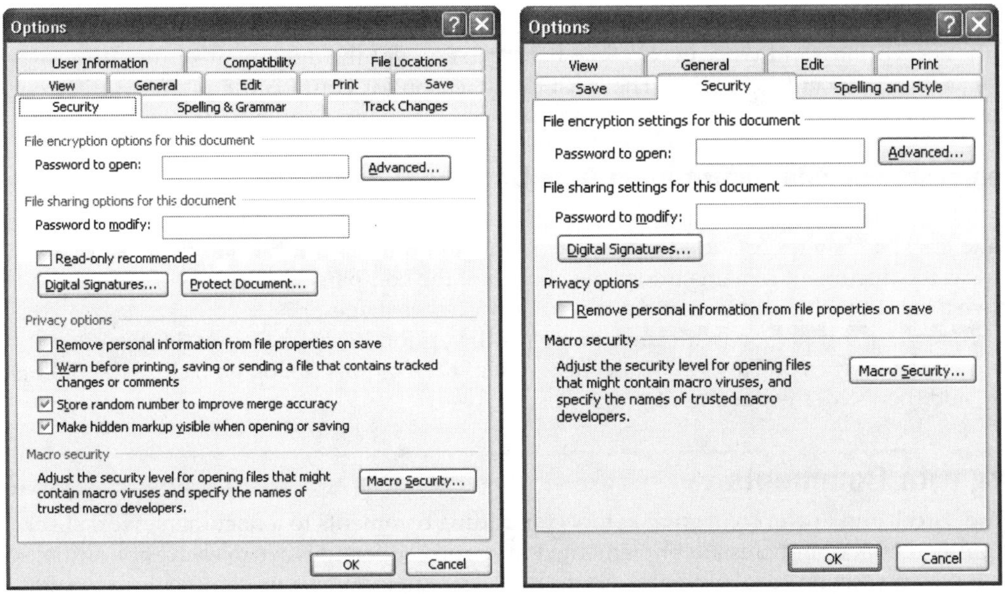

FIGURE 40-7   The Security tab of the Options dialog box for Word (left), Excel, and PowerPoint (right) offers key options for securing your documents.

Securing Documents with Passwords

To keep unauthorized users out of your documents, you can apply passwords for opening and modifying them. If you apply an opening password, users must enter the password to open the document at all. A modify password lets users open the document in read-only format without a password; to open the document for editing, they must supply the password.

To apply either kind of password, enter it in the appropriate box on the Security tab. When you close the Options dialog box, the application displays the Confirm Password dialog box to ensure that you typed the password accurately. After applying a password, save the document immediately.

The next time you (or other users) open the document, you'll be prompted for the password. In the case of a modify password, the application offers a Read Only button that you can click to open the document in read-only mode. You can then change the document and save the results under a new name. You can't save changes to the original document.

To remove the password, delete the password from the Security tab of the Options dialog box, and then save the document again.

Specifying an Encryption Type for a Document

By default, the Office applications use the Office 97/2000 Compatible encryption type, which provides reasonably effective protection against conventional attacks (such as password guessing) but can be cracked in short order by password-cracking utilities. (Some such utilities are sold for above-board purposes, such as recovering documents secured with passwords that have been forgotten or lost.)

Alternatively, you can apply another type of encryption by clicking Advanced on the Security tab of the Options dialog box and choosing the type in the Encryption Type dialog box. For some encryption types, you can specify a key length (a measure of the complexity of the encryption), and you can choose whether to encrypt the document's properties as well as the document's contents. The most likely reason for your needing to use a different type of encryption than Office's default is that your company's security policy requires it.

Removing Personal Information from Document Properties

By default, the Office applications save details of who created a document, last saved it, made tracked changes or added comments to it, and more. This information is useful as long as the document remains under the control of the company that created it, but it can prove a liability when the document is sent or posted elsewhere.

To remove this personal information, select the option Remove Personal Information from File Properties on Save on the Security tab of the Options dialog box, close the dialog box, and then save the document.

Working with Comments

Word, Excel, and PowerPoint contain tools for adding comments to a document, worksheet, or presentation. Comments are implemented in slightly different ways in each application, so the following sections deal with each application separately. However, comments in general behave in roughly the same way in each application, so we'll discuss their behavior first.

How Comments Work

A comment is a text note attached to a particular element in a document—for example, attached to a cell in an Excel worksheet, to a particular word in a Word document, or to a shape in a PowerPoint slide. In each of the applications, you can

- Insert a comment by choosing Insert | Comment or clicking the Insert Comment button on the Reviewing toolbar. The application inserts your username in boldface; you can delete this if you choose. Type the text of the comment, and then click elsewhere to deselect the comment.

- Display a temporarily hidden comment by hovering the mouse pointer over its marker (in PowerPoint) or the cell to which it is attached (in Excel).

- Edit a selected comment by right-clicking its marker or cell and choosing Edit Comment from the shortcut menu, or by clicking the Edit Comment button on the Reviewing toolbar.

- Delete a comment by selecting its frame and pressing DELETE or by clicking the Delete Comment button on the Reviewing toolbar.

- Navigate from one comment to another by clicking the Previous Comment button and Next Comment button on the Reviewing toolbar. (In PowerPoint, these buttons are called Previous Item and Next Item.)

- Format a comment by right-clicking it and choosing Format Comment, then working on the tabs of the Format Comment dialog box. A comment is a rectangular AutoShape, so you can format it in many of the ways that you can format most AutoShapes. For example, you can change the orientation of text in a comment by working on the Alignment tab of the Format Comment dialog box.

- Use many of the drawing commands discussed in Chapter 5 to manipulate comments. In normal use, you'll seldom need to do so, but occasionally you may find this capability useful. For example, you can group a comment with other AutoShapes, and you can use the Order submenu on the shortcut menu to change the comment's position within the sublayers of the drawing layer.

Using Comments in Word

In a Word document, you can attach a comment to a selection consisting of one or more characters or another element (for example, a graphic or a drawing object). You can't attach a comment to an empty selection (in other words, an individual point in the document)—if you do, Word selects the current word (if the selection is in a word) or the previous word (if the selection is between words). You also can't attach a comment to text in a text box.

Comments in Word are fully integrated with revisions, so you work with them largely as described earlier in this chapter. (In versions of Word up to Word 2000, comments appeared in a Comments pane of their own rather than in the Reviewing pane.) In all views, Word displays comments as red parentheses around the affected text. In Print Layout view and Web Layout view, Word displays comments in balloons attached to the parentheses. In Normal view and Outline view, Word displays comments in the Revisions pane.

To insert a comment, select the item you want it to refer to and choose Insert | Comment. Alternatively, if you have the Reviewing toolbar displayed, click the Insert Comment button. Word places red parentheses around the selection and displays a comment balloon (in Print Layout view or Web Layout view) or displays the Revisions pane (in other views). Type your comment in the balloon or in the Revisions pane.

Word numbers each reviewer's comment balloons with the reviewer's initials (set in the Initials box on the User Information tab of the Options dialog box) and a number indicating where the comment falls in the sequence of comments in the chapter—for example, PQM1, PQM2, PQM3. When you insert another comment before existing comments, or delete an existing comment, Word renumbers the comments automatically.

To delete a comment, right-click within the comment's brackets, or right-click the comment's balloon, or right-click the comment's header in the Revisions pane, and choose Delete Comment from the shortcut menu.

To navigate from one comment to another, use the Previous and Next buttons on the Reviewing toolbar, the balloons in the margin, or the entries in the Revisions pane.

Using Comments in Excel

In Excel, you can attach a comment to a cell. Any cell can have one comment attached to it at a time. You can add a comment by choosing Insert | Comment from the main menu, right-clicking the cell and choosing Insert Comment, or clicking the New Comment button on the Reviewing toolbar or the Formula Auditing toolbar.

To keep your worksheets readable, Excel's default settings for comments is to display only comment indicators—a red triangle marker in the upper-right corner of a cell that contains a comment.

You can control Excel's overall display settings for comments by choosing Tools | Options and selecting the appropriate option button in the Comments section of the View tab of the Options dialog box: None, Comment Indicator Only, or Comment & Indicator. The default setting is Comment Indicator Only, which makes Excel display a small red triangle in the upper-right corner to indicate that a cell has a comment attached to it. You can display the comment by hovering the mouse pointer over a cell with a comment indicator.

To toggle the display of a particular comment, right-click its cell and choose Show/Hide Comments from the shortcut menu or click the Show/Hide Comment button on the Reviewing toolbar. To toggle the display of all comments, click the Show/Hide All Comments button on the Reviewing toolbar.

Excel's Reviewing toolbar (Figure 40-8) provides self-explanatory commands for navigating through comments.

Using Comments in PowerPoint

PowerPoint provides a straightforward implementation of comments:

- You can attach a comment to a text object or a graphical object by choosing Insert | Comment from the main menu or by clicking the Insert Comment button on the Reviewing toolbar (Figure 40-9).

- PowerPoint displays a comment as a small box identified by the commentator's initials and the number of the comment—for example, PWS1. Hover the mouse pointer over the box, or click the box, to display a balloon containing the full text of the comment. Click elsewhere to hide the comment balloon again.

- To edit a comment, right-click the comment's box and choose Edit Comment from the shortcut menu. Alternatively, select the comment's box and click the Edit Comment button on the Reviewing toolbar.

- To copy the text of a comment so that you can paste it elsewhere, right-click the comment's box and choose Copy Text from the shortcut menu.

- To delete a comment, right-click the comment's box and choose Delete Comment from the shortcut menu.

- To delete all markup on the current slide, click the Delete drop-down button on the Reviewing toolbar and choose Delete All Markup on the Current Slide.

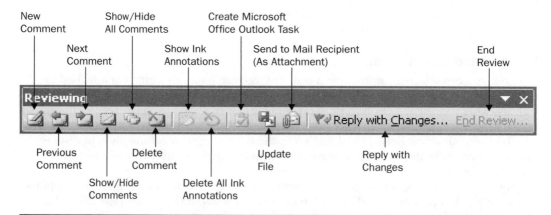

FIGURE 40-8   Use Excel's Reviewing toolbar to work your way through the edits, annotations, and comments in a workbook.

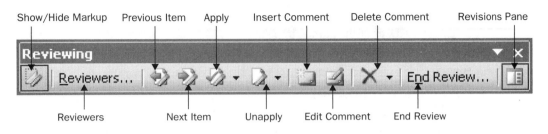

FIGURE 40-9   Use the Reviewing toolbar to work with comments in PowerPoint.

- To delete all markup in the presentation, click the Delete drop-down button on the Reviewing toolbar and choose Delete All Markup in This Presentation.
- To reposition a comment box, drag it to where you want it to appear.

Sending Documents in E-mail

Depending on the type of company or organization you work for, you may well need to send documents to your colleagues via e-mail. The Office applications provide a variety of commands for doing so. You can send a document for review, send a document as an attachment, or send a document with a routing slip attached so that it goes to two or more recipients in the order you specify.

Sending a Document for Review

Word, Excel, and PowerPoint enable you to send the active document to a colleague for review. When you send a document for review, the document is tagged so that it contains the information that it has been sent for review and should be returned to you via e-mail when the review is complete. (By contrast, a document you route goes to the specified people in sequence before returning to you.)

To send the active document for review, choose File | Send To | Mail Recipient (for Review). The application activates or launches Outlook (depending on whether it's running or not) and creates a new message, assigning the subject line "Please review" and the filename, and attaching the document to the message.

The application's default setting is to send the document as a "regular attachment." This means that each recipient receives a separate copy of the document. So if you send the same document to five people, and they return their copies, you'll need to integrate five sets of edits and changes with your master document.

The alternative is to send the document as a "shared attachment." This means that each recipient receives a separate copy of the document, as with a regular attachment, but Office also creates a copy in a document workspace. This copy can be automatically updated with the changes the recipients make to their individual copies of the document.

Making an Excel Workbook Shared so It Can Be Reviewed

To send an Excel workbook for review, you need to make it shared first:

1. Choose Tools | Share Workbook to display the Share Workbook dialog box.

2. On the Editing tab (shown on the left in Figure 40-10), select Allow Changes by More Than One User at the Same Time.

3. On the Advanced tab (shown on the right in Figure 40-10), choose the appropriate sharing options:

- **Track Changes**   Choose whether to keep the change history for a specified length of time (the default is 30 days) or not to keep the change history at all.

- **Update Changes**   Choose whether to update changes when the file is saved or update them automatically every so many minutes (the default is 15 minutes). If you choose automatic updating, choose whether to save your changes and see other people's changes or to see other users' changes only.

- **Conflicting Changes Between Users**   Choose what should happen when users make conflicting changes to the shared workbook. Excel's default setting is to ask you which changes win the conflict, but you can choose instead to have the changes being saved win the conflict.

- **Include in Personal View**   Choose whether to include print settings and filter settings in your view of the shared workbook.

4. Click OK.

Receiving and Returning a Document Sent for Review

When you receive a workbook sent for review, save it to the appropriate folder, and then open it from the application as usual (choose File | Open). The application automatically displays the Reviewing toolbar and makes the Reply with Changes button available.

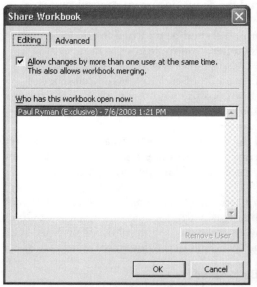

FIGURE 40-10   Before sending an Excel workbook for review, use the Editing tab (left) and Advanced tab (right) of the Share Workbook dialog box to enable and configure sharing.

After making your changes to the document, save it, and then click the Reply with Changes button on the Reviewing toolbar to create a reply to the sender with the document attached. Enter any necessary explanation, and then send the reply with its attachment.

Sending and Receiving a Document as an Attachment

If you want to send colleagues a document they can work with, but you don't need them to return it, send the document as an attachment. The process is almost identical to sending the document for review, except for these details:

- You choose File | Send To | Mail Recipient (As Attachment) instead of File | Send To | Mail Recipient (For Review).
- Outlook assigns the filename to the subject line of the message (without the words "Please review").

When you receive a document sent as an attachment, simply save it to the appropriate folder. You can then work with it as you would any other document.

Sending and Receiving a Word Document or Excel Worksheet in a Message

Word and Excel offer another capability for sharing a document or a worksheet if you're using Outlook as your default mail application. If you need to share a Word document or an Excel worksheet (as opposed to an entire workbook) with someone, you can send it as a message:

1. Open the document or workbook. In a workbook, activate the worksheet you want to send.

2. Choose File | Send To | Mail Recipient to display the mailing fields above the document or worksheet:

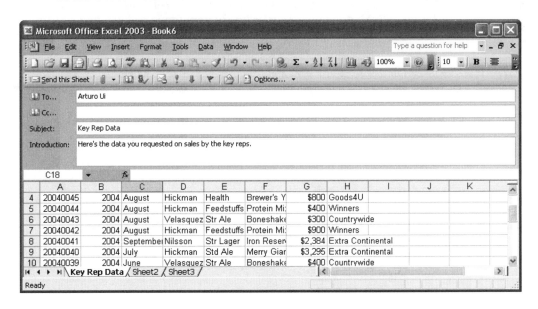

3. Enter the names of the recipients and any cc recipients, the subject, and any introduction necessary.

4. Click the Send a Copy button (in Word) or the Send This Sheet button in Excel to send the document or worksheet via Outlook.

When you receive a Word document or an Excel worksheet in a message, you can view the document or worksheet as you would any other message.

If you received an Excel worksheet, and you're using Outlook, you can insert the worksheet in a new workbook by opening it in a message window and then choosing Edit | Open in Microsoft Excel from the main menu.

Routing a Word Document or Excel Workbook Among a Group of People

Instead of sending a Word document or Excel workbook to a group of people for review (so that each receives a separate copy of the document or workbook, reviews it, and then returns it to you), you can route a single document or workbook among a specified group of people. Office's default method of routing a document or workbook makes the same copy of the document or workbook go to each recipient on the list in turn: the first recipient receives it, and sends it automatically to the second, who sends it to the third, and so forth. But you can also route a document or workbook so that it goes to each of the specified people at the same time, with each of the recipients receiving a separate copy of the document. This parallel routing has the same effect as sending the document or workbook to that same group of people for review.

A document or workbook you route via e-mail has a routing slip attached to it so that it is automatically routed. To create the routing slip and send the document from Word or the workbook from Excel:

1. Choose File | Send To | Routing Recipient to display the Routing Slip dialog box. Figure 40-11 shows the Routing Slip dialog box for an Excel workbook (on the left) and the Routing Slip dialog box for a Word document (on the right). As you can see, there are minor differences between the two.

NOTE   *If you're using Outlook as your e-mail application, you may see a Microsoft Office Outlook warning dialog box when Word or Excel tries to access the e-mail addresses stored in Outlook. If you've just issued the routing command, all is well. Click the Yes button to proceed. (If you haven't just issued the routing command or taken another action that involves borrowing functionality from your e-mail application, your computer might have a virus.)*

2. To add the addresses of the recipients to the routing slip, click the Address button, select the names or group in the Address Book dialog box, click the To button, and then click OK.

3. If necessary, use the two Move buttons to rearrange the order of the addresses in the To text box in the Routing Slip dialog box. You may also want to change the text in the Subject box. By default, Word enters "Routing:" and the contents of the document's Title field, whereas Excel enters "Routing:" and the filename (which is usually more helpful than the title).

FIGURE 40-11   In the Routing Slip dialog box, specify the recipients of the document or workbook and the order in which to route it to them. The left dialog box is for routing an Excel worksheet, while the right dialog box is for routing a Word document.

4. In the Message Text box, enter the text of any message you want to send with the routed document or workbook.

5. In the Route to Recipients section, select the One After Another option button (the default) or the All at Once option button, as appropriate. In most cases, you'll want to stay with the One After Another option.

6. By default, Word and Excel select the Return When Done check box. If you don't want the document or workbook returned to you at the end of the routing, clear this check box.

7. By default, Word and Excel select the Track Status check box. If you don't want to be able to track the status of this routed document or workbook by having it send e-mail messages reporting its progress, clear this check box.

8. In Word, select the type of protection you want for the document you're routing in the Protect For drop-down list. Your choices are Tracked Changes (the default), Comments, Forms, or (none).

9. Click the Add Slip button if you want to add the routing slip to the workbook without sending it now. Otherwise, click the Route button to route the workbook along the route you've just specified.

NOTE   *If you're using Outlook as your e-mail application, you may receive another warning at this point that "a program is trying to automatically send e-mail on your behalf." Click the Yes button to route the document or workbook.*

Receiving a Routed Document or Workbook

When you receive a routed document or workbook, the accompanying message warns you that it has a routing slip attached. Save the document or workbook to a folder, open it as usual (press CTRL-O and use the Open dialog box), and review it.

When you're finished with the document or workbook, choose File | Send To | Next Routing Recipient to display the smaller Routing Slip dialog box, leave the Route Document to *Recipient* option button selected (shown here), and click OK.

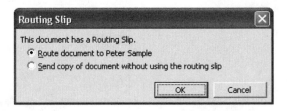

NOTE   *Once again, if you're using Outlook as your e-mail application, it may warn you that "a program is trying to automatically send e-mail on your behalf." Click the Yes button to send the workbook on its way.*

Instead of behaving as the routing's originator expected, you can also short-circuit the routing process by choosing File | Send To | Other Routing Recipient and using the full-sized Routing Slip dialog box to specify the recipient. In most cases, interfering with the routing isn't a good idea and won't endear you to the originator of the routing, but on other occasions you may need to tweak the routing to get a workbook reviewed in time—for example, if the next colleague on the routing list is unexpectedly out of the office.

If you close the document or workbook without routing it, Word or Excel reminds you to route it to the next recipient. Here's an example:

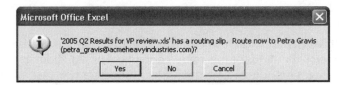

Click the Yes button to route the document or workbook, the No button to close the document or workbook without routing it, or the Cancel button to leave the document or workbook open so that you can finish reviewing it and then route it.

NOTE   *If you leave the Track Status check box selected in the Routing Slip dialog box, the routed document or workbook reports its progress back to you via e-mail each time it's forwarded. So if the document or workbook gets held up along its route, you'll know who's responsible.*

Using SharePoint Team Services

SharePoint Team Services is a Microsoft technology for collaborating with your colleagues via an intranet or the Internet. The SharePoint site runs on an Internet Information Services (IIS) web site that uses Microsoft Office Server extensions and functions as a shared workspace for a team. SharePoint also allows for threaded discussions (discussions in which messages on the same topic are linked in a thread) between team members. This feature can help improve communication among the team.

Anatomy of a SharePoint Site

A typical SharePoint site consists of these areas:

- **Home page**   The page displayed when you first access the SharePoint site. The home page contains areas for announcements, events, and favorite links, together with a search box and navigation links to all the major areas of the site.

- **Document libraries**   A document library is essentially a folder that you can open files from and save files to. Typically, a SharePoint site contains a document library for each different project the team is working on.

- **Picture libraries**   A picture library is a folder that contains pictures (as opposed to other types of documents). Again, a SharePoint site typically contains a picture library for each different project. You can open files from the picture library and save files to it.

- **Discussion boards**   A discussion board is an area in which the team members can hold discussions.

- **Tasks**   A list of the tasks assigned to the team. You can filter the list to display only a particular set of tasks—for example, those assigned to you.

- **Contacts**   A list of the team's contacts. You can import contacts from another application (for example, you can add contacts from your organizer to the SharePoint site) or link the site to contacts in Outlook.

- **Surveys**   Web-based surveys for polling web site users on a particular topic. A survey can either show respondents' names or be anonymous, and can permit multiple responses or only single responses.

- **Document workspaces**   An area of the SharePoint site set aside for working on a particular set of documents. An administrator can set unique permissions for each document workspace or can simply allow the SharePoint site permissions to cascade down to the document workspace.

- **Meeting workspaces**   An area of the SharePoint site set aside for preparing for a particular meeting: planning the meeting, organizing it, and tracking it.

A SharePoint site is implemented through an easy-to-use web-based interface that you can view and manipulate directly through Internet Explorer. You can also open documents from the SharePoint site and save documents to it from the Office applications.

Understanding Permissions on SharePoint Sites

In most cases, an administrator sets up your company's SharePoint sites and provides you with access information for the site you're supposed to use. The administrator also assigns you the appropriate level of privileges for the actions you need to take on the site. These are the available levels of privileges for a default site:

- **Reader**   Can view material on the site but cannot change it.
- **Contributor**   Can add content to the SharePoint site's existing libraries and lists but can't create lists or libraries.
- **Web Designer**   Can add content, create lists and libraries, and customize pages on the site.
- **Administrator**   Can add content, create lists and libraries, customize pages, and create and manage users.

Accessing a SharePoint Site

You can access a SharePoint site either through Internet Explorer or directly through an application. For example, when sending a document to your colleagues for review, you can choose to place a copy on your SharePoint site, and then make Word or Excel merge the changes your colleagues make to their copies of the documents into the copy saved on the SharePoint site.

To access a SharePoint site through Internet Explorer, simply enter the site's address in the Address bar and click Go. After accessing the site, you'll probably want to create a favorite for the site's home page and for pages you need to access frequently (for example, a particular library page or a discussion board) so that you can return to them quickly in the future without needing to type the address.

If necessary, you can access a SharePoint site directly through an application by entering the site's address in a common dialog box. But if you'll need to access the site more than once, create a network place for it, either automatically by accessing the site via Internet Explorer, or manually by choosing Start | My Network Places, double-clicking Add Network Place, and following through the steps of the Add Network Place wizard. After creating the network place, you can access the site quickly by clicking My Network Places on the Places bar in common dialog boxes (such as the Open dialog box and the Save As dialog box) and selecting the site from the resulting list.

NOTE   *The first time you try to access a SharePoint site, Windows displays the Connect To dialog box. Enter your username and password, select the Remember My Password option if appropriate (remembering the password is convenient, but it's a security risk), and click OK.*

Managing Documents Within SharePoint

When you access a SharePoint site through Internet Explorer, you can manipulate documents on the site by accessing them in the relevant document library and using the available links or the drop-down menu. Figure 40-12 shows an example of using a drop-down menu.

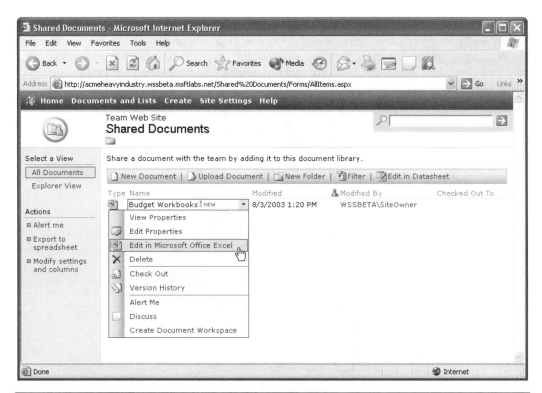

FIGURE 40-12   You can access a SharePoint site through Internet Explorer and open a document in one of the Office applications.

To upload a document to a document library, navigate to the library and click the Upload Document button. On the resulting screen, use the Browse button to navigate to and select the file, and then click Save and Close. To upload multiple files at once, click the Upload Multiple Files link and use the resulting Windows Explorer–like screen to select the files; then click Save and Close.

You can also upload documents to a document library by using a Windows Explorer window to open the network place for the SharePoint site, navigating to the appropriate folder, and then using conventional Windows techniques (such as Copy and Paste or drag-and-drop) to copy files from another Windows Explorer window. Because the folder structure of a SharePoint site can be confusing in a Windows Explorer window, it's usually easier to access the site via Internet Explorer and upload the file as described earlier in this section.

What you'll often want to do is open a document stored on a SharePoint site directly from one of the Office applications, or save a document from one of the applications directly to the SharePoint site. To open a document from a SharePoint site, display the Open dialog box (CTRL-O), click Network Places in the Places bar, open the site, and then open the document as usual. To save a document, display the Save As dialog box (File | Save As), click Network Places in the Places bar, open the site, and then save the document as usual.

When you open a document from a SharePoint site, the application displays the Shared Workspace task pane (shown here), which provides a readout of workspace information (the number of status messages, team members online, tasks, lists, and links), shows you which task members are online, and provides options for getting updates to open documents (discussed next).

Synchronizing Documents with SharePoint Sites

When you're working with documents from a shared workspace, it's important to keep them up-to-date. Start by clicking the Options link at the bottom of the Shared Workspace task pane and choosing settings for getting updates on the Shared Workspace tab of the Service Options dialog box (Figure 40-13). This tab contains options for specifying:

- When to display the Shared Workspace pane.
- When to get updates of a document you're opening and the workspace that contains it: always update, prompt to see if you agree, or never update. If you choose to get updates, you can customize the interval and choose whether to let Windows display desktop alerts about the updates.

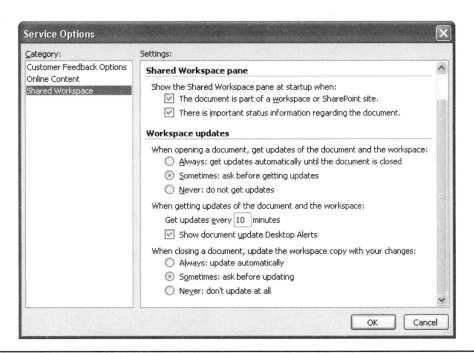

FIGURE 40-13   Configure updating for shared workspace files on the Shared Workspace tab of the Service Options dialog box.

- When to update the workspace copy of a document with your copy when you choose it: always update, prompt to see if you agree, or never update.

To update a document manually, click the Get Updates button at the bottom of the Shared Workspace task pane.

Macros and Visual Basic for Applications

CHAPTER 41:
Creating and Using Office Macros

CHAPTER 42
Using Visual Basic for Applications with Office

CHAPTER 43
Putting VBA and Macros to Work

PART

IX

Creating and Using
Office Macros

Most office jobs involve repetitive tasks, some on a grand scale, some on a more modest scale, and some on an entirely trivial scale. If you find yourself needing to perform the same task over and over in one of the Office applications, you should consider automating that task as much as possible. To automate a task, you can record a macro (as described in this chapter), or program in Visual Basic for Applications (VBA), as described in Chapters 42 and 43, or record a macro and then enhance it by programming in VBA.

In this chapter, after briefly discussing what macros are and what they're for, we explain the macro virus–protection features that Office uses. This may seem premature, but you need to understand these features in order to run even the most basic macro. Then we return to the basics of recording macros in Word, Excel, or PowerPoint, and testing, running, and storing the macros you record.

Understanding Macros

A *macro* is a sequence of commands, either recorded (by using a tool such as the Macro Recorder) or written down. For example, you might create a macro in Excel to format certain parts of a worksheet in a specific way. The macro can then be invoked when necessary, either by a user or by another macro or piece of code. (*Code* is the generic term for the program lines and program objects, such as custom dialog boxes, that you create with a programming language.) You could invoke your Excel macro manually to format a worksheet, or you could call the macro from another macro—for example, to perform the formatting as part of a series of tasks.

Macros in the Office applications are recorded or written in Visual Basic for Applications (VBA), a programming language developed by Microsoft. VBA is implemented in all the major Office applications, and it has become such a standard that many third-party companies have added it to their applications. By using VBA, you can make one application access another application; so you can create—for example—a macro in Word that accesses Excel, Visio, AutoCAD, WordPerfect, or another VBA-enabled application.

Understanding Office's Macro Virus–Protection Features

The inclusion of VBA and macro-recording capabilities in Office greatly increases Office's power, flexibility, and usefulness. Unfortunately, VBA and macros also expose the Office applications to the attentions of malefactors who create *macro viruses*—harmful code built using a macro language. Even if you've merely scanned the news during the last few years, you have most likely heard of macro viruses such as the Melissa virus, the I Love You virus or Love Bug, and Klez, each of which spread quickly and widely enough to raise serious concern.

Macro viruses can be contained in files that people exchange frequently, such as Word documents, PowerPoint presentations, or Excel workbooks, and can be triggered when the file is opened, closed, or otherwise manipulated. So whenever anyone sends you a file, you should check it for macro viruses.

Macro viruses can spread themselves in several ways. Some automatically add themselves surreptitiously to your existing documents and insert themselves in new documents you create. When you share a document with another user, that user's computer becomes infected with the virus as well, and can spread it further. Other macro viruses take a more aggressive approach, using a programmable e-mail application such as Outlook to send themselves to as many people as possible as an apparently normal or attractive document attached to a suitable e-mail message. For example, a macro virus designed to spread in a corporate environment might disguise itself as a routine document such as a memo or spreadsheet. A macro designed to spread anywhere might appeal to recipients' curiosity by pretending to contain—or actually containing—jokes or pornography.

NOTE   *VBA is far from being the only macro language that can be exploited by virus writers, but because Office and VBA are so widely used, they're the most popular target for malefactors. In particular, because Outlook can be controlled via VBA, it's one of the easiest ways to spread a virus—Outlook (or one of the other VBA-enabled applications) can be programmed to automatically send messages to every entry in its address book. This can generate enough e-mail to crash even powerful corporate mail servers in short order.*

To protect Office and its users against macro viruses, Microsoft has included antivirus features in Office. In order to use macros and VBA, you need to understand what these features are and how they work.

Understanding and Setting Security Levels

Office uses a three-part security mechanism for preventing harmful code from being run by an Office application:

- You can set different security levels to specify whether an installation of Office may or may not run code that might be harmful.

- You can sign a *VBA project* (a unit of VBA code) with a digital signature derived from a digital certificate to prove that you were the last person who changed that VBA project. This digital signature tells other people who the VBA project came from. In short, if other people have reason to trust you, they may trust the code you've signed.

- You can designate certain digital certificates as being *trusted sources* or *trusted publishers*—in effect, telling Office to trust any code signed with one of those digital certificates.

As you can see, these security measures are intertwined. The following sections discuss how you work with them.

Setting the Security Level

To set the security level used by Office for macros:

1. Choose Tools | Macro | Security to display the Security dialog box.

2. On the Security Level tab, select the option for the appropriate security level and click OK.

   - **High**   Office lets you run macros signed with digital signatures by sources that you or an administrator have designated as being trusted (trusted sources). Office disables macros signed by anyone else and macros that aren't signed with digital signatures. This setting is widely used in corporate environments in which administrators get to decide which users should be able to run which code. You can also use it to protect your computer in a standalone environment.

   - **Medium**   Office alerts you to macros that may be unsafe and lets you decide whether to run them. This setting is useful for more loosely controlled corporate environments and for SOHO (small office/home office) environments in which users make their own decisions about how to configure their computers and which code to run in their programmable applications.

   - **Low**   Office lets you run any macro, without warning you that it may be unsafe. This setting is useful for test computers that contain no valuable information and for computers thoroughly protected with other antivirus software. In other situations, you should avoid this setting.

NOTE   *In a corporate environment, an administrator is likely to set the security level centrally (probably to the High setting) and to prevent you from changing it and from adding trusted sources.*

Designating Trusted Publishers

The Trusted Publishers tab of the Security dialog box (Tools | Security), shown next, lists the publishers you or your administrator have specified as being trusted. You can view the details of publishers you've trusted, and you can remove any publisher you no longer wish to trust.

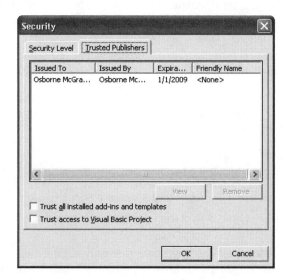

You can add trusted publishers to your installation of Windows by selecting the option Always Trust Content from *Publisher* (*Publisher* being their name) or the Always Trust Macros from This Publisher option in the Security Warning dialog box that Windows displays when you open an item signed by this publisher. The following illustration shows an example of a Word document that contains macros signed by an unauthenticated publisher.

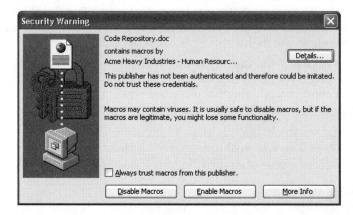

Office also offers an end around for circumventing the security mechanisms of digital signatures and trusted publishers. If you're certain that the templates and add-ins you've installed on your computer so far are harmless, you can tell Office to trust them by selecting the Trust All Installed Add-ins and Templates option on the Trusted Publishers tab of the Security dialog box. This option can save you a lot of time that you might spend manually specifying trusted sources individually or clicking through messages warning you that documents and templates may contain macros. But before you use this option, double-check the templates and add-ins already installed on your computer.

NOTE   *The Trust Access to Visual Basic Project option on the Trusted Publishers tab of the Security dialog box controls whether code can access Visual Basic project items. Leave this option deselected unless you have loaded an add-in that won't work without access to Visual Basic projects and that you know to be safe.*

Digital Signatures

As mentioned previously, Office uses a digital signature on a macro project to determine whether the source of the project is trusted (and, therefore, whether you can use the project). "Signing Your VBA Project" in Chapter 43 discusses how to use a digital certificate to apply a digital signature to a VBA project that you create and plan to distribute. Here, we'll cover the basics of what they are and how they are used.

What Digital Certificates Are and What They're For

A digital signature is derived from a *digital certificate,* an encrypted piece of code intended to identify its holder. That holder may be an individual, a group of individuals, a department, or an entire company. Different types of digital certificates are available, ranging from personal certificates (for purposes such as signing and encrypting e-mail messages), to software developer certificates (for signing macros and software), to corporate certificates (for identifying companies or parts of them).

Digital certificates aren't foolproof, but they provide reasonably effective security. Digital certificates are issued by *certification authorities* (CAs), and are only as reliable as the CAs choose to make them. For example, some CAs let you buy a personal digital certificate over the Web without providing any more verification than a credit card number and its current expiration date. This standard of verification is satisfactory for telephone and Internet mail order, because the physical address to which the goods are delivered provides further verification. But for proving identity via the Internet, this standard of verification is woefully unsatisfactory.

Software developer certificates and corporate certificates typically require better proof of identity than this, but again they typically leverage existing means of identification (for example, passports or other identity cards for individuals, business listings such as Dun & Bradstreet for companies) rather than checking rigorously from scratch. Another problem is that a digital certificate can be stolen from its holder, used by someone else without the holder's permission, applied inadvertently by its holder, or applied by *malware* (hostile software) running on the holder's computer.

Getting and Installing a Digital Certificate

The three main public sources of digital certificates at this writing are VeriSign (www.verisign.com), Thawte (www.thawte.com), and GlobalSign (www.globalsign.net). If your company requires you to use a digital certificate in your work, it may well run a CA of its own. For example, Windows 2000 Server and Windows 2003 Server provide CA features.

When you acquire a digital certificate, you'll need to install it on your computer before you can use it. The certificate-issuing routines used by some CAs automatically install the certificate for you. To install the certificate manually, double-click the certificate's file and follow the steps in the Certificate Import wizard that Windows launches.

Office includes a tool called Digital Certificate for VBA Projects for creating your own digital certificates for practicing signing code. This is a useful practice tool, but the certificate is effectively useless in the real world, because your identity isn't authenticated. As a result, Office will trust a certificate created with Digital Certificate for VBA Projects only on the computer that created the certificate.

Digital Certificate for VBA Projects is included in Complete installations of Office. For other installations, you may need to install it by running Office's Add or Remove Features function:

1. Choose Start | Control Panel | Add or Remove Programs, and then select Microsoft Office 2003.

2. Click Change, click Add or Remove Features, and click Choose Advanced Customization of Applications.

3. Expand the Office Shared Features category, and set the Digital Signature for VBA Projects item to Run from My Computer.

If your computer has the installation files cached, the Installer draws the files from the cache; if not, you'll need to supply your Office System CD or network installation source.

Once Digital Certificate for VBA Projects is installed, you can run it by choosing Start | All Programs | Microsoft Office | Microsoft Office Tools | Digital Certificate for VBA Projects. In the Create Digital Certificate dialog box, shown in the next illustration, enter the name you want to assign the certificate and click OK. The application displays a SelfCert Success dialog box (the application name is SelfCert.exe) telling you that the certificate was created.

Recording Macros

Word, Excel, and PowerPoint enable you to record macros by using a tool called the Macro Recorder that comes built into Office. When you're using Word as your e-mail editor for Outlook, Outlook can record macros by using Word's functionality. (Outlook can't record macros on its own.)

To record a macro:

1. Decide what the macro will do. Write the main points down if necessary so you don't forget them.

2. Open (or activate) the application in which you'll create the macro, and set it up ready for the actions you're about to perform. For example, if you're creating a macro to manipulate text in Word, prepare some suitable text. If you're creating a macro to reformat a presentation in PowerPoint, open a suitable presentation.

3. Choose Tools | Macro | Record New Macro to display the Record Macro dialog box. This dialog box contains the same basic options for each application but also contains options specific to the application. For example, the Record Macro dialog box for Word (shown here on the left) contains different options from the Record Macro dialog box for Excel (shown on the right).

4. The Macro Recorder enters a default name (such as Macro1) in the Macro Name box. You can accept this default name, but it's a much better idea to type a descriptive name of your own. Macro names have to start with a letter, after which they can be your choice of mixed letters, numbers, and underscores. The maximum length is 80 characters. Shorter names tend to be more practical, because you can see them in full in the Macros dialog box.

5. Enter a description of the macro's contents and purpose in the Description box. Either replace the Macro Recorder's default description or add to it.

6. Choose where to store the macro. Each application offers different options, but in most cases you'll do well to start with the default option:

   • Word offers to store macros you record in the Normal template (Normal.dot). These macros are then available whenever Word is running.

   • Excel offers to store macros you record in the active workbook. These macros are then available only when this workbook is open.

   • PowerPoint offers to store macros you record in the active presentation. These macros are then available only when this presentation is open.

NOTE   *For a full explanation of the options for storing a macro, see "Storing Your Macros," later in this chapter.*

   7. In Word or Excel, specify a way of running the macro:

   • Word lets you assign the macro to a menu item, shortcut menu item, toolbar button, or keyboard shortcut, by using the techniques described in "Customizing Toolbars and Menus" in Chapter 2.

   • Excel lets you assign the macro to a CTRL key shortcut or a CTRL-SHIFT key shortcut.

CAUTION   *Assign a way of running the macro only if you intend to leave the macro in the location in which the Macro Recorder places it. If you intend to move the macro to a better location (more on this in the next chapter), don't assign a way of running the macro now—assign it manually later instead.*

   8. Click OK to close the Record Macro dialog box. The application displays the Stop Recording toolbar (which contains one or more buttons for controlling and stopping recording, depending on the application), and starts the Macro Recorder working.

NOTE   *Word offers a Pause Recording button on the Stop Recording toolbar that lets you pause a recording to perform actions you don't want repeated in the macro. Excel offers a Relative References button on the Stop Recording toolbar that lets you switch between using relative references and absolute references.*

   9. Take the actions that you want the macro to record:

   • You can use either the keyboard or the mouse to choose menu commands.

   • For selecting objects, you can use the mouse only for maneuvers that unambiguously identify the object. For example, you can use the mouse to select a specific cell in an Excel worksheet, but you can't use the mouse to select a word in a Word document: the cell in the worksheet has a specific location (for example, the address GP286), but the word could appear almost anywhere in the Word document.

   10. Click the Stop Recording button on the Stop Recording toolbar (or, if you've lost track of it, choose Tools | Macro | Stop Recording).

NOTE   *Word displays a REC indicator in the status bar when you're recording a macro. Double-click this indicator to turn off recording.*

Testing and Running Your Macros

After recording a macro, test it immediately to make sure it works as it should. If it does, you're all set to use it in the future; if not, decide whether to edit the macro (as described in the next chapter) to fix its problems or to delete it and record it again in the hope of getting it right.

Remember that you may need to restore the application's environment to conditions suitable for the macro to run. In recording the macro, you may have created conditions in which the macro won't run. For example, if you create a macro to find certain items in a document and process them, you'll probably need to revert to the original document (rather than the processed version) before the macro will run successfully again.

Running a Macro from the Macros Dialog Box

The most basic way of running a macro is to use the Macros dialog box:

1. Press ALT-F8 or choose Tools | Macro | Macros.

2. Select the macro in the Macros dialog box, shown in the following illustration, either by scrolling to it or by typing in the text box enough of the first letters of the name to identify the macro. (If you can't locate the macro, it's probably because the Macros In drop-down list is set to display the wrong location. Change to the right location— for example, in Word, you might need to choose All Active Templates and Documents rather than the active document.)

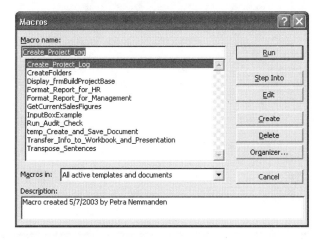

3. Click Run. The application closes the Macros dialog box and runs the macro.

This way of running macros is most suitable for macros you don't need to run frequently.

Running a Macro from an Interface Item

If you assigned the macro to an interface item (a toolbar, menu, or key combination) when you created it, you can run the macro directly from that item. If not, you can subsequently assign the macro to an interface item by using the techniques described in "Customizing Toolbars and Menus" in Chapter 2: choose Tools | Customize, select the Macros category on the Commands tab of the Customize dialog box, and drag the macro to the toolbar, menu, or context menu on which you want to make it available. Edit the display name to make it easy to understand, or assign a suitable button, or both.

NOTE   *Excel uses a different method of creating toolbar buttons and menu items for running macros. Select the Macros category on the Commands tab of the Customize dialog box, and then drag Custom Button or Custom Menu Item to the toolbar or menu to create the button or menu item. After creating it, click Modify Selection, choose Assign Macro, and use the Assign Macro dialog box to specify which macro to associate with the button or item.*

You can also set macros to run from a macro button in Word or from an object in Excel.

Creating a Macro Button in Word

In Word, you can also create a macro button—a button, embedded in a document, that runs a macro. Macro buttons can be a useful way of providing access to macros that the user might not easily find elsewhere in the interface (for example, on a toolbar, menu, or context menu).

To create a macro button:

1. Position the insertion point where you want the button to appear.

2. Choose Insert | Field to display the Field dialog box:

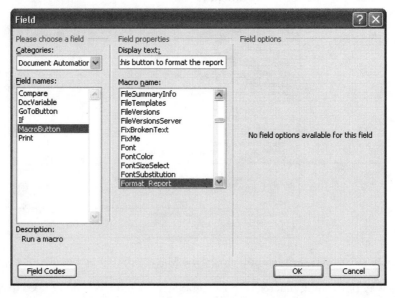

3. In the Please Choose a Field area, select Document Automation in the Categories list box, and then select MacroButton in the Field Names list box.

4. In the Field Properties area, type the text you want to appear on the macro button (for example, "Double-click this button to format the report"), and select the macro in the Macro Name list box. This box lists all the Word commands as well as your macros, so type the initial letters of the macro name to scroll down to the macro.

5. Click OK.

This produces a text button that the user can double-click to run the macro associated with it. A text button contains nothing but text, so you'll probably want to highlight it in some way to distinguish it and prevent it from getting lost in the document.

Alternatively, put a picture on a macro button. Insert the macro button as described in the preceding steps, and then toggle on the display of field codes for the field. Select the descriptive text, choose Insert | Field, and enter an INCLUDEPICTURE field with the full path to the picture you want to use. When you toggle off the display of field codes, you'll have a graphic that you (or the user) can double-click to run the macro associated with the macro button.

Assigning a Macro to an Object in Excel

In Excel, you can assign a macro to an object, such as a picture or AutoShape. Right-click the object and choose Assign Macro. Select the macro name in the Assign Macro dialog box, and click OK.

Storing Your Macros

As you saw in "Recording Macros," earlier in this chapter, Word, Excel, and PowerPoint let you store your macros in various locations. It's important to store your macros in a suitable location, because otherwise you won't be able to use them when you need them.

VBA stores code in storage containers called VBA projects. The term *project* is a little awkward in VBA, because each project is attached to an application file rather than being a self-standing project as it is in Visual Basic. For example, in Word, a document or template can contain a VBA project. Within a project, code is stored in modules, userforms, and classes, which we'll discuss in the next chapter. You can export and import modules, userforms, and classes individually, which enables you to copy or move them easily from one project to another. However, you can't apply protection to these individual elements—you have to apply protection to an entire project instead.

The following sections discuss your storage options, not just in Word, Excel, and PowerPoint, but in Access and Outlook as well.

While you're working in the Visual Basic Editor, you can save a project and its associated file by selecting its entry in the Project Explorer and pressing CTRL-S, clicking the Save button on the toolbar, or choosing File | Save *Project* from the menu. When you close the file that contains the project, the application will either prompt you to save any unsaved changes in the project or will save them automatically for you. For example, when you close a Word document that contains unsaved changes in its VBA project, Word prompts you to save changes to the document. When you close the Normal template, however, Word automatically saves changes to it and its VBA project (this is with Word's default settings).

You won't be able to tell whether the unsaved changes are in the VBA project section of the document or in the rest of the document. For example, if Excel prompts you to save a workbook when you close it, the changes could be in the VBA project, in the workbook itself, or in both.

Storing Your Macros in Word

Word offers the following options for storing your macros:

- **Normal template**   This global template is loaded all the time Word is running. Macros stored in Normal are available no matter which document or template you're working in (unless that document or template has been locked to prevent you from using macros). Storing macros in Normal is convenient when you're working with a modest number of macros. If you store too much code in Normal, it can grow bloated and detract from your computer's performance. You may also find it more efficient to store code only in the document or template it's used for.

- **Active template**   This is the template attached to the active document. If the active document is based on Normal, this option doesn't apply. Macros stored in a template are available whenever a document with that template attached is open, or when the template itself is open (for example, when you open the template directly to edit it). Storing macros in a template makes sense when they apply only to that particular template.

- **Active document**   Macros stored in a document are available only when that document is open. Choose this option for macros that apply only to that particular document.

You can also store macros in a global template other than Normal and then load that global template (by choosing Tools | Templates and Add-ins and clicking Add in the Templates and Add-ins dialog box) whenever you need the macros it contains. By separating your macros into different global templates like this, you can avoid making Normal too unwieldy, and you can keep macros out of the way when they're not needed.

While a global template other than Normal is loaded, you can't add macros to it. To store macros in a global template, open the global template as a conventional template (in other words, without loading it as a global template). Once you've done that, you can record macros into the template or move them manually by using Word's Organizer or the techniques discussed in the next chapter.

Storing Your Macros in Excel

Excel offers the following options for storing your macros:

- **Personal Macro Workbook**   The Personal Macro Workbook is Excel's central repository for macros you create. Macros in the Personal Macro Workbook are available whenever Excel is running. The Personal Macro Workbook is the \Application Data\Microsoft\Excel\XLSTART\PERSONAL.XLS file. Excel automatically creates this file when you first choose to store a macro in the Personal Macro Workbook.

- **This workbook**   Choose this option to store the macro in the active workbook. Macros stored in a workbook are available only when that workbook is open, so you will want to use this when macros apply only to a particular workbook.

- **New workbook**   Choose this option to create a new workbook and store the macro in it. The macro is available only when that workbook is open. This option is primarily useful for recording a quick macro that you want to use to manipulate a workbook but don't want to store in that workbook or in the Personal Macro Workbook. By closing the new workbook without saving changes to it, you can dispose of the new macro easily.

Storing Your Macros in PowerPoint

PowerPoint lets you store macros that you record in either the active presentation or in any other open presentation or template. Macros you store in any presentation or template are available only when that presentation or template is open.

PowerPoint has no analog to Word's Normal template or Excel's Personal Macro Workbook. However, you can make a macro available at any time by opening the presentation that contains it. For example, you might create a presentation that you use as a repository for all your general PowerPoint code. By opening this presentation during every PowerPoint session, you can make your macros available all the time.

Storing Your Macros in Access

Access lets you store written macros (you can't record macros in Access) in modules attached to a database, in reports and forms (which can be useful for automating those items), and in library database files.

Storing Your Macros in Outlook

Outlook stores all its macros and code in a single location that's available the whole time you're working with Outlook, so you don't need to choose a location for storing your VBA code in Outlook.

Recording the Sample Macros

To get some practice with macros, you'll use the Macro Recorder, first, to record a short macro in Word and then an even shorter macro in Excel. In the next chapter, you'll examine and edit those macros in the Visual Basic Editor. And in Chapter 43, you'll create a userform that works with the edited macros to give it greater power and usefulness.

Following through this example will familiarize you with the Visual Basic Editor and its features and give you skills that you can quickly build on to develop your understanding of VBA in the other Office applications.

Recording the Sample Macro in Word

Take the following steps to record a macro in Word that you'll subsequently build on:

1. Launch Word (for example, choose Start | All Programs | Microsoft Office | Microsoft Office Word).

2. Double-click the REC indicator on the status bar, or choose Tools | Macro | Record to display the Record Macro dialog box.

3. Replace the default macro name with **Create_Project_Log**.

4. Make sure that All Documents (Normal) is selected in the Store Macro In drop-down list.

5. Add the following text to the beginning of the automatically generated description: **Creates the project log document for the project.**

NOTE   *Don't use either of the options (Toolbars or Keyboard) in the Assign Macro To section of the dialog box. This is because when you edit the macro in the next chapter, you'll move the macro to a different module from the NewMacros module in which the Macro Recorder places it.*

---

6. Click OK to close the Record Macro dialog box. Word launches the Macro Recorder, displays the REC indicator on the status bar in black instead of its usual gray (to indicate that recording is active), and displays the Stop Recording toolbar.

7. Click the New button on the Standard toolbar to create a new blank document.

8. Type **Project Log created** and a space.

9. Choose Insert | Field to display the Field dialog box, select the (All) category if it's not already selected, select the CreateDate field, select the M/D/YYYY H:MM:SS A/P format (for example, 9/5/2003 4:15:07 PM), and click OK.

10. Type a period and press ENTER.

11. Issue a Save command (for example, press CTRL-S) to display the Save As dialog box.

12. Save the document under the name **Project Log.doc** in a folder of your choice. We'll use the folder Z:\Public for this example.

13. Choose File | Close to close the document.

14. Click the Stop Recording button on the Stop Recording toolbar, or double-click the REC indicator on the status bar, to stop the Macro Recorder.

If you like, test the sample macro by choosing Tools | Macro | Macros, selecting the macro name in the Macros dialog box, and clicking the Run button. VBA creates a new document, enters the text and field in it, saves the document (overwriting the previous document you created while recording the macro), and closes it.

Recording the Sample Macro in Excel

Take the following steps to record a macro in Excel that you'll build on in the next chapter and the chapter after that:

1. Launch Excel (for example, choose Start | All Programs | Microsoft Office | Microsoft Office Excel).

2. Choose Tools | Macro | Record to display the Record Macro dialog box.

3. Replace the default macro name with **Create_Budget_Workbook**.

4. In the Store Macro In drop-down list, select Personal Macro Workbook.

5. Add the following text to the beginning of the automatically generated description: **Creates the budget workbook for the project.**

6. Click OK to close the Record Macro dialog box. Excel launches the Macro Recorder and displays the Stop Recording toolbar.

7. Click the New button to create a new default workbook.

8. Issue a Save command (for example, press CTRL-S) to display the Save As dialog box.

9. Save the workbook under the name **Budget.xls** in a folder of your choice. Again, we'll use the folder Z:\Public for this example.

10. Choose File | Close to close the workbook.

11. Click the Stop Recording button on the Stop Recording toolbar, or choose Tools | Macro | Stop Recording, to stop the Macro Recorder.

Again, test the sample macro if you like: choose Tools | Macro | Macros (or press ALT-F8), select the macro name in the Macros dialog box, and click the Run button. VBA creates the workbook and saves it, overwriting the previous workbook. Notice that Excel warns you that you're about to overwrite the existing workbook, whereas Word didn't warn you.

Using Visual Basic for Applications with Office

The previous chapter discussed how to use the Macro Recorder included in Office to record macros in Word, Excel, and PowerPoint, and how to test and run those macros. This chapter shows you how to start working with Visual Basic for Applications (VBA) by using the Visual Basic Editor and the features it provides.

We'll start by explaining what you need to know about Visual Basic for Applications—what it is, what it's for, and what it consists of. You'll learn how to launch the Visual Basic Editor, navigate around it, and understand its key features. Then you'll open the macros you recorded in the previous chapter so that you can examine their contents and watch in the Visual Basic Editor as the code executes step by step.

Understanding VBA

Visual Basic for Applications is a powerful programming language developed by Microsoft and built into the Office applications. You can use VBA automatically via the Macro Recorder (discussed in the previous chapter) or manually via the Visual Basic Editor to create code that performs actions automatically.

VBA is derived from Microsoft's Visual Basic programming language. Visual Basic (VB for short) is designed to create *standalone* applications—applications that you run from an executable, the way you run most applications in Windows. By contrast, VBA is designed to run within a *host application* such as Word, Excel, or Outlook. The host application provides the environment that VBA needs, so the host application has to be running before VBA can work. This means that you can't create standalone applications with VBA (although, by various tricks, you can create the illusion of standalone applications if necessary).

If you learn to program one of the Office applications (or other applications) with VBA, you'll quickly learn how to program the others, because VBA works the same way in each application. The specifics of using VBA with each application are different, because the applications are different—for example, PowerPoint uses Slide objects to represent its slides, Excel uses Workbook objects to represent its workbooks, and Word uses Document objects to represent its documents—but the language structure and principles are the same. You'll also be in a good position to learn to use Visual Basic itself. Visual Basic works in a similar way to VBA, except without a host application and—again—with different objects.

Understanding Objects, Properties, and Methods

When you work with one of the Office applications (let's say PowerPoint) you probably consider it to be a unit that functions as a whole rather than a mass of different objects that interact with each other. (Microsoft would probably prefer that you consider PowerPoint to work as a unit, anyway.) VBA sees things the other way around: for VBA, PowerPoint consists of objects arranged in a hierarchy called the *object model* that provides access to each object.

The object model for most applications consists of an upside-down tree that has at its root (or top level) an Application object. This object represents the application as a whole and gives access to the objects contained in the application and to application-level properties. For example, the Application object in Word represents Word and gives access to its objects.

If the object model were implemented to its logical extreme, you'd need to go through the Application object in order to access just about anything in the application. This would be too clumsy to be effective. So most applications expose some top-level objects other than the Application object so that you can access them directly without going through the Application object. For example, Word exposes top-level objects such as the ActiveDocument object (which represents the active document), the Documents collection (which contains a Document object for each document that's currently open), and the Selection object (which represents the current selection).

Objects and Collections

VBA keeps objects of the same type together in *collections*. For example, VBA uses the Presentation object to represent a presentation in PowerPoint. The Presentation objects are organized into the Presentations collection. You can use a collection to access one of its objects—for example, a Presentations(1).Close statement tells VBA to close the first Presentation object currently in the Presentations collection—or to manipulate all the objects at once (for example, a Presentations.Count statement returns the number of Presentation objects currently in the collection).

Properties

Most objects have characteristics called *properties* that you can return (to see what the property's value is), set (to assign the property a specific value), or both. Properties that you can return are *read-only properties*; properties that you can set are *write-only properties*; and properties that you can both return and set are *read/write properties*. For example, as you just saw, the Presentations collection has a Count property that contains the number of Presentation objects in the collection. Count is a read-only property, because you can't change the number of Presentation objects by manipulating Count directly—instead, Count changes automatically as you open and close presentations.

Methods

Most objects have actions, called *methods*, that you can take with them. For example, the Presentation object in PowerPoint has a Close action that closes the specified presentation. As when closing a presentation manually, you can specify whether to save any unsaved changes the presentation contains. As in this example, many methods correspond closely to commands that you can issue in the application, although sometimes the correspondence is less direct. For example, the Selection.InlineShapes.AddPicture command is the VBA representation of inserting a picture in a document in Word.

VBA Projects and Their Components

As you learned in the previous chapter, VBA host applications store VBA code in VBA projects that are attached to files in the host applications. For example, Word can store VBA projects in the Normal template, in other templates, or in individual documents, while Outlook uses a single storage location.

No matter where they are stored, the main subcomponents of a VBA project are modules, procedures, and userforms.

Modules

In VBA, all code is stored in containers called *modules*. A module is a type of subcomponent of a VBA project. VBA organizes the modules in a project into the Modules collection, which you can access through the Project Explorer.

You can use modules to segregate code into logical sections so that related subprocedures are all stored in one place. You can export a module for backup or to copy or move the code it contains to another computer.

Userforms

A *userform* is a custom dialog box in a VBA project. A userform starts off as a blank sheet. You place controls such as command buttons, check boxes, option buttons, and text boxes on the userform to give it the required visual appearance. You then attach code to the userform itself and to such controls as require it to make the userform take the appropriate actions.

Classes

A *class* is a custom object built out of VBA code. Typical uses of classes are storing and processing information. Using classes is outside the scope of this book.

Procedures, Subprocedures, Macros, and Functions

A *procedure* is the generic term for a standalone section of code. Procedures are stored in modules, userforms, and classes.

There are two kinds of procedures: subprocedures and functions. A *subprocedure* is a standalone piece of code demarcated by the key words Sub (at the beginning, with the subprocedure name) and End Sub (at the end, on a line of its own). A subprocedure typically performs an action or a series of actions. A *macro* is another term for subprocedure. (Access uses the word "macro" differently from other VBA-enabled applications. We'll skip lightly over this exception.)

Here's what a macro or subprocedure looks like:

```
Sub Sample_Macro()
    MsgBox "This macro displays a message box."
End Sub
```

A *function* is a standalone piece of code that returns a value rather than performing an action. In VBA, a function is demarcated by the key words Function (at the beginning, with the function name) and End Function (at the end, on a line of its own), as in the following example:

```
Function CheckUserName(strInput As String)
    'contents of the function here
End Function
```

VBA includes a large number of functions that you can use as necessary. You can also create your own functions if you find VBA's functions don't meet your needs.

Using the Visual Basic Editor

The tool you use for editing and creating VBA macros and other code is the Visual Basic Editor. As its name suggests, the Editor is used in Visual Basic as well as in VBA.

Launching the Visual Basic Editor

The easiest way to launch the Visual Basic Editor for editing a specific macro is to open the Macros dialog box from the application (press ALT-F8 or choose Tools | Macro | Macros), select the macro, and click Edit. The application launches the Visual Basic Editor, which opens the module that contains the macro and displays the start of the macro. Use this method from Word to open the Create_Project_Log macro in a Code window.

You can also launch the Visual Basic Editor at any time by pressing ALT-F11 or choosing Tools | Macro | Visual Basic Editor from the menu. When you launch the Visual Basic Editor this way, it typically displays the module you were last working on, but it's not 100 percent reliable. You can then manually open or activate the module or window in which you want to work.

From Excel, press ALT-F11 to display the Visual Basic Editor. If this is the first time you've displayed the Visual Basic Editor from Excel, chances are that Excel won't display any Code windows. A little later in this chapter, we'll navigate to the macro you recorded in Chapter 41.

In the meantime, notice that each host application opens a separate instance of the Visual Basic Editor. This helps you keep your separate projects straight, but it means that on complex projects, you may have a handful of instances of the Visual Basic Editor on screen at the same time. The Windows taskbar typically shows the Visual Basic Editor's button as the button after the host application's button; occasionally, the taskbar displays the Visual Basic Editor's button *before* the host application's button.

NOTE   *If the Visual Basic Editor is already running, pressing* ALT-F11 *simply activates it. Pressing* ALT-F11 *from the Visual Basic Editor switches the focus back to the host application.*

Getting Acquainted with the Visual Basic Editor

The Visual Basic Editor's default configuration is to display three windows: the Project Explorer in the upper-left corner of the Editor window, the Properties window underneath the Project Explorer, and the Code window to the right of the Project Explorer and the Properties window. Figure 42-1 shows these windows in their default configuration.

Project Explorer   Code window   Userform window

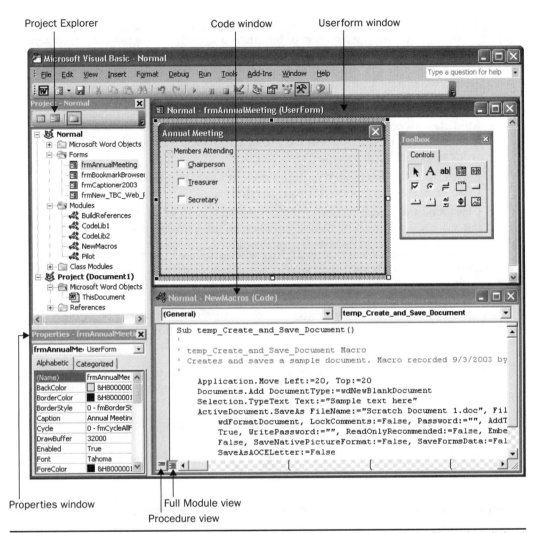

FIGURE 42-1   Use the Project Explorer to navigate the elements of a VBA project, the Properties window
to set properties for the current object, and the Code window to create and edit VBA code.

You can drag the shared boundaries of the windows to change how the space is allocated.
For example, drag the boundary between the Project Explorer and the Properties window
up or down to resize both those windows.

Understanding the Project Explorer Window

The Project Explorer window contains a collapsible list of the VBA projects available in the
host application. ("Storing Your Macros" in Chapter 41 explains what a VBA project is.)
Generally speaking, each file you have open in one of the Office applications can contain

a VBA project. For example, each Word document or template, each Excel workbook or template, each PowerPoint presentation or template, and each Access project can contain a VBA project. Outlook is a little different, in that it can have one VBA project or more than one, and its projects remain available all the time Outlook is running—you don't need to open a specific file to gain access to a project.

Each project can contain these three standard components:

- **Modules**   A collection of the code modules—storage units for macros, functions, and other code—in the project. This chapter shows you how to work with modules.

- **Forms**   A collection of all the userforms (custom dialog boxes) in the project. Chapter 43 shows you how to create userforms.

- **Class modules**   A collection of the classes (custom objects) in the project. This book doesn't discuss how to create classes, because this is an advanced topic.

VBA creates these collections automatically when you need them, so until you've created an object that needs storage, the collection doesn't exist and doesn't appear in the Project Explorer. For example, the first time you record a macro into a project that doesn't already have a Modules container, VBA creates the Modules container.

You can display or activate the Project Explorer by pressing CTRL-R or choosing View | Project Explorer. To close the Project Explorer, click its Close button (the X).

These are the key techniques for navigating in the Visual Basic Editor:

- Expand a project listing in the Project Explorer to see the project you want to work with, and then expand the category of item. For example, to work with macros, double-click the Modules entry in the appropriate project to expand it.

- Double-click an item in the Forms list, the Modules list, or the Class Modules list to display its Code window.

- Access a particular macro by choosing Tools | Macro, selecting the macro, and clicking Edit.

Display the Code window for the Excel macro you recorded in Chapter 41 by expanding the VBAProject (PERSONAL.XLS) item in the Project Explorer, expanding the Modules item, and double-clicking the Module1 item.

NOTE   *If the Module1 module doesn't contain the Create_Budget_Workbook macro, choose Tools | Macro, select the macro in the Macros dialog box, and click Edit.*

Understanding the Properties Window

The Properties window lists the properties of the object that's currently selected. In Figure 42-1 (earlier in this chapter), a userform is selected, so the Properties window shows the many properties you can set.

You can display or activate the Properties window by pressing F4 or choosing View | Properties Window. To close the Properties window, click the X.

Understanding the Code Window

The Code window is the window in which you create and edit VBA code. You open a Code window for a code module by double-clicking its item in the Modules list, or by right-clicking the item and choosing View Code. You open a Code window for a userform by right-clicking its item and choosing View Code. You open a Userform window (which also appears in the same area as the Code window) by double-clicking the userform's item in the Forms list or by right-clicking the item and choosing View Object.

You can navigate among your open Code windows by using the options on the Window menu (for example, choose the window from the list at the bottom of the menu, or tile or cascade the windows so you can see them) or by using the mouse to minimize, restore, maximize, and reposition windows.

By default, each Code window appears in Full Module view, in which it shows all the subprocedures in the module. You can switch to Procedure view, in which the Code window displays just the current procedure, by clicking the Procedure View button. Click the Full Module View button to switch back to Full Module view.

Returning to the Host Application

To switch focus back to the host application, press ALT-F11, or click the application's button on the Standard toolbar. (For example, to return to Excel from the Visual Basic Editor instance that Excel is hosting, click the Microsoft Excel button.)

To close the Visual Basic Editor and return to the host application, press ALT-Q, or choose File | Close and Return to *Application* from the menu.

Using the Visual Basic Editor's Features for Creating Code

The Visual Basic Editor contains a slew of features designed to simplify the task of navigating each application's object model and creating code with the correct parameters. We'll cover the features you're most likely to find helpful when getting started with VBA.

TIP   *You can toggle the Auto Syntax Check, Auto List Members, Auto Quick Info, Auto Data Tips, and Auto Indent features on and off from the Editor tab of the Options dialog box (Tools | Options). All these options are selected by default.*

Automatic Capitalization (in Most Cases)

The Visual Basic Editor automatically applies correct capitalization to most terms it recognizes—its own key words and variables that you declare explicitly. (The Visual Basic Editor misses some key words for unknown reasons.) This means you can save effort by typing in all lowercase (or uppercase, if you prefer) and let the Visual Basic Editor fix the capitalization for you. For example, if you type **activepresentation.close**, the Visual Basic Editor corrects it to ActivePresentation.Close.

Auto Syntax Check

VBA's Auto Syntax Check feature automatically checks the syntax of your code when you move to a different line—for example, by pressing ENTER, by pressing the UP ARROW or DOWN ARROW, or by using the mouse to move the insertion point. VBA highlights any problem it identifies with red and displays a message box explaining what the problem seems to be, for example:

Auto List Members

The Auto List Members feature displays a list of properties, methods, and constants as you type code in the Code window. For example, when you type the period after an object's name to indicate that you want to access a property or method of that object, VBA displays a list of the available items. Type down (type the initial letters of the item to identify it) or scroll through the list to select the item you want, and then take the appropriate action: press TAB to enter it and continue working on the same line, press . (the period key) to enter the item and display the list of items available to it, or press ENTER to enter the item and start a new line of code. The following illustrations show examples of the Auto List Members feature in action.

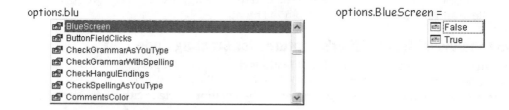

After entering a line of code, you can display the Auto List Members list of properties and methods by right-clicking the existing entry (BlueScreen in the preceding example) and choosing List Properties/Methods from the shortcut menu. You can display the Auto List Members list of constants by right-clicking the existing entry (True in the example). Select another entry from the list, and press TAB, ENTER, or . as appropriate.

Auto Quick Info

The Auto Quick Info feature displays ScreenTips containing a prompt about the syntax and arguments needed for the function or method you're currently working with. The following illustration shows an example of an Auto Quick Info ScreenTip. The bold item shows the point you've reached. You can return to your entries for an earlier argument by clicking its link in the ScreenTip. The Visual Basic Editor displays the link when you hover the mouse pointer over the argument.

ActiveWorkbook.SaveAs "z:\public\workbook\expenses.xls"|

> SaveAs([*Filename*], [***FileFormat***], [*Password*], [*WriteResPassword*],
> [*ReadOnlyRecommended*], [*CreateBackup*], [*AccessMode As*
> *XlSaveAsAccessMode* = *xlNoChange*], [*ConflictResolution*], [*AddToMru*],
> [*TextCodepage*], [*TextVisualLayout*], [*Local*])

Auto Data Tips

The Auto Data Tips feature displays a ScreenTip containing the value of a variable or expression when you hover the mouse pointer over it in Break mode, allowing you to check the value quickly. Here is an example:

```
Dim strSampleText As String
strSampleText = Selection.Text
```
strSampleText = "Acme Heavy Industries"

Complete Word

The Complete Word feature provides a list of VBA's matches for the key word or declared variable name you're typing when you press CTRL-SPACEBAR or choose Complete Word from the Edit menu or the context menu. If there's only one match, VBA enters it; if there's more than one, VBA displays a list from which you can select the correct item.

For example, say you've declared String variables named strDestinationCity, strDepartureCity, and strCustomerName. Typing **str** and pressing CTRL-SPACEBAR displays a Complete Word menu like that shown next for you to pick the correct item. As you can see, the menu starts with exact matches of VBA key words and variables and progresses to near misses. Typing **strcu** and pressing CTRL-SPACEBAR enters strCustomerName, because those letters uniquely identify the word.

```
Dim strDestinationCity As String
Dim strDepartureCity As String
Dim strCustomerName As String

str
```

str
Str
Str$
StrComp
StrConv
strCustomerName
strDepartureCity
strDestinationCity

Object Browser

The Object Browser is a tool for exploring the object models of VBA-enabled applications. Figure 42-2 shows the Object Browser with its key parts labeled and the Search Results pane displayed.

Many people find that it takes a while to get the hang of the Object Browser. Here are the basics of navigating through this tool:

1. Press F2 or choose View | Object Browser to display the Object Browser. You can resize it from a docked window to a floating window.

2. In the Project/Library box, select the application whose Object Browser you want to explore. VBA displays that application's commands in the Classes box.

NOTE   *If you need to work with object models other than that of the host application from which you launched the Visual Basic Editor, choose Tools | References, add references to the appropriate object models, and click OK.*

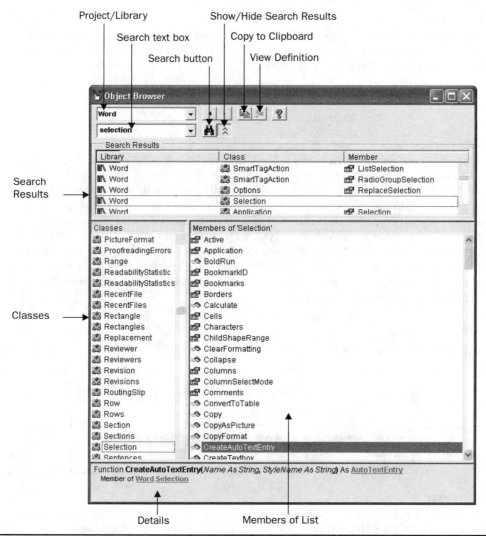

Project/Library
Search text box
Search button
Show/Hide Search Results
Copy to Clipboard
View Definition

Search
Results

Classes

Details   Members of List

FIGURE 42-2   The Object Browser enables you to browse through the object model of the applications available to VBA.

3. To search for an object, method, or property, enter the term in the Search text box, and press ENTER or click the Search button. (To toggle the display of the Search Results pane, click the Show/Hide Search Results button.)

4. Click an item to display its details in the Members Of list.

5. Select an item in the Members Of list to display its details in the Details pane.

Help Files

The most comprehensive source of information that VBA provides is in the help files, which typically contain a huge amount of information ranging from maps of the application's object model to examples of how to use many of the objects, properties, and methods. You can display help at any time by pressing F1 or choosing Help | Microsoft Visual Basic Help from the menu.

Running Code

As you saw in the previous chapter, you can run a macro from its host application by using the Macros dialog box or an interface customization (for example, a toolbar button). You can run a macro from the Macros dialog box (Tools | Macros) in the Visual Basic Editor as well, but the Visual Basic Editor also provides methods of running code one instruction or one group of instructions at a time so that you can keep track of exactly what the code does when.

The next few sections discuss the key techniques for running your code in the Visual Basic Editor. First, though, you need to understand the three modes in which code can exist in the Visual Basic Editor.

Design Mode, Run Mode, and Break Mode

The Visual Basic Editor recognizes three modes:

- **Run mode**   Code is running and has not been paused.
- **Break mode**   Code is running but has been paused.
- **Design mode**   Any time code isn't running—in other words, most of the time you're working in the Visual Basic Editor, writing code, designing userforms, or contemplating your next move.

Running a Macro from the Visual Basic Editor

In the Visual Basic Editor, you can run a subprocedure by placing the insertion point in the subprocedure's code in the Code window and doing any of the following:

- Press F5.
- Choose Run | Run Sub/UserForm from the menu.
- Click the Run Sub/UserForm button on the Standard toolbar.

NOTE   *You can also use these actions to launch a userform that's open in a Userform window.*

You can also run a subprocedure by choosing Tools | Macros, selecting the macro in the Macros dialog box, and clicking Run.

Interrupting Code When It's Running

To interrupt code when it's running, press CTRL-BREAK. This technique is primarily useful when a subprocedure seems to be stuck (for example, in an endless loop) and VBA won't return control of the host application to you. Pressing CTRL-BREAK puts the Visual Basic Editor into Break mode at the line of code that was running when you interrupted it.

Stepping into a Procedure

To see what your code does and to identify problems, you can run your code line by line or procedure by procedure instead of all at once. Working with code like this is called *stepping* and puts the Visual Basic Editor into Break mode.

You can *step into* a procedure—go through it one instruction at a time. You can *step over* a procedure called by another procedure—go through the called procedure at full speed, then return to step-by-step execution of the procedure that made the call. And you can *step out* of a procedure that you're stepping through—execute the rest of the instructions in the procedure at full speed once you've stepped through those instructions you needed to scrutinize.

- To step into a procedure, press F8.
- To step over a procedure, press SHIFT-F8.
- To step out of a procedure, press CTRL-SHIFT-F8.

You can also execute these commands from the Debug menu or from the Debug toolbar. But in most cases, the keyboard shortcuts are easiest.

Setting a Line of Code to Be the Next Statement

When you're running code in Break mode, you may need to skip back to an earlier line of code or skip ahead to a later line. To do so, select the line you want to use next, and press F8, or issue a Set Next Statement command from the Debug menu or the context menu.

Executing Code in the Immediate Window

For executing code one command at a time, you use the Immediate window. Executing code like this can be useful for testing the effect of a command or for changing the environment in which the code is running while the Visual Basic Editor is in Break mode. You can also use the Immediate window in Design mode to test the effect of a command.

Press CTRL-G or choose View | Immediate Window to display the Immediate window, shown here with code entered. By default, the Visual Basic Editor docks the Immediate window at the bottom of the window, but you can undock it so it floats. Type the command and press ENTER to execute it.

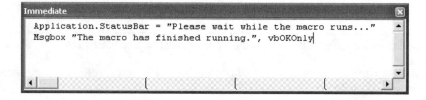

TIP   You can reuse an existing statement in the Immediate window by positioning the insertion point anywhere in the statement and pressing ENTER.

Following the Value of Expressions As Code Runs

To follow the value of expressions as your code runs, you can use the Locals window (View | Locals Window), shown next. The Locals window lists each expression, its current value, and its type. Expressions that have subobjects appear as collapsible trees. In the example, the Scratch_99 module has subobjects, as does the objExcel object.

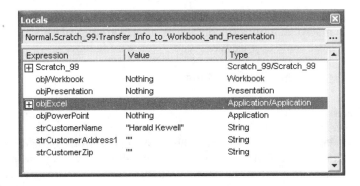

Another tool for tracking the value of expressions is the Watch window, which you can display by choosing View | Watch Window. The Watch window, shown on the left in the next illustration, lists the values of expressions that you select. The easiest way to add a watch is to right-click the variable or expression and choose Add Watch from the shortcut menu. In the Add Watch dialog box, shown on the right here, you can specify the settings for the watch and click OK.

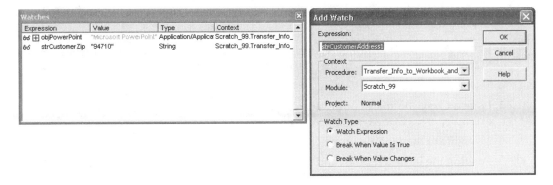

The key setting is the Watch Type option, which lets you create a basic watch expression or one that will break (go into Break mode) when the expression's value is True or break when the expression's value changes.

You can also create a watch with default settings by dragging the variable or expression to the Watch window. You can change the settings for an existing watch by right-clicking it in the Watch window and choosing Edit Watch. You can delete a watch by right-clicking it in the Watch window and choosing Delete Watch.

Managing Your Macros, Modules, Userforms, and Classes

After creating your macros, you may need to copy or move them—or the modules, userforms, or classes that contain them—to other projects. You may need to rename macros, modules, userforms, or classes. And when an item has outlived its usefulness, you'll need to delete it.

The following sections discuss how to perform these actions. But before you move or rename an item, be clear that doing so will break any interface customizations for running that macro or an item in that module, userform, or class. For example, if you've assigned a toolbar button to a macro, that button won't work after you move the macro to a different location. Obviously, the same applies when you delete a code item.

Creating a Module, Userform, or Class

To create a module, userform, or class, right-click the project in which you want to create it and choose Insert | Module, Insert | UserForm, or Insert | Class, as appropriate. (Alternatively, select the project, choose Insert, and then make the appropriate choice from the menu.) Press F4 to activate the Properties window, type to replace the default name (for example, Module2, UserForm3, or Class4) with a name of your choice, and press ENTER.

Names must start with a letter; can contain letters, numbers, and underscores (but no spaces or symbols); and can be up to 40 characters long. Each name has to be unique in the context it operates in. For example, each macro in a module needs a unique name, but macros in different modules can have the same name as each other, because they can be distinguished by the fully qualified name.

Copying or Moving a Macro

Copying and moving macros is such a basic task that you'd expect the Visual Basic Editor to provide an easy way of doing so. But it doesn't, and neither do most host applications. To copy or move a macro:

1. In the Visual Basic Editor, navigate to the macro. For example, choose Tools | Macros, select the macro in the Macros dialog box, and click Edit.

2. Select the macro.

3. Issue a Copy command (for example, press CTRL-INS) or a Cut command (for example, press CTRL-X) as appropriate.

4. Navigate to the module to which you want to copy or move the macro.

5. Position the insertion point and issue a Paste command (for example, press CTRL-V).

Renaming a Macro or Module

To rename a macro, navigate to it in the Visual Basic Editor's Code window, and then edit the Sub line to give the macro the new name.

To rename a module, select its entry in the Modules list, and press F4 to display or activate the Properties window. The Visual Basic Editor automatically activates the (Name) item. Type the new name and press ENTER.

Deleting a Macro or Module

You can delete a macro in any of the following ways:

- In the host application, press ALT-F8 or choose Tools | Macro | Macros, select the macro in the Macros dialog box, click Delete, and click Yes in the confirmation dialog box.
- In the Visual Basic Editor, choose Tools | Macros, select the macro in the Macros dialog box, and click Delete.
- In the Visual Basic Editor, navigate to the macro, select its code in the Code window, and press DELETE.

To delete a module, right-click it in the Project Explorer and choose Remove. The Visual Basic Editor suggests exporting the module before deleting it. Click Yes or No as appropriate.

Copying and Moving Modules, Userforms, or Classes

If you have both the source project and the destination project on your computer, and both are in the same type of project file, you can copy or move a module, userform, or class easily from one project to another in the Visual Basic Editor. Open both projects (for example, open both Excel workbook files), press ALT-F11 to display the Visual Basic Editor, and then drag the module from the source project to the destination project. The Visual Basic Editor copies the module. To effect a move rather than a copy operation, delete the module from the source project after copying it.

If you need to copy or move a module, userform, or class between applications or between computers, export the item from the source computer and import it on the destination computer, as described in the next section.

Exporting and Importing Modules, Userforms, and Classes

The Visual Basic Editor provides an Export command for exporting copies of modules, userforms, and classes to separate files. You can use the Export command (File | Export File, or press CTRL-E) to create backup copies of your vital code or to copy or move modules, userforms, and classes from one VBA project to another. After exporting a file, use the Import command (File | Import File, or press CTRL-M) on the destination application or destination computer to import the module, userform, or class into the appropriate VBA project.

Examining the Recorded Macros

Earlier in this chapter, you opened the Word macro and the Excel macro that you recorded in the previous chapter. We'll briefly discuss the contents of these two macros in light of what you've read so far in this chapter.

Examining and Editing the Word Macro

The Word macro you recorded should look something like this. We've added numbers to the beginning of the lines to make them easier to refer to, and broken the long lines so that they'll fit better in the book.

```
1.   Sub Create_Project_Log()
2.   '
3.   ' Create_Project_Log Macro
4.   ' Creates the project log document for the project. _
```

```
           Macro recorded 9/5/2003 by Petra Nemmanden
  5.  '
  6.       Documents.Add DocumentType:=wdNewBlankDocument
  7.       Selection.TypeText Text:="Project Log created "
  8.       Selection.Fields.Add Range:=Selection.Range, Type:=wdFieldEmpty, Text:= _
               "CREATEDATE  \@ ""M/d/yyyy h:mm:ss am/pm"" ", PreserveFormatting:=True
  9.       Selection.TypeText Text:="."
 10.       Selection.TypeParagraph
 11.       ActiveDocument.SaveAs FileName:="Project Log.doc", FileFormat:= _
             wdFormatDocument, LockComments:=False, Password:="", AddToRecentFiles:= _
             True, WritePassword:="", ReadOnlyRecommended:=False, EmbedTrueTypeFonts:= _
             False, SaveNativePictureFormat:=False, SaveFormsData:=False, _
             SaveAsAOCELetter:=False
 12.       ActiveDocument.Close
 13.  End Sub
```

Here's what the macro does:

- The Sub statement in line 1 starts the macro, and the End Sub statement in line 13 ends it.

- Lines 2, 3, 4, and 5 are comment lines, designated by the ' that begins them. These lines are for the benefit of human readers; VBA ignores them. Line 3 gives the macro's name and adds that it's a macro. Line 4 contains the description you entered while recording the macro.

- Line 6 uses the Add method of the Documents collection to add a new document. The DocumentType argument specifies the type of document to be created—wdNewBlankDocument, for a new blank document. wdNewBlankDocument is a constant. The first two letters ("wd") identify the constant as belonging to Word.

- Line 7 uses the TypeText method of the Selection object to enter the text you typed in the document. The Selection object represents the current selection, whether it has contents or is collapsed to an insertion point. The Text argument specifies the text string to be typed.

- Line 8 uses the Fields property of the Selection object to return the Fields collection (which contains all the Field objects in the document), then uses the Add method to add a field to the collection. The statement specifies the range at which to add the field (the Range property of the current Selection—in other words, where the insertion point currently is), the type of field (wdFieldEmpty—another Word constant), the text of the field, and that formatting should be preserved on the field during updates (PreserveFormatting:=True—a boolean argument).

NOTE   *Notice that the Macro Recorder has broken line 8 onto two lines by using the continuation character, an underscore preceded by a space. You can use the continuation character to break your lines of code to the width you want. Place the continuation character between code items rather than inside them.*

- Line 9 uses the TypeText method of the Selection object to enter the period you typed.

- Line 10 uses the TypeParagraph method of the Selection object to enter the paragraph you typed (the ENTER keypress).

- Line 11 uses the SaveAs method of the ActiveDocument object to save the active document under the filename you specified. Most of the arguments are easy to understand if you're familiar with the options that Word documents offer: the FileName argument is a String giving the filename, the FileFormat argument controls the document type (Word document, document template, web page, or whatever), and so on.

- Line 12 uses the Close method to close the document. You'll notice that this statement doesn't use any arguments, although Close does support three optional arguments. To see them, place the insertion point after Close, then press SPACEBAR to display the Auto Quick Info readout. The most useful of the three arguments is SaveChanges, which controls whether Word saves changes to the document being closed (SaveChanges:=wdSaveChanges) or not (SaveChanges:=wdDoNotSaveChanges). In this case, because the macro saved the document, you don't need to use the SaveChanges argument here.

So far, so good. But as mentioned earlier in this chapter, the NewMacros module isn't a great place to leave macros in Word. This is because the Macro Recorder in Word always records macros into the NewMacros module, so it quickly gets cluttered.

Move the macro to a new module by taking the following steps:

1. In the Code window for the NewMacros module, select all the lines of the Create_Project_Log macro and press CTRL-X to cut it to the Clipboard.

2. Right-click anywhere in the Normal listing in the Project Explorer, and choose Insert | Module from the context menu to create a new module. The Visual Basic Editor displays a Code window for the new module and activates it.

3. Press CTRL-V to paste the Create_Project_Log macro in.

4. Press F4 to activate the Properties window for the new module.

5. Type **BuildProjectBase** as the new name for the module, and press ENTER.

6. Press F7 to activate the Code window again.

After doing that, edit the macro as described in the following list. In the next chapter, the userform will need to pass to the macro a String argument that the macro will use to create the project log file in the appropriate folder.

1. Change the first line by adding the parenthetical element shown in the following line. This changes the macro to use the String argument named strProjectFolder that is passed to it. The ByVal key word specifies that VBA passes the value of the String to the macro.

```
Sub Create_Project_Log(ByVal strProjectFolder As String)
```

2. Change line 11 so that it reads like the following line by adding **strProjectFolder &** and the backslash. Note that all this should appear on one line in the Visual Basic Editor, even though the book shows it as two lines:

```
ActiveDocument.SaveAs FileName:=strProjectFolder
& "\Project Log.doc", FileFormat:= _
```

After making these changes, click the Save button on the Standard toolbar to save the VBA project and the template that contains it.

Examining the Excel Macro

The Excel macro you recorded should look something like this. Again, we've added numbers to the beginning of the lines for ease of reference.

```
1.   Sub Create_Budget_Workbook()
2.   '
3.   ' Create_Budget_Workbook Macro
4.   ' Creates the budget workbook for the project. _
        Macro recorded 9/5/2003 by Petra Nemmanden
5.   '
6.   '
7.      Workbooks.Add
8.      ActiveWorkbook.SaveAs Filename:= _
        "Z:\Public\Budget.xls", _
        FileFormat:=xlNormal, Password:="", WriteResPassword:="", _
        ReadOnlyRecommended:=False, CreateBackup:=False
9.       ActiveWorkbook.Close
10.  End Sub
```

Here's what the macro does:

- The Sub statement in line 1 starts the macro, and the End Sub statement in line 10 ends it.

- Lines 2, 3, 4, 5, and 6 are comment lines for humans, ignored by VBA. Line 3 states the macro's name and adds that it's a macro. Line 4 contains the description you entered while recording the macro.

- Line 7 uses the Add method of the Workbooks collection to create a new default workbook.

- Line 8 uses the SaveAs method of the ActiveWorkbook object to save the workbook under the name specified by the FileName argument. As with Word, the SaveAs method offers various other arguments for controlling choices, such as the file format used and whether Excel creates a backup of the file.

- Line 9 uses the Close method of the ActiveWorkbook object to close the workbook. As in the Word macro, Close here uses no arguments but offers three optional arguments. Again as with Word, the most useful of the arguments is SaveChanges, which controls whether Excel saves changes to the workbook being closed (SaveChanges:=xlSaveChanges) or not (SaveChanges:=xlDoNotSaveChanges). As you've probably guessed, Excel's VBA constants start with the letters "xl."

You'll notice that the actions this macro takes are very similar to those in the Word macro. The objects are different—Document objects and the Documents collection in Word, Workbook objects and the Workbooks collection in Excel—but many methods are the same (for example, VBA uses the Add method and the Close method in both applications). However, even when the methods are the same, the arguments used vary depending on the specifics of the application involved.

Putting VBA and Macros to Work

This chapter builds on the skills you have gained in the previous two chapters and shows you how to put those skills to work in the context of a practical VBA project. The project is to create a custom userform (dialog box) driven by code that sets up the folders and working documents for a corporate project.

We mix theory with practice in this chapter: we explain a key skill, then show you how to put it to use in the project. You'll learn how to declare variables for storing information, how to make decisions in your code, how to use message boxes to let the user of a macro decide between different courses of action, how to use loops to repeat actions, how to create custom dialog boxes, and how to distribute your macro projects. Along the way, you'll create a function for determining whether a given string is entirely alphanumeric or not, and you'll learn how to call one procedure from another procedure.

Working with Variables

For storing information while your code runs, you use *variables*—storage slots that hold information that changes (variable information), as opposed to information that stays the same. (For information that stays the same, you create and use *constants*.)

VBA's 12 Types of Variables

You can use 12 types of variables in VBA, which encompass all your needs for data storage. Table 43-1 explains the variable types in logical groups, together with the prefixes they're typically assigned in what's known as *Hungarian notation*. By assigning a prefix, anybody reading the code can see at a glance what data type a particular variable has without referring to wherever in the code a variable was declared.

Declaring and Using a Variable

To use a variable, you create it by *declaring* it or *dimensioning* it, which causes VBA to allocate memory for the variable. You can declare variables either explicitly or implicitly. Explicit declarations make your code much easier to read and debug, while implicit declarations take a little less effort up front.

Variable Type	Prefix	Explanation
Variant	v *or* var	Use this to contain any type of data, usually by including the appropriate subtype—for example, Variant/String for a Variant that contains string data.
String	s *or* str	Use this for storing a string of text.
Object	obj	Use this to refer to an object—for example, another application.
Boolean	b *or* bln	A Boolean variable can be either True or False.
Currency	c *or* cur	Used for currency, this variable can have up to 15 digits before the decimal point and 4 digits after it.
Date	dt	As discussed in "Date Format" in Chapter 16, VBA uses a numeric format for storing dates and times—for example, the serial date 37955 represents November 30, 2003, and 37955.25 represents 6:00 A.M. on that date. Date variables store dates in a similar format. The easiest way to enter a date or time in a Date variable is to type the literal value between pound signs—for example, #April 1, 2004#. VBA automatically converts your entry to a number and formats the display with the default date or time format set in Windows.
Byte	byt	Use this to store an integer number ranging from 0 to 255.
Integer	i *or* int	Use this to store an integer number ranging from −32,768 to 32,767.
Long	l	Use this to store an integer number ranging from −2,147,483,648 to 2,147,483,647.
Double	d	A double-precision floating-point number, the Double variable can store extremely large values and extremely small values.
Single	s	A single-precision floating-point number, the Single variable can store very large values and very small values. Single variables offer less precision than double variables but take up less memory.
Decimal	dec	A variant subtype used for storing numbers to a high level of accuracy, this can have between 0 and 28 decimal places.

TABLE 43-1   VBA's Variable Types

An explicit declaration uses the Dim keyword to dimension the variable. The following declaration declares the variable strLocation as the String data type:

```
Dim strLocation As String
```

After declaring the variable, you assign data to it:

```
strLocation = "Barcelona"
```

As you can see in the example, you enclose a string of text in double quotation marks. For most other data types, you simply use the equal sign and the data. Here's an example that creates a Currency variable named cIncome and assigns a value to it:

```
Dim cIncome As Currency
cIncome = 73924.77
```

For an Object variable, you need to use a Set statement to assign the data:

```
Dim objPowerPoint As Object
Set objPowerPoint = CreateObject("PowerPoint.Application")
```

These three declarations use what's called *strong typing*—the declaration specifies the data type (in this case, Object) to be assigned to the variable. The opposite of strong typing is *weak typing*, in which the declaration doesn't specify the data type. When you use weak typing, VBA creates the variable with the Variant data type and the Empty subtype (Variant/ Empty). When you assign data to the variable, VBA changes the variable to the appropriate subtype of Variant. For example, if you assign a variable the value True, VBA changes it to the Variant/Boolean subtype.

By contrast, an implicit declaration creates the variable and assigns the data in one statement. For example, the following statement creates the variable City and assigns the text "Walnut Creek" to it:

```
City = "Walnut Creek"
```

This statement creates a Variant/String variable because the data assigned to the variable is a string of text. But consider the following: the statement City = 1 creates a VariantInteger variable; the statement City = 100000 creates a Variant/Long variable; and the statement City = 100000.1 creates a Variant/Double variable. VBA applies each of the subtypes according to the data type it detects. If you're even a little careless and assign the wrong type of data to a variable, the variable's type may change during a macro, which can not only confuse you but also cause errors in your macro.

In VBA, the default scope for a variable is *Procedure* scope, which means that the variable is accessible only to the procedure that declares it. Procedure scope has a couple of important implications:

- You can use the same variable name in different procedures without confusing VBA.

- You can't use a Procedure variable to pass data between procedures.

Instead of Procedure scope, you can use Private scope or Public scope:

- *Private scope* makes a variable available to all procedures in the module that declares it. You can use Private variables to pass data between procedures in the same module. To create a Private variable, declare it using a Private statement in the declarations area of the appropriate code module—for example, Private strMyPrivateString As String. (You can also use a Dim statement in the declarations area, but Private is clearer.)

- *Public scope* makes a variable available to all procedures in all modules in the project that declares the variable. To create a Public variable, declare it using a Public statement in the declarations area of a code sheet in the appropriate project—for example, Public iPublicCount As Integer.

Recommendations for Declaring Variables Effectively

Here are four recommendations for declaring variables most effectively:

- Declare all your variables explicitly rather than implicitly. To force yourself to declare variables explicitly, enter an Option Explicit statement in the *declarations area*—the area at the beginning of a code sheet before any procedures. To make VBA enter the Option Explicit statement on new code modules you create, choose Tools | Options, select the Require Variable Declaration option on the Editor tab of the Options dialog box, and click OK. VBA will then highlight undefined variables with a "Compile Error: Variable Not Defined" error message when you try to run your code.

- Always use strong typing rather than weak typing. By using strong typing, you enlist VBA's help in making sure you put the correct type of data into a variable.

- Declare all your variables together at the beginning of a procedure rather than sprinkling declarations throughout your code. This will help you find the variables when you need to refer to them or add new variables.

- Declare each variable on a separate line for ease of reading.

TIP   *If you're not sure which data type to assign a variable, use weak typing to find out the type that VBA recommends. Create the variable, assign it the type of data it will hold, check the subtype listed in the Locals window, and then assign the corresponding data type. For example, if VBA assigns the Variant/Double subtype, assign the Double data type.*

Making Decisions with If and Select Case

A crucial skill in using VBA is deciding between different courses of action based on the conditions the macro finds or on user input in a message box, input box, or userform. VBA's main tools for making decisions are If statements and Select Case statements.

If Statements

VBA supports three kinds of If statements:

- If… Then statements test a single condition and run the subsequent code if it's met. The following code shows an example of an If… Then statement. The MsgBox statement displays a message box containing the specified text.

```
If Application.UserName = "Johann Schmidt" Then
    MsgBox "You're Johann Schmidt."
End If
```

NOTE   *If… Then statements are sometimes written as a single statement with no End If statement—for example, **If Application.UserName = "Johann Schmidt" Then MsgBox "You're Johann Schmidt."**. However, using the three-line structure just shown is easier for humans to read, because you can quickly see the End If statement that corresponds to the If statement.*

- If... Then... Else statements test a condition and specify an action to be performed if the condition isn't met. Here's an example:

```
If Application.UserName = "Johann Schmidt" Then
    MsgBox "You're Johann Schmidt."
Else
    MsgBox "You're not Johann Schmidt."
End If
```

- If... Then... ElseIf... Else statements enable you to test multiple conditions and take action accordingly. You can use as many ElseIf statements as necessary to test the extra conditions (but for testing many conditions, a Select Case statement is neater). This code shows an example of an If... Then... ElseIf... Else statement:

```
If Application.UserName = "Johann Schmidt" Then
    MsgBox "You're Johann Schmidt."
ElseIf Application.UserName = "Ana Benitez" Then
    MsgBox "You're Ana Benitez."
Else
    strUser = InputBox("Enter your name.")
    MsgBox "You're " & strUser & "."
End If
```

These examples are primitive to the point of being silly, but you see how they work. You'll see many examples of If conditions in use later in this chapter.

Select Case Structures

A Select Case structure is used for evaluating multiple conditions in a single maneuver. You can use a Select Case structure for evaluating a single condition, but typically Select Case structures are used for evaluating three, four, or more conditions, when If... Then... ElseIf... Else structures would become cumbersome.

A Select Case structure is easier for humans to read, which makes reviewing your code faster and less onerous, and typically runs a little faster than an If... Then... ElseIf... Else structure of the same length.

Here's an example of a Select Case structure:

```
Select Case Application.UserName
    Case "Johann Schmidt"
        MsgBox "You're Johann Schmidt."
    Case "Ana Benitez"
        MsgBox "You're Ana Benitez."
    Case "Steven Jones"
        MsgBox "You're Steven Jones."
    Case Else
        MsgBox "You're " & InputBox("Enter your name:") & "."
End Select
```

The Select Case structure starts with the Select Case statement and the item that's being tested (here, Application.UserName). The structure ends with the End Select statement. Each Case statement tests a different condition and runs code if met; if none of the conditions is met, the optional Case Else statement can run other code.

Using Message Boxes and Input Boxes

If you need to offer the users of your macro a straightforward choice, use a message box—a minimal, formalized dialog box that lets users choose which way to proceed by clicking one of two, three, or four command buttons. For example, you might use a message box at the beginning of a macro to double-check that the user chose to run the macro by design rather than by accident. Do this by displaying a Yes/No message box, and by making the No button the default button in case the user simply presses ENTER to dismiss the message box instead of giving it due attention.

VBA's syntax for displaying a message box is

```
VbMsgBoxResult = MsgBox(Prompt[, Buttons] [, Title] [, HelpFile] [, Context])
```

NOTE   *In VBA syntax, items in normal font (for example, MsgBox above) are keywords that don't change. Items in italic are arguments for which you specify the appropriate options. Commas separate one argument from another. Brackets indicate optional arguments. Where a comma appears inside a pair of brackets, it means the comma is necessary only if you use the optional argument.*

Here's what the components of that syntax mean:

- *VbMsgBoxResult*   Data representing the command button in the message box that the user clicked. You use this data to determine what the macro should do next.

- *Prompt*   A required argument that specifies the text to be displayed in the message box. The maximum length is 1023 characters, but most users will only read messages that are much shorter than that.

- *Buttons*   An optional argument that controls which command buttons and which icon are displayed in the message box, and which command button is the default. You can omit this argument to display a default message box that contains an OK command button and no icon.

- *Title*   An optional argument that specifies the text to be displayed in the title bar of the message box. Omitting this argument makes VBA display the application's name in the title bar—for example, "Microsoft PowerPoint."

- *HelpFile*   An optional argument that specifies the help file associated with the message box. Specifying a help file is an advanced topic, and this book doesn't discuss it.

- *Context*   An optional argument that specifies the topic in the help file specified by *HelpFile*. If you use this argument, you must use the *HelpFile* argument as well.

As you can see from the list, *Prompt* is the only required argument for the MsgBox function. But in most cases you'll want to use the *Title* argument to display descriptive or informative text in the message box's title bar, and the *Buttons* argument to control which button choices are available to the user.

The *Buttons* argument is complex, because it can consist of one, two, or three parts. The first part controls the buttons displayed, the second controls the icon displayed, and the third controls which button is the default.

Table 43-2 explains your options for the *Buttons* argument. For each option, you can enter either the constant or its corresponding value. The constants make your code easier to read,

Constant	Value	What It Does
Specifying the buttons in the message box		
vbOKOnly	0	Displays only the OK button (the default if *Buttons* is omitted)
vbOKCancel	1	Displays OK and Cancel buttons
vbAbortRetryIgnore	2	Displays Abort, Retry, and Ignore buttons
vbYesNoCancel	3	Displays Yes, No, and Cancel buttons
vbYesNo	4	Displays Yes and No buttons
vbRetryCancel	5	Displays Retry and Cancel buttons
Specifying the icon in the message box		
vbCritical	16	Displays the Stop icon
vbQuestion	32	Displays the Question icon
vbExclamation	48	Displays the Exclamation icon
vbInformation	64	Displays the Information icon
Specifying the default button in the message box		
[none]	[none]	Sets the first button as the default
vbDefaultButton1	0	Sets the first button as the default
vbDefaultButton2	256	Sets the second button as the default
vbDefaultButton3	512	Sets the third button as the default
vbDefaultButton4	768	Sets the fourth button as the default. (The fourth button is a Help button added to a three-button message box.)

TABLE 43-2   *Buttons* Argument Options

while the values make it more compact. VBA doesn't care if you mix constants and values in your code, but such mixing does human readers no favors.

For example, the following statement displays a message box (shown in the illustration) with Yes and No buttons, the Question icon, and the No button set as the default button:

```
lngClicked = MsgBox("Do you want to delete this object?", _
vbYesNo + vbQuestion + vbDefaultButton2, "Cleanup Macro")
```

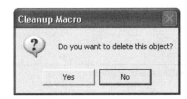

To find out which command button the user clicked in the message box, you check the data assigned to *VbMsgBoxResult* after the user has dismissed the message box. Table 43-3 explains the constants and values that can be assigned to *VbMsgBoxResult*.

We'll look at an example of checking the result of a message box and using it to direct the flow of code near the end of this chapter.

Input Boxes

An input box is a miniature dialog box that includes a single text field for soliciting input from the person using the macro, an OK button, and a Cancel button. You can display default text in the input box if you want—for example, to prompt users toward the type of information you're looking for, or to suggest a default value that they might want to accept. If you read "Making Decisions with If and Select Case," earlier in this chapter, you saw a couple of examples of using input boxes.

To display an input box, you enter an InputBox statement using this syntax:

```
String = InputBox(Prompt [, Title] [,Default] [, XPos] [, YPos],
[, HelpFile] [, Context]
```

Here's what the components of that syntax mean:

- *String*   The string of text the input box returns. If the user clicks Cancel or clicks OK without entering any text in the text box (and without default text being there), the input box returns an empty string, which VBA represents as "" (paired double quotation marks with nothing between them).

- *Prompt*   A required argument that specifies the text to be displayed in the input box. As with MsgBox, the maximum length is 1023 characters, but shorter messages are better.

- *Title*   An optional argument that specifies the text to be displayed in the title bar of the input box. Omitting this argument makes VBA display the application's name in the title bar—for example, "Microsoft Outlook."

- *XPos*   An optional argument for controlling the horizontal position of the left edge of the input box from the left edge of the screen. You'll seldom need to use XPos and

Constant	Value	Button Clicked
vbOK	1	OK
vbCancel	2	Cancel
vbAbort	3	Abort
vbRetry	4	Retry
vbIgnore	5	Ignore
vbYes	6	Yes
vbNo	7	No

TABLE 43-3   *VbMsgBoxResult* Constants and Values

YPos because the default position (midway across the screen and one-third of the way down) works well for most purposes.

- *YPos*   An optional argument for controlling the vertical position of the top of the input from the top of the screen.

- *HelpFile*   An optional argument that specifies the help file associated with the input box. Specifying a help file is advanced, and this book doesn't discuss it.

- *Context*   An optional argument that specifies the topic in the help file specified by *HelpFile*. If you use this argument, you must use the *HelpFile* argument as well.

You can assign the *String* that InputBox returns directly to a variable, or otherwise use it immediately in your code. (For example, you might insert the string in a document.) But for most purposes, you'll need to verify that the input box hasn't returned a blank string ("") before you try to do anything with that string. Here's an example for you to try:

```
Sub InputBoxExample()
    Dim strDogsName As String
    strDogsName = InputBox("Enter your dog's name:", "Example Input Box")
    If strDogsName <> "" Then MsgBox "Your dog's name is " & strDogsName
End Sub
```

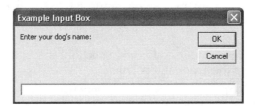

Using Loops to Repeat Actions

To repeat actions in VBA for a number of times, you use loop structures. VBA provides both fixed-iteration loops (which repeat for a fixed number of times) and indefinite loops (which repeat for a number of times that varies depending on conditions).

The type of loop you'll use in this chapter is the For… Next loop, a fixed-iteration loop. The basic form of For… Next takes the following syntax (there are a couple of options that we won't examine here):

```
For counter = start to end
'take actions here
Next counter
```

counter is either a numeric variable (typically an Integer variable) or an expression that returns a number. *start* is the starting value for *counter* and can be either a numeric variable or an expression that returns a number. *end* is the ending value for *counter* and can be either a numeric variable or an expression that returns a number. Each time the loop runs, VBA increments *counter* by 1.

For example, the following loop creates ten new default workbooks in Excel. The first line declares the Integer variable iWks. The second line starts the loop, which runs from iWks = 1 to iWks = 10, a total of ten times. Each time, it executes the Workbooks.Add statement, creating a new workbook. When execution reaches the Next statement, VBA evaluates the condition (whether or not iWks has reached its end value yet) and establishes whether to repeat the loop or not.

```
Dim iWks As Integer
For iWks = 1 to 10
    Workbooks.Add
Next iWks
```

Here's a summary of the other types of loops VBA offers. As you work further with VBA, you'll probably want to investigate these loops:

- For Each... Next loops are used for repeating actions for each of the members of a collection. For example, you could use a For Each... Next loop to perform intricate formatting on each Slide object in the Slides collection in a PowerPoint presentation.

- Do While... Loop loops are used for repeating actions while a condition is True. When the condition becomes False, the loop ends.

- Do Until... Loop loops are used for repeating actions until a condition becomes True. You can usually turn a Do While... Loop loop into a Do Until... Loop loop by reversing its condition.

- Do... Loop While loops are used for taking action, checking whether a condition is True, and repeating the action if it is True.

- Do... Loop Until loops are used for taking action, checking whether a condition is False, and repeating the action if it is False. You can usually turn a Do... Loop Until loop into a Do... Loop While loop by reversing its condition.

Creating the IsAlphanumeric Function

The userform you will create later in this chapter needs a function to determine whether a given string is alphanumeric—whether it contains only letters and numbers, or whether it contains other characters (such as symbols).

VBA includes an IsNumeric function that determines whether a string is numeric (the function returns True) or not (False). The IsAlphanumeric function uses this function to perform the numeric part of the check.

Enter the following function code in your BuildProjectBase code module (assuming you created it in Chapter 42). Omit the initial numbers (1., 2., etc.), which we've added to make the lines easier to refer to. When you press ENTER at the end of the Function statement, VBA enters the End Function line for you. The rest of the code you need to type for yourself.

```
1.    Function IsAlphanumeric(strMyString As String) As Boolean
2.        Dim i As Integer
3.        For i = 1 To Len(strMyString)
4.            If IsNumeric(Mid(strMyString, i, 1)) Then
5.                IsAlphanumeric = True
```

```
 6.            Else
 7.                If UCase(Mid(strMyString, i, 1)) < "A" _
                      Or UCase(Mid(strMyString, i, 1)) > "Z" Then
 8.                    IsAlphanumeric = False
 9.                Else
10.                    IsAlphanumeric = True
11.                End If
12.            End If
13.            If IsAlphanumeric = False Then Exit Function
14.        Next i
15.    End Function
```

Here's what the function does:

- Line 1 starts the function, and line 15 ends it. Line 1 declares the function as using a String argument named strMyString and as returning a Boolean value (True or False). When a subprocedure calls the function, the subprocedure passes to the function a string of text for evaluation. This string is stored in strMyString.

- Line 2 declares the variable i as the Integer data type. The function uses this variable to control the loop that checks each character.

- Line 3 starts a For… Next loop that line 14 ends. This loop starts with i having the value 1 and runs until i reaches the value returned by the expression Len(strMyString), which returns the length of the string—in other words, the number of characters in the string. So the loop runs once for each character in the string.

- Line 4 starts an If statement that ends in line 12. Line 4 uses VBA's built-in IsNumeric function to see if the character returned by the expression Mid(strMyString, i, 1) is numeric or not. Mid(strMyString, i, 1) selects from the String represented by strMyString the character represented by the current iteration of the loop—the first character in the string for the first iteration, the second character for the second iteration, and so on. Briefly, the Mid function returns the specified number of characters (here, 1) from the specified string (here, strMyString), starting at the specified character position (here, i).

- If the character tested is numeric, VBA executes line 5, setting the return value of IsAlphanumeric to True. In this case, execution jumps to line 12, which ends the outer If statement.

- If the character tested in line 4 isn't numeric, execution resumes at the Else statement in line 6. The nested If condition in lines 7 through 11 then tests if the character is alphabetical or not. Line 7 checks whether the uppercase version of the character returned by Mid(strMyString, i, 1) is either less than capital A or greater than capital Z. If it is, line 8 sets the return value of IsAlphanumeric to False. If it's not, line 10 sets the return value of IsAlphanumeric to True.

- Line 13 checks to see if IsAlphanumeric is already False; if so, the Exit Function returns execution to the subprocedure that called the function. This check is used because there's no point in checking any more characters after one character has been found to be nonalphanumeric.

To test the function, enter the short subprocedure shown here:

```
Sub TestAlphanumeric()
    Dim s1 As String
    s1 = InputBox("Enter the text to test:", _
        "Test Alphanumeric Function")
    MsgBox s1 & " is alphanumeric: " & IsAlphanumeric(s1), _
        vbOKOnly + vbInformation, "Test Alphanumeric"
End Sub
```

Click to place the insertion point in the TestAlphanumeric subprocedure, and press F8 to step into it. In the input box, enter one or more characters to evaluate, and click OK. The subprocedure uses the IsAlphanumeric function to test whether each character in the string you entered is alphanumeric. The subprocedure then displays True or False in the message box to tell you the result.

Calling One Procedure from Another Procedure

To enable you to keep your code modular and keep your macros and functions down to a manageable length, VBA lets you call one procedure from another procedure. If the procedures are in the same project, all you need to do is enter in the calling procedure the name of the procedure being called. For example, in the following code, the Example1 macro calls the CreateFolders macro:

```
Sub Example1()
    CreateFolders
End Sub

Sub CreateFolders()
    'contents of CreateFolders macro here
End Sub
```

Instead of simply using the name of the procedure being called, you can use a Call statement with the name (for example, Call CreateFolders). The advantage to using Call is that you can more easily see the calls (for example, by searching for them).

Adding a Reference to Another Project or Application

If your macro needs to call a procedure contained in a VBA project other than its own, you need to add a reference to that project so that your macro knows where to look for the procedure it calls. Similarly, if your macro needs to use code belonging to another application, you need to add a reference to that application. Your sample project requires the Normal template in Word to have a reference to Excel.

Add the reference to Excel as follows:

1. In the Project Explorer, select the Normal project (if it's not already selected).

2. Choose Tools | References to display the References dialog box:

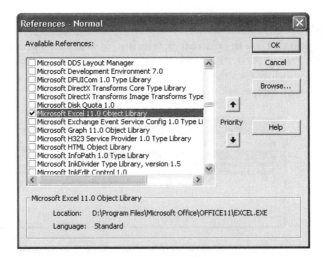

3. Add a reference to the appropriate project or object library:

- To add a reference to a project, click Browse, use the resulting Add Reference dialog box to select the file that contains the project (change the filter in the Files of Type drop-down list if necessary), and click Open.

- To add a reference to an object library, select the object library's check box in the Available References list box. In this case, select the Microsoft Excel 11.0 Object Library check box to add the reference to Excel.

4. Click OK.

After adding the reference, you can implement the call. The best way to do so is to use the fully qualified name of the procedure you're calling. The fully qualified name consists of the project name, the module name, and the procedure name, separated by periods—for example, Project1.Module2.Procedure3. As before, you can use a Call statement explicitly (Call Project1.Module2.Procedure3) or merely imply it by using the procedure's name.

Instead of using the fully qualified name, you can use just the procedure name. This makes your code harder to read and may cause VBA to take longer to identify the correct procedure.

Accessing Another Application

The easiest way for one host application to access another VBA-enabled application is to use the CreateObject function to create and return a reference to that application. The basic syntax of CreateObject, which we'll use in this chapter, is CreateObject(*class*), where *class* is the VBA name for the type of object you're trying to access. For example, the following statement uses CreateObject to create and return a reference to a PowerPoint Application object and assign it to the object variable objPPT:

```
Set objPPT = CreateObject("PowerPoint.Application")
```

You'll see an example of accessing another application via VBA later in this chapter.

Using the Call Stack Window to Track Procedure Calls

In Break mode, you can use the Call Stack window to see which procedure has called which other procedure. Press CTRL-L or choose View | Call Stack to display the Call Stack window, shown here. The window lists the active procedure calls, with the currently executing item at the top. To access a subprocedure, select it and click Show.

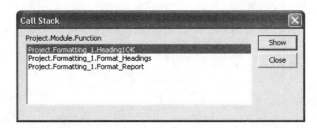

Creating Dialog Boxes

To create a dialog box using VBA, you create a userform. A userform is essentially a blank dialog box sheet on which you can place controls (such as command buttons, check boxes, and option buttons) to provide the features you need. You then create a subprocedure to display the userform, a subprocedure for each control that requires it, and any other subprocedures necessary to provide the functionality the userform needs.

To insert a userform in a project, you select the project in the Project Explorer and issue an Insert | UserForm command from the menu, from the context menu, or from the Insert button on the Standard toolbar. You then use the Toolbox (shown here), which the Visual Basic Editor displays when a userform is selected, to place controls on the userform. The Toolbox normally appears in a squarish format, but you can resize it as necessary. Here, we've resized it to show labels for the buttons more easily.

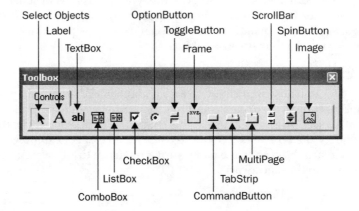

The best way to learn how to work with userforms is by creating them. In the following sections, you'll create the Build Project Base userform, shown in the following illustration, which will run the project you're building. As you can see, this userform contains option buttons for specifying the departments involved in the project; a text box for specifying the project code by which the project is classified; five check boxes (Invoices, Specifications, Memoranda, Presentations, and Other Documents) for choosing which subfolders to create for the project; two check boxes (Project Log Document and Project Budget Workbook) for specifying which standard project documents to create; and two command buttons (OK and Cancel) for proceeding with the form and canceling it, respectively. The controls are divided into three frames.

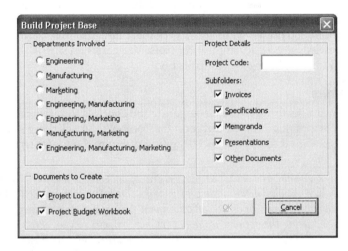

The userform's behavior is conventional, but the following points are worth noting:

- The option buttons act as a group, so only one option button can be selected at any time.
- All the check boxes are selected by default, so that users must actively deselect the check boxes for any subfolders and documents they don't want created for the current project.
- The contents of the Project Code text box are used to name the project folder, inside which the subfolders and documents are created. The Project Code text box is blank when the userform is displayed.
- The OK button is disabled until the user enters alphanumeric text in the Project Code text box, at which point VBA enables it. If the user enters nonalphanumeric text (for example, text that includes a symbol), VBA disables the OK button again.

Creating the Userform

Add the userform to the project by right-clicking anywhere in the Normal tree in the Project Explorer and choosing Insert | UserForm from the context menu. VBA creates the Forms collection (if this is the first userform to be added to this project) and adds a new userform called UserForm1.

Press F4 to activate the Properties window for the userform. You should find that VBA automatically selects the (Name) property in the Properties window, so you shouldn't need to select it manually. If VBA selects another property, select the (Name) property manually. Type the new name, **frmBuildProjectBase**, and press ENTER.

Press the DOWN ARROW to move the highlight down the Properties window to the Caption property, type **Build Project Base**, and press ENTER. The Visual Basic Editor enters the Caption property in the title bar of the userform as you type.

Press SHIFT-F7 to activate the userform again, and then drag its lower-right corner down and to the right to enlarge the userform from its modest default size. Alternatively, change the Height property and Width property in the Properties window to expand the form. The example form is about 360 points wide and 250 points high. You may want to set a bigger size to give you leeway for positioning the controls. You can then shrink the userform down to a snug-fitting size after placing the controls on it.

Adding the Frames

The sample userform uses three frames to separate the controls into logical groups. Place the first frame by clicking the Frame button on the Toolbox, then clicking at the upper-left corner of where you want it to appear and dragging down to the lower-right corner.

NOTE   *By default, the Visual Basic Editor displays a grid of dots on the userform to help you position the controls you place. Also by default, the Editor snaps controls to the grid so that you don't have to worry about them being a point or two off alignment. You can configure the grid by choosing Tools | Options and using the options in the Form Grid Settings section of the General tab of the Options dialog box. You can turn off the display of the grid, turn off snapping to the grid (whether displayed or not), and change the granularity of the grid from its default setting of six points.*

Press F4 to activate the Properties window for the frame. Set its (Name) property to **fraDepartmentsInvolved** and its Caption property to **Departments Involved**. The Caption property controls the text displayed at the top of the frame, so you'll see this text appear as you type. You may also want to adjust the Left property and the Top property to control where the frame appears on the userform.

With the frame still selected, hold down CTRL and drag the frame downward to create a copy of the frame underneath the original. Drag the selection handle at the bottom of the copy upward to reduce the height of the copy to about a third of the original's height.

Press F4 again to activate the Properties window for the new frame. Set its (Name) property to **fraDocumentsToCreate** and its Caption property to **Documents to Create**.

With the lower frame still selected, hold down CTRL and click the upper frame. VBA selects the upper frame and transfers the focus to it, so it has white selection handles and the lower frame has black selection handles. Choose Format | Align | Lefts to align the left edge of the lower frame with the left edge of the upper frame. (The frame with the focus stays still, while the other frame moves as necessary.)

Click the userform's title bar to deselect the selection. Then click the upper frame and CTRL-drag to create a copy of the frame positioned to the right of the original. Set the new frame's (Name) property to **fraProjectDetails** and its Caption property to **Project Details**.

Click the original frame to select it, SHIFT-click the Project Details frame to add it to the selection while retaining the focus on the original frame, and choose Format | Align | Tops to align the top of the Project Details frame with the top of the original frame.

Adding the Option Buttons

Next, add the six option buttons to the Departments Involved frame. The easiest way to do this is to create one option button with suitable settings, copy it five times, and then adjust the appropriate properties on the copies.

Click the OptionButton button in the Toolbox; then click toward the upper-left corner of the Departments Involved frame to position the first option button there. If necessary, adjust the option button's position by dragging or by setting its Top property and Left property in the Properties window.

With the first option button selected, press F4 and set the AutoSize property to True and the WordWrap property to False. (The default settings for option buttons, check boxes, and labels are False for AutoSize and True for WordWrap, which tend to produce controls that are either unnecessarily large or unnecessarily wrapped.)

After doing that, CTRL-drag the first option button down five times to create a stack of six option buttons in the Departments Involved frame. Click the first option button, hold down SHIFT, and click the last option button to select all the buttons in between. Choose Format | Align | Lefts to align the left edges of the option buttons with the top option button, and then choose Format | Vertical Spacing | Make Equal to make the Visual Basic Editor apply equal spacing to the option buttons. If the option buttons are too widely spaced, choose Format | Vertical Spacing | Decrease to bring them together a bit.

Set the following properties for the option buttons:

Option Button	Name	Accelerator	Caption
First	optEngineering	E	Engineering
Second	optManufacturing	M	Manufacturing
Third	optMarketing	k	Marketing
Fourth	optEngineeringManufacturing	n	Engineering, Manufacturing
Fifth	optManufacturingMarketing	f	Manufacturing, Marketing
Sixth	optEngineeringManufacturingMarketing	g	Engineering, Manufacturing, Marketing

The Name property is the name that VBA uses to refer to the control. The Caption property is the name that appears on screen to identify the control to the user. The Accelerator property controls the underlined letter in the name that appears on screen—the letter you can press with the ALT key to select the control. For best effect, the accelerator key should be different for each control that has one. Otherwise, the user will have to press ALT and the letter multiple times to navigate among the controls that share the accelerator key.

Adding the Check Boxes

Next, add the seven check boxes to the userform. Click the CheckBox button in the Toolbox, and then click near the upper-left corner of the Documents to Create frame to position the first check box there. If necessary, adjust the check box's position by dragging it or by setting its Top property and Left property in the Properties window.

Just as you did for the first option button, press F4 and set the AutoSize property to True and the WordWrap property to False. Then CTRL-drag the check box down once to create a second check box under it. CTRL-drag five more times to create a stack of five check boxes in the Project Details frame. Select each set of check boxes and use the layout commands on the Format menu to align and space them.

Set the following properties for the check boxes in the Documents to Create frame:

Check Box	Name	Accelerator	Caption
Upper	chkProjectLogDocument	P	Project Log Document
Lower	chkProjectBudgetWorkbook	B	Project Budget Workbook

Set the following properties for the check boxes in the Project Details frame:

Check Box	Name	Accelerator	Caption
First	chkInvoices	I	Invoices
Second	chkSpecifications	S	Specifications
Third	chkMemoranda	o	Memoranda
Fourth	chkPresentations	r	Presentations
Fifth	chkOtherDocuments	h	Other Documents

Creating the Initialize Subprocedure for the Userform

Select the userform (as opposed to any of its controls), press F7 to display its code sheet, and then create the Initialize subprocedure shown next. This subprocedure selects each of the check boxes in the userform so that the userform will create all of the folders and project items by default. It also selects the optEngineeringManufacturingMarketing option button to ensure that one of the option buttons is always selected. (Otherwise, the user could click the OK button without any option button selected.)

Here's the code for the Initialize subprocedure:

```
Private Sub UserForm_Initialize()
    chkInvoices.Value = True
    chkMemoranda.Value = True
    chkOtherDocuments.Value = True
    chkPresentations.Value = True
    chkSpecifications.Value = True
    chkProjectBudgetWorkbook.Value = True
    chkProjectLogDocument.Value = True
    optEngineeringManufacturingMarketing.Value = True
End Sub
```

You can enter this code in any of the ways you've learned so far. Here are a couple of suggestions:

- Create the first and last lines by selecting the UserForm item in the Object drop-down list. If the Visual Basic Editor creates a UserForm_Click subprocedure by default, select "Click" and type **Initialize** instead. If the Visual Basic Editor doesn't create the UserForm_Click subprocedure, choose the Initialize item from the Procedure drop-down list. (The Visual Basic Editor may also have created a Click subprocedure when you displayed the code sheet.)

- Create each of the check-box-related lines by typing **chk**, pressing CTRL-SPACEBAR, and then selecting the appropriate name from the list displayed by the Visual Basic Editor. The quickest way to do this is to type one or more identifying letters to select the appropriate item in the list (for example, type **m** for chkMemoranda), type the period to enter the name and display the Auto List Members list, type **v** to select the Value property, and type = to enter Value and the equal sign.

After creating this subprocedure, place the insertion point in it and press F8 to step through it. After the last statement, the userform appears on screen with the controls you've placed so far. Click the Close button (the X) to close the userform.

Adding the Label and Text Box

Create a label on the userform by clicking the Label button in the Toolbox and then clicking where you want the label to appear on the userform. Set the (Name) property to **lblProjectCode**, the Accelerator property to **j**, the AutoSize property to **True**, the Caption property to **Project Code:** (including the colon), and the WordWrap property to **False**. The Accelerator property for the label governs not the label itself, which the user shouldn't need to select, but the control next to it—in this case, the text box you're about to place.

Create a text box on the userform by clicking the TextBox button in the Toolbox and then clicking to the right of the label you just placed. Drag the right middle handle to reduce the width of the text box a bit; then set its (Name) property to **txtProjectCode** and its ControlTipText property to **Enter the alphanumeric project code here**. (VBA displays the ControlTipText contents as a ScreenTip when the user hovers the mouse pointer over the control.)

Select the label and the text box, place the focus on the label, and choose Format | Align | Middles to align the two controls vertically along their midpoints.

Adding the txtProjectCode_Change Subprocedure

As mentioned earlier in this chapter, the user's entry in the Project Code text box is used to create the main project folder. The project code entered must be alphanumeric both for the company's project-ID scheme to work and for Windows to be able to create the folder. So the txtProjectCode text box must check what the user enters to make sure it's alphanumeric. If so, the text box must enable the OK button; if not, the text box must disable the OK button.

To create the txtProjectCode_Change subprocedure, double-click the txtProjectCode text box. VBA displays the userform's code sheet and enters the stub automatically, because Change is the default event for a text box. Change is triggered by the user's making any change in the text box—for example, typing a character, backspacing, or pressing DELETE.

Complete the subprocedure by entering the If structure shown in the following code. This code uses the IsAlphanumeric function to check that the Text property of the txtProjectCode text box is alphanumeric. If so, the subprocedure sets the Enabled property of cmdOK (the OK button) to True; if not, the subprocedure sets this property to False.

```
Private Sub txtProjectCode_Change()
    If IsAlphanumeric(txtProjectCode.Text) Then
        cmdOK.Enabled = True
    Else
        cmdOK.Enabled = False
    End If
End Sub
```

Adding the Command Buttons

The last controls the userform needs are its two command buttons: OK and Cancel. To add the OK button, click the CommandButton button on the Toolbox, and then click at the bottom of the userform to place a command button of the default size.

Set the (Name) property to **cmdOK**, the Accelerator property to **O**, the Caption property to **OK**, and the Default property to **True**. You may want to adjust the Height property and the Width property to make the command button a little lower and narrower than its default width.

These settings produce a command button with the text OK, an underlined accelerator key on the *O* of OK, and the default focus for the userform. (The default button captures the user's pressing the ENTER key without moving the focus to a different control.)

To add the Cancel button, select the OK button, hold down CTRL, and drag it to the right to make a copy. As with the other controls you duplicated, the copy retains such properties as can be duplicated, including the height and width, but not the (Name) property, which must be unique within the userform.

Set the (Name) property to **cmdCancel**, the Accelerator property to **C**, the Caption property to **Cancel**, the Cancel property to **True**, and the Default property to **False**.

Creating the cmdOK_Click Subprocedure

You now need to add code to make the buttons perform the actions appropriate to their names and stations. To do so, you create a Click subprocedure for each button. This subprocedure is triggered by the user's clicking the button (or pressing ENTER with the focus on the button).

Double-click the cmdOK button to create a cmdOK_Click procedure on the userform's code sheet. This subprocedure takes most of the actions in the macro, so roll up your sleeves. Enter the following code in the stub (minus the initial numbers, which are there for reference as usual):

```
1.    Private Sub cmdOK_Click()
2.
3.        Dim strProjectFolder As String
4.        Dim objExcel As Excel.Application
5.
6.        frmBuildProjectBase.Hide
7.
```

```
8.      strProjectFolder = "Z:\Public\" & txtProjectCode.Text
9.      MkDir strProjectFolder
10.
11.     If optEngineering.Value = True Then
12.         MkDir strProjectFolder & "\Engineering"
13.     ElseIf optEngineeringManufacturing.Value = True Then
14.         MkDir strProjectFolder & "\Engineering"
15.         MkDir strProjectFolder & "\Manufacturing"
16.     ElseIf optEngineeringManufacturingMarketing.Value = True Then
17.         MkDir strProjectFolder & "\Engineering"
18.         MkDir strProjectFolder & "\Manufacturing"
19.         MkDir strProjectFolder & "\Marketing"
20.     ElseIf optEngineeringMarketing.Value = True Then
21.         MkDir strProjectFolder & "\Engineering"
22.         MkDir strProjectFolder & "\Marketing"
23.     ElseIf optManufacturing.Value = True Then
24.         MkDir strProjectFolder & "\Manufacturing"
25.     ElseIf optManufacturingMarketing.Value = True Then
26.         MkDir strProjectFolder & "\Manufacturing"
27.         MkDir strProjectFolder & "\Marketing"
28.     Else    'optMarketing is selected
29.         MkDir strProjectFolder & "\Marketing"
30.     End If
31.
32.     If chkInvoices.Value = True Then _
            MkDir strProjectFolder & "\Invoices"
33.     If chkMemoranda.Value = True Then _
            MkDir strProjectFolder & "\Memoranda"
34.     If chkPresentations.Value = True Then _
            MkDir strProjectFolder & "\Presentations"
35.     If chkSpecifications.Value = True Then _
            MkDir strProjectFolder & "\Specifications"
36.     If chkOtherDocuments.Value = True Then _
            MkDir strProjectFolder & "\Other Documents"
37.     If chkProjectBudgetWorkbook.Value = True Then
38.         Set objExcel = CreateObject("Excel.Application")
39.         With objExcel
40.             .Workbooks.Add
41.             .ActiveWorkbook.SaveAs strProjectFolder & "\Budget.xls"
42.             .ActiveWorkbook.Close
43.             .Quit
44.         End With
45.         Set objExcel = Nothing
46.     End If
47.     If chkProjectLogDocument.Value = True Then
48.         Create_Project_Log (strProjectFolder)
49.     End If
50.
51.     If chkProjectLogDocument.Value = True Then
52.         If MsgBox("The macro has finished running." & vbCr _
                & "Do you want to open the Project Log now?", _
                vbYesNo + vbQuestion, "Build Project Base") _
                = vbYes Then
```

```
53.                   Documents.Open strProjectFolder & "\Project Log.doc"
54.             End If
55.         Else
56.             MsgBox "The macro has finished running.", _
                vbOKOnly & vbInformation, "Build Project Base"
57.         End If
58.         Unload frmBuildProjectBase
59.     End Sub
```

As you'll notice when you're creating it, this subprocedure is very repetitive. Here are the main points, ignoring the spacer lines, which are there to make the code easier to read.

- Line 1 starts the subprocedure, and line 59 ends it.

- Line 3 declares the String variable strProjectFolder. Line 4 declares the objExcel object variable as being of the Excel.Application type. (You need to have added the reference to the Microsoft Excel 11.0 Object Library, as described in "Adding a Reference to Another Project or Application" earlier in this chapter, for this to work.)

- Line 6 uses the Hide method on frmBuildProjectBase to remove the userform from display.

- Line 8 assigns to the strProjectFolder String variable the path Z:\Public\ and the Text property of the txtProjectCode text box—in other words, the text the user entered in the text box. Line 9 then uses the MkDir command to create a directory using the string stored in strProjectFolder. So if the user entered P8392 in the Project Code text box, this statement would create the folder Z:\Public\P8392.

CAUTION   *MkDir fails if the folder it's trying to create already exists. When testing the macros in this userform, either use a different project code each time (which is what the code is intended to do) or delete the project folder and its subfolders after each test.*

- Line 11 begins an If... Then... ElseIf... Else structure that checks the Value property of each option button on the userform to determine which is selected. The code then uses MkDir statements to create the appropriate subfolders for each department involved. For example, if the optEngineeringMarketing option button is selected, the code creates an Engineering subfolder and a Marketing subfolder. If none of the other five option buttons are selected, the Else statement deduces that the optMarketing option button is selected and creates the Marketing subfolder.

- Lines 32 through 36 check the values of the five check boxes in the Project Details frame and create the appropriate subfolders if the check boxes are selected. For example, if the chkPresentations check box is selected, the code creates the Presentations subfolder. These lines use single-line If structures rather than three-line If structures (with End If statements) for compactness.

- Lines 37 through 46 contain an If structure that checks the Value property of the chkProjectBudgetWorkbook check box and creates the budget workbook in Excel if the value is True. Line 38 uses the CreateObject method to launch an instance of the

Excel.Application object and assigns it to the objExcel variable. Lines 39 through 44 contain a With… End With structure that works with the objExcel object. (A With structure lets you refer to subobjects of the specified object without naming them explicitly each time—for example, inside a With structure, you can use **.Workbooks .Add** instead of **objExcel.Workbooks.Add**.) Using slightly modified versions of the statements in the Excel macro you recorded in Chapter 41, lines 40, 41, and 42 create a new workbook, save it in the project folder, and close it. Line 43 uses the Quit method to exit the Excel application. Line 45 sets the value of the objExcel variable to **Nothing** to release the memory the variable occupied. (You only need to take this action with object variables.)

- Lines 47 through 49 contain an If structure that checks the Value property of the chkProjectLogDocument check box and runs the Create_Project_Log macro in the Normal.BuildProjectBase module in the Normal template if the value is True. Notice how the call to the Create_Project_Log subprocedure passes the String variable that the subprocedure uses.

- Lines 51 through 57 contain an If… Else structure that displays one of two message boxes depending on whether the user selected the chkProjectLogDocument check box. If the Value property of chkProjectLogDocument is True, line 52 displays a message box that tells the user that the macro has stopped running and asks if he or she wants to open the project log document. If the user clicks the Yes button, the message box returns vbYes, and line 53 uses the Open method of the Documents collection to open the project log document. If the Value property of chkProjectLogDocument is False, execution resumes at the Else statement in line 55, and line 56 displays an OK-only message box that tells the user that the macro has stopped running.

- Line 58 unloads the frmBuildProjectBase userform from memory because you've finished using it.

After creating this subprocedure, test it by placing the insertion point in it and pressing F5. When the userform appears, enter text in the Project Code text box and watch as VBA enables and disables the OK button for alphanumeric and nonalphanumeric text (respectively).

Enter alphanumeric text in the Project Code text box, and click the OK button to make the code execute. Open a Windows Explorer window to the location of the project folder, examine the subfolders and documents you chose to create, and delete them if appropriate.

Creating the cmdCancel_Click Subprocedure

Start a Click subprocedure for the cmdCancel button from the code sheet by selecting the cmdCancel item in the Object drop-down list. Inside the code stub inserted by the Visual Basic Editor, enter the middle two lines shown here:

```
Private Sub cmdCancel_Click()
    frmBuildProjectBase.Hide
    Unload frmBuildProjectBase
End Sub
```

The first statement after the Sub line hides the userform, and the second unloads it from memory.

Test this subprocedure quickly. Select the userform and press F5. When the userform appears, click the Cancel button.

Calling the Userform from the Macro

So far in your testing, you've been running the userform directly from the Visual Basic Editor's interface. To enable the user to run the macro from Word, create a short macro in the BuildProjectBase module in the Normal template:

1. Expand the Normal item in the Project Explorer if necessary, and then double-click the BuildProjectBase module to display its Code window.

2. Type the following macro:

```
Sub Display_frmBuild_Project_Base()
    frmBuildProjectBase.Show
End Sub
```

3. Create an interface customization (a toolbar button, a menu item, or a keyboard shortcut) so that users can run this macro easily. (Better still, create an interface customization of each type so that users can use their preferred method of running the macro.)

4. Click the Save button on the Standard toolbar in the Visual Basic Editor to save the Normal template.

You'll then be able to display the userform by using the interface customization or by running the Display_frmBuild_Project_Base macro from the Macros dialog box (ALT-F8).

Distributing a VBA Project

After creating a VBA project whose use goes beyond your desktop, you may well want to distribute it to other people. Before you do so, you should sign the project with a digital certificate to establish its provenance and lock it so that other people can't change its code.

Signing Your VBA Project

Before distributing a VBA project, you should sign it with a software developer certificate so that anyone who considers using the project can see who created it and decide whether they want to trust it.

To sign a VBA project:

1. In the host application, open the file that contains the project.

2. Press ALT-F11 or choose Tools | Macro | Visual Basic Editor to display the Visual Basic Editor.

3. Select the project's entry in the Project Explorer.

4. Choose Tools | Digital Signature to display the Digital Signature dialog box, shown on the left in the next illustration.

5. Click Choose to display the Select Certificate dialog box, shown on the right in the illustration.

6. Select the certificate and click OK to close the Select Certificate dialog box.

7. Click OK to close the Digital Signature dialog box.

To remove a digital signature from a project, display the Digital Signature dialog box and click Remove.

Locking Your VBA Project

Before distributing a VBA project, you should lock it against viewing and protect it with a password:

1. In the host application, open the file that contains the project.

2. Press ALT-F11 or choose Tools | Macro | Visual Basic Editor to display the Visual Basic Editor.

3. Right-click the project's entry in the Project Explorer, and choose Properties.

4. On the Protection tab of the project's Project Properties dialog box, select the Lock Project for Viewing option, and enter a strong password in the Password box and the Confirm Password box.

5. Click OK to close the Project Properties dialog box.

6. Save and close the file.

When you've locked a project, the Project Explorer in the Visual Basic Editor keeps this project collapsed until the user double-clicks it and enters the correct password in the Project Password dialog box. If the user can't supply the correct password, the project remains unviewable.

CAUTION *Be warned that password-cracking utilities that can crack protected VBA projects are widely available. (These utilities have legitimate uses—for example, when a programmer forgets a password or is frog-marched off the company's premises—as well as illegitimate uses.)*

PART

Appendixes

APPENDIX A
Keyboard Shortcuts

APPENDIX B
XML: The Underpinnings
of Office 2003

Keyboard Shortcuts

As you've seen throughout the book, the Office applications support many keyboard shortcuts for invoking commands from the keyboard rather than using the menus. You can save a lot of time and effort in your work by memorizing and using the keyboard shortcuts for the actions you take frequently with your hands on the keyboard; unless your job is wildly varied, you won't need to learn all the keyboard shortcuts.

This appendix summarizes the most important keyboard shortcuts in Office, concentrating on the applications you're likely to use the most and the actions you're most likely to need to take. The keyboard shortcuts are presented by category.

Note   Some actions have multiple keyboard shortcuts for historical reasons: Microsoft introduced new keyboard shortcuts for actions but didn't remove key combinations that users knew from older versions of the software. Some keyboard shortcuts cater to different keyboard layouts. For example, most keyboard shortcuts that use F11 or F12 are duplicated with shortcuts that don't use F11 or F12, because some keyboards don't have these two keys.

Table A-1 lists the keyboard shortcuts that apply to all (or almost all) of the Office applications.

TABLE A-1
Keyboard Shortcuts for (Almost) All the Office Applications

Action	Keyboard Shortcut
Opening and Saving Files	
Display the Open dialog box	CTRL-O, CTRL-F12, CTRL-ALT-F2
Display the Save As dialog box	F12
Save the active file	CTRL-S, SHIFT-F12, ALT-SHIFT-F2
Display the Print dialog box	CTRL-P, CTRL-SHIFT-F12
Moving and Resizing Windows	
Maximize the application window	ALT-F10
Maximize the active document window	CTRL-F10

TABLE A-1
Keyboard
Shortcuts for
(Almost) All the
Office Applications
(continued)

Action	Keyboard Shortcut
Moving and Resizing Windows	
Restore the application window	ALT-F5
Move the active document window	CTRL-F7
Restore the active document window	CTRL-F5
Resize the active document window	CTRL-F8
Close the active window or exit the application	ALT-F4
Close the active document window	CTRL-F4, CTRL-W
Switch to the next application	ALT-TAB
Switch to the previous application	ALT-SHIFT-TAB
Applying Basic Formatting	
Toggle boldface	CTRL-B
Toggle italic	CTRL-I
Toggle underline	CTRL-U
Apply left alignment	CTRL-L
Apply centering	CTRL-E
Apply right alignment	CTRL-R
Cutting, Copying, and Pasting	
Copy the current selection to the Clipboard	CTRL-C, CTRL-INSERT
Paste the current contents of the Clipboard	CTRL-V, SHIFT-INSERT
Cut the current selection to the Clipboard	CTRL-X, SHIFT-DELETE
Copy the screen to the Clipboard as a picture	PRTSCR
Copy the active window to the Clipboard as a picture	ALT-PRTSCR
Display the contents of the current or next Smart Tag	ALT-SHIFT-F10
Launching Help, the Visual Basic Editor, and the Microsoft Script Editor	
Launch Help	F1
Display the Visual Basic Editor	ALT-F11

TABLE A-1
Keyboard
Shortcuts for
(Almost) All the
Office Applications
(continued)

Action	Keyboard Shortcut
Launching Help, the Visual Basic Editor, and the Microsoft Script Editor	
Display the Microsoft Script Editor	ALT-SHIFT-F11
Display the Macros dialog box	ALT-F8
Repeating Actions and Invoking Tools	
Undo the previous action	CTRL-Z
Display the Find dialog box or Find tab	CTRL-F
Display the Replace dialog box or Replace tab	CTRL-H
Display the Insert Hyperlink dialog box	CTRL-K
Run the spell checker	F7
Display the Thesaurus dialog box (Word, PowerPoint)	SHIFT-F7
Research the word	ALT-click
Repeat the previous action (not in Outlook)	CTRL-Y

Table A-2 lists the most widely useful keyboard shortcuts for Word.

TABLE A-2
Keyboard
Shortcuts for Word

Action	Keyboard Shortcut
Creating and Saving Documents	
Create a new document using the default template	CTRL-N
Save the active document	CTRL-S
Changing the View	
Apply Normal view	CTRL-ALT-N
Apply Outline view	CTRL-ALT-O
Apply Print Layout view	CTRL-ALT-P
Toggle Print Preview	CTRL-F2, CTRL-ALT-I
Toggle the display of all nonprinting characters	CTRL-*

TABLE A-2
Keyboard
Shortcuts for
Word *(continued)*

Action	Keyboard Shortcut
Changing the View	
Close the active pane (for example, the Header pane), or remove the document window split	ALT-SHIFT-C
Split the active window horizontally	CTRL-ALT-S
Display the next document window	CTRL-F6, ALT-F6
Switch pane	F6, SHIFT-F6
Display the previous document window	CTRL-SHIFT-F6, ALT-SHIFT-F6
Navigating Through Documents	
Find the next occurrence of the search item	SHIFT-F4, CTRL-ALT-Y
Display the Go To tab of the Find and Replace dialog box	CTRL-G, F5
Select the next Browse object	CTRL-PAGE DOWN
Select the previous Browse object	CTRL-PAGE UP
Display the Bookmark dialog box	CTRL-SHIFT-F5
Editing Text	
Return to the previous editing point	SHIFT-F5, CTRL-ALT-Z
Repeat the previous action	CTRL-Y, F4, ALT-ENTER
Undo the previous action	CTRL-Z, ALT-BACKSPACE
Select all (select all the contents of the current object—for example, a document or a text box)	CTRL-A, CTRL-5 (on numeric keypad)
Cut the selection and add it to the Spike (a special AutoText entry)	CTRL-F3
Insert the contents of the Spike	CTRL-SHIFT-F3
Formatting Text	
Toggle all caps	CTRL-SHIFT-A
Toggle small caps	CTRL-SHIFT-K
Cycle the case of the selection	SHIFT-F3
Toggle boldface	CTRL-B, CTRL-SHIFT-B
Toggle underline	CTRL-U, CTRL-SHIFT-U
Toggle word underline	CTRL-SHIFT-W

TABLE A-2
Keyboard
Shortcuts for
Word *(continued)*

Action	Keyboard Shortcut
Formatting Text	
Toggle double underlining on the selection	CTRL-SHIFT-D
Toggle subscript	CTRL-=
Toggle superscript	CTRL-+
Toggle character and character code	ALT-X
Display the Font dialog box	CTRL-D
Select the Font Size drop-down list	CTRL-SHIFT-P
Apply the Symbol font	CTRL-SHIFT-Q
Display the Style dialog box or select the Style drop-down list (depending on the application)	CTRL-SHIFT-S
AutoFormat the document	CTRL-ALT-K
Increase the font size in jumps	CTRL->
Decrease the font size in jumps	CTRL-<
Increase the font size by one point	CTRL-]
Decrease the font size by one point	CTRL-[
Toggle the selection to or from hidden text	CTRL-SHIFT-H
Copy the formatting of the selection	CTRL-SHIFT-C
Apply the copied formatting to the selection	CTRL-SHIFT-V
Formatting Paragraphs	
Apply the specified heading level to the selection	CTRL-ALT-1 to 3
Apply the List Bullet style to the selection	CTRL-SHIFT-L
Apply the Normal style	CTRL-SHIFT-N, ALT-SHIFT-5 (on numeric keypad)
Apply or increase the hanging indent	CTRL-T
Decrease or remove the hanging indent	CTRL-SHIFT-T
Increase the left indent	CTRL-M
Decrease the left indent	CTRL-SHIFT-M

PART X

TABLE A-2
Keyboard
Shortcuts for
Word *(continued)*

Action	Keyboard Shortcut
Formatting Paragraphs	
Apply the default paragraph format of the current style	CTRL-Q
Distribute the paragraph (justify all lines, including the last line)	CTRL-SHIFT-J
Add or remove extra spacing on selected paragraphs	CTRL-0
Apply single line spacing	CTRL-1
Apply 1.5 line spacing	CTRL-5
Apply double line spacing	CTRL-2
Reset the formatting of the current paragraph or selection	CTRL-SPACEBAR, CTRL-SHIFT-Z
Working with Fields	
Lock the fields in the current selection	CTRL-3, CTRL-F11
Unlock the fields in the current selection	CTRL-4, CTRL-SHIFT-F11
Update the fields in the selection	F9, ALT-SHIFT-U
Unlink the fields in the current selection	CTRL-6, CTRL-SHIFT-F9
Copy the modifications in a linked object back to its source file	CTRL-SHIFT-F7
Toggle between field codes and field results	ALT-F9
Working with Outlines	
Display the level of heading indicated by the number	ALT-SHIFT-1 to ALT-SHIFT-9
Collapse the lowest subtext in the selection	ALT-_, ALT-SHIFT-– (on numeric keypad)
Expand the next level of subtext in the selection	ALT-+, ALT-SHIFT-+ (on numeric keypad)
Move the selection down one item in the outline	ALT-SHIFT-DOWN ARROW
Move the selection up one item in the outline	ALT-SHIFT-UP ARROW

TABLE A-2
Keyboard
Shortcuts for
Word *(continued)*

Action	Keyboard Shortcut
Working with Outlines	
Toggle the outline between displaying the first line of each paragraph and the full text of each paragraph	ALT-SHIFT-L
Display all headings and body text	ALT-SHIFT-A
Promote the selection by one heading level	ALT-SHIFT-LEFT ARROW
Demote the selection by one heading level	ALT-SHIFT-RIGHT ARROW
Inserting Items	
Insert an AutoText entry	F3, CTRL-ALT-V
Insert a column break at the insertion point	CTRL-SHIFT-ENTER
Insert an annotation at the insertion point	CTRL-ALT-M
Insert a date field in the default format at the insertion point	ALT-SHIFT-D
Insert an endnote at the insertion point	CTRL-ALT-D
Insert a footnote at the insertion point	CTRL-ALT-F
Insert a page-number field at the insertion point	ALT-SHIFT-P
Insert a time field in the default format at the insertion point	ALT-SHIFT-T
Checking Your Documents	
Run the spelling and grammar checker	F7
Find the next spelling error	ALT-F7
Toggle Track Changes on and off	CTRL-SHIFT-E
Update the document's word-count statistics	CTRL-SHIFT-R
Display the Translate pane	ALT-SHIFT-F7
Working with Tables	
Select all of the current table	ALT-5 (on the numeric keypad)
Update autoformatting on the selected table	CTRL-ALT-U

TABLE A-2
Keyboard
Shortcuts for
Word *(continued)*

Action	Keyboard Shortcut
Performing Mail Merge	
Insert a merge field	ALT-SHIFT-F
Check the mail merge	ALT-SHIFT-K
Open a mail-merge data source	ALT-SHIFT-E
Perform the mail merge to a document	ALT-SHIFT-N
Perform the mail merge to a printer	ALT-SHIFT-M

Table A-3 lists the most widely useful keyboard shortcuts for Excel.

TABLE A-3
Keyboard
Shortcuts for Excel

Action	Keyboard Shortcut
Creating and Displaying Workbooks	
Create a new default workbook	CTRL-N
Minimize the active workbook window	CTRL-F9
Restore or maximize the selected minimized workbook window	CTRL-F10
Navigating Worksheets	
Insert a new worksheet in the active workbook	SHIFT-F11, ALT-SHIFT-F1
Move to the next worksheet	CTRL-PAGE DOWN
Move to the previous worksheet	CTRL-PAGE UP
Select the current worksheet and the next worksheet	CTRL-SHIFT-PAGE DOWN
Select the current worksheet and the previous worksheet	CTRL-SHIFT-PAGE UP
Move to the specified edge of the data region	CTRL-UP ARROW, DOWN ARROW, LEFT ARROW, or RIGHT ARROW
Move to the first cell in the row	HOME
Move to the first cell in the worksheet	CTRL-HOME
Move to the last used cell in the worksheet	CTRL-END
Move down one screen	PAGE DOWN
Move up one screen	PAGE UP
Move to the right by one screen	ALT-PAGE DOWN

TABLE A-3
Keyboard
Shortcuts for
Excel *(continued)*

Action	Keyboard Shortcut
Navigating Worksheets	
Move to the left by one screen	ALT-PAGE UP
Scroll the workbook to display the active cell	CTRL-BACKSPACE
Display the Go To dialog box	CTRL-G
Selecting Items	
Select the current column	CTRL-SPACEBAR
Select the current row	SHIFT-SPACEBAR
Select all cells on the current worksheet	CTRL-A
Reduce the selection to the active cell	SHIFT-BACKSPACE
Select all the objects on the current worksheet while retaining the current selection	CTRL-SHIFT-SPACEBAR
Enter the time in the active cell	CTRL-SHIFT-:
Enter the date in the active cell	CTRL-;
Fill the selected cells with the current entry	CTRL-ENTER
Formatting Items	
Display the Style dialog box	ALT-'
Display the Format Cells dialog box	CTRL-1
Apply the General format	CTRL-SHIFT-~
Apply the two-decimal-place Currency format	CTRL-SHIFT-$
Apply the Percentage format (no decimal places)	CTRL-SHIFT-%
Apply the DD-MMM-YY date format	CTRL-SHIFT-#
Apply the HH:MM AM/PM time format	CTRL-SHIFT-@
Apply the two-decimal-place number format with the thousands separator	CTRL-SHIFT-!
Toggle strikethrough	CTRL-5
Apply an outline border	CTRL-SHIFT-&
Remove the outline border	CTRL-SHIFT-_

PART X

TABLE A-3
Keyboard
Shortcuts for
Excel *(continued)*

Action	Keyboard Shortcut
Hiding and Unhiding Rows and Columns	
Hide all selected rows	CTRL-9
Hide all selected columns	CTRL-0
Unhide hidden rows in the selection	CTRL-SHIFT-(
Unhide hidden columns in the selection	CTRL-SHIFT-)
Working in PivotTables	
Select the entire PivotTable	CTRL-SHIFT-*
Group the selected items	ALT-SHIFT-RIGHT ARROW
Ungroup the grouped items	ALT-SHIFT-LEFT ARROW
Creating a Chart	
Create a chart from the selected range	F11, ALT-F1

Table A-4 lists the most widely useful keyboard shortcuts for Outlook.

TABLE A-4
Keyboard
Shortcuts
for Outlook

Action	Keyboard Shortcut
Creating New Items	
Create a new mail message	CTRL-N
Create a new post in the current folder	CTRL-SHIFT-S
Create a new folder	CTRL-SHIFT-E
Create a new Search folder	CTRL-SHIFT-P
Create a new appointment	CTRL-SHIFT-A
Create a new contact	CTRL-SHIFT-C
Create a new distribution list	CTRL-SHIFT-L
Create a new task	CTRL-SHIFT-K
Create a new task request	CTRL-SHIFT-U
Create a new journal entry	CTRL-SHIFT-J
Create a new note	CTRL-SHIFT-N
Create a new fax	CTRL-SHIFT-X

TABLE A-4
Keyboard
Shortcuts
for Outlook
(continued)

Action	Keyboard Shortcut
Going to Categories	
Go to Mail	CTRL-1
Go to Calendar	CTRL-2
Go to Contacts	CTRL-3
Go to Tasks	CTRL-4
Go to Notes	CTRL-5
Go to Folder list	CTRL-6
Go to Shortcuts	CTRL-7
Go to Folder	CTRL-Y
Working with Messages	
Reply to the active message	CTRL-R
Reply to all recipients of the active message	CTRL-SHIFT-R
Forward the active message	CTRL-F
Mark the selected message as Read	CTRL-Q
Mark the selected message as Unread	CTRL-U
Send/receive all messages	F9
Mark to download the selected messages	CTRL-ALT-M
Unmark the selected headers	CTRL-ALT-U
Displaying Key Tools	
Display the Send/Receive Groups dialog box	CTRL-ALT-S
Display the Move to Folder dialog box	CTRL-SHIFT-V
Display the Find bar	CTRL-E
Display the Advanced Find dialog box	CTRL-SHIFT-F
Display the Address Book	CTRL-SHIFT-B
Opening and Deleting Items	
Open the selected items	CTRL-O
Delete the selected items	CTRL-D

PART X

Table A-5 lists some useful keyboard shortcuts for PowerPoint.

TABLE A-5
Keyboard
Shortcuts for
PowerPoint

Action	Keyboard Shortcut
Start a slide show	F5
Insert a new slide	CTRL-M
Duplicate the selected item	CTRL-D
Toggle Print Preview	CTRL-F2

XML: The Underpinnings of Office 2003

As you saw in Chapter 38, Word 2003 and Excel 2003 contain powerful features for creating and manipulating data formatted with the Extensible Markup Language (XML). Both applications can save their files in XML formats, enabling you to create Word documents using the XML Document format and Excel workbooks using the XML Spreadsheet format, that contain all the information stored in a Word document file or an Excel workbook file (with a few important exceptions). Both applications can also open XML data files attached to an external schema (a specification). This capability enables you to use Word and Excel as familiar front ends for manipulating data from a quite different source—for example, from a database.

Read this appendix if you need to understand what XML is, what it's for, and what the basic elements of an XML schema look like. Before you read further, be warned that there's a modest amount of theory—enough to make the appendix slow going compared to most of the chapters in the book. If your XML needs extend only as far as manipulating XML documents using schemas that other people have created and mapped to Word documents or Excel workbooks, consult Chapter 38 instead.

What Is XML?

XML is the abbreviation for *Extensible Markup Language*. As its name says, XML is a markup language—a language that uses tags to identify different parts of a document.

If you've created web pages, you've probably used HTML, the Hypertext Markup Language, either directly (typing codes) or indirectly (using a graphical interface that does the coding for you). If you've used HTML directly, coding by hand, you'll be familiar with the tags used to mark up elements. For example, the <title> tag denotes the start of a title, and the </title> tag denotes the end of a title. The tags are used in pairs, so a title might appear as <title>Here's the Title!</title> in an HTML document.

HTML is a formatting language: by using HTML tags, you can specify how a document appears on screen (allowing for the vagaries of the browser displaying the document and any overrides the user has programmed to take effect). By contrast, XML uses tags to describe not only formatting but also the contents of a document. XML can be used to create machine-readable documents attached to an external schema that explains what the contents of the document are and the types of data they should contain. This allows XML documents to be used for data transfer among disparate computer systems using XML-compatible applications. (If you want to be fully buzzword compliant, XML is *platform independent*—it can be used across different computer platforms. For example, XML can be used by Unix, Linux, and Macintosh applications as well as by Windows applications.)

XML is a simplified form of the Standard Generalized Markup Language (SGML) that has long been used for government documents and corporate documents. SGML provides rigid definitions of all the items an SGML document can contain. By contrast, XML is "extensible" in that XML documents can define custom tags to identify information rather than having to stick strictly with a predefined set of tags.

NOTE   *Like HTML files, XML files are plain text—and that includes XML schema files. So if you're feeling sufficiently hardcore, you can create or edit a schema in a text editor such as Notepad or vi. But generally speaking, your life will be easier and fuller if you use an XML editor that automates as much of creating the schema for you as possible.*

What Is XML For?

XML is for data exchange. Data exchange may sound like more of a priority for a company's IT department and developers than for end-users of applications, but in fact XML can greatly benefit end-users as well as developers:

- End-users can access their company's information-management system directly through the familiar interfaces of Word and Excel. For example, you can fill in an XML document (say, a travel-request form) by using Word, or an XML spreadsheet (say, a complex invoice) by using Excel and without having to learn to use a new application or new features.

- Developers can create documents and forms that can be deployed easily across different computing platforms and read by any XML-capable application. Various tools are available for creating such documents and forms. Microsoft's latest entry in the field is InfoPath, which enables administrators, developers, or power users to create XML-based templates. These templates can provide built-in help and extra commands to assist the user in filling them out and using them correctly.

- The IT department can extract the relevant details from such forms by using server-based tools. (For example, Microsoft's BizTalk Server has extensive capabilities for processing XML documents.)

- The company can share data with other companies without having to worry about operating-system or application compatibility.

What Benefits Does XML Offer?

At this writing, each typical company produces a large number of files in separate and proprietary formats: Word or WordPerfect documents, Excel or 1-2-3 spreadsheets,

PowerPoint or Keynote presentations, and so on. These files tend to behave as discrete islands of information rather than as a cohesive and accessible whole that can act as the company's knowledge base. This raises these problems:

- Searching for specific content in these files tends to be a slow and unwieldy process unless the company successfully enforces strict policies on file naming, folder locations, and key words. Windows and Office provide tools for searching for files by specific information, but such searches tend to produce multiple results that the searcher has to examine to find the right file.

- Extracting specific information from a file typically involves opening it manually in the associated application, locating the information by eye or by using the search feature, and copying the information out of the file. In some cases, developers can automate the extraction of information by creating VBA solutions for extracting specific parts of files. For example, a procedure might extract the contents of specific bookmarks from a Word document or specific ranges from worksheets in an Excel workbook. But in general, such automation tends to be labor intensive.

XML offers a neat solution to these problems for Word documents and Excel spreadsheets. By using XML documents and spreadsheets linked to external schemas, a company can automatically extract key information that would otherwise be stored in discrete documents.

Another strong component of XML's appeal is the validation it offers, which can provide a solution to the problems of formatting documents consistently and filling them in correctly. An XML document can validate its contents and formatting against the set of rules contained in the schema attached to it. For example, the schema for a text document might require each table to be followed by a caption; validation could identify tables missing their captions. Similarly, a schema might insist that a certain heading level be preceded by the heading level above it—for example, that each Heading 3 paragraph be preceded by a Heading 2 paragraph. Likewise, a schema attached to an invoice spreadsheet could ensure that cells mapped to specific elements contained data (rather than being empty) and that the data was of the required type.

How XML Is Implemented in Office

The versions of Word and Excel included in Office Professional 2003, and the standalone versions of Word 2003 and Excel 2003, can open XML data files attached to external schemas as well as save files in XML formats that support most of the features and formatting that Word and Excel offer. By contrast, the versions of Word and Excel included in other versions of Office 2003 can't open XML data files attached to external schemas.

For saving Word documents, Word uses the XML Document format, an XML file format that supports almost all of Word's formatting and features. The XML Document format uses an XML dialect called WordML (you'll also see it described as "Word XML" sometimes). Similarly, Excel uses the XML Spreadsheet format to encapsulate the data stored in an Excel workbook in an XML-compatible format. Excel workbooks saved in XML format can't contain VBA projects, AutoShapes, and some other objects. (If you try to save a workbook containing any unsupported items, Excel warns you of the problem, then strips out the items if you decide to continue.)

The XML Spreadsheet format is considerably more verbose than Excel's native format, but you can edit files saved in this format in any XML editor (or a text editor, if you have the energy). The XML Document format tends to be a little more verbose than Word's native format, but again, you can edit it using an XML editor or text editor.

For files saved in the XML Document format and the XML Spreadsheet format, Word and Excel can perform what's called *round-tripping*: saving a file and reopening it without any loss of data. Put in those terms, round-tripping doesn't sound like a big deal—after all, every application worth using can round-trip data in its own formats, and Word and Excel have been round-tripping files in their various native formats since the 1980s. But round-tripping data using XML is quite a different kettle of fish, because the files saved in XML can be read by any XML-compliant application. By contrast, files in the native Word and Excel formats need conversion when being read by other word processing and spreadsheet applications.

XML Terms and Components

Many people find XML nebulous, because you need to grasp various concepts before the whole makes sense. In the next few sections, you'll meet the key components of XML and see how they relate to each other.

XML Files

Like many things in life, XML files can have varying degrees of complexity, from as rudimentary as a farm track to as complex as a freeway junction. But all XML files, even the most rudimentary, must satisfy the following requirements:

- **Contain an XML declaration**   The XML declaration is a statement right at the beginning of the document that identifies the file as being written in XML (as opposed to, say, HTML), gives the XML version number used and the encoding type (for example, the UTF-8 character set), and states whether the file is a standalone file (one with an internal DTD) or a file linked to an external DTD or schema. Here's an example of an XML declaration:

```
<?xml version="1.0" encoding="UTF-8" standalone="no" ?>
```

NOTE   *Word documents saved in the XML Document format without a schema attached are standalone XML files. But in a corporate environment, most of the XML files you use are likely to have a schema attached, so they won't be standalone XML files.*

- **Contain a root element**   The *root element* is the first element identified in the XML file. The root element can contain *child elements* (subelements) but cannot be contained by any other element.

- **Be "well-formed"**   *Well-formed* in the XML sense refers not to shapeliness or comeliness but whether the XML file corresponds to the syntax rules of the XML specification. The stipulations of these syntax rules include the following: that the XML file contain a root element; that each start tag name have a corresponding end tag name; that all tags are correctly nested; and that attribute values have quotations placed around them.

XML Schemas and DTDs

An *XML schema* is the specification for an XML document. The schema is written in XML and specifies which elements and which data types can be used, which attributes can be used for each element, and which elements can be used in combination. The schema essentially specifies a class of document.

XML 1.0 used a syntax called a *document type definition* (*DTD*) to describe the structure and contents of an XML file. The DTD enables a validating XML parser to validate the information in the XML file against the defining information in the DTD. For example, if a personnel record requires an employee number, the DTD can validate that the required information is there and is in the specified format. This validation can greatly reduce errors in documents.

DTDs were derived from SGML, in which they worked well for applications such as electronic publishing, but they proved too restrictive for web-based development. DTDs have several problems for web-based development:

- DTD syntax itself isn't compliant with XML, so XML tools can't process DTDs.
- DTDs were created before namespaces, so DTDs don't contain features for describing namespaces. (Namespaces are discussed next.)
- DTDs contain a limited number of type identifiers for describing attributes. (For example, the ID type describes a unique name within a document.) These type identifiers aren't suitable for use with programming languages, and they're not extensible.

XML schemas (some people use "schemata" as the plural, which is technically more correct) were developed to get around the shortcomings of DTDs and offer the following advantages:

- A schema definition is an XML document, so it can be processed via XML tools.
- Schemas contain full features for describing namespaces.
- Schemas can describe attributes and are extensible.

Namespaces

Namespaces are the point at which most newcomers to XML get that unnerving sensation of the top of their head threatening to detach itself from its moorings. Briefly, a *namespace* is a collection of names used as element types and attribute names in an XML document. The namespace is identified using a uniform resource identifier, or URI, which is similar to the URL (uniform resource locator) used for web addresses. The namespace enables the creation of universal names with a scope extending beyond the document that contains them. (For example, the names apply to other documents that use the same XML schema.)

The namespace is typically declared in the root element of an XML schema. A declaration looks like this:

```
<xsd:schema xmlns:xsd="http://acmeheavyindustries.com/schema/XML01"
  targetNamespace="http://acmeheavyindustries.com/hr/"
  xmlns:tns="http://acmeheavyindustries.com/hr/">
  <!-- element definitions here -->
</xsd:schema>
```

The <xsd:schema> tag starts the schema declaration, and the </xsd:schema> ends it. The opening tag includes the assignment of the schema via the xmlns prefix, the target namespace, and the XML namespace. The comment line (<!-- element definitions here -->) indicates where element definitions would typically be placed in the schema.

The same XML file can use multiple namespaces at the same time. Here's an example from an XML Document file created by Microsoft Word that specifies eight namespaces.

```
<?mso-application progid="Word.Document"?>
<w:wordDocument xmlns:w="http://schemas.microsoft.com/office/
word/2003/2/wordml"
xmlns:v="urn:schemas-microsoft-com:vml"
xmlns:w10="urn:schemas-microsoft-com:office:word"
xmlns:SL="http://schemas.microsoft.com/schemaLibrary/2003/2/core"
xmlns:aml="http://schemas.microsoft.com/aml/2001/core"
xmlns:wx="http://schemas.microsoft.com/office/word/2003/2/auxHint"
xmlns:o="urn:schemas-microsoft-com:office:office"
xmlns:dt="uuid:C2F41010-65B3-11d1-A29F-00AA00C14882"
xml:space="preserve">
```

Each of the namespaces is identified by an abbreviation: w, v, w10, SL, aml, wx, o, and dt. These abbreviations are used to refer to the namespaces.

The xml:space="preserve" statement specifies that all the white space in the document be preserved rather than removed.

Names in the namespace can either be qualified or unqualified. *Qualified* names consist of the prefix identifying the namespace (the *namespace prefix*) and a local part. The two parts are separated by a colon. For example, the qualified name o:Author indicates that the Author element is part of the schemas-microsoft-com:office:office namespace in the previous example. *Unqualified* names don't have the prefix and are defined within the element they reference.

Elements

An *element* is an object defined by an XML schema. An element is declared using an xsd:element statement. For example, the following statement declares an element named first_name as being of the string type (a string of text—as opposed to, say, an integer number):

```
<xsd:element name="first_name" type="xsd:string"/>
```

That element is simple, consisting of only one component. But you can also define more complex elements—for example, elements that consist of a number of subelements in a particular sequence. Here's an example of such a complex element:

```
<xsd:element name="employee">
      <xsd:complexType>
            <xsd:sequence>
                  <xsd:element ref="first_name"/>
                  <xsd:element ref="middle_initial"/>
                  <xsd:element ref="last_name"/>
                  <xsd:element ref="employee_address"/>
                  <xsd:element ref="employee_number"/>
            </xsd:sequence>
```

```
        </xsd:complexType>
</xsd:element>
```

In this example, the employee element consists of the following child elements in the correct sequence: first_name, middle_initial, last_name, employee_address, and employee_number.

By placing an element declaration within the xsd:schema element, you automatically link the element to the associated namespace and make it available globally. If you don't need an element to be available globally within the schema, you can make it local by defining it within an element.

Attributes

An *attribute* is a piece of extra information associated with an element. An attribute is declared using an xsd:attribute statement. Here's an example of an attribute declaration:

```
<xsd:element name="manager">
<xsd:attribute name="managerID" type="xsd:string"/>
```

Comments

Like most programming languages, XML schemas can contain *comment* lines—lines that contain information for the human reader but which are ignored by computers. Comments are used to document or explain what an item does or is intended to do. Comments can be for the benefit of either the author of the XML schema file or others who may subsequently need to change it. The comments are hidden from users of the XML schema—they're visible only in an XML editor or a text editor.

To enter a comment, use this format:

```
<!-- here is a sample comment -->
```

NOTE *Comments can be placed anywhere after the XML declaration (which is the first entry in the XML file), even inside a document type declaration. However, comments cannot be nested.*

Index

References to figures and illustrations are in italics.

3-D shapes, 417–418

— A —

accented characters, 57–58
Access
    action queries, 505, 536–540
    append queries, 539–540
    AutoNumber fields, 518
    building a blank database, 497
    changing the working folder, 38–39
    converting databases, 499
    creating a project, 499–500
    creating objects, 507
    crosstab queries, 504, 534–535
    Crosstab Query wizard, 542–543
    Currency fields, 518, 524–525
    customizing, 508–511
    data access pages, 505
    data normalization, 526–530
    data types, 518–519
    database application wizards, 567–569
    database engine, 495–497
    database objects, 504–506
    database window, 506
    databases and projects, 497
    Date/Time fields, 518, 523–524
    default values, 525
    delete queries, 536–537
    editing in Design view, 507–508
    entering fields, 517–519
    file formats, 499, 503

    Find Duplicates Query wizard, 543
    Find Unmatched Query wizard, 544
    finding text, 76
    Format properties, 522–525
    forms, 505, 551–561
    Hyperlink fields, 519
    importing and exporting data, 501–503
    indexes, 520
    input masks, 520–522
    interface, *9*
    Jet engine, 496
    linking data, 503
    linking to external data, 576–577
    Lookup wizard, 519
    macros, 505–506
    make-table queries, 538–539
    Memo fields, 518, 523
    Microsoft's Templates home page, 568–569
    modules, 506
    non-normalized example, 527
    normal forms, 527
    normalized example, 528
    Number fields, 518, 524–525
    ODBC, 497
    OLE Object fields, 518
    overview, 8
    parameter queries, 505, 535–536
    primary keys, 519
    queries, 504–505
    Query Design view, 545–547
    query types, 531–540

Relationships window, 529–530
replicating a database, 577
reports, 505, 561–566
saving data access pages as web
    pages, 724
select queries, 504, 531–534
setting field properties, 519–526
Simple Query wizard, 541–542
spell checking, 29–31
SQL Server, 497
SQL Server 2000 Desktop Engine, 496
storing macros, 767
switchboards, 569–572
Table Design view, 516–517
table relationships, 528–530
Table wizard, 514–516
tables, 504
Text fields, 518, 523
update queries, 537–538
updating queries, 533–534
upsizing a database, 500–501
using a template wizard, 497–498
validation rules, 526
Yes/no (boolean) fields, 518, 523
See also database applications;
    databases; forms; querying;
    tables
accessibility features, 34
ACL files, 24
See also AutoCorrect
action queries, 505, 536–540
Add Network Place wizard, 43
add-ins, loading and unloading in Excel,
    256–257
alignment, 72–73, 145–146
    of shapes, 420
animation, 429, 431–432
appointments, 467, 468
    deleting, 491–492
    one-time, 469–470
    recurring, 470–471
    rescheduling a shared
        appointment, 490
    scheduling, 489–490

sending an e-mail to the
    appointment organizer, 491
archiving, in Outlook, 451–452
array formulas, 319–320
    See also formulas
attributes, 835
    See also XML
Auto Data Tips, 779
Auto List Members, 778
Auto Quick Info, 778
Auto Syntax Check, 777–778
AutoContent wizard, 384–386
AutoCorrect
    ACL files, 24
    configuring, 25
    creating and deleting entries, 26–27
    creating formatted entries in Word, 28
    exceptions, 27–28
    Formula AutoCorrect, 314
    how it works, 25–26
    overview, 24
    in PowerPoint, 399
    Smart Tags, 23–24
    tips for using effectively, 27
    undoing a correction, 27
    in Word, 125–126
AutoFill, 300–301
    creating custom lists, 301–302
AutoFilter, 363–365
AutoFormatting, 161–163
    entries, 164
    in Excel, 290–291
    table styles, 189–190
    See also formatting
AutoRecover, 50–51
    configuring, 51
AutoShapes
    3-D shapes, 417–418
    adding, 84
    adding text to, 86–87
    aligning, 420, *421*
    changing, 419
    changing fill color, 418–419
    connectors, 424–425
    copying and pasting, 420

in FrontPage, 609
in PowerPoint, 414–417
See also shapes
AutoText, 126
AutoComplete, 126
changing languages, 128
creating entries, 126–127
fields, 215
inserting, 127–128
organizing entries, 128–130

B

backgrounds, 201
formatting in FrontPage, 598–601
gradient, 202
pattern, 203
picture, 203
sounds, 601–602
texture, 202
See also watermarks
bookmarks, 224–225
borders, 73–74
in FrontPage, 598
in tables, 190
in Word, 198–199
browser compatibility, 645–647
bulleted lists
automatic, 137–139
customizing list formats, 140–141
multilevel outline lists, 141–142
outlines, 221–224
in PowerPoint, 395–397
removing bullets, 143
using Word's bullets and numbering
tools, 139
buttons
controlling appearance of, 21
customizing, 19

C

Calendar, *9*, 445, *446*, 467–474
accessing a shared calendar, 487–488
appointments, 467, 468–471, 489–492

events, 468, 473
hiding personal data, 488
management, 473–474
meetings, 468, 471–473, 489–492
reminders, 468, 473, *474*
sharing, 487–489
working with free/busy times,
488–489
cameras, importing pictures from, 95–96
capitalization
AutoCorrect options, 25
automatic, 777
changing case, 133–134
drop caps, 134
format switches, 208
small caps, 132
character styles, 165
charts
changing the chart type, 338
changing the plotting order of the
data series, 338–339
changing the scale of an axis, 339–340
changing the source data, 338
Chart toolbar, 337
Chart wizard, 332–335
choosing the right type of chart,
335–336
components of an Excel chart,
331–332, *333*
configuring options, 338
copying formatting from one chart
to another, 342
creating a conventional chart from
PivotTable data, 353–355
creating custom chart types, 343–344
creating in PowerPoint, 402–403
creating instantly using the
keyboard, 336
editing, 336–340
flow charts, 425–426
formatting individual elements,
341–342
formatting the chart area, 340–341
Microsoft Chart applet, 97
organization, 98, *99*, 100–102, 403–404

printing, 343
resizing, 340
selecting objects in a chart, 337
toggling between embedded and
chart sheet, 339
unlinking, 342
using an Excel chart in
PowerPoint, 403
clip art
adjusting contrast and brightness, 410
applying a line style, 411
Clip Art task pane, 106, 251
compressing, 411
cropping, 410–411
formatting pictures, 412
inserting, 78–82
Microsoft Clip Organizer, 81–82
moving, 410
positioning, 409
in PowerPoint, 407–409
in Publisher, 669–670
recoloring, 410
resizing, 409–410
rotating, 411
transparent color, 412
working with in FrontPage, 602–609
clipboards
Clipboard task pane, 106, 252
Office Clipboard, 67–69, 681–682
Windows Clipboard, 67–68, 681–682
clustering, 500
columns, 192–194
commands, rearranging, 19–20
comments, 738–739, 835
in Excel, 739–740
in PowerPoint, 740–741
in Word, 739
See also XML
connectors, 424–425
Contacts, 445
creating, 479–482
editing, 482–483
viewing, 482, *483*
working with, 483–484

context menus
customizing, 20–21
See also menus
copying
Office Clipboard, 67–69
Windows Clipboard, 67–68
cross-references, 234
formatting, 235
crosstab queries, 504, 534–535
customizing
menus, 17, 20–21
toolbars, 17–20
cutting
Office Clipboard, 67–69
Windows Clipboard, 67–68

D

data definition queries, 549
Data File Management, 448–450
data types, 518–519
database applications
adding custom menus and
toolbars, 572
building from scratch
linking to external data, 576–577
locking a database, 573–576
making MDE files, 576
replicating a database, 577
setting startup options, 572–573
switchboards, 569–572
wizards, 567–569
See also Access
databases, 357–358
AutoFilter, 363–365
building a blank database, 497
converting, 499
creating a project, 499–500
creating custom filters manually,
365–367
creating objects, 507
creating using a template wizard,
497–498
data access pages, 505

data entry forms, 359–361
database window, 506
editing in Design view, 507–508
entering data using standard
    techniques, 359
exporting data, 503
filtering a database, 363–367
finding and replacing data in, 363
forms, 505
importing data, 502
linking data, 503
linking to external databases, 367–373
macros, 505–506
modules, 506
MS Query, 371–373
multifield sorts, 362
objects, 504–506
queries, 504–505
Query wizard, 367–370
Quick Sort, 361
relational, 513
reports, 505
sorting, 361–363
sorting by custom sort order,
    362–363
tables, 504
upsizing, 500–501
See also Access
diagrams
    cycle, 98, *99*
    Diagram applet, 98–100
    Diagram toolbar, 99–100
    pyramid, 98, *99*
    radial, 98, *99*
    target, 98, *99*
    Venn, 98, *99*
dialog boxes, 802–812
dictation. *See* speech recognition
dictionaries
    custom, 31
    See also spell checking
digital certificates, 759–760
    and Contacts, 481
Document Actions task pane, 252

Document Map, 120
Document Recovery task pane, 52–54
document type definitions, 833
    See also XML
Document Updates task pane, 106, 252
downloading files, 715
drag and drop, entering text via, 61
drawing grid, configuring and displaying,
    89–90
drawing layer, 77–78
drawing objects
    aligning an object according to
        another object, 91
    dragging and nudging, 89
    grouping and ungrouping, 91–92
    layering, 92
    positioning, 89–92
    positioning using the Format dialog
        box, 90–91
    in PowerPoint, 405
    resizing and formatting, 87–88
    starting a drawing, 82–83
    text boxes, 92–93
    text-wrapping options, 92
    See also AutoShapes; clip art;
        graphics; shapes; WordArt
Drawing Pad, 36
Drawing toolbar, 78
    in FrontPage, 609–611
DTDs, 833
    See also XML

■■■ **E** ■■■

elements, 834–835
    See also XML
e-mail
    attachments, 457–460, 743
    automatically sending and receiving,
        462–463
    composing and responding to, 456–457
    flagging messages, 463–464
    junk, 465–466
    message rules, 466

opening a received attachment, 459–460

personal folders, 464–465

reading, 455–456

receiving and returning a document sent for review, 742–743

receiving a routed document or workbook, 746

routing document or workbook, 744–745

sending an attachment, 458

sending and receiving, 454–460

sending and receiving an attachment, 743

sending documents for review, 741–742

sending or receiving a Word document or Excel worksheet in a message, 743–744

setting up a mail account, 453–454

signatures, 461

standard options, 460

stationery, 461–462

viruses, 460

encryption, 737–738

endnotes, 235–236

envelopes, 244–246

See also labels; Letter wizard; mail merge

e-postage, 246

events, 468, 473

Excel

absolute references, 311

Accounting format, 282

adding worksheets, 277

add-ins, 256–257

alignment, 73

allowing users to edit ranges in a protected worksheet, 297–299

array formulas, 319–320

assigning a macro to an object, 765

attaching an XML schema to a workbook, 703–705

AutoCorrect options, 25

AutoFill, 300–302

AutoFormat, 290–291

borders, 74

Calculation options, 254

cell address, 257

changing formatting on default worksheets and workbooks, 279

changing the templates folder, 39

changing the working folder, 38–39

Chart toolbar, 337

charts, 331–344

checking for errors manually, 315

checking for invalid entries, 293–296

choosing print options, 274

choosing which items to include in the printout, 273–274

choosing XML options, 709

Collapse dialog button, 263

comments, 739–740

conditional formatting, 289–290

configuring error-checking options, 314–315

controlling automatic calculation, 308

converting data from other formats, 269–270

creating a conventional chart from PivotTable data, 353–355

creating XML files in Excel, 703–711

Currency format, 282

custom formats, 284–287

customizing options, 252–257

databases, 357–374

date and time functions, 323–324

Date format, 282

deleting worksheets, 278

displaying formulas, 311–312

Edit options, 255

entering data by drag and drop, 265

entering data manually, 264–265

entering data with Paste, Paste options and Paste Special, 265–267

External Data toolbar, 369–370

filtering data, 363–367

financial functions, 324–325

Find and Replace, 302–303
finding text, 76
formatting cells and ranges, 279–293
formatting rows and columns, 288–289
Formula AutoCorrect, 314
formulas, 305–312
Fraction format, 283
freezing to keep some rows and columns visible, 269
functions, 305–312, 315–319, 323–330
General number format, 281
General options, 255–256
Go To and Go To Special dialog boxes, 261–263
Goal Seek, 320–321
handling numbers, 308
headers and footers, 274–275
hiding formulas, 312
hiding windows, 268
hiding worksheets, 278
information functions, 326–327
instant printing with the default settings, 270
interface, 6
keyboard shortcuts, 824–826
linking across worksheets or workbooks, 267–268
locking a cell or range, 296
logical functions, 325–326
lookup and reference functions, 327
making a workbook shared for review, 741–742
mapping XML elements to an Excel worksheet, 706–708
margins, 273
mathematical and trigonometric functions, 327–328
mixed references, 311
moving or copying worksheets, 278–279
naming ranges, 260–261
navigating in worksheets, 258–259
Number format, 281–282

number formatting, 280–287
opening an XML data file, 702
opening an XML spreadsheet file, 701–702
operands, 306
operator precedence, 307–308
operators, 306
overview, 6
Percentage format, 283
PivotCharts, 352–353, 354
PivotTables, 344–352
Precision as Displayed option, 254
Print Preview, 270–271
printing worksheets, 270–275
protecting a workbook, 296
protecting workbooks with passwords, 299–300
protecting worksheets, 297
querying, 371–373
range names and labels, 309–310
recording the sample macro, 768–769
referring to cells and ranges in formulas, 308
referring to other worksheets in formulas, 308–309
relative references, 311
renaming worksheets, 279
repeating row or column titles on subsequent pages, 274
restricting data and protecting workbooks, 293–300
routing a workbook, 744–745
Save options, 256
saving Excel files in XML formats, 702
saving worksheets or workbooks as web pages, 721–722
scaling your worksheets to fit the paper, 274
Scientific format, 283
screen, 258, 259
selecting cells and ranges of cells, 260–263
selecting worksheets in workbooks, 263–264

sending a worksheet in an e-mail
message, 743–744
setting page breaks, 272
setting the print area, 271–272
Solver, 321–323
sorting database data, 361–363
Special format, 284
spell checking, 29–31
splitting the window, 268
statistical functions, 328–329
storing macros, 766–767
styles, 291–293
task pane, 251–252
Text format, 283–284
text functions, 329–330
Time format, 282–283
Track Changes, 730–733
Transition options, 256
troubleshooting formulas, 312–315
undoing actions, 264–265
using extra windows, 269
View options, 253–254
visual formatting, 287–288
Watch window, 319
web queries, 373–374
workbooks, 257
worksheets, 257–258
XML, 831–832
XML Source task pane, 705–706
zooming, 269
exporting
modules, userforms or classes, 785
Outlook data, 450–451
XML data, 711
Extensible Markup Language. *See* XML
External Data toolbar, 369–370

F

fields
AutoText, 215
basics, 207–213
capitalization format switches, 208
character format switches, 209
check box form fields, 217–218
common, 213–215
date and time, 213–214
date-time picture switch, 209–211
date-time switch symbols, 210–211
document properties fields, 214–215
drop-down form fields, 217
field code, 207–208
format switch, 208, 209
inserting, 211–212
keeping fields from updating, 213
lock result switch, 211
locking, 213
numeric format switches, 209
numeric picture switch, 208–209, 210
numeric switch symbols, 210
page numbering, 213, 214
switches, 208–211
text form fields, 216
toggling field codes, 212
unlinking, 213
updating field content, 213
Web form fields, 218
file formats
and Access, 499
Document format, 831–832
Single File Web Page format, 714
Spreadsheet format, 831–832
Web Page, Filtered format, 714
Web Page format, 714
XML Document format, 715
XML Spreadsheet format, 715
files
changing the templates folder, 39
changing the working folder, 38–39
creating a new default file, 43
creating from a template in Windows
Explorer, 45
creating from the New task pane,
43–45
creating your own templates, 45
finding, 45–50
My Documents folder, 37–38
storing on a network PC, 37

storing on a standalone PC, 37
See also templates
fills, 201
backgrounds, 201–203
changing a shape's fill color, 418–419
watermarks, 204, *205*
finding text, 74
in Access, 76
in Excel, 76
and replacing, 75, 302–303, 363
using wildcard characters, 75
in Word, 75–76
See also searching
flow charts, 425–426
folders
changing the templates folder, 39
changing the working folder, 38–39
My Network Places folder, 39, 42
Outlook's personal folders, 464–465
virtual, 38
See also files
Font dialog box, 65
fonts
custom font styles in FrontPage, 623–625
embedding in Publisher documents, 676
footers, 157–159, 436
in Excel, 274–275
footnotes, 235–236
formatting
alignment, 72–73, 145–146
AutoFormatting, 161–164, 290–291
borders, 73–74
charts, 340–342
conditional, 289–290
cross-references, 235
Formatting toolbar, 65
indentation, 149–153
line spacing, 146–148
paragraph, 72–74, 145–149
paragraph page flow, 148–149
PivotTables, 351
in PowerPoint, 392–394

rows and columns in Excel, 288–289
styles, 67
table content, 189–192
visual, 287–288
widows and orphans, 148
forms, 215–216
in Access, 551–561
adding form fields, 216–218
adding results to a database, 645
anatomy of, 552, *553*
AutoForm wizard, 554–555
check box form fields, 217–218
creating, 552–557
creating in Design view, 555–557
creating in FrontPage, 633–634
customizing, 557–559
drop-down form fields, 217
feedback, 634
form elements, 635–639
Form Page wizard, 639–642
Form wizard, 553–554
in FrontPage, 632–645
FrontPage form templates, 634
gathering form input, 642–645
guest book, 634
linked forms, 559–561
protecting, 218–220
search page, 634
Send to E-mail address, 644–645
Send to File, 644
subforms, 559–561
text form fields, 216
user registration, 634
Web forms, 218
See also Access
formulas
array formulas, 319–320
basic errors, 312, 313
components of, 305–308
defined, 305
displaying, 311–312
example, 309
formatting errors, 312–313
Formula AutoCorrect, 314

hiding from other users, 312
operator precedence, 307–308
operator precedence errors, 313
range change errors, 313
referring to cells and ranges in, 308
referring to other worksheets in, 308–309
troubleshooting, 312–315
using range names and labels in, 309–310
FrontPage
advanced buttons, 639
advanced controls, 615
alignment options, 608
Appearance tab, 607–609
assigning hyperlinks to an image, 619
assigning page titles, 602
AutoShapes, 609
background sounds, 601–602
border thickness, 608
borders and shading, 598
browser compatibility, 645–647
bullets and numbering, 597–598
check boxes, 636–637
choosing a design template, 583
choosing a Web provider, 648–650
clip art, 602–609
Code view, 628
color coding, 629, 630
Color Palette, 596
commercial components, 615
configuring theme colors, 621–623
confirmation page, 639, 640
creating a new theme, 620
creating a new web site, 581–587
creating forms, 633–634
creating new pages, 593–594
creating theme graphics, 625–626
custom font styles, 623–625
custom HTML, 629–630
deciding on a structure for the site, 583–584
detailed reports, 654–657
document libraries, 614
drawing a table, 618

Drawing toolbar, 609–611
drop-down boxes, 637–638
Dynamic Effects, 611
File Upload option, 636
finding and replacing text, 629
finding line numbers, 629
Form Page wizard, 639–642
form templates, 634
formatting a background, 598–601
formatting text, 596–598, 599
Formatting toolbar, 592
Group Box element, 637
grouping objects, 610–611
hit counters, 612
horizontal and vertical spacing, 608
HTML preferences, 630–632
hyperlinks, 619–620
image maps, 619–620
importing an existing site, 584–586
importing a table, 618–619
importing images, 605–606
included content, 614
Insert Table button, 616–617
inserting and defining a table, 617–618
inserting Web components, 615–616
interface, 10–11, 588–592
Label element, 639
link bars, 614, 615
list views, 614
option buttons, 637
overview, 10–11
Photo Gallery, 612–613
photos, 602–609
picture button, 639
Pictures toolbar, 603–605
positioning images, 607
publishing sites and pages, 647–652
push buttons, 638–639
report view options, 657–658
resizing images, 606–607
reveal tags, 630, 631
saving a web site, 587
Site Summary reports, 652–654
size options, 608–609

Split-Pane view, *11*, 628
spreadsheets and charts, 612
Standard toolbar, 590–592
tables, 616–619
tables of contents, 614
tags, 628–629
Text Area, 635–636
text boxes, 635
themes, 594–596, 620–626
Top 10 lists, 614
View options, 588–590
Web components, 611–616
Web Search, 612
WordArt, 610
working with HTML, 627–632
functions
components of, 316
database, 323
date and time, 323–324
defined, 305
editing, 319
entering, 316–317
financial, 324–325
information, 326–327
Insert Function dialog box, 317–318
logical, 325–326
lookup and reference, 327
mathematical and trigonometric, 327–328
nesting, 318
statistical, 328–329
text, 329–330

G

Getting Started task pane, 105, 251
hiding, 252
grammar checking
overview, 31–32
running a grammar check, 32–33
setting options, 33
turning on and off, 32
See also spell checking

graphics
adding to your document, 93–95
cropping pictures, 95
embedding, 93, 94
importing pictures from scanners
and cameras, 95–96
Insert and Link Command, 95
linking, 94
See also AutoShapes; clip art;
drawing objects; shapes; WordArt
gutter, 153–154

H

handouts
configuring print settings, 437
headers and footers, 436
printing a presentation, 439
using Print Preview, 437–439
hanging applications, closing, 51–52
headers, 157–159, 436
in Excel, 274–275
help
Help menu, 15–16
Help task pane, 106, 251
Microsoft support site, 16
Visual Basic Editor, 781
hidden slides, 433–434
highlighters
in PowerPoint, 434–435
in Word, 135
HTML, 713–714
custom, 629–630
preferences, 630–632
reveal tags, 630, *631*
tags, 628–629, 829
working in FrontPage, 627–632
Hungarian notation, 789
hyperlinks, 715–716
in FrontPage, 619–620
in PowerPoint, 405
Hypertext Markup Language. *See* HTML
hyphenation, 149, 195–196
in Publisher, 664

━━ **I** ━━

image maps, defining in FrontPage,
    619–620
importing
    an existing web site into FrontPage,
        584–586
    images in FrontPage, 605–606
    modules, userforms or classes, 785
    Outlook data, 450–451
    pictures from scanners and cameras,
        95–96
    tables in FrontPage, 618–619
    an XML data file into an existing
        XML mapping, 709–710
indentation, 149–153
indexes
    in Access, 520
    generating, 231–232
    preparing index entries, 230–231
    tables of authorities, 232–233
    tables of figures, 232, 233
ink, 34, 35
input masks, 520–521
    characters used to define, 521–522
    creating, 521
    examples, 522
Insert and Link Command, 95
installation
    Office, 12–15
    type of, 14
IntelliMouse, 34
Internet, using Office over the, 42–43

━━ **K** ━━

keyboard
    Correct Keyboard Settings option, 25
    installing different keyboard layouts
        or languages, 58–59
    On-Screen Standard Keyboard, 36
    On-Screen Symbol Keyboard, 36

    selecting text with the, 71–72
    special characters, 55–58
    switching among languages and
        keyboard layouts, 59
    symbols, 55–57
keyboard shortcuts, 57, 817
    for all Office applications, 817–819
    customizing in Word, 21–22
    for Excel, 824–826
    key combinations, 57–58
    for Outlook, 826–827
    for PowerPoint, 828
    for Word, 819–824

━━ **L** ━━

labels, 246–248
    using in formulas, 309–310
    See also envelopes; Letter wizard;
        mail merge
language
    AutoText, 128
    changing the language settings,
        58–59
    Correct Keyboard Settings option, 25
    using other languages with Office,
        59–60
Language bar, 35, 62
layers, 77–78
Letter wizard, 237–238
    See also envelopes; labels; mail merge
licensing, End-User License Agreement, 14
line spacing, 146–148
linking
    to external database data, 576–577
    Insert and Link Command, 95
    pictures, 94
lists
    bullets and numbering, 137–143,
        395–397
    styles, 165, 169–170
Lookup wizard, 519

═ **M** ═

macros, 505–506, 755
    assigning to an object in Excel, 765
    copying or moving in Visual Basic
      Editor, 784
    creating a macro button in Word,
      764–765
    deleting, 784–785
    examining and editing Word macros,
      785–787
    examining the Excel macro, 788
    macro virus-protection features,
      756–760
    recording, 760–762
    recording sample macros, 767–769
    renaming worksheets, 784
    running from an interface item,
      763–765
    running from the Macros dialog
      box, 763
    running from Visual Basic Editor, 781
    storing, 765–767
    testing, 762
mail merge, 238–241
    creating a database, 241–243
    e-postage, 246
    filtering a database, 243
    Letter wizard, 237–238
    Mail Merge task pane, 106
    sorting a database, 244
    See also envelopes
mapping
    configuring properties for an XML
      map, 708–709
    importing an XML data file into an
      existing XML mapping, 709–710
    a network drive to a local drive letter,
      40–42
    XML elements to an Excel worksheet,
      706–708
margins, 153–154

Master Documents, 225
    combining and splitting
      subdocuments, 227
    creating, 226
    page numbering, 227–228
    portability, 226
    working with subdocuments,
      226–227
MDE files, 576
meetings, 468, 471–473
    changing attendees, 491
    deleting, 491–492
    rescheduling a shared meeting, 490
    scheduling, 489–490
    sending an e-mail to the meeting
      organizer, 491
menus
    controlling appearance of menu
      items, 21
    customizing, 17, 20–21
Microsoft Clip Organizer, 81–82
Microsoft Office Application Recovery, 50
    closing a hung application, 51–52
Microsoft, support site, 16
Microsoft.com, Templates home page,
    568–569
mouse
    IntelliMouse, 34
    selecting text with, 71
MS Query, 371–373
multimedia, inserting in PowerPoint,
    427–428
My Documents folder, 37–38
My Network Places folder, 39, 42

═ **N** ═

namespaces, 833–834
    See also XML
networks
    accessing a network drive, 39–40
    Add Network Place wizard, 43

disconnecting a network drive, 42
mapping a network drive to a local
   drive letter, 40–42
My Network Places folder, 39, 42
universal naming convention, 40
using Office over, 39–42
New Document task pane, 106
New task panes, 43–45
New Workbook task pane, 252
notes
   changing a note's color, 485
   changing preferences, 485
   creating, 484
   viewing, 485
numbered lists
   automatic, 137–139
   customizing list formats, 140–141
   multilevel outline lists, 141–142
   outlines, 221–224
   in PowerPoint, 395–397
   removing numbering, 143
   using Word's bullets and numbering
      tools, 139

▬ O ▬

Object Browser, 121–122, 779–780
objects
   embedding and linking, 682–688
   layering, 671
   in PowerPoint, 405
   See also drawing objects
OCR, 62–64
Office, 3
   Clipboard, 67–69
   collaborative tools, 12
   customizing toolbars and menus,
      17–22
   End-User License Agreement, 14
   entering text via Paste and drag and
      drop, 60–61
   entering text with the keyboard, 55–60
   help, 15–16

improving accessibility, 34
installing, 12–15
keyboard shortcuts, 817–819
minimum requirements, 13
product key, 13
recovery options, 50–54
scanning and OCR, 62–64
speech recognition, 61–62
user information, 14
using on Tablet PCs, 34–36
using other languages with, 59–60
using over a network, 39–42
using over the Internet, 42–43
Office Clipboard, 67–69, 681–682
on-screen pen, in PowerPoint, 434–435
On-Screen Standard Keyboard, 36
On-Screen Symbol Keyboard, 36
operands, 306
operators, 306
   precedence, 307–308
optical character recognition. *See* OCR
organization charts, 98, *99*
   creating, 100–102
   in PowerPoint, 403–404
orphans, 148
outlines, 221
   changing outline level styles, 222–223
   combining outline tools, 223
   creating, 221–222
   rearranging and viewing, 223–224
Outlook
   Advanced toolbar, 447
   alignment, 73
   appointments, 467, 468–471, 489–492
   archiving data, 451–452
   attachments, 457–460
   automatically sending and receiving
      mail, 462–463
   borders, 74
   Calendar, *9*, 445, *446*, 467–474
   categories, 448
   composing and responding to e-mail,
      456–457

Contacts, 445, 479–484
customizing toolbars, 447
Data File Management, 448–450
drawing canvas, 82–83
events, 468, 473
flagging messages, 463–464
grammar checking, 31–33
importing and exporting data, 450–451
Insert and Link Command, 95
interface, *8*
junk e-mail, 465–466
keyboard shortcuts, 826–827
Mail, 443–445
meetings, 468, 471–473, 489–492
message rules, 466
notes, 484–485
opening a received attachment, 459–460
Outlook Today window, 443, *444*
overview, 7–8
personal folders, 464–465
Personal Folders dialog box, 450
reading e-mail, 455–456
Reading pane, 445
reminders, 468, 473, *474*
sending an attachment, 458
sending and receiving e-mail, 454–460
setting up a mail account, 453–454
sharing Calendars, 487–489
signatures, 461
spell checking, 29–31
standard options, 460
Standard toolbar, 446–447
stationery, 461–462
storing macros, 767
Tasks, 446, 474–477
text boxes, 92–93
themes, 180
Web toolbar, 447
overprinting settings, 675–676

P

Pack and Go, 676–677
page layout
advantages of using Publisher vs. Word, 197–198
borders, 198–199
fills and backgrounds, 201–204
horizontal rules, 200–201
shading, 199–200
text boxes, 92–93, 204–206
in Word, 197–206
page numbering, 159–160
fields, 213, 214
Master Documents, 227–228
in Publisher, 664
page orientation, 153–154
paragraph formatting, 72–74, 145–149
columns, 192–194
in PowerPoint, 394
paragraph styles, 165
parameter queries, 505, 535–536
passwords, 737
pasting
entering text via the Paste command, 60
Office Clipboard, 67–69
Paste Special, 69–70
Windows Clipboard, 67–68
pen input, configuring for, 35–36
permissions
read and write, 42, 715
SharePoint Services, 748
photo albums, 412–414
photos
and web publishing, 677–678
working with in FrontPage, 602–609
pictures. *See* graphics
Pictures toolbar, 603–605
PivotCharts, 352–353, *354*
PivotTables, 344
changing, 350
changing a field to a different function, 352

creating a conventional chart from
  PivotTable data, 353–355
defined, 345–346
formatting, 351
options, 352, *353*
PivotTable and PivotChart wizard,
  346–348
PivotTable toolbar, 351
PowerPoint
  3-D shapes, 417–418
  action buttons, 426–427
  adding slides, 389
  adjusting an AutoShape, 417
  adjusting a placeholder box, 397
  adjusting contrast and brightness
    of clip art, 410
  aligning a shape, 420, *421*
  alignment, 73
  animation, 429, 431–432
  applying a line style, 411
  arcs and other standard shapes, 423
  AutoContent wizard, 384–386
  AutoCorrect, 399
  AutoCorrect options, 25
  AutoShapes, 414–417
  Blank Presentation option, 382, *383*
  browsing a presentation, 386–387
  bullets and numbering, 395–397
  changing an AutoShape, 419
  changing a shape's fill color, 418–419
  changing slide design, 391–392
  changing slide layout, 392
  changing text on slides, 391
  changing the templates folder, 39
  changing the working folder, 38–39
  charts, 401–403
  clip art, 407–409
  comments, 740–741
  comparing and merging changes,
    735–736
  compressing pictures, 411
  connectors, 424–425
  Control Toolbox, 380
  copying and pasting shapes, 420

creating a photo album, 412–414
cropping an image, 410–411
From Design Template option,
  382–384
drawing basic shapes, 422
Drawing toolbar, 380, 414–421
editing line properties, 419
flow charts, 425–426
formatting paragraphs, 394
formatting pictures, 412
formatting text, 392–394
Formatting toolbar, 379, 392–394
grouping shapes, 423–424
hidden slides, 433–434
hyperlinks, 405
hyphenation, 664
inserting a photo, 412
inserting text on shapes, 424
interface, 7, 377–382
keyboard shortcuts, 828
managing placeholder layout, 398
menus, 377–379
modifying orientation, 416
moving clip art, 410
multimedia content, 427–428
objects, 405
on-screen pen or highlighter, 434–435
organization charts, 403–404
Outline/Slides pane, 381, 386–387
Outlining toolbar, 380
overview, 6–7
Picture toolbar, 380–381
placeholders, 397–398
positioning clip art, 409
printing speaker notes and handouts,
  436–439
recoloring clip art, 410
rehearsing your presentation, 433
removing slides, 390
reorganizing slides, 390
resizing clip art, 409–410
Reviewing toolbar, 381
Revisions pane, 381, 735–736
rotating clip art, 411

saving a presentation, 387
saving presentations as web pages,
  722–724
Set Up Show options, 435
spell checking, 29–31, 399
stack order, 420–421
Standard toolbar, 379
starting a presentation, 382–386
storing macros, 767
tables, 399–401
Tables and Borders toolbar, 381
task pane, 380
text boxes, 404
transitions, 429–431
transparent color, 412
viewing slide shows full screen, 432
Visual Basic toolbar, 381
Web toolbar, 381
WordArt toolbar, 381
work area, 381–382
precedence, 307–308
presentations
browsing, 386–387
rehearsing, 433
saving, 387
saving as web pages, 722–724
starting, 382–386
See also PowerPoint
previewing
Print Preview in Excel, 270–271
Web Page Preview, 719, *720*
primary keys, 519
printing
color, 674–675
embedding fonts, 676
Excel charts, 343
Excel worksheets, 270–275
PowerPoint presentations, 436–439
Publisher documents, 673, *674*
registration settings, 675–676
Word documents, 122–123
working with professional printers,
  673–677
product key, 13

Protect Document task pane, 106
Publisher
boxes, 665–666
color printing, 674–675
creating custom publications,
  661–671
creating publications with templates,
  659–661
custom colors, 664–665
Design Gallery objects, 670, *671*
entering personal information, 664
fonts, 676
interface, *12*
layout guides, 663–664
overprinting settings, 675–676
overview, 11–12
Pack and Go, 676–677
page numbering, 664
pictures, 669–670
printing on your home or office
  printer, 673, *674*
publishing to the Web, 677–678
registration settings, 675–676
shapes, 670
tables, 669
text boxes, 667–668
WordArt, 669
working with content, 665–671
working with professional printers,
  673–677

Q

qualified names, 834
Query wizard, 367–370
querying, 504–505
choosing fields, 545–546
choosing tables, 545
creating a custom query, 371–372
creating a parameter query, 372–373
defining query criteria, 546–547
with MS Query, 371–373
performing calculations, 547
Query Design view, 545–547

query types, 531–540
query wizards, 540–544
SQL queries, 547–549
updating queries, 533–534
web queries, 373–374
See also Access

━ **R** ━

recovery options, 50–51
AutoRecover, 50–51
closing a hung application, 51–52
configuring backup and recovery
options, 51
Document Recovery task pane, 52–54
Microsoft Office Application
Recovery, 50, 51–52
Redo button, 131
rehearsing presentations, 433
reminders, 473, *474*
repairing documents, 53
See also recovery options
replacing text, 75
See also finding text
replacing text as you type, 25
reports
calculating running sums, 566
creating using the Report wizard,
563–564
on files, 654–655
in FrontPage, 652–658
grouping and sorting records,
565–566
layout, 561–563
other Report wizards, 564–565
on problems, 656
setting view options, 657–658
shared content, 655
Site Summary reports, 652–654
usage, 657
workflow, 656–657
See also Access
Research task pane, 106, 251

Reveal Formatting task pane, 106
review tools, Track Changes, 725–730
Reviewing pane, 730, *731*
Reviewing toolbar, 729–730
round-tripping, 713–714, 832
routing, 744–746
See also e-mail
ruler, 152–153
rules, horizontal, 200–201

━ **S** ━

scanning, 62–64
importing pictures from scanners,
95–96
schemas, 830, 833
See also XML
scrolling, 34
Search Results task pane, 106, 251
searching, 45–46
advanced file searches, 47–49
basic file searches, 46–47
finding and replacing text, 75
finding text, 74
using wildcard characters, 75
working with the files you find,
49–50
security
digital certificates, 759–760
digital signatures, 759–760
encryption, 737–738
levels, 756–759
locking a database, 573–576
passwords, 737
removing personal information
from document properties, 738
Trusted Publishers, 757–759
select queries, 504, 531–534
SGML, 830
shading
in FrontPage, 598
in tables, 190
in Word, 199–200

shapes
    adding, 83
    arcs and other standard shapes, 423
    basic shapes, 422
    grouping, 423–424
    inserting text on, 424
    in Publisher, 670
    See also AutoShapes
Shared Workspace task pane, 106, 252
SharePoint Services, 747
    accessing a SharePoint site, 748
    anatomy of a SharePoint site, 747
    managing documents with, 748–750
    overview, 12
    permissions, 748
    synchronizing documents with
        SharePoint sites, 750–751
shell extensions, 38
shortcut menus
    customizing, 20–21
    See also menus
shortcuts. *See* keyboard shortcuts
signatures, 461
    See also digital certificates
smart quotes, 161
Smart Tags
    Paste Options Smart Tag, 69–70,
        265–266
    setting options, 23–24
sound
    background, 601–602
    See also multimedia
speaker notes
    configuring print settings, 437
    headers and footers, 436
    printing a presentation, 439
    using Print Preview, 437–439
special characters, 55–57, 135–136
    entering with key combinations,
        57–58
speech recognition, 61–62
spell checking
    AutoCorrect options, 25
    configuring options, 30

custom dictionaries, 31
in PowerPoint, 399
running a spell check, 29
    See also grammar checking
SQL queries, 505
    ANSI SQL query modes, 548–549
    data definition queries, 549
    union queries, 549
    using SQL as a record source, 547
Standard Generalized Markup Language.
    See SGML
styles, 67, 164–166
    applying, 166, 292
    character, 164
    controlling access to, 174–175
    creating, 166–168, 292
    in Excel, 291–293
    list, 165, 169–170
    merging styles from another
        workbook, 293
    modifying, 168–169, 293
    paragraph, 165
    Style Gallery, 175–176
    table, 165, 170
Styles and Formatting task pane, 106
subdocuments
    combining and splitting, 227
    working with, 226–227
    See also Master Documents
switchboards, 569
    Switchboard Manager, 570–572
symbols, 135–136
    entering, 55–57

━ **T** ━

table definitions, 504
tables
    and Access, 504
    in Access, 514–517
    Access' Table wizard, 514–516
    adjusting table properties, 186–188
    AutoSum button, 192
    changing borders and shading, 190

converting text to, 184–185
drawing, 183–184
formatting content, 189–192
formatting in PowerPoint, 400–401
formulas, 192
in FrontPage, 616–619
hiding grid lines, 189
inserting and deleting columns and
    rows, 186
inserting a Word table in
    PowerPoint, 401
inserting from the menu, 182–183
inserting from the toolbar, 183
inserting in PowerPoint, 399–401
manipulating, 185–189
many-to-many relationship, 529
math calculations, 192
merging and splitting cells, 188–189
nested, 181, 189
one-to-many relationship, 528–529
one-to-one relationship, 529
in Publisher, 669
relationships, 528–530
Relationships window, 529–530
repeating headings, 191
rotating text, 190–191
selecting elements, 186
sorting data, 191–192
splitting, 189
styles, 165, 170
table styles using AutoFormat,
    189–190
in Word, 181–192
See also Access; Word
tables of authorities, 232–233
tables of contents
    in FrontPage, 614
    in Word, 228–230
tables of figures, 232, 233
Tablet PCs, using Office on, 34–36
tabs, 150–152
tags, 713–714

Tasks, 446
    assigning, 476–477
    creating, 474–476
    recurring, 477
tear-off palettes, 89
templates, 170–171
    attaching, 171–173
    changing the templates folder, 39
    choosing a web site design
        template, 583
    creating a new template-based
        document, 171–172
    creating files from a template in
        Windows Explorer, 45
    creating your own, 45, 173
    form, 634
    Microsoft's Templates home page,
        568–569
    modifying the Normal template, 171
    Publisher, 659–661
    Template Help task pane, 252
text
    accented characters, 57–58
    adding to AutoShapes, 86–87
    AutoText, 126–130
    changing case, 133–134
    coloring and highlighting, 135
    columns, 192–194
    converting to tables, 184–185
    entering via Paste and drag and
        drop, 60–61
    entering via speech recognition,
        61–62
    entering with the keyboard, 55–60
    finding and replacing, 74–76
    formatting, 64–67, 131–135
    formatting in FrontPage, 596–598, *599*
    formatting in PowerPoint, 392–394
    hidden, 133
    hyphenation, 149, 195–196
    inserting on shapes, 424

installing different keyboard layouts
or languages, 58–59
key combinations, 57–58
repeating, 130–131
rotating, 190–191
scanning and OCR, 62–64
selecting with the keyboard, 71–72
selecting with the keyboard and
mouse, 72
selecting with the mouse, 71
special characters, 55–58, 135–136
switching among languages and
keyboard layouts, 59
symbols, 55–57, 135–136
text boxes, 92–93, 204–206, 404,
667–668, 807–808
wrapping options, 92
See also capitalization; language;
WordArt
themes
across applications, 180
applying and removing, 178, *179*
assets and liabilities, 177–178
backgrounds and graphics, 178
changing templates and styles, 177
converting into templates, 178–179
in FrontPage, 594–596, 620–626
in Word, 176–180
thumbnails, printing, 122–123
toolbars
Chart, 337
controlling appearance of buttons, 21
customizing, 17–20
Diagram, 99–100
displaying and moving, 18
Drawing, 78, 380, 609–611
External Data, 369–370
Formatting, 65, 379
FrontPage, 590–592
increasing size of buttons, 34
Outlook, 446–447
Pictures, 603–605

PivotTable, 351
PowerPoint, 379–381
Reviewing, 729–730
WordArt, 86, 381
Track Changes, 112, 725–726
controlling how Word displays
tracked changes, 727–729
in Excel, 730–733
Reviewing toolbar, 729–730
reviewing tracked changes in
Excel, 733
turning on and off in Excel, 731–732
turning on and off in Word, 727
working in Excel with, 732–733
transitions, 429–431
Trusted Publishers, 757–759

U

UNC. *See* universal naming convention
Undo button, 131
union queries, 549
universal naming convention, 40
unqualified names, 834
uploading files, 715
Upsizing wizard, 501
user information, 14
User-Level Security Wizard, 573–576

V

variables
declaring and using, 789–791
private scope, 791
public scope, 791
recommendations for declaring
effectively, 792
types of, 789, 790
VBA
accessing another application, 801
adding a reference to another project
or application, 800–801

Call Stack window, 802
calling one procedure from another,
    800–802
calling the userform from the
    macro, 812
check boxes, 805–806
classes, 773
collections, 772
command buttons, 808–812
creating the Initialize subprocedure
    for the userform, 806–807
dialog boxes, 802–812
frames, 804
functions, 773–774
If statements, 792–793
input boxes, 796–797
IsAlphanumeric function, 798–800
labels, 807–808
locking your VBA project, 813
loops, 797–800
macro viruses, 756–760
and macros, 755
macros, 773–774
message boxes, 794–796
methods, 772–773
modules, 773
objects, 772
option buttons, 805
overview, 771–773
procedures, 773–774
properties, 772
running code, 781–783
Select Case structure, 793
signing your VBA project, 812–813
subprocedures, 773–774
text boxes, 807–808
userforms, 773, 803–804
variables, 789–792
See also Visual Basic Editor
virtual folders, 38
viruses, 460
    macro virus-protection features,
        756–760

Visual Basic Editor
    Auto Data Tips, 779
    Auto List Members, 778
    Auto Quick Info, 778
    Auto Syntax Check, 777–778
    automatic capitalization, 777
    Code window, 777
    Complete Word, 779
    copying and moving modules,
        userforms, or classes, 785
    copying or moving a macro, 784
    creating a module, userform or
        class, 784
    deleting a macro or module, 784–785
    executing code in the Immediate
        window, 782
    exporting and importing modules,
        userforms or classes, 785
    following the value of expressions as
        code runs, 783
    getting acquainted with, 774–777
    help files, 781
    interrupting code when it's
        running, 781
    launching, 774
    modes, 781
    Object Browser, 779–780
    Project Explorer window, 775–776
    Properties window, 776
    renaming a macro or module, 784
    returning to the host application, 777
    running a macro, 781
    setting a line of code to be the next
        statement, 782
    stepping into a procedure, 782
Visual Basic for Applications. *See* VBA
Voice Command mode, 61–62

━ W ━

watermarks, 204, *205*
Web Digital Authoring and Versioning.
    See WebDAV

Web Options dialog box, 716–718
web pages
    assigning page titles, 602
    creating, 593–594
    publishing, 647–652
    saving Access data access pages, 724
    saving Excel worksheets or
        workbooks as, 721–722
    saving PowerPoint presentations as,
        722–724
    saving Word documents as, 719–720
    setting the title page, 719
    Web Page Preview, 719, *720*
    See also FrontPage
web providers, choosing, 648–650
web publishing, 677–678, 715
web queries, 373–374
web sites
    applying a theme to, 594–596
    choosing a design template, 583
    creating, 581–587
    deciding on a structure for the site,
        583–584
    importing an existing site into
        FrontPage, 584–586
    publishing, 647–652
    saving, 587
    updating, 651–652
    See also FrontPage
WebDAV, 715
widows, 148
wildcard characters, using in searches, 75
Windows Clipboard, 67–68, 681–682
wizards
    Add Network Place wizard, 43
    AutoContent, 384–386
    AutoForm wizard, 554–555
    Chart wizard, 332–335
    creating, 348–349
    Crosstab Query wizard, 542–543
    database application wizards,
        567–569
    Find Duplicates Query wizard, 543

    Find Unmatched Query wizard, 544
    Form Page wizard, 639–642
    Form wizard, 553–554
    Letter wizard, 237–238
    Lookup, 519
    Mail Merge wizard, 238–241
    PivotTable and PivotChart wizard,
        346–348
    Query, 367–370
    Report wizard, 563–565
    Simple Query wizard, 541–542
    Table, 514–516
    Upsizing wizard, 501
    User-Level Security Wizard, 573–576
Word
    alignment, 73, 145–146
    AutoComplete, 126
    AutoCorrect, 125–126
    AutoCorrect options, 25
    AutoFormatting, 161–164
    AutoText, 126–130
    bookmarks, 224–225
    borders, 74, 198–199
    bullets and numbering, 137–143
    changing case, 133–134
    changing the templates folder, 39
    changing the working folder, 38–39
    coloring and highlighting text, 135
    columns, 192–194
    comments, 739
    comparing and merging documents,
        733–735
    creating a macro button, 764–765
    creating formatted AutoCorrect
        entries, 28
    cross-references, 234–235
    customizing keyboard shortcuts,
        21–22
    customizing options, 107–112
    Document Map, 120
    document views, 112–119
    drawing canvas, 82–83
    drop caps, 134

Edit options, 109–110
envelopes, 244–246
e-postage, 246
Fast Save option, 111
fields, 207–220
fills, 201–204
finding text, 75–76
footnotes, 235–236
formatting marks, 108
formatting text, 131–135
forms, 215–220
General options, 108–109
grammar checking, 31–33
headers and footers, 157–159
hidden text, 133
hiding the task pane, 106–107
horizontal rules, 200–201
hyphenation, 149, 195–196
Include with Document options,
    110–111
indentation, 149–153
indexes, 230–233
Insert and Link Command, 95
interface, *4*
keyboard navigation, 119
keyboard shortcuts, 21–22, 819–824
labels, 246–248
Letter wizard, 237–238
line spacing, 146–148
mail merge, 238–244
margins, 153–154
Master Documents, 225–228
maximizing screen space, 118–119
mouse navigation, 120
Normal view, 113
Object Browser, 121–122
Outline view, 116–117
outlines, 221–224
overview, 4–6
page breaks, 148, 154–156
page numbering, 159–160
page orientation, 153–154
paragraph formatting, 145–149
paragraph page flow, 148–149

Print and Web Layout options, 108
Print Layout view, 114, *115*
Print options, 110–111
Print Preview, 122
printing, 122–123
printing thumbnails, 122–123
Reading Layout view, 114–116
recording the sample macro, 767–768
repeating text, 130–131
Reviewing toolbar, 729–730
routing a document, 744–745
ruler, 152–153
rules, 200–201
Save options, 111–112
saving documents as web pages,
    719–720
section breaks, 154–156
sending a document in an e-mail
    message, 743–744
shading, 199–200
small caps, 132
special characters, 135–136
spell checking, 29–31
splitting the document window,
    117–118
storing macros, 766
strikethrough and double
    strikethrough, 132
Style Area Width, 108
Style Gallery, 175–176
styles, 164–170, 174–175
superscript and subscript, 132
suppressing line numbers, 148
tables, 181–192
tables of contents, 228–230
tabs, 150–152
task pane, 105–107
templates, *5*, 170–175
text boxes, 92–93, 204–206
themes, 176–180
Track Changes, 112, 725–730
underlining, 132
undo and redo, 131
View options, 107–108

Web Layout view, 113–114
widows and orphans, 148–149
XML, 689–701, 831–832
zooming, 119
WordArt
adding to drawings, 84–86
in FrontPage, 610
in Publisher, 669
toolbar, 86
Write Anywhere feature, 36
Writing Pad, 34, *35*, 36
writing tools, 36

— **X** —

XML
adding a schema to the Schema
Library, 693–694
adding XML tags, 695–697
attaching an XML schema, 692–693
attaching an XML schema to a
workbook, 703–705
attributes, 835
benefits of, 830–831
comments, 835
configuring properties for an XML
map, 708–709
creating a new XML document, 692
creating XML documents in Word,
691–701
data binding, 709–711
declarations, 832
defined, 829–830
Document format, 831–832
document type definitions
(DTDs), 833
editing an XML document, 690
elements, 834–835
in Excel, 701–711
exporting XML data, 711
files, 832
implementing in Office, 831–832
importing an XML data file into an
existing XML mapping, 709–710

inserting an XML file into a Word
document, 700–701
mapping XML elements to an Excel
worksheet, 706–708
namespaces, 833–834
opening an XML data file in Excel, 702
opening an XML document, 689–690
opening an XML spreadsheet file,
701–702
options, 697–699, 709
overview, 688–689
platform independence, 830
protecting XML tags from being
deleted, 700
qualified names, 834
removing a schema, 694
removing XML tags, 697
root elements, 832
round-tripping, 832
saving a Word document in XML
format, 690–691
saving Excel files in XML formats, 702
saving only the data from an XML
document, 699
schemas, 830, 833
Spreadsheet format, 831–832
unqualified names, 834
uses for, 830
validating an XML document, 699
verifying a map for export, 711
well-formed files, 832
what you're likely to do with XML
files, 689
in Word, 689–691
XML Source task pane, 252, 705–706
XML Structure task pane, 106

— **Z** —

zooming, 34
in Excel, 269
in Word, 119

INTERNATIONAL CONTACT INFORMATION

AUSTRALIA
McGraw-Hill Book Company
Australia Pty. Ltd.
TEL +61-2-9900-1800
FAX +61-2-9878-8881
http://www.mcgraw-hill.com.au
books-it_sydney@mcgraw-hill.com

CANADA
McGraw-Hill Ryerson Ltd.
TEL +905-430-5000
FAX +905-430-5020
http://www.mcgraw-hill.ca

**GREECE, MIDDLE EAST, & AFRICA
(Excluding South Africa)**
McGraw-Hill Hellas
TEL +30-210-6560-990
TEL +30-210-6560-993
TEL +30-210-6560-994
FAX +30-210-6545-525

MEXICO (Also serving Latin America)
McGraw-Hill Interamericana Editores
S.A. de C.V.
TEL +525-1500-5108
FAX +525-117-1589
http://www.mcgraw-hill.com.mx
carlos_ruiz@mcgraw-hill.com

SINGAPORE (Serving Asia)
McGraw-Hill Book Company
TEL +65-6863-1580
FAX +65-6862-3354
http://www.mcgraw-hill.com.sg
mghasia@mcgraw-hill.com

SOUTH AFRICA
McGraw-Hill South Africa
TEL +27-11-622-7512
FAX +27-11-622-9045
robyn_swanepoel@mcgraw-hill.com

SPAIN
McGraw-Hill/
Interamericana de España, S.A.U.
TEL +34-91-180-3000
FAX +34-91-372-8513
http://www.mcgraw-hill.es
professional@mcgraw-hill.es

**UNITED KINGDOM, NORTHERN,
EASTERN, & CENTRAL EUROPE**
McGraw-Hill Education Europe
TEL +44-1-628-502500
FAX +44-1-628-770224
http://www.mcgraw-hill.co.uk
emea_queries@mcgraw-hill.com

ALL OTHER INQUIRIES Contact:
McGraw-Hill/Osborne
TEL +1-510-420-7700
FAX +1-510-420-7703
http://www.osborne.com
omg_international@mcgraw-hill.com

Microsoft
Office 2003
Answers for Everyone

Make the most of the entire Office system with help from these other books from Osborne

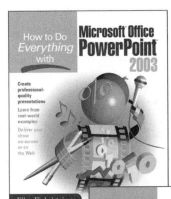

Sound Off!

Visit us at **www.osborne.com/bookregistration** and let us know what you thought of this book. While you're online you'll have the opportunity to register for newsletters and special offers from McGraw-Hill/Osborne.

We want to hear from you!

Sneak Peek

Visit us today at **www.betabooks.com** and see what's coming from McGraw-Hill/Osborne tomorrow!

Based on the successful software paradigm, Bet@Books™ allows computing professionals to view partial and sometimes complete text versions of selected titles online. Bet@Books™ viewing is free, invites comments and feedback, and allows you to "test drive" books in progress on the subjects that interest you the most.